Systematic Theology

Volume I - The Doctrine of God

By Augustus Hopkins Strong, D.D., LL.D.

President and Professor of Biblical Theology in the Rochester Theological Seminary

Edited by Anthony Uyl

Devoted Publishing
Woodstock, Ontario, 2017

Systematic Theology: Volume I - The Doctrine of God

A Compendium and Commonplace-Book
Designed For The Use Of Theological Students

By Augustus Hopkins Strong, D.D., LL.D. (1836-1921)

President and Professor of Biblical Theology in the Rochester Theological Seminary

Edited by Anthony Uyl

Revised and Enlarged In Three Volumes

The Judson Press
Philadelphia, Boston, Chicago, St. Louis, Los Angeles, Kansas City, Seattle, Toronto

Originally Published in 1907

The text of Systematic Theology: Volume I - The Doctrine of God is all in the Public Domain. This edition is published by Devoted Publishing a division of 2165467 Ontario Inc.

What kind of philosophies do you have?
Let us know!

Contact us at: devotedpub@hotmail.com
Visit our shop on Facebook: @DevotedPublishing

Published in Woodstock, Ontario, Canada 2017.

For bulk educational rates, please contact us at the above email address.

ISBN: 978-1-77356-037-3

Table of Contents

Christo Deo Salvatori

"THE EYE SEES ONLY THAT WHICH IT BRINGS WITH IT THE POWER OF SEEING."—Cicero.

"OPEN THOU MINE EYES, THAT I MAY BEHOLD WONDROUS THINGS OUT OF THY LAW."—Psalm 119:18.

"FOR WITH THEE IS THE FOUNTAIN OF LIFE: IN THY LIGHT SHALL WE SEE LIGHT."—Psalm 36:9.

"FOR WE KNOW IN PART, AND WE PROPHESY IN PART; BUT WHEN THAT WHICH IS PERFECT IS COME, THAT WHICH IS IN PART SHALL BE DONE AWAY."—1 Cor. 13:9, 10.

PREFACE

The present work is a revision and enlargement of my "Systematic Theology," first published in 1886. Of the original work there have been printed seven editions, each edition embodying successive corrections and supposed improvements. During the twenty years which have intervened since its first publication I have accumulated much new material, which I now offer to the reader. My philosophical and critical point of view meantime has also somewhat changed. While I still hold to the old doctrines, I interpret them differently and expound them more clearly, because I seem to myself to have reached a fundamental truth which throws new light upon them all. This truth I have tried to set forth in my book entitled "Christ in Creation," and to that book I refer the reader for further information.

That Christ is the one and only Revealer of God, in nature, in humanity, in history, in science, in Scripture, is in my judgment the key to theology. This view implies a monistic and idealistic conception of the world, together with an evolutionary idea as to its origin and progress. But it is the very antidote to pantheism, in that it recognizes evolution as only the method of the transcendent and personal Christ, who fills all in all, and who makes the universe teleological and moral from its centre to its circumference and from its beginning until now.

Neither evolution nor the higher criticism has any terrors to one who regards them as parts of Christ's creating and educating process. The Christ in whom are hid all the treasures of wisdom and knowledge himself furnishes all the needed safeguards and limitations. It is only because Christ has been forgotten that nature and law have been personified, that history has been regarded as unpurposed development, that Judaism has been referred to a merely human origin, that Paul has been thought to have switched the church off from its proper track even before it had gotten fairly started on its course, that superstition and illusion have come to seem the only foundation for the sacrifices of the martyrs and the triumphs of modern missions. I believe in no such irrational and atheistic evolution as this. I believe rather in him in whom all things consist, who is with his people even to the end of the world, and who has promised to lead them into all the truth.

Philosophy and science are good servants of Christ, but they are poor guides when they rule out the Son of God. As I reach my seventieth year and write these words on my birthday, I am thankful for that personal experience of union with Christ which has enabled me to see in science and philosophy the teaching of my Lord. But this same personal experience has made me even more alive to Christ's teaching in Scripture, has made me recognize in Paul and John a truth profounder than that disclosed by any secular writers, truth with regard to sin and atonement for sin, that satisfies the deepest wants of my nature and that is self-evidencing and divine.

I am distressed by some common theological tendencies of our time, because I believe them to be false to both science and religion. How men who have ever felt themselves to be lost sinners and who have once received pardon from their crucified Lord and Savior can thereafter seek to pare down his attributes, deny his deity and atonement, tear from his brow the crown of miracle and sovereignty, relegate him to the place of a merely moral teacher who influences us only as does Socrates by words spoken across a stretch of ages, passes my comprehension. Here is my test of orthodoxy: Do we pray to Jesus? Do we call upon the name of Christ, as did Stephen and all the early church? Is he our living Lord, omnipresent, omniscient, omnipotent? Is he divine only in the sense in which we are divine, or is he the only-begotten Son, God manifest in the flesh, in whom is all the fulness of the Godhead bodily? What think ye of the Christ? is still the critical question, and none are entitled to the name of Christian who, in the face of the evidence he has furnished us, cannot answer the question aright.

Under the influence of Ritschl and his Kantian relativism, many of our teachers and preachers have swung off into a practical denial of Christ's deity and of his atonement. We seem upon the verge of a second Unitarian defection, that will break up churches and compel secessions, in a worse manner than did that of Channing and Ware a century ago. American Christianity recovered from that disaster only by vigorously asserting the authority of Christ and the inspiration of the Scriptures. We need a new vision of the Savior like that which Paul saw on the way to Damascus and John saw on the isle of Patmos, to convince us that Jesus is lifted above space and time, that his existence antedated creation, that he conducted the march of Hebrew history, that he was born of a virgin, suffered on the cross, rose from the dead, and now lives forevermore, the Lord of the universe, the only God with whom we have to do, our Savior here and our Judge hereafter. Without a revival of this faith our churches will become secularized, mission enterprise will die out, and the candlestick will be removed out of its place as it was with the seven churches of Asia, and as it has been with the apostate churches of New England.

I print this revised and enlarged edition of my "Systematic Theology," in the hope that its publication may do something to stem this fast advancing tide, and to confirm the faith of God's elect. I make no doubt that the vast majority of Christians still hold the faith that was once for all delivered to the saints, and that they will sooner or later separate themselves from those who deny the Lord who bought them. When the enemy comes in like a flood, the Spirit of the Lord will raise up a standard against him. I would do my part in raising up such a standard. I would lead others to avow anew, as I do now, in spite of the supercilious assumptions of modern infidelity, my firm belief, only confirmed by the experience and reflection of a half-century, in the old doctrines of holiness as the fundamental attribute of God, of an original transgression and sin of the whole human race, in a divine preparation in Hebrew history for man's redemption, in the deity, preëxistence, virgin birth, vicarious atonement and bodily resurrection of Jesus Christ our Lord, and in his future coming to judge the quick and the dead. I believe that these are truths of science as well as truths of revelation; that the supernatural will yet be seen to be most truly natural; and that not the open-minded theologian but the narrow-minded scientist will be obliged to hide his head at Christ's coming.

The present volume, in its treatment of Ethical Monism, Inspiration, the Attributes of God, and the Trinity, contains an antidote to most of the false doctrine which now threatens the safety of the church. I desire especially to call attention to the section on Perfection, and the Attributes therein involved, because I believe that the recent merging of Holiness in Love, and the practical denial that Righteousness is fundamental in God's nature, are responsible for the utilitarian views of law and the superficial views of sin which now prevail in some systems of theology. There can be no proper doctrine of the atonement and no proper doctrine of retribution, so long as Holiness is refused its preëminence. Love must have a norm or standard, and this norm or standard can be found only in Holiness. The old conviction of sin and the sense of guilt that drove the convicted sinner to the cross are inseparable from a firm belief in the self-affirming attribute of God as logically prior to and as conditioning the self-communicating attribute. The theology of our day needs a new view of the Righteous One. Such a view will make it plain that God must be reconciled before man can be saved, and that the human conscience can be pacified only upon condition that propitiation is made to the divine Righteousness. In this volume I propound what I regard as the true Doctrine of God, because upon it will be based all that follows in the volumes on the Doctrine of Man, and the Doctrine of Salvation.

The universal presence of Christ, the Light that lighteth every man, in heathen as well as in Christian lands, to direct or overrule all movements of the human mind, gives me confidence that the recent attacks upon the Christian faith will fail of their purpose. It becomes evident at last that not only the outworks are assaulted, but the very citadel itself. We are asked to give up all belief in special revelation. Jesus Christ, it is said, has come in the flesh precisely as each one of us has come, and he was before Abraham only in the same sense that we were. Christian experience knows how to characterize such doctrine so soon as it is clearly stated. And the new theology will be of use in enabling even ordinary believers to recognize soul-destroying heresy even under the mask of professed orthodoxy.

I make no apology for the homiletical element in my book. To be either true or useful, theology must be a passion. Pectus est quod theologum facit, and no disdainful cries of "Pectoral Theology!" shall prevent me from maintaining that the eyes of the heart must be enlightened in order to perceive the truth of God, and that to know the truth it is needful to do the truth. Theology is a science which can be successfully cultivated only in connection with its practical application. I would therefore, in every discussion of its principles, point out its relations to Christian experience, and its power to awaken Christian emotions and lead to Christian decisions. Abstract theology is not really scientific. Only that theology is scientific which brings the student to the feet of Christ.

I would hasten the day when in the name of Jesus every knee shall bow. I believe that, if any man serve Christ, him the Father will honor, and that to serve Christ means to honor him as I honor the Father. I would not pride myself that I believe so little, but rather that I believe so much. Faith is God's measure of a man. Why should I doubt that God spoke to the fathers through the prophets? Why should I think it incredible that God should raise the dead? The things that are impossible with men are possible with God. When the Son of man comes, shall he find faith on the earth? Let him at least find faith in us who profess to be his followers. In the conviction that the present darkness is but temporary and that it will be banished by a glorious sunrising, I give this new edition of my "Theology" to the public with the prayer that whatever of good seed is in it may bring forth fruit, and that whatever plant the heavenly Father has not planted may be rooted up.

ROCHESTER THEOLOGICAL SEMINARY, ROCHESTER, N. Y., AUGUST 3, 1906.

PART I - PROLEGOMENA

Chapter I - Idea Of Theology

I. Definition of Theology

Theology is the science of God and of the relations between God and the universe.

Though the word "theology" is sometimes employed in dogmatic writings to designate that single department of the science which treats of the divine nature and attributes, prevailing usage, since Abelard (A. D. 1079-1142) entitled his general treatise "Theologia Christiana," has included under that term the whole range of Christian doctrine. Theology, therefore, gives account, not only of God, but of those relations between God and the universe in view of which we speak of Creation, Providence and Redemption.

John the Evangelist is called by the Fathers "the theologian," because he most fully treats of the internal relations of the persons of the Trinity. Gregory Nazianzen (328) received this designation because he defended the deity of Christ against the Arians. For a modern instance of this use of the term "theology" in the narrow sense, see the title of Dr. Hodge's first volume: "Systematic Theology, Vol. I: Theology." But theology is not simply "the science of God," nor even "the science of God and man." It also gives account of the relations between God and the universe.

If the universe were God, theology would be the only science. Since the universe is but a manifestation of God and is distinct from God, there are sciences of nature and of mind. Theology is "the science of the sciences," not in the sense of including all these sciences, but in the sense of using their results and of showing their underlying ground; (see Wardlaw, Theology, 1:1, 2). Physical science is not a part of theology. As a mere physicist, Humboldt did not need to mention the name of God in his "Cosmos" (but see Cosmos, 2:418, where Humboldt says: "Psalm 104 presents an image of the whole Cosmos"). Bishop of Carlisle: "Science is atheous, and therefore cannot be atheistic."

Only when we consider the relations of finite things to God, does the study of them furnish material for theology. Anthropology is a part of theology, because man's nature is the work of God and because God's dealings with man throw light upon the character of God. God is known through his works and his activities. Theology therefore gives account of these works and activities so far as they come within our knowledge. All other sciences require theology for their complete explanation. Proudhon: "If you go very deeply into politics, you are sure to get into theology." On the definition of theology, see Luthardt, Compendium der Dogmatik, 1:2; Blunt, Dict. Doct. and Hist. Theol., art.: Theology; H. B. Smith, Introd. to Christ. Theol., 44; cf. Aristotle, Metaph., 10, 7, 4; 11, 6, 4; and Lactantius, De Ira Dei, 11.

II. Aim of Theology.

The aim of theology is the ascertainment of the facts respecting God and the relations between God and the universe, and the exhibition of these facts in their rational unity, as connected parts of a formulated and organic system of truth.

In defining theology as a science, we indicate its aim. Science does not create; it discovers. Theology answers to this description of a science. It discovers facts and relations, but it does not create them. Fisher, Nature and Method of Revelation, 141—"Schiller, referring to the ardor of Columbus's faith, says that if the great discoverer had not found a continent, he would have created one. But faith is not creative. Had Columbus not found the land—had there been no real object answering to his belief— his faith would have been a mere fancy." Because theology deals with objective facts, we refuse to define it as "the science of religion"; versus Am. Theol. Rev., 1850:101-126, and Thornwell, Theology, 1:139. Both the facts and the relations with which theology has to deal have an existence independent of the subjective mental processes of the theologian.

Science is not only the observing, recording, verifying, and formulating of objective facts; it is also the recognition and explication of the relations between these facts, and the synthesis of both the facts and the rational principles which unite them in a comprehensive, rightly proportioned, and organic system. Scattered bricks and timbers are not a house; severed arms, legs, heads and trunks from a dissecting room are not living men; and facts alone do not constitute science. Science = facts +

relations; Whewell, Hist. Inductive Sciences, I, Introd., 43—"There may be facts without science, as in the knowledge of the common quarryman; there may be thought without science, as in the early Greek philosophy." A. MacDonald: "The a priori method is related to the a posteriori as the sails to the ballast of the boat: the more philosophy the better, provided there are a sufficient number of facts; otherwise, there is danger of upsetting the craft."

President Woodrow Wilson: " 'Give us the facts' is the sharp injunction of our age to its historians ... But facts of themselves do not constitute the truth. The truth is abstract, not concrete. It is the just idea, the right revelation, of what things mean. It is evoked only by such arrangements and orderings of facts as suggest meanings." Dove, Logic of the Christian Faith, 14—"The pursuit of science is the pursuit of relations." Everett, Science of Thought, 3—"'Logy' (e. g., in "theology"), from λόγος, = word + reason, expression + thought, fact + idea; cf. John 1:1—"In the beginning was the Word."

As theology deals with objective facts and their relations, so its arrangement of these facts is not optional, but is determined by the nature of the material with which it deals. A true theology thinks over again God's thoughts and brings them into God's order, as the builders of Solomon's temple took the stones already hewn, and put them into the places for which the architect had designed them; Reginald Heber: "No hammer fell, no ponderous axes rung; Like some tall palm, the mystic fabric sprung." Scientific men have no fear that the data of physics will narrow or cramp their intellects; no more should they fear the objective facts which are the data of theology. We cannot make theology, any more than we can make a law of physical nature. As the natural philosopher is "Naturæ minister et interpres," so the theologian is the servant and interpreter of the objective truth of God. On the Idea of Theology as a System, see H. B. Smith, Faith and Philosophy, 126-166.

III. Possibility of Theology.

The possibility of theology has a threefold ground: 1. In the existence of a God who has relations to the universe; 2. In the capacity of the human mind for knowing God and certain of these relations; and 3. In the provision of means by which God is brought into actual contact with the mind, or in other words, in the provision of a revelation.

Any particular science is possible only when three conditions combine, namely, the actual existence of the object with which the science deals, the subjective capacity of the human mind to know that object, and the provision of definite means by which the object is brought into contact with the mind. We may illustrate the conditions of theology from selenology—the science, not of "lunar politics," which John Stuart Mill thought so vain a pursuit, but of lunar physics. Selenology has three conditions: 1. the objective existence of the moon; 2. the subjective capacity of the human mind to know the moon; and 3. the provision of some means (e. g., the eye and the telescope) by which the gulf between man and the moon is bridged over, and by which the mind can come into actual cognizance of the facts with regard to the moon.

1. The existence of a God.

In the existence of a God who has relations to the universe.—It has been objected, indeed, that since God and these relations are objects apprehended only by faith, they are not proper objects of knowledge or subjects for science. We reply:

A. Faith is knowledge, and a higher sort of knowledge.—Physical science also rests upon faith— faith in our own existence, in the existence of a world objective and external to us, and in the existence of other persons than ourselves; faith in our primitive convictions, such as space, time, cause, substance, design, right; faith in the trustworthiness of our faculties and in the testimony of our fellow men. But physical science is not thereby invalidated, because this faith, though unlike sense-perception or logical demonstration, is yet a cognitive act of the reason, and may be defined as certitude with respect to matters in which verification is unattainable.

The objection to theology thus mentioned and answered is expressed in the words of Sir William Hamilton, Metaphysics, 44, 531—"Faith—belief—is the organ by which we apprehend what is beyond our knowledge." But science is knowledge, and what is beyond our knowledge cannot be matter for science. Pres. E. G. Robinson says well, that knowledge and faith cannot be severed from one another, like bulkheads in a ship, the first of which may be crushed in, while the second still keeps the vessel afloat. The mind is one,—"it cannot be cut in two with a hatchet." Faith is not antithetical to knowledge,—it is rather a larger and more fundamental sort of knowledge. It is never opposed to reason, but only to sight. Tennyson was wrong when he wrote: "We have but faith: we cannot know; For knowledge is of things we see" (In Memoriam, Introduction). This would make sensuous phenomena the only objects of knowledge. Faith in supersensible realities, on the contrary, is the highest exercise of reason.

Sir William Hamilton consistently declares that the highest achievement of science is the erection of an altar "To the Unknown God." This, however, is not the representation of Scripture. Cf. John 17:3—"this is life eternal, that they should know thee, the only true God"; and Jer. 9:24—"let him that glorieth glory in that he hath understanding and knoweth me." For criticism of Hamilton, see H. B. Smith, Faith and Philosophy, 297-336. Fichte: "We are born in faith." Even Goethe called himself a believer in the five senses. Balfour, Defence of Philosophic Doubt, 277-295, shows that intuitive beliefs in space, time, cause, substance, right, are presupposed in the acquisition of all other knowledge. Dove, Logic of the Christian Faith, 14—"If theology is to be overthrown because it starts from some primary terms and propositions, then all other sciences are overthrown with it." Mozley, Miracles, defines faith as "unverified reason." See A. H. Strong, Philosophy and Religion, 19-30.

B. Faith is a knowledge conditioned by holy affection.—The faith which apprehends God's being and working is not opinion or imagination. It is certitude with regard to spiritual realities, upon the testimony of our rational nature and upon the testimony of God. Its only peculiarity as a cognitive act of the reason is that it is conditioned by holy affection. As the science of æsthetics is a product of reason as including a power of recognizing beauty practically inseparable from a love for beauty, and as the science of ethics is a product of reason as including a power of recognizing the morally right practically inseparable from a love for the morally right, so the science of theology is a product of reason, but of reason as including a power of recognizing God which is practically inseparable from a love for God.

We here use the term "reason" to signify the mind's whole power of knowing. Reason in this sense includes states of the sensibility, so far as they are indispensable to knowledge. We cannot know an orange by the eye alone; to the understanding of it, taste is as necessary as sight. The mathematics of sound cannot give us an understanding of music; we need also a musical ear. Logic alone cannot demonstrate the beauty of a sunset, or of a noble character; love for the beautiful and the right precedes knowledge of the beautiful and the right. Ullman draws attention to the derivation of sapientia, wisdom, from sapěre, to taste. So we cannot know God by intellect alone; the heart must go with the intellect to make knowledge of divine things possible. "Human things," said Pascal, "need only to be known, in order to be loved; but divine things must first be loved, in order to be known." "This [religious] faith of the intellect," said Kant, "is founded on the assumption of moral tempers." If one were utterly indifferent to moral laws, the philosopher continues, even then religious truths "would be supported by strong arguments from analogy, but not by such as an obstinate, sceptical heart might not overcome."

Faith, then, is the highest knowledge, because it is the act of the integral soul, the insight, not of one eye alone, but of the two eyes of the mind, intellect and love to God. With one eye we can see an object as flat, but, if we wish to see around it and get the stereoptic effect, we must use both eyes. It is not the theologian, but the undevout astronomer, whose science is one-eyed and therefore incomplete. The errors of the rationalist are errors of defective vision. Intellect has been divorced from heart, that is, from a right disposition, right affections, right purpose in life. Intellect says: "I cannot know God"; and intellect is right. What intellect says, the Scripture also says: 1 Cor. 2:14—"the natural man receiveth not the things of the Spirit of God: for they are foolishness unto him; and he cannot know them, because they are spiritually judged"; 1:21—"in the wisdom of God the world through its wisdom knew not God."

The Scripture on the other hand declares that "by faith we know" (Heb. 11:3). By "heart" the Scripture means simply the governing disposition, or the sensibility + the will; and it intimates that the heart is an organ of knowledge: Ex. 35:25—"the women that were wise-hearted"; Ps. 34:8—"O taste and see that Jehovah is good" = a right taste precedes correct sight; Jer. 24:7—"I will give them a heart to know me"; Mat. 5:8—"Blessed are the pure in heart; for they shall see God"; Luke 24:25—"slow of heart to believe"; John 7:17—"If any man willeth to do his will, he shall know of the teaching, whether it is of God, or whether I speak from myself"; Eph. 1:18—"having the eyes of your heart enlightened, that ye may know"; 1 John 4:7, 8—"Every one that loveth is begotten of God, and knoweth God. He that loveth not knoweth not God." See Frank, Christian Certainty, 303-324; Clarke, Christ. Theol., 362; Illingworth, Div. and Hum. Personality, 114-137; R. T. Smith, Man's Knowledge of Man and of God, 6; Fisher, Nat. and Method of Rev., 6; William James, The Will to Believe, 1-31; Geo. T. Ladd, on Lotze's view that love is essential to the knowledge of God, in New World, Sept. 1895:401-406; Gunsaulus, Transfig. of Christ, 14, 15.

C. Faith, therefore, can furnish, and only faith can furnish, fit and sufficient material for a scientific theology.—As an operation of man's higher rational nature, though distinct from ocular vision or from reasoning, faith is not only a kind, but the highest kind, of knowing. It gives us understanding of realities which to sense alone are inaccessible, namely, God's existence, and some at least of the relations between God and his creation.

Philippi, Glaubenslehre, 1:50, follows Gerhard in making faith the joint act of intellect and will. Hopkins, Outline Study of Man, 77, 78, speaks not only of "the æsthetic reason" but of "the moral reason." Murphy, Scientific Bases of Faith, 91, 109, 145, 191—"Faith is the certitude concerning matter in which verification is unattainable." Emerson, Essays, 2:96—"Belief consists in accepting the affirmations of the soul—unbelief in rejecting them." Morell, Philos. of Religion, 38, 52, 53, quotes Coleridge: "Faith consists in the synthesis of the reason and of the individual will, ... and by virtue of the former (that is, reason), faith must be a light, a form of knowing, a beholding of truth." Faith, then, is not to be pictured as a blind girl clinging to a cross—faith is not blind—"Else the cross may just as well be a crucifix or an image of Gaudama." "Blind unbelief," not blind faith, "is sure to err, And scan his works in vain." As in conscience we recognize an invisible authority, and know the truth just in proportion to our willingness to "do the truth," so in religion only holiness can understand holiness, and only love can understand love (cf. John 3:21—"he that doeth the truth cometh to the light").

If a right state of heart be indispensable to faith and so to the knowledge of God, can there be any "theologia irregenitorum," or theology of the unregenerate? Yes, we answer; just as the blind man can have a science of optics. The testimony of others gives it claims upon him; the dim light penetrating the obscuring membrane corroborates this testimony. The unregenerate man can know God as power and justice, and can fear him. But this is not a knowledge of God's inmost character; it furnishes some material for a defective and ill-proportioned theology; but it does not furnish fit or sufficient material for a correct theology. As, in order to make his science of optics satisfactory and complete, the blind man must have the cataract removed from his eyes by some competent oculist, so, in order to any complete or satisfactory theology, the veil must be taken away from the heart by God himself (cf. 2 Cor. 3:15, 16—"a veil lieth upon their heart. But whensoever it [marg. 'a man'] shall turn to the Lord, the veil is taken away").

Our doctrine that faith is knowledge and the highest knowledge is to be distinguished from that of Ritschl, whose theology is an appeal to the heart to the exclusion of the head—to fiducia without notitia. But fiducia includes notitia, else it is blind, irrational, and unscientific. Robert Browning, in like manner, fell into a deep speculative error, when, in order to substantiate his optimistic faith, he stigmatized human knowledge as merely apparent. The appeal of both Ritschl and Browning from the head to the heart should rather be an appeal from the narrower knowledge of the mere intellect to the larger knowledge conditioned upon right affection. See A. H. Strong, The Great Poets and their Theology, 441. On Ritschl's postulates, see Stearns, Evidence of Christian Experience, 274-280, and Pfleiderer, Die Ritschl'sche Theologie. On the relation of love and will to knowledge, see Kaftan, in Am. Jour. Theology, 1900:717; Hovey, Manual Christ. Theol., 9; Foundations of our Faith, 12, 13; Shedd, Hist. Doct., 1:154-164; Presb. Quar., Oct. 1871, Oct. 1872, Oct. 1873; Calderwood, Philos. Infinite, 99, 117; Van Oosterzee, Dogmatics, 2-8; New Englander, July, 1873:481; Princeton Rev., 1864:122; Christlieb, Mod. Doubt, 124, 125; Grau, Glaube als höchste Vernunft, in Beweis des Glaubens, 1865:110; Dorner, Gesch. prot. Theol., 228; Newman, Univ. Sermons, 206; Hinton, Art of Thinking, Introd. by Hodgson, 5.

2. Man's capacity for the knowledge of God

In the capacity of the human mind for knowing God and certain of these relations.—But it has urged that such knowledge is impossible for the following reasons:

A. Because we can know only phenomena. We reply: (a) We know mental as well as physical phenomena. (b) In knowing phenomena, whether mental or physical, we know substance as underlying the phenomena, as manifested through them, and as constituting their ground of unity. (c) Our minds bring to the observation of phenomena not only this knowledge of substance, but also knowledge of time, space, cause, and right, realities which are in no sense phenomenal. Since these objects of knowledge are not phenomenal, the fact that God is not phenomenal cannot prevent us from knowing him.

What substance is, we need not here determine. Whether we are realists or idealists, we are compelled to grant that there cannot be phenomena without noumena, cannot be appearances without something that appears, cannot be qualities without something that is qualified. This something which underlies or stands under appearance or quality we call substance. We are Lotzeans rather than Kantians, in our philosophy. To say that we know, not the self, but only its manifestations in thought, is to confound self with its thinking and to teach psychology without a soul. To say that we know no external world, but only its manifestations in sensations, is to ignore the principle that binds these sensations together; for without a somewhat in which qualities inhere they can have no ground of unity. In like manner, to say that we know nothing of God but his manifestations, is to confound God with the world and practically to deny that there is a God.

Stählin, in his work on Kant, Lotze and Ritschl, 186-191, 218, 219, says well that "limitation of knowledge to phenomena involves the elimination from theology of all claim to know the objects of the Christian faith as they are in themselves." This criticism justly classes Ritschl with Kant, rather than with Lotze who maintains that knowing phenomena we know also the noumena manifested in them. While Ritschl professes to follow Lotze, the whole drift of his theology is in the direction of the Kantian identification of the world with our sensations, mind with our thoughts, and God with such activities of his as we can perceive. A divine nature apart from its activities, a preexistent Christ, an immanent Trinity, are practically denied. Assertions that God is self-conscious love and fatherhood become judgments of merely subjective value. On Ritschl, see the works of Orr, of Garvie, and of Swing; also Minton, in Pres. and Ref. Rev., Jan. 1902:162-169, and C. W. Hodge, ibid., Apl. 1902:321-326; Flint,

Agnosticism, 590-597; Everett, Essays Theol. and Lit., 92-99.

We grant that we can know God only so far as his activities reveal him, and so far as our minds and hearts are receptive of his revelation. The appropriate faculties must be exercised—not the mathematical, the logical, or the prudential, but the ethical and the religious. It is the merit of Ritschl that he recognizes the practical in distinction from the speculative reason; his error is in not recognizing that, when we do thus use the proper powers of knowing, we gain not merely subjective but also objective truth, and come in contact not simply with God's activities but also with God himself. Normal religious judgments, though dependent upon subjective conditions, are not simply "judgments of worth" or "value-judgments,"—they give us the knowledge of "things in themselves." Edward Caird says of his brother John Caird (Fund. Ideas of Christianity, Introd. cxxi)—"The conviction that God can be known and is known, and that, in the deepest sense, all our knowledge is knowledge of him, was the corner-stone of his theology."

Ritschl's phenomenalism is allied to the positivism of Comte, who regarded all so-called knowledge of other than phenomenal objects as purely negative. The phrase "Positive Philosophy" implies indeed that all knowledge of mind is negative; see Comte, Pos. Philosophy, Martineau's translation, 26, 28, 33—"In order to observe, your intellect must pause from activity—yet it is this very activity you want to observe. If you cannot effect the pause, you cannot observe; if you do effect it, there is nothing to observe." This view is refuted by the two facts; (1) consciousness, and (2) memory; for consciousness is the knowing of the self side by side with the knowing of its thoughts, and memory is the knowing of the self side by side with the knowing of its past; see Martineau, Essays Philos. and Theol., 1:24-40, 207-212. By phenomena we mean "facts, in distinction from their ground, principle, or law"; "neither phenomena nor qualities, as such, are perceived, but objects, percepts, or beings; and it is by an after-thought or reflex process that these are connected as qualities and are referred to as substances"; see Porter, Human Intellect, 51, 238, 520, 619-637, 640-645.

Phenomena may be internal, e. g., thoughts; in this case the noumenon is the mind, of which these thoughts are the manifestations. Or, phenomena may be external, e. g., color, hardness, shape, size; in this case the noumenon is matter, of which these qualities are the manifestations. But qualities, whether mental or material, imply the existence of a substance to which they belong: they can no more be conceived of as existing apart from substance, than the upper side of a plank can be conceived of as existing without an under side; see Bowne, Review of Herbert Spencer, 47, 207-217; Martineau, Types of Ethical Theory, 1; 455, 456—"Comte's assumption that mind cannot know itself or its states is exactly balanced by Kant's assumption that mind cannot know anything outside of itself.... It is precisely because all knowledge is of relations that it is not and cannot be of phenomena alone. The absolute cannot per se be known, because in being known it would ipso facto enter into relations and be absolute no more. But neither can the phenomenal per se be known, i. e., be known as phenomenal, without simultaneous cognition of what is non-phenomenal." McCosh, Intuitions, 138-154, states the characteristics of substance as (1) being, (2) power, (3) permanence. Diman, Theistic Argument, 337, 363—"The theory that disproves God, disproves an external world and the existence of the soul." We know something beyond phenomena, viz.: law, cause, force,—or we can have no science; see Tulloch, on Comte, in Modern Theories, 53-73; see also Bib. Sac., 1874:211; Alden, Philosophy, 44; Hopkins, Outline Study of Man, 87; Fleming, Vocab. of Philosophy, art.: Phenomena; New Englander, July, 1875:537-539.

B. Because we can know only that which bears analogy to our own nature or experience. We reply: (a) It is not essential to knowledge that there be similarity of nature between the knower and the known. We know by difference as well as by likeness. (b) Our past experience, though greatly facilitating new acquisitions, is not the measure of our possible knowledge. Else the first act of knowledge would be inexplicable, and all revelation of higher characters to lower would be precluded, as well as all progress to knowledge which surpasses our present attainments. (c) Even if knowledge depended upon similarity of nature and experience, we might still know God, since we are made in God's image, and there are important analogies between the divine nature and our own.

(a) The dictum of Empedocles, "Similia similibus percipiuntur," must be supplemented by a second dictum, "Similia dissimilibus percipiuntur." All things are alike, in being objects. But knowing is distinguishing, and there must be contrast between objects to awaken our attention. God knows sin, though it is the antithesis to his holy being. The ego knows the non-ego. We cannot know even self, without objectifying it, distinguishing it from its thoughts, and regarding it as another.

(b) Versus Herbert Spencer, First Principles, 79-82—"Knowledge is recognition and classification." But we reply that a thing must first be perceived in order to be recognized or compared with something else; and this is as true of the first sensation as of the later and more definite forms of knowledge,—indeed there is no sensation which does not involve, as its complement, an at least incipient perception; see Sir William Hamilton, Metaphysics, 351, 352; Porter, Human Intellect, 206.

(c) Porter, Human Intellect, 486—"Induction is possible only upon the assumption that the intellect of man is a reflex of the divine intellect, or that man is made in the image of God." Note, however, that man is made in God's image, not God in man's. The painting is the image of the landscape, not, vice versa, the landscape the image of the painting; for there is much in the landscape that has nothing corresponding to it in the painting. Idolatry perversely makes God in the image of man, and so deifies man's weakness and impurity. Trinity in God may have no exact counterpart in man's present constitution, though it may disclose to us the goal of man's future development and the meaning of the increasing differentiation of man's powers. Gore, Incarnation, 116—"If anthropomorphism as applied to God is false, yet theomorphism as applied to man is true; man is made in God's image, and his qualities are, not the measure of the divine, but their counterpart and real expression." See Murphy, Scientific Bases, 122; McCosh, in Internat. Rev., 1875:105; Bib. Sac., 1867:624; Martineau, Types of Ethical Theory, 2:4-8, and Study of Religion, 1:94.

C. Because we know only that of which we can conceive, in the sense of forming an adequate mental image. We reply: (a) It is true that we know only that of which we can conceive, if by the term "conceive" we mean our distinguishing in thought the object known from all other objects. But, (b) The objection confounds conception with that which is merely its occasional accompaniment and help, namely, the picturing of the object by the imagination. In this sense, conceivability is not a final test of truth. (c) That the formation of a mental image is not essential to conception or knowledge, is plain when we remember that, as a matter of fact, we both conceive and know many things of which we cannot form a mental image of any sort that in the least corresponds to the reality; for example, force, cause, law, space, our own minds. So we may know God, though we cannot form an adequate mental image of him.

The objection here refuted is expressed most clearly in the words of Herbert Spencer, First Principles, 25-36, 98—"The reality underlying appearances is totally and forever inconceivable by us." Mansel, Prolegomena Logica, 77, 78 (cf. 26) suggests the source of this error in a wrong view of the nature of the concept: "The first distinguishing feature of a concept, viz.: that it cannot in itself be depicted to sense or imagination." Porter, Human Intellect, 392 (see also 429, 656)—"The concept is not a mental image"—only the percept is. Lotze: "Color in general is not representable by any image; it looks neither green nor red, but has no look whatever." The generic horse has no particular color, though the individual horse may be black, white, or bay. So Sir William Hamilton speaks of "the unpicturable notions of the intelligence."

Martineau, Religion and Materialism, 39, 40—"This doctrine of Nescience stands in exactly the same relation to causal power, whether you construe it as Material Force or as Divine Agency. Neither can be observed; one or the other must be assumed. If you admit to the category of knowledge only what we learn from observation, particular or generalized, then is Force unknown; if you extend the word to what is imported by the intellect itself into our cognitive acts, to make them such, then is God known." Matter, ether, energy, protoplasm, organism, life,—no one of these can be portrayed to the imagination; yet Mr. Spencer deals with them as objects of Science. If these are not inscrutable, why should he regard the Power that gives unity to all things as inscrutable?

Herbert Spencer is not in fact consistent with himself, for in divers parts of his writings he calls the inscrutable Reality back of phenomena the one, eternal, ubiquitous, infinite, ultimate, absolute Existence, Power and Cause. "It seems," says Father Dalgairns, "that a great deal is known about the Unknowable." Chadwick, Unitarianism, 75—"The beggar phrase 'Unknowable' becomes, after Spencer's repeated designations of it, as rich as Croesus with all saving knowledge." Matheson: "To know that we know nothing is already to have reached a fact of knowledge." If Mr. Spencer intended to exclude God from the realm of Knowledge, he should first have excluded him from the realm of Existence; for to grant that he is, is already to grant that we not only may know him, but that we actually to some extent do know him; see D. J. Hill, Genetic Philosophy, 22; McCosh, Intuitions, 186-189 (Eng. ed., 214); Murphy, Scientific Bases, 133; Bowne, Review of Spencer, 30-34; New Englander, July, 1875:543, 544; Oscar Craig, in Presb. Rev., July, 1883:594-602.

D. Because we can know truly only that which we know in whole and not in part. We reply: (a) The objection confounds partial knowledge with the knowledge of a part. We know the mind in part, but we do not know a part of the mind. (b) If the objection were valid, no real knowledge of anything would be possible, since we know no single thing in all its relations. We conclude that, although God is a being not composed of parts, we may yet have a partial knowledge of him, and this knowledge, though not exhaustive, may yet be real, and adequate to the purposes of science.

(a) The objection mentioned in the text is urged by Mansel, Limits of Religious Thought, 97, 98, and is answered by Martineau, Essays, 1:291. The mind does not exist in space, and it has no parts: we cannot speak of its south-west corner, nor can we divide it into halves. Yet we find the material for mental science in partial knowledge of the mind. So, while we are not "geographers of the divine nature" (Bowne, Review of Spencer, 72), we may say with Paul, not "now know we a part of God," but "now I know [God], in part" (1 Cor. 13:12). We may know truly what we do not know exhaustively; see Eph. 3:19—"to know the love of Christ which passeth knowledge." I do not perfectly understand myself, yet I know myself in part; so I may know God, though I do not perfectly understand him.

(b) The same argument that proves God unknowable proves the universe unknowable also. Since every particle of matter in the universe attracts every other, no one particle can be exhaustively explained without taking account of all the rest. Thomas Carlyle: "It is a mathematical fact that the casting of this pebble from my hand alters the centre of gravity of the universe." Tennyson, Higher Pantheism: "Flower in the crannied wall, I pluck you out of the crannies; Hold you here, root and all, in my hand, Little flower; but if I could understand What you are, root and all, and all in all, I should know what God and man is." Schurman, Agnosticism, 119—"Partial as it is, this vision of the divine transfigures the life of man on earth." Pfleiderer, Philos. Religion, 1:167—"A faint-hearted agnosticism is worse than the arrogant and titanic gnosticism against which it protests."

E. Because all predicates of God are negative, and therefore furnish no real knowledge. We answer: (a) Predicates derived from our consciousness, such as spirit, love, and holiness, are positive. (b) The terms "infinite" and "absolute," moreover, express not merely a negative but a positive idea— the idea, in the former case, of the absence of all limit, the idea that the object thus described goes on and on forever; the idea, in the latter case, of entire self-sufficiency. Since predicates of God, therefore, are not merely negative, the argument mentioned above furnishes no valid reason why we may not know him.

Versus Sir William Hamilton, Metaphysics, 530—"The absolute and the infinite can each only be conceived as a negation of the thinkable; in other words, of the absolute and infinite we have no conception at all." Hamilton here confounds the infinite, or the absence of all limits, with the indefinite, or the absence of all known limits. Per contra, see Calderwood, Moral Philosophy, 248, and Philosophy of the Infinite, 272—"Negation of one thing is possible only by affirmation of another." Porter, Human Intellect, 652—"If the Sandwich Islanders, for lack of name, had called the ox a not-hog, the use of a negative appellation would not necessarily authorize the inference of a want of definite conceptions or positive knowledge." So with the infinite or not-finite, the unconditioned or not-conditioned, the independent or not-dependent,—these names do not imply that we cannot conceive and know it as something positive. Spencer, First Principles, 92—"Our consciousness of the Absolute, indefinite though it is, is positive, and not negative."

Schurman, Agnosticism, 100, speaks of "the farce of nescience playing at omniscience in setting the bounds of science." "The agnostic," he says, "sets up the invisible picture of a Grand Être, formless and colorless in itself, absolutely separated from man and from the world—blank within and void without—its very existence indistinguishable from its non-existence, and, bowing down before this idolatrous creation, he pours out his soul in lamentations over the incognizableness of such a mysterious and awful non-entity.... The truth is that the agnostic's abstraction of a Deity is unknown, only because it is unreal." See McCosh, Intuitions, 194, note; Mivart, Lessons from Nature, 363. God is not necessarily infinite in every respect. He is infinite only in every excellence. A plane which is unlimited in the one respect of length may be limited in another respect, such as breadth. Our doctrine here is not therefore inconsistent with what immediately follows.

F. Because to know is to limit or define. Hence the Absolute as unlimited, and the Infinite as undefined, cannot be known. We answer: (a) God is absolute, not as existing in no relation, but as existing in no necessary relation; and (b) God is infinite, not as excluding all coexistence of the finite with himself, but as being the ground of the finite, and so unfettered by it. (c) God is actually limited by the unchangeableness of his own attributes and personal distinctions, as well as by his self-chosen relations to the universe he has created and to humanity in the person of Christ. God is therefore limited and defined in such a sense as to render knowledge of him possible.

Versus Mansel, Limitations of Religious Thought, 75-84, 93-95; cf. Spinoza: "Omnis determinatio est negatio;" hence to define God is to deny him. But we reply that perfection is inseparable from limitation. Man can be other than he is: not so God, at least internally. But this limitation, inherent in his unchangeable attributes and personal distinctions, is God's perfection. Externally, all limitations upon God are self-limitations, and so are consistent with his perfection. That God should not be able thus to limit himself in creation and redemption would render all self-sacrifice in him impossible, and so would subject him to the greatest of limitations. We may say therefore that God's 1. Perfection involves his limitation to (a) personality, (b) trinity, (c) righteousness; 2. Revelation involves his self-limitation in (a) decree, (b) creation, (c) preservation, (d) government, (e) education of the world; 3. Redemption involves his infinite self-limitation in the (a) person and (b) work of Jesus Christ; see A. H. Strong, Christ in Creation, 87-101, and in Bap. Quar. Rev., Jan. 1891:521-532.

Bowne, Philos. of Theism, 135—"The infinite is not the quantitative all; the absolute is not the unrelated.... Both absolute and infinite mean only the independent ground of things." Julius Müller, Doct. Sin, Introduc., 10—"Religion has to do, not with an Object that must let itself be known because its very existence is contingent upon its being known, but with the Object in relation to whom we are truly subject, dependent upon him, and waiting until he manifest himself." James Martineau, Study of Religion, 1:346—"We must not confound the infinite with the total.... The self-abnegation of infinity is but a form of self-assertion, and the only form in which it can reveal itself.... However instantaneous the omniscient thought, however sure the almighty power, the execution has to be distributed in time, and must have an order of successive steps; on no other terms can the eternal become temporal, and the infinite articulately speak in the finite."

Perfect personality excludes, not self-determination, but determination from without, determination by another. God's self-limitations are the self-limitations of love, and therefore the evidences of his perfection. They are signs, not of weakness but of power. God has limited himself to the method of evolution, gradually unfolding himself in nature and in history. The government of sinners by a holy God involves constant self-repression. The education of the race is a long process of divine forbearance; Herder: "The limitations of the pupil are limitations of the teacher also." In inspiration, God limits himself by the human element through which he works. Above all, in the person and work of Christ, we have infinite self-limitation: Infinity narrows itself down to a point in the incarnation, and holiness endures the agonies of the Cross. God's promises are also self-limitations. Thus both nature and grace are self-imposed restrictions upon God, and these self-limitations are the means by which he reveals himself. See Pfleiderer, Die Religion, 1:189, 195; Porter, Human Intellect, 653; Murphy, Scientific Bases, 130; Calderwood, Philos. Infinite, 168; McCosh, Intuitions, 186; Hickok, Rational Cosmology, 85; Martineau, Study of Religion, 2:85, 86, 362; Shedd, Dogmatic Theology, 1:189-191.

G. Because all knowledge is relative to the knowing agent; that is, what we know, we know, not as it is objectively, but only as it is related to our own senses and faculties. In reply: (a) We grant that we can know only that which has relation to our faculties. But this is simply to say that we know only that which we come into mental contact with, that is, we know only what we know. But, (b) We deny that what we come into mental contact with is known by us as other than it is. So far as it is known at all, it is known as it is. In other words, the laws of our knowing are not merely arbitrary and regulative, but correspond to the nature of things. We conclude that, in theology, we are equally warranted in assuming that the laws of our thought are laws of God's thought, and that the results of normally conducted thinking with regard to God correspond to the objective reality.

Versus Sir Wm. Hamilton, Metaph., 96-116, and Herbert Spencer, First Principles, 68-97. This doctrine of relativity is derived from Kant, Critique of Pure Reason, who holds that a priori judgments are simply "regulative." But we reply that when our primitive beliefs are found to be simply regulative, they will cease to regulate. The forms of thought are also facts of nature. The mind does not, like the glass of a kaleidoscope, itself furnish the forms; it recognizes these as having an existence external to itself. The mind reads its ideas, not into nature, but in nature. Our intuitions are not green goggles, which make all the world seem green: they are the lenses of a microscope, which enable us to see what is objectively real (Royce, Spirit of Mod. Philos., 125). Kant called our understanding "the legislator of nature." But it is so, only as discoverer of nature's laws, not as creator of them. Human reason does impose its laws and forms upon the universe; but, in doing this, it interprets the real meaning of the universe.

Ladd, Philos. of Knowledge: "All judgment implies an objective truth according to which we judge, which constitutes the standard, and with which we have something in common, i. e., our minds are part of an infinite and eternal Mind." French aphorism: "When you are right, you are more right than you think you are." God will not put us to permanent intellectual confusion. Kant vainly wrote "No thoroughfare" over the reason in its highest exercise. Martineau, Study of Religion, 1:135, 136—"Over against Kant's assumption that the mind cannot know anything outside of itself, we may set Comte's equally unwarrantable assumption that the mind cannot know itself or its states. We cannot have philosophy without assumptions. You dogmatize if you say that the forms correspond with reality; but you equally dogmatize if you say that they do not.... 79—That our cognitive faculties correspond to things as they are, is much less surprising than that they should correspond to things as they are not." W. T. Harris, in Journ. Spec. Philos., 1:22, exposes Herbert Spencer's self-contradiction: "All knowledge is, not absolute, but relative; our knowledge of this fact however is, not relative, but absolute."

Ritschl, Justification and Reconciliation, 3:16-21, sets out with a correct statement of the nature of knowledge, and gives in his adhesion to the doctrine of Lotze, as distinguished from that of Kant. Ritschl's statement may be summarized as follows: "We deal, not with the abstract God of metaphysics, but with the God self-limited, who is revealed in Christ. We do not know either things or God apart from their phenomena or manifestations, as Plato imagined; we do not know phenomena or manifestations alone, without knowing either things or God, as Kant supposed; but we do know both things and God in their phenomena or manifestations, as Lotze taught. We hold to no mystical union with God, back of all experience in religion, as Pietism does; soul is always and only active, and religion is the activity of the human spirit, in which feeling, knowing and willing combine in an intelligible order."

But Dr. C. M. Mead, Ritschl's Place in the History of Doctrine, has well shown that Ritschl has not followed Lotze. His "value-judgments" are simply an application to theology of the "regulative" principle of Kant. He holds that we can know things not as they are in themselves, but only as they are for us. We reply that what things are worth for us depends on what they are in themselves. Ritschl regards the doctrines of Christ's preexistence, divinity and atonement as intrusions of metaphysics into theology, matters about which we cannot know, and with which we have nothing to do. There is no propitiation or mystical union with Christ; and Christ is our Example, but not our atoning Savior. Ritschl does well in recognizing that love in us gives eyes to the mind, and enables us to see the beauty of Christ and his truth. But our judgment is not, as he holds, a merely subjective value-judgment,—it is a coming in contact with objective fact. On the theory of knowledge held by Kant, Hamilton and Spencer, see Bishop Temple, Bampton Lectures for 1884:13; H. B. Smith, Faith and Philosophy, 297-336; J. S. Mill, Examination, 1:113-134; Herbert, Modern Realism Examined; M. B. Anderson, art.: "Hamilton," in Johnson's Encyclopædia; McCosh, Intuitions, 139-146, 340, 341, and Christianity and Positivism, 97-123; Maurice, What is Revelation? Alden, Intellectual Philosophy, 48-79, esp. 71-79; Porter, Hum. Intellect, 523; Murphy, Scientific Bases, 103; Bib. Sac. April, 1868:341; Princeton Rev., 1864:122; Bowne, Review of Herbert Spencer, 76; Bowen, in Princeton Rev., March, 1878:445-448; Mind, April, 1878:257; Carpenter, Mental Physiology, 117; Harris, Philos. Basis of Theism, 109-113; Iverach, in Present Day Tracts, 5: No. 29; Martineau, Study of Religion, 1:79, 120, 121, 135, 136.

3. God's revelation of himself to man.

In God's actual revelation of himself and certain of these relations.—As we do not in this place attempt a positive proof of God's existence or of man's capacity for the knowledge of God, so we do not now attempt to prove that God has brought himself into contact with man's mind by revelation. We shall consider the grounds of this belief hereafter. Our aim at present is simply to show that, granting the fact of revelation, a scientific theology is possible. This has been denied upon the following grounds:

A. That revelation, as a making known, is necessarily internal and subjective—either a mode of intelligence, or a quickening of man's cognitive powers—and hence can furnish no objective facts such as constitute the proper material for science.

Morell, Philos. Religion, 128-131, 143—"The Bible cannot in strict accuracy of language be called a revelation, since a revelation always implies an actual process of intelligence in a living mind." F. W. Newman, Phases of Faith, 152—"Of our moral and spiritual God we know nothing without—everything within." Theodore Parker: "Verbal revelation can never communicate a simple idea like that of God, Justice, Love, Religion"; see review of Parker in Bib. Sac., 18:24-27. James Martineau, Seat of Authority in Religion: "As many minds as there are that know God at first hand, so many revealing acts there have been, and as many as know him at second hand are strangers to revelation"; so, assuming external revelation to be impossible, Martineau subjects all the proofs of such revelation to unfair destructive criticism. Pfleiderer, Philos. Religion, 1:185—"As all revelation is originally an inner living experience, the springing up of religious truth in the heart, no external event can belong in itself to revelation, no matter whether it be naturally or supernaturally brought about." Professor George M. Forbes: "Nothing can be revealed to us which we do not grasp with our reason. It follows that, so far as reason acts normally, it is a part of revelation." Ritchie, Darwin and Hegel, 30—"The revelation of God is the growth of the idea of God."

In reply to this objection, urged mainly by idealists in philosophy, (a) We grant that revelation, to be effective, must be the means of inducing a new mode of intelligence, or in other words, must be understood. We grant that this understanding of divine things is impossible without a quickening of man's cognitive powers. We grant, moreover, that revelation, when originally imparted, was often internal and subjective.

Matheson, Moments on the Mount, 51-53, on Gal. 1:16—"to reveal his Son in me": "The revelation on the way to Damascus would not have enlightened Paul, had it been merely a vision to his eye. Nothing can be revealed to us which has not been revealed in us. The eye does not see the beauty of the landscape, nor the ear hear the beauty of music. So flesh and blood do not reveal Christ to us. Without the teaching of the Spirit, the external facts will be only like the letters of a book to a child that cannot read." We may say with Channing: "I am more sure that my rational nature is from God, than that any book is the expression of his will."

(b) But we deny that external revelation is therefore useless or impossible. Even if religious ideas sprang wholly from within, an external revelation might stir up the dormant powers of the mind. Religious ideas, however, do not spring wholly from within. External revelation can impart them. Man can reveal himself to man by external communications, and, if God has equal power with man, God can reveal himself to man in like manner.

Rogers, in his Eclipse of Faith, asks pointedly: "If Messrs. Morell and Newman can teach by a book, cannot God do the same?" Lotze, Microcosmos, 2:660 (book 9, chap. 4), speaks of revelation as "either contained in some divine act of historic occurrence, or continually repeated in men's hearts." But in fact there is no alternative here; the strength of the Christian creed is that God's revelation is both external and internal; see Gore, in Lux Mundi, 338. Rainy, in Critical Review, 1:1-21, well says that Martineau unwarrantably isolates the witness of God to the individual soul. The inward needs to be combined with the outward, in order to make sure that it is not a vagary of the imagination. We need to distinguish God's revelations from our own fancies. Hence, before giving the internal, God commonly gives us the external, as a standard by which to try our impressions. We are finite and sinful, and we need authority. The external revelation commends itself as authoritative to the heart which recognizes its own spiritual needs. External authority evokes the inward witness and gives added clearness to it, but only historical revelation furnishes indubitable proof that God is love, and gives us assurance that our longings after God are not in vain.

(c) Hence God's revelation may be, and, as we shall hereafter see, it is, in great part, an external revelation in works and words. The universe is a revelation of God; God's works in nature precede God's words in history. We claim, moreover, that, in many cases where truth was originally communicated internally, the same Spirit who communicated it has brought about an external record of it, so that the internal revelation might be handed down to others than those who first received it.

We must not limit revelation to the Scriptures. The eternal Word antedated the written word, and through the eternal Word God is made known in nature and in history. Internal revelation is preceded by, and conditioned upon, external revelation. In point of time earth comes before man, and sensation before perception. Action best expresses character, and historic revelation is more by deeds than by words. Dorner, Hist. Prot. Theol., 1:231-264—"The Word is not in the Scriptures alone. The whole creation reveals the Word. In nature God shows his power; in incarnation his grace and truth. Scripture testifies of these, but Scripture is not the essential Word. The Scripture is truly apprehended and appropriated when in it and through it we see the living and present Christ. It does not bind men to itself alone, but it points them to the Christ of whom it testifies. Christ is the authority. In the Scriptures he points us to himself and demands our faith in him. This faith, once begotten, leads us to new appropriation of Scripture, but also to new criticism of Scripture. We find Christ more and more in Scripture, and yet we judge Scripture more and more by the standard which we find in Christ."

Newman Smyth, Christian Ethics, 71-82: "There is but one authority—Christ. His Spirit works in many ways, but chiefly in two: first, the inspiration of the Scriptures, and, secondly, the leading of the church into the truth. The latter is not to be isolated or separated from the former. Scripture is law to the Christian consciousness, and Christian consciousness in time becomes law to the Scripture— interpreting, criticizing, verifying it. The word and the spirit answer to each other. Scripture and faith are coördinate. Protestantism has exaggerated the first; Romanism the second. Martineau fails to grasp the coördination of Scripture and faith."

(d) With this external record we shall also see that there is given under proper conditions a special influence of God's Spirit, so to quicken our cognitive powers that the external record reproduces in our minds the ideas with which the minds of the writers were at first divinely filled.

We may illustrate the need of internal revelation from Egyptology, which is impossible so long as the external revelation in the hieroglyphics is uninterpreted; from the ticking of the clock in a dark room, where only the lit candle enables us to tell the time; from the landscape spread out around the Rigi in Switzerland, invisible until the first rays of the sun touch the snowy mountain peaks. External revelation (φανέρωσις, Rom. 1:19, 20) must be supplemented by internal revelation (ἀποκάλυψις, 1 Cor. 2:10, 12). Christ is the organ of external, the Holy Spirit the organ of internal, revelation. In Christ (2 Cor. 1:20) are "the yea" and "the Amen"—the objective certainty and the subjective certitude, the reality and the realization.

Objective certainty must become subjective certitude in order to be a scientific theology. Before conversion we have the first, the external truth of Christ; only at conversion and after conversion do we have the second, "Christ formed in us" (Gal. 4:19). We have objective revelation at Sinai (Ex. 20:22); subjective revelation in Elisha's knowledge of Gehazi (2 K. 5:26). James Russell Lowell, Winter Evening Hymn to my Fire: "Therefore with thee I love to read Our brave old poets: at thy touch how stirs Life in the withered words! how swift recede Time's shadows! and how glows again Through its dead mass the incandescent verse, As when upon the anvil of the brain It glittering lay, cyclopically wrought By the fast throbbing hammers of the poet's thought!"

(e) Internal revelations thus recorded, and external revelations thus interpreted, both furnish objective facts which may serve as proper material for science. Although revelation in its widest sense may include, and as constituting the ground of the possibility of theology does include, both insight and illumination, it may also be used to denote simply a provision of the external means of knowledge, and theology has to do with inward revelations only as they are expressed in, or as they agree with, this objective standard.

We have here suggested the vast scope and yet the insuperable limitations of theology. So far as God is revealed, whether in nature, history, conscience, or Scripture, theology may find material for its structure. Since Christ is not simply the incarnate Son of God but also the eternal Word, the only Revealer of God, there is no theology apart from Christ, and all theology is Christian theology. Nature and history are but the dimmer and more general disclosures of the divine Being, of which the Cross is the culmination and the key. God does not intentionally conceal himself. He wishes to be known. He reveals himself at all times just as fully as the capacity of his creatures will permit. The infantile intellect cannot understand God's boundlessness, nor can the perverse disposition understand God's disinterested affection. Yet all truth is in Christ and is open to discovery by the prepared mind and heart.

The Infinite One, so far as he is unrevealed, is certainly unknowable to the finite. But the Infinite One, so far as he manifests himself, is knowable. This suggests the meaning of the declarations: John 1:18—"No man hath seen God at any time; the only begotten Son, who is in the bosom of the Father, he hath declared him"; 14:9—"he that hath seen me hath seen the Father"; 1 Tim. 6:16—"whom no man hath seen, nor can see." We therefore approve of the definition of Kaftan, Dogmatik, 1—"Dogmatics is the science of the Christian truth which is believed and acknowledged in the church upon the ground of the divine revelation"—in so far as it limits the scope of theology to truth revealed by God and apprehended by faith. But theology presupposes both God's external and God's internal revelations, and these, as we shall see, include nature, history, conscience and Scripture. On the whole subject, see Kahnis, Dogmatik, 3:37-43; Nitzsch, System Christ. Doct., 72; Luthardt, Fund. Truths, 193; Auberlen, Div. Rev., Introd., 29; Martineau, Essays, 1:171, 280; Bib. Sac., 1867:593, and 1872:428; Porter, Human Intellect, 373-375; C. M. Mead, in Boston Lectures, 1871:58.

B. That many of the truths thus revealed are too indefinite to constitute the material for science, because they belong to the region of the feelings, because they are beyond our full understanding, or because they are destitute of orderly arrangement.

We reply:

(a) Theology has to do with subjective feelings only as they can be defined, and shown to be effects of objective truth upon the mind. They are not more obscure than are the facts of morals or of psychology, and the same objection which would exclude such feelings from theology would make these latter sciences impossible.

See Jacobi and Schleiermacher, who regard theology as a mere account of devout Christian feelings, the grounding of which in objective historical facts is a matter of comparative indifference (Hagenbach, Hist. Doctrine, 2:401-403). Schleiermacher therefore called his system of theology "Der Christliche Glaube," and many since his time have called their systems by the name of "Glaubenslehre." Ritschl's "value-judgments," in like manner, render theology a merely subjective science, if any subjective science is possible. Kaftan improves upon Ritschl, by granting that we know, not only Christian feelings, but also Christian facts. Theology is the science of God, and not simply the science of faith. Allied to the view already mentioned is that of Feuerbach, to whom religion is a matter of subjective fancy; and that of Tyndall, who would remit theology to the region of vague feeling and aspiration, but would exclude it from the realm of science; see Feuerbach, Essence of Christianity, translated by Marian Evans (George Eliot); also Tyndall, Belfast Address.

(b) Those facts of revelation which are beyond our full understanding may, like the nebular hypothesis in astronomy, the atomic theory in chemistry, or the doctrine of evolution in biology, furnish a principle of union between great classes of other facts otherwise irreconcilable. We may define our concepts of God, and even of the Trinity, at least sufficiently to distinguish them from all other concepts; and whatever difficulty may encumber the putting of them into language only shows the importance of attempting it and the value of even an approximate success.

Horace Bushnell: "Theology can never be a science, on account of the infirmities of language." But this principle would render void both ethical and political science. Fisher, Nat. and Meth. of Revelation, 145—"Hume and Gibbon refer to faith as something too sacred to rest on proof. Thus religious beliefs are made to hang in mid-air, without any support. But the foundation of these beliefs is no less solid for the reason that empirical tests are not applicable to them. The data on which they rest are real, and the inferences from the data are fairly drawn." Hodgson indeed pours contempt on the whole intuitional method by saying: "Whatever you are totally ignorant of, assert to be the explanation of everything else!" Yet he would probably grant that he begins his investigations by assuming his own existence. The doctrine of the Trinity is not wholly comprehensible by us, and we accept it at the first upon the testimony of Scripture; the full proof of it is found in the fact that each successive doctrine of theology is bound up with it, and with it stands or falls. The Trinity is rational because it explains Christian experience as well as Christian doctrine.

(c) Even though there were no orderly arrangement of these facts, either in nature or in Scripture, an accurate systematizing of them by the human mind would not therefore be proved impossible, unless a principle were assumed which would show all physical science to be equally impossible. Astronomy and geology are constructed by putting together multitudinous facts which at first sight seem to have no order. So with theology. And yet, although revelation does not present to us a dogmatic system ready-made, a dogmatic system is not only implicitly contained therein, but parts of the system are wrought out in the epistles of the New Testament, as for example in Rom. 5:12-19; 1 Cor. 15:3, 4; 8:6; 1 Tim. 3:16; Heb. 6:1, 2.

We may illustrate the construction of theology from the dissected map, two pieces of which a father puts together, leaving his child to put together the rest. Or we may illustrate from the physical universe, which to the unthinking reveals little of its order. "Nature makes no fences." One thing seems to glide into another. It is man's business to distinguish and classify and combine. Origen: "God gives us truth in single threads, which we must weave into a finished texture." Andrew Fuller said of the doctrines of theology that "they are united together like chain-shot, so that, whichever one enters the heart, the others must certainly follow." George Herbert: "Oh that I knew how all thy lights combine, And the configuration of their glory; Seeing not only how each verse doth shine, But all the constellations of the story!"

Scripture hints at the possibilities of combination, in Rom. 5:12-19, with its grouping of the facts of sin and salvation about the two persons, Adam and Christ; in Rom. 4:24, 25, with its linking of the resurrection of Christ and our justification; in 1 Cor. 3:6, with its indication of the relations between the Father and Christ; in 1 Tim. 3:16, with its poetical summary of the facts of redemption (see Commentaries of DeWette, Meyer, Fairbairn); in Heb. 6:1, 2, with its statement of the first principles of the Christian faith. God's furnishing of concrete facts in theology, which we ourselves are left to systematize, is in complete accordance with his method of procedure with regard to the development of other sciences. See Martineau, Essays, 1:29, 40; Am. Theol. Rev., 1859:101-126—art. on the Idea, Sources and Uses of Christian Theology.

IV. Necessity of Theology

The necessity of theology has its grounds:

(a) In the organizing instinct of the human mind. This organizing principle is a part of our constitution. The mind cannot endure confusion or apparent contradiction in known facts. The tendency to harmonize and unify its knowledge appears as soon as the mind becomes reflective; just in proportion to its endowments and culture does the impulse to systematize and formulate increase. This is true of all departments of human inquiry, but it is peculiarly true of our knowledge of God. Since the truth with regard to God is the most important of all, theology meets the deepest want of man's rational nature. Theology is a rational necessity. If all existing theological systems were destroyed to-day, new systems would rise to-morrow. So inevitable is the operation of this law, that those who most decry theology show nevertheless that they have made a theology for themselves, and often one sufficiently meagre and blundering. Hostility to theology, where it does not originate in mistaken fears for the corruption of God's truth or in a naturally illogical structure of mind, often proceeds from a license of speculation which cannot brook the restraints of a complete Scriptural system.

President E. G. Robinson: "Every man has as much theology as he can hold." Consciously or unconsciously, we philosophize, as naturally as we speak prose. "Se moquer de la philosophie c'est vraiment philosopher." Gore, Incarnation, 21—"Christianity became metaphysical, only because man is rational. This rationality means that he must attempt 'to give account of things,' as Plato said, 'because he was a man, not merely because he was a Greek.' " Men often denounce systematic theology, while they extol the sciences of matter. Has God then left only the facts with regard to himself in so unrelated a state that man cannot put them together? All other sciences are valuable only as they contain or promote the knowledge of God. If it is praiseworthy to classify beetles, one science may be allowed to reason concerning God and the soul. In speaking of Schelling, Royce, Spirit of Modern Philosophy, 173, satirically exhorts us: "Trust your genius; follow your noble heart; change your doctrine whenever your heart changes, and change your heart often,—such is the practical creed of the romanticists." Ritchie, Darwin and Hegel, 3—"Just those persons who disclaim metaphysics are sometimes most apt to be infected with the disease they profess to abhor—and not to know when they have it." See Shedd, Discourses and Essays, 27-52; Murphy, Scientific Bases of Faith, 195-199.

(b) In the relation of systematic truth to the development of character. Truth thoroughly digested is essential to the growth of Christian character in the individual and in the church. All knowledge of God has its influence upon character, but most of all the knowledge of spiritual facts in their relations. Theology cannot, as has sometimes been objected, deaden the religious affections, since it only draws out from their sources and puts into rational connection with each other the truths which are best adapted to nourish the religions affections. On the other hand, the strongest Christians are those who have the firmest grasp upon the great doctrines of Christianity; the heroic ages of the church are those which have witnessed most consistently to them; the piety that can be injured by the systematic exhibition of them must be weak, or mystical, or mistaken.

Some knowledge is necessary to conversion—at least, knowledge of sin and knowledge of a Savior; and the putting together of these two great truths is a beginning of theology. All subsequent growth of character is conditioned upon the increase of this knowledge. Col. 1:10—αὐξανόμενοι τῇ ἐπιγνώσει τοῦ Θεοῦ [omit ἐν] = "increasing by the knowledge of God"—the instrumental dative represents the knowledge of God as the dew or rain which nurtures the growth of the plant; cf. 3 Pet. 3:18—"grow in the grace and knowledge of our Lord and Savior Jesus Christ." For texts which represent truth as nourishment, see Jer. 3:15—"feed you with knowledge and understanding"; Mat. 4:4—"Man shall not live by bread alone, but by every word that proceedeth out of the mouth of God"; 1

Cor. 3:1, 2—"babes in Christ ... I fed you with milk, not with meat"; Heb. 5:14—"but solid food is for full-grown men." Christian character rests upon Christian truth as its foundation; see 1 Cor. 3:10-15—"I laid a foundation, and another buildeth thereon." See Dorus Clarke, Saying the Catechism; Simon, on Christ Doct. and Life, in Bib. Sac., July, 1884:433-439.

Ignorance is the mother of superstition, not of devotion. Talbot W. Chambers:—"Doctrine without duty is a tree without fruits; duty without doctrine is a tree without roots." Christian morality is a fruit which grows only from the tree of Christian doctrine. We cannot long keep the fruits of faith after we have cut down the tree upon which they have grown. Balfour, Foundations of Belief, 82—"Naturalistic virtue is parasitic, and when the host perishes, the parasite perishes also. Virtue without religion will die." Kidd, Social Evolution, 214—"Because the fruit survives for a time when removed from the tree, and even mellows and ripens, shall we say that it is independent of the tree?" The twelve manner of fruits on the Christmas-tree are only tacked on,—they never grew there, and they can never reproduce their kind. The withered apple swells out under the exhausted receiver, but it will go back again to its former shrunken form; so the self-righteousness of those who get out of the atmosphere of Christ and have no divine ideal with which to compare themselves. W. M. Lisle: "It is the mistake and disaster of the Christian world that effects are sought instead of causes." George A. Gordon, Christ of To-day, 28—"Without the historical Christ and personal love for that Christ, the broad theology of our day will reduce itself to a dream, powerless to rouse a sleeping church."

(c) In the importance to the preacher of definite and just views of Christian doctrine. His chief intellectual qualification must be the power clearly and comprehensively to conceive, and accurately and powerfully to express, the truth. He can be the agent of the Holy Spirit in converting and sanctifying men, only as he can wield "the sword of the Spirit, which is the word of God" (Eph. 6:17), or, in other language, only as he can impress truth upon the minds and consciences of his hearers. Nothing more certainly nullifies his efforts than confusion and inconsistency in his statements of doctrine. His object is to replace obscure and erroneous conceptions among his hearers by those which are correct and vivid. He cannot do this without knowing the facts with regard to God in their relations—knowing them, in short, as parts of a system. With this truth he is put in trust. To mutilate it or misrepresent it, is not only sin against the Revealer of it,—it may prove the ruin of men's souls. The best safeguard against such mutilation or misrepresentation, is the diligent study of the several doctrines of the faith in their relations to one another, and especially to the central theme of theology, the person and work of Jesus Christ.

The more refined and reflective the age, the more it requires reasons for feeling. Imagination, as exercised in poetry and eloquence and as exhibited in politics or war, is not less strong than of old,—it is only more rational. Notice the progress from "Buncombe", in legislative and forensic oratory, to sensible and logical address. Bassanio in Shakespeare's Merchant of Venice, 1:1:113—"Gratiano speaks an infinite deal of nothing.... His reasons are as two grains of wheat hid in two bushels of chaff." So in pulpit oratory, mere Scripture quotation and fervid appeal are no longer sufficient. As well be a howling dervish, as to indulge in windy declamation. Thought is the staple of preaching. Feeling must be roused, but only by bringing men to "the knowledge of the truth" (2 Tim. 2:25). The preacher must furnish the basis for feeling by producing intelligent conviction. He must instruct before he can move. If the object of the preacher is first to know God, and secondly to make God known, then the study of theology is absolutely necessary to his success.

Shall the physician practice medicine without study of physiology, or the lawyer practice law without study of jurisprudence? Professor Blackie: "One may as well expect to make a great patriot out of a fencing-master, as to make a great orator out of a mere rhetorician." The preacher needs doctrine, to prevent his being a mere barrel-organ, playing over and over the same tunes. John Henry Newman: "The false preacher is one who has to say something; the true preacher is one who has something to say." Spurgeon, Autobiography, 1:167—"Constant change of creed is sure loss. If a tree has to be taken up two or three times a year, you will not need to build a very large loft in which to store the apples. When people are shifting their doctrinal principles, they do not bring forth much fruit.... We shall never have great preachers till we have great divines. You cannot build a man of war out of a currant-bush, nor can great soul-moving preachers be formed out of superficial students." Illustrate the harmfulness of ignorant and erroneous preaching, by the mistake in a physician's prescription; by the wrong trail at Lake Placid which led astray those ascending Whiteface; by the sowing of acorns whose crop was gathered only after a hundred years. Slight divergences from correct doctrine on our part may be ruinously exaggerated in those who come after us. Though the moth-miller has no teeth, its offspring has. 2 Tim. 2:2—"And the things which thou hast heard from me among many witnesses, the same commit thou to faithful men, who shall be able to teach others also."

(d) In the intimate connection between correct doctrine and the safety and aggressive power of the church. The safety and progress of the church is dependent upon her "holding the pattern of sound words" (2 Tim. 1:13), and serving as "pillar and ground of the truth" (1 Tim. 3:15). Defective understanding of the truth results sooner or later in defects of organization, of operation, and of life.

Thorough comprehension of Christian truth as an organized system furnishes, on the other hand, not only an invaluable defense against heresy and immorality, but also an indispensable stimulus and instrument in aggressive labor for the world's conversion.

The creeds of Christendom have not originated in mere speculative curiosity and logical hair-splitting. They are statements of doctrine in which the attacked and imperiled church has sought to express the truth which constitutes her very life. Those who deride the early creeds have small conception of the intellectual acumen and the moral earnestness which went to the making of them. The creeds of the third and fourth centuries embody the results of controversies which exhausted the possibilities of heresy with regard to the Trinity and the person of Christ, and which set up bars against false doctrine to the end of time. Mahaffy: "What converted the world was not the example of Christ's life,—it was the dogma of his death." Coleridge: "He who does not withstand, has no standing ground of his own." Mrs. Browning: "Entire intellectual toleration is the mark of those who believe nothing." E. G. Robinson, Christian Theology, 360-362—"A doctrine is but a precept in the style of a proposition; and a precept is but a doctrine in the form of a command.... Theology is God's garden; its trees are trees of his planting; and 'all the trees of the Lord are full of sap' (Ps. 104:16)."

Bose, Ecumenical Councils: "A creed is not catholic because a council of many or of few bishops decreed it, but because it expresses the common conviction of entire generations of men and women who turned their understanding of the New Testament into those forms of words." Dorner: "The creeds are the precipitate of the religious consciousness of mighty men and times." Foster, Christ. Life and Theol., 162—"It ordinarily requires the shock of some great event to startle men into clear apprehension and crystallization of their substantial belief. Such a shock was given by the rough and coarse doctrine of Arius, upon which the conclusion arrived at in the Council of Nice followed as rapidly as in chilled water the crystals of ice will sometimes form when the containing vessel receives a blow." Balfour, Foundations of Belief, 287—"The creeds were not explanations, but rather denials that the Arian and Gnostic explanations were sufficient, and declarations that they irremediably impoverished the idea of the Godhead. They insisted on preserving that idea in all its inexplicable fulness." Denny, Studies in Theology, 192—"Pagan philosophies tried to capture the church for their own ends, and to turn it into a school. In self-defense the church was compelled to become somewhat of a school on its own account. It had to assert its facts; it had to define its ideas; it had to interpret in its own way those facts which men were misinterpreting."

Professor Howard Osgood: "A creed is like a backbone. A man does not need to wear his backbone in front of him; but he must have a backbone, and a straight one, or he will be a flexible if not a humpbacked Christian." Yet we must remember that creeds are credita, and not credenda; historical statements of what the church has believed, not infallible prescriptions of what the church must believe. George Dana Boardman, The Church, 98—"Creeds are apt to become cages." Schurman, Agnosticism, 151—"The creeds were meant to be defensive fortifications of religion; alas, that they should have sometimes turned their artillery against the citadel itself." T. H. Green: "We are told that we must be loyal to the beliefs of the Fathers. Yes, but who knows what the Fathers believe now?" George A. Gordon, Christ of To-day, 60—"The assumption that the Holy Spirit is not concerned in the development of theological thought, nor manifest in the intellectual evolution of mankind, is the superlative heresy of our generation.... The metaphysics of Jesus are absolutely essential to his ethics.... If his thought is a dream, his endeavor for man is a delusion." See Schaff, Creeds of Christendom, 1:8, 15, 16; Storrs, Div. Origin of Christianity, 121; Ian Maclaren (John Watson), Cure of Souls, 152; Frederick Harrison, in Fortnightly Rev., Jan. 1889.

(e) In the direct and indirect injunctions of Scripture. The Scripture urges upon us the thorough and comprehensive study of the truth (John 5:39, marg.,—"Search the Scriptures"), the comparing and harmonizing of its different parts (1 Cor. 2:13—"comparing spiritual things with spiritual"), the gathering of all about the great central fact of revelation (Col. 1:27—"which is Christ in you, the hope of glory"), the preaching of it in its wholeness as well as in its due proportions (2 Tim. 4:2—"Preach the word"). The minister of the Gospel is called "a scribe who hath been made a disciple to the kingdom of heaven" (Mat. 13:52); the "pastors" of the churches are at the same time to be "teachers" (Eph. 4:11); the bishop must be "apt to teach" (1 Tim. 3:2), "handling aright the word of truth" (2 Tim. 2:15), "holding to the faithful word which is according to the teaching, that he may be able both to exhort in the sound doctrine and to convict the gainsayers" (Tit. 1:9).

As a means of instructing the church and of securing progress in his own understanding of Christian truth, it is well for the pastor to preach regularly each month a doctrinal sermon, and to expound in course the principal articles of the faith. The treatment of doctrine in these sermons should be simple enough to be comprehensible by intelligent youth; it should be made vivid and interesting by the help of brief illustrations; and at least one-third of each sermon should be devoted to the practical applications of the doctrine propounded. See Jonathan Edwards's sermon on the Importance of the Knowledge of Divine Truth, in Works, 4:1-15. The actual sermons of Edwards, however, are not models of doctrinal preaching for our generation. They are too scholastic in form, too metaphysical for substance; there is too little of Scripture and too little of illustration. The doctrinal preaching of the English Puritans in a similar manner addressed itself almost wholly to adults. The preaching of our Lord on the other hand was adapted also to children. No pastor should count himself faithful, who permits his young people to grow up without regular instruction from the pulpit in the whole circle of Christian doctrine. Shakespeare, K. Henry VI, 2nd part, 4:7—"Ignorance is the curse of God; knowledge the wing wherewith we fly to heaven."

V. Relation of Theology to Religion

Theology and religion are related to each other as effects, in different spheres, of the same cause. As theology is an effect produced in the sphere of systematic thought by the facts respecting God and the universe, so religion is an effect which these same facts produce in the sphere of individual and collective life. With regard to the term "religion", notice:

1. Derivation

(a) The derivation from religāre, "to bind back" (man to God), is negatived by the authority of Cicero and of the best modern etymologists; by the difficulty, on this hypothesis, of explaining such forms as religio, religens; and by the necessity, in that case, of presupposing a fuller knowledge of sin and redemption than was common to the ancient world.

(b) The more correct derivation is from relegĕre, "to go over again," "carefully to ponder." Its original meaning is therefore "reverent observance" (of duties due to the gods).

For advocacy of the derivation of religio, as meaning "binding duty," from religāre, see Lange, Dogmatik, 1:185-196. This derivation was first proposed by Lactantius, Inst. Div., 4:28, a Christian writer. To meet the objection that the form religio seems derived from a verb of the third conjugation, Lange cites rebellio, from rebellāre, and optio, from optāre. But we reply that these verbs of the first conjugation, like many others, are probably derived from obsolete verbs of the third conjugation. For the derivation favored in the text, see Curtius, Griechische Etymologie, 5te Aufl., 364; Fick, Vergl. Wörterb. der indoger. Spr., 2:227; Vanicek, Gr.-Lat. Etym. Wörterb., 2:829; Andrews, Latin Lexicon, in voce; Nitzsch, System of Christ. Doctrine, 7; Van Oosterzee, Dogmatics, 75-77; Philippi, Glaubenslehre, 1:6; Kahnis, Dogmatik, 3:18; Menzies, History of Religion, 11; Max Müller, Natural Religion, lect. 2.

2. False Conceptions

(a) Religion is not, as Hegel declared, a kind of knowing; for it would then be only an incomplete form of philosophy, and the measure of knowledge in each case would be the measure of piety.

In a system of idealistic pantheism, like that of Hegel, God is the subject of religion as well as its object. Religion is God's knowing of himself through the human consciousness. Hegel did not utterly ignore other elements in religion. "Feeling, intuition, and faith belong to it," he said, "and mere cognition is one-sided." Yet he was always looking for the movement of thought in all forms of life; God and the universe were but developments of the primordial idea. "What knowledge is worth knowing," he asked, "if God is unknowable? To know God is eternal life, and thinking is also true worship." Hegel's error was in regarding life as a process of thought, rather than in regarding thought as a process of life. Here was the reason for the bitterness between Hegel and Schleiermacher. Hegel rightly considered that feeling must become intelligent before it is truly religious, but he did not recognize the supreme importance of love in a theological system. He gave even less place to the will than he gave to the emotions, and he failed to see that the knowledge of God of which Scripture speaks is a knowing, not of the intellect alone, but of the whole man, including the affectional and voluntary nature.

Goethe: "How can a man come to know himself? Never by thinking, but by doing. Try to do your duty, and you will know at once what you are worth. You cannot play the flute by blowing alone,—you must use your fingers." So we can never come to know God by thinking alone. John 7:17—"If any man willeth to do his will, he will know of the teaching, whether it is of God." The Gnostics, Stapfer, Henry VIII, all show that there may be much theological knowledge without true religion. Chillingworth's maxim, "The Bible only, the religion of Protestants," is inadequate and inaccurate; for the Bible, without faith, love, and obedience, may become a fetich and a snare: John 5:39,40—"Ye search the Scriptures, ... and ye will not come to me, that ye may have life." See Sterrett, Studies in Hegel's Philosophy of Religion; Porter, Human Intellect, 59, 60, 412, 525-536, 589, 650; Morell, Hist. Philos., 476, 477; Hamerton, Intel. Life, 214; Bib. Sac., 9:374.

(b) Religion is not, as Schleiermacher held, the mere feeling of dependence; for such feeling of dependence is not religious, unless exercised toward God and accompanied by moral effort.

In German theology, Schleiermacher constitutes the transition from the old rationalism to the evangelical faith. "Like Lazarus, with the grave clothes of a pantheistic philosophy entangling his steps," yet with a Moravian experience of the life of God in the soul, he based religion upon the inner certainties of Christian feeling. But, as Principal Fairbairn remarks, "Emotion is impotent unless it speaks out of conviction; and where conviction is, there will be emotion which is potent to persuade." If Christianity is religious feeling alone, then there is no essential difference between it and other religions, for all alike are products of the religious sentiment. But Christianity is distinguished from other religions by its peculiar religious conceptions. Doctrine precedes life, and Christian doctrine, not mere religious feeling, is the cause of Christianity as a distinctive religion. Though faith begins in feeling, moreover, it does not end there. We see the worthlessness of mere feeling in the transient emotions of theatre-goers, and in the occasional phenomena of revivals.

Sabatier, Philos. Relig., 27, adds to Schleiermacher's passive element of dependence, the active element of prayer. Kaftan, Dogmatik, 10—"Schleiermacher regards God as the Source of our being, but forgets that he is also our End." Fellowship and progress are as important elements in religion as is dependence; and fellowship must come before progress—such fellowship as presupposes pardon and life. Schleiermacher apparently believed in neither a personal God nor his own personal immortality; see his Life and Letters, 2:77-90; Martineau, Study of Religion, 2:357. Charles Hodge compares him to a ladder in a pit—a good thing for those who wish to get out, but not for those who wish to get in. Dorner: "The Moravian brotherhood was his mother; Greece was his nurse." On Schleiermacher, see Herzog, Realencyclopädie, in voce; Bib. Sac., 1852:375; 1883:534; Liddon, Elements of Religion, lect. I; Ebrard, Dogmatik, 1:14; Julius Müller, Doctrine of Sin, 1:175; Fisher, Supernat. Origin of Christianity, 563-570; Caird, Philos. Religion, 160-186.

(c) Religion is not, as Kant maintained, morality or moral action; for morality is conformity to an abstract law of right, while religion is essentially a relation to a person, from whom the soul receives blessing and to whom it surrenders itself in love and obedience.

Kant, Kritik der praktischen Vernunft, Beschluss: "I know of but two beautiful things, the starry heavens above my head, and the sense of duty within my heart." But the mere sense of duty often distresses. We object to the word "obey" as the imperative of religion, because (1) it makes religion a matter of the will only; (2) will presupposes affection; (3) love is not subject to will; (4) it makes God all law, and no grace; (5) it makes the Christian a servant only, not a friend; cf. John 15:15—"No longer do I call you servants ... but I have called you friends"—a relation not of service but of love (Westcott, Bib. Com., in loco). The voice that speaks is the voice of love, rather than the voice of law. We object also to Matthew Arnold's definition: "Religion is ethics heightened, enkindled, lit up by feeling; morality touched with emotion." This leaves out of view the receptive element in religion, as well as its relation to a personal God. A truer statement would be that religion is morality toward God, as morality is religion toward man. Bowne, Philos. of Theism, 251—"Morality that goes beyond mere conscientiousness must have recourse to religion"; see Lotze, Philos. of Religion, 128-142. Goethe: "Unqualified activity, of whatever kind, leads at last to bankruptcy"; see also Pfleiderer, Philos. Religion, 1:65-69; Shedd, Sermons to the Natural Man, 244-246; Liddon, Elements of Religion, 19.

3. Essential Idea

Religion in its essential idea is a life in God, a life lived in recognition of God, in communion with God, and under control of the indwelling Spirit of God. Since it is a life, it cannot be described as consisting solely in the exercise of any one of the powers of intellect, affection, or will. As physical life involves the unity and coöperation of all the organs of the body, so religion, or spiritual life, involves the united working of all the powers of the soul. To feeling, however, we must assign the logical priority, since holy affection toward God, imparted in regeneration, is the condition of truly knowing God and of truly serving him.

See Godet, on the Ultimate Design of Man—"God in man, and man in God"—in Princeton Rev., Nov. 1880; Pfleiderer, Die Religion, 5-79, and Religionsphilosophie, 255—Religion is "Sache des ganzen Geisteslebens": Crane, Religion of To-morrow, 4—"Religion is the personal influence of the immanent God"; Sterrett, Reason and Authority in Religion, 31, 32—"Religion is the reciprocal relation or communion of God and man, involving (1) revelation, (2) faith"; Dr. J. W. A. Stewart: "Religion is fellowship with God"; Pascal: "Piety is God sensible to the heart"; Ritschl, Justif. and Reconcil., 13— "Christianity is an ellipse with two foci—Christ as Redeemer and Christ as King, Christ for us and Christ in us, redemption and morality, religion and ethics"; Kaftan, Dogmatik, 8—"The Christian religion is (1) the kingdom of God as a goal above the world, to be attained by moral development here, and (2) reconciliation with God permitting attainment of this goal in spite of our sins. Christian theology once grounded itself in man's natural knowledge of God; we now start with religion, i. e., that Christian knowledge of God which we call faith."

Herbert Spencer: "Religion is an a priori theory of the universe"; Romanes, Thoughts on Religion, 43, adds: "which assumes intelligent personality as the originating cause of the universe, science dealing with the How, the phenomenal process, religion dealing with the Who, the intelligent Personality who works through the process." Holland, in Lux Mundi, 27—"Natural life is the life in God which has not yet arrived at this recognition"—the recognition of the fact that God is in all things—"it is not yet, as such, religious; ... Religion is the discovery, by the son, of a Father who is in all his works, yet is distinct from them all." Dewey, Psychology, 283—"Feeling finds its absolutely universal expression in religious emotion, which is the finding or realization of self in a completely realized personality which unites in itself truth, or the complete unity of the relations of all objects, beauty or the complete unity of all ideal values, and rightness or the complete unity of all persons. The emotion which accompanies the religious life is that which accompanies the complete activity of ourselves; the self is realized and finds its true life in God." Upton, Hibbert Lectures, 262—"Ethics is simply the growing insight into, and the effort to actualize in society, the sense of fundamental kinship and identity of substance in all men; while religion is the emotion and the devotion which attend the realization in our self-consciousness of an inmost spiritual relationship arising out of that unity of substance which constitutes man the true son of the eternal Father." See Van Oosterzee, Dogmatics, 81-85; Julius Müller, Doct. Sin, 2:227; Nitzsch, Syst. of Christ. Doct., 10-28; Luthardt, Fund. Truths, 147; Twesten, Dogmatik, 1:12.

4. Inferences

From this definition of religion it follows:

(a) That in strictness there is but one religion. Man is a religious being, indeed, as having the capacity for this divine life. He is actually religious, however, only when he enters into this living relation to God. False religions are the caricatures which men given to sin, or the imaginations which men groping after light, form of this life of the soul in God.

Peabody, Christianity the Religion of Nature, 18—"If Christianity be true, it is not a religion, but the religion. If Judaism be also true, it is so not as distinct from but as coincident with Christianity, the one religion to which it can bear only the relation of a part to the whole. If there be portions of truth in other religious systems, they are not portions of other religions, but portions of the one religion which somehow or other became incorporated with fables and falsities." John Caird, Fund. Ideas of Christianity, 1:25—"You can never get at the true idea or essence of religion merely by trying to find out something that is common to all religions; and it is not the lower religions that explain the higher, but conversely the higher religion explains all the lower religions." George P. Fisher: "The recognition of certain elements of truth in the ethnic religions does not mean that Christianity has defects which are to be repaired by borrowing from them; it only means that the ethnic faiths have in fragments what Christianity has as a whole. Comparative religion does not bring to Christianity new truth; it provides illustrations of how Christian truth meets human needs and aspirations, and gives a full vision of that which the most spiritual and gifted among the heathen only dimly discerned."

Dr. C. H. Parkhurst, sermon on Proverbs 20:27—"The spirit of man is the lamp of Jehovah"—"a lamp, but not necessarily lighted; a lamp that can be lit only by the touch of a divine flame"—man has naturally and universally a capacity for religion, but is by no means naturally and universally religious. All false religions have some element of truth; otherwise they could never have gained or kept their hold upon mankind. We need to recognize these elements of truth in dealing with them. There is some silver in a counterfeit dollar, else it would deceive no one; but the thin washing of silver over the lead does not prevent it from being bad money. Clarke, Christian Theology, 8—"See Paul's methods of dealing with heathen religion, in Acts 14 with gross paganism and in Acts 17 with its cultured form. He treats it with sympathy and justice. Christian theology has the advantage of walking in the light of God's self-manifestation in Christ, while heathen religions grope after God and worship him in ignorance"; cf. Acts 14:16—"We ... bring you good tidings, that ye should turn from these vain things unto a living God"; 17:22—"I perceive that ye are more than usually reverent toward the divinities.... What therefore ye worship in ignorance, this I set forth unto you."

Matthew Arnold: "Children of men! the unseen Power whose eye Forever doth accompany mankind, Hath looked on no religion scornfully That man did ever find. Which has not taught weak wills how much they can? Which has not fallen on the dry heart like rain? Which has not cried to sunk, self-weary man, Thou must be born again?" Christianity is absolutely exclusive, because it is absolutely inclusive. It is not an amalgamation of other religions, but it has in it all that is best and truest in other religions. It is the white light that contains all the colored rays. God may have made disclosures of truth outside of Judaism, and did so in Balaam and Melchisedek, in Confucius and Socrates. But while other religions have a relative excellence, Christianity is the absolute religion that contains all excellencies. Matheson, Messages of the Old Religions, 328-342—"Christianity is reconciliation. Christianity includes the aspiration of Egypt; it sees, in this aspiration, God in the soul (Brahmanism); recognizes the evil power of sin with Parseeism; goes back to a pure beginning like China; surrenders itself to human brotherhood like Buddha; gets all things from within like Judaism; makes the present life beautiful like Greece; seeks a universal kingdom like Rome; shows a growth of divine life, like the Teuton. Christianity is the manifold wisdom of God." See also Van Oosterzee, Dogmatics, 88-93. Shakespeare: "There is some soul of goodness in things evil, Would men observingly distill it out"

(b) That the content of religion is greater than that of theology. The facts of religion come within the range of theology only so far as they can be definitely conceived, accurately expressed in language, and brought into rational relation to each other.

This principle enables us to define the proper limits of religious fellowship. It should be as wide as is religion itself. But it is important to remember what religion is. Religion is not to be identified with the capacity for religion. Nor can we regard the perversions and caricatures of religion as meriting our fellowship. Otherwise we might be required to have fellowship with devil-worship, polygamy, thuggery, and the inquisition; for all these have been dignified with the name of religion. True religion involves some knowledge, however rudimentary, of the true God, the God of righteousness; some sense of sin as the contrast between human character and the divine standard; some casting of the soul upon divine mercy and a divine way of salvation, in place of self-righteous earning of merit and reliance upon one's works and one's record; some practical effort to realize ethical principle in a pure life and in influence over others. Wherever these marks of true religion appear, even in Unitarians, Romanists, Jews or Buddhists, there we recognize the demand for fellowship. But we also attribute these germs of true religion to the inworking of the omnipresent Christ, "the light which lighteth every man" (John 1:9), and we see in them incipient repentance and faith, even though the Christ who is their object is yet unknown by name. Christian fellowship must have a larger basis in accepted Christian truth, and Church fellowship a still larger basis in common acknowledgment of N. T. teaching as to the church. Religious fellowship, in the widest sense, rests upon the fact that "God is no respecter of persons: but in every nation he that feareth him and worketh righteousness is acceptable to him" (Acts 10:34, 35).

(c) That religion is to be distinguished from formal worship, which is simply the outward expression of religion. As such expression, worship is "formal communion between God and his people." In it God speaks to man, and man to God. It therefore properly includes the reading of Scripture and preaching on the side of God, and prayer and song on the side of the people.

Sterrett, Reason and Authority in Religion, 166—"Christian worship is the utterance (outerance) of the spirit." But there is more in true love than can be put into a love-letter, and there is more in true religion than can be expressed either in theology or in worship. Christian worship is communion between God and man. But communion cannot be one-sided. Madame de Staël, whom Heine called "a whirlwind in petticoats," ended one of her brilliant soliloquies by saying: "What a delightful conversation we have had!" We may find a better illustration of the nature of worship in Thomas à Kempis's dialogues between the saint and his Savior, in the Imitation of Christ. Goethe: "Against the great superiority of another there is no remedy but love.... To praise a man is to put one's self on his level." If this be the effect of loving and praising man, what must be the effect of loving and praising God! Inscription in Grasmere Church: "Whoever thou art that enterest this church, leave it not without one prayer to God for thyself, for those who minister, and for those who worship here." In James 1:27— "Pure religion and undefiled before our God and Father is this, to visit the fatherless and widows in their affliction, and to keep oneself unspotted from the world"—"religion," θρησκεία, is cultus exterior; and the meaning is that "the external service, the outward garb, the very ritual of Christianity, is a life of purity, love and self-devotion. What its true essence, its inmost spirit may be, the writer does not say, but leaves this to be inferred." On the relation between religion and worship, see Prof. Day, in New Englander, Jan. 1882; Prof. T. Harwood Pattison, Public Prayer; Trench, Syn. N. T., 1; sec. 48; Coleridge, Aids to Reflection, Introd., Aphorism 23; Lightfoot, Gal., 351, note 2.

Chapter II - Material of Theology

I. Sources of Theology

God himself, in the last analysis, must be the only source of knowledge with regard to his own being and relations. Theology is therefore a summary and explanation of the content of God's self-revelations. These are, first, the revelation of God in nature; secondly and supremely, the revelation of God in the Scriptures.

Ambrose: "To whom shall I give greater credit concerning God than to God himself?" Von Baader: "To know God without God is impossible; there is no knowledge without him who is the prime source of knowledge." C. A. Briggs, Whither, 8—"God reveals truth in several spheres: in universal nature, in the constitution of mankind, in the history of our race, in the Sacred Scriptures, but above all in the person of Jesus Christ our Lord." F. H. Johnson, What is Reality? 399—"The teacher intervenes when needed. Revelation helps reason and conscience, but is not a substitute for them. But Catholicism affirms this substitution for the church, and Protestantism for the Bible. The Bible, like nature, gives many free gifts, but more in the germ. Growing ethical ideals must interpret the Bible." A. J. F. Behrends: "The Bible is only a telescope, not the eye which sees, nor the stars which the telescope brings to view. It is your business and mine to see the stars with our own eyes." Schurman, Agnosticism, 178—"The Bible is a glass through which to see the living God. But it is useless when you put your eyes out."

We can know God only so far as he has revealed himself. The immanent God is known, but the transcendent God we do not know any more than we know the side of the moon that is turned away from us. A. H. Strong, Christ in Creation, 118—"The word 'authority' is derived from auctor, augeo, 'to add.' Authority adds something to the truth communicated. The thing added is the personal element of witness. This is needed wherever there is ignorance which cannot be removed by our own effort, or unwillingness which results from our own sin. In religion I need to add to my own knowledge that which God imparts. Reason, conscience, church, Scripture, are all delegated and subordinate authorities; the only original and supreme authority is God himself, or Christ, who is only God revealed and made comprehensible by us." Gore, Incarnation, 181—"All legitimate authority represents the reason of God, educating the reason of man and communicating itself to it.... Man is made in God's image: he is, in his fundamental capacity, a son of God, and he becomes so in fact, and fully, through union with Christ. Therefore in the truth of God, as Christ presents it to him, he can recognize his own better reason,—to use Plato's beautiful expression, he can salute it by force of instinct as something akin to himself, before he can give intellectual account of it."

Balfour, Foundations of Belief, 332-337, holds that there is no such thing as unassisted reason, and that, even if there were, natural religion is not one of its products. Behind all evolution of our own reason, he says, stands the Supreme Reason. "Conscience, ethical ideals, capacity for admiration, sympathy, repentance, righteous indignation, as well as our delight in beauty and truth, are all derived from God." Kaftan, in Am. Jour. Theology, 1900; 718, 719, maintains that there is no other principle for dogmatics than Holy Scripture. Yet he holds that knowledge never comes directly from Scripture, but from faith. The order is not: Scripture, doctrine, faith; but rather, Scripture, faith, doctrine. Scripture is no more a direct authority than is the church. Revelation is addressed to the whole man, that is, to the will of the man, and it claims obedience from him. Since all Christian knowledge is mediated through faith, it rests on obedience to the authority of revelation, and revelation is self-manifestation on the part of God. Kaftan should have recognized more fully that not simply Scripture, but all knowable truth, is a revelation from God, and that Christ is "the light which lighteth every man" (John 1:9). Revelation is an organic whole, which begins in nature, but finds its climax and key in the historical Christ whom Scripture presents to us. See H. C. Minton's review of Martineau's Seat of Authority, in Presb. and Ref. Rev., Apr. 1900:203 sq.

1. Scripture and Nature

By nature we here mean not only physical facts, or facts with regard to the substances, properties, forces, and laws of the material world, but also spiritual facts, or facts with regard to the intellectual and moral constitution of man, and the orderly arrangement of human society and history.

We here use the word "nature" in the ordinary sense, as including man. There is another and more proper use of the word "nature," which makes it simply a complex of forces and beings under the law of cause and effect. To nature in this sense man belongs only as respects his body, while as immaterial and personal he is a supernatural being. Free will is not under the law of physical and mechanical causation. As Bushnell has said: "Nature and the supernatural together constitute the one system of God." Drummond, Natural Law in the Spiritual World, 232—"Things are natural or supernatural according to where we stand. Man is supernatural to the mineral; God is supernatural to the man." We shall in subsequent chapters use the term "nature" in the narrow sense. The universal use of the phrase "Natural Theology," however, compels us in this chapter to employ the word "nature" in its broader sense as including man, although we do this under protest, and with this explanation of the more proper meaning of the term. See Hopkins, in Princeton Review, Sept. 1882:183 sq.

E. G. Robinson: "Bushnell separates nature from the supernatural. Nature is a blind train of causes. God has nothing to do with it, except as he steps into it from without. Man is supernatural, because he is outside of nature, having the power of originating an independent train of causes." If this were the proper conception of nature, then we might be compelled to conclude with P. T. Forsyth, in Faith and Criticism, 100—"There is no revelation in nature. There can be none, because there is no forgiveness. We cannot be sure about her. She is only aesthetic. Her ideal is harmony, not reconciliation.... For the conscience, stricken or strong, she has no word.... Nature does not contain her own teleology, and for the moral soul that refuses to be fancy-fed, Christ is the one luminous smile on the dark face of the world." But this is virtually to confine Christ's revelation to Scripture or to the incarnation. As there was an astronomy without the telescope, so there was a theology before the Bible. George Harris, Moral Evolution, 411—"Nature is both evolution and revelation. As soon as the question How is answered, the questions Whence and Why arise. Nature is to God what speech is to thought." The title of Henry Drummond's book should have been: "Spiritual Law in the Natural World," for nature is but the free though regular activity of God; what we call the supernatural is simply his extraordinary working.

(a) Natural theology.—The universe is a source of theology. The Scriptures assert that God has revealed himself in nature. There is not only an outward witness to his existence and character in the constitution and government of the universe (Ps. 19; Acts 14:17; Rom. 1:20), but an inward witness to his existence and character in the heart of every man (Rom. 1:17, 18, 19, 20, 32; 2:15). The systematic exhibition of these facts, whether derived from observation, history or science, constitutes natural theology.

Outward witness: Ps.19:1-6—"The heavens declare the glory of God"; Acts 14:17—"he left not himself without witness, in that he did good, and gave you from heaven rains and fruitful seasons"; Rom. 1:20—"for the invisible things of him since the creation of the world are clearly seen, being perceived through the things that are made, even his everlasting power and divinity." Inward witness: Rom. 1:19—τὸ γνωστὸν τοῦ Θεοῦ = "that which is known of God is manifest in them." Compare the ἀποκαλύπτεται of the gospel in verse 17, with the ἀποκαλύπτεται of wrath in verse 18—two revelations, one of ὀργή, the other of χάρις; see Shedd, Homiletics, 11. Rom. 1:32—"knowing the ordinance of God"; 2:15—"they show the work of the law written in their hearts." Therefore even the heathen are "without excuse" (Rom. 1:20). There are two books: Nature and Scripture—one written, the other unwritten: and there is need of studying both. On the passages in Romans, see the Commentary of Hodge.

Spurgeon told of a godly person who, when sailing down the Rhine, closed his eyes, lest the beauty of the scene should divert his mind from spiritual themes. The Puritan turned away from the moss-rose, saying that he would count nothing on earth lovely. But this is to despise God's works. J. H. Barrows: "The Himalayas are the raised letters upon which we blind children put our fingers to spell out the name of God." To despise the works of God is to despise God himself. God is present in nature, and is now speaking. Ps. 19:1—"The heavens declare the glory of God, and the firmament showeth his handiwork"—present tenses. Nature is not so much a book, as a voice. Hutton, Essays, 2:236—"The direct knowledge of spiritual communion must be supplemented by knowledge of God's ways gained from the study of nature. To neglect the study of the natural mysteries of the universe leads to an arrogant and illicit intrusion of moral and spiritual assumptions into a different world. This is the lesson of the book of Job." Hatch, Hibbert Lectures, 85—"Man, the servant and interpreter of nature, is also, and is thereby, the servant and interpreter of the living God." Books of science are the record of man's past interpretations of God's works.

(b) Natural theology supplemented.—The Christian revelation is the chief source of theology. The Scriptures plainly declare that the revelation of God in nature does not supply all the knowledge which a sinner needs (Acts 17:23; Eph. 3:9). This revelation is therefore supplemented by another, in which divine attributes and merciful provisions only dimly shadowed forth in nature are made known to men. This latter revelation consists of a series of supernatural events and communications, the record of which is presented in the Scriptures.

Acts 17:23—Paul shows that, though the Athenians, in the erection of an altar to an unknown God, "acknowledged a divine existence beyond any which the ordinary rites of their worship recognized, that Being was still unknown to them; they had no just conception of his nature and perfections" (Hackett, in loco). Eph. 3:9—"the mystery which hath been hid in God"—this mystery is in the gospel made known for man's salvation. Hegel, in his Philosophy of Religion, says that Christianity is the only revealed religion, because the Christian God is the only one from whom a revelation can come. We may add that as science is the record of man's progressive interpretation of God's revelation in the realm of nature, so Scripture is the record of man's progressive interpretation of God's revelation in the realm of spirit. The phrase "word of God" does not primarily denote a record,—it is the spoken word, the doctrine, the vitalizing truth, disclosed by Christ; see Mat. 13:19—"heareth the word of the kingdom"; Luke 5:1—"heard the word of God"; Acts 8:25—"spoken the word of the Lord"; 13:48, 49—"glorified the word of God: ... the word of the Lord was spread abroad"; 19:10, 20—"heard the word of the Lord, ... mightily grew the word of the Lord"; 1 Cor. 1:18—"the word of the cross"—all designating not a document, but an unwritten word; cf. Jer. 1:4—"the word of Jehovah came unto me"; Ez. 1:3—"the word of Jehovah came expressly unto Ezekiel, the priest."

(c) The Scriptures the final standard of appeal.—Science and Scripture throw light upon each other. The same divine Spirit who gave both revelations is still present, enabling the believer to interpret the one by the other and thus progressively to come to the knowledge of the truth. Because of our finiteness and sin, the total record in Scripture of God's past communications is a more trustworthy source of theology than are our conclusions from nature or our private impressions of the teaching of the Spirit. Theology therefore looks to the Scripture itself as its chief source of material and its final standard of appeal.

There is an internal work of the divine Spirit by which the outer word is made an inner word, and its truth and power are manifested to the heart. Scripture represents this work of the Spirit, not as a giving of new truth, but as an illumination of the mind to perceive the fulness of meaning which lay wrapped up in the truth already revealed. Christ is "the truth" (John 14:6); "in whom are all the treasures of wisdom and knowledge hidden" (Col. 2:3); the Holy Spirit, Jesus says, "shall take of mine, and shall declare it unto you" (John 16:14). The incarnation and the Cross express the heart of God and the secret of the universe; all discoveries in theology are but the unfolding of truth involved in these facts. The Spirit of Christ enables us to compare nature with Scripture, and Scripture with nature, and to correct mistakes in interpreting the one by light gained from the other. Because the church as a whole, by which we mean the company of true believers in all lands and ages, has the promise that it shall be guided "into all the truth" (John 16:13), we may confidently expect the progress of Christian doctrine.

Christian experience is sometimes regarded as an original source of religious truth. Experience, however, is but a testing and proving of the truth objectively contained in God's revelation. The word "experience" is derived from experior, to test, to try. Christian consciousness is not "norma normans," but "norma normata." Light, like life, comes to us through the mediation of others. Yet the first comes from God as really as the last, of which without hesitation we say: "God made me," though we have human parents. As I get through the service-pipe in my house the same water which is stored in the reservoir upon the hillside, so in the Scriptures I get the same truth which the Holy Spirit originally communicated to prophets and apostles. Calvin, Institutes, book I, chap. 7—"As nature has an immediate manifestation of God in conscience, a mediate in his works, so revelation has an immediate manifestation of God in the Spirit, a mediate in the Scriptures." "Man's nature," said Spurgeon, "is not an organized lie, yet his inner consciousness has been warped by sin, and though once it was an infallible guide to truth and duty, sin has made it very deceptive. The standard of infallibility is not in man's consciousness, but in the Scriptures. When consciousness in any matter is contrary to the word of God, we must know that it is not God's voice within us, but the devil's." Dr. George A. Gordon says that "Christian history is a revelation of Christ additional to that contained in the New Testament." Should we not say "illustrative," instead of "additional"? On the relation between Christian experience and Scripture, see Stearns, Evidence of Christian Experience, 286-309: Twesten, Dogmatik, 1:344-348; Hodge, Syst. Theol., 1:15.

H. H. Bawden: "God is the ultimate authority, but there are delegated authorities, such as family, state, church; instincts, feelings, conscience; the general experience of the race, traditions, utilities; revelation in nature and in Scripture. But the highest authority available for men in morals and religion is the truth concerning Christ contained in the Christian Scriptures. What the truth concerning Christ is, is determined by: (1) the human reason, conditioned by a right attitude of the feelings and the will; (2) in the light of all the truth derived from nature, including man; (3) in the light of the history of Christianity; (4) in the light of the origin and development of the Scriptures themselves. The authority of the generic reason and the authority of the Bible are co-relative, since they both have been developed in the providence of God, and since the latter is in large measure but the reflection of the former. This view enables us to hold a rational conception of the function of the Scripture in religion. This view, further, enables us to rationalize what is called the inspiration of the Bible, the nature and extent of inspiration, the Bible as history—a record of the historic unfolding of revelation; the Bible as literature—a compend of life-principles, rather than a book of rules; the Bible Christocentric—an incarnation of the divine thought and will in human thought and language."

(d) The theology of Scripture not unnatural.—Though we speak of the systematized truths of nature as constituting natural theology, we are not to infer that Scriptural theology is unnatural. Since the Scriptures have the same author as nature, the same principles are illustrated in the one as in the other. All the doctrines of the Bible have their reason in that same nature of God which constitutes the basis of all material things. Christianity is a supplementary dispensation, not as contradicting, or correcting errors in, natural theology, but as more perfectly revealing the truth. Christianity is indeed the ground-plan upon which the whole creation is built—the original and eternal truth of which natural theology is but a partial expression. Hence the theology of nature and the theology of Scripture are mutually dependent. Natural theology not only prepares the way for, but it receives stimulus and aid from, Scriptural theology. Natural theology may now be a source of truth, which, before the Scriptures came, it could not furnish.

John Caird, Fund. Ideas of Christianity. 23—"There is no such thing as a natural religion or religion of reason distinct from revealed religion. Christianity is more profoundly, more comprehensively, rational, more accordant with the deepest principles of human nature and human thought than is natural religion; or, as we may put it, Christianity is natural religion elevated and transmuted into revealed." Peabody, Christianity the Religion of Nature, lecture 2—"Revelation is the unveiling, uncovering of what previously existed, and it excludes the idea of newness, invention, creation.... The revealed religion of earth is the natural religion of heaven." Compare Rev. 13:8—"the Lamb that hath been slain from the foundation of the world" = the coming of Christ was no make-shift; in a true sense the Cross existed in eternity; the atonement is a revelation of an eternal fact in the being of God.

Note Plato's illustration of the cave which can be easily threaded by one who has previously entered it with a torch. Nature is the dim light from the cave's mouth; the torch is Scripture. Kant to Jacobi, in Jacobi's Werke, 3:523—"If the gospel had not previously taught the universal moral laws, reason would not yet have obtained so perfect an insight into them." Alexander McLaren: "Non-Christian thinkers now talk eloquently about God's love, and even reject the gospel in the name of that love, thus kicking down the ladder by which they have climbed. But it was the Cross that taught the world the love of God, and apart from the death of Christ men may hope that there is a heart at the centre of the universe, but they can never be sure of it." The parrot fancies that he taught men to talk. So Mr. Spencer fancies that he invented ethics. He is only using the twilight, after his sun has gone down. Dorner, Hist. Prot. Theol., 252, 253—"Faith, at the Reformation, first gave scientific certainty; it had God sure: hence it proceeded to banish scepticism in philosophy and science." See also Dove, Logic of Christian Faith, 333; Bowen, Metaph. and Ethics, 442-463; Bib. Sac., 1874:436; A. H. Strong, Christ in Creation, 226, 227.

2. Scripture and Rationalism

Although the Scriptures make known much that is beyond the power of man's unaided reason to discover or fully to comprehend, their teachings, when taken together, in no way contradict a reason conditioned in its activity by a holy affection and enlightened by the Spirit of God. To reason in the large sense, as including the mind's power of cognizing God and moral relations—not in the narrow sense of mere reasoning, or the exercise of the purely logical faculty—the Scriptures continually appeal.

A. The proper office of reason, in this large sense, is: (a) To furnish us with those primary ideas of space, time, cause, substance, design, right, and God, which are the conditions of all subsequent knowledge. (b) To judge with regard to man's need of a special and supernatural revelation. (c) To examine the credentials of communications professing to be, or of documents professing to record, such a revelation. (d) To estimate and reduce to system the facts of revelation, when these have been found properly attested. (e) To deduce from these facts their natural and logical conclusions. Thus reason itself prepares the way for a revelation above reason, and warrants an implicit trust in such revelation when once given.

Dove, Logic of the Christian Faith, 318—"Reason terminates in the proposition: Look for revelation." Leibnitz: "Revelation is the viceroy who first presents his credentials to the provincial assembly (reason), and then himself presides." Reason can recognize truth after it is made known, as for example in the demonstrations of geometry, although it could never discover that truth for itself. See Calderwood's illustration of the party lost in the woods, who wisely take the course indicated by one at the tree-top with a larger view than their own (Philosophy of the Infinite, 126). The novice does well to trust his guide in the forest, at least till he learns to recognise for himself the marks blazed upon the trees. Luthardt, Fund. Truths, lect. viii—"Reason could never have invented a self-humiliating God, cradled in a manger and dying on a cross." Lessing, Zur Geschichte und Litteratur, 6:134—"What is the meaning of a revelation that reveals nothing?"

Ritschl denies the presuppositions of any theology based on the Bible as the infallible word of God on the one hand, and on the validity of the knowledge of God as obtained by scientific and philosophic processes on the other. Because philosophers, scientists, and even exegetes, are not agreed among themselves, he concludes that no trustworthy results are attainable by human reason. We grant that reason without love will fall into many errors with regard to God, and that faith is therefore the organ by which religious truth is to be apprehended. But we claim that this faith includes reason, and is itself reason in its highest form. Faith criticizes and judges the processes of natural science as well as the contents of Scripture. But it also recognizes in science and Scripture prior workings of that same Spirit of Christ which is the source and authority of the Christian life. Ritschl ignores Christ's world-relations and therefore secularizes and disparages science and philosophy. The faith to which he trusts as the source of theology is unwarrantably sundered from reason. It becomes a subjective and arbitrary standard, to which even the teaching of Scripture must yield precedence. We hold on the contrary, that there are ascertained results in science and in philosophy, as well as in the interpretation of Scripture as a whole, and that these results constitute an authoritative revelation. See Orr, The Theology of Ritschl; Dorner, Hist. Prot. Theol., 1:233—"The unreasonable in the empirical reason is taken captive by faith, which is the nascent true reason that despairs of itself and trustfully lays hold of objective Christianity."

B. Rationalism, on the other hand, holds reason to be the ultimate source of all religious truth, while Scripture is authoritative only so far as its revelations agree with previous conclusions of reason, or can be rationally demonstrated. Every form of rationalism, therefore, commits at least one of the following errors: (a) That of confounding reason with mere reasoning, or the exercise of the logical intelligence. (b) That of ignoring the necessity of a holy affection as the condition of all right reason in religious things. (c) That of denying our dependence in our present state of sin upon God's past revelations of himself. (d) That of regarding the unaided reason, even its normal and unbiased state, as capable of discovering, comprehending, and demonstrating all religious truth.

Reason must not be confounded with ratiocination, or mere reasoning. Shall we follow reason? Yes, but not individual reasoning, against the testimony of those who are better informed than we; nor by insisting on demonstration, where probable evidence alone is possible; nor by trusting solely to the evidence of the senses, when spiritual things are in question. Coleridge, in replying to those who argued that all knowledge comes to us from the senses, says: "At any rate we must bring to all facts the light in which we see them." This the Christian does. The light of love reveals much that would otherwise be invisible. Wordsworth, Excursion, book 5 (598)—"The mind's repose On evidence is not to be ensured By act of naked reason. Moral truth Is no mechanic structure, built by rule."

Rationalism is the mathematical theory of knowledge. Spinoza's Ethics is an illustration of it. It would deduce the universe from an axiom. Dr. Hodge very wrongly described rationalism as "an overuse of reason." It is rather the use of an abnormal, perverted, improperly conditioned reason; see Hodge, Syst. Theol., 1:34, 39, 55, and criticism by Miller, in his Fetich in Theology. The phrase "sanctified intellect" means simply intellect accompanied by right affections toward God, and trained to work under their influence. Bishop Butler: "Let reason be kept to, but let not such poor creatures as we are go on objecting to an infinite scheme that we do not see the necessity or usefulness of all its parts, and call that reasoning." Newman Smyth, Death's Place in Evolution, 86—"Unbelief is a shaft sunk down into the darkness of the earth. Drive the shaft deep enough, and it would come out into the sunlight on the earth's other side." The most unreasonable people in the world are those who depend solely upon reason, in the narrow sense. "The better to exalt reason, they make the world irrational." "The hen that has hatched ducklings walks with them to the water's edge, but there she stops, and she is amazed when they go on. So reason stops and faith goes on, finding its proper element in the invisible. Reason is the feet that stand on solid earth; faith is the wings that enable us to fly; and normal man is a creature with wings." Compare γνῶσις (1 Tim. 6:20—"the knowledge which is falsely so called") with ἐπίγνωσις (2 Pet. 1:2—"the knowledge of God and of Jesus our Lord" = full knowledge, or true knowledge). See Twesten, Dogmatik, 1:467-500; Julius Müller, Proof-texts, 4, 5; Mansel, Limits of Religious Thought, 96; Dawson, Modern Ideas of Evolution.

3. Scripture and Mysticism

As rationalism recognizes too little as coming from God, so mysticism recognizes too much.

A. True mysticism.—We have seen that there is an illumination of the minds of all believers by the Holy Spirit. The Spirit, however, makes no new revelation of truth, but uses for his instrument the truth already revealed by Christ in nature and in the Scriptures. The illuminating work of the Spirit is therefore an opening of men's minds to understand Christ's previous revelations. As one initiated into the mysteries of Christianity, every true believer may be called a mystic. True mysticism is that higher knowledge and fellowship which the Holy Spirit gives through the use of nature and Scripture as subordinate and principal means.

"Mystic" = one initiated, from μύω, "to close the eyes"—probably in order that the soul may have inward vision of truth. But divine truth is a "mystery," not only as something into which one must be initiated, but as ὑπερβάλλουσα τῆς γνώσεως (Eph. 3:19)—surpassing full knowledge, even to the believer; see Meyer on Rom. 11:25—"I would not, brethren, have you ignorant of this mystery." The

Germans have Mystik with a favorable sense, Mysticismus with an unfavorable sense,—corresponding respectively to our true and false mysticism. True mysticism is intimated in John 16:13—"the spirit of truth ... shall guide you into all the truth"; Eph. 3:9—"dispensation of the mystery"; 1 Cor. 2:10—"unto us God revealed them through the Spirit." Nitzsch, Syst. of Christ. Doct., 35—"Whenever true religion revives, there is an outcry against mysticism, i. e., higher knowledge, fellowship, activity through the Spirit of God in the heart." Compare the charge against Paul that he was mad, in Acts 26:24, 25, with his self-vindication in 2 Cor. 5:13—"whether we are beside ourselves, it is unto God."

Inge, Christian Mysticism, 21—"Harnack speaks of mysticism as rationalism applied to a sphere above reason. He should have said reason applied to a sphere above rationalism. Its fundamental doctrine is the unity of all existence. Man can realize his individuality only by transcending it and finding himself in the larger unity of God's being. Man is a microcosm. He recapitulates the race, the universe, Christ himself." Ibid., 5—Mysticism is "the attempt to realize in thought and feeling the immanence of the temporal in the eternal, and of the eternal in the temporal. It implies (1) that the soul can see and perceive spiritual truth; (2) that man, in order to know God, must be a partaker of the divine nature; (3) that without holiness no man can see the Lord; (4) that the true hierophant of the mysteries of God is love. The 'scala perfectionis' is (a) the purgative life; (b) the illuminative life; (c) the unitive life." Stevens, Johannine Theology, 239, 240—"The mysticism of John ... is not a subjective mysticism which absorbs the soul in self-contemplation and revery, but an objective and rational mysticism, which lives in a world of realities, apprehends divinely revealed truth, and bases its experience upon it. It is a mysticism which feeds, not upon its own feelings and fancies, but upon Christ. It involves an acceptance of him, and a life of obedience to him. Its motto is: Abiding in Christ." As the power press cannot dispense with the type, so the Spirit of God does not dispense with Christ's external revelations in nature and in Scripture. E. G. Robinson, Christian Theology, 364—"The word of God is a form or mould, into which the Holy Spirit delivers us when he creates us anew"; cf. Rom. 6:17—"ye became obedient from the heart to that form of teaching whereunto ye were delivered."

B. False mysticism.—Mysticism, however, as the term is commonly used, errs in holding to the attainment of religious knowledge by direct communication from God, and by passive absorption of the human activities into the divine. It either partially or wholly loses sight of (a) the outward organs of revelation, nature and the Scriptures; (b) the activity of the human powers in the reception of all religious knowledge; (c) the personality of man, and, by consequence, the personality of God.

In opposition to false mysticism, we are to remember that the Holy Spirit works through the truth externally revealed in nature and in Scripture (Acts 14:17—"he left not himself without witness"; Rom. 1:20—"the invisible things of him since the creation of the world are clearly seen"; Acts 7:51—"ye do always resist the Holy Spirit: as your fathers did, so do ye"; Eph. 6:17—"the sword of the Spirit, which is the word of God"). By this truth already given we are to test all new communications which would contradict or supersede it (1 John 4:1—"believe not every spirit, but prove the spirits, whether they are of God"; Eph. 5:10—"proving what is well pleasing unto the Lord"). By these tests we may try Spiritualism, Mormonism, Swedenborgianism. Note the mystical tendency in Francis de Sales, Thomas à Kempis, Madame Guyon, Thomas C. Upham. These writers seem at times to advocate an unwarrantable abnegation of our reason and will, and a "swallowing up of man in God." But Christ does not deprive us of reason and will; he only takes from us the perverseness of our reason and the selfishness of our will; so reason and will are restored to their normal clearness and strength. Compare Ps. 16:7—"Jehovah, who hath given me counsel; yea, my heart instructeth me in the night seasons"— God teaches his people through the exercise of their own faculties.

False mysticism is sometimes present though unrecognized. All expectation of results without the use of means partakes of it. Martineau, Seat of Authority, 288—"The lazy will would like to have the vision while the eye that apprehends it sleeps." Preaching without preparation is like throwing ourselves down from a pinnacle of the temple and depending on God to send an angel to hold us up. Christian Science would trust to supernatural agencies, while casting aside the natural agencies God has already provided; as if a drowning man should trust to prayer while refusing to seize the rope. Using Scripture "ad aperturam libri" is like guiding one's actions by a throw of the dice. Allen, Jonathan Edwards, 171, note—"Both Charles and John Wesley were agreed in accepting the Moravian method of solving doubts as to some course of action by opening the Bible at hazard and regarding the passage on which the eye first alighted as a revelation of God's will in the matter"; cf. Wedgwood, Life of Wesley, 193; Southey, Life of Wesley, 1:216. J. G. Paton, Life, 2:74—"After many prayers and wrestlings and tears, I went alone before the Lord, and on my knees cast lots, with a solemn appeal to God, and the answer came: 'Go home!' " He did this only once in his life, in overwhelming perplexity, and finding no light from human counsel. "To whomsoever this faith is given," he says, "let him obey it."

F. B. Meyer, Christian Living, 18—"It is a mistake to seek a sign from heaven; to run from counsellor to counsellor; to cast a lot; or to trust in some chance coincidence. Not that God may not reveal his will thus; but because it is hardly the behavior of a child with its Father. There is a more excellent way,"—namely, appropriate Christ who is wisdom, and then go forward, sure that we shall be guided, as each new step must be taken, or word spoken, or decision made. Our service is to be "rational service" (Rom. 12:1); blind and arbitrary action is inconsistent with the spirit of Christianity. Such action makes us victims of temporary feeling and a prey to Satanic deception. In cases of perplexity, waiting for light and waiting upon God will commonly enable us to make an intelligent decision, while "whatsoever is not of faith is sin" (Rom. 14:23).

"False mysticism reached its logical result in the Buddhistic theosophy. In that system man becomes most divine in the extinction of his own personality. Nirvana is reached by the eightfold path of right view, aspiration, speech, conduct, livelihood, effort, mindfulness, rapture; and Nirvana is the loss of ability to say: 'This is I,' and 'This is mine.' Such was Hypatia's attempt, by subjection of self, to be wafted away into the arms of Jove. George Eliot was wrong when she said: 'The happiest woman has no history.' Self-denial is not self-effacement. The cracked bell has no individuality. In Christ we become our complete selves." Col 2:9, 10—"For in him dwelleth all the fulness of the Godhead bodily, and in him ye are made full."

Royce, World and Individual, 2:248, 249—"Assert the spiritual man; abnegate the natural man. The fleshly self is the root of all evil; the spiritual self belongs to a higher realm. But this spiritual self lies at first outside the soul; it becomes ours only by grace. Plato rightly made the eternal Ideas the source of all human truth and goodness. Wisdom comes into a man, like Aristotle's νοῦς." A. H. Bradford, The Inner Light, in making the direct teaching of the Holy Spirit the sufficient if not the sole source of religious knowledge, seems to us to ignore the principle of evolution in religion. God builds upon the past. His revelation to prophets and apostles constitutes the norm and corrective of our individual experience, even while our experience throws new light upon that revelation. On Mysticism, true and false, see Inge, Christian Mysticism, 4, 5, 11; Stearns, Evidence of Christian Experience, 289-294; Dorner, Geschichte d. prot. Theol., 48-59, 243; Herzog, Encycl., art.: Mystik, by Lange; Vaughan, Hours with the Mystics, 1:199; Morell, Hist. Philos., 58, 191-215, 556-625, 726; Hodge, Syst. Theol., 1:61-69, 97, 104; Fleming, Vocab. Philos., in voce; Tholuck, Introd. to Blüthensammlung aus der morgenländischen Mystik; William James, Varieties of Religious Experience, 379-429.

4. Scripture and Romanism.

While the history of doctrine, as showing the progressive apprehension and unfolding by the church of the truth contained in nature and Scripture, is a subordinate source of theology, Protestantism recognizes the Bible as under Christ the primary and final authority.

Romanism, on the other hand, commits the two-fold error (a) Of making the church, and not the Scriptures, the immediate and sufficient source of religious knowledge; and (b) Of making the relation of the individual to Christ depend upon his relation to the church, instead of making his relation to the church depend upon, follow, and express his relation to Christ.

In Roman Catholicism there is a mystical element. The Scriptures are not the complete or final standard of belief and practice. God gives to the world from time to time, through popes and councils, new communications of truth. Cyprian: "He who has not the church for his mother, has not God for his Father." Augustine: "I would not believe the Scripture, unless the authority of the church also influenced me." Francis of Assisi and Ignatius Loyola both represented the truly obedient person as one dead, moving only as moved by his superior; the true Christian has no life of his own, but is the blind instrument of the church. John Henry Newman, Tracts, Theol. and Eccl., 287—"The Christian dogmas were in the church from the time of the apostles,—they were ever in their substance what they are now." But this is demonstrably untrue of the immaculate conception of the Virgin Mary; of the treasury of merits to be distributed in indulgences; of the infallibility of the pope (see Gore, Incarnation, 186). In place of the true doctrine, "Ubi Spiritus, ibi ecclesia," Romanism substitutes her maxim, "Ubi ecclesia, ibi Spiritus." Luther saw in this the principle of mysticism, when he said: "Papatus est merus enthusiasmus." See Hodge, Syst. Theol., 1:61-69.

In reply to the Romanist argument that the church was before the Bible, and that the same body that gave the truth at the first can make additions to that truth, we say that the unwritten word was before the church and made the church possible. The word of God existed before it was written down, and by that word the first disciples as well as the latest were begotten (1 Pet. 1:23—"begotten again ... through the word of God"). The grain of truth in Roman Catholic doctrine is expressed in 1 Tim. 3:15— "the church of the living God, the pillar and ground of the truth" = the church is God's appointed proclaimer of truth; cf. Phil. 2:16—"holding forth the word of life." But the church can proclaim the truth, only as it is built upon the truth. So we may say that the American Republic is the pillar and ground of liberty in the world; but this is true only so far as the Republic is built upon the principle of liberty as its foundation. When the Romanist asks: "Where was your church before Luther?" the Protestant may reply: "Where yours is not now—in the word of God. Where was your face before it was washed? Where was the fine flour before the wheat went to the mill?" Lady Jane Grey, three days before her execution, February 12, 1554, said: "I ground my faith on God's word, and not upon the church; for, if the church be a good church, the faith of the church must be tried by God's word, and not God's word by the church, nor yet my faith."

The Roman church would keep men in perpetual childhood—coming to her for truth instead of going directly to the Bible; "like the foolish mother who keeps her boy pining in the house lest he stub his toe, and would love best to have him remain a babe forever, that she might mother him still." Martensen, Christian Dogmatics, 30—"Romanism is so busy in building up a system of guarantees, that she forgets the truth of Christ which she would guarantee." George Herbert: "What wretchedness can give him any room, Whose house is foul while he adores his broom!" It is a semi-parasitic doctrine of safety without intelligence or spirituality. Romanism says: "Man for the machine!" Protestantism: "The machine for man!" Catholicism strangles, Protestantism restores, individuality. Yet the Romanist principle sometimes appears in so-called Protestant churches. The Catechism published by the League of the Holy Cross, in the Anglican Church, contains the following: "It is to the priest only that the child must acknowledge his sins, if he desires that God should forgive him. Do you know why? It is because God, when on earth, gave to his priests and to them alone the power of forgiving sins. Go to the priest, who is the doctor of your soul, and who cures you in the name of God." But this contradicts John 10:7—where Christ says "I am the door"; and 1 Cor. 3:11—"other foundation can no man lay than that which is laid, which is Jesus Christ" = Salvation is attained by immediate access to Christ, and there is no door between the soul and him. See Dorner, Gesch. prot. Theol., 227; Schleiermacher, Glaubenslehre, 1:24; Robinson, in Mad. Av. Lectures, 387; Fisher, Nat. and Method of Revelation, 10; Watkins, Bampton Lect. for 1890:149; Drummond, Nat. Law in Spir. World, 327.

II. Limitations of Theology

Although theology derives its material from God's two-fold revelation, it does not profess to give an exhaustive knowledge of God and of the relations between God and the universe. After showing what material we have, we must show what material we have not. We have indicated the sources of theology; we now examine its limitations. Theology has its limitations:

(a) In the finiteness of the human understanding. This gives rise to a class of necessary mysteries, or mysteries connected with the infinity and incomprehensibleness of the divine nature (Job 11:7; Rom. 11:33).

Job 11:7—"Canst thou by searching find out God? Canst thou find out the Almighty to perfection?" Rom. 11:33—"how unsearchable are his judgments, and his ways past finding out!" Every doctrine, therefore, has its inexplicable side. Here is the proper meaning of Tertullian's sayings: "Certum est, quia impossible est: quo absurdius, eo verius"; that of Anselm: "Credo, ut intelligam"; and that of Abelard: "Qui credit cito, levis corde est." Drummond, Nat. Law in Spir. World: "A science without mystery is unknown; a religion without mystery is absurd." E. G. Robinson: "A finite being cannot grasp even its own relations to the Infinite." Hovey, Manual of Christ. Theol., 7—"To infer from the perfection of God that all his works [nature, man, inspiration] will be absolutely and unchangeably perfect: to infer from the perfect love of God that there can be no sin or suffering in the world; to infer from the sovereignty of God that man is not a free moral agent;—all these inferences are rash; they are inferences from the cause to the effect, while the cause is imperfectly known." See Calderwood, Philos. of Infinite, 491; Sir Wm. Hamilton, Discussions, 22.

(b) In the imperfect state of science, both natural and metaphysical. This gives rise to a class of accidental mysteries, or mysteries which consist in the apparently irreconcilable nature of truths, which, taken separately, are perfectly comprehensible.

We are the victims of a mental or moral astigmatism, which sees a single point of truth as two. We see God and man, divine sovereignty and human freedom, Christ's divine nature and Christ's human nature, the natural and the supernatural, respectively, as two disconnected facts, when perhaps deeper insight would see but one. Astronomy has its centripetal and centrifugal forces, yet they are doubtless one force. The child cannot hold two oranges at once in its little hand. Negro preacher: "You can't carry two watermelons under one arm." Shakespeare, Antony and Cleopatra, 1:2—"In nature's infinite book of secresy, A little I can read." Cooke, Credentials of Science, 34—"Man's progress in knowledge has been so constantly and rapidly accelerated that more has been gained during the lifetime of men still living than during all human history before." And yet we may say with D'Arcy, Idealism and Theology, 248—"Man's position in the universe is eccentric. God alone is at the centre. To him alone is the orbit of truth completely displayed.... There are circumstances in which to us the onward movement of truth may seem a retrogression." William Watson, Collected Poems, 271—"Think not thy wisdom can illume away The ancient tanglement of night and day. Enough to acknowledge both, and both revere: They see not clearliest who see all things clear."

(c) In the inadequacy of language. Since language is the medium through which truth is expressed and formulated, the invention of a proper terminology in theology, as in every other science, is a condition and criterion of its progress. The Scriptures recognize a peculiar difficulty in putting spiritual truths into earthly language (1 Cor. 2:13; 2 Cor. 3:6; 12:4).

1 Cor. 2:13—"not in words which man's wisdom teacheth"; 2 Cor. 3:6—"the letter killeth"; 12:4—"unspeakable words." God submits to conditions of revelation; cf. John 16:12—"I have yet many

things to say into you, but ye cannot bear them now." Language has to be created. Words have to be taken from a common, and to be put to a larger and more sacred, use, so that they "stagger under their weight of meaning"—e. g., the word "day," in Genesis 1, and the word ἀγάπη in 1 Cor. 13. See Gould, in Amer. Com., on 1 Cor. 13:12—"now we see in a mirror, darkly"—in a metallic mirror whose surface is dim and whose images are obscure = Now we behold Christ, the truth, only as he is reflected in imperfect speech—"but then face to face" = immediately, without the intervention of an imperfect medium. "As fast as we tunnel into the sandbank of thought, the stones of language must be built into walls and arches, to allow further progress into the boundless mine."

(d) In the incompleteness of our knowledge of the Scriptures. Since it is not the mere letter of the Scriptures that constitutes the truth, the progress of theology is dependent upon hermeneutics, or the interpretation of the word of God.

Notice the progress in commenting, from homiletical to grammatical, historical, dogmatic, illustrated in Scott, Ellicott, Stanley, Lightfoot. John Robinson: "I am verily persuaded that the Lord hath more truth yet to break forth from his holy word." Recent criticism has shown the necessity of studying each portion of Scripture in the light of its origin and connections. There has been an evolution of Scripture, as truly as there has been an evolution of natural science, and the Spirit of Christ who was in the prophets has brought about a progress from germinal and typical expression to expression that is complete and clear. Yet we still need to offer the prayer of Ps. 119:18—"Open thou mine eyes, that I may behold wondrous things out of thy law." On New Testament Interpretation, see A. H. Strong, Philosophy and Religion, 334-336.

(e) In the silence of written revelation. For our discipline and probation, much is probably hidden from us, which we might even with our present powers comprehend.

Instance the silence of Scripture with regard to the life and death of Mary the Virgin, the personal appearance of Jesus and his occupations in early life, the origin of evil, the method of the atonement, the state after death. So also as to social and political questions, such as slavery, the liquor traffic, domestic virtues, governmental corruption. "Jesus was in heaven at the revolt of the angels, yet he tells us little about angels or about heaven. He does not discourse about Eden, or Adam, or the fall of man, or death as the result of Adam's sin; and he says little of departed spirits, whether they are lost or saved." It was better to inculcate principles, and trust his followers to apply them. His gospel is not intended to gratify a vain curiosity. He would not divert men's minds from pursuing the one thing needful; cf. Luke 13:23, 24—"Lord, are they few that are saved? And he said unto them, Strive to enter in by the narrow door; for many, I say unto you, shall seek to enter in, and shall not be able." Paul's silence upon speculative questions which he must have pondered with absorbing interest is a proof of his divine inspiration. John Foster spent his life, "gathering questions for eternity"; cf. John 13:7—"What I do thou knowest not now; but thou shalt understand hereafter." The most beautiful thing in a countenance is that which a picture can never express. He who would speak well must omit well. Story: "Of every noble work the silent part is best; Of all expressions that which cannot be expressed." Cf. 1 Cor. 2:9—"Things which eye saw not, and ear heard not, And which entered not into the heart of man, Whatsoever things God prepared for them that love him"; Deut 29:29—"The secret things belong unto Jehovah our God: but the things that are revealed belong unto us and to our children." For Luther's view, see Hagenbach, Hist. Doctrine, 2:388. See also B. D. Thomas, The Secret of the Divine Silence.

(f) In the lack of spiritual discernment caused by sin. Since holy affection is a condition of religious knowledge, all moral imperfection in the individual Christian and in the church serves as a hindrance to the working out of a complete theology.

John 3:3—"Except one be born anew, he cannot see the kingdom of God." The spiritual ages make most progress in theology,—witness the half-century succeeding the Reformation, and the half-century succeeding the great revival in New England in the time of Jonathan Edwards. Ueberweg, Logic (Lindsay's transl.), 514—"Science is much under the influence of the will; and the truth of knowledge depends upon the purity of the conscience. The will has no power to resist scientific evidence; but scientific evidence is not obtained without the continuous loyalty of the will." Lord Bacon declared that man cannot enter the kingdom of science, any more than he can enter the kingdom of heaven, without becoming a little child. Darwin describes his own mind as having become a kind of machine for grinding general laws out of large collections of facts, with the result of producing "atrophy of that part of the brain on which the higher tastes depend." But a similar abnormal atrophy is possible in the case of the moral and religious faculty (see Gore, Incarnation, 37). Dr. Allen said in his Introductory Lecture at Lane Theological Seminary: "We are very glad to see you if you wish to be students; but the professors' chairs are all filled."

(a) A perfect system of theology is impossible. We do not expect to construct such a system. All science but reflects the present attainment of the human mind. No science is complete or finished. However it may be with the sciences of nature and of man, the science of God will never amount to an exhaustive knowledge. We must not expect to demonstrate all Scripture doctrines upon rational grounds, or even in every case to see the principle of connection between them. Where we cannot do this, we must, as in every other science, set the revealed facts in their places and wait for further light, instead of ignoring or rejecting any of them because we cannot understand them or their relation to other parts of our system.

Three problems left unsolved by the Egyptians have been handed down to our generation: (1) the duplication of the cube; (2) the trisection of the angle; (3) the quadrature of the circle. Dr. Johnson: "Dictionaries are like watches; the worst is better than none; and the best cannot be expected to go quite true." Hood spoke of Dr. Johnson's "Contradictionary," which had both "interiour" and "exterior." Sir William Thompson (Lord Kelvin) at the fiftieth anniversary of his professorship said: "One word characterizes the most strenuous of the efforts for the advancement of science which I have made perseveringly through fifty-five years: that word is failure; I know no more of electric and magnetic force, or of the relations between ether, electricity and ponderable matter, or of chemical affinity, than I knew and tried to teach my students of natural philosophy fifty years ago in my first session as professor." Allen, Religious Progress, mentions three tendencies. "The first says: Destroy the new! The second says: Destroy the old! The third says: Destroy nothing! Let the old gradually and quietly grow into the new, as Erasmus wished. We should accept contradictions, whether they can be intellectually reconciled or not. The truth has never prospered by enforcing some 'via media.' Truth lies rather in the union of opposite propositions, as in Christ's divinity and humanity, and in grace and freedom. Blanco White went from Rome to infidelity; Orestes Brownson from infidelity to Rome; so the brothers John Henry Newman and Francis W. Newman, and the brothers George Herbert of Bemerton and Lord Herbert of Cherbury. One would secularize the divine, the other would divinize the secular. But if one is true, so is the other. Let us adopt both. All progress is a deeper penetration into the meaning of old truth, and a larger appropriation of it."

(b) Theology is nevertheless progressive. It is progressive in the sense that our subjective understanding of the facts with regard to God, and our consequent expositions of these facts, may and do become more perfect. But theology is not progressive in the sense that its objective facts change, either in their number or their nature. With Martineau we may say: "Religion has been reproached with not being progressive; it makes amends by being imperishable." Though our knowledge may be imperfect, it will have great value still. Our success in constructing a theology will depend upon the proportion which clearly expressed facts of Scripture bear to mere inferences, and upon the degree in which they all cohere about Christ, the central person and theme.

The progress of theology is progress in apprehension by man, not progress in communication by God. Originality in astronomy is not man's creation of new planets, but man's discovery of planets that were never seen before, or the bringing to light of relations between them that were never before suspected. Robert Kerr Eccles: "Originality is a habit of recurring to origins—the habit of securing personal experience by personal application to original facts. It is not an eduction of novelties either from nature, Scripture, or inner consciousness; it is rather the habit of resorting to primitive facts, and of securing the personal experiences which arise from contact with these facts." Fisher, Nat. and Meth. of Revelation, 48—"The starry heavens are now what they were of old; there is no enlargement of the stellar universe, except that which comes through the increased power and use of the telescope." We must not imitate the green sailor who, when set to steer, said he had "sailed by that star."

Martineau, Types, 1:492, 493—"Metaphysics, so far as they are true to their work, are stationary, precisely because they have in charge, not what begins and ceases to be, but what always is.... It is absurd to praise motion for always making way, while disparaging space for still being what it ever was: as if the motion you prefer could be, without the space which you reproach." Newman Smyth, Christian Ethics, 45, 67-70, 79—"True conservatism is progress which takes direction from the past and fulfils its good; false conservatism is a narrowing and hopeless reversion to the past, which is a betrayal of the promise of the future. So Jesus came not 'to destroy the law or the prophets'; he 'came not to destroy, but to fulfil' (Mat. 5:17).... The last book on Christian Ethics will not be written before the Judgment Day." John Milton, Areopagitica: "Truth is compared in the Scripture to a streaming fountain; if her waters flow not in a perpetual progression, they sicken into a muddy pool of conformity and tradition. A man may be a heretic in the truth." Paul in Rom. 2:16, and in 2 Tim. 2:8—speaks of "my gospel." It is the duty of every Christian to have his own conception of the truth, while he respects the conceptions of others. Tennyson, Locksley Hall: "I that rather held it better men should perish one by one, Than that earth should stand at gaze like Joshua's moon at Ajalon." We do not expect any new worlds, and we need not expect any new Scriptures; but we may expect progress in the interpretation of both. Facts are final, but interpretation is not.

Chapter III - Method Of Theology

I. Requisites to the study of Theology

The requisites to the successful study of theology have already in part been indicated in speaking of its limitations. In spite of some repetition, however, we mention the following:

(a) A disciplined mind. Only such a mind can patiently collect the facts, hold in its grasp many facts at once, educe by continuous reflection their connecting principles, suspend final judgment until its conclusions are verified by Scripture and experience.

Robert Browning, Ring and Book, 175 (Pope, 228)—"Truth nowhere lies, yet everywhere, in these; Not absolutely in a portion, yet Evolveable from the whole: evolved at last Painfully, held tenaciously by me." Teachers and students may be divided into two classes: (1) those who know enough already; (2) those wish to learn more than they now know. Motto of Winchester School in England: "Disce, aut discede." Butcher, Greek Genius, 213, 230—"The Sophists fancied that they were imparting education, when they were only imparting results. Aristotle illustrates their method by the example of a shoemaker who, professing to teach the art of making painless shoes, puts into the apprentice's hand a large assortment of shoes ready-made. A witty Frenchman classes together those who would make science popular, metaphysics intelligible, and vice respectable. The word σχόλη, which first meant 'leisure,' then 'philosophical discussion,' and finally 'school,' shows the pure love of learning among the Greeks." Robert G. Ingersoll said that the average provincial clergyman is like the land of the upper Potomac spoken of by Tom Randolph, as almost worthless in its original state, and rendered wholly so by cultivation. Lotze, Metaphysics, 1:16—"the constant whetting of the knife is tedious, if it is not proposed to cut anything with it." "To do their duty is their only holiday," is the description of Athenian character given by Thucydides. Chitty asked a father inquiring as to his son's qualifications for the law: "Can your son eat sawdust without any butter?" On opportunities for culture in the Christian ministry, see New Englander, Oct. 1875:644; A. H. Strong, Philosophy and Religion, 273-275; Christ in Creation, 318-320.

(b) An intuitional as distinguished from a merely logical habit of mind,—or, trust in the mind's primitive convictions, as well as in its processes of reasoning. The theologian must have insight as well as understanding. He must accustom himself to ponder spiritual facts as well as those which are sensible and material; to see things in their inner relations as well as in their outward forms; to cherish confidence in the reality and the unity of truth.

Vinet, Outlines of Philosophy, 39, 40—"If I do not feel that good is good, who will ever prove it to me?" Pascal: "Logic, which is an abstraction, may shake everything. A being purely intellectual will be incurably sceptical." Calvin: "Satan is an acute theologian." Some men can see a fly on a barn door a mile away, and yet can never see the door. Zeller, Outlines of Greek Philosophy, 93—"Gorgias the Sophist was able to show metaphysically that nothing can exist; that what does exist cannot be known by us; and that what is known by us cannot be imparted to others" (quoted by Wenley, Socrates and Christ, 28). Aristotle differed from those moderate men who thought it impossible to go over the same river twice,—he held that it could not be done even once (cf. Wordsworth, Prelude, 536). Dove, Logic of the Christian Faith, 1-29, and especially 25, gives a demonstration of the impossibility of motion: A thing cannot move in the place where it is; it cannot move in the places where it is not; but the place where it is and the places where it is not are all the places that there are; therefore a thing cannot move at all. Hazard, Man a Creative First Cause, 109, shows that the bottom of a wheel does not move, since it goes backward as fast as the top goes forward. An instantaneous photograph makes the upper part a confused blur, while the spokes of the lower part are distinctly visible. Abp. Whately: "Weak arguments are often thrust before my path; but, although they are most unsubstantial, it is not easy to destroy them. There is not a more difficult feat known than to cut through a cushion with a sword." Cf. 1 Tim. 6:20—"oppositions of the knowledge which is falsely so called"; 3:2—"the bishop therefore must be ... sober-minded"—σώφρων = "well balanced." The Scripture speaks of "sound [ὑγιής = healthful] doctrine" (1 Tim. 1:10). Contrast 1 Tim. 6:4—[νοσῶν = ailing] "diseased about questionings and disputes of words."

(c) An acquaintance with physical, mental, and moral science. The method of conceiving and expressing Scripture truth is so affected by our elementary notions of these sciences, and the weapons with which theology is attacked and defended are so commonly drawn from them as arsenals, that the student cannot afford to be ignorant of them.

Goethe explains his own greatness by his avoidance of metaphysics: "Mein Kind, Ich habe es klug gemacht: Ich habe nie über's Denken gedacht"—"I have been wise in never thinking about thinking"; he would have been wiser, had he pondered more deeply the fundamental principles of his philosophy; see A. H. Strong, The Great Poets and their Theology, 296-299, and Philosophy and Religion, 1-18; also in Baptist Quarterly, 2:393 sq. Many a theological system has fallen, like the Campanile at Venice, because its foundations were insecure. Sir William Hamilton: "No difficulty arises in theology which has not first emerged in philosophy." N. W. Taylor: "Give me a young man in metaphysics, and I care not who has him in theology." President Samson Talbot: "I love metaphysics, because they have to do with realities." The maxim "Ubi tres medici, ibi duo athei," witnesses to the truth of Galen's words: ἄριστος ἰατρὸς καὶ φιλόσοφος—"the best physician is also a philosopher." Theology cannot dispense with science, any more than science can dispense with philosophy. E. G. Robinson: "Science has not invalidated any fundamental truth of revelation, though it has modified the statement of many.... Physical Science will undoubtedly knock some of our crockery gods on the head, and the sooner the better." There is great advantage to the preacher in taking up, as did Frederick W. Robertson, one science after another. Chemistry entered into his mental structure, as he said, "like iron into the blood."

(d) A knowledge of the original languages of the Bible. This is necessary to enable us not only to determine the meaning of the fundamental terms of Scripture, such as holiness, sin, propitiation, justification, but also to interpret statements of doctrine by their connections with the context.

Emerson said that the man who reads a book in a strange tongue, when he can have a good translation, is a fool. Dr. Behrends replied that he is a fool who is satisfied with the substitute. E. G. Robinson: "Language is a great organism, and no study so disciplines the mind as the dissection of an organism." Chrysostom: "This is the cause of all our evils—our not knowing the Scriptures." Yet a modern scholar has said: "The Bible is the most dangerous of all God's gifts to men." It is possible to adore the letter, while we fail to perceive its spirit. A narrow interpretation may contradict its meaning. Much depends upon connecting phrases, as for example, the διὰ τοῦτο and ἐφ' ᾧ, in Rom. 5:12. Professor Philip Lindsley of Princeton, 1813-1853, said to his pupils: "One of the best preparations for death is a thorough knowledge of the Greek grammar." The youthful Erasmus: "When I get some money, I will get me some Greek books, and, after that, some clothes." The dead languages are the only really living ones—free from danger of misunderstanding from changing usage. Divine Providence has put revelation into fixed forms in the Hebrew and the Greek. Sir William Hamilton, Discussions, 330—"To be a competent divine is in fact to be a scholar." On the true idea of a Theological Seminary Course, see A. H. Strong, Philos. and Religion, 302-313.

(e) A holy affection toward God. Only the renewed heart can properly feel its need of divine revelation, or understand that revelation when given.

Ps. 25:14—"The secret of Jehovah is with them that fear him"; Rom. 12:2—"prove what is the ... will of God"; cf. Ps. 36:1—"the transgression of the wicked speaks in his heart like an oracle." "It is the heart and not the brain That to the highest doth attain." To "learn by heart" is something more than to learn by mind, or by head. All heterodoxy is preceded by heteropraxy. In Bunyan's Pilgrim's Progress, Faithful does not go through the Slough of Despond, as Christian did; and it is by getting over the fence to find an easier road, that Christian and Hopeful get into Doubting Castle and the hands of Giant Despair. "Great thoughts come from the heart," said Vauvenargues. The preacher cannot, like Dr. Kane, kindle fire with a lens of ice. Aristotle: "The power of attaining moral truth is dependent upon our acting rightly." Pascal: "We know truth, not only by the reason, but by the heart.... The heart has its reasons, which the reason knows nothing of." Hobbes: "Even the axioms of geometry would be disputed, if men's passions were concerned in them." Macaulay: "The law of gravitation would still be controverted, if it interfered with vested interests." Nordau, Degeneracy: "Philosophic systems simply furnish the excuses reason demands for the unconscious impulses of the race during a given period of time."

Lord Bacon: "A tortoise on the right path will beat a racer on the wrong path." Goethe: "As are the inclinations, so also are the opinions.... A work of art can be comprehended by the head only with the assistance of the heart.... Only law can give us liberty." Fichte: "Our system of thought is very often only the history of our heart.... Truth is descended from conscience.... Men do not will according to their reason, but they reason according to their will." Neander's motto was: "Pectus est quod theologum facit"—"It is the heart that makes the theologian." John Stirling: "That is a dreadful eye which can be divided from a living human heavenly heart, and still retain its all-penetrating vision,—such was the eye of the Gorgons." But such an eye, we add, is not all-penetrating. E. G. Robinson: "Never study theology in cold blood." W. C. Wilkinson: "The head is a magnetic needle with truth for its pole. But the heart is a hidden mass of magnetic iron. The head is drawn somewhat toward its natural pole, the truth; but more it is drawn by that nearer magnetism." See an affecting instance of Thomas Carlyle's enlightenment, after the death of his wife, as to the meaning of the Lord's Prayer, in Fisher, Nat. and Meth. of Revelation, 165. On the importance of feeling, in association of ideas, see Dewey, Psychology, 106, 107.

(f) The enlightening influence of the Holy Spirit. As only the Spirit fathoms the things of God, so only he can illuminate our minds to apprehend them.

1 Cor. 2:11, 12—"the things of God none knoweth, save the Spirit of God. But we received ... the Spirit which is from God; that we might know." Cicero, Nat. Deorum, 66—"Nemo igitur vir magnus sine aliquo adfiatu divino unquam fuit." Professor Beck of Tübingen: "For the student, there is no privileged path leading to the truth; the only one which leads to it is also that of the unlearned; it is that of regeneration and of gradual illumination by the Holy Spirit; and without the Holy Spirit, theology is not only a cold stone, it is a deadly poison." As all the truths of the differential and integral calculus are wrapped up in the simplest mathematical axiom, so all theology is wrapped up in the declaration that God is holiness and love, or in the protevangelium uttered at the gates of Eden. But dull minds cannot of themselves evolve the calculus from the axiom, nor can sinful hearts evolve theology from the first prophecy. Teachers are needed to demonstrate geometrical theorems, and the Holy Spirit is needed to show us that the "new commandment" illustrated by the death of Christ is only an "old commandment which ye had from the beginning" (1 John 2:7). The Principia of Newton is a revelation of Christ, and so are the Scriptures. The Holy Spirit enables us to enter into the meaning of Christ's revelations in both Scripture and nature; to interpret the one by the other; and so to work out original demonstrations and applications of the truth; Mat. 13:52—"Therefore every scribe who hath been made a disciple of the kingdom of heaven is like unto a man that is a householder, who bringeth forth out of his treasure things new and old." See Adolph Monod's sermons on Christ's Temptation, addressed to the theological students of Montauban, in Select Sermons from the French and German, 117-179.

II. Divisions of Theology

Theology is commonly divided into Biblical, Historical, Systematic, and Practical.

1. Biblical Theology aims to arrange and classify the facts of revelation, confining itself to the Scriptures for its material, and treating of doctrine only so far as it was developed at the close of the apostolic age.

Instance DeWette, Biblische Theologie; Hofmann, Schriftbeweis; Nitzsch, System of Christian Doctrine. The last, however, has more of the philosophical element than properly belongs to Biblical Theology. The third volume of Ritschl's Justification and Reconciliation is intended as a system of Biblical Theology, the first and second volumes being little more than an historical introduction. But metaphysics, of a Kantian relativity and phenomenalism, enter so largely into Ritschl's estimates and interpretations, as to render his conclusions both partial and rationalistic. Notice a questionable use of the term Biblical Theology to designate the theology of a part of Scripture severed from the rest, as Steudel's Biblical Theology of the Old Testament; Schmidt's Biblical Theology of the New Testament; and in the common phrases: Biblical Theology of Christ, or of Paul. These phrases are objectionable as intimating that the books of Scripture have only a human origin. Upon the assumption that there is no common divine authorship of Scripture, Biblical Theology is conceived of as a series of fragments, corresponding to the differing teachings of the various prophets and apostles, and the theology of Paul is held to be an unwarranted and incongruous addition to the theology of Jesus. See Reuss, History of Christian Theology in the Apostolic Age.

2. Historical Theology traces the development of the Biblical doctrines from the time of the apostles to the present day, and gives account of the results of this development in the life of the church.

By doctrinal development we mean the progressive unfolding and apprehension, by the church, of the truth explicitly or implicitly contained in Scripture. As giving account of the shaping of the Christian faith into doctrinal statements, Historical Theology is called the History of Doctrine. As describing the resulting and accompanying changes in the life of the church, outward and inward, Historical Theology is called Church History. Instance Cunningham's Historical Theology; Hagenbach's and Shedd's Histories of Doctrine; Neander's Church History. There is always a danger that the historian will see his own views too clearly reflected in the history of the church. Shedd's History of Christian Doctrine has been called "The History of Dr. Shedd's Christian Doctrine." But if Dr. Shedd's Augustinianism colors his History, Dr. Sheldon's Arminianism also colors his. G. P. Fisher's History of Christian Doctrine is unusually lucid and impartial. See Neander's Introduction and Shedd's Philosophy of History.

3. Systematic Theology takes the material furnished by Biblical and by Historical Theology, and with this material seeks to build up into an organic and consistent whole all our knowledge of God and of the relations between God and the universe, whether this knowledge be originally derived from nature or from the Scriptures.

Systematic Theology is therefore theology proper, of which Biblical and Historical Theology are the incomplete and preparatory stages. Systematic Theology is to be clearly distinguished from Dogmatic Theology. Dogmatic Theology is, in strict usage, the systematizing of the doctrines as expressed in the symbols of the church, together with the grounding of these in the Scriptures, and the exhibition, so far as may be, of their rational necessity. Systematic Theology begins, on the other hand, not with the symbols, but with the Scriptures. It asks first, not what the church has believed, but what is the truth of God's revealed word. It examines that word with all the aids which nature and the Spirit have given it, using Biblical and Historical Theology as its servants and helpers, but not as its masters. Notice here the technical use of the word "symbol," from συμβάλλω, = a brief throwing together, or condensed statement of the essentials of Christian doctrine. Synonyms are: Confession, creed, consensus, declaration, formulary, canons, articles of faith.

Dogmatism argues to foregone conclusions. The word is not, however, derived from "dog," as Douglas Jerrold facetiously suggested, when he said that "dogmatism is puppyism full grown," but from δοκέω to think, to opine. Dogmatic Theology has two principles: (1) The absolute authority of creeds, as decisions of the church: (2) The application to these creeds of formal logic, for the purpose of demonstrating their truth to the understanding. In the Roman Catholic Church, not the Scripture but the church, and the dogma given by it, is the decisive authority. The Protestant principle, on the contrary, is that Scripture decides, and that dogma is to be judged by it. Following Schleiermacher, Al. Schweizer thinks that the term "Dogmatik" should be discarded as essentially unprotestant, and that "Glaubenslehre" should take its place; and Harnack, Hist. Dogma, 6, remarks that "dogma has ever, in the progress of history, devoured its own progenitors." While it is true that every new and advanced thinker in theology has been counted a heretic, there has always been a common faith—"the faith which was once for all delivered unto the saints" (Jude 3)—and the study of Systematic Theology has been one of the chief means of preserving this faith in the world. Mat. 15:13, 14—"Every plant which my heavenly Father planted not, shall be rooted up. Let them alone: they are blind guides" = there is truth planted by God, and it has permanent divine life. Human errors have no permanent vitality and they perish of themselves. See Kaftan, Dogmatik, 2, 3.

4. Practical Theology is the system of truth considered as a means of renewing and sanctifying men, or, in other words, theology in its publication and enforcement.

To this department of theology belong Homiletics and Pastoral Theology, since these are but scientific presentations of the right methods of unfolding Christian truth, and of bringing it to bear upon men individually and in the church. See Van Oosterzee, Practical Theology; T. Harwood Pattison, The Making of the Sermon, and Public Prayer; Yale Lectures on Preaching by H. W. Beecher, R. W. Dale, Phillips Brooks, E. G. Robinson, A. J. F. Behrends, John Watson, and others; and the work on Pastoral Theology, by Harvey.

It is sometimes asserted that there are other departments of theology not included in those above mentioned. But most of these, if not all, belong to other spheres of research, and cannot properly be classed under theology at all. Moral Theology, so called, or the science of Christian morals, ethics, or theological ethics, is indeed the proper result of theology, but is not to be confounded with it. Speculative theology, so called, respecting, as it does, such truth as is mere matter of opinion, is either extra-scriptural, and so belongs to the province of the philosophy of religion, or is an attempt to explain truth already revealed, and so falls within the province of Systematic Theology. "Speculative theology starts from certain a priori principles, and from them undertakes to determine what is and must be. It deduces its scheme of doctrine from the laws of mind or from axioms supposed to be inwrought into its constitution." Bib. Sac., 1852:376—"Speculative theology tries to show that the dogmas agree with the laws of thought, while the philosophy of religion tries to show that the laws of thought agree with the dogmas." Theological Encyclopædia (the word signifies "instruction in a circle") is a general introduction to all the divisions of Theology, together with an account of the relations between them. Hegel's Encyclopædia was an attempted exhibition of the principles and connections of all the sciences. See Crooks and Hurst, Theological Encyclopædia and Methodology; Zöckler, Handb. der theol. Wissenschaften, 2:606-769.

The relations of theology to science and philosophy have been variously stated, but by none better than by H. B. Smith, Faith and Philosophy, 18—"Philosophy is a mode of human knowledge—not the whole of that knowledge, but a mode of it—the knowing of things rationally." Science asks: "What do I know?" Philosophy asks: "What can I know?" William James, Psychology, 1:145—"Metaphysics means nothing but an unusually obstinate effort to think clearly." Aristotle: "The particular sciences are toiling workmen, while philosophy is the architect. The workmen are slaves, existing for the free master. So philosophy rules the sciences." With regard to philosophy and science Lord Bacon remarks: "Those who have handled knowledge have been too much either men of mere observation or abstract reasoners. The former are like the ant: they only collect material and put it to immediate use. The abstract reasoners are like spiders, who make cobwebs out of their own substance. But the bee takes a middle course: it gathers its material from the flowers of the garden and the field, while it transforms and digests what it gathers by a power of its own. Not unlike this is the work of the philosopher." Novalis: "Philosophy can bake no bread; but it can give us God, freedom and immortality." Prof. DeWitt of Princeton: "Science, philosophy, and theology are the three great modes of organizing the universe into an intellectual system. Science never goes below second causes; if it does, it is no longer science,—it becomes philosophy. Philosophy views the universe as a unity, and the goal it is always seeking to reach is the source and centre of this unity—the Absolute, the First Cause. This goal of philosophy is the point of departure for theology. What philosophy is striving to find, theology asserts has been found. Theology therefore starts with the Absolute, the First Cause." W. N. Clarke, Christian Theology, 48—"Science examines and classifies facts; philosophy inquires concerning spiritual meanings. Science seeks to know the universe; philosophy to understand it."

Balfour, Foundations of Belief, 7—"Natural science has for its subject matter things and events. Philosophy is the systematic exhibition of the grounds of our knowledge. Metaphysics is our knowledge respecting realities which are not phenomenal, e. g., God and the soul." Knight, Essays in Philosophy, 81—"The aim of the sciences is increase of knowledge, by the discovery of laws within which all phenomena may be embraced and by means of which they may be explained. The aim of philosophy, on the other hand, is to explain the sciences, by at once including and transcending them. Its sphere is substance and essence." Bowne, Theory of Thought and Knowledge, 3-5—"Philosophy = doctrine of knowledge (is mind passive or active in knowing?—Epistemology) + doctrine of being (is fundamental being mechanical and unintelligent, or purposive and intelligent?—Metaphysics). The systems of Locke, Hume, and Kant are preëminently theories of knowing; the systems of Spinoza and Leibnitz are preëminently theories of being. Historically theories of being come first, because the object is the only determinant for reflective thought. But the instrument of philosophy is thought itself. First then, we must study Logic, or the theory of thought; secondly, Epistemology, or the theory of knowledge; thirdly, Metaphysics, or the theory of being."

Professor George M. Forbes on the New Psychology: "Locke and Kant represent the two tendencies in philosophy—the empirical, physical, scientific, on the one hand, and the rational, metaphysical, logical, on the other. Locke furnishes the basis for the associational schemes of Hartley, the Mills, and Bain; Kant for the idealistic scheme of Fichte, Schelling, and Hegel. The two are not contradictory, but complementary, and the Scotch Reid and Hamilton combine them both, reacting against the extreme empiricism and scepticism of Hume. Hickok, Porter, and McCosh represented the Scotch school in America. It was exclusively analytical; its psychology was the faculty-psychology; it represented the mind as a bundle of faculties. The unitary philosophy of T. H. Green, Edward Caird, in Great Britain, and in America, of W. T. Harris, George S. Morris, and John Dewey, was a reaction against this faculty-psychology, under the influence of Hegel. A second reaction under the influence of the Herbartian doctrine of apperception substituted function for faculty, making all processes phases of apperception. G. F. Stout and J. Mark Baldwin represent this psychology. A third reaction comes from the influence of physical science. All attempts to unify are relegated to a metaphysical Hades. There is nothing but states and processes. The only unity is the laws of their coëxistence and succession. There is nothing a priori. Wundt identifies apperception with will, and regards it as the unitary principle. Külpe and Titchener find no self, or will, or soul, but treat these as inferences little warranted. Their psychology is psychology without a soul. The old psychology was exclusively static, while the new emphasizes the genetic point of view. Growth and development are the leading ideas of Herbert Spencer, Preyer, Tracy and Stanley Hall. William James is explanatory, while George T. Ladd is descriptive. Cattell, Scripture, and Münsterberg apply the methods of Fechner, and the Psychological Review is their organ. Their error is in their negative attitude. The old psychology is needed to supplement the new. It has greater scope and more practical significance." On the relation of theology to philosophy and to science, see Luthardt, Compend. der Dogmatik, 4; Hagenbach, Encyclopädie, 109.

III. History of Systematic Theology

1. In the Eastern Church, Systematic Theology may be said to have had its beginning and end in John of Damascus (700-760).

Ignatius († 115—Ad Trall., c. 9) gives us "the first distinct statement of the faith drawn up in a series of propositions. This systematizing formed the basis of all later efforts" (Prof. A. H. Newman). Origen of Alexandria (186-254) wrote his Περὶ Ἀρχῶν; Athanasius of Alexandria (300-373) his Treatises on the Trinity and the Deity of Christ; and Gregory of Nyssa in Cappadocia (332-398) his Λόγος κατηχητικὸς ὁ μέγας. Hatch, Hibbert Lectures, 323, regards the "De Principiis" of Origen as the "first complete system of dogma," and speaks of Origen as "the disciple of Clement of Alexandria, the first great teacher of philosophical Christianity." But while the Fathers just mentioned seem to have conceived the plan of expounding the doctrines in order and of showing their relation to one another, it was John of Damascus (700-760) who first actually carried out such a plan. His Ἔκδοσις ἀκριβὴς τῆς ὀρθοδόξου Πίστεως, or Summary of the Orthodox Faith, may be considered the earliest work of Systematic Theology. Neander calls it "the most important doctrinal text-book of the Greek Church." John, like the Greek Church in general, was speculative, theological, semi-pelagian, sacramentarian. The Apostles' Creed, so called, is, in its present form, not earlier than the fifth century; see Schaff, Creeds of Christendom, 1:19. Mr. Gladstone suggested that the Apostles' Creed was a development of the baptismal formula. McGiffert, Apostles' Creed, assigns to the meagre original form a date of the third quarter of the second century, and regards the Roman origin of the symbol as proved. It was framed as a baptismal formula, but specifically in opposition to the teachings of Marcion, which were at that time causing much trouble at Rome. Harnack however dates the original Apostles' Creed at 150, and Zahn places it at 120. See also J. C. Long, in Bap. Quar. Rev., Jan. 1892: 89-101.

2. In the Western Church, we may (with Hagenbach) distinguish three periods:

(a) The period of Scholasticism,—introduced by Peter Lombard (1100-1160), and reaching its culmination in Thomas Aquinas (1221-1274) and Duns Scotus (1265-1308).

Though Systematic Theology had its beginning in the Eastern Church, its development has been confined almost wholly to the Western. Augustine (353-430) wrote his "Encheiridion ad Laurentium" and his "De Civitate Dei," and John Scotus Erigena († 850), Roscelin (1092-1122), and Abelard (1079-1142), in their attempts at the rational explanation of the Christian doctrine foreshadowed the works of the great scholastic teachers. Anselm of Canterbury (1034-1109), with his "Proslogion de Dei Existentia" and his "Cur Deus Homo," has sometimes, but wrongly, been called the founder of Scholasticism. Allen, in his Continuity of Christian Thought, represents the transcendence of God as the controlling principle of the Augustinian and of the Western theology. The Eastern Church, he maintains, had founded its theology on God's immanence. Paine, in his Evolution of Trinitarianism, shows that this is erroneous. Augustine was a theistic monist. He declares that "Dei voluntas rerum natura est," and regards God's upholding as a continuous creation. Western theology recognized the immanence of God as well as his transcendence.

Peter Lombard, however, (1100-1160), the "magister sententiarum," was the first great systematizer of the Western Church, and his "Libri Sententiarum Quatuor" was the theological text-book of the Middle Ages. Teachers lectured on the "Sentences" (Sententia = sentence, Satz, locus, point, article of faith), as they did on the books of Aristotle, who furnished to Scholasticism its impulse and guide. Every doctrine was treated in the order of Aristotle's four causes: the material, the formal, the efficient, the final. ("Cause" here = requisite: (1) matter of which a thing consists, e. g., bricks and mortar; (2) form it assumes, e. g., plan or design; (3) producing agent, e. g., builder; (4) end for which made, e. g., house.) The organization of physical as well as of theological science was due to Aristotle. Dante called him "the master of those who know." James Ten Broeke, Bap. Quar. Rev., Jan. 1892:1-26—"The Revival of Learning showed the world that the real Aristotle was much broader than the Scholastic Aristotle—information very unwelcome to the Roman Church." For the influence of Scholasticism, compare the literary methods of Augustine and of Calvin,—the former giving us his materials in disorder, like soldiers bivouacked for the night; the latter arranging them like those same soldiers drawn up in battle array; see A. H. Strong, Philosophy and Religion, 4, and Christ in Creation, 188, 189.

Candlish, art.: Dogmatic, in Encycl. Brit., 7:340—"By and by a mighty intellectual force took hold of the whole collected dogmatic material, and reared out of it the great scholastic systems, which have been compared to the grand Gothic cathedrals that were the work of the same ages." Thomas Aquinas (1221-1274), the Dominican, "doctor angelicus," Augustinian and Realist,—and Duns Scotus (1265-1308), the Franciscan, "doctor subtilis,"—wrought out the scholastic theology more fully, and left behind them, in their Summæ, gigantic monuments of intellectual industry and acumen. Scholasticism aimed at the proof and systematizing of the doctrines of the Church by means of Aristotle's philosophy. It became at last an illimitable morass of useless subtilities and abstractions, and it finally ended in the nominalistic scepticism of William of Occam (1270-1347). See Townsend, The Great Schoolmen of the Middle Ages.

(b) The period of Symbolism,—represented by the Lutheran theology of Philip Melanchthon (1497-1560), and the Reformed theology of John Calvin (1509-1564); the former connecting itself with the Analytic theology of Calixtus (1585-1656), and the latter with the Federal theology of Cocceius (1603-1669).

The Lutheran Theology.—Preachers precede theologians, and Luther (1485-1546) was preacher rather than theologian. But Melanchthon (1497-1560), "the preceptor of Germany," as he was called, embodied the theology of the Lutheran church in his "Loci Communes" = points of doctrine common to believers (first edition Augustinian, afterwards substantially Arminian; grew out of lectures on the Epistle to the Romans). He was followed by Chemnitz (1522-1586), "clear and accurate," the most learned of the disciples of Melanchthon. Leonhard Hutter (1563-1616), called "Lutherus redivivus," and John Gerhard (1582-1637) followed Luther rather than Melanchthon. "Fifty years after the death of Melanchthon, Leonhard Hutter, his successor in the chair of theology at Wittenberg, on an occasion when the authority of Melanchthon was appealed to, tore down from the wall the portrait of the great Reformer, and trampled it under foot in the presence of the assemblage" (E. D. Morris, paper at the 60th Anniversary of Lane Seminary). George Calixtus (1586-1656) followed Melanchthon rather than Luther. He taught a theology which recognized the good element in both the Reformed and the Romanist doctrine and which was called "Syncretism." He separated Ethics from Systematic Theology, and applied the analytical method of investigation to the latter, beginning with the end, or final cause, of all things, viz.: blessedness. He was followed in his analytic method by Dannhauer (1603-1666), who treated theology allegorically, Calovius (1612-1686), "the most uncompromising defender of Lutheran orthodoxy and the most drastic polemicist against Calixtus," Quenstedt (1617-1688), whom Hovey calls "learned, comprehensive and logical," and Hollaz († 1730). The Lutheran theology aimed to purify the existing church, maintaining that what is not against the gospel is for it. It emphasized the material principle of the Reformation, justification by faith; but it retained many Romanist customs not expressly forbidden in Scripture. Kaftan, Am. Jour. Theol., 1900:716—"Because the mediæval school-philosophy mainly held sway, the Protestant theology representing the new faith was meanwhile necessarily accommodated to forms of knowledge thereby conditioned, that is, to forms essentially Catholic."

The Reformed Theology.—The word "Reformed" is here used in its technical sense, as designating that phase of the new theology which originated in Switzerland. Zwingle, the Swiss reformer (1484-1531), differing from Luther as to the Lord's Supper and as to Scripture, was more than Luther entitled to the name of systematic theologian. Certain writings of his may be considered the beginning of Reformed theology. But it was left to John Calvin (1509-1564), after the death of Zwingle, to arrange the principles of that theology in systematic form. Calvin dug channels for Zwingle's flood to flow in, as Melanchthon did for Luther's. His Institutes ("Institutio Religionis Christianæ"), is one of the great works in theology (superior as a systematic work to Melanchthon's "Loci"). Calvin was followed by Peter Martyr (1500-1562), Chamier (1565-1621), and Theodore Beza (1519-1605). Beza carried Calvin's doctrine of predestination to an extreme supralapsarianism, which is hyper-Calvinistic rather than Calvinistic. Cocceius (1603-1669), and after him Witsius (1626-1708), made theology centre about the idea of the covenants, and founded the Federal theology. Leydecker (1642-1721) treated theology in the order of the persons of the Trinity. Amyraldus (1596-1664) and Placeus of Saumur (1596-1632) modified the Calvinistic doctrine, the latter by his theory of mediate imputation, and the former by advocating the hypothetic universalism of divine grace. Turretin (1671-1737), a clear and strong theologian whose work is still a text-book at Princeton, and Pictet (1655-1725), both of them Federalists, showed the influence of the Cartesian philosophy. The Reformed theology aimed to build a new church, affirming that what is not derived from the Bible is against it. It emphasized the formal principle of the Reformation, the sole authority of Scripture.

In general, while the line between Catholic and Protestant in Europe runs from west to east, the line between Lutheran and Reformed runs from south to north, the Reformed theology flowing with the current of the Rhine northward from Switzerland to Holland and to England, in which latter country the Thirty-nine Articles represent the Reformed faith, while the Prayer-book of the English Church is substantially Arminian; see Dorner, Gesch. prot. Theologie, Einleit., 9. On the difference between Lutheran and Reformed doctrine, see Schaff, Germany, its Universities, Theology and Religion, 167-177. On the Reformed Churches of Europe and America, see H. B. Smith, Faith and Philosophy, 87-124.

(c) The period of Criticism and Speculation,—in its three divisions: the Rationalistic, represented by Semler (1725-1791); the Transitional, by Schleiermacher (1768-1834); the Evangelical, by Nitzsch, Müller, Tholuck and Dorner.

First Division. Rationalistic theologies: Though the Reformation had freed theology in great part from the bonds of scholasticism, other philosophies after a time took its place. The Leibnitz- (1646-1754) Wolffian (1679-1754) exaggeration of the powers of natural religion prepared the way for rationalistic systems of theology. Buddeus (1667-1729) combated the new principles, but Semler's (1725-1791) theology was built upon them, and represented the Scriptures as having a merely local and temporary character. Michaelis (1716-1784) and Doederlein (1714-1789) followed Semler, and the tendency toward rationalism was greatly assisted by the critical philosophy of Kant (1724-1804), to whom "revelation was problematical, and positive religion merely the medium through which the practical truths of reason are communicated" (Hagenbach, Hist. Doct., 2:397). Ammon (1766-1850) and Wegscheider (1771-1848) were representatives of this philosophy. Daub, Marheinecke and Strauss (1808-1874) were the Hegelian dogmatists. The system of Strauss resembled "Christian theology as a cemetery resembles a town." Storr (1746-1805), Reinhard (1753-1812), and Knapp (1753-1825), in the main evangelical, endeavored to reconcile revelation with reason, but were more or less influenced by this rationalizing spirit. Bretschneider (1776-1828) and De Wette (1780-1849) may be said to have held middle ground.

Second Division. Transition to a more Scriptural theology. Herder (1744-1803) and Jacobi (1743-1819), by their more spiritual philosophy, prepared the way for Schleiermacher's (1768-1834) grounding of doctrine in the facts of Christian experience. The writings of Schleiermacher constituted an epoch, and had great influence in delivering Germany from the rationalistic toils into which it had fallen. We may now speak of a

Third Division—and in this division we may put the names of Neander and Tholuck, Twesten and Nitzsch, Müller and Luthardt, Dorner and Philippi, Ebrard and Thomasius, Lange and Kahnis, all of them exponents of a far more pure and evangelical theology than was common in Germany a century ago. Two new forms of rationalism, however, have appeared in Germany, the one based upon the philosophy of Hegel, and numbering among its adherents Strauss and Baur, Biedermann, Lipsius and Pfleiderer; the other based upon the philosophy of Kant, and advocated by Ritschl and his followers, Harnack, Hermann and Kaftan; the former emphasizing the ideal Christ, the latter emphasizing the historical Christ; but neither of the two fully recognizing the living Christ present in every believer (see Johnson's Cyclopædia, art.: Theology, by A. H. Strong).

3. Among theologians of views diverse from the prevailing Protestant faith, may be mentioned:

(a) Bellarmine (1542-1621), the Roman Catholic.

Besides Bellarmine, "the best controversial writer of his age" (Bayle), the Roman Catholic Church numbers among its noted modern theologians:—Petavius (1583-1652), whose dogmatic theology Gibbon calls "a work of incredible labor and compass"; Melchior Canus (1523-1560), an opponent of the Jesuits and their scholastic method; Bossuet (1627-1704), who idealized Catholicism in his Exposition of Doctrine, and attacked Protestantism in his History of Variations of Protestant Churches; Jansen (1585-1638), who attempted, in opposition to the Jesuits, to reproduce the theology of Augustine, and who had in this the powerful assistance of Pascal (1623-1662). Jansenism, so far as the doctrines of grace are concerned, but not as respects the sacraments, is virtual Protestantism within the Roman Catholic Church. Moehler's Symbolism, Perrone's "Prelectiones Theologicæ," and Hurter's "Compendium Theologiæ Dogmaticæ" are the latest and most approved expositions of Roman Catholic doctrine.

(b) Arminius (1560-1609), the opponent of predestination.

Among the followers of Arminius (1560-1609) must be reckoned Episcopius (1583-1643), who carried Arminianism to almost Pelagian extremes; Hugo Grotius (1553-1645), the jurist and statesman, author of the governmental theory of the atonement; and Limborch (1633-1712), the most thorough expositor of the Arminian doctrine.

(c) Laelius Socinus (1525-1562), and Faustus Socinus (1539-1604), the leaders of the modern Unitarian movement.

The works of Laelius Socinus (1525-1562) and his nephew, Faustus Socinus (1539-1604) constituted the beginnings of modern Unitarianism. Laelius Socinus was the preacher and reformer, as Faustus Socinus was the theologian; or, as Baumgarten Crusius expresses it: "the former was the spiritual founder of Socinianism, and the latter the founder of the sect." Their writings are collected in the Bibliotheca Fratrum Polonorum. The Racovian Catechism, taking its name from the Polish town Racow, contains the most succinct exposition of their views. In 1660, the Unitarian church of the Socini in Poland was destroyed by persecution, but its Hungarian offshoot has still more than a hundred congregations.

4. British Theology, represented by:

(a) The Baptists, John Bunyan (1628-1688), John Gill (1697-1771), and Andrew Fuller (1754-1815).

Some of the best British theology is Baptist. Among John Bunyan's works we may mention his "Gospel Truths Opened," though his "Pilgrim's Progress" and "Holy War" are theological treatises in allegorical form. Macaulay calls Milton and Bunyan the two great creative minds of England during the latter part of the 17th century. John Gill's "Body of Practical Divinity" shows much ability, although the Rabbinical learning of the author occasionally displays itself in a curious exegesis, as when on the word "Abba" he remarks: "You see that this word which means 'Father' reads the same whether we read forward or backward; which suggests that God is the same whichever way we look at him." Andrew Fuller's "Letters on Systematic Divinity" is a brief compend of theology. His treatises upon special doctrines are marked by sound judgment and clear insight. They were the most influential factor in rescuing the evangelical churches of England from antinomianism. They justify the epithets which Robert Hall, one of the greatest of Baptist preachers, gives him: "sagacious," "luminous," "powerful."

(b) The Puritans, John Owen (1616-1683), Richard Baxter (1615-1691), John Howe (1630-1705), and Thomas Ridgeley (1666-1734).

Owen was the most rigid, as Baxter was the most liberal, of the Puritans. The Encyclopædia Britannica remarks: "As a theological thinker and writer, John Owen holds his own distinctly defined place among those titanic intellects with which the age abounded. Surpassed by Baxter in point and pathos, by Howe in imagination and the higher philosophy, he is unrivaled in his power of unfolding the rich meanings of Scripture. In his writings he was preëminently the great theologian." Baxter wrote a "Methodus Theologiæ," and a "Catholic Theology"; John Howe is chiefly known by his "Living Temple"; Thomas Ridgeley by his "Body of Divinity." Charles H. Spurgeon never ceased to urge his students to become familiar with the Puritan Adams, Ambrose, Bowden, Manton and Sibbes.

(c) The Scotch Presbyterians, Thomas Boston (1676-1732), John Dick (1764-1833), and Thomas Chalmers (1780-1847).

Of the Scotch Presbyterians, Boston is the most voluminous, Dick the most calm and fair, Chalmers the most fervid and popular.

(d) The Methodists, John Wesley (1703-1791), and Richard Watson (1781-1833).

Of the Methodists, John Wesley's doctrine is presented in "Christian Theology," collected from his writings by the Rev. Thornley Smith. The great Methodist text-book, however, is the "Institutes" of Watson, who systematized and expounded the Wesleyan theology. Pope, a recent English theologian, follows Watson's modified and improved Arminianism, while Whedon and Raymond, recent American writers, hold rather to a radical and extreme Arminianism.

(e) The Quakers, George Fox (1624-1691), and Robert Barclay (1648-1690).

As Jesus, the preacher and reformer, preceded Paul the theologian; as Luther preceded Melanchthon; as Zwingle preceded Calvin; as Laelius Socinus preceded Faustus Socinus; as Wesley preceded Watson; so Fox preceded Barclay. Barclay wrote an "Apology for the true Christian Divinity," which Dr. E. G. Robinson described as "not a formal treatise of Systematic Theology, but the ablest exposition of the views of the Quakers." George Fox was the reformer, William Penn the social founder, Robert Barclay the theologian, of Quakerism.

(f) The English Churchmen, Richard Hooker (1553-1600), Gilbert Burnet (1643-1715), and John Pearson (1613-1686).

The English church has produced no great systematic theologian (see reasons assigned in Dorner, Gesch. prot. Theologie, 470). The "judicious" Hooker is still its greatest theological writer, although his work is only on "Ecclesiastical Polity." Bishop Burnet is the author of the "Exposition of the XXXIX Articles," and Bishop Pearson of the "Exposition of the Creed." Both these are common English text-books. A recent "Compendium of Dogmatic Theology," by Litton, shows a tendency to return from the usual Arminianism of the Anglican church to the old Augustinianism; so also Bishop Moule's "Outlines of Christian Doctrine," and Mason's "Faith of the Gospel."

5. American theology, running in two lines:

(a) The Reformed system of Jonathan Edwards (1703-1758), modified successively by Joseph Bellamy (1719-1790), Samuel Hopkins (1721-1803), Timothy Dwight (1752-1817), Nathanael Emmons (1745-1840), Leonard Woods (1774-1854), Charles G. Finney (1792-1875), Nathaniel W. Taylor (1786-1858), and Horace Bushnell (1802-1876). Calvinism, as thus modified, is often called the New England, or New School, theology.

Jonathan Edwards, one of the greatest of metaphysicians and theologians, was an idealist who held that God is the only real cause, either in the realm of matter or in the realm of mind. He regarded the chief good as happiness—a form of sensibility. Virtue was voluntary choice of this good. Hence union with Adam in acts and exercises was sufficient. Thus God's will made identity of being with Adam. This led to the exercise-system of Hopkins and Emmons, on the one hand, and to Bellamy's and Dwight's denial of any imputation of Adam's sin or of inborn depravity, on the other—in which last denial agree many other New England theologians who reject the exercise-scheme, as for example, Strong, Tyler, Smalley, Burton, Woods, and Park. Dr. N. W. Taylor added a more distinctly Arminian element, the power of contrary choice—and with this tenet of the New Haven theology, Charles G. Finney, of Oberlin, substantially agreed. Horace Bushnell held to a practically Sabellian view of the Trinity, and to a moral-influence theory of the atonement. Thus from certain principles admitted by Edwards, who held in the main to an Old School theology, the New School theology has been gradually developed.

Robert Hall called Edwards "the greatest of the sons of men." Dr. Chalmers regarded him as the "greatest of theologians." Dr. Fairbairn says: "He is not only the greatest of all the thinkers that America has produced, but also the highest speculative genius of the eighteenth century. In a far higher degree than Spinoza, he was a 'God-intoxicated man.'" His fundamental notion that there is no causality except the divine was made the basis of a theory of necessity which played into the hands of the deists whom he opposed and was alien not only to Christianity but even to theism. Edwards could not have gotten his idealism from Berkeley; it may have been suggested to him by the writings of Locke or Newton, Cudworth or Descartes, John Norris or Arthur Collier. See Prof. H. N. Gardiner, in Philos. Rev., Nov. 1900:573-596; Prof. E. C. Smyth, in Am. Jour. Theol., Oct. 1897:956; Allen, Jonathan Edwards, 16, 308-310, and in Atlantic Monthly, Dec. 1891:767; Sanborn, in Jour. Spec. Philos., Oct. 1883:401-420; G. P. Fisher, Edwards on the Trinity, 18, 19.

(b) The older Calvinism, represented by Charles Hodge the father (1797-1878) and A. A. Hodge the son (1823-1886), together with Henry B. Smith (1815-1877), Robert J. Breckinridge (1800-1871), Samuel J. Baird, and William G. T. Shedd (1820-1894). All these, although with minor differences, hold to views of human depravity and divine grace more nearly conformed to the doctrine of Augustine and Calvin, and are for this reason distinguished from the New England theologians and their followers by the popular title of Old School.

Old School theology, in its view of predestination, exalts God; New School theology, by emphasizing the freedom of the will, exalts man. It is yet more important to notice that Old School theology has for its characteristic tenet the guilt of inborn depravity. But among those who hold this view, some are federalists and creationists, and justify God's condemnation of all men upon the ground that Adam represented his posterity. Such are the Princeton theologians generally, including Charles

Hodge, A. A. Hodge, and the brothers Alexander. Among those who hold to the Old School doctrine of the guilt of inborn depravity, however, there are others who are traducians, and who explain the imputation of Adam's sin to his posterity upon the ground of the natural union between him and them. Baird's "Elohim Revealed" and Shedd's essay on "Original Sin" (Sin a Nature and that Nature Guilt) represent this realistic conception of the relation of the race to its first father. R. J. Breckinridge, R. L. Dabney, and J. H. Thornwell assert the fact of inherent corruption and guilt, but refuse to assign any rationale for it, though they tend to realism. H. B. Smith holds guardedly to the theory of mediate imputation.

On the history of Systematic Theology in general, see Hagenbach, History of Doctrine (from which many of the facts above given are taken), and Shedd, History of Doctrine; also, Ebrard, Dogmatik, 1:44-100; Kahnis, Dogmatik, 1:15-128; Hase, Hutterus Redivivus, 24-52. Gretillat, Théologie Systématique, 3:24-120, has given an excellent history of theology, brought down to the present time. On the history of New England theology, see Fisher, Discussions and Essays, 285-354.

IV. Order of Treatment in Systematic Theology.

1. Various methods of arranging the topics of a theological system.

(a) The Analytical method of Calixtus begins with the assumed end of all things, blessedness, and thence passes to the means by which it is secured. (b) The Trinitarian method of Leydecker and Martensen regards Christian doctrine as a manifestation successively of the Father, Son and Holy Spirit. (c) The Federal method of Cocceius, Witsius, and Boston treats theology under the two covenants. (d) The Anthropological method of Chalmers and Rothe; the former beginning with the Disease of Man and passing to the Remedy; the latter dividing his Dogmatik into the Consciousness of Sin and the Consciousness of Redemption. (e) The Christological method of Hase, Thomasius and Andrew Fuller treats of God, man, and sin, as presuppositions of the person and work of Christ. Mention may also be made of (f) The Historical method, followed by Ursinus, and adopted in Jonathan Edwards's History of Redemption; and (g) The Allegorical method of Dannhauer, in which man is described as a wanderer, life as a road, the Holy Spirit as a light, the church as a candlestick, God as the end, and heaven as the home; so Bunyan's Holy War, and Howe's Living Temple.

See Calixtus, Epitome Theologiæ; Leydecker, De Œconomia trium Personarum in Negotio Salutis humanæ; Martensen (1808-1884), Christian Dogmatics; Cocceius, Summa Theologiæ, and Summa Doctrinæ de Fœdere et Testamento Dei, in Works, vol. vi; Witsius, The Economy of the Covenants; Boston, A Complete Body of Divinity (in Works, vol. 1 and 2), Questions in Divinity (vol. 6), Human Nature in its Fourfold State (vol. 8); Chalmers, Institutes of Theology; Rothe (1799-1867), Dogmatik, and Theologische Ethik; Hase (1800-1890), Evangelische Dogmatik; Thomasius (1802-1875), Christi Person und Werk; Fuller, Gospel Worthy of all Acceptation (in Works, 2:328-416), and Letters on Systematic Divinity (1:684-711); Ursinus (1534-1583), Loci Theologici (in Works, 1:426-909); Dannhauer (1603-1666) Hodosophia Christiana, seu Theologia Positiva in Methodum redacta. Jonathan Edwards's so-called History of Redemption was in reality a system of theology in historical form. It "was to begin and end with eternity, all great events and epochs in time being viewed 'sub specie eternitatis.' The three worlds—heaven, earth and hell—were to be the scenes of this grand drama. It was to include the topics of theology as living factors, each in its own place," and all forming a complete and harmonious whole; see Allen, Jonathan Edwards, 379, 380.

2. The Synthetic Method, which we adopt in this compendium, is both the most common and the most logical method of arranging the topics of theology. This method proceeds from causes to effects, or, in the language of Hagenbach (Hist. Doctrine, 2:152), "starts from the highest principle, God, and proceeds to man, Christ, redemption, and finally to the end of all things." In such a treatment of theology we may best arrange our topics in the following order:

1st. The existence of God. 2d. The Scriptures a revelation from God. 3d. The nature, decrees and works of God. 4th. Man, in his original likeness to God and subsequent apostasy. 5th. Redemption, through the work of Christ and of the Holy Spirit. 6th. The nature and laws of the Christian church. 7th. The end of the present system of things.

V. Text-Books in Theology

1. Confessions: Schaff, Creeds of Christendom.

2. Compendiums: H. B. Smith, System of Christian Theology; A. A. Hodge, Outlines of Theology; E. H. Johnson, Outline of Systematic Theology; Hovey, Manual of Theology and Ethics; W. N. Clarke, Outline of Christian Theology; Hase, Hutterus Redivivus; Luthardt, Compendium der Dogmatik; Kurtz, Religionslehre.

3. Extended Treatises: Dorner, System of Christian Doctrine; Shedd, Dogmatic Theology; Calvin, Institutes; Charles Hodge, Systematic Theology; Van Oosterzee, Christian Dogmatics; Baird, Elohim Revealed; Luthardt, Fundamental, Saving, and Moral Truths; Phillippi, Glaubenslehre; Thomasius, Christi Person und Werk.

4. Collected Works: Jonathan Edwards; Andrew Fuller.

5. Histories of Doctrine: Harnack; Hagenbach; Shedd; Fisher; Sheldon; Orr, Progress of Dogma.

6. Monographs: Julius Müller, Doctrine of Sin; Shedd, Discourses and Essays; Liddon, Our Lord's Divinity; Dorner, History of the Doctrine of the Person of Christ; Dale, Atonement; Strong, Christ in Creation; Upton, Hibbert Lectures.

7. Theism: Martineau, Study of Religion; Harris, Philosophical Basis of Theism; Strong, Philosophy and Religion; Bruce, Apologetics; Drummond, Ascent of Man; Griffith-Jones, Ascent through Christ.

8. Christian Evidences: Butler, Analogy of Natural and Revealed Religion; Fisher, Grounds of Theistic and Christian Belief; Row, Bampton Lectures for 1877; Peabody, Evidences of Christianity; Mair, Christian Evidences; Fairbairn, Philosophy of the Christian Religion; Matheson, Spiritual Development of St. Paul.

9. Intellectual Philosophy: Stout, Handbook of Psychology; Bowne, Metaphysics; Porter, Human Intellect; Hill, Elements of Psychology; Dewey, Psychology.

10. Moral Philosophy: Robinson, Principles and Practice of Morality; Smyth, Christian Ethics; Porter, Elements of Moral Science; Calderwood, Moral Philosophy; Alexander, Moral Science; Robins, Ethics of the Christian Life.

11. General Science: Todd, Astronomy; Wentworth and Hill, Physics; Remsen, Chemistry; Brigham, Geology; Parker, Biology; Martin, Physiology; Ward, Fairbanks, or West, Sociology; Walker, Political Economy.

12. Theological Encyclopædias: Schaff-Herzog (English); McClintock and Strong; Herzog (Second German Edition).

13. Bible Dictionaries: Hastings; Davis; Cheyne; Smith (edited by Hackett).

14. Commentaries: Meyer, on the New Testament; Philippi, Lange, Shedd, Sanday, on the Epistle to the Romans; Godet, on John's Gospel; Lightfoot, on Philippians and Colossians; Expositor's Bible, on the Old Testament books.

15. Bibles: American Revision (standard edition); Revised Greek-English New Testament (published by Harper & Brothers); Annotated Paragraph Bible (published by the London Religious Tract Society) Stier and Theile, Polyglotten-Bibel.

An attempt has been made, in the list of text-books given above, to put first in each class the book best worth purchasing by the average theological student, and to arrange the books that follow this first one in the order of their value. German books, however, when they are not yet accessible in an English translation, are put last, simply because they are less likely to be used as books of reference by the average student.

PART II - THE EXISTENCE OF GOD

Chapter I - Origin Of Our Idea Of God's Existence

God is the infinite and perfect Spirit in whom all things have their source, support, and end.

On the definition of the term God, see Hodge, Syst. Theol., 1:366. Other definitions are those of Calovius: "Essentia spiritualis infinite"; Ebrard: "The eternal source of all that is temporal"; Kahnis: "The infinite Spirit"; John Howe: "An eternal, uncaused, independent, necessary Being, that hath active power, life, wisdom, goodness, and whatsoever other supposable excellency, in the highest perfection, in and of itself"; Westminster Catechism: "A Spirit infinite, eternal and unchangeable in his being, wisdom, power, holiness, justice, goodness and truth"; Andrew Fuller: "The first cause and last end of all things."

The existence of God is a first truth; in other words, the knowledge of God's existence is a rational intuition. Logically, it precedes and conditions all observation and reasoning. Chronologically, only reflection upon the phenomena of nature and of mind occasions its rise in consciousness.

The term intuition means simply direct knowledge. Lowndes (Philos. of Primary Beliefs, 78) and Mansel (Metaphysics, 52) would use the term only of our direct knowledge of substances, as self and body; Porter applies it by preference to our cognition of first truths, such as have been already mentioned. Harris (Philos. Basis of Theism, 44-151, but esp. 45, 46) makes it include both. He divides intuitions into two classes: 1. Presentative intuitions, as self-consciousness (in virtue of which I perceive the existence of spirit and already come in contact with the supernatural), and sense-perception (in virtue of which I perceive the existence of matter, at least in my own organism, and come in contact with nature); 2. Rational intuitions, as space, time, substance, cause, final cause, right, absolute being. We may accept this nomenclature, using the terms "first truths" and "rational intuitions" as equivalent to each other, and classifying rational intuitions under the heads of (1) intuitions of relations, as space and time; (2) intuitions of principles, as substance, cause, final cause, right; and (3) intuition of absolute Being, Power, Reason, Perfection, Personality, as God. We hold that, as upon occasion of the senses cognizing (a) extended matter, (b) succession, (c) qualities, (d) change, (e) order, (f) action, respectively, the mind cognizes (a) space, (b) time, (c) substance, (d) cause, (e) design, (f) obligation, so upon occasion of our cognizing our finiteness, dependence and responsibility, the mind directly cognizes the existence of an Infinite and Absolute Authority, Perfection, Personality, upon whom we are dependent and to whom we are responsible.

Bowne, Theory of Thought and Knowledge, 60—"As we walk in entire ignorance of our muscles, so we often think in entire ignorance of the principles which underlie and determine thinking. But as anatomy reveals that the apparently simple act of walking involves a highly complex muscular activity, so analysis reveals that the apparently simple act of thinking involves a system of mental principles." Dewey, Psychology, 238, 244—"Perception, memory, imagination, conception—each of these is an act of intuition.... Every concrete act of knowledge involves an intuition of God." Martineau, Types, 1:459—The attempt to divest experience of either percepts or intuitions is "like the attempt to peel a bubble in search for its colors and contents: in tenuem ex oculis evanuit auram"; Study, 1:199—"Try with all your might to do something difficult, e. g., to shut a door against a furious wind, and you recognize Self and Nature—causal will, over against external causality"; 201—"Hence our fellow-feeling with Nature"; 65—"As Perception gives us Will in the shape of Causality over against us in the non-ego, so Conscience gives us Will in the shape of Authority over against us in the non-ego"; Types, 2:5—"In perception it is self and nature, in morals it is self and God, that stand face to face in the subjective and objective antithesis"; Study, 2:2, 3—"In volitional experience we meet with objective causality; in moral experience we meet with objective authority,—both being objects of immediate knowledge, on the same footing of certainty with the apprehension of the external material world. I know of no logical advantage which the belief in finite objects around us can boast over the belief in the infinite and righteous Cause of all"; 51—"In recognition of God as Cause, we raise the University; in recognition of God as Authority, we raise the Church."

Kant declares that the idea of freedom is the source of our idea of personality,—personality consists in the freedom of the whole soul from the mechanism of nature. Lotze, Metaphysics, § 244—

"So far as, and so long as, the soul knows itself as the identical subject of inward experience, it is, and is named simply for that reason, substance." Illingworth, Personality, Human and Divine, 32—"Our conception of substance is derived, not from the physical, but from the mental world. Substance is first of all that which underlies our mental affections and manifestations." James, Will to Believe, 80— "Substance, as Kant says, means 'das Beharrliche,' the abiding, that which will be as it has been, because its being is essential and eternal." In this sense we have an intuitive belief in an abiding substance which underlies our own thoughts and volitions, and this we call the soul. But we also have an intuitive belief in an abiding substance which underlies all natural phenomena and all the events of history, and this we call God. Among those who hold to this general view of an intuitive knowledge of God may be mentioned the following:—Calvin, Institutes, book I, chap. 3; Nitzsch, System of Christian Doctrine, 15-26, 133-140; Julius Müller, Doctrine of Sin, 1:78-84; Ulrici, Leib und Seele, 688-725; Porter, Human Intellect, 497; Hickok, Rational Cosmology, 58-89; Farrar, Science in Theology, 27-29; Bib. Sac., July, 1872:533, and January, 1873:204; Miller, Fetich in Theology, 110-122; Fisher, Essays, 565-572; Tulloch, Theism, 314-336; Hodge, Systematic Theology, 1:191-203; Christlieb, Mod. Doubt and Christian Belief, 75, 76; Raymond, Syst. Theology, 1:247-262; Bascom, Science of Mind, 246, 247; Knight, Studies in Philos. and Lit., 155-224; A. H. Strong, Philosophy and Religion, 76-89.

I. First Truths in General

1. Their nature

A. Negatively.—A first truth is not (a) Truth written prior to consciousness upon the substance of the soul—for such passive knowledge implies a materialistic view of the soul; (b) Actual knowledge of which the soul finds itself in possession at birth—for it cannot be proved that the soul has such knowledge; (c) An idea, undeveloped at birth, but which has the power of self-development apart from observation and experience—for this is contrary to all we know of the laws of mental growth.

Cicero, De Natura Deorum, 1:17—"Intelligi necesse est esse deos, quoniam insitas eorum vel potius innatas cogitationes habemus." Origen, Adv. Celsum, 1:4—"Men would not be guilty, if they did not carry in their minds common notions of morality, innate and written in divine letters." Calvin, Institutes, 1:3:3—"Those who rightly judge will always agree that there is an indelible sense of divinity engraven upon men's minds." Fleming, Vocab. of Philosophy, art.: "Innate Ideas"—"Descartes is supposed to have taught (and Locke devoted the first book of his Essays to refuting the doctrine) that these ideas are innate or connate with the soul; i. e., the intellect finds itself at birth, or as soon as it wakes to conscious activity, to be possessed of ideas to which it has only to attach the appropriate names, or of judgments which it only needs to express in fit propositions—i. e., prior to any experience of individual objects."

Royce, Spirit of Modern Philosophy, 77—"In certain families, Descartes teaches, good breeding and the gout are innate. Yet, of course, the children of such families have to be instructed in deportment, and the infants just learning to walk seem happily quite free from gout. Even so geometry is innate in us, but it does not come to our consciousness without much trouble"; 79—Locke found no innate ideas. He maintained, in reply, that "infants, with their rattles, showed no sign of being aware that things which are equal to the same thing are equal to each other." Schopenhauer said that "Jacobi had the trifling weakness of taking all he had learned and approved before his fifteenth year for inborn ideas of the human mind." Bowne, Principles of Ethics, 5—"That the rational ideas are conditioned by the sense experience and are sequent to it, is unquestioned by any one; and that experience shows a successive order of manifestation is equally undoubted. But the sensationalist has always shown a curious blindness to the ambiguity of such a fact. He will have it that what comes after must be a modification of what went before; whereas it might be that, and it might be a new, though conditioned, manifestation of an immanent nature or law. Chemical affinity is not gravity, although affinity cannot manifest itself until gravity has brought the elements into certain relations."

Pfleiderer, Philosophy of Religion, 1:103—"This principle was not from the beginning in the consciousness of men; for, in order to think ideas, reason must be clearly developed, which in the first of mankind it could just as little be as in children. This however does not exclude the fact that there was from the beginning the unconscious rational impulse which lay at the basis of the formation of the belief in God, however manifold may have been the direct motives which co-operated with it." Self is implied in the simplest act of knowledge. Sensation gives us two things, e. g., black and white; but I cannot compare them without asserting difference for me. Different sensations make no knowledge, without a self to bring them together. Upton, Hibbert Lectures, lecture 2—"You could as easily prove the existence of an external world to a man who had no senses to perceive it, as you could prove the existence of God to one who had no consciousness of God."

B. Positively.—A first truth is a knowledge which, though developed upon occasion of observation and reflection, is not derived from observation and reflection,—a knowledge on the contrary which has such logical priority that it must be assumed or supposed, in order to make any observation or reflection possible. Such truths are not, therefore, recognized first in order of time; some of them are assented to somewhat late in the mind's growth; by the great majority of men they are never consciously formulated at all. Yet they constitute the necessary assumptions upon which all other knowledge rests, and the mind has not only the inborn capacity to evolve them so soon as the proper occasions are presented, but the recognition of them is inevitable so soon as the mind begins to give account to itself of its own knowledge.

Mansel, Metaphysics, 52, 279—"To describe experience as the cause of the idea of space would be as inaccurate as to speak of the soil in which it was planted as the cause of the oak—though the planting in the soil is the condition which brings into manifestation the latent power of the acorn." Coleridge: "We see before we know that we have eyes; but when once this is known, we perceive that eyes must have preëxisted in order to enable us to see." Coleridge speaks of first truths as "those necessities of mind or forms of thinking, which, though revealed to us by experience, must yet have preëxisted in order to make experience possible." McCosh, Intuitions, 48, 49—Intuitions are "like flower and fruit, which are in the plant from its embryo, but may not be actually formed till there have been a stalk and branches and leaves." Porter, Human Intellect, 501, 519—"Such truths cannot be acquired or assented to first of all." Some are reached last of all. The moral intuition is often developed late, and sometimes, even then, only upon occasion of corporal punishment. "Every man is as lazy as circumstances will admit." Our physical laziness is occasional; our mental laziness frequent; our moral laziness incessant. We are too lazy to think, and especially to think of religion. On account of this depravity of human nature we should expect the intuition of God to be developed last of all. Men shrink from contact with God and from the thought of God. In fact, their dislike for the intuition of God leads them not seldom to deny all their other intuitions, even those of freedom and of right. Hence the modern "psychology without a soul."

Schurman, Agnosticism and Religion, 105-115—"The idea of God ... is latest to develop into clear consciousness ... and must be latest, for it is the unity of the difference of the self and the not-self, which are therefore presupposed." But "it has not less validity in itself, it gives no less trustworthy assurance of actuality, than the consciousness of the self, or the consciousness of the not-self.... The consciousness of God is the logical prius of the consciousness of self and of the world. But not, as already observed, the chronological; for, according to the profound observation of Aristotle, what in the nature of things is first, is in the order of development last. Just because God is the first principle of being and knowing, he is the last to be manifested and known.... The finite and the infinite are both known together, and it is as impossible to know one without the other as it is to apprehend an angle without the sides which contain it." For account of the relation of the intuitions to experience, see especially Cousin, True, Beautiful and Good, 39-64, and History of Philosophy, 2:199-245. Compare Kant, Critique of Pure Reason, Introd., 1. See also Bascom, in Bib. Sac., 23:1-47; 27:68-90.

2. Their criteria. The criteria by which first truths are to be tested are three

A. Their universality. By this we mean, not that all men assent to them or understand them when propounded in scientific form, but that all men manifest a practical belief in them by their language, actions, and expectations.

B. Their necessity. By this we mean, not that it is impossible to deny these truths, but that the mind is compelled by its very constitution to recognize them upon the occurrence of the proper conditions, and to employ them in its arguments to prove their non-existence.

C. Their logical independence and priority. By this we mean that these truths can be resolved into no others, and proved by no others; that they are presupposed in the acquisition of all other knowledge, and can therefore be derived from no other source than an original cognitive power of the mind.

Instances of the professed and formal denial of first truths:—the positivist denies causality; the idealist denies substance; the pantheist denies personality; the necessitarian denies freedom; the nihilist denies his own existence. A man may in like manner argue that there is no necessity for an atmosphere; but even while he argues, he breathes it. Instance the knock-down argument to demonstrate the freedom of the will. I grant my own existence in the very doubting of it; for "cogito, ergo sum," as Descartes himself insisted, really means "cogito, scilicet sum"; H. B. Smith: "The statement is analysis, not proof." Ladd, Philosophy of Knowledge, 59—"The cogito, in barbarous Latin = cogitans sum: thinking is self-conscious being." Bentham: "The word ought is an authoritative imposture, and ought to be banished from the realm of morals." Spinoza and Hegel really deny self-consciousness when they make man a phenomenon of the infinite. Royce likens the denier of personality to the man who goes outside of his own house and declares that no one lives there because, when he looks in at the window, he sees no one inside.

Professor James, in his Psychology, assumes the reality of a brain, but refuses to assume the reality of a soul. This is essentially the position of materialism. But this assumption of a brain is metaphysics, although the author claims to be writing a psychology without metaphysics. Ladd, Philosophy of Mind, 3—"The materialist believes in causation proper so long as he is explaining the origin of mind from matter, but when he is asked to see in mind the cause of physical change he at once becomes a mere phenomenalist." Royce, Spirit of Modern Philosophy, 400—"I know that all beings, if only they can count, must find that three and two make five. Perhaps the angels cannot count; but, if they can, this axiom is true for them. If I met an angel who declared that his experience had occasionally shown him a three and two that did not make five, I should know at once what sort of an angel he was." On the criteria of first truths, see Porter, Human Intellect, 510, 511. On denial of them, see Shedd, Dogmatic Theology, 1:213.

II. The Existence of God a first truth

1. Its universality

That the knowledge of God's existence answers the first criterion of universality, is evident from the following considerations:

A. It is an acknowledged fact that the vast majority of men have actually recognized the existence of a spiritual being or beings, upon whom they conceived themselves to be dependent.

The Vedas declare: "There is but one Being—no second." Max Müller, Origin and Growth of Religion, 34—"Not the visible sun, moon and stars are invoked, but something else that cannot be seen." The lowest tribes have conscience, fear death, believe in witches, propitiate or frighten away evil fates. Even the fetich-worshiper, who calls the stone or the tree a god, shows that he has already the idea of a God. We must not measure the ideas of the heathen by their capacity for expression, any more than we should judge the child's belief in the existence of his father by his success in drawing the father's picture. On heathenism, its origin and nature, see Tholuck, in Bib. Repos., 1832:86; Scholz, Götzendienst und Zauberwesen.

B. Those races and nations which have at first seemed destitute of such knowledge have uniformly, upon further investigation, been found to possess it, so that no tribe of men with which we have thorough acquaintance can be said to be without an object of worship. We may presume that further knowledge will show this to be true of all.

Moffat, who reported that certain African tribes were destitute of religion, was corrected by the testimony of his son-in-law, Livingstone: "The existence of God and of a future life is everywhere recognized in Africa." Where men are most nearly destitute of any formulated knowledge of God, the conditions for the awakening of the idea are most nearly absent. An apple-tree may be so conditioned that it never bears apples. "We do not judge of the oak by the stunted, flowerless specimens on the edge of the Arctic Circle." The presence of an occasional blind, deaf or dumb man does not disprove the definition that man is a seeing, hearing and speaking creature. Bowne, Principles of Ethics, 154—"We need not tremble for mathematics, even if some tribes should be found without the multiplication-table.... Sub-moral and sub-rational existence is always with us in the case of young children; and, if we should find it elsewhere, it would have no greater significance."

Victor Hugo: "Some men deny the Infinite; some, too, deny the sun; they are the blind." Gladden, What is Left? 148—"A man may escape from his shadow by going into the dark; if he comes under the light of the sun, the shadow is there. A man may be so mentally undisciplined that he does not recognize these ideas; but let him learn the use of his reason, let him reflect on his own mental processes, and he will know that they are necessary ideas." On an original monotheism, see Diestel, in Jahrbuch für deutsche Theologie, 1860, and vol. 5:669; Max Müller, Chips, 1:337; Rawlinson, in Present Day Tracts, No. 11; Legge, Religions of China, 8-11; Shedd, Dogmatic Theology, 1:201-208. Per contra, see Asmus, Indogerm. Relig., 2:1-8; and synopsis in Bib. Sac., Jan. 1877:167-172.

C. This conclusion is corroborated by the fact that those individuals, in heathen or in Christian lands, who profess themselves to be without any knowledge of a spiritual power or powers above them, do yet indirectly manifest the existence of such an idea in their minds and its positive influence over them.

Comte said that science would conduct God to the frontier and then bow him out, with thanks for his provisional services. But Herbert Spencer affirms the existence of a "Power to which no limit in time or space is conceivable, of which all phenomena as presented in consciousness are manifestations." The intuition of God, though formally excluded, is implicitly contained in Spencer's system, in the shape of the "irresistible belief" in Absolute Being, which distinguishes his position from that of Comte; see H. Spencer, who says: "One truth must ever grow clearer—the truth that there is an inscrutable existence everywhere manifested, to which we can neither find nor conceive beginning or end—the one absolute certainty that we are ever in the presence of an infinite and eternal energy from which all things proceed." Mr. Spencer assumes unity in the underlying Reality. Frederick Harrison sneeringly asks him: "Why not say 'forces,' instead of 'force'?" While Harrison gives us a supreme moral ideal without a metaphysical ground, Spencer gives us an ultimate metaphysical principle without a final moral purpose. The idea of God is the synthesis of the two,—"They are but broken lights of Thee, And thou, O Lord, art more than they" (Tennyson, In Memoriam).

Solon spoke of ὁ θεός and of τὸ θεῖον, and Sophocles of ὁ μέγας θεός. The term for "God" is identical in all the Indo-European languages, and therefore belonged to the time before those languages separated; see Shedd, Dogm. Theol., 1:201-208. In Virgil's Æneid, Mezentius is an atheist, a despiser of the gods, trusting only in his spear and in his right arm; but, when the corpse of his son is brought to him, his first act is to raise his hands to heaven. Hume was a sceptic, but he said to Ferguson, as they walked on a starry night: "Adam, there is a God!" Voltaire prayed in an Alpine thunderstorm. Shelley wrote his name in the visitors' book of the inn at Montanvert, and added: "Democrat, philanthropist, atheist"; yet he loved to think of a "fine intellectual spirit pervading the universe"; and he also wrote: "The One remains, the many change and pass; Heaven's light forever shines, Earth's shadows fly." Strauss worships the Cosmos, because "order and law, reason and goodness" are the soul of it. Renan trusts in goodness, design, ends. Charles Darwin, Life, 1:274—"In my most extreme fluctuations, I have never been an atheist, in the sense of denying the existence of a God."

D. This agreement among individuals and nations so widely separated in time and place can be most satisfactorily explained by supposing that it has its ground, not in accidental circumstances, but in the nature of man as man. The diverse and imperfectly developed ideas of the supreme Being which prevail among men are best accounted for as misinterpretations and perversions of an intuitive conviction common to all.

Huxley, Lay Sermons, 163—"There are savages without God, in any proper sense of the word; but there are none without ghosts." Martineau, Study, 2:353, well replies: "Instead of turning other people into ghosts, and then appropriating one to ourselves [and attributing another to God, we may add] by way of imitation, we start from the sense of personal continuity, and then predicate the same of others, under the figures which keep most clear of the physical and perishable." Grant Allen describes the higher religions as "a grotesque fungoid growth," that has gathered about a primitive thread of ancestor-worship. But this is to derive the greater from the less. Sayce, Hibbert Lectures, 358—"I can find no trace of ancestor-worship in the earliest literature of Babylonia which has survived to us"—this seems fatal to Huxley's and Allen's view that the idea of God is derived from man's prior belief in spirits of the dead. C. M. Tyler, in Am. Jour. Theo., Jan. 1899:144—"It seems impossible to deify a dead man, unless there is embryonic in primitive consciousness a prior concept of Deity."

Renouf, Religion of Ancient Egypt, 93—"The whole mythology of Egypt ... turns on the histories of Ra and Osiris.... Texts are discovered which identify Osiris and Ra.... Other texts are known wherein Ra, Osiris, Amon, and all other gods disappear, except as simple names, and the unity of God is asserted in the noblest language of monotheistic religion." These facts are earlier than any known ancestor-worship. "They point to an original idea of divinity above humanity" (see Hill, Genetic Philosophy, 317). We must add the idea of the superhuman, before we can turn any animism or ancestor-worship into a religion. This superhuman element was suggested to early man by all he saw of nature about him, especially by the sight of the heavens above, and by what he knew of causality within. For the evidence of a universal recognition of a superior power, see Flint, Anti-theistic Theories, 250-289, 522-533; Renouf, Hibbert Lectures for 1879:100; Bib. Sac., Jan. 1884:132-157; Peschel, Races of Men, 261; Ulrici, Leib und Seele, 688, and Gott und die Natur, 658-670, 758; Tylor, Primitive Culture, 1:377, 381, 418; Alexander, Evidences of Christianity, 22; Calderwood, Philosophy of the Infinite, 512; Liddon, Elements of Religion, 50; Methodist Quar. Rev., Jan. 1875:1; J. F. Clark, Ten Great Religions, 2:17-21.

2. Its necessity

That the knowledge of God's existence answers the second criterion of necessity, will be seen by considering:

A. That men, under circumstances fitted to call forth this knowledge, cannot avoid recognizing the existence of God. In contemplating finite existence, there is inevitably suggested the idea of an infinite Being as its correlative. Upon occasion of the mind's perceiving its own finiteness, dependence, responsibility, it immediately and necessarily perceives the existence of an infinite and unconditioned Being upon whom it is dependent and to whom it is responsible.

We could not recognize the finite as finite, except by comparing it with an already existing standard—the Infinite. Mansel, Limits of Religious Thought, lect. 3—"We are compelled by the constitution of our minds to believe in the existence of an Absolute and Infinite Being—a belief which appears forced upon us as the complement of our consciousness of the relative and finite." Fisher, Journ. Chr. Philos., Jan. 1883:113—"Ego and non-ego, each being conditioned by the other, presuppose unconditioned being on which both are dependent. Unconditioned being is the silent presupposition of all our knowing." Perceived dependent being implies an independent; independent being is perfectly self-determining; self-determination is personality; perfect self-determination is infinite Personality. John Watson, in Philos. Rev., Sept. 1893:526—"There is no consciousness of self apart from the consciousness of other selves and things; and no consciousness of the world apart from the consciousness of the single Reality presupposed in both." E. Caird, Evolution of Religion, 64-68—In every act of consciousness the primary elements are implied: "the idea of the object, or not-self; the idea of the subject, or self; and the idea of the unity which is presupposed in the difference of the self and not-self, and within which they act and react on each other." See Calderwood, Philos. of Infinite, 46, and Moral Philos., 77; Hopkins, Outline Study of Man, 283-285; Shedd, Dogm. Theol., 1:211.

B. That men, in virtue of their humanity, have a capacity for religion. This recognized capacity for religion is proof that the idea of God is a necessary one. If the mind upon proper occasion did not evolve this idea, there would be nothing in man to which religion could appeal.

"It is the suggestion of the Infinite that makes the line of the far horizon, seen over land or sea, so much more impressive than the beauties of any limited landscape." In times of sudden shock and danger, this rational intuition becomes a presentative intuition,—men become more conscious of God's existence than of the existence of their fellow-men and they instinctively cry to God for help. In the commands and reproaches of the moral nature the soul recognizes a Lawgiver and Judge whose voice conscience merely echoes. Aristotle called man "a political animal"; it is still more true, as Sabatier declares, that "man is incurably religious." St. Bernard: "Noverim me, noverim te." O. P. Gifford: "As milk, from which under proper conditions cream does not rise, is not milk, so the man, who upon proper occasion shows no knowledge of God, is not man, but brute." We must not however expect cream from frozen milk. Proper environment and conditions are needed.

It is the recognition of a divine Personality in nature which constitutes the greatest merit and charm of Wordsworth's poetry. In his Tintern Abbey, he speaks of "A presence that disturbs me with the joy Of elevated thoughts; a sense sublime Of something far more deeply interfused, Whose dwelling is the light of setting suns, And the round ocean and the living air, And the blue sky and in the mind of man: A motion and a spirit that impels All thinking things, all objects of all thought, And rolls through all things." Robert Browning sees God in humanity, as Wordsworth sees God in nature. In his Hohenstiel-Schwangau he writes: "This is the glory, that in all conceived Or felt or known, I recognize a Mind—Not mine, but like mine—for the double joy Making all things for me, and me for Him." John Ruskin held that the foundation of beauty in the world is the presence of God in it. In his youth he tells us that he had "a continual perception of sanctity in the whole of nature, from the slightest thing to the vastest—an instinctive awe mixed with delight, an indefinable thrill such as we sometimes imagine to indicate the presence of a disembodied spirit." But it was not a disembodied, but an embodied, Spirit that he saw. Nitzsch, Christian Doctrine, § 7—"Unless education and culture were preceded by an innate consciousness of God as an operative predisposition, there would be nothing for education and culture to work upon." On Wordsworth's recognition of a divine personality in nature, see Knight, Studies, 282-317, 405-426; Hutton, Essays, 2:113.

C. That he who denies God's existence must tacitly assume that existence in his very argument, by employing logical processes whose validity rests upon the fact of God's existence. The full proof of this belongs under the next head.

"I am an atheist, God knows"—was the absurd beginning of an argument to disprove the divine existence. Cutler, Beginnings of Ethics, 22—"Even the Nihilists, whose first principle is that God and duty are great bugbears to be abolished, assume that God and duty exist, and they are impelled by a sense of duty to abolish them." Mrs. Browning, The Cry of the Human: " 'There is no God,' the foolish saith; But none, 'There is no sorrow'; And nature oft the cry of faith In bitter need will borrow: Eyes which the preacher could not school By wayside graves are raised; And lips say, 'God be pitiful,' Who ne'er said, 'God be praised.' " Dr. W. W. Keen, when called to treat an Irishman's aphasia, said: "Well, Dennis, how are you?" "Oh, doctor, I cannot spake!" "But, Dennis, you are speaking." "Oh, doctor, it's many a word I cannot spake!" "Well, Dennis, now I will try you. See if you cannot say, 'Horse.' " "Oh, doctor dear, 'horse' is the very word I cannot spake!" On this whole section, see A. M. Fairbairn, Origin and Development of the Idea of God, in Studies in Philos. of Relig. and History; Martineau, Religion and Materialism, 45; Bishop Temple, Bampton Lectures, 1884:37-65.

3. Its logical independence and priority

That the knowledge of God's existence answers the third criterion of logical independence and priority, may be shown as follows:

A. It is presupposed in all other knowledge as its logical condition and foundation. The validity of the simplest mental acts, such as sense-perception, self-consciousness, and memory, depends upon the assumption that a God exists who has so constituted our minds that they give us knowledge of things as they are.

Pfleiderer, Philos. of Religion, 1:88—"The ground of science and of cognition generally is to be found neither in the subject nor in the object per se, but only in the divine thinking that combines the two, which, as the common ground of the forms of thinking in all finite minds, and of the forms of being in all things, makes possible the correspondence or agreement between the former and the latter, or in a word makes knowledge of truth possible." 91—"Religious belief is presupposed in all scientific knowledge as the basis of its possibility." This is the thought of Psalm 36:10—"In thy light shall we see light." A. J. Balfour, Foundations of Belief, 303—"The uniformity of nature cannot be proved from experience, for it is what makes proof from experience possible.... Assume it, and we shall find that facts conform to it.... 309—The uniformity of nature can be established only by the aid of that principle itself, and is necessarily involved in all attempts to prove it.... There must be a God, to justify our confidence in innate ideas."

Bowne, Theory of Thought and Knowledge, 276—"Reflection shows that the community of individual intelligences is possible only through an all-embracing Intelligence, the source and creator of finite minds." Science rests upon the postulate of a world-order. Huxley: "The object of science is the discovery of the rational order which pervades the universe." This rational order presupposes a rational Author. Dubois, in New Englander, Nov. 1890:468—"We assume uniformity and continuity, or we can have no science. An intelligent Creative Will is a genuine scientific hypothesis [postulate?], suggested by analogy and confirmed by experience, not contradicting the fundamental law of uniformity but accounting for it." Ritchie, Darwin and Hegel, 18—"That nature is a system, is the assumption underlying the earliest mythologies: to fill up this conception is the aim of the latest science." Royce, Relig. Aspect of Philosophy, 435—"There is such a thing as error; but error is inconceivable unless there be such a thing as truth; and truth is inconceivable unless there be a seat of truth, an infinite all-including Thought or Mind; therefore such a Mind exists."

B. The more complex processes of the mind, such as induction and deduction, can be relied on only by presupposing a thinking Deity who has made the various parts of the universe and the various aspects of truth to correspond to each other and to the investigating faculties of man.

We argue from one apple to the others on the tree. Newton argued from the fall of an apple to gravitation in the moon and throughout the solar system. Rowland argued from the chemistry of our world to that of Sirius. In all such argument there is assumed a unifying thought and a thinking Deity. This is Tyndall's "scientific use of the imagination." "Nourished," he says, "by knowledge partially won, and bounded by coöperant reason, imagination is the mightiest instrument of the physical discoverer." What Tyndall calls "imagination", is really insight into the thoughts of God, the great Thinker. It prepares the way for logical reasoning,—it is not the product of mere reasoning. For this reason Goethe called imagination "die Vorschule des Denkens," or "thought's preparatory school."

Peabody, Christianity the Religion of Nature, 23—"Induction is syllogism, with the immutable attributes of God for a constant term." Porter, Hum. Intellect, 492—"Induction rests upon the assumption, as it demands for its ground, that a personal or thinking Deity exists"; 658—"It has no meaning or validity unless we assume that the universe is constituted in such a way as to presuppose an absolute and unconditioned originator of its forces and laws"; 662—"We analyze the several processes of knowledge into their underlying assumptions, and we find that the assumption which underlies them all is that of a self-existent Intelligence who not only can be known by man, but must be known by man in order that man may know anything besides"; see also pages 486, 508, 509, 518, 519, 585, 616. Harris, Philos. Basis of Theism, 81—"The processes of reflective thought imply that the universe is grounded in, and is the manifestation of, reason"; 560—"The existence of a personal God is a necessary datum of scientific knowledge." So also, Fisher, Essays on Supernat. Origin of Christianity, 564, and in Journ. Christ. Philos., Jan. 1883:129, 130.

C. Our primitive belief in final cause, or, in other words, our conviction that all things have their ends, that design pervades the universe, involves a belief in God's existence. In assuming that there is a universe, that the universe is a rational whole, a system of thought-relations, we assume the existence of an absolute Thinker, of whose thought the universe is an expression.

Pfleiderer, Philos. of Religion, 1:81—"The real can only be thinkable if it is realized thought, a thought previously thought, which our thinking has only to think again. Therefore the real, in order to be thinkable for us, must be the realized thought of the creative thinking of an eternal divine Reason which is presented to our cognitive thinking." Royce, World and Individual, 2:41—"Universal teleology constitutes the essence of all facts." A. H. Bradford, The Age of Faith, 142—"Suffering and sorrow are universal. Either God could prevent them and would not, and therefore he is neither beneficent nor loving; or else he cannot prevent them and therefore something is greater than God, and therefore there is no God? But here is the use of reason in the individual reasoning. Reasoning in the individual necessitates the absolute or universal reason. If there is the absolute reason, then the universe and history are ordered and administered in harmony with reason; then suffering and sorrow can be neither meaningless nor final, since that would be the contradiction of reason. That cannot be possible in the universal and absolute which contradicts reason in man."

D. Our primitive belief in moral obligation, or, in other words, our conviction that right has universal authority, involves the belief in God's existence. In assuming that the universe is a moral whole, we assume the existence of an absolute Will, of whose righteousness the universe is an expression.

Pfleiderer, Philos. of Religion, 1:88—"The ground of moral obligation is found neither in the subject nor in society, but only in the universal or divine Will that combines both.... 103—The idea of God is the unity of the true and the good, or of the two highest ideas which our reason thinks as theoretical reason, but demands as practical reason.... In the idea of God we find the only synthesis of the world that is—the world of science, and of the world that ought to be—the world of religion." Seth, Ethical Principles, 425—"This is not a mathematical demonstration. Philosophy never is an exact science. Rather is it offered as the only sufficient foundation of the moral life.... The life of goodness ... is a life based on the conviction that its source and its issues are in the Eternal and the Infinite." As finite truth and goodness are comprehensible only in the light of some absolute principle which furnishes for them an ideal standard, so finite beauty is inexplicable except as there exists a perfect standard with which it may be compared. The beautiful is more than the agreeable or the useful. Proportion, order, harmony, unity in diversity—all these are characteristics of beauty. But they all imply an intellectual and spiritual Being, from whom they proceed and by whom they can be measured. Both physical and moral beauty, in finite things and beings, are symbols and manifestations of Him who is the author and lover of beauty, and who is himself the infinite and absolute Beauty. The beautiful in nature and in art shows that the idea of God's existence is logically independent and prior. See Cousin, The True, the Beautiful, and the Good, 140-153; Kant, Metaphysic of Ethics, who holds that belief in God is the necessary presupposition of the belief in duty.

To repeat these four points in another form—the intuition of an Absolute Reason is (a) the necessary presupposition of all other knowledge, so that we cannot know anything else to exist except by assuming first of all that God exists; (b) the necessary basis of all logical thought, so that we cannot put confidence in any one of our reasoning processes except by taking for granted that a thinking Deity has constructed our minds with reference to the universe and to truth; (c) the necessary implication of our primitive belief in design, so that we can assume all things to exist for a purpose, only by making the prior assumption that a purposing God exists—can regard the universe as a thought, only by postulating the existence of an absolute Thinker; and (d) the necessary foundation of our conviction of moral obligation, so that we can believe in the universal authority of right, only by assuming that there exists a God of righteousness who reveals his will both in the individual conscience and in the moral universe at large. We cannot prove that God is; but we can show that, in order to show the existence of any knowledge, thought, reason, conscience, in man, man must assume that God is.

As Jacobi said of the beautiful: "Es kann gewiesen aber nicht bewiesen werden"—it can be shown, but not proved. Bowne, Metaphysics, 472—"Our objective knowledge of the finite must rest upon ethical trust in the infinite"; 480—"Theism is the absolute postulate of all knowledge, science and philosophy"; "God is the most certain fact of objective knowledge." Ladd, Bib. Sac., Oct. 1877:611-616—"Cogito, ergo Deus est. We are obliged to postulate a not-ourselves which makes for rationality, as well as for righteousness." W. T. Harris: "Even natural science is impossible, where philosophy has not yet taught that reason made the world, and that nature is a revelation of the rational." Whately, Logic, 270; New Englander, Oct. 1871, art. on Grounds of Confidence in Inductive Reasoning; Bib. Sac., 7:415-425; Dorner, Glaubenslehre, 1:197; Trendelenburg, Logische Untersuchungen, ch. "Zweck"; Ulrici, Gott und die Natur, 540-626; Lachelier, Du Fondement de l'Induction, 78. Per contra, see Janet, Final Causes, 174, note, and 457-464, who holds final cause to be, not an intuition, but the result of applying the principle of causality to cases which mechanical laws alone will not explain.

Pascal: "Nature confounds the Pyrrhonist, and Reason confounds the Dogmatist. We have an incapacity of demonstration, which the former cannot overcome; we have a conception of truth which the latter cannot disturb." "There is no Unbelief! Whoever says. 'To-morrow,' 'The Unknown,' 'The Future,' trusts that Power alone. Nor dares disown." Jones, Robert Browning, 314—"We cannot indeed prove God as the conclusion of a syllogism, for he is the primary hypothesis of all proof." Robert Browning, Hohenstiel-Schwangau: "I know that he is there, as I am here, By the same proof, which seems no proof at all, It so exceeds familiar forms of proof"; Paracelsus, 27—"To know Rather consists in opening out a way Whence the imprisoned splendor may escape Than in effecting entrance for a light Supposed to be without." Tennyson, Holy Grail: "Let visions of the night or day Come as they will, and many a time they come.... In moments when he feels he cannot die, And knows himself no vision to himself, Nor the high God a vision, nor that One Who rose again"; The Ancient Sage, 548—"Thou canst not prove the Nameless, O my son! Nor canst thou prove the world thou movest in. Thou canst not prove that thou art body alone, Nor canst Thou prove that thou art spirit alone, Nor canst thou prove that thou art both in one. Thou canst not prove that thou art immortal, no, Nor yet that thou art mortal. Nay, my son, thou canst not prove that I, who speak with thee, Am not thyself in converse with thyself. For nothing worthy proving can be proven, Nor yet disproven: Wherefore be thou wise, Cleave ever to the sunnier side of doubt, And cling to Faith beyond the forms of Faith."

Our proof that the idea of God's existence is a rational intuition will not be complete, until we show that attempts to account in other ways for the origin of the idea are insufficient, and require as their presupposition the very intuition which they would supplant or reduce to a secondary place. We claim that it cannot be derived from any other source than an original cognitive power of the mind.

1. Not from external revelation,—whether communicated (a) through the Scriptures, or (b)through tradition; for, unless man had from another source a previous knowledge of the existence of a God from whom such a revelation might come, the revelation itself could have no authority for him.

(a) See Gillespie, Necessary Existence of God, 10; Ebrard, Dogmatik, 1:117; H. B. Smith, Faith and Philosophy, 18—"A revelation takes for granted that he to whom it is made has some knowledge of God, though it may enlarge and purify that knowledge." We cannot prove God from the authority of the Scriptures, and then also prove the Scriptures from the authority of God. The very idea of Scripture as a revelation presupposes belief in a God who can make it. Newman Smyth, in New Englander, 1878:355—We cannot derive from a sun-dial our knowledge of the existence of a sun. The sun-dial presupposes the sun, and cannot be understood without previous knowledge of the sun. Wuttke, Christian Ethics, 2:103—"The voice of the divine ego does not first come to the consciousness of the individual ego from without; rather does every external revelation presuppose already this inner one; there must echo out from within man something kindred to the outer revelation, in order to its being recognized and accepted as divine."

Fairbairn, Studies in Philos. of Relig. and Hist., 21, 22—"If man is dependent on an outer revelation for his idea of God, then he must have what Schelling happily termed 'an original atheism of consciousness.' Religion cannot, in that case, be rooted in the nature of man,—it must be implanted from without." Schurman, Belief in God, 78—"A primitive revelation of God could only mean that God had endowed man with the capacity of apprehending his divine original. This capacity, like every other, is innate, and like every other, it realizes itself only in the presence of appropriate conditions." Clarke, Christian Theology, 112—"Revelation cannot demonstrate God's existence, for it must assume it; but it will manifest his existence and character to men, and will serve them as the chief source of certainty concerning him, for it will teach them what they could not know by other means."

(b) Nor does our idea of God come primarily from tradition, for "tradition can perpetuate only what has already been originated" (Patton). If the knowledge thus handed down is the knowledge of a primitive revelation, then the argument just stated applies—that very revelation presupposed in those who first received it, and presupposes in those to whom it is handed down, some knowledge of a Being from whom such a revelation might come. If the knowledge thus handed down is simply knowledge of the results of the reasonings of the race, then the knowledge of God comes originally from reasoning—an explanation which we consider further on. On the traditive theory of religion, see Flint, Theism, 23, 338; Cocker, Christianity and Greek Philosophy, 86-96; Fairbairn, Studies in Philos. of Relig. and Hist., 14, 15; Bowen, Metaph. and Ethics, 453, and in Bib. Sac., Oct. 1876; Pfleiderer, Religionsphilos., 312-322.

Similar answers must be returned to many common explanations of man's belief in God: "Primus in orbe deos fecit timor"; Imagination made religion; Priests invented religion; Religion is a matter of imitation and fashion. But we ask again: What caused the fear? Who made the imagination? What made priests possible? What made imitation and fashion natural? To say that man worships, merely because he sees other men worshiping, is as absurd as to say that a horse eats hay because he sees other horses eating it. There must be a hunger in the soul to be satisfied, or external things would never attract man to worship. Priests could never impose upon men so continuously, unless there was in human nature a universal belief in a God who might commission priests as his representatives. Imagination itself requires some basis of reality, and a larger basis as civilization advances. The fact that belief in God's existence gets a wider hold upon the race with each added century, shows that, instead of fear having caused belief in God, the truth is that belief in God has caused fear; indeed, "the fear of Jehovah is the beginning of wisdom" (Ps. 111:10).

2. Not from experience,—whether this mean (a) the sense-perception and reflection of the individual (Locke), (b) the accumulated results of the sensations and associations of past generations of the race (Herbert Spencer), or (c) the actual contact of our sensitive nature with God, the supersensible reality, through the religious feeling (Newman Smyth).

The first form of this theory is inconsistent with the fact that the idea of God is not the idea of a sensible or material object, nor a combination of such ideas. Since the spiritual and infinite are direct opposites of the material and finite, no experience of the latter can account for our idea of the former.

With Locke (Essay on Hum. Understanding, 2:1:4), experience is the passive reception of ideas by sensation or by reflection. Locke's "tabula rasa" theory mistakes the occasion of our primitive ideas for their cause. To his statement: "Nihil est in intellectu nisi quod ante fuerit in sensu," Leibnitz replied: "Nisi intellectus ipse." Consciousness is sometimes called the source of our knowledge of God. But consciousness, as simply an accompanying knowledge of ourselves and our states, is not properly the source of any other knowledge. The German Gottesbewusstsein = not "consciousness of God," but "knowledge of God"; Bewusstsein here = not a "conknowing," but a "beknowing"; see Porter, Human Intellect, 86; Cousin, True, Beautiful and Good, 48, 49.

Fraser, Locke, 143-147—Sensations are the bricks, and association the mortar, of the mental house. Bowne, Theory of Thought and Knowledge, 47—"Develope language by allowing sounds to associate and evolve meaning for themselves? Yet this is the exact parallel of the philosophy which aims to build intelligence out of sensation....52—One who does not know how to read would look in vain for meaning in a printed page, and in vain would he seek to help his failure by using strong spectacles." Yet even if the idea of God were a product of experience, we should not be warranted in rejecting it as irrational. See Brooks, Foundations of Zoölogy, 132—"There is no antagonism between those who attribute knowledge to experience and those who attribute it to our innate reason; between those who attribute the development of the germ to mechanical conditions and those who attribute it to the inherent potency of the germ itself; between those who hold that all nature was latent in the cosmic vapor and those who believe that everything in nature is immediately intended rather than predetermined." All these may be methods of the immanent God.

The second form of the theory is open to the objection that the very first experience of the first man, equally with man's latest experience, presupposes this intuition, as well as the other intuitions, and therefore cannot be the cause of it. Moreover, even though this theory of its origin were correct, it would still be impossible to think of the object of the intuition as not existing, and the intuition would still represent to us the highest measure of certitude at present attainable by man. If the evolution of ideas is toward truth instead of falsehood, it is the part of wisdom to act upon the hypothesis that our primitive belief is veracious.

Martineau, Study, 2:26—"Nature is as worthy of trust in her processes, as in her gifts." Bowne, Examination of Spencer, 163, 164—"Are we to seek truth in the minds of pre-human apes, or in the blind stirrings of some primitive pulp? In that case we can indeed put away all our science, but we must put away the great doctrine of evolution along with it. The experience-philosophy cannot escape this alternative: either the positive deliverances of our mature consciousness must be accepted as they stand, or all truth must be declared impossible." See also Harris, Philos. Basis Theism, 137-142.

Charles Darwin, in a letter written a year before his death, referring to his doubts as to the existence of God, asks: "Can we trust to the convictions of a monkey's mind?" We may reply: "Can we trust the conclusions of one who was once a baby?" Bowne, Ethics, 3—"The genesis and emergence of an idea are one thing; its validity is quite another. The logical value of chemistry cannot be decided by reciting its beginnings in alchemy; and the logical value of astronomy is independent of the fact that it began in astrology.... 11—Even if man came from the ape, we need not tremble for the validity of the multiplication-table or of the Golden Rule. If we have moral insight, it is no matter how we got it; and if we have no such insight, there is no help in any psychological theory.... 159—We must not appeal to savages and babies to find what is natural to the human mind.... In the case of anything that is under the law of development we can find its true nature, not by going back to its crude beginnings, but by studying the finished outcome." Dawson, Mod. Ideas of Evolution, 13—"If the idea of God be the phantom of an apelike brain, can we trust to reason or conscience in any other matter? May not science and philosophy themselves be similar phantasies, evolved by mere chance and unreason?" Even though man came from the ape, there is no explaining his ideas by the ideas of the ape: "A man 's a man for a' that."

We must judge beginnings by endings, not endings by beginnings. It matters not how the development of the eye took place nor how imperfect was the first sense of sight, if the eye now gives us correct information of external objects. So it matters not how the intuitions of right and of God originated, if they now give us knowledge of objective truth. We must take for granted that evolution of ideas is not from sense to nonsense. G. H. Lewes, Study of Psychology, 122—"We can understand the amœba and the polyp only by a light reflected from the study of man." Seth, Ethical Principles, 429—"The oak explains the acorn even more truly than the acorn explains the oak." Sidgwick: "No one appeals from the artist's sense of beauty to the child's. Higher mathematics are no less true, because they can be apprehended only by trained intellect. No strange importance attaches to what was first felt or thought." Robert Browning, Paracelsus: "Man, once descried, imprints forever His presence on all lifeless things.... A supplementary reflux of light Illustrates all the inferior grades, explains Each back step in the circle." Man, with his higher ideas, shows the meaning and content of all that led up to him. He is the last round of the ascending ladder, and from this highest product and from his ideas we may infer what his Maker is.

Bixby, Crisis in Morals, 162, 245—"Evolution simply gave man such height that he could at last discern the stars of moral truth which had previously been below the horizon. This is very different from saying that moral truths are merely transmitted products of the experiences of utility.... The germ of the idea of God, as of the idea of right, must have been in man just so soon as he became man,—the brute's gaining it turned him into man. Reason is not simply a register of physical phenomena and of experiences of pleasure and pain: it is creative also. It discerns the oneness of things and the supremacy of God." Sir Charles Lyell: "The presumption is enormous that all our faculties, though liable to err, are true in the main and point to real objects. The religious faculty in man is one of the strongest of all. It existed in the earliest ages, and instead of wearing out before advancing civilization, it grows stronger and stronger, and is to-day more developed among the highest races than it ever was before. I think we may safely trust that it points to a great truth." Fisher, Nat. and Meth. of Rev., 137, quotes Augustine: "Securus judicat orbis terrarum," and tells us that the intellect is assumed to be an organ of knowledge, however the intellect may have been evolved. But if the intellect is worthy of trust, so is the moral nature. George A. Gordon, The Christ of To-day, 103—"To Herbert Spencer, human history is but an incident of natural history, and force is supreme. To Christianity nature is only the beginning, and man the consummation. Which gives the higher revelation of the life of the tree—the seed, or the fruit?"

The third form of the theory seems to make God a sensuous object, to reverse the proper order of knowing and feeling, to ignore the fact that in all feeling there is at least some knowledge of an object, and to forget that the validity of this very feeling can be maintained only by previously assuming the existence of a rational Deity.

Newman Smyth tells us that feeling comes first; the idea is secondary. Intuitive ideas are not denied, but they are declared to be direct reflections, in thought, of the feelings. They are the mind's immediate perception of what it feels to exist. Direct knowledge of God by intuition is considered to be idealistic, reaching God by inference is regarded as rationalistic, in its tendency. See Smyth, The Religious Feeling; reviewed by Harris, in New Englander, Jan., 1878: reply by Smyth, in New Englander, May, 1878.

We grant that, even in the case of unregenerate men, great peril, great joy, great sin often turn the rational intuition of God into a presentative intuition. The presentative intuition, however, cannot be affirmed to be common to all men. It does not furnish the foundation or explanation of a universal capacity for religion. Without the rational intuition, the presentative would not be possible, since it is only the rational that enables man to receive and to interpret the presentative. The very trust that we put in feeling presupposes an intuitive belief in a true and good God. Tennyson said in 1869: "Yes, it is true that there are moments when the flesh is nothing to me; when I know and feel the flesh to be the vision; God and the spiritual is the real; it belongs to me more than the hand and the foot. You may tell me that my hand and my foot are only imaginary symbols of my existence,—I could believe you; but you never, never can convince me that the I is not an eternal Reality, and that the spiritual is not the real and true part of me."

3. Not from reasoning,—because

(a) The actual rise of this knowledge in the great majority of minds is not the result of any conscious process of reasoning. On the other hand, upon occurrence of the proper conditions, it flashes upon the soul with the quickness and force of an immediate revelation.

(b) The strength of men's faith in God's existence is not proportioned to the strength of the reasoning faculty. On the other hand, men of greatest logical power are often inveterate sceptics, while men of unwavering faith are found among those who cannot even understand the arguments for God's existence.

(c) There is more in this knowledge than reasoning could ever have furnished. Men do not limit their belief in God to the just conclusions of argument. The arguments for the divine existence, valuable as they are for purposes to be shown hereafter, are not sufficient by themselves to warrant our conviction that there exists an infinite and absolute Being. It will appear upon examination that the a priori argument is capable of proving only an abstract and ideal proposition, but can never conduct us to the existence of a real Being. It will appear that the a posteriori arguments, from merely finite existence, can never demonstrate the existence of the infinite. In the words of Sir Wm. Hamilton (Discussions, 23)—"A demonstration of the absolute from the relative is logically absurd, as in such a syllogism we must collect in the conclusion what is not distributed in the premises"—in short, from finite premises we cannot draw an infinite conclusion.

Whately, Logic, 290-292; Jevons, Lessons in Logic, 81; Thompson, Outline Laws of Thought, sections 82-92; Calderwood, Philos. of Infinite, 60-69, and Moral Philosophy, 238; Turnbull, in Bap. Quarterly, July, 1872:271; Van Oosterzee, Dogmatics, 239; Dove, Logic of Christian Faith, 21. Sir Wm. Hamilton: "Departing from the particular, we admit that we cannot, in our highest generalizations, rise above the finite." Dr. E. G. Robinson: "The human mind turns out larger grists than are ever put in at the hopper." There is more in the idea of God than could have come out so small a knot-hole as human reasoning. A single word, a chance remark, or an attitude of prayer, suggests the idea to a child. Helen Keller told Phillips Brooks that she had always known that there was a God, but that she had not known his name. Ladd, Philosophy of Mind, 119—"It is a foolish assumption that nothing can be certainly known unless it be reached as the result of a conscious syllogistic process, or that the more complicated and subtle this process is, the more sure is the conclusion. Inferential knowledge is always dependent upon the superior certainty of immediate knowledge." George M. Duncan, in Memorial of Noah Porter,

246—"All deduction rests either on the previous process of induction, or on the intuitions of time and space which involve the Infinite and Absolute."

(d) Neither do men arrive at the knowledge of God's existence by inference; for inference is condensed syllogism, and, as a form of reasoning, is equally open to the objection just mentioned. We have seen, moreover, that all logical processes are based upon the assumption of God's existence. Evidently that which is presupposed in all reasoning cannot itself be proved by reasoning.

By inference, we of course mean mediate inference, for in immediate inference (e. g., "All good rulers are just; therefore no unjust rulers are good") there is no reasoning, and no progress in thought. Mediate inference is reasoning—is condensed syllogism; and what is so condensed may be expanded into regular logical form. Deductive inference: "A negro is a fellow-creature; therefore he who strikes a negro strikes a fellow-creature." Inductive inference: "The first finger is before the second; therefore it is before the third." On inference, see Martineau, Essays, 1:105-108; Porter, Human Intellect, 444-448; Jevons, Principles of Science, 1:14, 136-139, 168, 262.

Flint, in his Theism, 77, and Herbert, in his Mod. Realism Examined, would reach the knowledge of God's existence by inference. The latter says God is not demonstrable, but his existence is inferred, like the existence of our fellow men. But we reply that in this last case we infer only the finite from the finite, while the difficulty in the case of God is in inferring the infinite from the finite. This very process of reasoning, moreover, presupposes the existence of God as the absolute Reason, in the way already indicated.

Substantially the same error is committed by H. B. Smith, Introd. to Chr. Theol., 84-133, and by Diman, Theistic Argument, 316, 364, both of whom grant an intuitive element, but use it only to eke out the insufficiency of reasoning. They consider that the intuition gives us only an abstract idea, which contains in itself no voucher for the existence of an actual being corresponding to the idea, and that we reach real being only by inference from the facts of our own spiritual natures and of the outward world. But we reply, in the words of McCosh, that "the intuitions are primarily directed to individual objects." We know, not the infinite in the abstract, but infinite space and time, and the infinite God. See McCosh, Intuitions, 26, 199, who, however, holds the view here combated.

Schurman, Belief in God, 43—"I am unable to assign to our belief in God a higher certainty than that possessed by the working hypotheses of science.... 57—The nearest approach made by science to our hypothesis of the existence of God lies in the assertion of the universality of law ... based on the conviction of the unity and systematic connection of all reality.... 64—This unity can be found only in self-conscious spirit." The fault of this reasoning is that it gives us nothing necessary or absolute. Instances of working hypotheses are the nebular hypothesis in astronomy, the law of gravitation, the atomic theory in chemistry, the principle of evolution. No one of these is logically independent or prior. Each of them is provisional, and each may be superseded by new discovery. Not so with the idea of God. This idea is presupposed by all the others, as the condition of every mental process and the guarantee of its validity.

IV. Contents of this Intuition

1. In this fundamental knowledge that God is, it is necessarily implied that to some extent men know intuitively what God is, namely, (a) a Reason in which their mental processes are grounded; (b) a Power above them upon which they are dependent; (c) a Perfection which imposes law upon their moral natures; (d) a Personality which they may recognize in prayer and worship.

In maintaining that we have a rational intuition of God, we by no means imply that a presentative intuition of God is impossible. Such a presentative intuition was perhaps characteristic of unfallen man; it does belong at times to the Christian; it will be the blessing of heaven (Mat. 5:8—"the pure in heart ... shall see God"; Rev. 22:4—"they shall see his face"). Men's experiences of face-to-face apprehension of God, in danger and guilt, give some reason to believe that a presentative knowledge of God is the normal condition of humanity. But, as this presentative intuition of God is not in our present state universal, we here claim only that all men have a rational intuition of God.

It is to be remembered, however, that the loss of love to God has greatly obscured even this rational intuition, so that the revelation of nature and the Scriptures is needed to awaken, confirm and enlarge it, and the special work of the Spirit of Christ to make it the knowledge of friendship and communion. Thus from knowing about God, we come to know God (John 17:3—"This is life eternal, that they should know thee"; 2 Tim. 1:12—"I know him whom I have believed").

Plato said, for substance, that there can be no ὅτι οἶδεν without something of the ἁ οἶδεν. Harris, Philosophical Basis of Theism, 208—"By rational intuition man knows that absolute Being exists; his knowledge of what it is, is progressive with his progressive knowledge of man and of nature." Hutton, Essays: "A haunting presence besets man behind and before. He cannot evade it. It gives new meanings to his thoughts, new terror to his sins. It becomes intolerable. He is moved to set up some idol, carved out of his own nature, that will take its place—a non-moral God who will not disturb his dream of rest. It is a righteous Life and Will, and not the mere idea of righteousness that stirs men so." Porter, Hum.

Int., 661—"The Absolute is a thinking Agent." The intuition does not grow in certainty; what grows is the mind's quickness in applying it and power of expressing it. The intuition is not complex; what is complex is the Being intuitively cognized. See Calderwood, Moral Philosophy, 232; Lowndes, Philos. of Primary Beliefs, 108-112; Luthardt, Fund. Truths, 157—Latent faculty of speech is called forth by speech of others; the choked-up well flows again when debris is cleared away. Bowen, in Bib. Sac., 33:740-754; Bowne, Theism, 79.

Knowledge of a person is turned into personal knowledge by actual communication or revelation. First, comes the intuitive knowledge of God possessed by all men—the assumption that there exists a Reason, Power, Perfection, Personality, that makes correct thinking and acting possible. Secondly, comes the knowledge of God's being and attributes which nature and Scripture furnish. Thirdly, comes the personal and presentative knowledge derived from actual reconciliation and intercourse with God, through Christ and the Holy Spirit. Stearns, Evidence of Christian Experience, 208—"Christian experience verifies the claims of doctrine by experiment,—so transforming probable knowledge into real knowledge." Biedermann, quoted by Pfleiderer, Grundriss, 18—"God reveals himself to the human spirit, 1. as its infinite Ground, in the reason; 2. as its infinite Norm, in the conscience; 3. as its infinite Strength, in elevation to religious truth, blessedness, and freedom."

Shall I object to this Christian experience, because only comparatively few have it, and I am not among the number? Because I have not seen the moons of Jupiter, shall I doubt the testimony of the astronomer to their existence? Christian experience, like the sight of the moons of Jupiter, is attainable by all. Clarke, Christian Theology, 113—"One who will have full proof of the good God's reality must put it to the experimental test. He must take the good God for real, and receive the confirmation that will follow. When faith reaches out after God, it finds him.... They who have found him will be the sanest and truest of their kind, and their convictions will be among the safest convictions of man.... Those who live in fellowship with the good God will grow in goodness, and will give practical evidence of his existence aside from their oral testimony."

2. The Scriptures, therefore, do not attempt to prove the existence of God, but, on the other hand, both assume and declare that the knowledge that God is, is universal (Rom. 1:19-21, 28, 32; 2:15). God has inlaid the evidence of this fundamental truth in the very nature of man, so that nowhere is he without a witness. The preacher may confidently follow the example of Scripture by assuming it. But he must also explicitly declare it, as the Scripture does. "For the invisible things of him since the creation of the world are clearly seen" (καθορᾶται—spiritually viewed); the organ given for this purpose is the νοῦς (νοούμενα); but then—and this confirms the transition to our next division of the subject—they are "perceived through the things that are made" (τοῖς ποιήμασιν, Rom. 1:20).

On Rom. 1:19-21, see Weiss, Bib. Theol. des N. T., 251, note; also commentaries of Meyer, Alford, Tholuck, and Wordsworth; τὸ γνωστὸν τοῦ θεοῦ = not "that which may be known" (Rev. Vers.) but "that which is known" of God; νοούμενα καθορᾶται = are clearly seen in that they are perceived by the reason—νοούμενα expresses the manner of the καθορᾶται (Meyer); compare John 1:9; Acts 17:27; Rom. 1:28; 2:15. On 1 Cor. 15:34, see Calderwood, Philos. of Inf., 466—ἀγνωσίαν Θεοῦ τινὲς ἔχουσι = do not possess the specially exalted knowledge of God which belongs to believers in Christ (cf. 1 Jo. 4:7—"every one that loveth is begotten of God, and knoweth God"). On Eph. 2:12, see Pope, Theology, 1:240—ἄθεοι ἐν τῷ κόσμῳ is opposed to being in Christ, and signifies rather forsaken of God, than denying him or entirely ignorant of him. On Scripture passages, see Schmid, Bib. Theol. des N. T., 486; Hofmann, Schriftbeweis, 1:62.

E. G. Robinson: "The first statement of the Bible is, not that there is a God, but that 'In the beginning God created the heavens and the earth' (Gen. 1:1). The belief in God never was and never can be the result of logical argument, else the Bible would give us proofs." Many texts relied upon as proofs of God's existence are simply explications of the idea of God, as for example: Ps. 94:9, 10—"He that planted the ear, shall he not hear? He that formed the eye, shall he not see? He that chastiseth the nations, shall not he correct, even he that teacheth man knowledge?" Plato says that God holds the soul by its roots,—he therefore does not need to demonstrate to the soul the fact of his existence. Martineau, Seat of Authority, 308, says well that Scripture and preaching only interpret what is already in the heart which it addresses: "Flinging a warm breath on the inward oracles hid in invisible ink, it renders them articulate and dazzling as the handwriting on the wall. The divine Seer does not convey to you his revelation, but qualifies you to receive your own. This mutual relation is possible only through the common presence of God in the conscience of mankind." Shedd, Dogmatic Theology, 1:195-220—"The earth and sky make the same sensible impressions on the organs of a brute that they do upon those of a man; but the brute never discerns the 'invisible things' of God, his 'eternal power and godhood' (Rom. 1:20)."

Our subconscious activity, so far as it is normal, is under the guidance of the immanent Reason. Sensation, before it results in thought, has in it logical elements which are furnished by mind—not ours, but that of the Infinite One. Christ, the Revealer of God, reveals God in every man's mental life, and the Holy Spirit may be the principle of self-consciousness in man as in God. Harris, God the Creator, tells us that "man finds the Reason that is eternal and universal revealing itself in the exercise of his own reason." Savage, Life after Death, 268—"How do you know that your subliminal consciousness does not tap Omniscience, and get at the facts of the universe?" Savage negatives this suggestion, however, and wrongly favors the spirit-theory. For his own experience, see pages 295-329 of his book.

C. M. Barrows, in Proceedings of Soc. for Psychical Research, vol. 12, part 30, pages 34-36—"There is a subliminal agent. What if this is simply one intelligent Actor, filling the universe with his presence, as the ether fills space; the common Inspirer of all mankind, a skilled Musician, presiding over many pipes and keys, and playing through each what music he will? The subliminal self is a universal fountain of energy, and each man is an outlet of the stream. Each man's personal self is contained in it, and thus each man is made one with every other man. In that deep Force, the last fact behind which analysis cannot go, all psychical and bodily effects find their common origin." This statement needs to be qualified by the assertion of man's ethical nature and distinct personality; see section of this work on Ethical Monism, in chapter III. But there is truth here like that which Coleridge sought to express in his Æolian Harp: "And what if all of animated Nature Be but organic harps diversely framed, That tremble into thought, as o'er them sweeps, Plastic and vast, one intellectual breeze, At once the soul of each, and God of all?" See F. W. H. Myers, Human Personality.

Dorner, System of Theology, 1:75—"The consciousness of God is the true fastness of our self-consciousness.... Since it is only in the God-conscious man that the innermost personality comes to light, in like manner, by means of the interweaving of that consciousness of God and of the world, the world is viewed in God ('sub specie eternitatis'), and the certainty of the world first obtains its absolute security for the spirit." Royce, Spirit of Mod. Philosophy, synopsis in N. Y. Nation: "The one indubitable fact is the existence of an infinite self, a Logos or World-mind (345). That it exists is clear, I. Because idealism shows that real things are nothing more nor less than ideas, or 'possibilities of experience'; but a mere 'possibility', as such, is nothing, and a world of 'possible' experiences, in so far as it is real, must be a world of actual experience to some self (367). If then there be a real world, it has all the while existed as ideal and mental, even before it became known to the particular mind with which we conceive it as coming into connection (368). II. But there is such a real world; for, when I think of an object, when I mean it, I do not merely have in mind an idea resembling it, for I aim at the object, I pick it out, I already in some measure possess it. The object is then already present in essence to my hidden self (370). As truth consists in knowledge of the conformity of a cognition to its object, that alone can know a truth which includes within itself both idea and object. This inclusive Knower is the Infinite Self (374). With this I am in essence identical (371); it is my larger self (372); and this larger self alone is (379). It includes all reality, and we know other finite minds, because we are one with them in its unity" (409).

The experience of George John Romanes is instructive. For years he could recognize no personal Intelligence controlling the universe. He made four mistakes: 1. He forgot that only love can see, that God is not disclosed to the mere intellect, but only to the whole man, to the integral mind, to what the Scripture calls "the eyes of your heart" (Eph. 1:18). Experience of life taught him at last the weakness of mere reasoning, and led him to depend more upon the affections and intuitions. Then, as one might say, he gave the X-rays of Christianity a chance to photograph God upon his soul. 2. He began at the wrong end, with matter rather than with mind, with cause and effect rather than with right and wrong, and so got involved in the mechanical order and tried to interpret the moral realm by it. The result was that instead of recognizing freedom, responsibility, sin, guilt, he threw them out as pretenders. But study of conscience and will set him right. He learned to take what be found instead of trying to turn it into something else, and so came to interpret nature by spirit, instead of interpreting spirit by nature. 3. He took the Cosmos by bits, instead of regarding it as a whole. His early thinking insisted on finding design in each particular part, or nowhere. But his more mature thought recognized wisdom and reason in the ordered whole. As he realized that this is a universe, he could not get rid of the idea of an organizing Mind. He came to see that the Universe, as a thought, implies a Thinker. 4. He fancied that nature excludes God, instead of being only the method of God's working. When he learned how a thing was done, he at first concluded that God had not done it. His later thought recognized that God and nature are not mutually exclusive. So he came to find no difficulty even in miracles and inspiration; for the God who is in man and of whose mind and will nature is only the expression, can reveal himself, if need be, in special ways. So George John Romanes came back to prayer, to Christ, to the church.

On the general subject of intuition as connected with our idea of God, see Ladd, in Bib. Sac., 1877:1-36, 611-616; 1878:619; Fisher, on Final Cause and Intuition, in Journ. Christ. Philos., Jan. 1883:113-134; Patton, on Genesis of Idea of God, in Jour. Christ. Philos., Apl. 1883:283-307; McCosh, Christianity and Positivism, 124-140; Mansel, in Encyc. Brit., 8th ed., vol. 14:604 and 615; Robert Hall, sermon on Atheism; Hutton, on Atheism, in Essays, 1:3-37; Shairp, in Princeton Rev., March, 1881:264.

Chapter II - Corroborative Evidences Of God's Existence

Although the knowledge of God's existence is intuitive, it may be explicated and confirmed by arguments drawn from the actual universe and from the abstract ideas of the human mind.

Remark 1. These arguments are probable, not demonstrative. For this reason they supplement each other, and constitute a series of evidences which is cumulative in its nature. Though, taken singly, none of them can be considered absolutely decisive, they together furnish a corroboration of our primitive conviction of God's existence, which is of great practical value, and is in itself sufficient to bind the moral action of men.

Butler, Analogy, Introd., Bohn's ed., 72—Probable evidence admits of degrees, from the highest moral certainty to the lowest presumption. Yet probability is the guide of life. In matters of morals and religion, we are not to expect mathematical or demonstrative, but only probable, evidence, and the slightest preponderance of such evidence may be sufficient to bind our moral action. The truth of our religion, like the truth of common matters, is to be judged by the whole evidence taken together; for probable proofs, by being added, not only increase the evidence, but multiply it. Dove, Logic of Christ. Faith, 24—Value of the arguments taken together is much greater than that of any single one. Illustrated from water, air and food, together but not separately, supporting life; value of £1000 note, not in paper, stamp, writing, signature, taken separately. A whole bundle of rods cannot be broken, though each rod in the bundle may be broken separately. The strength of the bundle is the strength of the whole. Lord Bacon, Essay on Atheism: "A little philosophy inclineth man's mind to atheism, but depth in philosophy bringeth men's minds about to religion. For while the mind of man looketh upon second causes scattered, it may sometimes rest in them and go no further, but, when it beholdeth the chain of them confederate and linked together, it must needs fly to Providence and Deity." Murphy, Scientific Bases of Faith, 221-223—"The proof of a God and of a spiritual world which is to satisfy us must consist in a number of different but converging lines of proof."

In a case where only circumstantial evidence is attainable, many lines of proof sometimes converge, and though no one of the lines reaches the mark, the conclusion to which they all point becomes the only rational one. To doubt that there is a London, or that there was a Napoleon, would indicate insanity; yet London and Napoleon are proved by only probable evidence. There is no constraining efficacy in the arguments for God's existence; but the same can be said of all reasoning that is not demonstrative. Another interpretation of the facts is possible, but no other conclusion is so satisfactory, as that God is; see Fisher, Nature and Method of Revelation, 129. Prof. Rogers: "If in practical affairs we were to hesitate to act until we had absolute and demonstrative certainty, we should never begin to move at all." For this reason an old Indian official advised a young Indian judge "always to give his verdict, but always to avoid giving the grounds of it."

Bowne, Philos. of Theism, 11-14—"Instead of doubting everything that can be doubted, let us rather doubt nothing until we are compelled to doubt.... In society we get on better by assuming that men are truthful, and by doubting only for special reasons, than we should if we assumed that all men are liars, and believed them only when compelled. So in all our investigations we make more progress if we assume the truthfulness of the universe and of our own nature than we should if we doubted both.... The first method seems the more rigorous, but it can be applied only to mathematics, which is a purely subjective science. When we come to deal with reality, the method brings thought to a standstill.... The law the logician lays down is this: Nothing may be believed which is not proved. The law the mind actually follows is this: Whatever the mind demands for the satisfaction of its subjective interests and tendencies may be assumed as real, in default of positive disproof."

Remark 2. A consideration of these arguments may also serve to explicate the contents of an intuition which has remained obscure and only half conscious for lack of reflection. The arguments, indeed, are the efforts of the mind that already has a conviction of God's existence to give to itself a formal account of its belief. An exact estimate of their logical value and of their relation to the intuition which they seek to express in syllogistic form, is essential to any proper refutation of the prevalent atheistic and pantheistic reasoning.

Diman, Theistic Argument, 363—"Nor have I claimed that the existence, even, of this Being can be demonstrated as we demonstrate the abstract truths of science. I have only claimed that the universe, as a great fact, demands a rational explanation, and that the most rational explanation that can possibly be given is that furnished in the conception of such a Being. In this conclusion reason rests, and refuses to rest in any other." Rückert: "Wer Gott nicht fühlt in sich und allen Lebenskreisen, Dem werdet ihr nicht ihn beweisen mit Beweisen." Harris, Philos. Basis of Theism, 307—"Theology depends on noetic and empirical science to give the occasion on which the idea of the Absolute Being arises, and to give content to the idea." Andrew Fuller, Part of Syst. of Divin., 4:283, questions "whether argumentation in favor of the existence of God has not made more sceptics than believers." So far as this is true, it is due to an overstatement of the arguments and an exaggerated notion of what is to be expected from them. See Nitzsch, Christian Doctrine, translation, 140; Ebrard, Dogmatik, 1:119, 120; Fisher, Essays on Supernatural Origin of Christianity, 572, 573; Van Oosterzee, 238, 241.

"Evidences of Christianity?" said Coleridge, "I am weary of the word." The more Christianity was proved, the less it was believed. The revival of religion under Whitefield and Wesley did what all the apologists of the eighteenth century could not do,—it quickened men's intuitions into life, and made them practically recognize God. Martineau, Types, 2:231—Men can "bow the knee to the passing Zeitgeist, while turning the back to the consensus of all the ages"; Seat of Authority, 312—"Our reasonings lead to explicit Theism because they start from implicit Theism." Illingworth, Div. and Hum. Personality, 81—"The proofs are ... attempts to account for and explain and justify something that already exists; to decompose a highly complex though immediate judgment into its constituent elements, none of which when isolated can have the completeness or the cogency of the original conviction taken as a whole."

Bowne, Philos. of Theism, 31, 32—"Demonstration is only a makeshift for helping ignorance to insight.... When we come to an argument in which the whole nature is addressed, the argument must seem weak or strong, according as the nature is feebly, or fully, developed. The moral argument for theism cannot seem strong to one without a conscience. The argument from cognitive interests will be empty when there is no cognitive interest. Little souls find very little that calls for explanation or that excites surprise, and they are satisfied with a correspondingly small view of life and existence. In such a case we cannot hope for universal agreement. We can only proclaim the faith that is in us, in hope that this proclamation may not be without some response in other minds and hearts.... We have only probable evidence for the uniformity of nature or for the affection of friends. We cannot logically prove either. The deepest convictions are not the certainties of logic, but the certainties of life."

Remark 3. The arguments for the divine existence may be reduced to four, namely: I. The Cosmological; II. The Teleological; III. The Anthropological; and IV. The Ontological. We shall examine these in order, seeking first to determine the precise conclusions to which they respectively lead, and then to ascertain in what manner the four may be combined.

I. The Cosmological Argument, or Argument from Change in Nature

This is not properly an argument from effect to cause; for the proposition that every effect must have a cause is simply identical, and means only that every caused event must have a cause. It is rather an argument from begun existence to a sufficient cause of that beginning, and may be accurately stated as follows:

Everything begun, whether substance or phenomenon, owes its existence to some producing cause. The universe, at least so far as its present form is concerned, is a thing begun, and owes its existence to a cause which is equal to its production. This cause must be indefinitely great.

It is to be noticed that this argument moves wholly in the realm of nature. The argument from man's constitution and beginning upon the planet is treated under another head (see Anthropological Argument). That the present form of the universe is not eternal in the past, but has begun to be, not only personal observation but the testimony of geology assures us. For statements of the argument, see Kant, Critique of Pure Reason (Bohn's transl.), 370; Gillespie, Necessary Existence of God, 8:34-44; Bib. Sac., 1849:613; 1850:613; Porter, Hum. Intellect, 570; Herbert Spencer, First Principles, 93. It has often been claimed, as by Locke, Clarke, and Robert Hall, that this argument is sufficient to conduct the mind to an Eternal and Infinite First Cause. We proceed therefore to mention

1. The defects of the Cosmological Argument.

A. It is impossible to show that the universe, so far as its substance is concerned, has had a beginning. The law of causality declares, not that everything has a cause—for then God himself must have a cause—but rather that everything begun has a cause, or in other words, that every event or change has a cause.

Hume, Philos. Works, 2:411 sq., urges with reason that we never saw a world made. Many philosophers in Christian lands, as Martineau, Essays, 1:206, and the prevailing opinions of ante-Christian times, have held matter to be eternal. Bowne, Metaphysics, 107—"For being itself, the reflective reason never asks a cause, unless the being show signs of dependence. It is change that first gives rise to the demand for cause." Martineau, Types, 1:291—"It is not existence, as such, that demands a cause, but the coming into existence of what did not exist before. The intellectual law of causality is a law for phenomena, and not for entity." See also McCosh, Intuitions, 225-241; Calderwood, Philos. of Infinite, 61. Per contra, see Murphy, Scient. Bases of Faith, 49, 195, and Habit and Intelligence, 1:55-67; Knight, Lect. on Metaphysics, lect. ii, p. 19.

B. Granting that the universe, so far as its phenomena are concerned, has had a cause, it is impossible to show that any other cause is required than a cause within itself, such as the pantheist supposes.

Flint, Theism, 65—"The cosmological argument alone proves only force, and no mere force is God. Intelligence must go with power to make a Being that can be called God." Diman, Theistic Argument: "The cosmological argument alone cannot decide whether the force that causes change is permanent self-existent mind, or permanent self-existent matter." Only intelligence gives the basis for an answer. Only mind in the universe enables us to infer mind in the maker. But the argument from intelligence is not the Cosmological, but the Teleological, and to this last belong all proofs of Deity from order and combination in nature.

Upton, Hibbert Lectures, 201-296—Science has to do with those changes which one portion of the visible universe causes in another portion. Philosophy and theology deal with the Infinite Cause which brings into existence and sustains the entire series of finite causes. Do we ask the cause of the stars? Science says: Fire-mist, or an infinite regress of causes. Theology says: Granted; but this infinite regress demands for its explanation the belief in God. We must believe both in God, and in an endless series of finite causes. God is the cause of all causes, the soul of all souls: "Centre and soul of every sphere, Yet to each loving heart how near!" We do not need, as mere matter of science, to think of any beginning.

C. Granting that the universe most have had a cause outside of itself, it is impossible to show that this cause has not itself been caused, i. e., consists of an infinite series of dependent causes. The principle of causality does not require that everything begun should be traced back to an uncaused cause; it demands that we should assign a cause, but not that we should assign a first cause.

So with the whole series of causes. The materialist is bound to find a cause for this series, only when the series is shown to have had a beginning. But the very hypothesis of an infinite series of causes excludes the idea of such a beginning. An infinite chain has no topmost link (versus Robert Hall); an uncaused and eternal succession does not need a cause (versus Clarke and Locke). See Whately, Logic, 270; New Englander, Jan. 1874:75; Alexander, Moral Science, 221; Pfleiderer, Die Religion, 1:160-164; Calderwood, Moral Philos., 225; Herbert Spencer, First Principles, 37—criticized by Bowne, Review of H. Spencer, 36. Julius Müller, Doct. Sin, 2:128, says that the causal principle is not satisfied till by regress we come to a cause which is not itself an effect—to one who is causa sui; Aids to Study of German Theology, 15-17—Even if the universe be eternal, its contingent and relative nature requires us to postulate an eternal Creator; Diman, Theistic Argument, 86—"While the law of causation does not lead logically up to the conclusion of a first cause, it compels us to affirm it." We reply that it is not the law of causation which compels us to affirm it, for this certainly "does not lead logically up to the conclusion." If we infer an uncaused cause, we do it, not by logical process, but by virtue of the intuitive belief within us. So substantially Secretan, and Whewell, in Indications of a Creator, and in Hist. of Scientific Ideas, 2:321, 322—"The mind takes refuge, in the assumption of a First Cause, from an employment inconsistent with its own nature"; "we necessarily infer a First Cause, although the palætiological sciences only point toward it, but do not lead us to it."

D. Granting that the cause of the universe has not itself been caused, it is impossible to show that this cause is not finite, like the universe itself. The causal principle requires a cause no greater than just sufficient to account for the effect.

We cannot therefore infer an infinite cause, unless the universe is infinite—which cannot be proved, but can only be assumed—and this is assuming an infinite in order to prove an infinite. All we know of the universe is finite. An infinite universe implies infinite number. But no number can be infinite, for to any number, however great, a unit can be added, which shows that it was not infinite before. Here again we see that the most approved forms of the Cosmological Argument are obliged to avail themselves of the intuition of the infinite, to supplement the logical process. Versus Martineau, Study, 1:416—"Though we cannot directly infer the infinitude of God from a limited creation, indirectly we may exclude every other position by resort to its unlimited scene of existence (space)." But this would equally warrant our belief in the infinitude of our fellow men. Or, it is the argument of Clarke and Gillespie (see Ontological Argument below). Schiller, Die Grösse der Welt, seems to hold to a boundless universe. He represents a tired spirit as seeking the last limit of creation. A second pilgrim meets him from the spaces beyond with the words: "Steh! du segelst umsonst,—vor dir Unendlichkeit"—"Hold! thou journeyest in vain,—before thee is only Infinity." On the law of parsimony, see Sir Wm. Hamilton, Discussions, 628.

2. The value of the Cosmological Argument, then, is simply this,—it proves the existence of some cause of the universe indefinitely great. When we go beyond this and ask whether this cause is a cause of being, or merely a cause of change, to the universe; whether it is a cause apart from the universe, or one with it; whether it is an eternal cause, or a cause dependent upon some other cause; whether it is

intelligent or unintelligent, infinite or finite, one or many,—this argument cannot assure us.

On the whole argument, see Flint, Theism, 93-130; Mozley, Essays, Hist. and Theol., 2:414-444; Hedge, Ways of the Spirit, 148-154; Studien und Kritiken, 1876:9-31.

II. The Teleological Argument, or Argument from Order and Useful Collocation in Nature

This is not properly an argument from design to a designer; for that design implies a designer is simply an identical proposition. It may be more correctly stated as follows: Order and useful collocation pervading a system respectively imply intelligence and purpose as the cause of that order and collocation. Since order and useful collocation pervade the universe, there must exist an intelligence adequate to the production of this order, and a will adequate to direct this collocation to useful ends.

Etymologically, "teleological argument" = argument to ends or final causes, that is, "causes which, beginning as a thought, work themselves out into a fact as an end or result" (Porter, Hum. Intellect, 592-618);—health, for example, is the final cause of exercise, while exercise is the efficient cause of health. This definition of the argument would be broad enough to cover the proof of a designing intelligence drawn from the constitution of man. This last, however, is treated as a part of the Anthropological Argument, which follows this, and the Teleological Argument covers only the proof of a designing intelligence drawn from nature. Hence Kant, Critique of Pure Reason (Bohn's trans.), 381, calls it the physico-theological argument. On methods of stating the argument, see Bib. Sac., Oct. 1867:625. See also Hedge, Ways of the Spirit, 155-185; Mozley, Essays Hist. and Theol., 2:365-413.

Hicks, in his Critique of Design-Arguments, 347-389, makes two arguments instead of one: (1) the argument from order to intelligence, to which he gives the name Eutaxiological; (2) the argument from adaptation to purpose, to which he would restrict the name Teleological. He holds that teleology proper cannot prove intelligence, because in speaking of "ends" at all, it must assume the very intelligence which it seeks to prove; that it actually does prove simply the intentional exercise of an intelligence whose existence has been previously established. "Circumstances, forces or agencies converging to a definite rational result imply volition—imply that this result is intended—is an end. This is the major premise of this new teleology." He objects to the term "final cause." The end is not a cause at all—it is a motive. The characteristic element of cause is power to produce an effect. Ends have no such power. The will may choose them or set them aside. As already assuming intelligence, ends cannot prove intelligence.

With this in the main we agree, and count it a valuable help to the statement and understanding of the argument. In the very observation of order, however, as well as in arguing from it, we are obliged to assume the same all-arranging intelligence. We see no objection therefore to making Eutaxiology the first part of the Teleological Argument, as we do above. See review of Hicks, in Meth. Quar. Rev., July, 1883:569-576. We proceed however to certain

1. Further explanations

A. The major premise expresses a primitive conviction. It is not invalidated by the objections: (a) that order and useful collocation may exist without being purposed—for we are compelled by our very mental constitution to deny this in all cases where the order and collocation pervade a system: (b) that order and useful collocation may result from the mere operation of physical forces and laws—for these very forces and laws imply, instead of excluding, an originating and superintending intelligence and will.

Janet, in his work on Final Causes, 8, denies that finality is a primitive conviction, like causality, and calls it the result of an induction. He therefore proceeds from (1) marks of order and useful collocation to (2) finality in nature, and then to (3) an intelligent cause of this finality or "pre-conformity to future event." So Diman, Theistic Argument, 105, claims simply that, as change requires cause, so orderly change requires intelligent cause. We have shown, however, that induction and argument of every kind presupposes intuitive belief in final cause. Nature does not give us final cause; but no more does she give us efficient cause. Mind gives us both, and gives them as clearly upon one experience as after a thousand. Ladd: "Things have mind in them: else they could not be minded by us." The Duke of Argyll told Darwin that it seemed to him wholly impossible to ascribe the adjustments of nature to any other agency than that of mind. "Well," said Darwin, "that impression has often come upon me with overpowering force. But then, at other times, it all seems—;" and then he passed his hands over his eyes, as if to indicate the passing of a vision out of sight. Darwinism is not a refutation of ends in nature, but only of a particular theory with regard to the way in which ends are realized in the organic world. Darwin would begin with an infinitesimal germ, and make all the subsequent development unteleological; see Schurman, Belief in God, 193.

(a) Illustration of unpurposed order in the single throwing of "double sixes,"—constant throwing of double sixes indicates design. So arrangement of detritus at mouth of river, and warming pans sent to the West Indies,—useful but not purposed. Momerie, Christianity and Evolution, 72—"It is only within narrow limits that seemingly purposeful arrangements are produced by chance. And therefore, as the signs of purpose increase, the presumption in favor of their accidental origin diminishes." Elder, Ideas from Nature, 81, 82—"The uniformity of a boy's marbles shows them to be products of design. A single one might be accidental, but a dozen cannot be. So atomic uniformity indicates manufacture." Illustrations of purposed order, in Beattie's garden, Tillotson's blind men, Kepler's salad. Dr. Carpenter: "The atheist is like a man examining the machinery of a great mill, who, finding that the whole is moved by a shaft proceeding from a brick wall, infers that the shaft is a sufficient explanation of what he sees, and that there is no moving power behind it." Lord Kelvin: "The atheistic idea is nonsensical." J. G. Paton, Life, 2:191—The sinking of a well on the island of Aniwa convinces the cannibal chief Namakei that Jehovah God exists, the invisible One. See Chauncey Wright, in N. Y. Nation, Jan. 15, 1874; Murphy, Scientific Bases of Faith, 208.

(b) Bowne, Review of Herbert Spencer, 231-247—"Law is method, not cause. A man cannot offer the very fact to be explained, as its sufficient explanation." Martineau, Essays, 1:144—"Patterned damask, made not by the weaver, but by the loom?" Dr. Stevenson: "House requires no architect, because it is built by stone-masons and carpenters?" Joseph Cook: "Natural law without God behind it is no more than a glove without a hand in it, and all that is done by the gloved hand of God in nature is done by the hand and not by the glove. Evolution is a process, not a power; a method of operation, not an operator. A book is not written by the laws of spelling and grammar, but according to those laws. So the book of the universe is not written by the laws of heat, electricity, gravitation, evolution, but according to those laws." G. F. Wright, Ant. and Orig. of Hum. Race, lecture IX—"It is impossible for evolution to furnish evidence which shall drive design out of nature. It can only drive it back to an earlier point of entrance, thereby increasing our admiration for the power of the Creator to accomplish ulterior designs by unlikely means."

Evolution is only the method of God. It has to do with the how, not with the why, of phenomena, and therefore is not inconsistent with design, but rather is a new and higher illustration of design. Henry Ward Beecher: "Design by wholesale is greater than design by retail." Frances Power Cobbe: "It is a singular fact that, whenever we find out how a thing is done, our first conclusion seems to be that God did not do it." Why should we say: "The more law, the less God?" The theist refers the phenomena to a cause that knows itself and what it is doing; the atheist refers them to a power which knows nothing of itself and what it is doing (Bowne). George John Romanes said that, if God be immanent, then all natural causation must appear to be mechanical, and it is no argument against the divine origin of a thing to prove it due to natural causation: "Causes in nature do not obviate the necessity of a cause in nature." Shaler, Interpretation of Nature, 47—Evolution shows that the direction of affairs is under control of something like our own intelligence: "Evolution spells Purpose." Clarke, Christ. Theology, 105—"The modern doctrine of evolution has been awake to the existence of innumerable ends within the universe, but not to the one great end for the universe itself." Huxley, Critiques and Addresses, 274, 275, 307—"The teleological and mechanical views of the universe are not mutually exclusive." Sir William Hamilton, Metaphysics: "Intelligence stands first in the order of existence. Efficient causes are preceded by final causes." See also Thornton, Old Fashioned Ethics, 199-265; Archbp. Temple, Bampton Lect., 1884:99-123; Owen, Anat. of Vertebrates, 3:796; Peirce, Ideality in the Physical Sciences, 1-35; Newman Smyth, Through Science to Faith, 96; Fisher, Nat. and Meth. of Rev., 135.

B. The minor premise expresses a working-principle of all science, namely, that all things have their uses, that order pervades the universe, and that the methods of nature are rational methods. Evidences of this appear in the correlation of the chemical elements to each other; in the fitness of the inanimate world to be the basis and support of life; in the typical forms and unity of plan apparent in the organic creation; in the existence and coöperation of natural laws; in cosmical order and compensations.

This minor premise is not invalidated by the objections: (a) That we frequently misunderstand the end actually subserved by natural events and objects; for the principle is, not that we necessarily know the actual end, but that we necessarily believe that there is some end, in every case of systematic order and collocation. (b) That the order of the universe is manifestly imperfect; for this, if granted, would argue, not absence of contrivance, but some special reason for imperfection, either in the limitations of the contriving intelligence itself, or in the nature of the end sought (as, for example, correspondence with the moral state and probation of sinners).

The evidences of order and useful collocation are found both in the indefinitely small and the indefinitely great. The molecules are manufactured articles; and the compensations of the solar system which provide that a secular flattening of the earth's orbit shall be made up for by a secular rounding of that same orbit, alike show an intelligence far transcending our own; see Cooke, Religion and Chemistry, and Credentials of Science, 23—"Beauty is the harmony of relations which perfect fitness produces; law is the prevailing principle which underlies that harmony. Hence both beauty and law imply design. From energy, fitness, beauty, order, sacrifice, we argue might, skill, perfection, law, and love in a Supreme Intelligence. Christianity implies design, and is the completion of the design argument." Pfleiderer, Philos. Religion, 1:168—"A good definition of beauty is immanent purposiveness, the teleological ideal background of reality, the shining of the Idea through phenomena."

Bowne, Philos. Theism, 85—"Design is never causal. It is only ideal, and it demands an efficient cause for its realization. If ice is not to sink, and to freeze out life, there must be some molecular structure which shall make its bulk greater than that of an equal weight of water." Jackson, Theodore Parker, 355—"Rudimentary organs are like the silent letters in many words,—both are witnesses to a past history; and there is intelligence in their preservation." Diman, Theistic Argument: "Not only do we observe in the world the change which is the basis of the Cosmological Argument, but we perceive that this change proceeds according to a fixed and invariable rule. In inorganic nature, general order, or regularity; in organic nature, special order or adaptation." Bowne, Review of H. Spencer, 113-115, 224-230: "Inductive science proceeds upon the postulate that the reasonable and the natural are one." This furnished the guiding clue to Harvey and Cuvier; see Whewell, Hist. Induct. Sciences, 2:489-491. Kant: "The anatomist must assume that nothing in man is in vain." Aristotle: "Nature makes nothing in vain." On molecules as manufactured articles, see Maxfield, in Nature, Sept. 25, 1873. See also Tulloch, Theism, 116, 120; LeConte, Religion and Science, lect. 2 and 3; McCosh, Typical Forms, 81, 420; Agassiz, Essay on Classification, 9, 10; Bib. Sac., 1849:626 and 1850:613; Hopkins, in Princeton Review, 1882:181.

(a) Design, in fact that rivers always run by large towns? that springs are always found at gambling places? Plants made for man, and man for worms? Voltaire: "Noses are made for spectacles— let us wear them!" Pope: "While man exclaims 'See all things for my use,' 'See man for mine,' replies the pampered goose." Cherries do not ripen in the cold of winter when they do not taste as well, and grapes do not ripen in the heat of summer when the new wine would turn to vinegar? Nature divides melons into sections for convenience in family eating? Cork-tree made for bottle-stoppers? The child who was asked the cause of salt in the ocean, attributed it to codfish, thus dimly confounding final cause with efficient cause. Teacher: "What are marsupials?" Pupil: "Animals that have pouches in their stomachs." Teacher: "And what do they have pouches for?" Pupil: "To crawl into and conceal themselves in, when they are pursued." Why are the days longer in summer than in winter? Because it is the property of all natural objects to elongate under the influence of heat. A Jena professor held that doctors do not exist because of disease, but that diseases exist precisely in order that there may be doctors. Kepler was an astronomical Don Quixote. He discussed the claims of eleven different damsels to become his second wife, and he likened the planets to huge animals rushing through the sky. Many of the objections to design arise from confounding a part of the creation with the whole, or a structure in the process of development with a structure completed. For illustrations of mistaken ends, see Janet, Final Causes.

(b) Alphonso of Castile took offense at the Ptolemaic System, and intimated that, if he had been consulted at the creation, he could have suggested valuable improvements. Lange, in his History of Materialism, illustrates some of the methods of nature by millions of gun barrels shot in all directions to kill a single hare; by ten thousand keys bought at haphazard to get into a shut room; by building a city in order to obtain a house. Is not the ice a little overdone about the poles? See John Stuart Mill's indictment of nature, in his posthumous Essays on Religion, 29—"Nature impales men, breaks men as if on a wheel, casts them to be devoured by wild beasts, crushes them with stones like the first Christian martyr, starves them with hunger, freezes them with cold, poisons them with the quick or slow venom of her exhalations, and has hundreds of other hideous deaths in reserve, such as the ingenious cruelty of a Nabis or a Domitian never surpassed." So argue Schopenhauer and Von Hartmann.

The doctrine of evolution answers many of these objections, by showing that order and useful collocation in the system as a whole is necessarily and cheaply purchased by imperfection and suffering in the initial stages of development. The question is: Does the system as a whole imply design? My opinion is of no value as to the usefulness of an intricate machine the purpose of which I do not know. If I stand at the beginning of a road and do not know whither it leads, it is presumptuous in me to point out a more direct way to its destination. Bowne, Philos. of Theism, 20-22—"In order to counterbalance the impressions which apparent disorder and immorality in nature make upon us, we have to assume that the universe at its root is not only rational, but good. This is faith, but it is an act on which our whole moral life depends." Metaphysics, 165—"The same argument which would deny mind in nature denies mind in man." Fisher, Nat. and Meth. of Rev., 264—"Fifty years ago, when the crane stood on top of the tower of unfinished Cologne Cathedral, was there no evidence of design in the whole structure?" Yet we concede that, so long as we cannot with John Stuart Mill explain the imperfections of the universe by any limitations in the Intelligence which contrived it, we are shut up to regarding them as intended to correspond with the moral state and probation of sinners which God foresaw and provided for at the creation. Evil things in the universe are symbols of sin, and helps to its overthrow. See Bowne, Review of H. Spencer, 264, 265; McCosh, Christ. and Positivism, 82 sq.; Martineau, Essays, 1:50, and Study, 1:351-398; Porter, Hum. Intellect, 599; Mivart, Lessons from Nature, 366-371; Princeton Rev., 1878:272-303; Shaw, on Positivism.

2. Defects of the Teleological Argument. These attach not to the premises but to the conclusion sought to be drawn therefrom

A. The argument cannot prove a personal God. The order and useful collocations of the universe may be only the changing phenomena of an impersonal intelligence and will, such as pantheism supposes. The finality may be only immanent finality.

There is such a thing as immanent and unconscious finality. National spirit, without set purpose, constructs language. The bee works unconsciously to ends. Strato of Lampsacus regarded the world as a vast animal. Aristotle, Phys., 2:8—"Plant the ship-builder's skill within the timber itself, and you have the mode in which nature produces." Here we see a dim anticipation of the modern doctrine of development from within instead of creation from without. Neander: "The divine work goes on from within outward." John Fiske: "The argument from the watch has been superseded by the argument from the flower." Iverach, Theism, 91—"The effect of evolution has been simply to transfer the cause from a mere external influence working from without to an immanent rational principle." Martineau, Study, 1:349, 350—"Theism is in no way committed to the doctrine of a God external to the world ... nor does intelligence require, in order to gain an object, to give it externality."

Newman Smyth, Place of Death, 62-80—"The universe exists in some all-pervasive Intelligence. Suppose we could see a small heap of brick, scraps of metal, and pieces of mortar, gradually shaping themselves into the walls and interior structure of a building, adding needed material as the work advanced, and at last presenting in its completion a factory furnished with varied and finely wrought machinery. Or, a locomotive carrying a process of self-repair to compensate for wear, growing and increasing in size, detaching from itself at intervals pieces of brass or iron endowed with the power of growing up step by step into other locomotives capable of running themselves and of reproducing new locomotives in their turn." So nature in its separate parts may seem mechanical, but as a whole it is rational. Weismann does not "disown a directive power,"—only this power is "behind the mechanism as its final cause ... it must be teleological."

Impressive as are these evidences of intelligence in the universe as a whole, and increased in number as they are by the new light of evolution, we must still hold that nature alone cannot prove that this intelligence is personal. Hopkins, Miscellanies, 18-36—"So long as there is such a thing as impersonal and adapting intelligence in the brute creation, we cannot necessarily infer from unchanging laws a free and personal God." See Fisher, Supernat. Origin of Christianity, 576-578. Kant shows that the argument does not prove intelligence apart from the world (Critique, 370). We must bring mind to the world, if we would find mind in it. Leave out man, and nature cannot be properly interpreted: the intelligence and will in nature may still be unconscious. But, taking in man, we are bound to get our idea of the intelligence and will in nature from the highest type of intelligence and will we know, and that is man's. "Nullus in microcosmo spiritus, nullus in macrocosmo Deus." "We receive but what we give, And in our life alone does Nature live."

The Teleological Argument therefore needs to be supplemented by the Anthropological Argument, or the argument from the mental and moral constitution of man. By itself, it does not prove a Creator. See Calderwood, Moral Philosophy, 26; Ritter, Hist. Anc. Philos., bk. 9, chap. 6; Foundations of our Faith, 38; Murphy, Scientific Bases, 215; Habit and Intelligence, 2:6, and chap. 27. On immanent finality, see Janet, Final Causes, 345-415; Diman, Theistic Argument, 201-203. Since righteousness belongs only to personality, this argument cannot prove righteousness in God. Flint, Theism, 66—"Power and Intelligence alone do not constitute God, though they be infinite. A being may have these, and, if lacking righteousness, may be a devil." Here again we see the need of the Anthropological Argument to supplement this.

B. Even if this argument could prove personality in the intelligence and will that originated the order of the universe, it could not prove either the unity, the eternity, or the infinity of God; not the unity—for the useful collocations of the universe might be the result of oneness of counsel, instead of oneness of essence, in the contriving intelligence; not the eternity—for a created demiurge might conceivably have designed the universe; not the infinity—since all marks of order and collocation within our observation are simply finite.

Diman asserts (Theistic Argument, 114) that all the phenomena of the universe must be due to the same source—since all alike are subject to the same method of sequence, e. g., gravitation—and that the evidence points us irresistibly to some one explanatory cause. We can regard this assertion only as the utterance of a primitive belief in a first cause, not as the conclusion of logical demonstration, for we know only an infinitesimal part of the universe. From the point of view of the intuition of an Absolute Reason, however, we can cordially assent to the words of F. L. Patton: "When we consider Matthew Arnold's 'stream of tendency,' Spencer's 'unknowable,' Schopenhauer's 'world as will,' and Hartmann's elaborate defence of finality as the product of unconscious intelligence, we may well ask if the theists, with their belief in one personal God, are not in possession of the only hypothesis that can save the language of these writers from the charge of meaningless and idiotic raving" (Journ. Christ. Philos., April, 1883:283-307).

The ancient world, which had only the light of nature, believed in many gods. William James, Will to Believe, 44—"If there be a divine Spirit of the universe, nature, such as we know her, cannot possibly be its ultimate word to man. Either there is no spirit revealed in nature, or else it is inadequately revealed there; and (as all the higher religions have assumed) what we call visible nature, or this world, must be but a veil and surface-show whose full meaning resides in a supplementary unseen, or other world." Bowne, Theory of Thought and Knowledge, 234—"But is not intelligence itself the mystery of mysteries?... No doubt, intellect is a great mystery.... But there is a choice in mysteries. Some mysteries leave other things clear, and some leave things as dark and impenetrable as ever. The former is the case with the mystery of intelligence. It makes possible the comprehension of everything but itself."

3. The value of the Teleological Argument is simply this,—it proves from certain useful collocations and instances of order which have clearly had a beginning, or in other words, from the present harmony of the universe, that there exists an intelligence and will adequate to its contrivance. But whether this intelligence and will is personal or impersonal, creator or only fashioner, one or many, finite or infinite, eternal or owing its being to another, necessary or free, this argument cannot assure us.

In it, however, we take a step forward. The causative power which we have proved by the Cosmological Argument has now become an intelligent and voluntary power.

John Stuart Mill, Three Essays on Theism, 168-170—"In the present state of our knowledge, the adaptations in nature afford a large balance of probability in favor of causation by intelligence." Ladd holds that, whenever one being acts upon its like, each being undergoes changes of state that belong to its own nature under the circumstances. Action of one body on another never consists in transferring the state of one being to another. Therefore there is no more difficulty in beings that are unlike acting on one another than in beings that are like. We do not transfer ideas to other minds,—we only rouse them to develop their own ideas. So force also is positively not transferable. Bowne, Philos. of Theism, 49, begins with "the conception of things interacting according to law and forming an intelligible system. Such a system cannot be construed by thought without the assumption of a unitary being which is the fundamental reality of the system. 53—No passage of influences or forces will avail to bridge the gulf, so long as the things are regarded as independent. 56—The system itself cannot explain this interaction, for the system is only the members of it. There must be some being in them which is their reality, and of which they are in some sense phases or manifestations. In other words, there must be a basal monism." All this is substantially the view of Lotze, of whose philosophy see criticism in Stählin's Kant, Lotze, and Ritschl, 116-156, and especially 123. Falckenberg, Gesch. der neueren Philosophie, 454, shows as to Lotze's view that his assumption of monistic unity and continuity does not explain how change of condition in one thing should, as equalization or compensation, follow change of condition in another thing. Lotze explains this actuality by the ethical conception of an all-embracing Person. On the whole argument, see Bib. Sac., 1849:634; Murphy, Sci. Bases, 216; Flint, Theism, 131-210; Pfleiderer, Die Religion, 1:164-174; W. R. Benedict, on Theism and Evolution, in Andover Rev., 1886:307-350, 607-622.

III. The Anthropological Argument, or Argument from Man's Mental and Moral Nature

This is an argument from the mental and moral condition of man to the existence of an Author, Lawgiver, and End. It is sometimes called the Moral Argument.

The common title "Moral Argument" is much too narrow, for it seems to take account only of conscience in man, whereas the argument which this title so imperfectly designates really proceeds from man's intellectual and emotional, as well as from his moral, nature. In choosing the designation we have adopted, we desire, moreover, to rescue from the mere physicist the term "Anthropology"—a term to which he has attached altogether too limited a signification, and which, in his use of it, implies that man is a mere animal,—to him Anthropology is simply the study of la bête humaine. Anthropology means, not simply the science of man's physical nature, origin, and relations, but also the science which treats of his higher spiritual being. Hence, in Theology, the term Anthropology designates that division of the subject which treats of man's spiritual nature and endowments, his original state and his subsequent apostasy. As an argument, therefore, from man's mental and moral nature, we can with perfect propriety call the present argument the Anthropological Argument.

The argument is a complex one, and may be divided into three parts.

1. Man's intellectual and moral nature must have had for its author an intellectual and moral Being. The elements of the proof are as follows:—(a) Man, as an intellectual and moral being, has had a beginning upon the planet. (b) Material and unconscious forces do not afford a sufficient cause for man's reason, conscience, and free will. (c) Man, as an effect, can be referred only to a cause possessing self-consciousness and a moral nature, in other words, personality.

This argument is is part an application to man of the principles of both the Cosmological and the Teleological Arguments. Flint, Theism, 74—"Although causality does not involve design, nor design goodness, yet design involves causality, and goodness both causality and design." Jacobi: "Nature conceals God; man reveals him."

Man is an effect. The history of the geologic ages proves that man has not always existed, and even if the lower creatures were his progenitors, his intellect and freedom are not eternal a parte ante. We consider man, not as a physical, but as a spiritual, being. Thompson, Christian Theism, 75—"Every true cause must be sufficient to account for the effect." Locke, Essay, book 4, chap. 10—"Cogitable existence cannot be produced out of incogitable." Martineau, Study of Religion, 1:258 sq.

Even if man had always existed, however, we should not need to abandon the argument. We might start, not from beginning of existence, but from beginning of phenomena. I might see God in the world, just as I see thought, feeling, will, in my fellow men. Fullerton, Plain Argument for God: I do not infer you, as cause of the existence of your body: I recognize you as present and working through your body. Its changes of gesture and speech reveal a personality behind them. So I do not need to argue back to a Being who once caused nature and history; I recognize a present Being, exercising wisdom and power, by signs such as reveal personality in man. Nature is itself the Watchmaker manifesting himself in the very process of making the watch. This is the meaning of the noble Epilogue to Robert Browning's Dramatis Personæ, 252—"That one Face, far from vanish, rather grows, Or decomposes but to recompose, Become my universe that feels and knows." "That Face," said Mr. Browning to Mrs. Orr, "That Face is the face of Christ; that is how I feel him." Nature is an expression of the mind and will of Christ, as my face is an expression of my mind and will. But in both cases, behind and above the face is a personality, of which the face is but the partial and temporary expression.

Bowne, Philos. Theism, 104, 107—"My fellow beings act as if they had thought, feeling, and will. So nature looks as if thought, feeling, and will were behind it. If we deny mind in nature, we must deny mind in man. If there be no controlling mind in nature, moreover, there can be none in man, for if the basal power is blind and necessary, then all that depends upon it is necessitated also." LeConte, in Royce's Conception of God, 44—"There is only one place in the world where we can get behind physical phenomena, behind the veil of matter, namely, in our own brain, and we find there a self, a person. Is it not reasonable that, if we could get behind the veil of nature, we should find the same, that is, a Person? But if so, we must conclude, an infinite Person, and therefore the only complete Personality that exists. Perfect personality is not only self-conscious, but self-existent. They are only imperfect images, and, as it were, separated fragments, of the infinite Personality of God."

Personality = self-consciousness + self-determination in view of moral ends. The brute has intelligence and will, but has neither self-consciousness, conscience, nor free-will. See Julius Müller, Doctrine of Sin, 1:76 sq. Diman, Theistic Argument, 91, 251—"Suppose 'the intuitions of the moral faculty are the slowly organized results of experience received from the race'; still, having found that the universe affords evidence of a supremely intelligent cause, we may believe that man's moral nature affords the highest illustration of its mode of working"; 358—"Shall we explain the lower forms of will by the higher, or the higher by the lower?"

2. Man's moral nature proves the existence of a holy Lawgiver and Judge. The elements of the proof are:—(a) Conscience recognizes the existence of a moral law which has supreme authority. (b) Known violations of this moral law are followed by feelings of ill-desert and fears of judgment. (c) This moral law, since it is not self-imposed, and these threats of judgment, since they are not self-executing, respectively argue the existence of a holy will that has imposed the law, and of a punitive power that will execute the threats of the moral nature.

See Bishop Butler's Sermons on Human Nature, in Works, Bohn's ed., 385-414. Butler's great discovery was that of the supremacy of conscience in the moral constitution of man: "Had it strength as it has right, had it power as it has manifest authority, it would absolutely govern the world." Conscience = the moral judiciary of the soul—not law, nor sheriff, but judge; see under Anthropology. Diman, Theistic Argument, 251—"Conscience does not lay down a law; it warns us of the existence of a law; and not only of a law, but of a purpose—not our own, but the purpose of another, which it is our mission to realize." See Murphy, Scientific Bases of Faith, 218 sq. It proves personality in the Lawgiver, because its utterances are not abstract, like those of reason, but are in the nature of command; they are not in the indicative, but in the imperative, mood; it says, "thou shalt" and "thou shalt not." This argues will.

Hutton, Essays, 1:11—"Conscience is an ideal Moses, and thunders from an invisible Sinai"; "the Atheist regards conscience not as a skylight, opened to let in upon human nature an infinite dawn from above, but as a polished arch or dome, completing and reflecting the whole edifice beneath." But conscience cannot be the mere reflection and expression of human nature, for it represses and condemns nature. Tulloch, Theism: "Conscience, like the magnetic needle, indicates the existence of an unknown Power which from afar controls its vibrations and at whose presence it trembles." Nero spends nights of terror in wandering through the halls of his Golden House. Kant holds that faith in duty requires faith in a God who will defend and reward duty—see Critique of Pure Reason, 359-387. See also Porter, Human Intellect, 524.

Kant, in his Metaphysic of Ethics, represents the action of conscience as like "conducting a case before a court," and he adds: "Now that he who is accused before his conscience should be figured to be just the same person as his judge, is an absurd representation of a tribunal; since, in such an event, the accuser would always lose his suit. Conscience must therefore represent to itself always some other than itself as Judge, unless it is to arrive at a contradiction with itself." See also his Critique of the Practical Reason, Werke, 8:214—"Duty, thou sublime and mighty name, that hast in thee nothing to attract or win, but challengest submission; and yet dost threaten nothing to sway the will by that which may arouse natural terror or aversion, but merely holdest forth a Law; a Law which of itself finds entrance into the mind, and even while we disobey, against our will compels our reverence, a Law in presence of which all inclinations grow dumb, even while they secretly rebel; what origin is there worthy of thee? Where can we find the root of thy noble descent, which proudly rejects all kinship with the inclinations?" Archbishop Temple answers, in his Bampton Lectures, 58, 59, "This eternal Law is the Eternal himself, the almighty God." Robert Browning: "The sense within me that I owe a debt Assures me—Somewhere must be Somebody, Ready to take his due. All comes to this: Where due is, there acceptance follows: find Him who accepts the due."

Salter, Ethical Religion, quoted in Pfleiderer's article on Religionless Morality, Am. Jour. Theol., 3:237—"The earth and the stars do not create the law of gravitation which they obey; no more does man, or the united hosts of rational beings in the universe, create the law of duty." The will expressed in the moral imperative is superior to ours, for otherwise it would issue no commands. Yet it is one with ours as the life of an organism is one with the life of its members. Theonomy is not heteronomy but the highest autonomy, the guarantee of our personal freedom against all servitude of man. Seneca: "Deo parere libertas est." Knight, Essays in Philosophy, 272—"In conscience we see an 'alter ego', in us yet not of us, another Personality behind our own." Martineau, Types, 2:105—"Over a person only a person can have authority.... A solitary being, with no other sentient nature in the universe, would feel no duty"; Study, 1:26—"As Perception gives us Will in the shape of Causality over against us in the Non-Ego, so Conscience gives us Will in the shape of Authority over against us in the Non-Ego.... 2:7—We cannot deduce the phenomena of character from an agent who has none." Hutton, Essays, 1:41, 42—"When we disobey conscience, the Power which has therein ceased to move us has retired only to observe—to keep watch over us as we mould ourselves." Cardinal Newman, Apologia, 377—"Were it not for the voice speaking so clearly in my conscience and my heart, I should be an atheist, or a pantheist, or a polytheist, when I looked into the world."

3. Man's emotional and voluntary nature proves the existence of a Being who can furnish in himself a satisfying object of human affection and an end which will call forth man's highest activities and ensure his highest progress.

Only a Being of power, wisdom, holiness, and goodness, and all these indefinitely greater than any that we know upon the earth, can meet this demand of the human soul. Such a Being must exist. Otherwise man's greatest need would be unsupplied, and belief in a lie be more productive of virtue than belief in the truth.

Feuerbach calls God "the Brocken-shadow of man himself"; "consciousness of God = self-consciousness"; "religion is a dream of the human soul"; "all theology is anthropology"; "man made God in his own image." But conscience shows that man does not recognize in God simply his like, but also his opposite. Not as Galton: "Piety = conscience + instability." The finest minds are of the leaning type; see Murphy, Scientific Bases, 370; Augustine, Confessions, 1:1—"Thou hast made us for thyself, and our heart is restless till it finds rest in thee." On John Stuart Mill—"a mind that could not find God, and a heart that could not do without him"—see his Autobiography, and Browne, in Strivings for the Faith (Christ. Ev. Socy.), 259-287. Comte, in his later days, constructed an object of worship in Universal Humanity, and invented a ritual which Huxley calls "Catholicism minus Christianity." See also Tyndall, Belfast Address: "Did I not believe, said a great man to me once, that an Intelligence exists at the heart of things, my life on earth would be intolerable." Martineau, Types of Ethical Theory, 1:505,506.

The last line of Schiller's Pilgrim reads: "Und das Dort ist niemals hier." The finite never satisfies. Tennyson, Two Voices: "'Tis life, whereof our nerves are scant, Oh life, not death, for which we pant; More life, and fuller, that I want." Seth, Ethical Principles, 419—"A moral universe, an absolute moral Being, is the indispensable environment of the ethical life, without which it cannot attain to its perfect growth.... There is a moral God, or this is no universe." James, Will to Believe, 116—"A God is the most adequate possible object for minds framed like our own to conceive as lying at the root of the universe. Anything short of God is not a rational object, anything more than God is not possible, if man needs an object of knowledge, feeling, and will."

Romanes, Thoughts on Religion, 41—"To speak of the Religion of the Unknowable, the Religion of Cosmism, the Religion of Humanity, where the personality of the First Cause is not recognized, is as unmeaning as it would be to speak of the love of a triangle or the rationality of the equator." It was said of Comte's system that, "the wine of the real presence being poured out, we are asked to adore the empty cup." "We want an object of devotion, and Comte presents us with a looking-glass" (Martineau). Huxley said he would as soon adore a wilderness of apes as the Positivist's rationalized conception of humanity. It is only the ideal in humanity, the divine element in humanity that can be worshiped. And when we once conceive of this, we cannot be satisfied until we find it somewhere realized, as in Jesus Christ.

Upton, Hibbert Lectures, 265-272—Huxley believes that Evolution is "a materialized logical process"; that nothing endures save the flow of energy and "the rational order which pervades it." In the earlier part of this process, nature, there is no morality or benevolence. But the process ends by producing man, who can make progress only by waging moral war against the natural forces which impel him. He must be benevolent and just. Shall we not say, in spite of Mr. Huxley, that this shows what the nature of the system is, and that there must be a benevolent and just Being who ordained it? Martineau, Seat of Authority, 63-68—"Though the authority of the higher incentive is self-known, it cannot be self-created; for while it is in me, it is above me.... This authority to which conscience introduces me, though emerging in consciousness, is yet objective to us all, and is necessarily referred to the nature of things, irrespective of the accidents of our mental constitution. It is not dependent on us, but independent. All minds born into the universe are ushered into the presence of a real righteousness, as surely as into a scene of actual space. Perception reveals another than ourselves; conscience reveals a higher than ourselves."

We must freely grant, however, that this argument from man's aspirations has weight only upon the supposition that a wise, truthful, holy, and benevolent God exists, who has so constituted our minds that their thinking and their affections correspond to truth and to himself. An evil being might have so constituted us that all logic would lead us into error. The argument is therefore the development and expression of our intuitive idea of God. Luthardt, Fundamental Truths: "Nature is like a written document containing only consonants. It is we who must furnish the vowels that shall decipher it. Unless we bring with us the idea of God, we shall find nature but dumb." See also Pfleiderer, Die Religion, 1:174.

A. The defects of the Anthropological Argument are: (a) It cannot prove a creator of the material universe. (b) It cannot prove the infinity of God, since man from whom we argue is finite. (c) It cannot prove the mercy of God. But,

B. The value of the Argument is, that it assures us of the existence of a personal Being, who rules us in righteousness, and who is the proper object of supreme affection and service. But whether this Being is the original creator of all things, or merely the author of our own existence, whether he is infinite or finite, whether he is a Being of simple righteousness or also of mercy, this argument cannot assure us.

Among the arguments for the existence of God, however, we assign to this the chief place, since it adds to the ideas of causative power (which we derived from the Cosmological Argument) and of contriving intelligence (which we derived from the Teleological Argument), the far wider ideas of personality and righteous lordship.

Sir Wm. Hamilton, Works of Reid, 2:974, note U; Lect. on Metaph., 1:33—"The only valid arguments for the existence of God and for the immortality of the soul rest upon the ground of man's moral nature"; "theology is wholly dependent upon psychology, for with the proof of the moral nature of man stands or falls the proof of the existence of a Deity." But Diman, Theistic Argument, 244, very properly objects to making this argument from the nature of man the sole proof of Deity: "It should be rather used to show the attributes of the Being whose existence has been already proved from other sources"; "hence the Anthropological Argument is as dependent upon the Cosmological and Teleological Arguments as they are upon it."

Yet the Anthropological Argument is needed to supplement the conclusions of the two others. Those who, like Herbert Spencer, recognize an infinite and absolute Being, Power and Cause, may yet fail to recognize this being as spiritual and personal, simply because they do not recognize themselves as spiritual and personal beings, that is, do not recognize reason, conscience and free-will in man. Agnosticism in philosophy involves agnosticism in religion. R. K. Eccles: "All the most advanced languages capitalize the word 'God,' and the word 'I.' " See Flint, Theism, 68; Mill, Criticism of Hamilton, 2:266; Dove, Logic of Christian Faith, 211-236, 261-299; Martineau, Types, Introd., 3; Cooke, Religion and Chemistry: "God is love; but nature could not prove it, and the Lamb was slain from the foundation of the world in order to attest it."

Everything in philosophy depends on where we begin, whether with nature or with self, whether with the necessary or with the free. In one sense, therefore, we should in practice begin with the Anthropological Argument, and then use the Cosmological and Teleological Arguments as warranting the application to nature of the conclusions which we have drawn from man. As God stands over against man in Conscience, and says to him: "Thou"; so man stands over against God in Nature, and may say to him: "Thou." Mulford, Republic of God, 28—"As the personality of man has its foundation in the personality of God, so the realization by man of his own personality always brings man nearer to God."

Robert Browning: "Quoth a young Sadducee: 'Reader of many rolls, Is it so certain we Have, as they tell us, souls?' 'Son, there is no reply!' The Rabbi bit his beard: 'Certain, a soul have I—We may have none,' he sneered. Thus Karshook, the Hiram's Hammer, The Right-hand Temple-column, Taught babes in grace their grammar, And struck the simple, solemn."

It is very common at this place to treat of what are called the Historical and the Biblical Arguments for the existence of God—the former arguing, from the unity of history, the latter arguing, from the unity of the Bible, that this unity must in each case have for its cause and explanation the existence of God. It is a sufficient reason for not discussing these arguments, that, without a previous belief in the existence of God, no one will see unity either in history or in the Bible. Turner, the painter, exhibited a picture which seemed all mist and cloud until he put a dab of scarlet into it. That gave the true point of view, and all the rest became intelligible. So Christ's coming and Christ's blood make intelligible both the Scriptures and human history. He carries in his girdle the key to all mysteries. Schopenhauer, knowing no Christ, admitted no philosophy of history. He regarded history as the mere fortuitous play of individual caprice. Pascal: "Jesus Christ is the centre of everything, and the object of everything, and he that does not know him knows nothing of nature, and nothing of himself."

IV. The Ontological Argument, or Argument from our Abstract and Necessary Ideas

This argument infers the existence of God from the abstract and necessary ideas of the human mind. It has three forms:

1. That of Samuel Clarke. Space and time are attributes of substance or being. But space and time are respectively infinite and eternal. There must therefore be an infinite and eternal substance or Being to whom these attributes belong.

Gillespie states the argument somewhat differently. Space and time are modes of existence. But space and time are respectively infinite and eternal. There must therefore be an infinite and eternal Being who subsists in these modes. But we reply:

Space and time are neither attributes of substance nor modes of existence. The argument, if valid, would prove that God is not mind but matter, for that could not be mind, but only matter, of which space and time were either attributes or modes.

The Ontological Argument is frequently called the a priori argument, that is, the argument from that which is logically prior, or earlier than experience, viz., our intuitive ideas. All the forms of the Ontological Argument are in this sense a priori. Space and time are a priori ideas. See Samuel Clarke, Works, 2:521; Gillespie, Necessary Existence of God. Per contra, see Kant, Critique of Pure Reason, 364: Calderwood, Moral Philosophy, 226—"To begin, as Clarke did, with the proposition that 'something has existed from eternity,' is virtually to propose an argument after having assumed what is to be proved. Gillespie's form of the a priori argument, starting with the proposition 'infinity of extension is necessarily existing,' is liable to the same objection, with the additional disadvantage of attributing a property of matter to the Deity."

H. B. Smith says that Brougham misrepresented Clarke: "Clarke's argument is in his sixth proposition, and supposes the existence proved in what goes before. He aims here to establish the infinitude and omnipresence of this First Being. He does not prove existence from immensity." But we reply, neither can he prove the infinity of God from the immensity of space. Space and time are neither substances nor attributes, but are rather relations; see Calderwood, Philos. of Infinite, 331-335; Cocker, Theistic Conception of the World, 66-96. The doctrine that space and time are attributes or modes of God's existence tends to materialistic pantheism like that of Spinoza, who held that "the one and simple substance" (substantia una et unica) is known to us through the two attributes of thought and extension; mind = God in the mode of thought; matter = God in the mode of extension. Dove, Logic of the Christian Faith, 127, says well that an extended God is a material God; "space and time are attributes neither of matter nor mind"; "we must carry the moral idea into the natural world, not the natural idea into the moral world." See also, Blunt, Dictionary Doct. and Hist. Theol., 740; Porter, Human Intellect, 567. H. M. Stanley, on Space and Science, in Philos. Rev., Nov. 1898:615—"Space is not full of things, but things are spaceful.... Space is a form of dynamic appearance." Prof. C. A. Strong: "The world composed of consciousness and other existences is not in space, though it may be in something of which space is the symbol."

2. That of Descartes. We have the idea of an infinite and perfect Being. This idea cannot be derived from imperfect and finite things. There must therefore be an infinite and perfect Being who is its cause.

But we reply that this argument confounds the idea of the infinite with an infinite idea. Man's idea of the infinite is not infinite but finite, and from a finite effect we cannot argue an infinite cause.

This form of the Ontological Argument, while it is a priori, as based upon a necessary idea of the human mind, is, unlike the other forms of the same argument, a posteriori, as arguing from this idea, as an effect, to the existence of a Being who is its cause. A posteriori argument = from that which is later to that which is earlier, that is, from effect to cause. The Cosmological, Teleological, and

Anthropological Arguments are arguments a posteriori. Of this sort is the argument of Descartes; see Descartes, Meditation 3: "Hæc idea quæ in nobis est requirit Deum pro causa; Deusque proinde existit." The idea in men's minds is the impression of the workman's name stamped indelibly on his work—the shadow cast upon the human soul by that unseen One of whose being and presence it dimly informs us. Blunt, Dict. of Theol., 739; Saisset, Pantheism, 1:54—"Descartes sets out from a fact of consciousness, while Anselm sets out from an abstract conception"; "Descartes's argument might be considered a branch of the Anthropological or Moral Argument, but for the fact that this last proceeds from man's constitution rather than from his abstract ideas." See Bib. Sac., 1849:637.

3. That of Anselm. We have the idea of an absolutely perfect Being. But existence is an attribute of perfection. An absolutely perfect Being must therefore exist.

But we reply that this argument confounds ideal existence with real existence. Our ideas are not the measure of external reality.

Anselm, Proslogion, 2—"Id, quo majus cogitari nequit, non potest esse in intellectu solo." See translation of the Proslogion, in Bib. Sac., 1851:529, 699; Kant, Critique, 368. The arguments of Descartes and Anselm, with Kant's reply, are given in their original form by Harris, in Journ. Spec. Philos., 15:420-428. The major premise here is not that all perfect ideas imply the existence of the object which they represent, for then, as Kant objects, I might argue from my perfect idea of a $100 bill that I actually possessed the same, which would be far from the fact. So I have a perfect idea of a perfectly evil being, of a centaur, of nothing,—but it does not follow that the evil being, that the centaur, that nothing, exists. The argument is rather from the idea of absolute and perfect Being—of "that, no greater than which can be conceived." There can be but one such being, and there can be but one such idea.

Yet, even thus understood, we cannot argue from the idea to the actual existence of such a being. Case, Physical Realism, 173—"God is not an idea, and consequently cannot be inferred from mere ideas." Bowne, Philos. Theism, 43—The Ontological Argument "only points out that the idea of the perfect must include the idea of existence; but there is nothing to show that the self-consistent idea represents an objective reality." I can imagine the Sea-serpent, the Jinn of the Thousand and One Nights, "The Anthropophagi, and men whose heads Do grow beneath their shoulders." The winged horse of Uhland possessed every possible virtue, and only one fault,—it was dead. If every perfect idea implied the reality of its object, there might be horses with ten legs, and trees with roots in the air.

"Anselm's argument implies," says Fisher, in Journ. Christ. Philos., Jan. 1883:114, "that existence in re is a constituent of the concept. It would conclude the existence of a being from the definition of a word. This inference is justified only on the basis of philosophical realism." Dove, Logic of the Christ. Faith, 141—"The Ontological Argument is the algebraic formula of the universe, which leads to a valid conclusion with regard to real existence, only when we fill it in with objects with which we become acquainted in the arguments a posteriori." See also Shedd, Hist. Doct., 1:331, Dogm. Theol., 1:221-241, and in Presb. Rev., April, 1884:212-227 (favoring the argument); Fisher, Essays, 574; Thompson, Christian Theism, 171; H. B. Smith, Introd. to Christ. Theol., 122; Pfleiderer, Die Religion, 1:181-187; Studien und Kritiken, 1875:611-655.

Dorner, in his Glaubenslehre, 1:197, gives us the best statement of the Ontological Argument: "Reason thinks of God as existing. Reason would not be reason, if it did not think of God as existing. Reason only is, upon the assumption that God is." But this is evidently not argument, but only vivid statement of the necessary assumption of the existence of an absolute Reason which conditions and gives validity to ours.

Although this last must be considered the most perfect form of the Ontological Argument, it is evident that it conducts us only to an ideal conclusion, not to real existence. In common with the two preceding forms of the argument, moreover, it tacitly assumes, as already existing in the human mind, that very knowledge of God's existence which it would derive from logical demonstration. It has value, therefore, simply as showing what God must be, if he exists at all.

But the existence of a Being indefinitely great, a personal Cause, Contriver and Lawgiver, has been proved by the preceding arguments; for the law of parsimony requires us to apply the conclusions of the first three arguments to one Being, and not to many. To this one Being we may now ascribe the infinity and perfection, the idea of which lies at the basis of the Ontological Argument—ascribe them, not because they are demonstrably his, but because our mental constitution will not allow us to think otherwise. Thus clothing him with all perfections which the human mind can conceive, and these in illimitable fullness, we have one whom we may justly call God.

McCosh, Div. Govt., 12, note—"It is at this place, if we do not mistake, that the idea of the Infinite comes in. The capacity of the human mind to form such an idea, or rather its intuitive belief in an Infinite of which it feels that it cannot form an adequate conception, may be no proof (as Kant maintains) of the existence of an infinite Being; but it is, we are convinced, the means by which the mind is enabled to invest the Deity, shown on other grounds to exist, with the attributes of infinity, i. e., to look on his being, power, goodness, and all his perfections, as infinite." Even Flint, Theism, 68, who holds that we reach the existence of God by inference, speaks of "necessary conditions of thought and feeling, and ineradicable aspirations, which force on us ideas of absolute existence, infinity, and perfection, and will neither permit us to deny these perfections to God, nor to ascribe them to any other being." Belief in God is not the conclusion of a demonstration, but the solution of a problem. Calderwood, Moral Philosophy, 226—"Either the whole question is assumed in starting, or the Infinite is not reached in concluding."

Clarke, Christian Theology, 97-114, divides his proof into two parts: I. Evidence of the existence of God from the intellectual starting-point: The discovery of Mind in the universe is made, 1. through the intelligibleness of the universe to us; 2. through the idea of cause; 3. through the presence of ends in the universe. II. Evidence of the existence of God from the religious starting-point: The discovery of the good God is made, 1. through the religious nature of man; 2. through the great dilemma—God the best, or the worst; 3. through the spiritual experience of men, especially in Christianity. So far as Dr. Clarke's proof is intended to be a statement, not of a primitive belief, but of a logical process, we must hold it to be equally defective with the three forms of proof which we have seen to furnish some corroborative evidence of God's existence. Dr. Clarke therefore does well to add: "Religion was not produced by proof of God's existence, and will not be destroyed by its insufficiency to some minds. Religion existed before argument; in fact, it is the preciousness of religion that leads to the seeking for all possible confirmations of the reality of God."

The three forms of proof already mentioned—the Cosmological, the Teleological, and the Anthropological Arguments—may be likened to the three arches of a bridge over a wide and rushing river. The bridge has only two defects, but these defects are very serious. The first is that one cannot get on to the bridge; the end toward the hither bank is wholly lacking; the bridge of logical argument cannot be entered upon except by assuming the validity of logical processes; this assumption takes for granted at the outset the existence of a God who has made our faculties to act correctly; we get on to the bridge, not by logical process, but only by a leap of intuition, and by assuming at the beginning the very thing which we set out to prove. The second defect of the so-called bridge of argument is that when one has once gotten on, he can never get off. The connection with the further bank is also lacking. All the premises from which we argue being finite, we are warranted in drawing only a finite conclusion. Argument cannot reach the Infinite, and only an infinite Being is worthy to be called God. We can get off from our logical bridge, not by logical process, but only by another and final leap of intuition, and by once more assuming the existence of the infinite Being whom we had so vainly sought to reach by mere argument. The process seems to be referred to in Job 11:7—"Canst thou by searching find out God? Canst thou find out the Almighty unto perfection?"

As a logical process this is indeed defective, since all logic as well as all observation depends for its validity upon the presupposed existence of God, and since this particular process, even granting the validity of logic in general, does not warrant the conclusion that God exists, except upon a second assumption that our abstract ideas of infinity and perfection are to be applied to the Being to whom argument has actually conducted us.

But although both ends of the logical bridge are confessedly wanting, the process may serve and does serve a more useful purpose than that of mere demonstration, namely, that of awakening, explicating, and confirming a conviction which, though the most fundamental of all, may yet have been partially slumbering for lack of thought.

Morell, Philos. Fragments, 177, 179—"We can, in fact, no more prove the existence of a God by a logical argument, than we can prove the existence of an external world; but none the less may we obtain as strong a practical conviction of the one, as of the other." "We arrive at a scientific belief in the existence of God just as we do at any other possible human truth. We assume it, as a hypothesis absolutely necessary to account for the phenomena of the universe; and then evidences from every quarter begin to converge upon it, until, in process of time, the common sense of mankind, cultivated and enlightened by ever accumulating knowledge, pronounces upon the validity of the hypothesis with a voice scarcely less decided and universal than it does in the case of our highest scientific convictions."

Fisher, Supernat. Origin of Christianity, 572—"What then is the purport and force of the several arguments for the existence of God? We reply that these proofs are the different modes in which faith expresses itself and seeks confirmation. In them faith, or the object of faith, is more exactly conceived and defined, and in them is found a corroboration, not arbitrary but substantial and valuable, of that faith which springs from the soul itself. Such proofs, therefore, are neither on the one hand sufficient to create and sustain faith, nor are they on the other hand to be set aside as of no value." A. J. Barrett: "The arguments are not so much a bridge in themselves, as they are guys, to hold firm the great suspension-bridge of intuition, by which we pass the gulf from man to God. Or, while they are not a ladder by which we may reach heaven, they are the Ossa on Pelion, from whose combined height we may descry heaven."

Anselm: "Negligentia mihi videtur, si postquam confirmati sumus in fide non studemus quod credimus intelligere." Bradley, Appearance and Reality: "Metaphysics is the finding of bad reasons for what we believe upon instinct; but to find these reasons is no less an instinct." Illingworth, Div. and Hum. Personality, lect. III—"Belief in a personal God is an instinctive judgment, progressively justified by reason." Knight, Essays in Philosophy, 241—The arguments are "historical memorials of the efforts of the human race to vindicate to itself the existence of a reality of which it is conscious, but which it cannot perfectly define." H. Fielding, The Hearts of Men, 313—"Creeds are the grammar of religion. They are to religion what grammar is to speech. Words are the expression of our wants; grammar is the theory formed afterwards. Speech never proceeded from grammar, but the reverse. As speech progresses and changes from unknown causes, grammar must follow." Pascal: "The heart has reasons of its own which the reason does not know." Frances Power Cobbe: "Intuitions are God's tuitions." On the whole subject, see Cudworth, Intel. System, 3:42; Calderwood, Philos. of Infinite, 150 sq.; Curtis, Human Element in Inspiration, 242; Peabody, in Andover Rev., July, 1884; Hahn, History of Arguments for Existence of God; Lotze, Philos. of Religion, 8-34; Am. Jour. Theol., Jan. 1906:53-71.

Hegel, in his Logic, page 3, speaking of the disposition to regard the proofs of God's existence as the only means of producing faith in God, says: "Such a doctrine would find its parallel, if we said that eating was impossible before we had acquired a knowledge of the chemical, botanical and zoölogical qualities of our food; and that we must delay digestion till we had finished the study of anatomy and physiology." It is a mistake to suppose that there can be no religious life without a correct theory of life. Must I refuse to drink water or to breathe air, until I can manufacture both for myself? Some things are given to us. Among these things are "grace and truth" (John 1:17; cf. 9). But there are ever those who are willing to take nothing as a free gift, and who insist on working out all knowledge, as well as all salvation, by processes of their own. Pelagianism, with its denial of the doctrines of grace, is but the further development of a rationalism which refuses to accept primitive truths unless these can be logically demonstrated. Since the existence of the soul, of the world, and of God cannot be proved in this way, rationalism is led to curtail, or to misinterpret, the deliverances of consciousness, and hence result certain systems now to be mentioned.

Chapter III - Erroneous Explanations, And Conclusion

Any correct explanation of the universe must postulate an intuitive knowledge of the existence of the external world, of self, and of God. The desire for scientific unity, however, has occasioned attempts to reduce these three factors to one, and according as one or another of the three has been regarded as the all-inclusive principle, the result has been Materialism, Materialistic Idealism, or Idealistic Pantheism. This scientific impulse is better satisfied by a system which we may designate as Ethical Monism.

We may summarize the present chapter as follows: 1. Materialism: Universe = Atoms. Reply: Atoms can do nothing without force, and can be nothing (intelligible) without ideas. 2. Materialistic Idealism: Universe = Force + Ideas. Reply: Ideas belong to Mind, and Force can be exerted only by Will. 3. Idealistic Pantheism: Universe = Immanent and Impersonal Mind and Will. Reply: Spirit in man shows that the Infinite Spirit must be Transcendent and Personal Mind and Will. We are led from these three forms of error to a conclusion which we may denominate 4. Ethical Monism: Universe = Finite, partial, graded manifestation of the divine Life; Matter being God's self-limitation under the law of necessity, Humanity being God's self-limitation under the law of freedom, Incarnation and Atonement being God's self-limitations under the law of grace. Metaphysical Monism, or the doctrine of one Substance, Principle, or Ground of Being, is consistent with Psychological Dualism, or the doctrine that the soul is personally distinct from matter on the one hand and from God on the other.

I. Materialism

Materialism is that method of thought which gives priority to matter, rather than to mind, in its explanations of the universe. Upon this view, material atoms constitute the ultimate and fundamental reality of which all things, rational and irrational, are but combinations and phenomena. Force is regarded as a universal and inseparable property of matter.

The element of truth in materialism is the reality of the external world. Its error is in regarding the external world as having original and independent existence, and in regarding mind as its product.

Materialism regards atoms as the bricks of which the material universe, the house we inhabit, is built. Sir William Thomson (Lord Kelvin) estimates that, if a drop of water were magnified to the size of our earth, the atoms of which it consists would certainly appear larger than boy's marbles, and yet would be smaller than billiard balls. Of these atoms, all things, visible and invisible, are made. Mind, with all its activities, is a combination or phenomenon of atoms. "Man ist was er iszt: ohne Phosphor kein Gedanke"—"One is what he eats: without phosphorus, no thought." Ethics is a bill of fare; and worship, like heat, is a mode of motion. Agassiz, however, wittily asked: "Are fishermen, then, more intelligent than farmers, because they eat so much fish, and therefore take in more phosphorus?"

It is evident that much is here attributed to atoms which really belongs to force. Deprive atoms of force, and all that remains is extension, which = space = zero. Moreover, "if atoms are extended, they cannot be ultimate, for extension implies divisibility, and that which is conceivably divisible cannot be a philosophical ultimate. But, if atoms are not extended, then even an infinite multiplication and combination of them could not produce an extended substance. Furthermore, an atom that is neither extended substance nor thinking substance is inconceivable. The real ultimate is force, and this force cannot be exerted by nothing, but, as we shall hereafter see, can be exerted only by a personal Spirit, for this alone possesses the characteristics of reality, namely, definiteness, unity, and activity."

Not only force but also intelligence must be attributed to atoms, before they can explain any operation of nature. Herschel says not only that "the force of gravitation seems like that of a universal will," but that the atoms themselves, in recognizing each other in order to combine, show a great deal of "presence of mind." Ladd, Introd. to Philosophy, 269—"A distinguished astronomer has said that every body in the solar system is behaving as if it knew precisely how it ought to behave in consistency with its own nature, and with the behavior of every other body in the same system.... Each atom has danced countless millions of miles, with countless millions of different partners, many of which required an important modification of its mode of motion, without ever departing from the correct step or the right time." J. P. Cooke, Credentials of Science, 104, 177, suggests that something more than atoms is needed to explain the universe. A correlating Intelligence and Will must be assumed. Atoms by themselves would be like a heap of loose nails which need to be magnetized if they are to hold together. All structures would be resolved, and all forms of matter would disappear, if the Presence which sustains them were withdrawn. The atom, like the monad of Leibnitz, is "parvus in suo genere deus"—"a little god in its nature"—only because it is the expression of the mind and will of an immanent God.

Plato speaks of men who are "dazzled by too near a look at material things." They do not perceive that these very material things, since they can be interpreted only in terms of spirit, must themselves be essentially spiritual. Materialism is the explanation of a world of which we know something—the world of mind—by a world of which we know next to nothing—the world of matter. Upton, Hibbert Lectures, 297, 298—"How about your material atoms and brain-molecules? They have no real existence save as objects of thought, and therefore the very thought, which you say your atoms produce, turns out to be the essential precondition of their own existence." With this agree the words of Dr. Ladd: "Knowledge of matter involves repeated activities of sensation and reflection, of inductive and deductive inference, of intuitional belief in substance. These are all activities of mind. Only as the mind has a self-conscious life, is any knowledge of what matter is, or can do, to be gained.... Everything is real which is the permanent subject of changing states. That which touches, feels, sees, is more real than that which is touched, felt, seen."

H. N. Gardner, Presb. Rev., 1885:301, 665, 666—"Mind gives to matter its chief meaning,— hence matter alone can never explain the universe." Gore, Incarnation, 31—"Mind is not the product of nature, but the necessary constituent of nature, considered as an ordered knowable system." Fraser, Philos. of Theism: "An immoral act must originate in the immoral agent; a physical effect is not known to originate in its physical cause." Matter, inorganic and organic, presupposes mind; but it is not true that mind presupposes matter. LeConte: "If I could remove your brain cap, what would I see? Only physical changes. But you—what do you perceive? Consciousness, thought, emotion, will. Now take external nature, the Cosmos. The observer from the outside sees only physical phenomena. But must there not be in this case also—on the other side—psychical phenomena, a Self, a Person, a Will?"

The impossibility of finding in matter, regarded as mere atoms, any of the attributes of a cause, has led to a general abandonment of this old Materialism of Democritus, Epicurus, Lucretius, Condillac, Holbach, Feuerbach, Büchner; and Materialistic Idealism has taken its place, which instead of regarding force as a property of matter, regards matter as a manifestation of force. From this section we therefore pass to Materialistic Idealism, and inquire whether the universe can be interpreted simply as a system of force and of ideas. A quarter of a century ago, John Tyndall, in his opening address as President of the British Association at Belfast, declared that in matter was to be found the promise and potency of every form of life. But in 1898, Sir William Crookes, in his address as President of that same British Association, reversed the apothegm, and declared that in life he saw the promise and potency of every form of matter. See Lange, History of Materialism; Janet, Materialism; Fabri, Materialismus; Herzog, Encyclopädie, art.: Materialismus; but esp., Stallo, Modern Physics, 148-170.

In addition to the general error indicated above, we object to this system as follows:

1. In knowing matter, the mind necessarily judges itself to be different in kind, and higher in rank, than the matter which it knows.

We here state simply an intuitive conviction. The mind, in using its physical organism and through it bringing external nature into its service, recognizes itself as different from and superior to matter. See Martineau, quoted in Brit. Quar., April, 1882:173, and the article of President Thomas Hill in the Bibliotheca Sacra, April, 1852:353—"All that is really given by the act of sense-perception is the existence of the conscious self, floating in boundless space and boundless time, surrounded and sustained by boundless power. The material moved, which we at first think the great reality, is only the shadow of a real being, which is immaterial." Harris, Philos. Basis of Theism, 317—"Imagine an infinitesimal being in the brain, watching the action of the molecules, but missing the thought. So science observes the universe, but misses God." Hebberd, in Journ. Spec. Philos., April, 1886:135.

Robert Browning, "the subtlest assertor of the soul in song," makes the Pope, in The Ring and the Book, say: "Mind is not matter, nor from matter, but above." So President Francis Wayland: "What is mind?" "No matter." "What is matter?" "Never mind." Sully, The Human Mind, 2:369— "Consciousness is a reality wholly disparate from material processes, and cannot therefore be resolved into these. Materialism makes that which is immediately known (our mental states) subordinate to that which is only indirectly or inferentially known (external things). Moreover, a material entity existing per se out of relation to a cogitant mind is an absurdity." As materialists work out their theory, their so-called matter grows more and more ethereal, until at last a stage is reached when it cannot be distinguished from what others call spirit. Martineau: "The matter they describe is so exceedingly clever that it is up to anything, even to writing Hamlet and discovering its own evolution. In short, but for the spelling of its name, it does not seem to differ appreciably from our old friends, Mind and God." A. W. Momerie, in Christianity and Evolution, 54—"A being conscious of his unity cannot possibly be formed out of a number of atoms unconscious of their diversity. Any one who thinks this possible is capable of asserting that half a dozen fools might be compounded into a single wise man."

2. Since the mind's attributes of (a) continuous identity, (b) self-activity, (c) unrelatedness to space, are different in kind and higher in rank than the attributes of matter, it is rational to conclude that mind is itself different in kind from matter and higher in rank than matter.

This is an argument from specific qualities to that which underlies and explains the qualities. (a) Memory proves personal identity. This is not an identity of material atoms, for atoms change. The molecules that come cannot remember those that depart. Some immutable part in the brain? organized or unorganized? Organized decays; unorganized = soul. (b) Inertia shows that matter is not self-moving. It acts only as it is acted upon. A single atom would never move. Two portions are necessary, and these, in order to useful action, require adjustment by a power which does not belong to matter. Evolution of the universe inexplicable, unless matter were first moved by some power outside itself. See Duke of Argyll, Reign of Law, 92. (c) The highest activities of mind are independent of known physical conditions. Mind controls and subdues the body. It does not cease to grow when the growth of the body ceases. When the body nears dissolution, the mind often asserts itself most strikingly.

Kant: "Unity of apprehension is possible on account of the transcendental unity of self-consciousness." I get my idea of unity from the indivisible self. Stout, Manual of Psychology, 53—"So far as matter exists independently of its presentation to a cognitive subject, it cannot have material properties, such as extension, hardness, color, weight, etc.... The world of material phenomena presupposes a system of immaterial agency. In this immaterial system the individual consciousness originates. This agency, some say, is thought, others will." A. J. Dubois, in Century Magazine, Dec. 1894:228—Since each thought involves a molecular movement in the brain, and this moves the whole universe, mind is the secret of the universe, and we should interpret nature as the expression of underlying purpose. Science is mind following the traces of mind. There can be no mind without antecedent mind. That all human beings have the same mental modes shows that these modes are not due simply to environment. Bowne: "Things act upon the mind and the mind reacts with knowledge. Knowing is not a passive receiving, but an active construing." Wundt: "We are compelled to admit that the physical development is not the cause, but much more the effect, of psychical development."

Paul Carus, Soul of Man, 52-64, defines soul as "the form of an organism," and memory as "the psychical aspect of the preservation of form in living substance." This seems to give priority to the organism rather than to the soul, regardless of the fact that without soul no organism is conceivable. Clay cannot be the ancestor of the potter, nor stone the ancestor of the mason, nor wood the ancestor of the carpenter. W. N. Clarke, Christian Theology, 99—"The intelligibleness of the universe to us is strong and ever present evidence that there is an all-pervading rational Mind, from which the universe received its character." We must add to the maxim, "Cogito, ergo sum," the other maxim, "Intelligo, ergo Deus est." Pfleiderer, Philos. Relig., 1:273—"The whole idealistic philosophy of modern times is in fact only the carrying out and grounding of the conviction that Nature is ordered by Spirit and for Spirit, as a subservient means for its eternal ends; that it is therefore not, as the heathen naturalism thought, the one and all, the last and highest of things, but has the Spirit, and the moral Ends over it, as its Lord and Master." The consciousness by which things are known precedes the things themselves, in the order of logic, and therefore cannot be explained by them or derived from them. See Porter, Human Intellect, 22, 131, 132. McCosh, Christianity and Positivism, chap. on Materialism; Divine Government, 71-94; Intuitions, 140-145. Hopkins, Study of Man, 53-56; Morell, Hist. of Philosophy, 318-334; Hickok, Rational Cosmology, 403; Theol. Eclectic, 6:555; Appleton, Works, 1:151-154; Calderwood, Moral Philos., 235; Ulrici, Leib und Seele, 688-725, and synopsis, in Bap. Quar., July, 1873:380.

3. Mind rather than matter must therefore be regarded as the original and independent entity, unless it can be scientifically demonstrated that mind is material in its origin and nature. But all attempts to explain the psychical from the physical, or the organic from the inorganic, are acknowledged failures. The most that can be claimed is, that psychical are always accompanied by physical changes, and that the inorganic is the basis and support of the organic. Although the precise connection between the mind and the body is unknown, the fact that the continuity of physical changes is unbroken in times of psychical activity renders it certain that mind is not transformed physical force. If the facts of sensation indicate the dependence of mind upon body, the facts of volition equally indicate the dependence of body upon mind.

The chemist can produce organic, but not organized, substances. The life cannot be produced from matter. Even in living things progress is secured only by plan. Multiplication of desired advantage, in the Darwinian scheme, requires a selecting thought; in other words the natural selection is artificial selection after all. John Fiske, Destiny of the Creature, 109—"Cerebral physiology tells us that, during the present life, although thought and feeling are always manifested in connection with a peculiar form of matter, yet by no possibility can thought and feeling be in any sense the product of matter. Nothing could be more grossly unscientific than the famous remark of Cabanis, that the brain secretes thought as the liver secretes bile. It is not even correct to say that thought goes on in the brain. What goes on in the brain is an amazingly complex series of molecular movements, with which thought and feeling are in some unknown way correlated, not as effects or as causes, but as concomitants."

Leibnitz's "preëstablished harmony" indicates the difficulty of defining the relation between mind and matter. They are like two entirely disconnected clocks, the one of which has a dial and indicates the hour by its hands, while the other without a dial simultaneously indicates the same hour by its striking apparatus. To Leibnitz the world is an aggregate of atomic souls leading absolutely separate lives. There is no real action of one upon another. Everything in the monad is the development of its individual unstimulated activity. Yet there is a preëstablished harmony of them all, arranged from the beginning by the Creator. The internal development of each monad is so adjusted to that of all the other monads, as to produce the false impression that they are mutually influenced by each other (see Johnson, in Andover Rev., Apl. 1890:407, 408). Leibnitz's theory involves the complete rejection of the freedom of the human will in the libertarian sense. To escape from this arbitrary connection of mind and matter in Leibnitz's preëstablished harmony, Spinoza rejected the Cartesian doctrine of two God-created substances, and maintained that there is but one fundamental substance, namely, God himself (see Upton, Hibbert Lectures, 172).

There is an increased flow of blood to the head in times of mental activity. Sometimes, in intense heat of literary composition, the blood fairly surges through the brain. No diminution, but further increase, of physical activity accompanies the greatest efforts of mind. Lay a man upon a balance; fire a pistol shot or inject suddenly a great thought into his mind; at once he will tip the balance, and tumble upon his head. Romanes, Mind and Motion, 21—"Consciousness causes physical changes, but not vice versa. To say that mind is a function of motion is to say that mind is a function of itself, since motion exists only for mind. Better suppose the physical and the psychical to be only one, as in the violin sound and vibration are one. Volition is a cause in nature because it has cerebration for its obverse and inseparable side. But if there is no motion without mind, then there can be no universe without God."... 34—"Because within the limits of human experience mind is only known as associated with brain, it does not follow that mind cannot exist without brain. Helmholtz's explanation of the effect of one of Beethoven's sonatas on the brain may be perfectly correct, but the explanation of the effect given by a musician may be equally correct within its category."

Herbert Spencer, Principles of Psychology, 1:§ 56—"Two things, mind and nervous action, exist together, but we cannot imagine how they are related" (see review of Spencer's Psychology, in N. Englander, July, 1873). Tyndall, Fragments of Science, 120—"The passage from the physics of the brain to the facts of consciousness is unthinkable." Schurman, Agnosticism and Religion, 95—"The metamorphosis of vibrations into conscious ideas is a miracle, in comparison with which the floating of iron or the turning of water into wine is easily credible." Bain, Mind and Body, 131—There is no break in the physical continuity. See Brit. Quar., Jan. 1874; art. by Herbert, on Mind and the Science of Energy; McCosh, Intuitions, 145; Talbot, in Bap. Quar., Jan. 1871. On Geulincx's "occasional causes" and Descartes's dualism, see Martineau, Types, 144, 145, 156-158, and Study, 2:77.

4. The materialistic theory, denying as it does the priority of spirit, can furnish no sufficient cause for the highest features of the existing universe, namely, its personal intelligences, its intuitive ideas, its free-will, its moral progress, its beliefs in God and immortality.

Herbert, Modern Realism Examined: "Materialism has no physical evidence of the existence of consciousness in others. As it declares our fellow men to be destitute of free volition, so it should declare them destitute of consciousness; should call them, as well as brutes, pure automata. If physics are all, there is no God, but there is also no man, existing." Some of the early followers of Descartes used to kick and beat their dogs, laughing meanwhile at their cries and calling them the "creaking of the machine." Huxley, who calls the brutes "conscious automata," believes in the gradual banishment, from all regions of human thought, of what we call spirit and spontaneity: "A spontaneous act is an absurdity; it is simply an effect that is uncaused."

James, Psychology, 1:149—"The girl in Midshipman Easy could not excuse the illegitimacy of her child by saying that 'it was a very small one.' And consciousness, however small, is an illegitimate birth in any philosophy that starts without it, and yet professes to explain all facts by continued evolution.... Materialism denies reality to almost all the impulses which we most cherish. Hence it will fail of universal adoption." Clerk Maxwell, Life, 391—"The atoms are a very tough lot, and can stand a great deal of knocking about, and it is strange to find a number of them combining to form a man of feeling.... 426—I have looked into most philosophical systems, and I have seen none that will work without a God." President E. B. Andrews: "Mind is the only substantive thing in this universe, and all else is adjective. Matter is not primordial, but is a function of spirit." Theodore Parker: "Man is the highest product of his own history. The discoverer finds nothing so tall or grand as himself, nothing so valuable to him. The greatest star is at the small end of the telescope—the star that is looking, not looked after, nor looked at."

Materialism makes men to be "a serio-comic procession of wax figures or of cunning casts in clay" (Bowne). Man is "the cunningest of clocks." But if there were nothing but matter, there could be no materialism, for a system of thought, like materialism, implies consciousness. Martineau, Types, preface, xii, xiii—"It was the irresistible pleading of the moral consciousness which first drove me to rebel against the limits of the merely scientific conception. It became incredible to me that nothing was possible except the actual.... Is there then no ought to be, other than what is?" Dewey, Psychology, 84—"A world without ideal elements would be one in which the home would be four walls and a roof to keep out cold and wet; the table a mess for animals; and the grave a hole in the ground." Omar Khayyám, Rubaiyat, stanza 72—"And that inverted bowl they call the Sky, Whereunder crawling coop'd we live and die, Lift not your hands to It for help—for it As impotently moves as you or I." Victor Hugo: "You say the soul is nothing but the resultant of bodily powers? Why then is my soul more luminous when my bodily powers begin to fail? Winter is on my head, and eternal spring is in my heart.... The nearer I approach the end, the plainer I hear the immortal symphonies of the worlds which invite me."

Diman, Theistic Argument, 348—"Materialism can never explain the fact that matter is always combined with force. Coördinate principles? then dualism, instead of monism. Force cause of matter? then we preserve unity, but destroy materialism; for we trace matter to an immaterial source. Behind multiplicity of natural forces we must postulate some single power—which can be nothing but coördinating mind." Mark Hopkins sums up Materialism in Princeton Rev., Nov. 1879:490—"1. Man, who is a person, is made by a thing, i. e., matter. 2. Matter is to be worshiped as man's maker, if anything is to be (Rom. 1:25). 3. Man is to worship himself—his God is his belly." See also Martineau, Religion and Materialism, 25-31, Types, 1: preface, xii, xiii, and Study, 1:248, 250, 345; Christlieb, Modern Doubt and Christian Belief, 145-161; Buchanan, Modern Atheism, 247, 248; McCosh, in International Rev., Jan. 1895; Contemp. Rev., Jan. 1875, art.: Man Transcorporeal; Calderwood, Relations of Mind and Brain; Laycock, Mind and Brain; Diman, Theistic Argument, 358; Wilkinson, in Present Day Tracts, 3:no. 17; Shedd, Dogm. Theol., 1:487-499; A. H. Strong, Philos. and Relig., 31-38.

II. Materialistic Idealism

Idealism proper is that method of thought which regards all knowledge as conversant only with affections of the percipient mind.

Its element of truth is the fact that these affections of the percipient mind are the conditions of our knowledge. Its error is in denying that through these and in these we know that which exists independently of our consciousness.

The idealism of the present day is mainly a materialistic idealism. It defines matter and mind alike in terms of sensation, and regards both as opposite sides or successive manifestations of one underlying and unknowable force.

Modern subjective idealism is the development of a principle found as far back as Locke. Locke derived all our knowledge from sensation; the mind only combines ideas which sensation furnishes, but gives no material of its own. Berkeley held that externally we can be sure only of sensations,—cannot be sure that any external world exists apart from mind. Berkeley's idealism, however, was objective; for he maintained that while things do not exist independently of consciousness, they do exist independently of our consciousness, namely, in the mind of God, who in a correct philosophy takes the place of a mindless external world as the cause of our ideas. Kant, in like manner, held to existences outside of our own minds, although he regarded these existences as unknown and unknowable. Over against these forms of objective idealism we must put the subjective idealism of Hume, who held that internally also we cannot be sure of anything but mental phenomena; we know thoughts, feelings and volitions, but we do not know mental substance within, any more than we know material substance without; our ideas are a string of beads, without any string; we need no cause for these ideas, in an external world, a soul, or God. Mill, Spencer, Bain and Tyndall are Humists, and it is their subjective idealism which we oppose.

All these regard the material atom as a mere centre of force, or a hypothetical cause of sensations. Matter is therefore a manifestation of force, as to the old materialism force was a property of matter. But if matter, mind and God are nothing but sensations, then the body itself is nothing but sensations. There is no body to have the sensations, and no spirit, either human or divine, to produce them. John Stuart Mill, in his Examination of Sir William Hamilton, 1:234-253, makes sensations the only original sources of knowledge. He defines matter as "a permanent possibility of sensation," and mind as "a series of feelings aware of itself." So Huxley calls matter "only a name for the unknown cause of the states of consciousness"; although he also declares: "If I am compelled to choose between the materialism of a man like Büchner and the idealism of Berkeley, I would have to agree with Berkeley." He would hold to the priority of matter, and yet regard matter as wholly ideal. Since John Stuart Mill, of all the materialistic idealists, gives the most precise definitions of matter and of mind, we attempt to show the inadequacy of his treatment.

The most complete refutation of subjective idealism is that of Sir William Hamilton, in his Metaphysics, 348-372, and Theories of Sense-perception—the reply to Brown. See condensed statement of Hamilton's view, with estimate and criticism, in Porter, Human Intellect, 236-240, and on Idealism, 129, 132. Porter holds that original perception gives us simply affections of our own sensorium; as cause of these, we gain knowledge of extended externality. So Sir William Hamilton: "Sensation proper has no object but a subject-object." But both Porter and Hamilton hold that through these sensations we know that which exists independently of our sensations. Hamilton's natural realism, however, was an exaggeration of the truth. Bowne, Introd. to Psych. Theory, 257, 258—"In Sir William Hamilton's desire to have no go-betweens in perception, he was forced to maintain that every sensation is felt where it seems to be, and hence that the mind fills out the entire body. Likewise he had to affirm that the object in vision is not the thing, but the rays of light, and even the object itself had, at last, to be brought into consciousness. Thus he reached the absurdity that the true object in perception is something of which we are totally unconscious." Surely we cannot be immediately conscious of what is outside of consciousness. James, Psychology, 1:11—"The terminal organs are telephones, and brain-cells are the receivers at which the mind listens." Berkeley's view is to be found in his Principles of Human Knowledge, § 18 sq. See also Presb. Rev., Apl. 1885:301-315; Journ. Spec. Philos., 1884:246-260, 383-399; Tulloch, Mod. Theories, 360, 361; Encyc. Britannica, art.: Berkeley.

There is, however, an idealism which is not open to Hamilton's objections, and to which most recent philosophers give their adhesion. It is the objective idealism of Lotze. It argues that we know nothing of the extended world except through the forces which impress our nervous organism. These forces take the form of vibrations of air or ether, and we interpret them as sound, light, or motion, according as they affect our nerves of hearing, sight, or touch. But the only force which we immediately know is that of our own wills, and we can either not understand matter at all or we must understand it as the product of a will comparable to our own. Things are simply "concreted laws of action," or divine ideas to which permanent reality has been given by divine will. What we perceive in the normal exercise of our faculties has existence not only for us but for all intelligent beings and for God himself: in other words, our idealism is not subjective, but objective. We have seen in the previous section that atoms cannot explain the universe,—they presuppose both ideas and force. We now see that this force presupposes will, and these ideas presuppose mind. But, as it still may be claimed that this mind is not self-conscious mind and that this will is not personal will, we pass in the next section to consider Idealistic Pantheism, of which these claims are characteristic. Materialistic Idealism, in truth, is but a half-way house between Materialism and Pantheism, in which no permanent lodging is to be found by the logical intelligence.

Lotze, Outlines of Metaphysics, 152—"The objectivity of our cognition consists therefore in this, that it is not a meaningless play of mere seeming; but it brings before us a world whose coherency is ordered in pursuance of the injunction of the sole Reality in the world, to wit, the Good. Our cognition thus possesses more of truth than if it copied exactly a world that has no value in itself. Although it does not comprehend in what manner all that is phenomenon is presented to the view, still it understands what is the meaning of it all; and is like to a spectator who comprehends the æsthetic significance of that which takes place on the stage of a theatre, and would gain nothing essential if he were to see besides the machinery by means of which the changes are effected on the stage." Professor C. A. Strong: "Perception is a shadow thrown upon the mind by a thing-in-itself. The shadow is the symbol of the thing; and, as shadows are soulless and dead, physical objects may seem soulless and dead, while the reality symbolized is never so soulful and alive. Consciousness is reality. The only existence of which we can conceive is mental in its nature. All existence for consciousness is existence of consciousness. The horse's shadow accompanies him, but it does not help him to draw the cart. The brain-event is simply the mental state itself regarded from the point of view of the perception."

Aristotle: "Substance is in its nature prior to relation" = there can be no relation without things to be related. Fichte: "Knowledge, just because it is knowledge, is not reality,—it comes not first, but second." Veitch, Knowing and Being, 216, 217, 292, 293—"Thought can do nothing, except as it is a synonym for Thinker.... Neither the finite nor the infinite consciousness, alone or together, can constitute an object external, or explain its existence. The existence of a thing logically precedes the perception of it. Perception is not creation. It is not the thinking that makes the ego, but the ego that makes the thinking." Seth, Hegelianism and Personality: "Divine thoughts presuppose a divine Being. God's thoughts do not constitute the real world. The real force does not lie in them,—it lies in the divine Being, as living, active Will." Here was the fundamental error of Hegel, that he regarded the Universe as mere Idea, and gave little thought to the Love and the Will that constitute it. See John Fiske, Cosmic Philosophy, 1:75; 2:80; Contemp. Rev., Oct. 1872: art. on Huxley; Lowndes, Philos. Primary Beliefs, 115-143; Atwater (on Ferrier), in Princeton Rev., 1857:258, 280; Cousin, Hist. Philosophy, 2:239-343; Veitch's Hamilton, (Blackwood's Philos. Classics,) 176, 191; A. H. Strong, Philosophy and Religion, 58-74.

To this view we make the following objections:

1. Its definition of matter as a "permanent possibility of sensation" contradicts our intuitive judgment that, in knowing the phenomena of matter, we have direct knowledge of substance as underlying phenomena, as distinct from our sensations, and as external to the mind which experiences these sensations.

Bowne, Metaphysics, 432—"How the possibility of an odor and a flavor can be the cause of the yellow color of an orange is probably unknowable, except to a mind that can see that two and two may make five." See Iverach's Philosophy of Spencer Examined, in Present Day Tracts, 5: no. 29. Martineau, Study, 1:102-112—"If external impressions are telegraphed to the brain, intelligence must receive the message at the beginning as well as deliver it at the end.... It is the external object which gives the possibility, not the possibility which gives the external object. The mind cannot make both its cognita and its cognitio. It cannot dispense with standing-ground for its own feet, or with atmosphere for its own wings." Professor Charles A. Strong: "Kant held to things-in-themselves back of physical phenomena, as well as to things-in-themselves back of mental phenomena; he thought things-in-themselves back of physical might be identical with things-in-themselves back of mental phenomena. And since mental phenomena, on this theory, are not specimens of reality, and reality manifests itself indifferently through them and through physical phenomena, he naturally concluded that we have no ground for supposing reality to be like either—that we must conceive of it as 'weder Materie noch ein denkend Wesen'—'neither matter nor a thinking being'—a theory of the Unknowable. Would that it had been also the Unthinkable and the Unmentionable!" Ralph Waldo Emerson was a subjective idealist; but, when called to inspect a farmer's load of wood, he said to his company: "Excuse me a moment, my friends; we have to attend to these matters, just as if they were real." See Mivart, On Truth, 71-141.

2. Its definition of mind as a "series of feelings aware of itself" contradicts our intuitive judgment that, in knowing the phenomena of mind, we have direct knowledge of a spiritual substance of which these phenomena are manifestations, which retains its identity independently of our consciousness, and which, in its knowing, instead of being the passive recipient of impressions from without, always acts from within by a power of its own.

James, Psychology, 1:226—"It seems as if the elementary psychic fact were not thought, or this thought, or that thought, but my thought, every thought being owned. The universal conscious fact is not 'feelings and thoughts exist,' but 'I think,' and 'I feel.' " Professor James is compelled to say this, even though he begins his Psychology without insisting upon the existence of a soul. Hamilton's Reid, 443—"Shall I think that thought can stand by itself? or that ideas can feel pleasure or pain?" R. T. Smith, Man's Knowledge, 44—"We say 'my notions and my passions,' and when we use these phrases we imply that our central self is felt to be something different from the notions or passions which belong to it or characterize it for a time." Lichtenberg: "We should say, 'It thinks;' just as we say, 'It lightens,' or 'It rains.' In saying 'Cogito,' the philosopher goes too far if he translates it, 'I think.' " Are the faculties, then, an army without a general, or an engine without a driver? In that case we should not have sensations,—we should only be sensations.

Professor C. A. Strong: "I have knowledge of other minds. This non-empirical knowledge— transcendent knowledge of things-in-themselves, derived neither from experience nor reasoning, and assuming that like consequents (intelligent movements) must have like antecedents (thoughts and feelings), and also assuming instinctively that something exists outside of my own mind—this refutes the post-Kantian phenomenalism. Perception and memory also involve transcendence. In both I transcend the bounds of experience, as truly as in my knowledge of other minds. In memory I recognize a past, as distinguished from the present. In perception I cognize a possibility of other experiences like the present, and this alone gives the sense of permanence and reality. Perception and memory refute phenomenalism. Things-in-themselves must be assumed in order to fill the gaps between individual minds, and to give coherence and intelligibility to the universe, and so to avoid pluralism. If matter can influence and even extinguish our minds, it must have some force of its own, some existence in itself. If consciousness is an evolutionary product, it must have arisen from simpler mental facts. But these simpler mental facts are only another name for things-in-themselves. A deep prerational instinct compels us to recognize them, for they cannot be logically demonstrated. We must assume them in order to give continuity and intelligibility to our conceptions of the universe." See, on Bain's Cerebral Psychology, Martineau's Essays, 1:265. On the physiological method of mental philosophy, see Talbot, in Bap. Quar., 1871:1; Bowen, in Princeton Rev., March, 1878:423-450; Murray, Psychology, 279-287.

3. In so far as this theory regards mind as the obverse side of matter, or as a later and higher development from matter, the mere reference of both mind and matter to an underlying force does not save the theory from any of the difficulties of pure materialism already mentioned; since in this case, equally with that, force is regarded as purely physical, and the priority of spirit is denied.

Herbert Spencer, Psychology, 2:80—"Mind and nervous action are the subjective and objective faces of the same thing. Yet we remain utterly incapable of seeing, or even of imagining, how the two are related. Mind still continues to us a something without kinship to other things." Owen, Anatomy of Vertebrates, quoted by Talbot, Bap. Quar., Jan. 1871:5— "All that I know of matter and mind in themselves is that the former is an external centre of force, and the latter an internal centre of force." New Englander, Sept. 1883:636—"If the atom be a mere centre of force and not a real thing in itself, then the atom is a supersensual essence, an immaterial being. To make immaterial matter the source of conscious mind is to make matter as wonderful as an immortal soul or a personal Creator." See New Englander, July, 1875:532-535; Martineau, Study, 102-130, and Relig. and Mod. Materialism, 25—"If it takes mind to construe the universe, how can the negation of mind constitute it?"

David J. Hill, in his Genetic Philosophy, 200, 201, seems to deny that thought precedes force, or that force precedes thought: "Objects, or things in the external world, may be elements of a thought-process in a cosmic subject, without themselves being conscious.... A true analysis and a rational genesis require the equal recognition of both the objective and the subjective elements of experience, without priority in time, separation in space or disruption of being. So far as our minds can penetrate reality, as disclosed in the activities of thought, we are everywhere confronted with a Dynamic Reason." In Dr. Hill's account of the genesis of the universe, however, the unconscious comes first, and from it the conscious seems to be derived. Consciousness of the object is only the obverse side of the object of consciousness. This is, as Martineau, Study, 1:341, remarks, "to take the sea on board the boat." We greatly prefer the view of Lotze, 2:641—"Things are acts of the Infinite wrought within minds alone, or states which the Infinite experiences nowhere but in minds.... Things and events are the sum of those actions which the highest Principle performs in all spirits so uniformly and coherently, that to these spirits there must seem to be a world of substantial and efficient things existing in space outside themselves." The data from which we draw our inferences as to the nature of the external world being mental and spiritual, it is more rational to attribute to that world a spiritual reality than a kind of reality of which our experience knows nothing. See also Schurman, Belief in God, 208, 225.

4. In so far as this theory holds the underlying force of which matter and mind are manifestations to be in any sense intelligent or voluntary, it renders necessary the assumption that there is an intelligent and voluntary Being who exerts this force. Sensations and ideas, moreover, are explicable only as manifestations of Mind.

Many recent Christian thinkers, as Murphy, Scientific Bases of Faith, 13-15, 29-36, 42-52, would define mind as a function of matter, matter as a function of force, force as a function of will, and therefore as the power of an omnipresent and personal God. All force, except that of man's free will, is the will of God. So Herschel, Lectures, 460; Argyll, Reign of Law, 121-127; Wallace on Nat. Selection, 363-371; Martineau, Essays, 1:63, 121, 145, 265; Bowen, Metaph. and Ethics, 146-162. These writers are led to their conclusion in large part by the considerations that nothing dead can be a proper cause; that will is the only cause of which we have immediate knowledge; that the forces of nature are intelligible only when they are regarded as exertions of will. Matter, therefore, is simply centres of force—the regular and, as it were, automatic expression of God's mind and will. Second causes in nature are only secondary activities of the great First Cause.

This view is held also by Bowne, in his Metaphysics. He regards only personality as real. Matter is phenomenal, although it is an activity of the divine will outside of us. Bowne's phenomenalism is therefore an objective idealism, greatly preferable to that of Berkeley who held to God's energizing indeed, but only within the soul. This idealism of Bowne is not pantheism, for it holds that, while there are no second causes in nature, man is a second cause, with a personality distinct from that of God, and lifted above nature by his powers of free will. Royce, however, in his Religious Aspect of Philosophy, and in his The World and the Individual, makes man's consciousness a part or aspect of a universal consciousness, and so, instead of making God come to consciousness in man, makes man come to consciousness in God. While this scheme seems, in one view, to save God's personality, it may be doubted whether it equally guarantees man's personality or leaves room for man's freedom, responsibility, sin and guilt. Bowne, Philos. Theism, 175—" 'Universal reason' is a class-term which denotes no possible existence, and which has reality only in the specific existences from which it is abstracted." Bowne claims that the impersonal finite has only such otherness as a thought or act has to its subject. There is no substantial existence except in persons. Seth, Hegelianism and Personality: "Neo-Kantianism erects into a God the mere form of self-consciousness in general, that is, confounds consciousness überhaupt with a universal consciousness."

Bowne, Theory of Thought and Knowledge, 318-343, esp. 328—"Is there anything in existence but myself? Yes. To escape solipsism I must admit at least other persons. Does the world of apparent objects exist for me only? No; it exists for others also, so that we live in a common world. Does this common world consist in anything more than a similarity of impressions in finite minds, so that the world apart from these is nothing? This view cannot be disproved, but it accords so ill with the impression of our total experience that it is practically impossible. Is then the world of things a continuous existence of some kind independent of finite thought and consciousness? This claim cannot be demonstrated, but it is the only view that does not involve insuperable difficulties. What is the nature and where is the place of this cosmic existence? That is the question between Realism and Idealism. Realism views things as existing in a real space, and as true ontological realities. Idealism views both them and the space in which they are supposed to be existing as existing only in and for a cosmic Intelligence, and apart from which they are absurd and contradictory. Things are independent of our thought, but not independent of all thought, in a lumpish materiality which is the antithesis and negation of consciousness." Sec also Martineau, Study, 1:214-230, 341. For advocacy of the substantive existence of second causes, see Porter, Hum. Intellect, 582-588; Hodge, Syst. Theol., 1:596; Alden, Philosophy, 48-80; Hodgson, Time and Space, 149-218; A. J. Balfour, in Mind, Oct. 1893: 430.

III. Idealistic Pantheism

Pantheism is that method of thought which conceives of the universe as the development of one intelligent and voluntary, yet impersonal, substance, which reaches consciousness only in man. It therefore identifies God, not with each individual object in the universe, but with the totality of things. The current Pantheism of our day is idealistic.

The elements of truth in Pantheism are the intelligence and voluntariness of God, and his immanence in the universe; its error lies in denying God's personality and transcendence.

Pantheism denies the real existence of the finite, at the same time that it deprives the Infinite of self-consciousness and freedom. See Hunt, History of Pantheism; Manning, Half-truths and the Truth; Bayne, Christian Life, Social and Individual, 21-53; Hutton, on Popular Pantheism, in Essays, 1:55-76—"The pantheist's 'I believe in God', is a contradiction. He says: 'I perceive the external as different from myself; but on further reflection, I perceive that this external was itself the percipient agency.' So the worshiped is really the worshiper after all." Harris, Philosophical Basis of Theism, 173—"Man is a bottle of the ocean's water, in the ocean, temporarily distinguishable by its limitation within the bottle, but lost again in the ocean, so soon as these fragile limits are broken." Martineau, Types, 1:23—Mere immanency excludes Theism; transcendency leaves it still possible; 211-225—Pantheism declares that "there is nothing but God; he is not only sole cause but entire effect; he is all in all." Spinoza has been falsely called "the God-intoxicated man." "Spinoza, on the contrary, translated God into the universe; it was Malebranche who transfigured the universe into God."

The later Brahmanism is pantheistic. Rowland Williams, Christianity and Hinduism, quoted in Mozley on Miracles, 284—"In the final state personality vanishes. You will not, says the Brahman, accept the term 'void' as an adequate description of the mysterious nature of the soul, but you will clearly apprehend soul, in the final state, to be unseen and ungrasped being, thought, knowledge, joy—no other than very God." Flint, Theism, 69—"Where the will is without energy, and rest is longed for as the end of existence, as among the Hindus, there is marked inability to think of God as cause or will, and constant inveterate tendency to pantheism."

Hegel denies God's transcendence: "God is not a spirit beyond the stars; he is spirit in all spirit"; which means that God, the impersonal and unconscious Absolute, comes to consciousness only in man. If the eternal system of abstract thoughts were itself conscious, finite consciousness would disappear; hence the alternative is either no God, or no man. Stirling: "The Idea, so conceived, is a blind, dumb, invisible idol, and the theory is the most hopeless theory that has ever been presented to humanity." It is practical autolatry, or self-deification. The world is reduced to a mere process of logic; thought thinks; there is thought without a thinker. To this doctrine of Hegel we may well oppose the remarks of Lotze: "We cannot make mind the equivalent of the infinitive to think,—we feel that it must be that which thinks; the essence of things cannot be either existence or activity,—it must be that which exists and that which acts. Thinking means nothing, if it is not the thinking of a thinker; acting and working mean nothing, if we leave out the conception of a subject distinguishable from them and from which they proceed." To Hegel, Being is Thought; to Spinoza, Being has Thought + Extension; the truth seems to be that Being has Thought + Will, and may reveal itself in Extension and Evolution (Creation).

By other philosophers, however, Hegel is otherwise interpreted. Prof. H. Jones, in Mind, July, 1893: 289-306, claims that Hegel's fundamental Idea is not Thought, but Thinking: "The universe to him was not a system of thoughts, but a thinking reality, manifested most fully in man.... The fundamental reality is the universal intelligence whose operation we should seek to detect in all things. All reality is ultimately explicable as Spirit, or Intelligence,—hence our ontology must be a Logic, and the laws of things must be laws of thinking." Sterrett, in like manner, in his Studies in Hegel's Philosophy of Religion, 17, quotes Hegel's Logic, Wallace's translation, 89, 91, 236: "Spinoza's Substance is, as it were, a dark, shapeless abyss, which devours all definite content as utterly null, and produces from itself nothing that has positive subsistence in itself.... God is Substance,—he is, however, no less the Absolute Person." This is essential to religion, but this, says Hegel, Spinoza never perceived: "Everything depends upon the Absolute Truth being perceived, not merely as Substance, but as Subject." God is self-conscious and self-determining Spirit. Necessity is excluded. Man is free and immortal. Men are not mechanical parts of God, nor do they lose their identity, although they find themselves truly only in him. With this estimate of Hegel's system, Caird, Erdmann and Mulford substantially agree. This is Tennyson's "Higher Pantheism."

Seth, Ethical Principles, 440—"Hegel conceived the superiority of his system to Spinozism to lie in the substitution of Subject for Substance. The true Absolute must contain, instead of abolishing, relations; the true Monism must include, instead of excluding, Pluralism. A One which, like Spinoza's

Substance, or the Hegelian Absolute, does not enable us to think the Many, cannot be the true One—the unity of the Manifold.... Since evil exists, Schopenhauer substituted for Hegel's Panlogism, which asserted the identity of the rational and the real, a blind impulse of life,—for absolute Reason he substituted a reasonless Will"—a system of practical pessimism. Alexander, Theories of Will, 5—"Spinoza recognized no distinction between will and intellectual affirmation or denial." John Caird, Fund. Ideas of Christianity, 1:107—"As there is no reason in the conception of pure space why any figures or forms, lines, surfaces, solids, should arise in it, so there is no reason in the pure colorless abstraction of Infinite Substance why any world of finite things and beings should ever come into existence. It is the grave of all things, the productive source of nothing." Hegel called Schelling's Identity or Absolute "the infinite night in which all cows are black"—an allusion to Goethe's Faust, part 2, act 1, where the words are added: "and cats are gray." Although Hegel's preference of the term Subject, instead of the term Substance, has led many to maintain that he believed in a personality of God distinct from that of man, his over-emphasis of the Idea, and his comparative ignoring of the elements of Love and Will, leave it still doubtful whether his Idea was anything more than unconscious and impersonal intelligence—less materialistic than that of Spinoza indeed, yet open to many of the same objections.

We object to this system as follows:

1. Its idea of God is self-contradictory, since it makes him infinite, yet consisting only of the finite; absolute, yet existing in necessary relation to the universe; supreme, yet shut up to a process of self-evolution and dependent for self-consciousness on man; without self-determination, yet the cause of all that is.

Saisset, Pantheism, 148—"An imperfect God, yet perfection arising from imperfection." Shedd, Hist. Doctrine, 1:13—"Pantheism applies to God a principle of growth and imperfection, which belongs only to the finite." Calderwood, Moral Philos., 245—"Its first requisite is moment, or movement, which it assumes, but does not account for." Caro's sarcasm applies here: "Your God is not yet made—he is in process of manufacture." See H. B. Smith, Faith and Philosophy, 25. Pantheism is practical atheism, for impersonal spirit is only blind and necessary force. Angelus Silesius: "Wir beten 'Es gescheh, mein Herr und Gott, dein Wille'; Und sieh', Er hat nicht Will',—Er ist ein ew'ge Stille"—which Max Müller translates as follows: "We pray, 'O Lord our God, Do thou thy holy Will'; and see! God has no will; He is at peace and still." Angelus Silesius consistently makes God dependent for self-consciousness on man: "I know that God cannot live An instant without me; He must give up the ghost, If I should cease to be." Seth, Hegelianism and Personality: "Hegelianism destroys both God and man. It reduces man to an object of the universal Thinker, and leaves this universal Thinker without any true personality." Pantheism is a game of solitaire, in which God plays both sides.

2. Its assumed unity of substance is not only without proof, but it directly contradicts our intuitive judgments. These testify that we are not parts and particles of God, but distinct personal subsistences.

Martineau, Essays, 1:158—"Even for immanency, there must be something wherein to dwell, and for life, something whereon to act." Many systems of monism contradict consciousness; they confound harmony between two with absorption in one. "In Scripture we never find the universe called τὸ πᾶν, for this suggests the idea of a self-contained unity: we have everywhere τὰ πάντα instead." The Bible recognizes the element of truth in pantheism—God is "through all"; also the element of truth in mysticism—God is "in you all"; but it adds the element of transcendence which both these fail to recognize—God is "above all" (Eph. 4:6). See Fisher, Essays on Supernat. Orig. of Christianity, 539. G. D. B. Pepper: "He who is over all and in all is yet distinct from all. If one is over a thing, he is not that very thing which he is over. If one is in something, he must be distinct from that something. And so the universe, over which and in which God is, must be thought of as something distinct from God. The creation cannot be identical with God, or a mere form of God." We add, however, that it may be a manifestation of God and dependent upon God, as our thoughts and acts are manifestations of our mind and will and dependent upon our mind and will, yet are not themselves our mind and will.

Pope wrote: "All are but parts of one stupendous whole, Whose body nature is and God the soul." But Case, Physical Realism, 193, replies: "Not so. Nature is to God as works are to a man; and as man's works are not his body, so neither is nature the body of God." Matthew Arnold, On Heine's Grave: "What are we all but a mood, A single mood of the life Of the Being in whom we exist, Who alone is all things in one?" Hovey, Studies, 51—"Scripture recognizes the element of truth in pantheism, but it also teaches the existence of a world of things, animate and inanimate, in distinction from God. It represents men as prone to worship the creature more than the Creator. It describes them as sinners worthy of death ... moral agents.... It no more thinks of men as being literally parts of God, than it thinks of children as being parts of their parents, or subjects as being parts of their king." A. J. F. Behrends: "The true doctrine lies between the two extremes of a crass dualism which makes God and the world two self-contained entities, and a substantial monism in which the universe has only a phenomenal existence. There is no identity of substance nor division of the divine substance. The universe is eternally dependent, the product of the divine Word, not simply manufactured. Creation is primarily a spiritual act." Prof. George M. Forbes: "Matter exists in subordinate dependence upon God; spirit in coördinate dependence upon God. The body of Christ was Christ externalized, made manifest to sense-perception. In apprehending matter, I am apprehending the mind and will of God. This is the highest sort of reality. Neither matter nor finite spirits, then, are mere phenomena."

3. It assigns no sufficient cause for that fact of the universe which is highest in rank, and therefore most needs explanation, namely, the existence of personal intelligences. A substance which is itself unconscious, and under the law of necessity, cannot produce beings who are self-conscious and free.

Gess, Foundations of our Faith, 36—"Animal instinct, and the spirit of a nation working out its language, might furnish analogies, if they produced personalities as their result, but not otherwise. Nor were these tendencies self-originated, but received from an external source." McCosh, Intuitions, 215, 393, and Christianity and Positivism, 180. Seth, Freedom as an Ethical Postulate, 47—"If man is an 'imperium in imperio,' not a person, but only an aspect or expression of the universe or God, then he cannot be free. Man may be depersonalized either into nature or into God. Through the conception of our own personality we reach that of God. To resolve our personality into that of God would be to negate the divine greatness itself by invalidating the conception through which it was reached." Bradley, Appearance and Reality, 551, is more ambiguous: "The positive relation of every appearance as an adjective to Reality; and the presence of Reality among its appearances in different degrees and with diverse values; this double truth we have found to be the centre of philosophy." He protests against both "an empty transcendence" and "a shallow pantheism." Hegelian immanence and knowledge, he asserts, identified God and man. But God is more than man or man's thought. He is spirit and life—best understood from the human self, with its thoughts, feelings, volitions. Immanence needs to be qualified by transcendence. "God is not God till he has become all-in-all, and a God which is all-in-all is not the God of religion. God is an aspect, and that must mean but an appearance of the Absolute." Bradley's Absolute, therefore, is not so much personal as super-personal; to which we reply with Jackson, James Martineau, 416—"Higher than personality is lower; beyond it is regression from its height. From the equator we may travel northward, gaining ever higher and higher latitudes; but, if ever the pole is reached, pressing on from thence will be descending into lower latitudes, not gaining higher.... Do I say, I am a pantheist? Then, ipso facto, I deny pantheism; for, in the very assertion of the Ego, I imply all else as objective to me."

4. It therefore contradicts the affirmations of our moral and religious natures by denying man's freedom and responsibility; by making God to include in himself all evil as well as all good; and by precluding all prayer, worship, and hope of immortality.

Conscience is the eternal witness against pantheism. Conscience witnesses to our freedom and responsibility, and declares that moral distinctions are not illusory. Renouf, Hibbert Lect., 234—"It is only out of condescension to popular language that pantheistic systems can recognize the notions of right and wrong, of iniquity and sin. If everything really emanates from God, there can be no such thing as sin. And the ablest philosophers who have been led to pantheistic views have vainly endeavored to harmonize these views with what we understand by the notion of sin or moral evil. The great systematic work of Spinoza is entitled 'Ethica'; but for real ethics we might as profitably consult the Elements of Euclid." Hodge, System. Theology, 1:299-320—"Pantheism is fatalistic. On this theory, duty = pleasure; right = might; sin = good in the making. Satan, as well as Gabriel, is a self-development of God. The practical effects of pantheism upon popular morals and life, wherever it has prevailed, as in Buddhist India and China, demonstrate its falsehood." See also Dove, Logic of the Christian Faith, 118; Murphy, Scientific Bases of Faith, 202; Bib. Sac., Oct. 1867:603-615; Dix, Pantheism, Introd., 12. On the fact of sin as refuting the pantheistic theory, see Bushnell, Nature and the Supernat., 140-164.

Wordsworth: "Look up to heaven! the industrious sun Already half his course hath run; He cannot halt or go astray; But our immortal spirits may." President John H. Harris; "You never ask a cyclone's opinion of the ten commandments." Bowne, Philos. of Theism, 245—"Pantheism makes man an automaton. But how can an automaton have duties?" Principles of Ethics, 18—"Ethics is defined as the science of conduct, and the conventions of language are relied upon to cover up the fact that there is no 'conduct' in the case. If man be a proper automaton, we might as well speak of the conduct of the winds as of human conduct; and a treatise on planetary motions is as truly the ethics of the solar system as a treatise on human movements is the ethics of man." For lack of a clear recognition of personality, either human or divine, Hegel's Ethics is devoid of all spiritual nourishment,—his "Rechtsphilosophie" has been called "a repast of bran." Yet Professor Jones, in Mind, July, 1893:304, tells us that Hegel's task was "to discover what conception of the single principle or fundamental unity which alone is, is adequate to the differences which it carries within it. 'Being,' he found, leaves no room for differences,—it is overpowered by them.... He found that the Reality can exist only as absolute Self-consciousness, as a Spirit, who is universal, and who knows himself in all things. In all this he is dealing, not simply with thoughts, but with Reality." Prof. Jones's vindication of Hegel, however, still leaves it undecided whether that philosopher regarded the divine self-consciousness as distinct from that of finite beings, or as simply inclusive of theirs. See John Caird, Fund. Ideas of Christianity, 1:109.

5. Our intuitive conviction of the existence of a God of absolute perfection compels us to conceive of God as possessed of every highest quality and attribute of men, and therefore, especially, of that which constitutes the chief dignity of the human spirit, its personality.

Diman, Theistic Argument, 328—"We have no right to represent the supreme Cause as inferior to ourselves, yet we do this when we describe it under phrases derived from physical causation." Mivart, Lessons from Nature, 351—"We cannot conceive of anything as impersonal, yet of higher nature than our own,—any being that has not knowledge and will must be indefinitely inferior to one who has them." Lotze holds truly, not that God is supra-personal, but that man is infra-personal, seeing that in the infinite Being alone is self-subsistence, and therefore perfect personality. Knight, Essays in Philosophy, 224—"The radical feature of personality is the survival of a permanent self, under all the fleeting or deciduous phases of experience; in other words, the personal identity that is involved in the assertion 'I am.'... Is limitation a necessary adjunct of that notion?" Seth, Hegelianism: "As in us there is more for ourselves than for others, so in God there is more of thought for himself than he manifests to us. Hegel's doctrine is that of immanence without transcendence." Heinrich Heine was a pupil and intimate friend of Hegel. He says: "I was young and proud, and it pleased my vain-glory when I learned from Hegel that the true God was not, as my grandmother believed, the God who lived in heaven, but was rather myself upon the earth." John Fiske, Idea of God, xvi—"Since our notion of force is purely a generalization from our subjective sensations of overcoming resistance, there is scarcely less anthropomorphism in the phrase 'Infinite Power' than in the phrase 'Infinite Person.' We must symbolize Deity in some form that has meaning to us; we cannot symbolize it as physical; we are bound to symbolize it as psychical. Hence we may say, God is Spirit. This implies God's personality."

6. Its objection to the divine personality, that over against the Infinite there can be in eternity past no non-ego to call forth self-consciousness, is refuted by considering that even man's cognition of the non-ego logically presupposes knowledge of the ego, from which the non-ego is distinguished; that, in an absolute mind, self-consciousness cannot be conditioned, as in the case of finite mind, upon contact with a not-self; and that, if the distinguishing of self from a not-self were an essential condition of divine self-consciousness, the eternal personal distinctions in the divine nature or the eternal states of the divine mind might furnish such a condition.

Pfleiderer, Die Religion, 1:163, 190 sq.—"Personal self-consciousness is not primarily a distinguishing of the ego from the non-ego, but rather a distinguishing of itself from itself, i. e., of the unity of the self from the plurality of its contents.... Before the soul distinguishes self from the not-self, it must know self—else it could not see the distinction. Its development is connected with the knowledge of the non-ego, but this is due, not to the fact of personality, but to the fact of finite personality. The mature man can live for a long time upon his own resources. God needs no other, to stir him up to mental activity. Finiteness is a hindrance to the development of our personality. Infiniteness is necessary to the highest personality." Lotze, Microcosmos, vol. 3, chapter 4; transl. in N. Eng., March, 1881:191-200—"Finite spirit, not having conditions of existence in itself, can know the ego only upon occasion of knowing the non-ego. The Infinite is not so limited. He alone has an independent existence, neither introduced nor developed through anything not himself, but, in an inward activity without beginning or end, maintains himself in himself." See also Lotze, Philos. of Religion, 55-69; H. N. Gardiner on Lotze, in Presb. Rev., 1885:669-673; Webb, in Jour. Theol. Studies, 2:49-61.

Dorner, Glaubenslehre: "Absolute Personality = perfect consciousness of self, and perfect power over self. We need something external to waken our consciousness—yet self-consciousness comes [logically] before consciousness of the world. It is the soul's act. Only after it has distinguished self from self, can it consciously distinguish self from another." British Quarterly, Jan. 1874:32, note; July, 1884:108—"The ego is thinkable only in relation to the non-ego; but the ego is liveable long before any such relation." Shedd, Dogm. Theol., 1:185, 186—In the pantheistic scheme, "God distinguishes himself from the world, and thereby finds the object required by the subject; ... in the Christian scheme, God distinguishes himself from himself, not from something that is not himself." See Julius Müller, Doctrine of Sin, 2:122-126; Christlieb, Mod. Doubt and Christ. Belief, 161-190; Hanne, Idee der absoluten Persönlichkeit; Eichhorn, Die Persönlichkeit Gottes; Seth, Hegelianism and Personality; Knight, on Personality and the Infinite, in Studies in Philos. and Lit., 70-118.

On the whole subject of Pantheism, see Martineau, Study of Religion, 2:141-194, esp. 192—"The personality of God consists in his voluntary agency as free cause in an unpledged sphere, that is, a sphere transcending that of immanent law. But precisely this also it is that constitutes his infinity, extending his sway, after it has filled the actual, over all the possible, and giving command over indefinite alternatives. Though you might deny his infinity without prejudice to his personality, you cannot deny his personality without sacrificing his infinitude: for there is a mode of action—the preferential, the very mode which distinguishes rational beings—from which you exclude him"; 341— "The metaphysicians who, in their impatience of distinction, insist on taking the sea on board the boat, swamp not only it but the thought it holds, and leave an infinitude which, as it can look into no eye and whisper into no ear, they contradict in the very act of affirming." Jean Paul Richter's "Dream": "I wandered to the farthest verge of Creation, and there I saw a Socket, where an Eye should have been, and I heard the shriek of a Fatherless World" (quoted in David Brown's Memoir of John Duncan, 49-70). Shelley, Beatrice Cenci: "Sweet Heaven, forgive weak thoughts! If there should be No God, no Heaven, no Earth, in the void world—The wide, grey, lampless, deep, unpeopled world!"

For the opposite view, see Biedermann, Dogmatik, 638-647—"Only man, as finite spirit, is personal; God, as absolute spirit, is not personal. Yet in religion the mutual relations of intercourse and communion are always personal.... Personality is the only adequate term by which we can represent the theistic conception of God." Bruce, Providential Order, 76—"Schopenhauer does not level up cosmic force to the human, but levels down human will-force to the cosmic. Spinoza held intellect in God to be no more like man's than the dog-star is like a dog. Hartmann added intellect to Schopenhauer's will, but the intellect is unconscious and knows no moral distinctions." See also Bruce, Apologetics, 71-90; Bowne, Philos. of Theism, 128-134, 171-186; J. M. Whiton, Am. Jour. Theol., Apl. 1901:306—Pantheism = God consists in all things; Theism = All things consist in God, their ground, not their sum. Spirit in man shows that the infinite Spirit must be personal and transcendent Mind and Will.

IV. Ethical Monism

Ethical Monism is that method of thought which holds to a single substance, ground, or principle of being, namely, God, but which also holds to the ethical facts of God's transcendence as well as his immanence, and of God's personality as distinct from, and as guaranteeing, the personality of man.

Although we do not here assume the authority of the Bible, reserving our proof of this to the next following division on The Scriptures a Revelation from God, we may yet cite passages which show that our doctrine is not inconsistent with the teachings of holy Writ. The immanence of God is implied in all statements of his omnipresence, as for example: Ps. 139:7 sq.—"Whither shall I go from thy spirit? Or whither shall I flee from thy presence?" Jer. 23:23, 24—"Am I a God at hand, saith Jehovah, and not a God afar off?... Do not I fill heaven and earth?" Acts 17:27, 28—"he is not far from each one of us: for in him we live, and move, and have our being." The transcendence of God is implied in such passages as: 1 Kings 8:27—"the heaven and the heaven of heavens cannot contain thee"; Ps. 113:5—"that hath his seat on high"; Is. 57:15—"the high and lofty One that inhabiteth eternity."

This is the faith of Augustine: "O God, thou hast made us for thyself, and our heart is restless till it find rest in thee.... I could not be, O my God, could not be at all, wert thou not in me; rather, were not I in thee, of whom are all things, by whom are all things, in whom are all things." And Anselm, in his Proslogion, says of the divine nature: "It is the essence of the being, the principle of the existence, of all things.... Without parts, without differences, without accidents, without changes, it might be said in a certain sense alone to exist, for in respect to it the other things which appear to be have no existence. The unchangeable Spirit is all that is, and it is this without limit, simply, interminably. It is the perfect and absolute Existence. The rest has come from non-entity, and thither returns if not supported by God. It does not exist by itself. In this sense the Creator alone exists; created things do not."

1. While Ethical Monism embraces the one element of truth contained in Pantheism—the truth that God is in all things and that all things are in God—it regards this scientific unity as entirely consistent with the facts of ethics—man's freedom, responsibility, sin, and guilt; in other words, Metaphysical Monism, or the doctrine of one substance, ground, or principle of being, is qualified by Psychological Dualism, or the doctrine that the soul is personally distinct from matter on the one hand, and from God on the other.

Ethical Monism is a monism which holds to the ethical facts of the freedom of man and the transcendence and personality of God; it is the monism of free-will, in which personality, both human and divine, sin and righteousness, God and the world, remain—two in one, and one in two—in their moral antithesis as well as their natural unity. Ladd, Introd. to Philosophy: "Dualism is yielding, in history and in the judgment-halls of reason, to a monistic philosophy.... Some form of philosophical monism is indicated by the researches of psycho-physics, and by that philosophy of mind which builds upon the principles ascertained by these researches. Realities correlated as are the body and the mind must have, as it were, a common ground.... They have their reality in the ultimate one Reality; they have their interrelated lives as expressions of the one Life which is immanent in the two.... Only some form of monism that shall satisfy the facts and truths to which both realism and idealism appeal can occupy the place of the true and final philosophy.... Monism must so construct its tenets as to preserve, or at least as not to contradict and destroy, the truths implicated in the distinction between the me and the not-me, ... between the morally good and the morally evil. No form of monism can persistently maintain itself which erects its system upon the ruins of fundamentally ethical principles and ideals."... Philosophy of Mind, 411—"Dualism must be dissolved in some ultimate monistic solution. The Being of the world, of which all particular beings are but parts, must be so conceived of as that in it can be found the one ground of all interrelated existences and activities.... This one Principle is an Other and an Absolute Mind."

Dorner, Hist. Doct. Person of Christ, II, 3:101, 231—"The unity of essence in God and man is the great discovery of the present age.... The characteristic feature of all recent Christologies is the endeavor to point out the essential unity of the divine and human. To the theology of the present day, the divine and human are not mutually exclusive, but are connected magnitudes.... Yet faith postulates a difference between the world and God, between whom religion seeks an union. Faith does not wish to be a relation merely to itself, or to its own representations and thoughts; that would be a monologue,—faith desires a dialogue. Therefore it does not consort with a monism which recognizes only God, or only the world; it opposes such a monism as this. Duality is, in fact, a condition of true and vital unity. But duality is not dualism. It has no desire to oppose the rational demand for unity." Professor Small of Chicago: "With rare exceptions on each side, all philosophy to-day is monistic in its ontological presumptions; it is dualistic in its methodological procedures." A. H. Bradford, Age of Faith, 71—"Men and God are the same in substance, though not identical as individuals." The theology of fifty years ago was merely individualistic, and ignored the complementary truth of solidarity. Similarly we think of the continents and islands of our globe as disjoined from one another. The dissociable sea is regarded as an absolute barrier between them. But if the ocean could be dried, we should see that all the while there had been submarine connections, and the hidden unity of all lands would appear. So the individuality of human beings, real as it is, is not the only reality. There is the profounder fact of a common life. Even the great mountain-peaks of personality are superficial distinctions, compared with the organic oneness in which they are rooted, into which they all dip down, and from which they all, like volcanoes, receive at times quick and overflowing impulses of insight, emotion and energy; see A. H. Strong, Christ in Creation and Ethical Monism, 189, 190.

2. In contrast then with the two errors of Pantheism—the denial of God's transcendence and the denial of God's personality—Ethical Monism holds that the universe, instead of being one with God and conterminous with God, is but a finite, partial and progressive manifestation of the divine Life: Matter being God's self-limitation under the law of Necessity; Humanity being God's self-limitation under the law of Freedom; Incarnation and Atonement being God's self-limitations under the law of Grace.

The universe is related to God as my thoughts are related to me, the thinker. I am greater than my thoughts, and my thoughts vary in moral value. Ethical Monism traces the universe back to a beginning, while Pantheism regards the universe as coëternal with God. Ethical Monism asserts God's transcendence, while Pantheism regards God as imprisoned in the universe. Ethical Monism asserts that the heaven of heavens cannot contain him, but that contrariwise the whole universe taken together, with its elements and forces, its suns and systems, is but a light breath from his mouth, or a drop of dew upon the fringe of his garment. Upton, Hibbert Lectures: "The Eternal is present in every finite thing, and is felt and known to be present in every rational soul; but still is not broken up into individualities, but ever remains one and the same eternal substance, one and the same unifying principle, immanently and indivisibly present in every one of that countless plurality of finite individuals into which man's analyzing understanding dissects the Cosmos." James Martineau, in 19th Century, Apl. 1895:559— "What is Nature but the province of God's pledged and habitual causality? And what is Spirit, but the province of his free causality, responding to the needs and affections of his children?... God is not a retired architect, who may now and then be called in for repairs. Nature is not self-active, and God's agency is not intrusive." Calvin: Pie hoc potest dici, Deum esse Naturam.

With this doctrine many poets show their sympathy. "Every fresh and new creation, A divine improvisation, From the heart of God proceeds." Robert Browning asserts God's immanence; Hohenstiel-Schwangau: "This is the glory that, in all conceived Or felt, or known, I recognize a Mind— Not mine, but like mine—for the double joy, Making all things for me, and me for him"; Ring and Book, Pope: "O thou, as represented to me here In such conception as my soul allows—Under thy measureless, my atom-width! Man's mind, what is it but a convex glass, Wherein are gathered all the scattered points Picked out of the immensity of sky, To reunite there, be our heaven for earth, Our Known Unknown, our God revealed to man?" But Browning also asserts God's transcendence: in Death in the Desert, we read: "Man is not God, but hath God's end to serve, A Master to obey, a Cause to take, Somewhat to cast off, somewhat to become"; in Christmas Eve, the poet derides "The important stumble Of adding, he, the sage and humble, Was also one with the Creator"; he tells us that it was God's plan to make man in his image: "To create man, and then leave him Able, his own word saith, to grieve him; But able to glorify him too, As a mere machine could never do That prayed or praised, all unaware Of its fitness for aught but praise or prayer, Made perfect as a thing of course.... God, whose pleasure brought Man into being, stands away, As it were, a hand-breadth off, to give Room for the newly made to live And look at him from a place apart And use his gifts of brain and heart"; "Life's business being just the terrible choice."

So Tennyson's Higher Pantheism: "The sun, the moon, the stars, the seas, the hills, and the plains, Are not these, O soul, the vision of Him who reigns? Dark is the world to thee; thou thyself art the reason why; For is not He all but thou, that hast power to feel 'I am I'? Speak to him, thou, for he hears, and spirit with spirit can meet; Closer is he than breathing, and nearer than hands and feet. And the ear of man cannot hear, and the eye of man cannot see; But if we could see and hear, this vision—were it not He?" Also Tennyson's Ancient Sage: "But that one ripple on the boundless deep Feels that the deep is boundless, and itself Forever changing form, but evermore One with the boundless motion of the deep"; and In Memoriam: "One God, one law, one element, And one far-off divine event, Toward which the whole creation moves." Emerson: "The day of days, the greatest day in the feast of life, is that in which the inward eye opens to the unity of things"; "In the mud and scum of things Something always, always sings." Mrs. Browning: "Earth is crammed with heaven, And every common bush afire with God; But only he who sees takes off his shoes." So manhood is itself potentially a divine thing. All life, in all its vast variety, can have but one Source. It is either one God, above all, through all, and in all, or it is no God at all. E. M. Poteat, On Chesapeake Bay: "Night's radiant glory overhead, A softer glory there below, Deep answered unto deep, and said: A kindred fire in us doth glow. For life is one— of sea and stars, Of God and man, of earth and heaven—And by no theologic bars Shall my scant life from God's be riven." See Professor Henry Jones, Robert Browning.

3. The immanence of God, as the one substance, ground and principle of being, does not destroy, but rather guarantees, the individuality and rights of each portion of the universe, so that there is variety of rank and endowment. In the case of moral beings, worth is determined by the degree of their voluntary recognition and appropriation of the divine. While God is all, he is also in all; so making the universe a graded and progressive manifestation of himself, both in his love for righteousness and his opposition to moral evil.

It has been charged that the doctrine of monism necessarily involves moral indifference; that the divine presence in all things breaks down all distinctions of rank and makes each thing equal to every other; that the evil as well as the good is legitimated and consecrated. Of pantheistic monism all this is true,—it is not true of ethical monism; for ethical monism is the monism that recognizes the ethical fact of personal intelligence and will in both God and man, and with these God's purpose in making the universe a varied manifestation of himself. The worship of cats and bulls and crocodiles in ancient Egypt, and the deification of lust in the Brahmanic temples of India, were expressions of a non-ethical monism, which saw in God no moral attributes, and which identified God with his manifestations. As an illustration of the mistakes into which the critics of monism may fall for lack of discrimination between monism that is pantheistic and monism that is ethical, we quote from Emma Marie Caillard: "Integral parts of God are, on monistic premises, liars, sensualists, murderers, evil livers and evil thinkers of every description. Their crimes and their passions enter intrinsically into the divine experience. The infinite Individual in his wholeness may reject them indeed, but none the less are these evil finite individuals constituent parts of him, even as the twigs of a tree, though they are not the tree, and though the tree transcends any or all of them, are yet constituent parts of it. Can he whose universal consciousness includes and defines all finite consciousnesses be other than responsible for all finite actions and motives?"

To this indictment we may reply in the words of Bowne, The Divine Immanence, 130-133— "Some weak heads have been so heated by the new wine of immanence as to put all things on the same level, and make men and mice of equal value. But there is nothing in the dependence of all things on God to remove their distinctions of value. One confused talker of this type was led to say that he had no trouble with the notion of a divine man, as he believed in a divine oyster. Others have used the doctrine to cancel moral differences; for if God be in all things, and if all things represent his will, then whatever is is right. But this too is hasty. Of course even the evil will is not independent of God, but lives and moves and has its being in and through the divine. But through its mysterious power of selfhood and self-determination the evil will is able to assume an attitude of hostility to the divine law, which forthwith vindicates itself by appropriate reactions.

"These reactions are not divine in the highest or ideal sense. They represent nothing which God desires or in which he delights; but they are divine in the sense that they are things to be done under the circumstances. The divine reaction in the case of the good is distinct from the divine reaction against evil. Both are divine as representing God's action, but only the former is divine in the sense of representing God's approval and sympathy. All things serve, said Spinoza. The good serve, and are furthered by their service. The bad also serve and are used up in the serving. According to Jonathan Edwards, the wicked are useful 'in being acted upon and disposed of.' As 'vessels of dishonor' they may reveal the majesty of God. There is nothing therefore in the divine immanence, in its only tenable form, to cancel moral distinctions or to minify retribution. The divine reaction against iniquity is even more solemn in this doctrine. The besetting God is the eternal and unescapable environment; and only as we are in harmony with him can there be any peace.... What God thinks of sin, and what his will is concerning it can be plainly seen in the natural consequences which attend it.... In law itself we are face to face with God; and natural consequences have a supernatural meaning."

4. Since Christ is the Logos of God, the immanent God, God revealed in Nature, in Humanity, in Redemption, Ethical Monism recognizes the universe as created, upheld, and governed by the same Being who in the course of history was manifest in human form and who made atonement for human sin

by his death on Calvary. The secret of the universe and the key to its mysteries are to be found in the Cross.

John 1:1-4 (marg.), 14, 18—"In the beginning was the Word, and the Word was with God, and the Word was God. The same was in the beginning with God. All things were made through him; and without him was not any thing made. That which hath been made was life in him; and the life was the light of men.... And the Word became flesh, and dwelt among us.... No man hath seen God at any time; the only begotten Son, who is in the bosom of the Father, he hath declared him." Col. 1:16, 17—"for in him were all things created, in the heavens and upon the earth, things visible and things invisible, whether thrones or dominions or principalities or powers; all things have been created through him and unto him; and he is before all things, and in him all things consist." Heb. 1:2, 3—"his Son ... through whom also he made the worlds ... upholding all things by the word of his power"; Eph. 1:22, 23—"the church, which is his body, the fulness of him that filleth all in all" = fills all things with all that they contain of truth, beauty, and goodness; Col. 2:2, 3, 9—"the mystery of God, even Christ, in whom are all the treasures of wisdom and knowledge hidden ... for in him dwelleth all the fulness of the Godhead bodily."

This view of the relation of the universe to God lays the foundation for a Christian application of recent philosophical doctrine. Matter is no longer blind and dead, but is spiritual in its nature, not in the sense that it is spirit, but in the sense that it is the continual manifestation of spirit, just as my thoughts are a living and continual manifestation of myself. Yet matter does not consist simply in ideas, for ideas, deprived of an external object and of an internal subject, are left suspended in the air. Ideas are the product of Mind. But matter is known only as the operation of force, and force is the product of Will. Since this force works in rational ways, it can be the product only of Spirit. The system of forces which we call the universe is the immediate product of the mind and will of God; and, since Christ is the mind and will of God in exercise, Christ is the Creator and Upholder of the universe. Nature is the omnipresent Christ, manifesting God to creatures.

Christ is the principle of cohesion, attraction, interaction, not only in the physical universe, but in the intellectual and moral universe as well. In all our knowing, the knower and known are "connected by some Being who is their reality," and this being is Christ, "the Light which lighteth every man" (John 1:9). We know in Christ, just as "in him we live, and move, and have our being" (Acts 17:28). As the attraction of gravitation and the principle of evolution are only other names for Christ, so he is the basis of inductive reasoning and the ground of moral unity in the creation. I am bound to love my neighbor as myself because he has in him the same life that is in me, the life of God in Christ. The Christ in whom all humanity is created, and in whom all humanity consists, holds together the moral universe, drawing all men to himself and so drawing them to God. Through him God "reconciles all things unto himself ... whether things upon the earth, or things in the heavens" (Col. 1:20).

As Pantheism = exclusive immanence = God imprisoned, so Deism = exclusive transcendence = God banished. Ethical Monism holds to the truth contained in each of these systems, while avoiding their respective errors. It furnishes the basis for a new interpretation of many theological as well as of many philosophical doctrines. It helps our understanding of the Trinity. If within the bounds of God's being there can exist multitudinous finite personalities, it becomes easier to comprehend how within those same bounds there can be three eternal and infinite personalities,—indeed, the integration of plural consciousnesses in an all-embracing divine consciousness may find a valid analogy in the integration of subordinate consciousnesses in the unit-personality of man; see Baldwin, Handbook of Psychology, Feeling and Will, 53, 54.

Ethical Monism, since it is ethical, leaves room for human wills and for their freedom. While man could never break the natural bond which united him to God, he could break the spiritual bond and introduce into creation a principle of discord and evil. Tie a cord tightly about your finger; you partially isolate the finger, diminish its nutrition, bring about atrophy and disease. So there has been given to each intelligent and moral agent the power, spiritually to isolate himself from God while yet he is naturally joined to God. As humanity is created in Christ and lives only in Christ, man's self-isolation is his moral separation from Christ. Simon, Redemption of Man, 339—"Rejecting Christ is not so much refusal to become one with Christ as it is refusal to remain one with him, refusal to let him be our life." All men are naturally one with Christ by physical birth, before they become morally one with him by spiritual birth. They may set themselves against him and may oppose him forever. This our Lord intimates, when he tells us that there are natural branches of Christ, which do not "abide in the vine" or "bear fruit," and so are "cast forth," "withered," and "burned" (John 15:4-6).

Ethical Monism, however, since it is Monism, enables us to understand the principle of the Atonement. Though God's holiness binds him to punish sin, the Christ who has joined himself to the sinner must share the sinner's punishment. He who is the life of humanity must take upon his own heart the burden of shame and penalty that belongs to his members. Tie the cord about your finger; not only the finger suffers pain, but also the heart; the life of the whole system rouses itself to put away the evil, to untie the cord, to free the diseased and suffering member. Humanity is bound to Christ, as the finger to the body. Since human nature is one of the "all things" that "consist" or hold together in Christ (Col 1:17), and man's sin is a self-perversion of a part of Christ's own body, the whole must be injured by the self-inflicted injury of the part, and "it must needs be that Christ should suffer" (Acts 17:3). Simon, Redemption of Man, 321—"If the Logos is the Mediator of the divine immanence in creation, especially in man; if men are differentiations of the effluent divine energy; and if the Logos is the immanent controlling principle of all differentiation—i. e., the principle of all form—must not the self-perversion of these human differentiations react on him who is their constitutive principle?" A more full explanation of the relations of Ethical Monism to other doctrines must be reserved to our separate treatment of the Trinity, Creation, Sin, Atonement, Regeneration. Portions of the subject are treated by Upton, Hibbert Lectures; Le Conte, in Royce's Conception of God, 43-50; Bowne, Theory of Thought and Knowledge, 297-301, 311-317, and Immanence of God, 5-32, 116-153; Ladd, Philos. of Knowledge, 574-590, and Theory of Reality, 525-529; Edward Caird, Evolution of Religion, 2:48; Ward, Naturalism and Agnosticism, 2:258-283; Göschel, quoted in Dorner, Hist. Doct. Person of Christ, 5:170. An attempt has been made to treat the whole subject by A. H. Strong, Christ in Creation and Ethical Monism, 1-86, 141-162, 166-180, 186-208.

PART III - THE SCRIPTURES A REVELATION FROM GOD

Chapter I - Preliminary Considerations

I. Reasons a priori for expecting a Revelation from God

1. Needs of man's nature. Man's intellectual and moral nature requires, in order to preserve it from constant deterioration, and to ensure its moral growth and progress, an authoritative and helpful revelation of religious truth, of a higher and completer sort than any to which, in its present state of sin, it can attain by the use of its unaided powers. The proof of this proposition is partly psychological, and partly historical.

A. Psychological proof.—(a) Neither reason nor intuition throws light upon certain questions whose solution is of the utmost importance to us; for example, Trinity, atonement, pardon, method of worship, personal existence after death. (b) Even the truth to which we arrive by our natural powers needs divine confirmation and authority when it addresses minds and wills perverted by sin. (c) To break this power of sin, and to furnish encouragement to moral effort, we need a special revelation of the merciful and helpful aspect of the divine nature.

(a) Bremen Lectures, 72, 73; Plato, Second Alcibiades, 22, 23; Phædo, 85—λόγου θείου τινός. Iamblicus, περὶ τοῦ Πυθαγορικοῦ βίου, chap. 28. Æschylus, in his Agamemnon, shows how completely reason and intuition failed to supply the knowledge of God which man needs: "Renown is loud," he says, "and not to lose one's senses is God's greatest gift.... The being praised outrageously Is grave; for at the eyes of such a one Is launched, from Zeus, the thunder-stone. Therefore do I decide For so much and no more prosperity Than of his envy passes unespied." Though the gods might have favorites, they did not love men as men, but rather, envied and hated them. William James, Is Life Worth Living? in Internat. Jour. Ethics, Oct. 1895:10—"All we know of good and beauty proceeds from nature, but none the less all we know of evil.... To such a harlot we owe no moral allegiance.... If there be a divine Spirit of the universe, nature, such as we know her, cannot possibly be its ultimate word to man. Either there is no Spirit revealed in nature, or else it is inadequately revealed there; and, as all the higher religions have assumed, what we call visible nature, or this world, must be but a veil and surface-show whose full meaning resides in a supplementary unseen or other world."

(b) Versus Socrates: Men will do right, if they only know the right. Pfleiderer, Philos. Relig., 1:219—"In opposition to the opinion of Socrates that badness rests upon ignorance, Aristotle already called the fact to mind that the doing of the good is not always combined with the knowing of it, seeing that it depends also on the passions. If badness consisted only in the want of knowledge, then those who are theoretically most cultivated must also be morally the best, which no one will venture to assert." W. S. Lilly, On Shibboleths: "Ignorance is often held to be the root of all evil. But mere knowledge cannot transform character. It cannot minister to a mind diseased. It cannot convert the will from bad to good. It may turn crime into different channels, and render it less easy to detect. It does not change man's natural propensities or his disposition to gratify them at the expense of others. Knowledge makes the good man more powerful for good, the bad man more powerful for evil. And that is all it can do." Gore, Incarnation, 174—"We must not depreciate the method of argument, for Jesus and Paul occasionally used it in a Socratic fashion, but we must recognize that it is not the basis of the Christian system nor the primary method of Christianity." Martineau, in Nineteenth Century, 1:331, 531, and Types, 1:112— "Plato dissolved the idea of the right into that of the good, and this again was indistinguishably mingled with that of the true and the beautiful." See also Flint, Theism, 305.

(c) Versus Thomas Paine: "Natural religion teaches us, without the possibility of being mistaken, all that is necessary or proper to be known." Plato, Laws, 9:854, c, for substance: "Be good; but, if you cannot, then kill yourself." Farrar, Darkness and Dawn, 75—"Plato says that man will never know God until God has revealed himself in the guise of suffering man, and that, when all is on the verge of destruction, God sees the distress of the universe, and, placing himself at the rudder, restores it to order." Prometheus, the type of humanity, can never be delivered "until some god descends for him into the black depths of Tartarus." Seneca in like manner teaches that man cannot save himself. He says:

"Do you wonder that men go to the gods? God comes to men, yes, into men." We are sinful, and God's thoughts are not as our thoughts, nor his ways as our ways. Therefore he must make known his thoughts to us, teach us what we are, what true love is, and what will please him. Shaler, Interpretation of Nature, 227—"The inculcation of moral truths can be successfully effected only in the personal way; ... it demands the influence of personality; ... the weight of the impression depends upon the voice and the eye of a teacher." In other words, we need not only the exercise of authority, but also the manifestation of love.

B. Historical proof.—(a) The knowledge of moral and religious truth possessed by nations and ages in which special revelation is unknown is grossly and increasingly imperfect. (b) Man's actual condition in ante-Christian times, and in modern heathen lands, is that of extreme moral depravity. (c) With this depravity is found a general conviction of helplessness, and on the part of some nobler natures, a longing after, and hope of, aid from above.

Pythagoras: "It is not easy to know [duties], except men were taught them by God himself, or by some person who had received them from God, or obtained the knowledge of them through some divine means." Socrates: "Wait with patience, till we know with certainty how we ought to behave ourselves toward God and man." Plato: "We will wait for one, be he a God or an inspired man, to instruct us in our duties and to take away the darkness from our eyes." Disciple of Plato: "Make probability our raft, while we sail through life, unless we could have a more sure and safe conveyance, such as some divine communication would be." Plato thanked God for three things: first, that he was born a rational soul; secondly, that he was born a Greek; and, thirdly, that he lived in the days of Socrates. Yet, with all these advantages, he had only probability for a raft, on which to navigate strange seas of thought far beyond his depth, and he longed for "a more sure word of prophecy" (2 Pet. 1:19). See references and quotations in Peabody, Christianity the Religion of Nature, 35, and in Luthardt, Fundamental Truths, 156-172, 335-338; Farrar, Seekers after God; Garbett, Dogmatic Faith, 187.

2. Presumption of supply. What we know of God, by nature, affords ground for hope that these wants of our intellectual and moral being will be met by a corresponding supply, in the shape of a special divine revelation. We argue this:

(a) From our necessary conviction of God's wisdom. Having made man a spiritual being, for spiritual ends, it may be hoped that he will furnish the means needed to secure these ends. (b) From the actual, though incomplete, revelation already given in nature. Since God has actually undertaken to make himself known to men, we may hope that he will finish the work he has begun. (c) From the general connection of want and supply. The higher our needs, the more intricate and ingenious are, in general, the contrivances for meeting them. We may therefore hope that the highest want will be all the more surely met. (d) From analogies of nature and history. Signs of reparative goodness in nature and of forbearance in providential dealings lead us to hope that, while justice is executed, God may still make known some way of restoration for sinners.

(a) There were two stages in Dr. John Duncan's escape from pantheism: 1. when he came first to believe in the existence of God, and "danced for joy upon the brig o' Dee"; and 2. when, under Malan's influence, he came also to believe that "God meant that we should know him." In the story in the old Village Reader, the mother broke completely down when she found that her son was likely to grow up stupid, but her tears conquered him and made him intelligent. Laura Bridgman was blind, deaf and dumb, and had but small sense of taste or smell. When her mother, after long separation, went to her in Boston, the mother's heart was in distress lest the daughter should not recognize her. When at last, by some peculiar mother's sign, she pierced the veil of insensibility, it was a glad time for both. So God, our Father, tries to reveal himself to our blind, deaf and dumb souls. The agony of the Cross is the sign of God's distress over the insensibility of humanity which sin has caused. If he is the Maker of man's being, he will surely seek to fit it for that communion with himself for which it was designed.

(b) Gore, Incarnation, 52, 53—"Nature is a first volume, in itself incomplete, and demanding a second volume, which is Christ." (c) R. T. Smith, Man's Knowledge of Man and of God, 228—"Mendicants do not ply their calling for years in a desert where there are no givers. Enough of supply has been received to keep the sense of want alive." (d) In the natural arrangements for the healing of bruises in plants and for the mending of broken bones in the animal creation, in the provision of remedial agents for the cure of human diseases, and especially in the delay to inflict punishment upon the transgressor and the space given him for repentance, we have some indications, which, if uncontradicted by other evidence, might lead us to regard the God of nature as a God of forbearance and mercy. Plutarch's treatise "De Sera Numinis Vindicta" is proof that this thought had occurred to the heathen. It may be doubted, indeed, whether a heathen religion could even continue to exist, without embracing in it some element of hope. Yet this very delay in the execution of the divine judgments gave its own occasion for doubting the existence of a God who was both good and just. "Truth forever on the scaffold, Wrong forever on the throne," is a scandal to the divine government which only the sacrifice of Christ can fully remove.

The problem presents itself also in the Old Testament. In Job 21, and in Psalms, 17, 37, 49, 73, there are partial answers; see Job 21:7—"Wherefore do the wicked live, Become old, yea, wax mighty in power?" 24:1—"Why are not judgment times determined by the Almighty? And they that know him, why see they not his days?" The New Testament intimates the existence of a witness to God's goodness among the heathen, while at the same time it declares that the full knowledge of forgiveness and salvation is brought only by Christ. Compare Acts 14:17—"And yet he left not himself without witness, in that he did good, and gave you from heaven rains and fruitful seasons, filling your hearts with food and gladness"; 17:25-27—"he himself giveth to all life, and breath, and all things; and he made of one every nation of men ... that they should seek God, if haply they might feel after him and find him"; Rom. 2:4—"the goodness of God leadeth thee to repentance"; 3:25—"the passing over of the sins done aforetime, in the forbearance of God"; Eph. 3:9—"to make all men see what is the dispensation of the mystery which for ages hath been hid in God"; 2 Tim. 1:10—"our Savior Christ Jesus, who abolished death, and brought life and incorruption to light through the gospel." See Hackett's edition of the treatise of Plutarch, as also Bowen, Metaph. and Ethics, 462-487; Diman, Theistic Argument, 371.

We conclude this section upon the reasons a priori for expecting a revelation from God with the acknowledgment that the facts warrant that degree of expectation which we call hope, rather than that larger degree of expectation which we call assurance; and this, for the reason that, while conscience gives proof that God is a God of holiness, we have not, from the light of nature, equal evidence that God is a God of love. Reason teaches man that, as a sinner, he merits condemnation; but he cannot, from reason alone, know that God will have mercy upon him and provide salvation. His doubts can be removed only by God's own voice, assuring him of "redemption ... the forgiveness of ... trespasses" (Eph. 1:7) and revealing to him the way in which that forgiveness has been rendered possible.

Conscience knows no pardon, and no Savior. Hovey, Manual of Christian Theology, 9, seems to us to go too far when he says: "Even natural affection and conscience afford some clue to the goodness and holiness of God, though much more is needed by one who undertakes the study of Christian theology." We grant that natural affection gives some clue to God's goodness, but we regard conscience as reflecting only God's holiness and his hatred of sin. We agree with Alexander McLaren: "Does God's love need to be proved? Yes, as all paganism shows. Gods vicious, gods careless, gods cruel, gods beautiful, there are in abundance; but where is there a god who loves?"

II. Marks of the Revelation man may expect

1. As to its substance. We may expect this later revelation not to contradict, but to confirm and enlarge, the knowledge of God which we derive from nature, while it remedies the defects of natural religion and throws light upon its problems.

Isaiah's appeal is to God's previous communications of truth: Is. 8:20—"To the law and to the testimony! if they speak not according to this word, surely there is no morning for them." And Malachi follows the example of Isaiah; Mal. 4:4—"Remember ye the law of Moses my servant." Our Lord himself based his claims upon the former utterances of God: Luke 24:27—"beginning from Moses and from all the prophets, he interpreted to them in all the scriptures the things concerning himself."

2. As to its method. We may expect it to follow God's methods of procedure in other communications of truth.

Bishop Butler (Analogy, part ii, chap. iii) has denied that there is any possibility of judging a priori how a divine revelation will be given. "We are in no sort judges beforehand," he says, "by what methods, or in what proportion, it were to be expected that this supernatural light and instruction would be afforded us." But Bishop Butler somewhat later in his great work (part ii, chap. iv) shows that God's progressive plan in revelation has its analogy in the slow, successive steps by which God accomplishes his ends in nature. We maintain that the revelation in nature affords certain presumptions with regard to the revelation of grace, such for example as those mentioned below.

Leslie Stephen, in Nineteenth Century, Feb. 1891:180—"Butler answered the argument of the deists, that the God of Christianity was unjust, by arguing that the God of nature was equally unjust. James Mill, admitting the analogy, refused to believe in either God. Dr. Martineau has said, for similar reasons, that Butler 'wrote one of the most terrible persuasives to atheism ever produced.' So J. H. Newman's 'kill or cure' argument is essentially that God has either revealed nothing, or has made revelations in some other places than in the Bible. His argument, like Butler's, may be as good a persuasive to scepticism as to belief." To this indictment by Leslie Stephen we reply that it has cogency only so long as we ignore the fact of human sin. Granting this fact, our world becomes a world of discipline, probation and redemption, and both the God of nature and the God of Christianity are cleared from all suspicion of injustice. The analogy between God's methods in the Christian system and his methods in nature becomes an argument in favor of the former.

(a) That of continuous historical development,—that it will be given in germ to early ages, and will be more fully unfolded as the race is prepared to receive it.

Instances of continuous development in God's impartations are found in geological history; in the growth of the sciences; in the progressive education of the individual and of the race. No other religion but Christianity shows "a steady historical progress of the vision of one infinite Character unfolding itself to man through a period of many centuries." See sermon by Dr. Temple, on the Education of the World, in Essays and Reviews; Rogers, Superhuman Origin of the Bible, 374-384; Walker, Philosophy of the Plan of Salvation. On the gradualness of revelation, see Fisher, Nature and Method of Revelation, 46-86; Arthur H. Hallam, in John Brown's Rab and his Friends, 282—"Revelation is a gradual approximation of the infinite Being to the ways and thoughts of finite humanity." A little fire can kindle a city or a world; but ten times the heat of that little fire, if widely diffused, would not kindle anything.

(b) That of original delivery to a single nation, and to single persons in that nation, that it may through them be communicated to mankind.

Each nation represents an idea. As the Greek had a genius for liberty and beauty, and the Roman a genius for organization and law, so the Hebrew nation had a "genius for religion" (Renan); this last, however, would have been useless without special divine aid and superintendence, as witness other productions of this same Semitic race, such as Bel and the Dragon, in the Old Testament Apocrypha; the gospels of the Apocryphal New Testament; and later still, the Talmud and the Koran.

The O. T. Apocrypha relates that, when Daniel was thrown a second time into the lions' den, an angel seized Habakkuk in Judea by the hair of his head and carried him with a bowl of pottage to give to Daniel for his dinner. There were seven lions, and Daniel was among them seven days and nights. Tobias starts from his father's house to secure his inheritance, and his little dog goes with him. On the banks of the great river a great fish threatens to devour him, but he captures and despoils the fish. He finally returns successful to his father's house, and his little dog goes in with him. In the Apocryphal Gospels, Jesus carries water in his mantle when his pitcher is broken; makes clay birds on the Sabbath, and, when rebuked, causes them to fly; strikes a youthful companion with death, and then curses his accusers with blindness; mocks his teachers, and resents control. Later Moslem legends declare that Mohammed caused darkness at noon; whereupon the moon flew to him, went seven times around the Kaāba, bowed, entered his right sleeve, split into two halves after slipping out at the left, and the two halves, after retiring to the extreme east and west, were reunited. These products of the Semitic race show that neither the influence of environment nor a native genius for religion furnishes an adequate explanation of our Scriptures. As the flame on Elijah's altar was caused, not by the dead sticks, but by the fire from heaven, so only the inspiration of the Almighty can explain the unique revelation of the Old and New Testaments.

The Hebrews saw God in conscience. For the most genuine expression of their life we "must look beneath the surface, in the soul, where worship and aspiration and prophetic faith come face to face with God" (Genung, Epic of the Inner Life, 28). But the Hebrew religion needed to be supplemented by the sight of God in reason, and in the beauty of the world. The Greeks had the love of knowledge, and the æsthetic sense. Butcher, Aspects of the Greek Genius, 34—"The Phœnicians taught the Greeks how to write, but it was the Greeks who wrote." Aristotle was the beginner of science, and outside the Aryan race none but the Saracens ever felt the scientific impulse. But the Greek made his problem clear by striking all the unknown quantities out of it. Greek thought would never have gained universal currency and permanence if it had not been for Roman jurisprudence and imperialism. England has contributed her constitutional government, and America her manhood suffrage and her religious freedom. So a definite thought of God is incorporated in each nation, and each nation has a message to every other. Acts 17:26—God "made of one every nation of men to dwell on all the face of the earth, having determined their appointed seasons, and the bounds of their habitation"; Rom. 3:12—"What advantage then hath the Jew?... first of all, that they were entrusted with the oracles of God." God's choice of the Hebrew nation, as the repository and communicator of religious truth, is analogous to his choice of other nations, as the repositories and communicators of æsthetic, scientific, governmental truth.

Hegel: "No nation that has played a weighty and active part in the world's history has ever issued from the simple development of a single race along the unmodified lines of blood-relationship. There must be differences, conflicts, a composition of opposed forces." The conscience of the Hebrew, the thought of the Greek, the organization of the Latin, the personal loyalty of the Teuton, must all be united to form a perfect whole. "While the Greek church was orthodox, the Latin church was Catholic; while the Greek treated of the two wills in Christ, the Latin treated of the harmony of our wills with God; while the Latin saved through a corporation, the Teuton saved through personal faith." Brereton, in Educational Review, Nov. 1901:339—"The problem of France is that of the religious orders; that of Germany, the construction of society; that of America, capital and labor." Pfleiderer, Philos. Religion, 1:183, 184—"Great ideas never come from the masses, but from marked individuals. These ideas, when propounded, however, awaken an echo in the masses, which shows that the ideas had been slumbering unconsciously in the souls of others." The hour strikes, and a Newton appears, who interprets God's will in nature. So the hour strikes, and a Moses or a Paul appears, who interprets God's will in morals and religion. The few grains of wheat found in the clasped hand of the Egyptian mummy would have been utterly lost if one grain had been sown in Europe, a second in Asia, a third in Africa, and a fourth in America; all being planted together in a flower-pot, and their product in a garden-bed, and the still later fruit in a farmer's field, there came at last to be a sufficient crop of new Mediterranean wheat to distribute to all the world. So God followed his ordinary method in giving religious truth first to a single nation and to chosen individuals in that nation, that through them it might be given to all mankind. See British Quarterly, Jan. 1874: art.: Inductive Theology.

(c) That of preservation in written and accessible documents, handed down from those to whom the revelation is first communicated.

Alphabets, writing, books, are our chief dependence for the history of the past; all the great religions of the world are book-religions; the Karens expected their teachers in the new religion to bring to them a book. But notice that false religions have scriptures, but not Scripture; their sacred books lack the principle of unity which is furnished by divine inspiration. H. P. Smith, Biblical Scholarship and Inspiration, 68—"Mohammed discovered that the Scriptures of the Jews were the source of their religion. He called them a 'book-people,' and endeavored to construct a similar code for his disciples. In it God is the only speaker; all its contents are made known to the prophet by direct revelation; its Arabic style is perfect; its text is incorruptible; it is absolute authority in law, science and history." The Koran is a grotesque human parody of the Bible; its exaggerated pretensions of divinity, indeed, are the best proof that it is of purely human origin. Scripture, on the other hand, makes no such claims for itself, but points to Christ as the sole and final authority. In this sense we may say with Clarke, Christian Theology, 20—"Christianity is not a book-religion, but a life-religion. The Bible does not give us Christ, but Christ gives us the Bible." Still it is true that for our knowledge of Christ we are almost wholly dependent upon Scripture. In giving his revelation to the world, God has followed his ordinary method of communicating and preserving truth by means of written documents. Recent investigations, however, now render it probable that the Karen expectation of a book was the survival of the teaching of the Nestorian missionaries, who as early as the eighth century penetrated the remotest parts of Asia, and left in the wall of the city of Singwadu in Northwestern China a tablet as a monument of their labors. On book-revelation, see Rogers, Eclipse of Faith, 73-96, 281-304.

3. As to its attestation. We may expect that this revelation will be accompanied by evidence that its author is the same being whom we have previously recognized as God of nature. This evidence must constitute (a) a manifestation of God himself; (b) in the outward as well as the inward world; (c) such as only God's power or knowledge can make; and (d) such as cannot be counterfeited by the evil, or mistaken by the candid, soul. In short, we may expect God to attest by miracles and by prophecy, the divine mission and authority of those to whom he communicates a revelation. Some such outward sign would seem to be necessary, not only to assure the original recipient that the supposed revelation is not a vagary of his own imagination, but also to render the revelation received by a single individual authoritative to all (compare Judges 6:17, 36-40—Gideon asks a sign, for himself; 1 K. 18:36-38—Elijah asks a sign, for others). But in order that our positive proof of a divine revelation may not be embarrassed by the suspicion that the miraculous and prophetic elements in the Scripture history create a presumption against its credibility, it will be desirable to take up at this point the general subject of miracles and prophecy.

III. *Miracles, as attesting a Divine Revelation.*

1. Definition of Miracle

A. Preliminary Definition.—A miracle is an event palpable to the senses, produced for a religious purpose by the immediate agency of God; an event therefore which, though not contravening any law of nature, the laws of nature, if fully known, would not without this agency of God be competent to explain.

This definition corrects several erroneous conceptions of the miracle:—(a) A miracle is not a suspension or violation of natural law; since natural law is in operation at the time of the miracle just as much as before. (b) A miracle is not a sudden product of natural agencies—a product merely foreseen, by him who appears to work it; it is the effect of a will outside of nature. (c) A miracle is not an event without a cause; since it has for its cause a direct volition of God. (d) A miracle is not an irrational or capricious act of God; but an act of wisdom, performed in accordance with the immutable laws of his being, so that in the same circumstances the same course would be again pursued. (e) A miracle is not contrary to experience; since it is not contrary to experience for a new cause to be followed by a new effect. (f) A miracle is not a matter of internal experience, like regeneration or illumination; but is an event palpable to the senses, which may serve as an objective proof to all that the worker of it is divinely commissioned as a religious teacher.

For various definitions of miracles, see Alexander, Christ and Christianity, 302. On the whole subject, see Mozley, Miracles; Christlieb, Mod. Doubt and Christ. Belief, 285-339; Fisher, in Princeton Rev., Nov. 1880, and Jan. 1881; A. H. Strong, Philosophy and Religion, 129-147, and in Baptist Review, April, 1879. The definition given above is intended simply as a definition of the miracles of the Bible, or, in other words, of the events which profess to attest a divine revelation in the Scriptures. The

New Testament designates these events in a two-fold way, viewing them either subjectively, as producing effects upon men, or objectively, as revealing the power and wisdom of God. In the former aspect they are called τέρατα, "wonders," and σημεῖα, "signs," (John 4:48; Acts 2:22). In the latter aspect they are called δυνάμεις, "powers," and ἔργα, "works," (Mat 7:22; John 14:11). See H. B. Smith, Lect. on Apologetics, 90-116, esp. 94—"σημεῖον, sign, marking the purpose or object, the moral end, placing the event in connection with revelation." The Bible Union Version uniformly and properly renders τέρας by "wonder," δυνάμις by "miracle," ἔργον by "work," and σημεῖον by "sign." Goethe, Faust: "Alles Vergängliche ist nur ein Gleichniss: Das Unzulängliche wird hier Ereigniss"— "Everything transitory is but a parable; The unattainable appears as solid fact." So the miracles of the New Testament are acted parables,—Christ opens the eyes of the blind to show that he is the Light of the world, multiplies the loaves to show that he is the Bread of Life, and raises the dead to show that he lifts men up from the death of trespasses and sins. See Broadus on Matthew, 175.

A modification of this definition of the miracle, however, is demanded by a large class of Christian physicists, in the supposed interest of natural law. Such a modification is proposed by Babbage, in the Ninth Bridgewater Treatise, chap. viii. Babbage illustrates the miracle by the action of his calculating machine, which would present to the observer in regular succession the series of units from one to ten million, but which would then make a leap and show, not ten million and one, but a hundred million; Ephraim Peabody illustrates the miracle from the cathedral clock which strikes only once in a hundred years; yet both these results are due simply to the original construction of the respective machines. Bonnet held this view; see Dorner, Glaubenslehre, 1:591, 592; Eng. translation, 2:155, 156; so Matthew Arnold, quoted in Bruce, Miraculous Element in Gospels, 52; see also A. H. Strong, Philosophy and Religion, 129-147. Babbage and Peabody would deny that the miracle is due to the direct and immediate agency of God, and would regard it as belonging to a higher order of nature. God is the author of the miracle only in the sense that he instituted the laws of nature at the beginning and provided that at the appropriate time miracle should be their outcome. In favor of this view it has been claimed that it does not dispense with the divine working, but only puts it further back at the origination of the system, while it still holds God's work to be essential, not only to the upholding of the system, but also to the inspiring of the religious teacher or leader with the knowledge needed to predict the unusual working of the system. The wonder is confined to the prophecy, which may equally attest a divine revelation. See Matheson, in Christianity and Evolution, 1-26.

But it is plain that a miracle of this sort lacks to a large degree the element of "signality" which is needed, if it is to accomplish its purpose. It surrenders the great advantage which miracle, as first defined, possessed over special providence, as an attestation of revelation—the advantage, namely, that while special providence affords some warrant that this revelation comes from God, miracle gives full warrant that it comes from God. Since man may by natural means possess himself of the knowledge of physical laws, the true miracle which God works, and the pretended miracle which only man works, are upon this theory far less easy to distinguish from each other: Cortez, for example, could deceive Montezuma by predicting an eclipse of the sun. Certain typical miracles, like the resurrection of Lazarus, refuse to be classed as events within the realm of nature, in the sense in which the term nature is ordinarily used. Our Lord, moreover, seems clearly to exclude such a theory as this, when he says: "If I by the finger of God cast out demons" (Luke 11:20); Mark 1:41—"I will; be thou made clean." The view of Babbage is inadequate, not only because it fails to recognize any immediate exercise of will in the miracle, but because it regards nature as a mere machine which can operate apart from God—a purely deistic method of conception. On this view, many of the products of mere natural law might be called miracles. The miracle would be only the occasional manifestation of a higher order of nature, like the comet occasionally invading the solar system. William Elder, Ideas from Nature: "The century-plant which we have seen growing from our childhood may not unfold its blossoms until our old age comes upon us, but the sudden wonder is natural notwithstanding." If, however, we interpret nature dynamically, rather than mechanically, and regard it as the regular working of the divine will instead of the automatic operation of a machine, there is much in this view which we may adopt. Miracle may be both natural and supernatural. We may hold, with Babbage, that it has natural antecedents, while at the same time we hold that it is produced by the immediate agency of God. We proceed therefore to an alternative and preferable definition, which in our judgment combines the merits of both that have been mentioned. On miracles as already defined, see Mozley, Miracles, preface, ix-xxvi, 7, 143-166; Bushnell, Nature and Supernatural, 333-336; Smith's and Hastings' Dict. of Bible, art.: Miracles; Abp. Temple, Bampton Lectures for 1884:193-221; Shedd, Dogm. Theology, 1:541, 542.

B. Alternative and Preferable Definition.—A miracle is an event in nature, so extraordinary in itself and so coinciding with the prophecy or command of a religious teacher or leader, as fully to warrant the conviction, on the part of those who witness it, that God has wrought it with the design of certifying that this teacher or leader has been commissioned by him.

This definition has certain marked advantages as compared with the preliminary definition given above:—(a) It recognizes the immanence of God and his immediate agency in nature, instead of assuming an antithesis between the laws of nature and the will of God. (b) It regards the miracle as simply an extraordinary act of that same God who is already present in all natural operations and who in them is revealing his general plan. (c) It holds that natural law, as the method of God's regular activity, in no way precludes unique exertions of his power when these will best secure his purpose in creation. (d) It leaves it possible that all miracles may have their natural explanations and may hereafter be traced to natural causes, while both miracles and their natural causes may be only names for the one and self-same will of God. (e) It reconciles the claims of both science and religion: of science, by permitting any possible or probable physical antecedents of the miracle; of religion, by maintaining that these very antecedents together with the miracle itself are to be interpreted as signs of God's special commission to him under whose teaching or leadership the miracle is wrought.

Augustine, who declares that "Dei voluntas rerum natura est," defines the miracle in De Civitate Dei, 21:8—"Portentum ergo fit non contra naturam, sed contra quam est nota natura." He says also that a birth is more miraculous than a resurrection, because it is more wonderful that something that never was should begin to be, than that something that was and ceased to be should begin again. E. G. Robinson, Christ. Theology, 104—"The natural is God's work. He originated it. There is no separation between the natural and the supernatural. The natural is supernatural. God works in everything. Every end, even though attained by mechanical means, is God's end as truly as if he wrought by miracle." Shaler, Interpretation of Nature, 141, regards miracle as something exceptional, yet under the control of natural law; the latent in nature suddenly manifesting itself; the revolution resulting from the slow accumulation of natural forces. In the Windsor Hotel fire, the heated and charred woodwork suddenly burst into flame. Flame is very different from mere heat, but it may be the result of a regularly rising temperature. Nature may be God's regular action, miracle its unique result. God's regular action may be entirely free, and yet its extraordinary result may be entirely natural. With these qualifications and explanations, we may adopt the statement of Biedermann, Dogmatik, 581-591—"Everything is miracle,—therefore faith sees God everywhere; Nothing is miracle,—therefore science sees God nowhere."

Miracles are never considered by the Scripture writers as infractions of law. Bp. Southampton, Place of Miracles, 18—"The Hebrew historian or prophet regarded miracles as only the emergence into sensible experience of that divine force which was all along, though invisibly, controlling the course of nature." Hastings, Bible Dictionary, 4:117—"The force of a miracle to us, arising from our notion of law, would not be felt by a Hebrew, because he had no notion of natural law." Ps. 77:19, 20—"Thy way was in the sea, And thy paths in the great waters, And thy footsteps were not known"—They knew not, and we know not, by what precise means the deliverance was wrought, or by what precise track the passage through the Red Sea was effected; all we know is that "Thou leddest thy people like a flock, By the hand of Moses and Aaron." J. M. Whiton, Miracles and Supernatural Religion: "The supernatural is in nature itself, at its very heart, at its very life; ... not an outside power interfering with the course of nature, but an inside power vitalizing nature and operating through it." Griffith-Jones, Ascent through Christ, 35—"Miracle, instead of spelling 'monster', as Emerson said, simply bears witness to some otherwise unknown or unrecognized aspect of the divine character." Shedd, Dogm. Theol., 1:533—"To cause the sun to rise and to cause Lazarus to rise, both demand omnipotence; but the manner in which omnipotence works in one instance is unlike the manner in the other."

Miracle is an immediate operation of God; but, since all natural processes are also immediate operations of God, we do not need to deny the use of these natural processes, so far as they will go, in miracle. Such wonders of the Old Testament as the overthrow of Sodom and Gomorrah, the partings of the Red Sea and of the Jordan, the calling down of fire from heaven by Elijah and the destruction of the army of Sennacherib, are none the less works of God when regarded as wrought by the use of natural means. In the New Testament Christ took water to make wine, and took the five loaves to make bread, just as in ten thousand vineyards to-day he is turning the moisture of the earth into the juice of the grape, and in ten thousand fields is turning carbon into corn. The virgin-birth of Christ may be an extreme instance of parthenogenesis, which Professor Loeb of Chicago has just demonstrated to take place in other than the lowest forms of life and which he believes to be possible in all. Christ's resurrection may be an illustration of the power of the normal and perfect human spirit to take to itself a proper body, and so may be the type and prophecy of that great change when we too shall lay down our life and take it again. The scientist may yet find that his disbelief is not only disbelief in Christ, but also disbelief in science. All miracle may have its natural side, though we now are not able to discern it; and, if this were true, the Christian argument would not one whit be weakened, for still miracle would evidence the extraordinary working of the immanent God, and the impartation of his knowledge to the prophet or apostle who was his instrument.

This view of the miracle renders entirely unnecessary and irrational the treatment accorded to the Scripture narratives by some modern theologians. There is a credulity of scepticism, which minimizes the miraculous element in the Bible and treats it as mythical or legendary, in spite of clear evidence that it belongs to the realm of actual history. Pfleiderer, Philos. Relig., 1:295—"Miraculous legends arise in two ways, partly out of the idealizing of the real, and partly out of the realizing of the ideal.... Every occurrence may obtain for the religious judgment the significance of a sign or proof of the world-governing power, wisdom, justice or goodness of God.... Miraculous histories are a poetic realizing of religious ideas." Pfleiderer quotes Goethe's apothegm: "Miracle is faith's dearest child." Foster, Finality of the Christian Religion, 128-138—"We most honor biblical miraculous narratives when we seek to understand them as poesies." Ritschl defines miracles as "those striking natural occurrences with which the experience of God's special help is connected." He leaves doubtful the bodily resurrection of Christ, and many of his school deny it; see Mead, Ritschl's Place in the History of Doctrine, 11. We do not need to interpret Christ's resurrection as a mere appearance of his spirit to the disciples. Gladden, Seven Puzzling Books, 202—"In the hands of perfect and spiritual man, the forces of nature are pliant and tractable as they are not in ours. The resurrection of Christ is only a sign of the superiority of the life of the perfect spirit over external conditions. It may be perfectly in accordance with nature." Myers, Human Personality, 2:288—"I predict that, in consequence of the new evidence, all reasonable men, a century hence, will believe the resurrection of Christ." We may add that Jesus himself intimates that the working of miracles is hereafter to be a common and natural manifestation of the new life which he imparts: John 14:12—"He that believeth on me, the works that I do shall he do also; and greater works than these shall he do, because I go unto the Father."

We append a number of opinions, ancient and modern, with regard to miracles, all tending to show the need of so defining them as not to conflict with the just claims of science. Aristotle: "Nature is not full of episodes, like a bad tragedy." Shakespeare, All's Well that Ends Well, 2:3:1—"They say miracles are past; and we have our philosophical persons to make modern and familiar things supernatural and causeless. Hence it is that we make trifles of terrors, ensconcing ourselves into seeming knowledge, when we should submit ourselves to an unknown fear." Keats, Lamia: "There was an awful rainbow once in heaven; We know her woof, her texture: she is given In the dull catalogue of common things." Hill, Genetic Philosophy, 334—"Biological and psychological science unite in affirming that every event, organic or psychic, is to be explained in the terms of its immediate antecedents, and that it can be so explained. There is therefore no necessity, there is even no room, for interference. If the existence of a Deity depends upon the evidence of intervention and supernatural agency, faith in the divine seems to be destroyed in the scientific mind." Theodore Parker: "No whim in God,—therefore no miracle in nature." Armour, Atonement and Law, 15-33—"The miracle of redemption, like all miracles, is by intervention of adequate power, not by suspension of law. Redemption is not 'the great exception.' It is the fullest revelation and vindication of law." Gore, in Lux Mundi, 320—"Redemption is not natural but supernatural—supernatural, that is, in view of the false nature which man made for himself by excluding God. Otherwise, the work of redemption is only the reconstitution of the nature which God had designed." Abp. Trench: "The world of nature is throughout a witness for the world of spirit, proceeding from the same hand, growing out of the same root, and being constituted for this very end. The characters of nature which everywhere meet the eye are not a common but a sacred writing,—they are the hieroglyphics of God." Pascal: "Nature is the image of grace." President Mark Hopkins: "Christianity and perfect Reason are identical." See Mead, Supernatural Revelation, 97-123; art.: Miracle, by Bernard, in Hastings' Dictionary of the Bible. The modern and improved view of the miracle is perhaps best presented by T. H. Wright, The Finger of God; and by W. N. Rice, Christian Faith in an Age of Science, 336.

2. Possibility of Miracle

An event in nature may be caused by an agent in nature yet above nature. This is evident from the following considerations:

(a) Lower forces and laws in nature are frequently counteracted and transcended by the higher (as mechanical forces and laws by chemical, and chemical by vital), while yet the lower forces and laws are not suspended or annihilated, but are merged in the higher, and made to assist in accomplishing purposes to which they are altogether unequal when left to themselves.

By nature we mean nature in the proper sense—not "everything that is not God," but "everything that is not God or made in the image of God"; see Hopkins, Outline Study of Man, 258, 259. Man's will does not belong to nature, but is above nature. On the transcending of lower forces by higher, see Murphy, Habit and Intelligence, 1:88. James Robertson, Early Religion of Israel, 23—"Is it impossible that there should be unique things in the world? Is it scientific to assert that there are not?" Ladd, Philosophy of Knowledge, 406—"Why does not the projecting part of the coping-stone fall, in obedience to the law of gravitation, from the top of yonder building? Because, as physics declares, the forces of cohesion, acting under quite different laws, thwart and oppose for the time being the law of gravitation.... But now, after a frosty night, the coping-stone actually breaks off and tumbles to the ground; for that unique law which makes water forcibly expand at 32° Fahrenheit has contradicted the laws of cohesion and has restored to the law of gravitation its temporarily suspended rights over this mass of matter." Gore, Incarnation, 48—"Evolution views nature as a progressive order in which there are new departures, fresh levels won, phenomena unknown before. When organic life appeared, the future did not resemble the past. So when man came. Christ is a new nature—the creative Word made flesh. It is to be expected that, as new nature, he will exhibit new phenomena. New vital energy will radiate from him, controlling the material forces. Miracles are the proper accompaniments of his person." We may add that, as Christ is the immanent God, he is present in nature while at the same time he is above nature, and he whose steady will is the essence of all natural law can transcend all past exertions of that will. The infinite One is not a being of endless monotony. William Elder, Ideas from Nature, 156—"God is not bound hopelessly to his process, like Ixion to his wheel."

(b) The human will acts upon its physical organism, and so upon nature, and produces results which nature left to herself never could accomplish, while yet no law of nature is suspended or violated. Gravitation still operates upon the axe, even while man holds it at the surface of the water—for the axe still has weight (cf. 2 K. 6:5-7).

Versus Hume, Philos. Works, 4:130—"A miracle is a violation of the laws of nature." Christian apologists have too often needlessly embarrassed their argument by accepting Hume's definition. The stigma is entirely undeserved. If man can support the axe at the surface of the water while gravitation still acts upon it, God can certainly, at the prophet's word, make the iron to swim, while gravitation still acts upon it. But this last is miracle. See Mansel, Essay on Miracles, in Aids to Faith, 26, 27: After the greatest wave of the season has landed its pebble high up on the beach, I can move the pebble a foot further without altering the force of wind or wave or climate in a distant continent. Fisher, Supernat. Origin of Christianity, 471; Hamilton, Autology, 685-690; Bowen, Metaph. and Ethics, 445; Row, Bampton Lectures on Christian Evidences, 54-74; A. A. Hodge: Pulling out a new stop of the organ does not suspend the working or destroy the harmony of the other stops. The pump does not suspend the law of gravitation, nor does our throwing a ball into the air. If gravitation did not act, the upward velocity of the ball would not diminish and the ball would never return. "Gravitation draws iron down. But the magnet overcomes that attraction and draws the iron up. Yet here is no suspension or violation of law, but rather a harmonious working of two laws, each in its sphere. Death and not life is the order of nature. But men live notwithstanding. Life is supernatural. Only as a force additional to mere nature works against nature does life exist. So spiritual life uses and transcends the laws of nature" (Sunday School Times). Gladden, What Is Left? 60—"Wherever you find thought, choice, love, you find something that is not under the dominion of fixed law. These are the attributes of a free personality." William James: "We need to substitute the personal view of life for the impersonal and mechanical view. Mechanical rationalism is narrowness and partial induction of facts,—it is not science."

(c) In all free causation, there is an acting without means. Man acts upon external nature through his physical organism, but, in moving his physical organism, he acts directly upon matter. In other words, the human will can use means, only because it has the power of acting initially without means.

See Hopkins, on Prayer-gauge, 10, and in Princeton Review, Sept. 1882:188. A. J. Balfour, Foundations of Belief, 311—"Not Divinity alone intervenes in the world of things. Each living soul, in its measure and degree, does the same." Each soul that acts in any way on its surroundings does so on the principle of the miracle. Phillips Brooks, Life, 2:350—"The making of all events miraculous is no more an abolition of miracle than the flooding of the world with sunshine is an extinction of the sun." George Adam Smith, on Is. 33:14—"devouring fire ... everlasting burnings": "If we look at a conflagration through smoked glass, we see buildings collapsing, but we see no fire. So science sees results, but not the power which produces them; sees cause and effect, but does not see God." P. S. Henson: "The current in an electric wire is invisible so long as it circulates uniformly. But cut the wire and insert a piece of carbon between the two broken ends, and at once you have an arc-light that drives away the darkness. So miracle is only the momentary interruption in the operation of uniform laws, which thus gives light to the ages,"—or, let us say rather, the momentary change in the method of their operation whereby the will of God takes a new form of manifestation. Pfleiderer, Grundriss, 100— "Spinoza leugnete ihre metaphysische Möglichkeit, Hume ihre geschichtliche Erkennbarkeit, Kant ihre practische Brauchbarkeit, Schleiermacher ihre religiöse Bedeutsamkeit, Hegel ihre geistige Beweiskraft, Fichte ihre wahre Christlichkeit, und die kritische Theologie ihre wahre Geschichtlichkeit."

(d) What the human will, considered as a supernatural force, and what the chemical and vital forces of nature itself, are demonstrably able to accomplish, cannot be regarded as beyond the power of God, so long as God dwells in and controls the universe. If man's will can act directly upon matter in his own physical organism, God's will can work immediately upon the system which he has created and which he sustains. In other words, if there be a God, and if he be a personal being, miracles are possible. The impossibility of miracles can be maintained only upon principles of atheism or pantheism.

See Westcott, Gospel of the Resurrection, 19; Cox, Miracles, an Argument and a Challenge: "Anthropomorphism is preferable to hylomorphism." Newman Smyth, Old Faiths in a New Light, ch. 1—"A miracle is not a sudden blow struck in the face of nature, but a use of nature, according to its inherent capacities, by higher powers." See also Gloatz, Wunder und Naturgesetz, in Studien und Kritiken, 1886:403-546; Gunsaulus, Transfiguration of Christ, 18, 19, 26; Andover Review, on "Robert

Elsmere," 1888:303; W. E. Gladstone, in Nineteenth Century, 1888:766-788; Dubois, on Science and Miracle, in New Englander, July, 1889:1-32—Three postulates: (1) Every particle attracts every other in the universe; (2) Man's will is free; (3) Every volition is accompanied by corresponding brain-action. Hence every volition of ours causes changes throughout the whole universe; also, in Century Magazine, Dec. 1894:229—Conditions are never twice the same in nature; all things are the results of will, since we know that the least thought of ours shakes the universe; miracle is simply the action of will in unique conditions; the beginning of life, the origin of consciousness, these are miracles, yet they are strictly natural; prayer and the mind that frames it are conditions which the Mind in nature cannot ignore. Cf. Ps. 115:3—"our God is in the heavens: He hath done whatsoever he pleased" = his almighty power and freedom do away with all a priori objections to miracles. If God is not a mere force, but a person, then miracles are possible.

(e) This possibility of miracles becomes doubly sure to those who see in Christ none other than the immanent God manifested to creatures. The Logos or divine Reason who is the principle of all growth and evolution can make God known only by means of successive new impartations of his energy. Since all progress implies increment, and Christ is the only source of life, the whole history of creation is a witness to the possibility of miracle.

See A. H. Strong, Christ in Creation, 163-166—"This conception of evolution is that of Lotze. That great philosopher, whose influence is more potent than any other in present thought, does not regard the universe as a plenum to which nothing can be added in the way of force. He looks upon the universe rather as a plastic organism to which new impulses can be imparted from him of whose thought and will it is an expression. These impulses, once imparted, abide in the organism and are thereafter subject to its law. Though these impulses come from within, they come not from the finite mechanism but from the immanent God. Robert Browning's phrase, 'All's love, but all's law,' must be interpreted as meaning that the very movements of the planets and all the operations of nature are revelations of a personal and present God, but it must not be interpreted as meaning that God runs in a rut, that he is confined to mechanism, that he is incapable of unique and startling manifestations of power.

"The idea that gives to evolution its hold upon thinking minds is the idea of continuity. But absolute continuity is inconsistent with progress. If the future is not simply a reproduction of the past, there must be some new cause of change. In order to progress there must be either a new force, or a new combination of forces, and the new combination of forces can be explained only by some new force that causes the combination. This new force, moreover, must be intelligent force, if the evolution is to be toward the better instead of toward the worse. The continuity must be continuity not of forces but of plan. The forces may increase, nay, they must increase, unless the new is to be a mere repetition of the old. There must be additional energy imparted, the new combination brought about, and all this implies purpose and will. But through all there runs one continuous plan, and upon this plan the rationality of evolution depends.

"A man builds a house. In laying the foundation he uses stone and mortar, but he makes the walls of wood and the roof of tin. In the superstructure he brings into play different laws from those which apply to the foundation. There is continuity, not of material, but of plan. Progress from cellar to garret requires breaks here and there, and the bringing in of new forces; in fact, without the bringing in of these new forces the evolution of the house would be impossible. Now substitute for the foundation and superstructure living things like the chrysalis and the butterfly; imagine the power to work from within and not from without; and you see that true continuity does not exclude but involves new beginnings.

"Evolution, then, depends on increments of force plus continuity of plan. New creations are possible because the immanent God has not exhausted himself. Miracle is possible because God is not far away, but is at hand to do whatever the needs of his moral universe may require. Regeneration and answers to prayer are possible for the very reason that these are the objects for which the universe was built. If we were deists, believing in a distant God and a mechanical universe, evolution and Christianity would be irreconcilable. But since we believe in a dynamical universe, of which the personal and living God is the inner source of energy, evolution is but the basis, foundation and background of Christianity, the silent and regular working of him who, in the fulness of time, utters his voice in Christ and the Cross."

Lotze's own statement of his position may be found in his Microcosmos, 2:479 sq. Professor James Ten Broeke has interpreted him as follows: "He makes the possibility of the miracle depend upon the close and intimate action and reaction between the world and the personal Absolute, in consequence of which the movements of the natural world are carried on only through the Absolute, with the possibility of a variation in the general course of things, according to existing facts and the purpose of the divine Governor."

3. Probability of Miracles

A. We acknowledge that, so long as we confine our attention to nature, there is a presumption against miracles. Experience testifies to the uniformity of natural law. A general uniformity is needful, in order to make possible a rational calculation of the future, and a proper ordering of life.

See Butler, Analogy, part ii, chap. ii; F. W. Farrar, Witness of History to Christ, 3-45; Modern Scepticism, 1:179-227; Chalmers, Christian Revelation, 1:47. G. D. B. Pepper: "Where there is no law, no settled order, there can be no miracle. The miracle presupposes the law, and the importance assigned to miracles is the recognition of the reign of law. But the making and launching of a ship may be governed by law, no less than the sailing of the ship after it is launched. So the introduction of a higher spiritual order into a merely natural order constitutes a new and unique event." Some Christian apologists have erred in affirming that the miracle was antecedently as probable as any other event, whereas only its antecedent improbability gives it value as a proof of revelation. Horace: "Nec deus intersit, nisi dignus vindice nodus Inciderit."

B. But we deny that this uniformity of nature is absolute and universal. (a) It is not a truth of reason that can have no exceptions, like the axiom that a whole is greater than its parts. (b) Experience could not warrant a belief in absolute and universal uniformity, unless experience were identical with absolute and universal knowledge. (c) We know, on the contrary, from geology, that there have been breaks in this uniformity, such as the introduction of vegetable, animal and human life, which cannot be accounted for, except by the manifestation in nature of a supernatural power.

(a) Compare the probability that the sun will rise to-morrow morning with the certainty that two and two make four. Huxley, Lay Sermons, 158, indignantly denies that there is any "must" about the uniformity of nature: "No one is entitled to say a priori that any given so-called miraculous event is impossible." Ward, Naturalism and Agnosticism, 1:84—"There is no evidence for the statement that the mass of the universe is a definite and unchangeable quantity"; 108, 109—"Why so confidently assume that a rigid and monotonous uniformity is the only, or the highest, indication of order, the order of an ever living Spirit, above all? How is it that we depreciate machine-made articles, and prefer those in which the artistic impulse, or the fitness of the individual case, is free to shape and to make what is literally manufactured, hand-made?... Dangerous as teleological arguments in general may be, we may at least safely say the world was not designed to make science easy.... To call the verses of a poet, the politics of a statesman, or the award of a judge mechanical, implies, as Lotze has pointed out, marked disparagement, although it implies, too, precisely those characteristics—exactness and invariability—in which Maxwell would have us see a token of the divine." Surely then we must not insist that divine wisdom must always run in a rut, must ever repeat itself, must never exhibit itself in unique acts like incarnation and resurrection. See Edward Hitchcock, in Bib. Sac., 20:489-561, on "The Law of Nature's Constancy Subordinate to the Higher Law of Change"; Jevons, Principles of Science, 2:430-438; Mozley, Miracles, 26.

(b) S. T. Coleridge, Table Talk, 18 December, 1831—"The light which experience gives us is a lantern on the stern of the ship, which shines only on the waves behind us." Hobbes: "Experience concludeth nothing universally." Brooks, Foundations of Zoölogy, 131—"Evidence can tell us only what has happened, and it can never assure us that the future must be like the past; 132—Proof that all nature is mechanical would not be inconsistent with the belief that everything in nature is immediately sustained by Providence, and that my volition counts for something in determining the course of events." Royce, World and Individual, 2:204—"Uniformity is not absolute. Nature is a vaster realm of life and meaning, of which we men form a part, and of which the final unity is in God's life. The rhythm of the heart-beat has its normal regularity, yet its limited persistence. Nature may be merely the habits of free will. Every region of this universally conscious world may be a centre whence issues new conscious life for communication to all the worlds." Principal Fairbairn: "Nature is Spirit." We prefer to say: "Nature is the manifestation of spirit, the regularities of freedom."

(c) Other breaks in the uniformity of nature are the coming of Christ and the regeneration of a human soul. Harnack, What is Christianity, 18, holds that though there are no interruptions to the working of natural law, natural law is not yet fully known. While there are no miracles, there is plenty of the miraculous. The power of mind over matter is beyond our present conceptions. Bowne, Philosophy of Theism, 210—The effects are no more consequences of the laws than the laws are consequences of the effects = both laws and effects are exercises of divine will. King, Reconstruction in Theology, 56—We must hold, not to the uniformity of law, but to the universality of law; for evolution has successive stages with new laws coming in and becoming dominant that had not before appeared. The new and higher stage is practically a miracle from the point of view of the lower. See British Quarterly Review, Oct. 1881:154; Martineau, Study, 2:200, 203, 209.

C. Since the inworking of the moral law into the constitution and course of nature shows that nature exists, not for itself, but for the contemplation and use of moral beings, it is probable that the God of nature will produce effects aside from those of natural law, whenever there are sufficiently important moral ends to be served thereby.

Beneath the expectation of uniformity is the intuition of final cause; the former may therefore give way to the latter. See Porter, Human Intellect, 592-615—Efficient causes and final causes may conflict, and then the efficient give place to the final. This is miracle. See Hutton, in Nineteenth Century, Aug. 1885, and Channing, Evidences of Revealed Religion, quoted in Shedd, Dogm. Theol., 1:534, 535—"The order of the universe is a means, not an end, and like all other means must give way when the end can be best promoted without it. It is the mark of a weak mind to make an idol of order and method; to cling to established forms of business when they clog instead of advancing it." Balfour, Foundations of Belief, 357—"The stability of the heavens is in the sight of God of less importance than the moral growth of the human spirit." This is proved by the Incarnation. The Christian sees in this little earth the scene of God's greatest revelation. The superiority of the spiritual to the physical helps us to see our true dignity in the creation, to rule our bodies, to overcome our sins. Christ's suffering shows us that God is no indifferent spectator of human pain. He subjects himself to our conditions, or rather in this subjection reveals to us God's own eternal suffering for sin. The atonement enables us to solve the problem of sin.

D. The existence of moral disorder consequent upon the free acts of man's will, therefore, changes the presumption against miracles into a presumption in their favor. The non-appearance of miracles, in this case, would be the greatest of wonders.

Stearns, Evidence of Christian Experience, 331-335—So a man's personal consciousness of sin, and above all his personal experience of regenerating grace, will constitute the best preparation for the study of miracles. "Christianity cannot be proved except to a bad conscience." The dying Vinet said well: "The greatest miracle that I know of is that of my conversion. I was dead, and I live; I was blind, and I see; I was a slave, and I am free; I was an enemy of God, and I love him; prayer, the Bible, the society of Christians, these were to me a source of profound ennui; whilst now it is the pleasures of the world that are wearisome to me, and piety is the source of all my joy. Behold the miracle! And if God has been able to work that one, there are none of which he is not capable."

Yet the physical and the moral are not "sundered as with an axe." Nature is but the lower stage or imperfect form of the revelation of God's truth and holiness and love. It prepares the way for the miracle by suggesting, though more dimly, the same essential characteristics of the divine nature. Ignorance and sin necessitate a larger disclosure. G. S. Lee, The Shadow Christ, 84—"The pillar of cloud was the dim night-lamp that Jehovah kept burning over his infant children, to show them that he was there. They did not know that the night itself was God." Why do we have Christmas presents in Christian homes? Because the parents do not love their children at other times? No; but because the mind becomes sluggish in the presence of merely regular kindness, and special gifts are needed to wake it to gratitude. So our sluggish and unloving minds need special testimonies of the divine mercy. Shall God alone be shut up to dull uniformities of action? Shall the heavenly Father alone be unable to make special communications of love? Why then are not miracles and revivals of religion constant and uniform? Because uniform blessings would be regarded simply as workings of a machine. See Mozley, Miracles, preface, xxiv; Turner, Wish and Will, 291-315; N. W. Taylor, Moral Government, 2:388-423.

E. As belief in the possibility of miracles rests upon our belief in the existence of a personal God, so belief in the probability of miracles rests upon our belief that God is a moral and benevolent being. He who has no God but a God of physical order will regard miracles as an impertinent intrusion upon that order. But he who yields to the testimony of conscience and regards God as a God of holiness, will see that man's unholiness renders God's miraculous interposition most necessary to man and most becoming to God. Our view of miracles will therefore be determined by our belief in a moral, or in a non-moral, God.

Philo, in his Life of Moses, 1:88, speaking of the miracles of the quails and of the water from the rock, says that "all these unexpected and extraordinary things are amusements or playthings of God." He believes that there is room for arbitrariness in the divine procedure. Scripture however represents miracle as an extraordinary, rather than as an arbitrary, act. It is "his work, his strange work ... his act, his strange act" (Is. 28:21). God's ordinary method is that of regular growth and development. Chadwick, Unitarianism, 72—"Nature is economical. If she wants an apple, she develops a leaf; if she wants a brain, she develops a vertebra. We always thought well of backbone; and, if Goethe's was a sound suggestion, we think better of it now."

It is commonly, but very erroneously, taken for granted that miracle requires a greater exercise of power than does God's upholding of the ordinary processes of nature. But to an omnipotent Being our measures of power have no application. The question is not a question of power, but of rationality and love. Miracle implies self-restraint, as well as self-unfolding, on the part of him who works it. It is therefore not God's common method of action; it is adopted only when regular methods will not suffice; it often seems accompanied by a sacrifice of feeling on the part of Christ Mat. 17:17—"O faithless and perverse generation, how long shall I be with you? how long shall I bear with you? bring him hither to me"; Mark 7:34—"looking up to heaven, he sighed, and saith unto him, Ephphatha, that is, Be opened"; cf. Mat. 12:39—"An evil and adulterous generation seeketh after a sign; and there shall no sign be given to it but the sign of Jonah the prophet."

F. From the point of view of ethical monism the probability of miracle becomes even greater. Since God is not merely the intellectual but the moral Reason of the world, the disturbances of the world-order which are due to sin are the matters which most deeply affect him. Christ, the life of the whole system and of humanity as well, must suffer; and, since we have evidence that he is merciful as well as just, it is probable that he will rectify the evil by extraordinary means, when merely ordinary means do not avail.

Like creation and providence, like inspiration and regeneration, miracle is a work in which God limits himself, by a new and peculiar exercise of his power,—limits himself as part of a process of condescending love and as a means of teaching sense-environed and sin-burdened humanity what it would not learn in any other way. Self-limitation, however, is the very perfection and glory of God, for without it no self-sacrificing love would be possible (see page 9, F.). The probability of miracles is therefore argued not only from God's holiness but also from his love. His desire to save men from their sins must be as infinite as his nature. The incarnation, the atonement, the resurrection, when once made known to us, commend themselves, not only as satisfying our human needs, but as worthy of a God of moral perfection.

An argument for the probability of the miracle might be drawn from the concessions of one of its chief modern opponents, Thomas H. Huxley. He tells us in different places that the object of science is "the discovery of the rational order that pervades the universe," which in spite of his professed agnosticism is an unconscious testimony to Reason and Will at the basis of all things. He tells us again that there is no necessity in the uniformities of nature: "When we change 'will' into 'must,' we introduce an idea of necessity which has no warrant in the observed facts, and has no warranty that I can discover elsewhere." He speaks of "the infinite wickedness that has attended the course of human history." Yet he has no hope in man's power to save himself: "I would as soon adore a wilderness of apes," as the Pantheist's rationalized conception of humanity. He grants that Jesus Christ is "the noblest ideal of humanity which mankind has yet worshiped." Why should he not go further and concede that Jesus Christ most truly represents the infinite Reason at the heart of things, and that his purity and love, demonstrated by suffering and death, make it probable that God will use extraordinary means for man's deliverance? It is doubtful whether Huxley recognized his own personal sinfulness as fully as he recognized the sinfulness of humanity in general. If he had done so, he would have been willing to accept miracle upon even a slight preponderance of historical proof. As a matter of fact, he rejected miracle upon the grounds assigned by Hume, which we now proceed to mention.

4. Amount of Testimony necessary to prove a Miracle

The amount of testimony necessary to prove a miracle is no greater than that which is requisite to prove the occurrence of any other unusual but confessedly possible event.

Hume, indeed, argued that a miracle is so contradictory of all human experience that it is more reasonable to believe any amount of testimony false than to believe a miracle to be true.

The original form of the argument can be found in Hume's Philosophical Works, 4:124-150. See also Bib. Sac., Oct. 1867:615. For the most recent and plausible statement of it, see Supernatural Religion, 1:55-94. The argument maintains for substance that things are impossible because improbable. It ridicules the credulity of those who "thrust their fists against the posts, And still insist they see the ghosts," and holds with the German philosopher who declared that he would not believe in a miracle, even if he saw one with his own eyes. Christianity is so miraculous that it takes a miracle to make one believe it.

The argument is fallacious, because

(a) It is chargeable with a petitio principii, in making our own personal experience the measure of all human experience. The same principle would make the proof of any absolutely new fact impossible. Even though God should work a miracle, he could never prove it.

(b) It involves a self-contradiction, since it seeks to overthrow our faith in human testimony by adducing to the contrary the general experience of men, of which we know only from testimony. This general experience, moreover, is merely negative, and cannot neutralize that which is positive, except upon principles which would invalidate all testimony whatever.

(c) It requires belief in a greater wonder than those which it would escape. That multitudes of intelligent and honest men should unite against all their interests unite in deliberate and persistent falsehood, under the circumstances narrated in the New Testament record, involves a change in the sequences of nature far more incredible than the miracles of Christ and his apostles.

(a) John Stuart Mill, Essays on Theism, 216-241, grants that, even if a miracle were wrought, it would be impossible to prove it. In this he only echoes Hume, Miracles, 112—"The ultimate standard by which we determine all disputes that may arise is always derived from experience and observation." But here our own personal experience is made the standard by which to judge all human experience. Whately, Historic Doubts relative to Napoleon Buonaparte, shows that the same rule would require us to deny the existence of the great Frenchman, since Napoleon's conquests were contrary to all experience, and civilized nations had never before been so subdued. The London Times for June 18, 1888, for the first time in at least a hundred years or in 31,200 issues, was misdated, and certain pages read June 17, although June 17 was Sunday. Yet the paper would have been admitted in a court of justice as evidence of a marriage. The real wonder is, not the break in experience, but the continuity without the break.

(b) Lyman Abbott: "If the Old Testament told the story of a naval engagement between the Jewish people and a pagan people, in which all the ships of the pagan people were absolutely destroyed and not a single man was killed among the Jews, all the sceptics would have scorned the narrative. Every one now believes it, except those who live in Spain." There are people who in a similar way refuse to investigate the phenomena of hypnotism, second sight, clairvoyance, and telepathy, declaring a priori that all these things are impossible. Prophecy, in the sense of prediction, is discredited. Upon the same principle wireless telegraphy might be denounced as an imposture. The son of Erin charged with murder defended himself by saying: "Your honor, I can bring fifty people who did not see me do it." Our faith in testimony cannot be due to experience.

(c) On this point, see Chalmers, Christian Revelation, 3:70; Starkie on Evidence, 739; De Quincey, Theological Essays, 1:162-188; Thornton, Old-fashioned Ethics, 143-153; Campbell on Miracles. South's sermon on The Certainty of our Savior's Resurrection had stated and answered this objection long before Hume propounded it.

5. Evidential force of Miracles

(a) Miracles are the natural accompaniments and attestations of new communications from God. The great epochs of miracles—represented by Moses, the prophets, the first and second comings of Christ—are coincident with the great epochs of revelation. Miracles serve to draw attention to new truth, and cease when this truth has gained currency and foothold.

Miracles are not scattered evenly over the whole course of history. Few miracles are recorded during the 2500 years from Adam to Moses. When the N. T. Canon is completed and the internal evidence of Scripture has attained its greatest strength, the external attestations by miracle are either wholly withdrawn or begin to disappear. The spiritual wonders of regeneration remain, and for these the way has been prepared by the long progress from the miracles of power wrought by Moses to the miracles of grace wrought by Christ. Miracles disappeared because newer and higher proofs rendered them unnecessary. Better things than these are now in evidence. Thomas Fuller: "Miracles are the swaddling-clothes of the infant church." John Foster: "Miracles are the great bell of the universe, which draws men to God's sermon." Henry Ward Beecher: "Miracles are the midwives of great moral truths; candles lit before the dawn but put out after the sun has risen." Illingworth, in Lux Mundi, 210—"When we are told that miracles contradict experience, we point to the daily occurrence of the spiritual miracle of regeneration and ask: 'Which is easier to say, Thy sins are forgiven; or to say, Arise and walk?' (Mat. 9:5)."

Miracles and inspiration go together; if the former remain in the church, the latter should remain also; see Marsh, in Bap. Quar. Rev., 1887:225-242. On the cessation of miracles in the early church, see Henderson, Inspiration, 443-490; Bückmann, in Zeitsch. f. luth. Theol. u. Kirche, 1878:216. On miracles in the second century, see Barnard, Literature of the Second Century, 139-180. A. J. Gordon, Ministry of the Spirit, 167—"The apostles were commissioned to speak for Christ till the N. T. Scriptures, his authoritative voice, were completed. In the apostolate we have a provisional inspiration; in the N. T. a stereotyped inspiration; the first being endowed with authority ad interim to forgive sins, and the second having this authority in perpetuo." Dr. Gordon draws an analogy between coal, which is fossil sunlight, and the New Testament, which is fossil inspiration. Sabatier, Philos. Religion, 74—"The Bible is very free from the senseless prodigies of oriental mythology. The great prophets, Isaiah, Amos, Micah, Jeremiah, John the Baptist, work no miracles. Jesus' temptation in the wilderness is a victory of the moral consciousness over the religion of mere physical prodigy." Trench says that miracles cluster about the foundation of the theocratic kingdom under Moses and Joshua, and about the restoration of that kingdom under Elijah and Elisha. In the O. T., miracles confute the gods of Egypt under Moses, the Phœnician Baal under Elijah and Elisha, and the gods of Babylon under Daniel. See Diman, Theistic Argument, 376, and art.: Miracle, by Bernard, in Hastings' Bible Dictionary.

(b) Miracles generally certify to the truth of doctrine, not directly, but indirectly; otherwise a new miracle must needs accompany each new doctrine taught. Miracles primarily and directly certify to the divine commission and authority of a religious teacher, and therefore warrant acceptance of his doctrines and obedience to his commands as the doctrines and commands of God, whether these be communicated at intervals or all together, orally or in written documents.

The exceptions to the above statement are very few, and are found only in cases where the whole commission and authority of Christ, and not some fragmentary doctrine, are involved. Jesus appeals to his miracles as proof of the truth of his teaching in Mat. 9:5, 6—"Which is easier to say, Thy sins are forgiven; or to say, Arise and walk? But that ye may know that the Son of man hath authority on earth to forgive sins (then saith he to the sick of the palsy), Arise, and take up thy bed, and go unto thy house"; 12:28—"if I by the spirit of God cast out demons, then is the kingdom of God come upon you." So Paul in Rom. 1:4, says that Jesus "was declared to be the Son of God with power, ... by the resurrection from the dead." Mair, Christian Evidences, 223, quotes from Natural Religion, 181—"It is said that the theo-philanthropist Larévellière-Lépeaux once confided to Talleyrand his disappointment at the ill success of his attempt to bring into vogue a sort of improved Christianity, a sort of benevolent rationalism which he had invented to meet the wants of a benevolent age. 'His propaganda made no way,' he said. 'What was he to do?' he asked. The ex-bishop Talleyrand politely condoled with him, feared it was a difficult task to found a new religion, more difficult than he had imagined, so difficult that he hardly knew what to advise. 'Still,'—so he went on after a moment's reflection,—'there is one plan which you might at least try: I should recommend you to be crucified, and to rise again the third day.' " See also Murphy, Scientific Bases of Faith, 147-167; Farrar, Life of Christ, 1:168-172.

(c) Miracles, therefore, do not stand alone as evidences. Power alone cannot prove a divine commission. Purity of life and doctrine must go with the miracles to assure us that a religious teacher has come from God. The miracles and the doctrine in this manner mutually support each other, and form parts of one whole. The internal evidence for the Christian system may have greater power over certain minds and over certain ages than the external evidence.

Pascal's aphorism that "doctrines must be judged by miracles, miracles by doctrine," needs to be supplemented by Mozley's statement that "a supernatural fact is the proper proof of a supernatural doctrine, while a supernatural doctrine is not the proper proof of a supernatural fact." E. G. Robinson, Christian Theology, 107, would "defend miracles, but would not buttress up Christianity by them.... No amount of miracles could convince a good man of the divine commission of a known bad man; nor, on the other hand, could any degree of miraculous power suffice to silence the doubts of an evil-minded man.... The miracle is a certification only to him who can perceive its significance.... The Christian church has the resurrection written all over it. Its very existence is proof of the resurrection. Twelve men could never have founded the church, if Christ had remained in the tomb. The living church is the burning bush that is not consumed." Gore, Incarnation, 57—"Jesus did not appear after his resurrection to unbelievers, but to believers only,—which means that this crowning miracle was meant to confirm an existing faith, not to create one where it did not exist."

Christian Union, July 11, 1891—"If the anticipated resurrection of Joseph Smith were to take place, it would add nothing whatever to the authority of the Mormon religion." Schurman, Agnosticism and Religion, 57—"Miracles are merely the bells to call primitive peoples to church. Sweet as the music they once made, modern ears find them jangling and out of tune, and their dissonant notes scare away pious souls who would fain enter the temple of worship." A new definition of miracle which recognizes their possible classification as extraordinary occurrences in nature, yet sees in all nature the working of the living God, may do much to remove this prejudice. Bishop of Southampton, Place of Miracle, 53—"Miracles alone could not produce conviction. The Pharisees ascribed them to Beelzebub. Though Jesus had done so many signs, yet they believed not.... Though miracles were frequently wrought, they were rarely appealed to as evidence of the truth of the gospel. They are simply signs of God's presence in his world. By itself a miracle had no evidential force. The only test for distinguishing divine from Satanic miracles is that of the moral character and purpose of the worker; and therefore miracles depend for all their force upon a previous appreciation of the character and personality of Christ (79). The earliest apologists make no use of miracles. They are of no value except in connection with prophecy. Miracles are the revelation of God, not the proof of revelation." Versus Supernatural Religion, 1:23, and Stearns, in New Englander, Jan. 1882:80. See Mozley, Miracles, 15; Nicoll, Life of Jesus Christ, 133; Mill, Logic, 374-382; H. B. Smith, Int. to Christ. Theology, 167-169; Fisher, in Journ. Christ. Philos., April, 1883:270-283.

(d) Yet the Christian miracles do not lose their value as evidence in the process of ages. The loftier the structure of Christian life and doctrine the greater need that its foundation be secure. The authority of Christ as a teacher of supernatural truth rests upon his miracles, and especially upon the miracle of his resurrection. That one miracle to which the church looks back as the source of her life carries with it irresistibly all the other miracles of the Scripture record; upon it alone we may safely rest the proof that the Scriptures are an authoritative revelation from God.

The miracles of Christ are simple correlates of the Incarnation—proper insignia of his royalty and divinity. By mere external evidence however we can more easily prove the resurrection than the incarnation. In our arguments with sceptics, we should not begin with the ass that spoke to Balaam, or the fish that swallowed Jonah, but with the resurrection of Christ; that conceded, all other Biblical miracles will seem only natural preparations, accompaniments, or consequences. G. F. Wright, in Bib. Sac., 1889:707—"The difficulties created by the miraculous character of Christianity may be compared to those assumed by a builder when great permanence is desired in the structure erected. It is easier to lay the foundation of a temporary structure than of one which is to endure for the ages." Pressensé: "The empty tomb of Christ has been the cradle of the church, and if in this foundation of her faith the church has been mistaken, she must needs lay herself down by the side of the mortal remains, I say, not of a man, but of a religion."

President Schurman believes the resurrection of Christ to be "an obsolete picture of an eternal truth—the fact of a continued life with God." Harnack, Wesen des Christenthums, 102, thinks no consistent union of the gospel accounts of Christ's resurrection can be attained; apparently doubts a literal and bodily rising; yet traces Christianity back to an invincible faith in Christ's conquering of death and his continued life. But why believe the gospels when they speak of the sympathy of Christ, yet disbelieve them when they speak of his miraculous power? We have no right to trust the narrative when it gives us Christ's words "Weep not" to the widow of Nain, (Luke 7:13), and then to distrust it when it tells us of his raising the widow's son. The words "Jesus wept" belong inseparably to a story of which "Lazarus, come forth!" forms a part (John 11:35, 43). It is improbable that the disciples should have believed so stupendous a miracle as Christ's resurrection, if they had not previously seen other manifestations of miraculous power on the part of Christ. Christ himself is the great miracle. The conception of him as the risen and glorified Savior can be explained only by the fact that he did so rise. E. G. Robinson, Christ. Theology, 109—"The Church attests the fact of the resurrection quite as much as the resurrection attests the divine origin of the church. Resurrection, as an evidence, depends on the existence of the church which proclaims it."

(e) The resurrection of our Lord Jesus Christ—by which we mean his coming forth from the sepulchre in body as well as in spirit—is demonstrated by evidence as varied and as conclusive as that which proves to us any single fact of ancient history. Without it Christianity itself is inexplicable, as is shown by the failure of all modern rationalistic theories to account for its rise and progress.

In discussing the evidence of Jesus' resurrection, we are confronted with three main rationalistic theories:

I. The Swoon-theory of Strauss. This holds that Jesus did not really die. The cold and the spices of the sepulchre revived him. We reply that the blood and water, and the testimony of the centurion (Mark 15:45), proved actual death (see Bib. Sac., April, 1889:228; Forrest, Christ of History and Experience, 137-170). The rolling away of the stone, and Jesus' power immediately after, are inconsistent with immediately preceding swoon and suspended animation. How was his life preserved? where did he go? when did he die? His not dying implies deceit on his own part or on that of his disciples.

II. The Spirit-theory of Keim. Jesus really died, but only his spirit appeared. The spirit of Jesus gave the disciples a sign of his continued life, a telegram from heaven. But we reply that the telegram was untrue, for it asserted that his body had risen from the tomb. The tomb was empty and the linen cloths showed an orderly departure. Jesus himself denied that he was a bodiless spirit: "a spirit hath not flesh and bones, as ye see me having" (Luke 24:39). Did "his flesh see corruption" (Acts 2:31)? Was the penitent thief raised from the dead as much as he? Godet, Lectures in Defence of the Christian Faith, lect. i: A dilemma for those who deny the fact of Christ's resurrection: Either his body remained in the hands of his disciples, or it was given up to the Jews. If the disciples retained it, they were impostors: but this is not maintained by modern rationalists. If the Jews retained it, why did they not produce it as conclusive evidence against the disciples?

III. The Vision-theory of Renan. Jesus died, and there was no objective appearance even of his spirit. Mary Magdalene was the victim of subjective hallucination, and her hallucination became contagious. This was natural because the Jews expected that the Messiah would work miracles and would rise from the dead. We reply that the disciples did not expect Jesus' resurrection. The women went to the sepulchre, not to see a risen Redeemer, but to embalm a dead body. Thomas and those at Emmaus had given up all hope. Four hundred years had passed since the days of miracles; John the Baptist "did no miracle" (John 10:41); the Sadducees said "there is no resurrection" (Mat. 22:23). There were thirteen different appearances, to: 1. the Magdalen; 2. other women; 3. Peter; 4. Emmaus; 5. the Twelve; 6. the Twelve after eight days; 7. Galilee seashore; 8. Galilee mountain; 9. Galilee five hundred; 10. James; 11. ascension at Bethany; 12. Stephen; 13. Paul on way to Damascus. Paul describes Christ's appearance to him as something objective, and he implies that Christ's previous appearances to others were objective also: "last of all [these bodily appearances], ... he appeared to me also" (1 Cor. 15:8). Bruce, Apologetics, 396—"Paul's interest and intention in classing the two together was to level his own vision [of Christ] up to the objectivity of the early Christophanies. He believed that the eleven, that Peter in particular, had seen the risen Christ with the eye of the body, and he meant to claim for himself a vision of the same kind." Paul's was a sane, strong nature. Subjective visions do not transform human lives; the resurrection moulded the apostles; they did not create the resurrection (see Gore, Incarnation, 76). These appearances soon ceased, unlike the law of hallucinations, which increase in frequency and intensity. It is impossible to explain the ordinances, the Lord's day, or Christianity itself, if Jesus did not rise from the dead.

The resurrection of our Lord teaches three important lessons: (1) It showed that his work of atonement was completed and was stamped with the divine approval; (2) It showed him to be Lord of all and gave the one sufficient external proof of Christianity; (3) It furnished the ground and pledge of our own resurrection, and thus "brought life and immortality to light" (2 Tim. 1:10). It must be remembered that the resurrection was the one sign upon which Jesus himself staked his claims—"the sign of Jonah" (Luke 11:29); and that the resurrection is proof, not simply of God's power, but of Christ's own power: John 10:18—"I have power to lay it down, and I have power to take it again"; 2:19—"Destroy this temple, and in three days I will raise it up".... 21—"he spake of the temple of his body." See Alexander, Christ and Christianity, 9, 158-224, 302; Mill, Theism, 216; Auberlen, Div. Revelation, 56; Boston Lectures, 203-239; Christlieb, Modern Doubt and Christian Belief, 448-503; Row, Bampton Lectures, 1887:358-423; Hutton, Essays, 1:119; Schaff, in Princeton Rev., May, 1880; 411-419; Fisher, Christian Evidences, 41-46, 82-85; West, in Defence and Conf. of Faith, 80-129; also special works on the Resurrection of our Lord, by Milligan, Morrison, Kennedy, J. Baldwin Brown.

6. Counterfeit Miracles

Since only an act directly wrought by God can properly be called a miracle, it follows that surprising events brought about by evil spirits or by men, through the use of natural agencies beyond our knowledge, are not entitled to this appellation. The Scriptures recognize the existence of such, but denominate them "lying wonders" (2 Thess. 2:9).

These counterfeit miracles in various ages argue that the belief in miracles is natural to the race, and that somewhere there must exist the true. They serve to show that not all supernatural occurrences are divine, and to impress upon us the necessity of careful examination before we accept them as divine.

False miracles may commonly be distinguished from the true by (a) their accompaniments of immoral conduct or of doctrine contradictory to truth already revealed—as in modern spiritualism; (b) their internal characteristics of inanity and extravagance—as in the liquefaction of the blood of St. Januarius, or the miracles of the Apocryphal New Testament; (c) the insufficiency of the object which they are designed to further—as in the case of Apollonius of Tyana, or of the miracles said to accompany the publication of the doctrines of the immaculate conception and of the papal infallibility; (d) their lack of substantiating evidence—as in mediæval miracles, so seldom attested by contemporary and disinterested witnesses; (e) their denial or undervaluing of God's previous revelation of himself in nature—as shown by the neglect of ordinary means, in the cases of Faith-cure and of so-called Christian Science.

Only what is valuable is counterfeited. False miracles presuppose the true. Fisher, Nature and Method of Revelation, 283—"The miracles of Jesus originated faith in him, while mediæval miracles follow established faith. The testimony of the apostles was given in the face of incredulous Sadducees. They were ridiculed and maltreated on account of it. It was no time for devout dreams and the invention of romances." The blood of St. Januarius at Naples is said to be contained in a vial, one side of which is of thick glass, while the other side is of thin. A similar miracle was wrought at Hales in Gloucestershire. St. Alban, the first martyr of Britain, after his head is cut off, carries it about in his hand. In Ireland the place is shown where St. Patrick in the fifth century drove all the toads and snakes over a precipice into the nether regions. The legend however did not become current until some hundreds of years after the saint's bones had crumbled to dust at Saul, near Downpatrick (see Hemphill, Literature of the Second Century, 180-182). Compare the story of the book of Tobit (6-8), which relates the expulsion of a demon by smoke from the burning heart and liver of a fish caught in the Tigris, and the story of the Apocryphal New Testament (I, Infancy), which tells of the expulsion of Satan in the form of a mad dog from Judas by the child Jesus. On counterfeit miracles in general, see Mozley, Miracles, 15, 161; F. W. Farrar, Witness of History to Christ, 72; A. S. Farrar, Science and Theology, 208; Tholuck, Vermischte Schriften, 1:27; Hodge, Syst. Theol., 1:630; Presb. Rev., 1881:687-719.

Some modern writers have maintained that the gift of miracles still remains in the church. Bengel: "The reason why many miracles are not now wrought is not so much because faith is established, as because unbelief reigns." Christlieb: "It is the want of faith in our age which is the greatest hindrance to the stronger and more marked appearance of that miraculous power which is working here and there in quiet concealment. Unbelief is the final and most important reason for the retrogression of miracles." Edward Irving, Works, 5:464—"Sickness is sin apparent in the body, the presentiment of death, the forerunner of corruption. Now, as Christ came to destroy death, and will yet redeem the body from the bondage of corruption, if the church is to have a first fruits or earnest of this power, it must be by receiving power over diseases that are the first fruits and earnest of death." Dr. A. J. Gordon, in his Ministry of Healing, held to this view. See also Boys, Proofs of the Miraculous in the Experience of the Church; Bushnell, Nature and the Supernatural, 446-492; Review of Gordon, by Vincent, in Presb. Rev., 1883:473-502; Review of Vincent, in Presb. Rev., 1884:49-79.

In reply to the advocates of faith-cure in general, we would grant that nature is plastic in God's hand; that he can work miracle when and where it pleases him; and that he has given promises which, with certain Scriptural and rational limitations, encourage believing prayer for healing in cases of sickness. But we incline to the belief that in these later ages God answers such prayer, not by miracle, but by special providence, and by gifts of courage, faith and will, thus acting by his Spirit directly upon the soul and only indirectly upon the body. The laws of nature are generic volitions of God, and to ignore them and disuse means is presumption and disrespect to God himself. The Scripture promise to faith is always expressly or impliedly conditioned upon our use of means: we are to work out our own salvation, for the very reason that it is God who works in us; it is vain for the drowning man to pray, so long as he refuses to lay hold of the rope that is thrown to him. Medicines and physicians are the rope thrown to us by God; we cannot expect miraculous help, while we neglect the help God has already given us; to refuse this help is practically to deny Christ's revelation in nature. Why not live without eating, as well as recover from sickness without medicine? Faith-feeding is quite as rational as faith-healing. To except cases of disease from this general rule as to the use of means has no warrant either in reason or in Scripture. The atonement has purchased complete salvation, and some day salvation shall be ours. But death and depravity still remain, not as penalty, but as chastisement. So disease remains also. Hospitals for Incurables, and the deaths even of advocates of faith-cure, show that they too are compelled to recognize some limit to the application of the New Testament promise.

In view of the preceding discussion we must regard the so-called Christian Science as neither Christian nor scientific. Mrs. Mary Baker G. Eddy denies the authority of all that part of revelation which God has made to man in nature, and holds that the laws of nature may be disregarded with impunity by those who have proper faith; see G. F. Wright, in Bib. Sac., April, 1899:375. Bishop Lawrence of Massachusetts: "One of the errors of Christian Science is its neglect of accumulated knowledge, of the fund of information stored up for these Christian centuries. That knowledge is just as much God's gift as is the knowledge obtained from direct revelation. In rejecting accumulated knowledge and professional skill, Christian Science rejects the gift of God." Most of the professed cures of Christian Science are explicable by the influence of the mind upon the body, through hypnosis or suggestion; (see A. A. Bennett, in Watchman, Feb. 13, 1903). Mental disturbance may make the mother's milk a poison to the child; mental excitement is a common cause of indigestion; mental depression induces bowel disorders; depressed mental and moral conditions render a person more susceptible to grippe, pneumonia, typhoid fever. Reading the account of an accident in which the body is torn or maimed, we ourselves feel pain in the same spot; when the child's hand is crushed, the mother's hand, though at a distance, becomes swollen; the mediæval stigmata probably resulted from continuous brooding upon the sufferings of Christ (see Carpenter, Mental Physiology, 676-690).

But mental states may help as well as harm the body. Mental expectancy facilitates cure in cases of sickness. The physician helps the patient by inspiring hope and courage. Imagination works wonders, especially in the case of nervous disorders. The diseases said to be cured by Christian Science are commonly of this sort. In every age fakirs, mesmerists, and quacks have availed themselves of these underlying mental forces. By inducing expectancy, imparting courage, rousing the paralyzed will, they have indirectly caused bodily changes which have been mistaken for miracle. Tacitus tells us of the healing of a blind man by the Emperor Vespasian. Undoubted cures have been wrought by the royal touch in England. Since such wonders have been performed by Indian medicine-men, we cannot regard them as having any specific Christian character, and when, as in the present case, we find them used to aid in the spread of false doctrine with regard to sin, Christ, atonement, and the church, we must class them with the "lying wonders" of which we are warned in 2 Thess. 2:9. See Harris, Philosophical Basis of Theism, 381-386; Buckley, Faith-Healing, and in Century Magazine, June, 1886:221-236; Bruce, Miraculous Element in Gospels, lecture 8; Andover Review, 1887:249-264.

IV. Prophecy as Attesting a Divine Revelation

We here consider prophecy in its narrow sense of mere prediction, reserving to a subsequent chapter the consideration of prophecy as interpretation of the divine will in general.

1. Definition. Prophecy is the foretelling of future events by virtue of direct communication from God—a foretelling, therefore, which, though not contravening any laws of the human mind, those laws, if fully known, would not, without this agency of God, be sufficient to explain.

In discussing the subject of prophecy, we are met at the outset by the contention that there is not, and never has been, any real foretelling of future events beyond that which is possible to natural prescience. This is the view of Kuenen, Prophets and Prophecy in Israel. Pfleiderer, Philos. Relig., 2:42, denies any direct prediction. Prophecy in Israel, he intimates, was simply the consciousness of God's righteousness, proclaiming its ideals of the future, and declaring that the will of God is the moral ideal of the good and the law of the world's history, so that the fates of nations are conditioned by their bearing toward this moral purpose of God: "The fundamental error of the vulgar apologetics is that it confounds prophecy with heathen soothsaying—national salvation without character." W. Robertson Smith, in Encyc. Britannica, 19:821, tells us that "detailed prediction occupies a very secondary place in the writings of the prophets; or rather indeed what seem to be predictions in detail are usually only free poetical illustrations of historical principles, which neither received nor demanded exact fulfilment."

As in the case of miracles, our faith in an immanent God, who is none other than the Logos or larger Christ, gives us a point of view from which we may reconcile the contentions of the naturalists and supernaturalists. Prophecy is an immediate act of God; but, since all natural genius is also due to God's energizing, we do not need to deny the employment of man's natural gifts in prophecy. The instances of telepathy, presentiment, and second sight which the Society for Psychical Research has demonstrated to be facts show that prediction, in the history of divine revelation, may be only an intensification, under the extraordinary impulse of the divine Spirit, of a power that is in some degree latent in all men. The author of every great work of creative imagination knows that a higher power than his own has possessed him. In all human reason there is a natural activity of the divine Reason or Logos, and he is "the light which lighteth every man" (John 1:9). So there is a natural activity of the Holy Spirit, and he who completes the circle of the divine consciousness completes also the circle of human consciousness, gives self-hood to every soul, makes available to man the natural as well as the spiritual gifts of Christ; cf. John 16:14—"he shall take of mine, and shall declare it unto you." The same Spirit who in the beginning "brooded over the face of the waters" (Gen. 1:2) also broods over humanity, and it is he who, according to Christ's promise, was to "declare unto you the things that are to come" (John 16:13). The gift of prophecy may have its natural side, like the gift of miracles, yet may be finally explicable only as the result of an extraordinary working of that Spirit of Christ who to some degree manifests himself in the reason and conscience of every man; cf. 1 Pet 1:11—"searching what time or what manner of time the Spirit of Christ which was in them did point unto, when it testified beforehand the sufferings of Christ, and the glories that should follow them." See Myers, Human Personality, 2:262-292.

A. B. Davidson, in his article on Prophecy and Prophets, in Hastings' Bible Dictionary, 4:120, 121, gives little weight to this view that prophecy is based on a natural power of the human mind: "The arguments by which Giesebrecht, Berufsgabung, 13 ff., supports the theory of a 'faculty of presentiment' have little cogency. This faculty is supposed to reveal itself particularly on the approach of death (Gen. 28 and 49). The contemporaries of most great religious personages have attributed to them a prophetic gift. The answer of John Knox to those who credited him with such a gift is worth reading: 'My assurances are not marvels of Merlin, nor yet the dark sentences of profane prophecy. But first, the plain truth of God's word; second, the invincible justice of the everlasting God; and third, the ordinary course of his punishments and plagues from the beginning, are my assurances and grounds.' " While Davidson grants the fulfilment of certain specific predictions of Scripture, to be hereafter mentioned, he holds that "such presentiments as we can observe to be authentic are chiefly products of the conscience or moral reason. True prophecy is based on moral grounds. Everywhere the menacing future is connected with the evil past by 'therefore' (Micah 3:12; Is. 5:13; Amos 1:2)." We hold with Davidson to the moral element in prophecy, but we also recognize a power in normal humanity which he would minimize or deny. We claim that the human mind even in its ordinary and secular working gives occasional signs of transcending the limitations of the present. Believing in the continual activity of the divine Reason in the reason of man, we have no need to doubt the possibility of an extraordinary insight into the future, and such insight is needed at the great epochs of religious history. Expositor's Gk. Test., 2:34—"Savonarola foretold as early as 1496 the capture of Rome, which happened in 1527, and he did this not only in general terms but in detail; his words were realized to the letter when the sacred churches of St. Peter and St. Paul became, as the prophet foretold, stables for the conquerors' horses." On the general subject, see Payne-Smith, Prophecy a Preparation for Christ; Alexander, Christ and Christianity; Farrar, Science and Theology, 106; Newton on Prophecy; Fairbairn on Prophecy.

2. Relation of Prophecy to Miracles. Miracles are attestations of revelation proceeding from divine power; prophecy is an attestation of revelation proceeding from divine knowledge. Only God can know the contingencies of the future. The possibility and probability of prophecy may be argued upon the same grounds upon which we argue the possibility and probability of miracles. As an evidence of divine revelation, however, prophecy possesses two advantages over miracles, namely: (a) The proof, in the case of prophecy, is not derived from ancient testimony, but is under our eyes. (b) The evidence of miracles cannot become stronger, whereas every new fulfilment adds to the argument from prophecy.

3. Requirements in Prophecy, considered as an Evidence of Revelation. (a) The utterance must be distant from the event. (b) Nothing must exist to suggest the event to merely natural prescience. (c) The utterance must be free from ambiguity. (d) Yet it must not be so precise as to secure its own fulfilment. (e) It must be followed in due time by the event predicted.

Hume: "All prophecies are real miracles, and only as such can be admitted as proof of any revelation." See Wardlaw, Syst. Theol., 1:347. (a) Hundreds of years intervened between certain of the O. T. predictions and their fulfilment. (b) Stanley instances the natural sagacity of Burke, which enabled him to predict the French Revolution. But Burke also predicted in 1793 that France would be partitioned like Poland among a confederacy of hostile powers. Canning predicted that South American colonies would grow up as the United States had grown. D'Israeli predicted that our Southern Confederacy would become an independent nation. Ingersoll predicted that within ten years there would be two theatres for one church. (c) Illustrate ambiguous prophecies by the Delphic oracle to Crœsus: "Crossing the river, thou destroyest a great nation"—whether his own or his enemy's the oracle left undetermined. "Ibis et redibis nunquam peribis in bello." (d) Strauss held that O. T. prophecy itself determined either the events or the narratives of the gospels. See Greg, Creed of Christendom, chap. 4. (e) Cardan, the Italian mathematician, predicted the day and hour of his own death, and committed suicide at the proper time to prove the prediction true. Jehovah makes the fulfilment of his predictions the proof of his deity in the controversy with false gods: Is. 41:23—"Declare the things that are to come hereafter, that we may know that ye are gods"; 42:9—"Behold, the former things are come to pass and new things do I declare: before they spring forth I tell you of them."

4. General Features of Prophecy in the Scriptures. (a) Its large amount—occupying a great portion of the Bible, and extending over many hundred years. (b) Its ethical and religious nature—the events of the future being regarded as outgrowths and results of men's present attitude toward God. (c) Its unity in diversity—finding its central point in Christ the true servant of God and deliverer of his people. (d) Its actual fulfilment as regards many of its predictions—while seeming non-fulfilments are explicable from its figurative and conditional nature.

A. B. Davidson, in Hastings' Bible Dictionary, 4:125, has suggested reasons for the apparent non-fulfilment of certain predictions. Prophecy is poetical and figurative; its details are not to be pressed; they are only drapery, needed for the expression of the idea. In Isa. 13:16—"Their infants shall be dashed in pieces ... and their wives ravished"—the prophet gives an ideal picture of the sack of a city; these things did not actually happen, but Cyrus entered Babylon "in peace." Yet the essential truth remained that the city fell into the enemy's hands. The prediction of Ezekiel with regard to Tyre, Ez. 26:7-14, is recognized in Ez. 29:17-20 as having been fulfilled not in its details but in its essence—the actual event having been the breaking of the power of Tyre by Nebuchadnezzar. Is. 17:1—"Behold, Damascus is taken away from being a city, and it shall be a ruinous heap"—must be interpreted as predicting the blotting out of its dominion, since Damascus has probably never ceased to be a city. The conditional nature of prophecy explains other seeming non-fulfilments. Predictions were often threats, which might be revoked upon repentance. Jer. 26:13—"amend your ways ... and the Lord will repent him of the evil which he hath pronounced against you." Jonah 3:4—"Yet forty days, and Nineveh shall be overthrown ..." 10—God saw their works, that they turned from their evil way; and God repented of the evil, which he said he would do unto them; and he did it not; cf. Jer. 18:8; 26:19.

Instances of actual fulfilment of prophecy are found, according to Davidson, in Samuel's prediction of some things that would happen to Saul, which the history declares did happen (1 Sam. 1 and 10). Jeremiah predicted the death of Hananiah within the year, which took place (Jer. 28). Micaiah predicted the defeat and death of Ahab at Ramoth-Gilead (1 Kings 22). Isaiah predicted the failure of the northern coalition to subdue Jerusalem (Is. 7); the overthrow in two or three years of Damascus and Northern Israel before the Assyrians (Is. 8 and 17); the failure of Sennacherib to capture Jerusalem, and the melting away of his army (Is. 37:34-37). "And in general, apart from details, the main predictions of the prophets regarding Israel and the nations were verified in history, for example, Amos 1 and 2. The chief predictions of the prophets relate to the imminent downfall of the kingdoms of Israel and Judah; to what lies beyond this, namely, the restoration of the kingdom of God; and to the state of the people in their condition of final felicity." For predictions of the exile and the return of Israel, see especially Amos 9:9—"For, lo, I will command, and I will sift the house of Israel among all the nations, like as grain is sifted in a sieve, yet shall not the least kernel fall upon the earth.... 14—And I will bring again the captivity of my people Israel, and they shall build the waste cities and inhabit them." Even if we accept the theory of composite authorship of the book of Isaiah, we still have a foretelling of the sending back of the Jews from Babylon, and a designation of Cyrus as God's agent, in Is. 44:28—"that saith of Cyrus, He is my shepherd, and shall perform all my pleasure: even saying of Jerusalem, She shall be built; and of the temple, Thy foundation shall be laid"; see George Adam Smith, in Hastings' Bible Dictionary, 2:493. Frederick the Great said to his chaplain: "Give me in one word a proof of the divine origin of the Bible"; and the chaplain well replied: "The Jews, your Majesty." In the case of the Jews we have even now the unique phenomena of a people without a land, and a land without a people,—yet both these were predicted centuries before the event.

5. Messianic Prophecy in general. (a) Direct predictions of events—as in Old Testament prophecies of Christ's birth, suffering and subsequent glory. (b) General prophecy of the Kingdom in the Old Testament, and of its gradual triumph. (c) Historical types in a nation and in individuals—as Jonah and David. (d) Prefigurations of the future in rites and ordinances—as in sacrifice, circumcision, and the passover.

6. Special Prophecies uttered by Christ. (a) As to his own death and resurrection. (b) As to events occurring between his death and the destruction of Jerusalem (multitudes of impostors; wars and rumors of wars; famine and pestilence). (c) As to the destruction of Jerusalem and the Jewish polity (Jerusalem compassed with armies; abomination of desolation in the holy place; flight of Christians; misery; massacre; dispersion). (d) As to the world-wide diffusion of his gospel (the Bible already the most widely circulated book in the world).

The most important feature in prophecy is its Messianic element; see Luke 24:27—"beginning from Moses and from all the prophets, he interpreted to them in all the scriptures the things concerning himself"; Acts 10:43—"to him bear all the prophets witness"; Rev. 19:10—"the testimony of Jesus is the spirit of prophecy." Types are intended resemblances, designed prefigurations; for example, Israel is a type of the Christian church; outside nations are types of the hostile world; Jonah and David are types of Christ. The typical nature of Israel rests upon the deeper fact of the community of life. As the life of God the Logos lies at the basis of universal humanity and interpenetrates it in every part, so out of this universal humanity grows Israel in general; out of Israel as a nation springs the spiritual Israel, and out of spiritual Israel Christ according to the flesh,—the upward rising pyramid finds its apex and culmination in him. Hence the predictions with regard to "the servant of Jehovah" (Is. 42:1-7), and "the Messiah" (Is. 61:1; John 1:41), have partial fulfilment in Israel, but perfect fulfilment only in Christ; so Delitzsch, Oehler, and Cheyne on Isaiah, 2:253. Sabatier, Philos. Religion, 59—"If humanity were not potentially and in some degree Immanuel, God with us, there would never have issued from its bosom he who bore and revealed this blessed name." Gardiner, O. T. and N. T. in their Mutual Relations, 170-194.

In the O. T., Jehovah is the Redeemer of his people. He works through judges, prophets, kings, but he himself remains the Savior; "it is only the Divine in them that saves"; "Salvation is of Jehovah" (Jonah 2:9). Jehovah is manifested in the Davidic King under the monarchy; in Israel, the Servant of the Lord, during the exile; and in the Messiah, or Anointed One, in the post-exilian period. Because of its conscious identification with Jehovah, Israel is always a forward-looking people. Each new judge, king, prophet is regarded as heralding the coming reign of righteousness and peace. These earthly deliverers are saluted with rapturous expectation; the prophets express this expectation in terms that transcend the possibilities of the present; and, when this expectation fails to be fully realized, the Messianic hope is simply transferred to a larger future. Each separate prophecy has its drapery furnished by the prophet's immediate surroundings, and finds its occasion in some event of contemporaneous history. But by degrees it becomes evident that only an ideal and perfect King and Savior can fill out the requirements of prophecy. Only when Christ appears, does the real meaning of the various Old Testament predictions become manifest. Only then are men able to combine the seemingly inconsistent prophecies of a priest who is also a king (Psalm 110), and of a royal but at the same time a suffering Messiah (Isaiah 53). It is not enough for us to ask what the prophet himself meant, or what his earliest hearers understood, by his prophecy. This is to regard prophecy as having only a single, and that a human, author. With the spirit of man coöperated the Spirit of Christ, the Holy Spirit (1 Pet. 1:11—"the Spirit of Christ which was in them"; 2 Pet. 1:21—"no prophecy ever came by the will of man; but men spake from God, being moved by the Holy Spirit"). All prophecy has a twofold authorship, human and divine; the same Christ who spoke through the prophets brought about the fulfilment of their words.

It is no wonder that he who through the prophets uttered predictions with regard to himself should, when he became incarnate, be the prophet par excellence (Deut. 18:15; Acts 3:22—"Moses indeed said, A prophet shall the Lord God raise up from among your brethren, like unto me; to him shall ye hearken"). In the predictions of Jesus we find the proper key to the interpretation of prophecy in general, and the evidence that while no one of the three theories—the preterist, the continuist, the futurist— furnishes an exhaustive explanation, each one of these has its element of truth. Our Lord made the fulfilment of the prediction of his own resurrection a test of his divine commission: it was "the sign of Jonah the prophet" (Mat. 12:39). He promised that his disciples should have prophetic gifts: John 15:15—"No longer do I call you servants; for the servant knoweth not what his lord doeth: but I have called you friends; for all things that I heard from my Father I have made known unto you"; 16:13— "the Spirit of truth ... he shall declare unto you the things that are to come." Agabus predicted the famine and Paul's imprisonment (Acts 11:28; 21:10); Paul predicted heresies (Acts 20:29, 30), shipwreck (Acts 27:10, 21-26), "the man of sin" (2 Thess. 2:3), Christ's second coming, and the resurrection of the saints (1 Thess. 4:15-17).

7. On the double sense of Prophecy.

(a) Certain prophecies apparently contain a fulness of meaning which is not exhausted by the event to which they most obviously and literally refer. A prophecy which had a partial fulfilment at a time not remote from its utterance, may find its chief fulfilment in an event far distant. Since the principles of God's administration find ever recurring and ever enlarging illustration in history, prophecies which have already had a partial fulfilment may have whole cycles of fulfilment yet before them.

In prophecy there is an absence of perspective; as in Japanese pictures the near and the far appear equally distant; as in dissolving views, the immediate future melts into a future immeasurably far away. The candle that shines through a narrow aperture sends out its light through an ever-increasing area; sections of the triangle correspond to each other, but the more distant are far greater than the near. The châlet on the mountain-side may turn out to be only a black cat on the woodpile, or a speck upon the window pane. "A hill which appears to rise close behind another is found on nearer approach to have receded a great way from it." The painter, by foreshortening, brings together things or parts that are relatively distant from each other. The prophet is a painter whose foreshortenings are supernatural; he seems freed from the law of space and time, and, rapt into the timelessness of God, he views the events of history "sub specie eternitatis." Prophecy was the sketching of an outline-map. Even the prophet could not fill up the outline. The absence of perspective in prophecy may account for Paul's being misunderstood by the Thessalonians, and for the necessity of his explanations in 2 Thess. 2:1, 2. In Isaiah 10 and 11, the fall of Lebanon (the Assyrian) is immediately connected with the rise of the Branch (Christ); in Jeremiah 51:41, the first capture and the complete destruction of Babylon are connected with each other, without notice of the interval of a thousand years between them.

Instances of the double sense of prophecy may be found in Is. 7:14-16; 9:6, 7—"a virgin shall conceive and bear a son, ... unto us a son is given"—compared with Mat. 1:22, 23, where the prophecy is applied to Christ (see Meyer, in loco); Hos. 11:1—"I ... called my son out of Egypt"—referring originally to the calling of the nation out of Egypt—is in Mat. 2:15 referred to Christ, who embodied and consummated the mission of Israel; Psalm 118:22, 23—"The stone which the builders rejected is become the head of the corner"—which primarily referred to the Jewish nation, conquered, carried away, and flung aside as of no use, but divinely destined to a future of importance and grandeur, is in Mat. 21:42 referred by Jesus to himself, as the true embodiment of Israel. William Arnold Stevens, on The Man of Sin, in Bap. Quar. Rev., July, 1889:328-360—As in Daniel 11:36, the great enemy of the faith, who "shall exalt himself, and magnify himself above every god," is the Syrian King, Antiochus Epiphanes, so "the man of lawlessness" described by Paul in 2 Thess. 2:3 is the corrupt and impious Judaism of the apostolic age. This had its seat in the temple of God, but was doomed to destruction when the Lord should come at the fall of Jerusalem. But even this second fulfilment of the prophecy does not preclude a future and final fulfilment. Broadus on Mat., page 480—In Isaiah 41:8 to chapter 53, the predictions with regard to "the servant of Jehovah" make a gradual transition from Israel to the Messiah, the former alone being seen in 41:8, the Messiah also appearing in 42:1 sq., and Israel quite sinking out of sight in chapter 53.

The most marked illustration of the double sense of prophecy however is to be found in Matthew 24 and 25, especially 24:34 and 25:31, where Christ's prophecy of the destruction of Jerusalem passes into a prophecy of the end of the world. Adamson, The Mind in Christ, 183—"To him history was the robe of God, and therefore a constant repetition of positions really similar, kaleidoscopic combining of a few truths, as the facts varied in which they were to be embodied." A. J. Gordon: "Prophecy has no sooner become history, than history in turn becomes prophecy." Lord Bacon: "Divine prophecies have springing and germinant accomplishment through many ages, though the height or fulness of them may refer to some one age." In a similar manner there is a manifoldness of meaning in Dante's Divine Comedy. C. E. Norton, Inferno, xvi—"The narrative of the poet's spiritual journey is so vivid and consistent that it has all the reality of an account of an actual experience; but within and beneath runs a stream of allegory not less consistent and hardly less continuous than the narrative itself." A. H. Strong, The Great Poets and their Theology, 116—"Dante himself has told us that there are four separate senses which he intends his story to convey. There are the literal, the allegorical, the moral, and the analogical. In Psalm 114:1 we have the words, 'When Israel went forth out of Egypt.' This, says the poet, may be taken literally, of the actual deliverance of God's ancient people; or allegorically, of the redemption of the world through Christ; or morally, of the rescue of the sinner from the bondage of his sin; or anagogically, of the passage of both soul and body from the lower life of earth to the higher life of heaven. So from Scripture Dante illustrates the method of his poem." See further, our treatment of Eschatology. See also Dr. Arnold of Rugby, Sermons on the Interpretation of Scripture, Appendix A, pages 441-454; Aids to Faith, 449-462; Smith's Bible Dict., 4:2727. Per contra, see Elliott, Horæ Apocalypticæ, 4:662. Gardiner, O. T. and N. T., 262-274, denies double sense, but affirms manifold applications of a single sense. Broadus, on Mat. 24:1, denies double sense, but affirms the use of types.

(b) The prophet was not always aware of the meaning of his own prophecies (1 Pet. 1:11). It is enough to constitute his prophecies a proof of divine revelation, if it can be shown that the correspondences between them and the actual events are such as to indicate divine wisdom and purpose in the giving of them—in other words, it is enough if the inspiring Spirit knew their meaning, even though the inspired prophet did not.

It is not inconsistent with this view, but rather confirms it, that the near event, and not the distant fulfilment, was often chiefly, if not exclusively, in the mind of the prophet when he wrote. Scripture declares that the prophets did not always understand their own predictions: 1 Pet. 1:11—"searching what time or what manner of time the Spirit of Christ which was in them did point unto, when it testified beforehand the sufferings of Christ, and the glories that should follow them." Emerson: "Himself from God he could not free; He builded better than he knew." Keble: "As little children lisp and tell of heaven, So thoughts beyond their thoughts to those high bards were given." Westcott: Preface to Com. on Hebrews, vi—"No one would limit the teaching of a poet's words to that which was definitely present to his mind. Still less can we suppose that he who is inspired to give a message of

God to all ages sees himself the completeness of the truth which all life serves to illuminate." Alexander McLaren: "Peter teaches that Jewish prophets foretold the events of Christ's life and especially his sufferings; that they did so as organs of God's Spirit; that they were so completely organs of a higher voice that they did not understand the significance of their own words, but were wiser than they knew and had to search what were the date and the characteristics of the strange things which they foretold; and that by further revelation they learned that 'the vision is yet for many days' (Is. 24:22; Dan. 10:14). If Peter was right in his conception of the nature of Messianic prophecy, a good many learned men of to-day are wrong." Matthew Arnold, Literature and Dogma: "Might not the prophetic ideals be poetic dreams, and the correspondence between them and the life of Jesus, so far as real, only a curious historical phenomenon?" Bruce, Apologetics, 359, replies: "Such scepticism is possible only to those who have no faith in a living God who works out purposes in history." It is comparable only to the unbelief of the materialist who regards the physical constitution of the universe as explicable by the fortuitous concourse of atoms.

8. Purpose of Prophecy—so far as it is yet unfulfilled. (a) Not to enable us to map out the details of the future; but rather (b) To give general assurance of God's power and foreseeing wisdom, and of the certainty of his triumph; and (c) To furnish, after fulfilment, the proof that God saw the end from the beginning.

Dan. 12:8, 9—"And I heard, but I understood not; then said I, O my Lord, what shall be the issue of these things? And he said, Go thy way, Daniel; for the words are shut up and sealed till the time of the end"; 2 Pet. 1:19—prophecy is "a lamp shining in a dark place, until the day dawn"—not until day dawns can distant objects be seen; 20—"no prophecy of scripture is of private interpretation"—only God, by the event, can interpret it. Sir Isaac Newton: "God gave the prophecies, not to gratify men's curiosity by enabling them to foreknow things, but that after they were fulfilled they might be interpreted by the event, and his own providence, not the interpreter's, be thereby manifested to the world." Alexander McLaren: "Great tracts of Scripture are dark to us till life explains them, and then they come on us with the force of a new revelation, like the messages which of old were sent by a strip of parchment coiled upon a bâton and then written upon, and which were unintelligible unless the receiver had a corresponding bâton to wrap them round." A. H. Strong, The Great Poets and their Theology, 23—"Archilochus, a poet of about 700 B. C., speaks of 'a grievous scytale'—the scytale being the staff on which a strip of leather for writing purposes was rolled slantwise, so that the message inscribed upon the strip could not be read until the leather was rolled again upon another staff of the same size; since only the writer and the receiver possessed staves of the proper size, the scytale answered all the ends of a message in cypher."

Prophecy is like the German sentence,—it can be understood only when we have read its last word. A. J. Gordon, Ministry of the Spirit, 48—"God's providence is like the Hebrew Bible; we must begin at the end and read backward, in order to understand it." Yet Dr. Gordon seems to assert that such understanding is possible even before fulfilment: "Christ did not know the day of the end when here in his state of humiliation; but he does know now. He has shown his knowledge in the Apocalypse, and we have received 'The Revelation of Jesus Christ, which God gave him to show unto his servants, even the things which must shortly come to pass' (Rev. 1:1)." A study however of the multitudinous and conflicting views of the so-called interpreters of prophecy leads us to prefer to Dr. Gordon's view that of Briggs, Messianic Prophecies, 49—"The first advent is the resolver of all Old Testament prophecy; ... the second advent will give the key to New Testament prophecy. It is 'the Lamb that hath been slain' (Rev. 5:12) ... who alone opens the sealed book, solves the riddles of time, and resolves the symbols of prophecy."

Nitzsch: "It is the essential condition of prophecy that it should not disturb man's relation to history." In so far as this is forgotten, and it is falsely assumed that the purpose of prophecy is to enable us to map out the precise events of the future before they occur, the study of prophecy ministers to a diseased imagination and diverts attention from practical Christian duty. Calvin: "Aut insanum inveniet aut faciet"; or, as Lord Brougham translated it: "The study of prophecy either finds a man crazy, or it leaves him so." Second Adventists do not often seek conversions. Dr. Cumming warned the women of his flock that they must not study prophecy so much as to neglect their household duties. Paul has such in mind in 2 Thess. 2:1, 2—"touching the coming of our Lord Jesus Christ ... that ye be not quickly shaken from your mind ... as that the day of the Lord is just at hand"; 3:11—"For we hear of some that walk among you disorderly."

9. Evidential force of Prophecy—so far as it is fulfilled. Prophecy, like miracles, does not stand alone as evidence of the divine commission of the Scripture writers and teachers. It is simply a corroborative attestation, which unites with miracles to prove that a religious teacher has come from God and speaks with divine authority. We cannot, however, dispense with this portion of the evidences,—for unless the death and resurrection of Christ are events foreknown and foretold by himself, as well as by the ancient prophets, we lose one main proof of his authority as a teacher sent from God.

Stearns, Evidence of Christian Experience, 338—"The Christian's own life is the progressive fulfilment of the prophecy that whoever accepts Christ's grace shall be born again, sanctified, and saved. Hence the Christian can believe in God's power to predict, and in God's actual predictions." See Stanley Leathes, O. T. Prophecy, xvii—"Unless we have access to the supernatural, we have no access to God." In our discussions of prophecy, we are to remember that before making the truth of Christianity stand or fall with any particular passage that has been regarded as prediction, we must be certain that the passage is meant as prediction, and not as merely figurative description. Gladden, Seven Puzzling Bible Books, 195—"The book of Daniel is not a prophecy,—it is an apocalypse.... The author [of such books] puts his words into the mouth of some historical or traditional writer of eminence. Such are the Book of Enoch, the Assumption of Moses, Baruch, 1 and 2 Esdras, and the Sibylline Oracles. Enigmatic form indicates persons without naming them, and historic events as animal forms or as operations of nature.... The book of Daniel is not intended to teach us history. It does not look forward from the sixth century before Christ, but backward from the second century before Christ. It is a kind of story which the Jews called Haggada. It is aimed at Antiochus Epiphanes, who, from his occasional fits of melancholy, was called Epimanes, or Antiochus the Mad."

Whatever may be our conclusion as to the authorship of the book of Daniel, we must recognize in it an element of prediction which has been actually fulfilled. The most radical interpreters do not place its date later than 163 B. C. Our Lord sees in the book clear reference to himself (Mat. 26:64—"the Son of man, sitting at the right hand of Power, and coming on the clouds of heaven"; cf. Dan. 7:13); and he repeats with emphasis certain predictions of the prophet which were yet unfulfilled (Mat. 24:15—"When ye see the abomination of desolation, which was spoken of through Daniel the prophet"; cf. Dan. 9:27; 11:31; 12:11). The book of Daniel must therefore be counted profitable not only for its moral and spiritual lessons, but also for its actual predictions of Christ and of the universal triumph of his kingdom (Dan. 2:45—"a stone cut out of the mountain without hands"). See on Daniel, Hastings' Bible Dictionary; Farrar, in Expositor's Bible. On the general subject see Annotated Paragraph Bible, Introd. to Prophetical Books; Cairns, on Present State of Christian Argument from Prophecy, in Present Day Tracts, 5: no. 27; Edersheim, Prophecy and History; Briggs, Messianic Prophecy; Redford, Prophecy, its Nature and Evidence; Willis J. Beecher, the Prophet and the Promise; Orr, Problem of the O. T., 455-465.

Having thus removed the presumption originally existing against miracles and prophecy, we may now consider the ordinary laws of evidence and determine the rules to be followed in estimating the weight of the Scripture testimony.

V. Principles of Historical Evidence applicable to the Proof of a Divine Revelation

PRINCIPLES OF HISTORICAL EVIDENCE APPLICABLE TO THE PROOF OF A DIVINE REVELATION (mainly derived from Greenleaf, Testimony of the Evangelists, and from Starkie on Evidence).

1. As to documentary evidence

(a) Documents apparently ancient, not bearing upon their face the marks of forgery, and found in proper custody, are presumed to be genuine until sufficient evidence is brought to the contrary. The New Testament documents, since they are found in the custody of the church, their natural and legitimate depository, must by this rule be presumed to be genuine.

The Christian documents were not found, like the Book of Mormon, in a cave, or in the custody of angels. Martineau, Seat of Authority, 322—"The Mormon prophet, who cannot tell God from devil close at hand, is well up with the history of both worlds, and commissioned to get ready the second promised land." Washington Gladden, Who wrote the Bible?—"An angel appeared to Smith and told him where he would find this book; he went to the spot designated and found in a stone box a volume six inches thick, composed of thin gold plates, eight inches by seven, held together by three gold rings; these plates were covered with writing, in the 'Reformed Egyptian tongue'; with this book were the 'Urim and Thummim', a pair of supernatural spectacles, by means of which he was able to read and translate this 'Reformed Egyptian' language." Sagebeer, The Bible in Court, 113—"If the ledger of a business firm has always been received and regarded as a ledger, its value is not at all impeached if it is impossible to tell which particular clerk kept this ledger.... The epistle to the Hebrews would be no less valuable as evidence, if shown not to have been written by Paul." See Starkie on Evidence, 480 sq.; Chalmers, Christian Revelation, in Works, 3:147-171.

(b) Copies of ancient documents, made by those most interested in their faithfulness, are presumed to correspond with the originals, even although those originals no longer exist. Since it was the church's interest to have faithful copies, the burden of proof rests upon the objector to the Christian documents.

Upon the evidence of a copy of its own records, the originals having been lost, the House of Lords decided a claim to the peerage; see Starkie on Evidence, 51. There is no manuscript of Sophocles earlier than the tenth century, while at least two manuscripts of the N. T. go back to the fourth century. Frederick George Kenyon, Handbook to Textual Criticism of N. T.: "We owe our knowledge of most of the great works of Greek and Latin literature—Æschylus, Sophocles, Thucydides, Horace, Lucretius, Tacitus, and many more—to manuscripts written from 900 to 1500 years after their authors' deaths; while of the N. T. we have two excellent and approximately complete copies at an interval of only 250 years. Again, of the classical writers we have as a rule only a few score of copies (often less), of which one or two stand out as decisively superior to all the rest; but of the N. T. we have more than 3000 copies (besides a very large number of versions), and many of these have distinct and independent value." The mother of Tischendorf named him Lobgott, because her fear that her babe would be born blind had not come true. No man ever had keener sight than he. He spent his life in deciphering old manuscripts which other eyes could not read. The Sinaitic manuscript which he discovered takes us back within three centuries of the time of the apostles.

(c) In determining matters of fact, after the lapse of considerable time, documentary evidence is to be allowed greater weight than oral testimony. Neither memory nor tradition can long be trusted to give absolutely correct accounts of particular facts. The New Testament documents, therefore, are of greater weight in evidence than tradition would be, even if only thirty years had elapsed since the death of the actors in the scenes they relate.

See Starkie on Evidence, 51, 730. The Roman Catholic Church, in its legends of the saints, shows how quickly mere tradition can become corrupt. Abraham Lincoln was assassinated in 1865, yet sermons preached to-day on the anniversary of his birth make him out to be Unitarian, Universalist, or Orthodox, according as the preacher himself believes.

2. As to testimony in general

(a) In questions as to matters of fact, the proper inquiry is not whether it is possible that the testimony may be false, but whether there is sufficient probability that it is true. It is unfair, therefore, to allow our examination of the Scripture witnesses to be prejudiced by suspicion, merely because their story is a sacred one.

There must be no prejudice against, there must be open-mindedness to, truth; there must be a normal aspiration after the signs of communication from God. Telepathy, forty days fasting, parthenogenesis, all these might once have seemed antecedently incredible. Now we see that it would have been more rational to admit their existence on presentation of appropriate evidence.

(b) A proposition of fact is proved when its truth is established by competent and satisfactory evidence. By competent evidence is meant such evidence as the nature of the thing to be proved admits. By satisfactory evidence is meant that amount of proof which ordinarily satisfies an unprejudiced mind beyond a reasonable doubt. Scripture facts are therefore proved when they are established by that kind and degree of evidence which would in the affairs of ordinary life satisfy the mind and conscience of a common man. When we have this kind and degree of evidence it is unreasonable to require more.

In matters of morals and religion competent evidence need not be mathematical or even logical. The majority of cases in criminal courts are decided upon evidence that is circumstantial. We do not determine our choice of friends or of partners in life by strict processes of reasoning. The heart as well as the head must be permitted a voice, and competent evidence includes considerations arising from the moral needs of the soul. The evidence, moreover, does not require to be demonstrative. Even a slight balance of probability, when nothing more certain is attainable, may suffice to constitute rational proof and to bind our moral action.

(c) In the absence of circumstances which generate suspicion, every witness is to be presumed credible, until the contrary is shown; the burden of impeaching his testimony lying upon the objector. The principle which leads men to give true witness to facts is stronger than that which leads them to give false witness. It is therefore unjust to compel the Christian to establish the credibility of his witnesses before proceeding to adduce their testimony, and it is equally unjust to allow the uncorroborated testimony of a profane writer to outweigh that of a Christian writer. Christian witnesses should not be considered interested, and therefore untrustworthy; for they became Christians against their worldly interests, and because they could not resist the force of testimony. Varying accounts among them should be estimated as we estimate the varying accounts of profane writers.

John's account of Jesus differs from that of the synoptic gospels; but in a very similar manner, and probably for a very similar reason, Plato's account of Socrates differs from that of Xenophon. Each saw and described that side of his subject which he was by nature best fitted to comprehend,—compare the Venice of Canaletto with the Venice of Turner, the former the picture of an expert draughtsman, the latter the vision of a poet who sees the palaces of the Doges glorified by air and mist and distance. In Christ there was a "hiding of his power" (Hab. 3:4); "how small a whisper do we hear of him!" (Job 26:14); he, rather than Shakespeare, is "the myriad-minded"; no one evangelist can be expected to know or describe him except "in part" (1 Cor. 13:12). Frances Power Cobbe, Life, 2:402—"All of us human beings resemble diamonds, in having several distinct facets to our characters; and, as we always turn one of these to one person and another to another, there is generally some fresh side to be seen in a particularly brilliant gem." E. P. Tenney, Coronation, 45—"The secret and powerful life he [the hero of the story] was leading was like certain solitary streams, deep, wide, and swift, which run unseen through vast and unfrequented forests. So wide and varied was this man's nature, that whole courses of life might thrive in its secret places,—and his neighbors might touch him and know him only on that side on which he was like them."

(d) A slight amount of positive testimony, so long as it is uncontradicted, outweighs a very great amount of testimony that is merely negative. The silence of a second witness, or his testimony that he did not see a certain alleged occurrence, cannot counterbalance the positive testimony of a first witness that he did see it. We should therefore estimate the silence of profane writers with regard to facts narrated in Scripture precisely as we should estimate it if the facts about which they are silent were narrated by other profane writers, instead of being narrated by the writers of Scripture.

Egyptian monuments make no mention of the destruction of Pharaoh and his army; but then, Napoleon's dispatches also make no mention of his defeat at Trafalgar. At the tomb of Napoleon in the Invalides of Paris, the walls are inscribed with names of a multitude of places where his battles were fought, but Waterloo, the scene of his great defeat, is not recorded there. So Sennacherib, in all his monuments, does not refer to the destruction of his army in the time of Hezekiah. Napoleon gathered 450,000 men at Dresden to invade Russia. At Moscow the soft-falling snow conquered him. In one night 20,000 horses perished with cold. Not without reason at Moscow, on the anniversary of the retreat of the French, the exultation of the prophet over the fall of Sennacherib is read in the churches. James Robertson, Early History of Israel, 395, note—"Whately, in his Historic Doubts, draws attention to the fact that the principal Parisian journal in 1814, on the very day on which the allied armies entered Paris as conquerors, makes no mention of any such event. The battle of Poictiers in 732, which effectually checked the spread of Mohammedanism across Europe, is not once referred to in the monastic annals of the period. Sir Thomas Browne lived through the Civil Wars and the Commonwealth, yet there is no syllable in his writings with regard to them. Sale says that circumcision is regarded by Mohammedans as an ancient divine institution, the rite having been in use many years before Mohammed, yet it is not so much as once mentioned in the Koran."

Even though we should grant that Josephus does not mention Jesus, we should have a parallel in Thucydides, who never once mentions Socrates, the most important character of the twenty years embraced in his history. Wieseler, however, in Jahrbuch f. d. Theologie, 23:98, maintains the essential genuineness of the commonly rejected passage with regard to Jesus in Josephus, Antiq., 18:3:3, omitting, however, as interpolations, the phrases: "if it be right to call him man"; "this was the Christ"; "he appeared alive the third day according to prophecy"; for these, if genuine, would prove Josephus a Christian, which he, by all ancient accounts, was not. Josephus lived from A. D. 34 to possibly 114. He does elsewhere speak of Christ; for he records (20:9:1) that Albinus "assembled the Sanhedrim of judges, and brought before them the brother of Jesus who was called Christ, whose name was James, and some others ... and delivered them to be stoned." See Niese's new edition of Josephus; also a monograph on the subject by Gustav Adolph Müller, published at Innsbruck, 1890. Rush Rhees, Life of Jesus of Nazareth, 22—"To mention Jesus more fully would have required some approval of his life and teaching. This would have been a condemnation of his own people whom he desired to commend to Gentile regard, and he seems to have taken the cowardly course of silence concerning a matter more noteworthy, for that generation, than much else of which he writes very fully."

(e) "The credit due to the testimony of witnesses depends upon: first, their ability; secondly, their honesty; thirdly, their number and the consistency of their testimony; fourthly, the conformity of their testimony with experience; and fifthly, the coincidence of their testimony with collateral circumstances." We confidently submit the New Testament witnesses to each and all of these tests.

See Starkie on Evidence, 726.

Chapter II - Positive Proofs That The Scriptures Are A Divine Revelation

I. Genuineness of the Christian Documents

THE GENUINENESS OF THE CHRISTIAN DOCUMENTS, or proof that the books of the Old and New Testaments were written at the age to which they are assigned and by the men or class of men to whom they are ascribed.

Our present discussion comprises the first part, and only the first part, of the doctrine of the Canon (κανών, a measuring-reed; hence, a rule, a standard). It is important to observe that the determination of the Canon, or list of the books of sacred Scripture, is not the work of the church as an organized body. We do not receive these books upon the authority of Fathers or Councils. We receive them, only as the Fathers and Councils received them, because we have evidence that they are the writings of the men, or class of men, whose names they bear, and that they are also credible and inspired. If the previous epistle alluded to in 1 Cor. 5:9 should be discovered and be universally judged authentic, it could be placed with Paul's other letters and could form part of the Canon, even though it has been lost for 1800 years. Bruce, Apologetics, 321—"Abstractly the Canon is an open question. It can never be anything else on the principles of Protestantism which forbid us to accept the decisions of church councils, whether ancient or modern, as final. But practically the question of the Canon is closed." The Westminster Confession says that the authority of the word of God "does not rest upon historic evidence; it does not rest upon the authority of Councils; it does not rest upon the consent of the past or the excellence of the matter; but it rests upon the Spirit of God bearing witness to our hearts concerning its divine authority." Clarke, Christian Theology, 24—"The value of the Scriptures to us does not depend upon our knowing who wrote them. In the O. T. half its pages are of uncertain authorship. New dates mean new authorship. Criticism is a duty, for dates of authorship give means of interpretation. The Scriptures have power because God is in them, and because they describe the entrance of God into the life of man."

Saintine, Picciola, 782—"Has not a feeble reed provided man with his first arrow, his first pen, his first instrument of music?" Hugh Macmillan: "The idea of stringed instruments was first derived from the twang of the well strung bow, as the archer shot his arrows; the lyre and the harp which discourse the sweetest music of peace were invented by those who first heard this inspiring sound in the excitement of battle. And so there is no music so delightful amid the jarring discord of the world, turning everything to music and harmonizing earth and heaven, as when the heart rises out of the gloom of anger and revenge, and converts its bow into a harp, and sings to it the Lord's song of infinite forgiveness." George Adam Smith, Mod. Criticism and Preaching of O. T., 5—"The church has never renounced her liberty to revise the Canon. The liberty at the beginning cannot be more than the liberty thereafter. The Holy Spirit has not forsaken the leaders of the church. Apostolic writers nowhere define the limits of the Canon, any more than Jesus did. Indeed, they employed extra-canonical writings. Christ and the apostles nowhere bound the church to believe all the teachings of the O. T. Christ discriminates, and forbids the literal interpretation of its contents. Many of the apostolic interpretations challenge our sense of truth. Much of their exegesis was temporary and false. Their judgment was that much in the O. T. was rudimentary. This opens the question of development in revelation, and justifies the attempt to fix the historic order. The N. T. criticism of the O. T. gives the liberty of criticism, and the need, and the obligation of it. O. T. criticism is not, like Baur's of the N. T., the result of a priori Hegelian reasoning. From the time of Samuel we have real history. The prophets do not appeal to miracles. There is more gospel in the book of Jonah, when it is treated as a parable. The O. T. is a gradual ethical revelation of God. Few realize that the church of Christ has a higher warrant for her Canon of the O. T. than she has for her Canon of the N. T. The O. T. was the result of criticism in the widest sense of that word. But what the church thus once achieved, the church may at any time revise."

We reserve to a point somewhat later the proof of the credibility and the inspiration of the Scriptures. We now show their genuineness, as we would show the genuineness of other religious books, like the Koran, or of secular documents, like Cicero's Orations against Catiline. Genuineness, in the sense in which we use the term, does not necessarily imply authenticity (i. e., truthfulness and authority); see Blunt, Dict. Doct. and Hist. Theol., art.: Authenticity. Documents may be genuine which are written in whole or in part by persons other than they whose names they bear, provided these persons belong to the same class. The Epistle to the Hebrews, though not written by Paul, is genuine, because it proceeds from one of the apostolic class. The addition of Deut. 34, after Moses' death, does not invalidate the genuineness of the Pentateuch; nor would the theory of a later Isaiah, even if it were established, disprove the genuineness of that prophecy; provided, in both cases, that the additions were made by men of the prophetic class. On the general subject of the genuineness of the Scripture documents, see Alexander, McIlvaine, Chalmers, Dodge, and Peabody, on the Evidences of Christianity; also Archibald, The Bible Verified.

1. Genuineness of the Books of the New Testament

We do not need to adduce proof of the existence of the books of the New Testament as far back as the third century, for we possess manuscripts of them which are at least fourteen hundred years old, and, since the third century, references to them have been inwoven into all history and literature. We begin our proof, therefore, by showing that these documents not only existed, but were generally accepted as genuine, before the close of the second century.

Origen was born as early as 186 A. D.; yet Tregelles tells us that Origen's works contain citations embracing two-thirds of the New Testament. Hatch, Hibbert Lectures, 12—"The early years of Christianity were in some respects like the early years of our lives.... Those early years are the most important in our education. We learn then, we hardly know how, through effort and struggle and innocent mistakes, to use our eyes and ears, to measure distance and direction, by a process which ascends by unconscious steps to the certainty which we feel in our maturity.... It was in some such unconscious way that the Christian thought of the early centuries gradually acquired the form which we find when it emerges as it were into the developed manhood of the fourth century."

A. All the books of the New Testament, with the single exception of 2 Peter, were not only received as genuine, but were used in more or less collected form, in the latter half of the second century. These collections of writings, so slowly transcribed and distributed, imply the long continued previous existence of the separate books, and forbid us to fix their origin later than the first half of the second century.

(a) Tertullian (160-230) appeals to the "New Testament" as made up of the "Gospels" and "Apostles." He vouches for the genuineness of the four gospels, the Acts, 1 Peter, 1 John, thirteen epistles of Paul, and the Apocalypse; in short, to twenty-one of the twenty-seven books of our Canon.

Sanday, Bampton Lectures for 1893, is confident that the first three gospels took their present shape before the destruction of Jerusalem. Yet he thinks the first and third gospels of composite origin, and probably the second. Not later than 125 A. D. the four gospels of our Canon had gained a recognized and exceptional authority. Andover Professors, Divinity of Jesus Christ, 40—"The oldest of our gospels was written about the year 70. The earlier one, now lost, a great part of which is preserved in Luke and Matthew, was probably written a few years earlier."

(b) The Muratorian Canon in the West and the Peshito Version in the East (having a common date of about 160) in their catalogues of the New Testament writings mutually complement each other's slight deficiencies, and together bear witness to the fact that at that time every book of our present New Testament, with the exception of 2 Peter, was received as genuine.

Hovey, Manual of Christian Theology, 50—"The fragment on the Canon, discovered by Muratori in 1738, was probably written about 170 A. D., in Greek. It begins with the last words of a sentence which must have referred to the Gospel of Mark, and proceeds to speak of the Third Gospel as written by Luke the physician, who did not see the Lord, and then of the Fourth Gospel as written by John, a disciple of the Lord, at the request of his fellow disciples and his elders." Bacon, N. T. Introduction, 50, gives the Muratorian Canon in full; 30—"Theophilus of Antioch (181-190) is the first to cite a gospel by name, quoting John 1:1 as from 'John, one of those who were vessels of the Spirit.' " On the Muratorian Canon, see Tregelles, Muratorian Canon. On the Peshito Version, see Schaff, Introd. to Rev. Gk.-Eng. N. T., xxxvii; Smith's Bible Dict., pp. 3388, 3389.

(c) The Canon of Marcion (140), though rejecting all the gospels but that of Luke, and all the epistles but ten of Paul's, shows, nevertheless, that at that early day "apostolic writings were regarded as a complete original rule of doctrine." Even Marcion, moreover, does not deny the genuineness of those writings which for doctrinal reasons he rejects.

Marcion, the Gnostic, was the enemy of all Judaism, and regarded the God of the O. T. as a restricted divinity, entirely different from the God of the N. T. Marcion was "ipso Paulo paulinior"—"plus loyal que le roi." He held that Christianity was something entirely new, and that it stood in opposition to all that went before it. His Canon consisted of two parts: the "Gospel" (Luke, with its text curtailed by omission of the Hebraistic elements) and the Apostolicon (the epistles of Paul). The epistle to Diognetus by an unknown author, and the epistle of Barnabas, shared the view of Marcion. The name of the Deity was changed from Jehovah to Father, Son, and Holy Ghost. If Marcion's view had prevailed, the Old Testament would have been lost to the Christian Church. God's revelation would have been deprived of its proof from prophecy. Development from the past, and divine conduct of

Jewish history, would have been denied. But without the Old Testament, as H. W. Beecher maintained, the New Testament would lack background; our chief source of knowledge with regard to God's natural attributes of power, wisdom, and truth would be removed: the love and mercy revealed in the New Testament would seem characteristics of a weak being, who could not enforce law or inspire respect. A tree has as much breadth below ground as there is above; so the O. T. roots of God's revelation are as extensive and necessary as are its N. T. trunk and branches and leaves. See Allen, Religious Progress, 81; Westcott, Hist. N. T. Canon, and art.: Canon, in Smith's Bible Dictionary. Also Reuss, History of Canon; Mitchell, Critical Handbook, part I.

B. The Christian and Apostolic Fathers who lived in the first half of the second century not only quote from these books and allude to them, but testify that they were written by the apostles themselves. We are therefore compelled to refer their origin still further back, namely, to the first century, when the apostles lived.

(a) Irenæus (120-200) mentions and quotes the four gospels by name, and among them the gospel according to John: "Afterwards John, the disciple of the Lord, who also leaned upon his breast, he likewise published a gospel, while he dwelt in Ephesus in Asia." And Irenæus was the disciple and friend of Polycarp (80-166), who was himself a personal acquaintance of the Apostle John. The testimony of Irenæus is virtually the evidence of Polycarp, the contemporary and friend of the Apostle, that each of the gospels was written by the person whose name it bears.

To this testimony it is objected that Irenæus says there are four gospels because there are four quarters of the world and four living creatures in the cherubim. But we reply that Irenæus is here stating, not his own reason for accepting four and only four gospels, but what he conceives to be God's reason for ordaining that there should be four. We are not warranted in supposing that he accepted the four gospels on any other ground than that of testimony that they were the productions of apostolic men.

Chrysostom, in a similar manner, compares the four gospels to a chariot and four: When the King of Glory rides forth in it, he shall receive the triumphal acclamations of all peoples. So Jerome: God rides upon the cherubim, and since there are four cherubim, there must be four gospels. All this however is an early attempt at the philosophy of religion, and not an attempt to demonstrate historical fact. L. L. Paine, Evolution of Trinitarianism, 319-367, presents the radical view of the authorship of the fourth gospel. He holds that John the apostle died A. D. 70, or soon after, and that Irenæus confounded the two Johns whom Papias so clearly distinguished—John the Apostle and John the Elder. With Harnack, Paine supposes the gospel to have been written by John the Elder, a contemporary of Papias. But we reply that the testimony of Irenæus implies a long continued previous tradition. R. W. Dale, Living Christ and Four Gospels, 145—"Religious veneration such as that with which Irenæus regarded these books is of slow growth. They must have held a great place in the Church as far back as the memory of living men extended." See Hastings' Bible Dictionary, 2:695.

(b) Justin Martyr (died 148) speaks of "memoirs (ἀπομνημονεύματα) of Jesus Christ," and his quotations, though sometimes made from memory, are evidently cited from our gospels.

To this testimony it is objected: (1) That Justin Martyr uses the term "memoirs" instead of "gospels." We reply that he elsewhere uses the term "gospels" and identifies the "memoirs" with them: Apol., 1:66—"The apostles, in the memoirs composed by them, which are called gospels," i. e., not memoirs, but gospels, was the proper title of his written records. In writing his Apology to the heathen Emperors, Marcus Aurelius and Marcus Antoninus, he chooses the term "memoirs", or "memorabilia", which Xenophon had used as the title of his account of Socrates, simply in order that he may avoid ecclesiastical expressions unfamiliar to his readers and may commend his writing to lovers of classical literature. Notice that Matthew must be added to John, to justify Justin's repeated statement that there were "memoirs" of our Lord "written by apostles," and that Mark and Luke must be added to justify his further statement that these memoirs were compiled by "his apostles and those who followed them." Analogous to Justin's use of the word "memoirs" is his use of the term "Sunday", instead of Sabbath: Apol. 1:67—"On the day called Sunday, all who live in cities or in the country gather together to one place, and the memoirs of the apostles or the writings of the prophets are read." Here is the use of our gospels in public worship, as of equal authority with the O. T. Scriptures; in fact, Justin constantly quotes the words and acts of Jesus' life from a written source, using the word γέγραπται. See Morison, Com. on Mat., ix; Hemphill, Literature of Second Century, 234.

To Justin's testimony it is objected: (2) That in quoting the words spoken from heaven at the Savior's baptism, he makes them to be: "My son, this day have I begotten thee," so quoting Psalm 2:7, and showing that he was ignorant of our present gospel, Mat. 3:17. We reply that this was probably a slip of the memory, quite natural in a day when the gospels existed only in the cumbrous form of manuscript rolls. Justin also refers to the Pentateuch for two facts which it does not contain; but we should not argue from this that he did not possess our present Pentateuch. The plays of Terence are quoted by Cicero and Horace, and we require neither more nor earlier witnesses to their genuineness,— yet Cicero and Horace wrote a hundred years after Terence. It is unfair to refuse similar evidence to the gospels. Justin had a way of combining into one the sayings of the different evangelists—a hint which

Tatian, his pupil, probably followed out in composing his Diatessaron. On Justin Martyr's testimony, see Ezra Abbot, Genuineness of the Fourth Gospel, 49, note. B. W. Bacon, Introd. to N. T., speaks of Justin as "writing circa 155 A. D."

(c) Papias (80-164), whom Irenæus calls a "hearer of John," testifies that Matthew "wrote in the Hebrew dialect the sacred oracles (τὰ λόγια)," and that "Mark, the interpreter of Peter, wrote after Peter, (ὕστερον Πέτρῳ) [or under Peter's direction], an unsystematic account (οὐ τάξει)" of the same events and discourses.

To this testimony it is objected: (1) That Papias could not have had our gospel of Matthew, for the reason that this is Greek. We reply, either with Bleek, that Papias erroneously supposed a Hebrew translation of Matthew, which he possessed, to be the original; or with Weiss, that the original Matthew was in Hebrew, while our present Matthew is an enlarged version of the same. Palestine, like modern Wales, was bilingual; Matthew, like James, might write both Hebrew and Greek. While B. W. Bacon gives to the writing of Papias a date so late as 145-160 A. D., Lightfoot gives that of 130 A. D. At this latter date Papias could easily remember stories told him so far back as 80 A. D., by men who were youths at the time when our Lord lived, died, rose and ascended. The work of Papias had for its title Λογίων κυριακῶν ἐξήγησις—"Exposition of Oracles relating to the Lord" = Commentaries on the Gospels. Two of these gospels were Matthew and Mark. The view of Weiss mentioned above has been criticized upon the ground that the quotations from the O. T. in Jesus' discourses in Matthew are all taken from the Septuagint and not from the Hebrew. Westcott answers this criticism by suggesting that, in translating his Hebrew gospel into Greek, Matthew substituted for his own oral version of Christ's discourses the version of these already existing in the oral common gospel. There was a common oral basis of true teaching, the "deposit"—τὴν παραθήκην—committed to Timothy (1 Tim. 6:20; 2 Tim. 1:12, 14), the same story told many times and getting to be told in the same way. The narratives of Matthew, Mark and Luke are independent versions of this apostolic testimony. First came belief; secondly, oral teaching; thirdly, written gospels. That the original gospel was in Aramaic seems probable from the fact that the Oriental name for "tares," zawān, (Mat. 13:25) has been transliterated into Greek, ζιζάνια. Morison, Com. on Mat., thinks that Matthew originally wrote in Hebrew a collection of Sayings of Jesus Christ, which the Nazarenes and Ebionites added to, partly from tradition, and partly from translating his full gospel, till the result was the so-called Gospel of the Hebrews; but that Matthew wrote his own gospel in Greek after he had written the Sayings in Hebrew. Professor W. A. Stevens thinks that Papias probably alluded to the original autograph which Matthew wrote in Aramaic, but which he afterwards enlarged and translated into Greek. See Hemphill, Literature of the Second Century, 267.

To the testimony of Papias it is also objected: (2) That Mark is the most systematic of all evangelists, presenting events as a true annalist, in chronological order. We reply that while, so far as chronological order is concerned, Mark is systematic, so far as logical order is concerned he is the most unsystematic of the evangelists, showing little of the power of historical grouping which is so discernible in Matthew. Matthew aimed to portray a life, rather than to record a chronology. He groups Jesus' teachings in chapters 5, 6, and 7; his miracles in chapters 8 and 9; his directions to the apostles in chapter 10; chapters 11 and 12 describe the growing opposition; chapter 13 meets this opposition with his parables; the remainder of the gospel describes our Lord's preparation for his death, his progress to Jerusalem, the consummation of his work in the Cross and in the resurrection. Here is true system, a philosophical arrangement of material, compared with which the method of Mark is eminently unsystematic. Mark is a Froissart, while Matthew has the spirit of J. R. Green. See Bleek, Introd. to N. T., 1:108, 126; Weiss, Life of Jesus, 1:27-39.

(d) The Apostolic Fathers,—Clement of Rome (died 101), Ignatius of Antioch (martyred 115), and Polycarp (80-166),—companions and friends of the apostles, have left us in their writings over one hundred quotations from or allusions to the New Testament writings, and among these every book, except four minor epistles (2 Peter, Jude, 2 and 3 John) is represented.

Although these are single testimonies, we must remember that they are the testimonies of the chief men of the churches of their day, and that they express the opinion of the churches themselves. "Like banners of a hidden army, or peaks of a distant mountain range, they represent and are sustained by compact, continuous bodies below." In an article by P. W. Calkins, McClintock and Strong's Encyclopædia, 1:315-317, quotations from the Apostolic Fathers in great numbers are put side by side with the New Testament passages from which they quote or to which they allude. An examination of these quotations and allusions convinces us that these Fathers were in possession of all the principal books of our New Testament. See Ante-Nicene Library of T. and T. Clark; Thayer, in Boston Lectures for 1871:324; Nash, Ethics and Revelation, 11—"Ignatius says to Polycarp: 'The times call for thee, as the winds call for the pilot.' So do the times call for reverent, fearless scholarship in the church." Such scholarship, we are persuaded, has already demonstrated the genuineness of the N. T. documents.

(e) In the synoptic gospels, the omission of all mention of the fulfilment of Christ's prophecies with regard to the destruction of Jerusalem is evidence that these gospels were written before the occurrence of that event. In the Acts of the Apostles, universally attributed to Luke, we have an allusion to "the former treatise", or the gospel by the same author, which must, therefore, have been written before the end of Paul's first imprisonment at Rome, and probably with the help and sanction of that apostle.

Acts 1:1—"The former treatise I made, O Theophilus, concerning all that Jesus began both to do and to teach." If the Acts was written A. D. 63, two years after Paul's arrival at Rome, then "the former treatise," the gospel according to Luke, can hardly be dated later than 60; and since the destruction of Jerusalem took place in 70, Matthew and Mark must have published their gospels at least as early as the year 68, when multitudes of men were still living who had been eye-witnesses of the events of Jesus' life. Fisher, Nature and Method of Revelation, 180—"At any considerably later date [than the capture of Jerusalem] the apparent conjunction of the fall of the city and the temple with the Parousia would have been avoided or explained.... Matthew, in its present form, appeared after the beginning of the mortal struggle of the Romans with the Jews, or between 65 and 70. Mark's gospel was still earlier. The language of the passages relative to the Parousia, in Luke, is consistent with the supposition that he wrote after the fall of Jerusalem, but not with the supposition that it was long after." See Norton, Genuineness of the Gospels; Alford, Greek Testament, Prolegomena, 30, 31, 36, 45-47.

C. It is to be presumed that this acceptance of the New Testament documents as genuine, on the part of the Fathers of the churches, was for good and sufficient reasons, both internal and external, and this presumption is corroborated by the following considerations:

(a) There is evidence that the early churches took every care to assure themselves of the genuineness of these writings before they accepted them.

Evidences of care are the following:—Paul, in 2 Thess. 2:2, urged the churches to use care, "to the end that ye be not quickly shaken from your mind, nor yet be troubled, either by spirit, or by word, or by epistle as from us"; 1 Cor. 5:9—"I wrote unto you in my epistle to have no company with fornicators"; Col. 4:16—"when this epistle hath been read among you, cause that it be read also in the church of the Laodiceans; and that ye also read the epistle from Laodicea." Melito (169), Bishop of Sardis, who wrote a treatise on the Revelation of John, went as far as Palestine to ascertain on the spot the facts relating to the Canon of the O. T., and as a result of his investigations excluded the Apocrypha. Ryle, Canon of O. T., 203—"Melito, the Bishop of Sardis, sent to a friend a list of the O. T. Scriptures which he professed to have obtained from accurate inquiry, while traveling in the East, in Syria. Its contents agree with those of the Hebrew Canon, save in the omission of Esther." Serapion, Bishop of Antioch (191-213, Abbot), says: "We receive Peter and other apostles as Christ, but as skilful men we reject those writings which are falsely ascribed to them." Geo. H. Ferris, Baptist Congress, 1899:94— "Serapion, after permitting the reading of the Gospel of Peter in public services, finally decided against it, not because he thought there could be no fifth gospel, but because he thought it was not written by Peter." Tertullian (160-230) gives an example of the deposition of a presbyter in Asia Minor for publishing a pretended work of Paul; see Tertullian, De Baptismo, referred to by Godet on John, Introduction; Lardner, Works, 2:304, 305; McIlvaine, Evidences, 92.

(b) The style of the New Testament writings, and their complete correspondence with all we know of the lands and times in which they profess to have been written, affords convincing proof that they belong to the apostolic age.

Notice the mingling of Latin and Greek, as in σπεκουλάτωρ (Mark 6:27) and κεντυρίων (Mark 15:39); of Greek and Aramæan, as in πρασιαὶ πρασιαί (Mark 6:40) and βδέλυγμα τῆς ἐρημώσεως (Mat. 24:15); this could hardly have occurred after the first century. Compare the anachronisms of style and description in Thackeray's "Henry Esmond," which, in spite of the author's special studies and his determination to exclude all words and phrases that had originated in his own century, was marred by historical errors that Macaulay in his most remiss moments would hardly have made. James Russell Lowell told Thackeray that "different to" was not a century old. "Hang it, no!" replied Thackeray. In view of this failure, on the part of an author of great literary skill, to construct a story purporting to be written a century before his time and that could stand the test of historical criticism, we may well regard the success of our gospels in standing such tests as a practical demonstration that they were written in, and not after, the apostolic age. See Alexander, Christ and Christianity, 27-37; Blunt, Scriptural Coincidences, 244-354.

(c) The genuineness of the fourth gospel is confirmed by the fact that Tatian (155-170), the Assyrian, a disciple of Justin, repeatedly quoted it without naming the author, and composed a Harmony of our four gospels which he named the Diatessaron; while Basilides (130) and Valentinus (150), the Gnostics, both quote from it.

The sceptical work entitled "Supernatural Religion" said in 1874; "No one seems to have seen Tatian's Harmony, probably for the very simple reason that there was no such work"; and "There is no evidence whatever connecting Tatian's Gospel with those of our Canon." In 1876, however, there was published in a Latin form in Venice the Commentary of Ephraem Syrus on Tatian, and the commencement of it was: "In the beginning was the Word" (John 1:1). In 1888, the Diatessaron itself was published in Rome in the form of an Arabic translation made in the eleventh century from the Syriac. J. Rendel Harris, in Contemp. Rev., 1893:800 sq., says that the recovery of Tatian's Diatessaron has indefinitely postponed the literary funeral of St. John. Advanced critics, he intimates, are so called, because they run ahead of the facts they discuss. The gospels must have been well established in the Christian church when Tatian undertook to combine them. Mrs. A. S. Lewis, in S. S. Times, Jan. 23, 1904—"The gospels were translated into Syriac before A. D. 160. It follows that the Greek document from which they were translated was older still, and since the one includes the gospel of St. John, so did the other." Hemphill, Literature of the Second Century, 183-231, gives the birth of Tatian about 120, and the date of his Diatessaron as 172 A. D.

The difference in style between the Revelation and the gospel of John is due to the fact that the Revelation was written during John's exile in Patmos, under Nero, in 67 or 68, soon after John had left Palestine and had taken up his residence at Ephesus. He had hitherto spoken Aramæan, and Greek was comparatively unfamiliar to him. The gospel was written thirty years after, probably about 97, when Greek had become to him like a mother tongue. See Lightfoot on Galatians, 343, 347; per contra, see Milligan, Revelation of St. John. Phrases and ideas which indicate a common authorship of the Revelation and the gospel are the following: "the Lamb of God," "the Word of God," "the True" as an epithet applied to Christ, "the Jews" as enemies of God, "manna," "him whom they pierced"; see Elliott, Horæ Apocalypticæ, 1:4, 5. In the fourth gospel we have ἀμνός, in Apoc. ἀρνίον, perhaps better to distinguish "the Lamb" from the diminutive τὸ θηρίον, "the beast." Common to both Gospel and Rev. are ποιεῖν, "to do" [the truth]; περιπατεῖν, of moral conduct; ἀληθινός, "genuine"; διψᾷν, πεινᾷν, of the higher wants of the soul; σκηνοῦν ἐν, ποιμαίνειν, ὁδηγεῖν; also "overcome," "testimony," "Bridegroom," "Shepherd," "Water of life." In the Revelation there are grammatical solecisms: nominative for genitive, 1:4—ἀπὸ ὁ ὤν; nominative for accusative, 7:9—εῖδον ... ὄχλος πολύς; accusative for nominative, 20:2—τὸν δράκοντα ὁ ὄφις. Similarly we have in Rom. 12:5—τὸ δὲ καθ' εῖς instead of τὸ δὲ καθ' ἕνα, where κατὰ has lost its regimen—a frequent solecism in later Greek writers; see Godet on John, 1:269, 270. Emerson reminded Jones Very that the Holy Ghost surely writes good grammar. The Apocalypse seems to show that Emerson was wrong.

The author of the fourth gospel speaks of John in the third person, "and scorned to blot it with a name." But so does Cæsar speak of himself in his Commentaries. Harnack regards both the fourth gospel and the Revelation as the work of John the Presbyter or Elder, the former written not later than about 110 A. D.; the latter from 93 to 96, but being a revision of one or more underlying Jewish apocalypses. Vischer has expounded this view of the Revelation; and Porter holds substantially the same, in his article on the Book of Revelation in Hastings' Bible Dictionary, 4:239-266. "It is the obvious advantage of the Vischer-Harnack hypothesis that it places the original work under Nero and its revised and Christianized edition under Domitian." (Sanday, Inspiration, 371, 372, nevertheless dismisses this hypothesis as raising worse difficulties than it removes. He dates the Apocalypse between the death of Nero and the destruction of Jerusalem by Titus.) Martineau, Seat of Authority, 227, presents the moral objections to the apostolic authorship, and regards the Revelation, from chapter 4:1 to 22:5, as a purely Jewish document of the date 66-70, supplemented and revised by a Christian, and issued not earlier than 136: "How strange that we should ever have thought it possible for a personal attendant upon the ministry of Jesus to write or edit a book mixing up fierce Messianic conflicts, in which, with the sword, the gory garment, the blasting flame, the rod of iron, as his emblems, he leads the war-march, and treads the winepress of the wrath of God until the deluge of blood rises to the horses' bits, with the speculative Christology of the second century, without a memory of his life, a feature of his look, a word from his voice, or a glance back at the hillsides of Galilee, the courts of Jerusalem, the road to Bethany, on which his image must be forever seen!"

The force of this statement, however, is greatly broken if we consider that the apostle John, in his earlier days, was one of the "Boanerges; which is, Sons of thunder" (Mark 3:17), but became in his later years the apostle of love: 1 John 4:7—"Beloved, let us love one another, for love is of God." The likeness of the fourth gospel to the epistle, which latter was undoubtedly the work of John the apostle, indicates the same authorship for the gospel. Thayer remarks that "the discovery of the gospel according to Peter sweeps away half a century of discussion. Brief as is the recovered fragment, it attests indubitably all four of our canonical books." Riddle, in Popular Com., 1:25—"If a forger wrote the fourth gospel, then Beelzebub has been casting out devils for these eighteen hundred years." On the genuineness of the fourth gospel, see Bleek, Introd. to N. T., 1:250; Fisher, Essays on Supernat. Origin of Christianity, 33, also Beginnings of Christianity, 320-362, and Grounds of Theistic and Christian Belief, 245-309; Sanday, Authorship of the Fourth Gospel, Gospels in the Second Century, and Criticism of the Fourth Gospel; Ezra Abbott, Genuineness of the Fourth Gospel, 52, 80-87; Row, Bampton Lectures on Christian Evidences, 249-287; British Quarterly, Oct. 1872:216; Godet, in Present Day Tracts, 5: no. 25; Westcott, in Bib. Com. on John's Gospel, Introd., xxviii-xxxii; Watkins, Bampton Lectures for 1890; W. L. Ferguson, in Bib. Sac., 1896:1-27.

(d) The epistle to the Hebrews appears to have been accepted during the first century after it was written (so Clement of Borne, Justin Martyr, and the Peshito Version witness). Then for two centuries, especially in the Roman and North African churches, and probably because its internal characteristics were inconsistent with the tradition of a Pauline authorship, its genuineness was doubted (so Tertullian, Cyprian, Irenæus, Muratorian Canon). At the end of the fourth century, Jerome examined the evidence and decided in its favor; Augustine did the same; the third Council of Carthage formally recognized it (397); from that time the Latin churches united with the East in receiving it, and thus the doubt was finally and forever removed.

The Epistle to the Hebrews, the style of which is so unlike that of the Apostle Paul, was possibly written by Apollos, who was an Alexandrian Jew, "a learned man" and "mighty in the Scriptures" (Acts 18:24); but it may notwithstanding have been written at the suggestion and under the direction of Paul, and so be essentially Pauline. A. C. Kendrick, in American Commentary on Hebrews, points out that while the style of Paul is prevailingly dialectic, and only in rapt moments becomes rhetorical or poetic, the style of the Epistle to the Hebrews is prevailingly rhetorical, is free from anacolutha, and is always dominated by emotion. He holds that these characteristics point to Apollos as its author. Contrast also Paul's method of quoting the O. T.: "it is written" (Rom. 11:8; 1 Cor. 1:31; Gal. 3:10) with that of the Hebrews: "he saith" (8:5, 13), "he hath said" (4:4). Paul quotes the O. T. fifty or sixty times, but never in this latter way. Heb. 2:3—"which having at the first been spoken by the Lord, was confirmed unto us by them that heard"—shows that the writer did not receive the gospel at first hand. Luther and Calvin rightly saw in this a decisive proof that Paul was not the author, for he always insisted on the primary and independent character of his gospel. Harnack formerly thought the epistle written by Barnabas to Christians at Rome, A. D. 81-96. More recently however he attributes it to Priscilla, the wife of Aquila, or to their joint authorship. The majesty of its diction, however, seems unfavorable to this view. William T. C. Hanna: "The words of the author ... are marshalled grandly, and move with the tread of an army, or with the swell of a tidal wave"; see Franklin Johnson, Quotations in N. T. from O. T., xii. Plumptre, Introd. to N. T., 37, and in Expositor, Vol. I, regards the author of this epistle as the same with that of the Apocryphal Wisdom of Solomon, the latter being composed before, the former after, the writer's conversion to Christianity. Perhaps our safest conclusion is that of Origen: "God only knows who wrote it." Harnack however remarks: "The time in which our ancient Christian literature, the N. T. included, was considered as a web of delusions and falsifications, is past. The oldest literature of the church is, in its main points, and in most of its details, true and trustworthy." See articles on Hebrews, in Smith's and in Hastings' Bible Dictionaries.

(e) As to 2 Peter, Jude, and 2 and 3 John, the epistles most frequently held to be spurious, we may say that, although we have no conclusive external evidence earlier than A. D. 160, and in the case of 2 Peter none earlier than A. D. 230-250, we may fairly urge in favor of their genuineness not only their internal characteristics of literary style and moral value, but also the general acceptance of them all since the third century as the actual productions of the men or class of men whose names they bear.

Firmilianus (250), Bishop of Cæsarea in Cappadocia, is the first clear witness to 2 Peter. Origen (230) names it, but, in naming it, admits that its genuineness is questioned. The Council of Laodicea (372) first received it into the Canon. With this very gradual recognition and acceptance of 2 Peter, compare the loss of the later works of Aristotle for a hundred and fifty years after his death, and their recognition as genuine so soon as they were recovered from the cellar of the family of Neleus in Asia; De Wette's first publication of certain letters of Luther after the lapse of three hundred years, yet without occasioning doubt as to their genuineness; or the concealment of Milton's Treatise on Christian Doctrine, among the lumber of the State Paper Office in London, from 1677 to 1823; see Mair, Christian Evidences, 95. Sir William Hamilton complained that there were treatises of Cudworth, Berkeley and Collier, still lying unpublished and even unknown to their editors, biographers and fellow metaphysicians, but yet of the highest interest and importance; see Mansel, Letters, Lectures and Reviews, 381; Archibald, The Bible Verified, 27. 2 Peter was probably sent from the East shortly before Peter's martyrdom; distance and persecution may have prevented its rapid circulation in other countries. Sagebeer, The Bible in Court, 114—"A ledger may have been lost, or its authenticity for a long time doubted, but when once it is discovered and proved, it is as trustworthy as any other part of the res gestæ." See Plumptre, Epistles of Peter, Introd., 73-81; Alford on 2 Peter, 4: Prolegomena, 157; Westcott, on Canon, in Smith's Bib. Dict., 1:370, 373; Blunt, Dict. Doct. and Hist. Theol., art.: Canon.

It is urged by those who doubt the genuineness of 2 Peter that the epistle speaks of "your apostles" (3:2), just as Jude 17 speaks of "the apostles," as if the writer did not number himself among them. But 2 Peter begins with "Simon Peter, a servant and apostle of Jesus Christ," and Jude, "brother of James" (verse 1) was a brother of our Lord, but not an apostle. Hovey, Introd. to N. T., xxxi—"The earliest passage manifestly based upon 2 Peter appears to be in the so-called Second Epistle of the Roman Clement, 16:3, which however is now understood to be a Christian homily from the middle of the second century." Origen (born 186) testifies that Peter left one epistle, "and perhaps a second, for that is disputed." He also says: "John wrote the Apocalypse, and an epistle of very few lines; and, it may be, a second and a third; since all do not admit them to be genuine." He quotes also from James and from

Jude, adding that their canonicity was doubted.

Harnack regards 1 Peter, 2 Peter, James, and Jude, as written respectively about 160, 170, 130, and 130, but not by the men to whom they are ascribed—the ascriptions to these authors being later additions. Hort remarks: "If I were asked, I should say that the balance of the argument was against 2 Peter, but the moment I had done so I should begin to think I might be in the wrong." Sanday, Oracles of God, 73 note, considers the arguments in favor of 2 Peter unconvincing, but also the arguments against. He cannot get beyond a non liquet. He refers to Salmon, Introd. to N. T., 529-559, ed. 4, as expressing his own view. But the later conclusions of Sanday are more radical. In his Bampton Lectures on Inspiration, 348, 399, he says: 2 Peter "is probably at least to this extent a counterfeit, that it appears under a name which is not that of its true author."

Chase, in Hastings' Bib. Dict., 3:806-817, says that "the first piece of certain evidence as to 2 Peter is the passage from Origen quoted by Eusebius, though it hardly admits of doubt that the Epistle was known to Clement of Alexandria.... We find no trace of the epistle in the period when the tradition of apostolic days was still living.... It was not the work of the apostle but of the second century ... put forward without any sinister motive ... the personation of the apostle an obvious literary device rather than a religious or controversial fraud. The adoption of such a verdict can cause perplexity only when the Lord's promise of guidance to his Church is regarded as a charter of infallibility." Against this verdict we would urge the dignity and spiritual value of 2 Peter—internal evidence which in our judgment causes the balance to incline in favor of its apostolic authorship.

(f) Upon no other hypothesis than that of their genuineness can the general acceptance of these four minor epistles since the third century, and of all the other books of the New Testament since the middle of the second century, be satisfactorily accounted for. If they had been mere collections of floating legends, they could not have secured wide circulation as sacred books for which Christians must answer with their blood. If they had been forgeries, the churches at large could neither have been deceived as to their previous non-existence, nor have been induced unanimously to pretend that they were ancient and genuine. Inasmuch, however, as other accounts of their origin, inconsistent with their genuineness, are now current, we proceed to examine more at length the most important of these opposing views.

The genuineness of the New Testament as a whole would still be demonstrable, even if doubt should still attach to one or two of its books. It does not matter that 2nd Alcibiades was not written by Plato, or Pericles by Shakespeare. The Council of Carthage in 397 gave a place in the Canon to the O. T. Apocrypha, but the Reformers tore it out. Zwingli said of the Revelation: "It is not a Biblical book," and Luther spoke slightingly of the Epistle of James. The judgment of Christendom at large is more trustworthy than the private impressions of any single Christian scholar. To hold the books of the N. T. to be written in the second century by other than those whose names they bear is to hold, not simply to forgery, but to a conspiracy of forgery. There must have been several forgers at work, and, since their writings wonderfully agree, there must have been collusion among them. Yet these able men have been forgotten, while the names of far feebler writers of the second century have been preserved.

G. F. Wright, Scientific Aspects of Christian Evidences, 343—"In civil law there are 'statutes of limitations' which provide that the general acknowledgment of a purported fact for a certain period shall be considered as conclusive evidence of it. If, for example, a man has remained in undisturbed possession of land for a certain number of years, it is presumed that he has a valid claim to it, and no one is allowed to dispute his claim." Mair, Evidences, 99—"We probably have not a tenth part of the evidence upon which the early churches accepted the N. T. books as the genuine productions of their authors. We have only their verdict." Wynne, in Literature of the Second Century, 58—"Those who gave up the Scriptures were looked on by their fellow Christians as 'traditores,' traitors, who had basely yielded up what they ought to have treasured as dearer than life. But all their books were not equally sacred. Some were essential, and some were non-essential to the faith. Hence arose the distinction between canonical and non-canonical. The general consciousness of Christians grew into a distinct registration." Such registration is entitled to the highest respect, and lays the burden of proof upon the objector. See Alexander, Christ and Christianity, Introduction; Hovey, General Introduction to American Commentary on N. T.

D. Rationalistic Theories as to the origin of the gospels. These are attempts to eliminate the miraculous element from the New Testament records, and to reconstruct the sacred history upon principles of naturalism.

Against them we urge the general objection that they are unscientific in their principle and method. To set out in an examination of the New Testament documents with the assumption that all history is a mere natural development, and that miracles are therefore impossible, is to make history a matter, not of testimony, but of a priori speculation. It indeed renders any history of Christ and his apostles impossible, since the witnesses whose testimony with regard to miracles is discredited can no longer be considered worthy of credence in their account of Christ's life or doctrine.

In Germany, half a century ago, "a man was famous according as he had lifted up axes upon the thick trees" (Ps. 74:5, A. V.), just as among the American Indians he was not counted a man who could not show his scalps. The critics fortunately scalped each other; see Tyler, Theology of Greek Poets, 79—on Homer. Nicoll, The Church's One Foundation, 15—"Like the mummers of old, sceptical critics send one before them with a broom to sweep the stage clear of everything for their drama. If we assume at the threshold of the gospel study that everything of the nature of miracle is impossible, then the specific questions are decided before the criticism begins to operate in earnest." Matthew Arnold: "Our popular religion at present conceives the birth, ministry and death of Christ as altogether steeped in prodigy, brimful of miracle,—and miracles do not happen." This presupposition influences the investigations of Kuenen, and of A. E. Abbott, in his article on the Gospels in the Encyc. Britannica. We give special attention to four of the theories based upon this assumption.

1st. The Myth-theory of Strauss (1808-1874).

According to this view, the gospels are crystallizations into story of Messianic ideas which had for several generations filled the minds of imaginative men in Palestine. The myth is a narrative in which such ideas are unconsciously clothed, and from which the element of intentional and deliberate deception is absent.

This early view of Strauss, which has become identified with his name, was exchanged in late years for a more advanced view which extended the meaning of the word "myths" so as to include all narratives that spring out of a theological idea, and it admitted the existence of "pious frauds" in the gospels. Baur, he says, first convinced him that the author of the fourth gospel had "not unfrequently composed mere fables, knowing them to be mere fictions." The animating spirit of both the old view and the new is the same. Strauss says: "We know with certainty what Jesus was not, and what he has not done, namely, nothing superhuman and supernatural." "No gospel can claim that degree of historic credibility that would be required in order to make us debase our reason to the point of believing miracles." He calls the resurrection of Christ "ein weltgeschichtlicher Humbug." "If the gospels are really historical documents, we cannot exclude miracle from the life-story of Jesus;" see Strauss, Life of Jesus, 17; New Life of Jesus, 1: preface, xii. Vatke, Einleitung in A. T., 210, 211, distinguishes the myth from the saga or legend: The criterion of the pure myth is that the experience is impossible, while the saga is a tradition of remote antiquity; the myth has in it the element only of belief, the saga has in it an element of history. Sabatier, Philos. Religion, 37—"A myth is false in appearance only. The divine Spirit can avail himself of the fictions of poetry as well as of logical reasonings. When the heart was pure, the veils of fable always allowed the face of truth to shine through. And does not childhood run on into maturity and old age?"

It is very certain that childlike love of truth was not the animating spirit of Strauss. On the contrary, his spirit was that of remorseless criticism and of uncompromising hostility to the supernatural. It has been well said that he gathered up all the previous objections of sceptics to the gospel narrative and hurled them in one mass, just as if some Sadducee at the time of Jesus' trial had put all the taunts and gibes, all the buffetings and insults, all the shame and spitting, into one blow delivered straight into the face of the Redeemer. An octogenarian and saintly German lady said unsuspectingly that "somehow she never could get interested" in Strauss's Leben Jesu, which her sceptical son had given her for religious reading. The work was almost altogether destructive, only the last chapter suggesting Strauss's own view of what Jesus was.

If Luther's dictum is true that "the heart is the best theologian," Strauss must be regarded as destitute of the main qualification for his task. Encyc. Britannica, 22:592—"Strauss's mind was almost exclusively analytical and critical, without depth of religious feeling, or philosophical penetration, or historical sympathy. His work was rarely constructive, and, save when he was dealing with a kindred spirit, he failed as a historian, biographer, and critic, strikingly illustrating Goethe's profoundly true principle that loving sympathy is essential for productive criticism." Pfleiderer, Strauss's Life of Jesus, xix—"Strauss showed that the church formed the mythical traditions about Jesus out of its faith in him as the Messiah; but he did not show how the church came by the faith that Jesus of Nazareth was the Messiah." See Carpenter, Mental Physiology, 362; Grote, Plato, 1:249.

We object to the Myth-theory of Strauss, that

(a) The time between the death of Christ and the publication of the gospels was far too short for the growth and consolidation of such mythical histories. Myths, on the contrary, as the Indian, Greek, Roman and Scandinavian instances bear witness, are the slow growth of centuries.

(b) The first century was not a century when such formation of myths was possible. Instead of being a credulous and imaginative age, it was an age of historical inquiry and of Sadduceeism in matters of religion.

Horace, in Odes 1:34 and 3:6, denounces the neglect and squalor of the heathen temples, and Juvenal, Satire 2:150, says that "Esse aliquid manes et subterranea regna Nec pueri credunt." Arnold of Rugby: "The idea of men writing mythic histories between the times of Livy and of Tacitus, and of St. Paul mistaking them for realities!" Pilate's sceptical inquiry, "What is truth?" (John 18:38), better represented the age. "The mythical age is past when an idea is presented abstractly—apart from narrative." The Jewish sect of the Sadducees shows that the rationalistic spirit was not confined to Greeks or Romans. The question of John the Baptist, Mat. 11:3—"Art thou he that cometh, or look we for another?" and our Lord's answer, Mat. 11:4, 5—"Go and tell John the thing which ye hear and see: the blind receive their sight ... the dead are raised up," show that the Jews expected miracles to be wrought by the Messiah; yet John 10:41—"John indeed did no sign" shows also no irresistible inclination to invest popular teachers with miraculous powers; see E. G. Robinson, Christian Evidences, 22; Westcott, Com. on John 10:41; Rogers, Superhuman Origin of the Bible, 61; Cox, Miracles, 50.

(c) The gospels cannot be a mythical outgrowth of Jewish ideas and expectations, because, in their main features, they run directly counter to these ideas and expectations. The sullen and exclusive nationalism of the Jews could not have given rise to a gospel for all nations, nor could their expectations of a temporal monarch have led to the story of a suffering Messiah.

The O. T. Apocrypha shows how narrow was the outlook of the Jews. 2 Esdras 6:55, 56 says the Almighty has made the world "for our sakes"; other peoples, though they "also come from Adam," to the Eternal "are nothing, but be like unto spittle." The whole multitude of them are only, before him, "like a single foul drop that oozes out of a cask" (C. Geikie, in S. S. Times). Christ's kingdom differed from that which the Jews expected, both in its spirituality and its universality (Bruce, Apologetics, 3). There was no missionary impulse in the heathen world; on the other hand, it was blasphemy for an ancient tribesman to make known his god to an outsider (Nash, Ethics and Revelation, 106). The Apocryphal gospels show what sort of myths the N. T. age would have elaborated: Out of a demoniac young woman Satan is said to depart in the form of a young man (Bernard, in Literature of the Second Century, 99-136).

(d) The belief and propagation of such myths are inconsistent with what we know of the sober characters and self-sacrificing lives of the apostles.

(e) The mythical theory cannot account for the acceptance of the gospels among the Gentiles, who had none of the Jewish ideas and expectations.

(f) It cannot explain Christianity itself, with its belief in Christ's crucifixion and resurrection, and the ordinances which commemorate these facts.

(d) Witness Thomas's doubting, and Paul's shipwrecks and scourgings. Cf. 2 Pet. 1:16—οὐ γὰρ σεσοφισμένοις μύθοις ἐξακολουθήσαντες = "we have not been on the false track of myths artificially elaborated." See F. W. Farrar, Witness of History to Christ, 49-88. (e) See the two books entitled: If the Gospel Narratives are Mythical,—What Then? and, But How,—if the Gospels are Historic? (f) As the existence of the American Republic is proof that there was once a Revolutionary War, so the existence of Christianity is proof of the death of Christ. The change from the seventh day to the first, in Sabbath observance, could never have come about in a nation so Sabbatarian, had not the first day been the celebration of an actual resurrection. Like the Jewish Passover and our own Independence Day, Baptism and the Lord's Supper cannot be accounted for, except as monuments and remembrances of historical facts at the beginning of the Christian church. See Muir, on the Lord's Supper an abiding Witness to the Death of Christ, In Present Day Tracts, 6: no. 36. On Strauss and his theory, see Hackett, in Christian Rev., 48; Weiss, Life of Jesus, 155-163; Christlieb, Mod. Doubt and Christ. Belief, 379-425; Maclear, in Strivings for the Faith, 1-136; H. B. Smith, in Faith and Philosophy, 442-468; Bayne, Review of Strauss's New Life, in Theol. Eclectic, 4:74; Row, in Lectures on Modern Scepticism, 305-360; Bibliotheca Sacra, Oct. 1871: art. by Prof. W. A. Stevens; Burgess, Antiquity and Unity of Man, 263, 264; Curtis on Inspiration, 62-67; Alexander, Christ and Christianity, 92-126; A. P. Peabody, in Smith's Bible Dict., 2:954-958.

2nd. The Tendency-theory of Baur (1792-1860).

This maintains that the gospels originated in the middle of the second century, and were written under assumed names as a means of reconciling opposing Jewish and Gentile tendencies in the church. "These great national tendencies find their satisfaction, not in events corresponding to them, but in the elaboration of conscious fictions."

Baur dates the fourth gospel at 160-170 A. D.; Matthew at 130; Luke at 150; Mark at 150-160. Baur never inquires who Christ was. He turns his attention from the facts to the documents. If the documents be proved unhistorical, there is no need of examining the facts, for there are no facts to examine. He indicates the presupposition of his investigations, when he says: "The principal argument for the later origin of the gospels must forever remain this, that separately, and still more when taken together, they give an account of the life of Jesus which involves impossibilities"—i. e., miracles. He would therefore remove their authorship far enough from Jesus' time to permit regarding the miracles as inventions. Baur holds that in Christ were united the universalistic spirit of the new religion, and the particularistic form of the Jewish Messianic idea; some of his disciples laid emphasis on the one, some on the other; hence first conflict, but finally reconciliation; see statement of the Tübingen theory and of the way in which Baur was led to it, in Bruce, Apologetics, 360. E. G. Robinson interprets Baur as follows: "Paul = Protestant; Peter = sacramentarian; James = ethical; Paul + Peter + James = Christianity. Protestant preaching should dwell more on the ethical—cases of conscience—and less on mere doctrine, such as regeneration and justification."

Baur was a stranger to the needs of his own soul, and so to the real character of the gospel. One of his friends and advisers wrote, after his death, in terms that were meant to be laudatory: "His was a completely objective nature. No trace of personal needs or struggles is discernible in connection with his investigations of Christianity." The estimate of posterity is probably expressed in the judgment with regard to the Tübingen school by Harnack: "The possible picture it sketched was not the real, and the key with which it attempted to solve all problems did not suffice for the most simple.... The Tübingen views have indeed been compelled to undergo very large modifications. As regards the development of the church in the second century, it may safely be said that the hypotheses of the Tübingen school have proved themselves everywhere inadequate, very erroneous, and are to-day held by only a very few scholars." See Baur, Die kanonischen Evangelien; Canonical Gospels (Eng. transl.), 530; Supernatural Religion, 1:212-444 and vol. 2: Pfleiderer, Hibbert Lectures for 1885. For accounts of Baur's position, see Herzog, Encyclopädie, art.: Baur; Clarke's transl. of Hase's Life of Jesus, 34-36; Farrar, Critical History of Free Thought, 227, 228.

We object to the Tendency-theory of Baur, that

(a) The destructive criticism to which it subjects the gospels, if applied to secular documents, would deprive us of any certain knowledge of the past, and render all history impossible.

The assumption of artifice is itself unfavorable to a candid examination of the documents. A perverse acuteness can descry evidences of a hidden animus in the most simple and ingenuous literary productions. Instance the philosophical interpretation of "Jack and Jill."

(b) The antagonistic doctrinal tendencies which it professes to find in the several gospels are more satisfactorily explained as varied but consistent aspects of the one system of truth held by all the apostles.

Baur exaggerates the doctrinal and official differences between the leading apostles. Peter was not simply a Judaizing Christian, but was the first preacher to the Gentiles, and his doctrine appears to have been subsequently influenced to a considerable extent by Paul's (see Plumptre on 1 Pet., 68-69). Paul was not an exclusively Hellenizing Christian, but invariably addressed the gospel to the Jews before he turned to the Gentiles. The evangelists give pictures of Jesus from different points of view. As the Parisian sculptor constructs his bust with the aid of a dozen photographs of his subject, all taken from different points of view, so from the four portraits furnished us by Matthew, Mark, Luke and John we are to construct the solid and symmetrical life of Christ. The deeper reality which makes reconciliation of the different views possible is the actual historical Christ. Marcus Dods, Expositor's Greek Testament, 1:675—"They are not two Christs, but one, which the four Gospels depict: diverse as the profile and front face, but one another's complement rather than contradiction."

Godet, Introd. to Gospel Collection, 272—Matthew shows the greatness of Jesus—his full-length portrait; Mark his indefatigable activity; Luke his beneficent compassion; John his essential divinity. Matthew first wrote Aramæan Logia. This was translated into Greek and completed by a narrative of the ministry of Jesus for the Greek churches founded by Paul. This translation was not made by Matthew and did not make use of Mark (217-224). E. D. Burton: Matthew = fulfilment of past prophecy; Mark = manifestation of present power. Matthew is argument from prophecy; Mark is argument from miracle. Matthew, as prophecy, made most impression on Jewish readers; Mark, as power, was best adapted to Gentiles. Prof. Burton holds Mark to be based upon oral tradition alone; Matthew upon his Logia (his real earlier Gospel) and other fragmentary notes; while Luke has a fuller origin in manuscripts and in Mark. See Aids to the Study of German Theology, 148-155; F. W. Farrar, Witness of History to Christ, 61.

(c) It is incredible that productions of such literary power and lofty religious teaching as the gospels should have sprung up in the middle of the second century, or that, so springing up, they should have been published under assumed names and for covert ends.

The general character of the literature of the second century is illustrated by Ignatius's fanatical desire for martyrdom, the value ascribed by Hermas to ascetic rigor, the insipid allegories of Barnabas, Clement of Rome's belief in the phœnix, and the absurdities of the Apocryphal Gospels. The author of the fourth gospel among the writers of the second century would have been a mountain among mole-hills. Wynne, Literature of the Second Century, 60—"The apostolic and the sub-apostolic writers differ from each other as a nugget of pure gold differs from a block of quartz with veins of the precious metal gleaming through it." Dorner, Hist. Doct. Person Christ, 1:1:92—"Instead of the writers of the second century marking an advance on the apostolic age, or developing the germ given them by the apostles, the second century shows great retrogression,—its writers were not able to retain or comprehend all that had been given them." Martineau, Seat of Authority, 291—"Writers not only barbarous in speech and rude in art, but too often puerile in conception, passionate in temper, and credulous in belief. The legends of Papias, the visions of Hermas, the imbecility of Irenæus, the fury of Tertullian, the rancor and indelicacy of Jerome, the stormy intolerance of Augustine, cannot fail to startle and repel the student; and, if he turns to the milder Hippolytus, he is introduced to a brood of thirty heresies which sadly dissipate his dream of the unity of the church." We can apply to the writers of the second century the question of R. G. Ingersoll in the Shakespeare-Bacon controversy: "Is it possible that Bacon left the best children of his brain on Shakespeare's doorstep, and kept only the deformed ones at home?" On the Apocryphal Gospels, see Cowper, in Strivings for the Faith, 73-108.

(d) The theory requires us to believe in a moral anomaly, namely, that a faithful disciple of Christ in the second century could be guilty of fabricating a life of his master, and of claiming authority for it on the ground that the author had been a companion of Christ or his apostles.

"A genial set of Jesuitical religionists"—with mind and heart enough to write the gospel according to John, and who at the same time have cold-blooded sagacity enough to keep out of their writings every trace of the developments of church authority belonging to the second century. The newly discovered "Teaching of the Twelve Apostles," if dating from the early part of that century, shows that such a combination is impossible. The critical theories assume that one who knew Christ as a man could not possibly also regard him as God. Lowrie, Doctrine of St. John, 12—"If St. John wrote, it is not possible to say that the genius of St. Paul foisted upon the church a conception which was strange to the original apostles." Fairbairn has well shown that if Christianity had been simply the ethical teaching of the human Jesus, it would have vanished from the earth like the sects of the Pharisees and of the Sadducees; if on the other hand it had been simply the Logos-doctrine, the doctrine of a divine Christ, it would have passed away like the speculations of Plato or Aristotle; because Christianity unites the idea of the eternal Son of God with that of the incarnate Son of man, it is fitted to be and it has become an universal religion; see Fairbairn, Philosophy of the Christian Religion, 4, 15—"Without the personal charm of the historical Jesus, the œcumenical creeds would never have been either formulated or tolerated, and without the metaphysical conception of Christ the Christian religion would long ago have ceased to live.... It is not Jesus of Nazareth who has so powerfully entered into history: it is the deified Christ who has been believed, loved and obeyed as the Savior of the world.... The two parts of Christian doctrine are combined in the one name 'Jesus Christ.' "

(e) This theory cannot account for the universal acceptance of the gospels at the end of the second century, among widely separated communities where reverence for writings of the apostles was a mark of orthodoxy, and where the Gnostic heresies would have made new documents instantly liable to suspicion and searching examination.

Abbot, Genuineness of the Fourth Gospel, 52, 80, 88, 89. The Johannine doctrine of the Logos, if first propounded in the middle of the second century, would have ensured the instant rejection of that gospel by the Gnostics, who ascribed creation, not to the Logos, but to successive "Æons." How did the Gnostics, without "peep or mutter," come to accept as genuine what had only in their own time been first sprung upon the churches? While Basilides (130) and Valentinus (150), the Gnostics, both quote from the fourth gospel, they do not dispute its genuineness or suggest that it was of recent origin. Bruce, in his Apologetics, says of Baur "He believed in the all-sufficiency of the Hegelian theory of development through antagonism. He saw tendency everywhere. Anything additional, putting more contents into the person and teaching of Jesus than suits the initial stage of development, must be reckoned spurious. If we find Jesus in any of the gospels claiming to be a supernatural being, such texts can with the utmost confidence be set aside as spurious, for such a thought could not belong to the initial stage of Christianity." But such a conception certainly existed in the second century, and it directly antagonized the speculations of the Gnostics. F. W. Farrar, on Hebrews 1:2—"The word æon was used by the later Gnostics to describe the various emanations by which they tried at once to widen and to bridge over the gulf between the human and the divine. Over that imaginary chasm John threw the arch of the Incarnation, when he wrote: 'The Word became flesh' (John 1:14)." A document which so contradicted the Gnostic teachings could not in the second century have been quoted by the Gnostics themselves without dispute as to its genuineness, if it had not been long recognized in the churches as a work of the apostle John.

(f) The acknowledgment by Baur that the epistles to the Romans, Galatians and Corinthians were written by Paul in the first century is fatal to his theory, since these epistles testify not only to miracles at the period at which they were written, but to the main events of Jesus' life and to the miracle of his resurrection, as facts already long acknowledged in the Christian church.

Baur, Paulus der Apostel, 276—"There never has been the slightest suspicion of unauthenticity cast on these epistles (Gal., 1 and 2 Cor., Rom.), and they bear so incontestably the character of Pauline originality, that there is no conceivable ground for the assertion of critical doubts in their case." Baur, in discussing the appearance of Christ to Paul on the way to Damascus, explains the outward from the inward: Paul translated intense and sudden conviction of the truth of the Christian religion into an outward scene. But this cannot explain the hearing of the outward sound by Paul's companions. On the evidential value of the epistles here mentioned, see Lorimer, in Strivings for the Faith, 109-144; Howson, in Present Day Tracts, 4: no. 24; Row, Bampton Lectures for 1877:289-356. On Baur and his theory in general, see Weiss, Life of Jesus, 1:157 sq.; Christlieb, Mod. Doubt and Christ. Belief, 504-549; Hutton, Essays, 1:176-215; Theol. Eclectic, 5:1-42; Auberlen, Div. Revelation; Bib. Sac., 19:75;

Answers to Supernatural Religion, in Westcott, Hist. N. T. Canon, 4th ed., Introd.; Lightfoot, in Contemporary Rev., Dec. 1874, and Jan. 1875; Salmon, Introd. to N. T., 6-31; A. B. Bruce, in Present Day Tracts, 7: no. 38.

3d. The Romance-theory of Renan (1823-1892).

This theory admits a basis of truth in the gospels and holds that they all belong to the century following Jesus' death. "According to" Matthew, Mark, etc., however, means only that Matthew, Mark, etc., wrote these gospels in substance. Renan claims that the facts of Jesus' life were so sublimated by enthusiasm, and so overlaid with pious fraud, that the gospels in their present form cannot be accepted as genuine,—in short, the gospels are to be regarded as historical romances which have only a foundation in fact.

The animus of this theory is plainly shown in Renan's Life of Jesus, preface to 13th ed.—"If miracles and the inspiration of certain books are realities, my method is detestable. If miracles and the inspiration of books are beliefs without reality, my method is a good one. But the question of the supernatural is decided for us with perfect certainty by the single consideration that there is no room for believing in a thing of which the world offers no experimental trace." "On the whole," says Renan, "I admit as authentic the four canonical gospels. All, in my opinion, date from the first century, and the authors are, generally speaking, those to whom they are attributed." He regards Gal., 1 and 2 Cor., and Rom., as "indisputable and undisputed." He speaks of them as "being texts of an absolute authenticity, of complete sincerity, and without legends" (Les Apôtres, xxix; Les Évangiles, xi). Yet he denies to Jesus "sincerity with himself"; attributes to him "innocent artifice" and the toleration of pious fraud, as for example in the case of the stories of Lazarus and of his own resurrection. "To conceive the good is not sufficient: it must be made to succeed; to accomplish this, less pure paths must be followed.... Not by any fault of his own, his conscience lost somewhat of its original purity,—his mission overwhelmed him.... Did he regret his too lofty nature, and, victim of his own greatness, mourn that he had not remained a simple artizan?" So Renan "pictures Christ's later life as a misery and a lie, yet he requests us to bow before this sinner and before his superior, Sakya-Mouni, as demigods" (see Nicoll, The Church's One Foundation, 62, 63). Of the highly wrought imagination of Mary Magdalene, he says: "O divine power of love! sacred moments, in which the passion of one whose senses were deceived gives us a resuscitated God!" See Renan, Life of Jesus, 21.

To this Romance-theory of Renan, we object that

(a) It involves an arbitrary and partial treatment of the Christian documents. The claim that one writer not only borrowed from others, but interpolated ad libitum, is contradicted by the essential agreement of the manuscripts as quoted by the Fathers, and as now extant.

Renan, according to Mair, Christian Evidences, 153, dates Matthew at 84 A. D.; Mark at 76; Luke at 94; John at 125. These dates mark a considerable retreat from the advanced positions taken by Baur. Mair, in his chapter on Recent Reverses in Negative Criticism, attributes this result to the late discoveries with regard to the Epistle of Barnabas, Hippolytus's Refutation of all Heresies, the Clementine Homilies, and Tatian's Diatessaron: "According to Baur and his immediate followers, we have less than one quarter of the N. T. belonging to the first century. According to Hilgenfeld, the present head of the Baur school, we have somewhat less than three quarters belonging to the first century, while substantially the same thing may be said with regard to Holzmann. According to Renan, we have distinctly more than three quarters of the N. T. falling within the first century, and therefore within the apostolic age. This surely indicates a very decided and extraordinary retreat since the time of Baur's grand assault, that is, within the last fifty years." We may add that the concession of authorship within the apostolic age renders nugatory Renan's hypothesis that the N. T. documents have been so enlarged by pious fraud that they cannot be accepted as trustworthy accounts of such events as miracles. The oral tradition itself had attained so fixed a form that the many manuscripts used by the Fathers were in substantial agreement in respect to these very events, and oral tradition in the East hands down without serious alteration much longer narratives than those of our gospels. The Pundita Ramabai can repeat after the lapse of twenty years portions of the Hindu sacred books exceeding in amount the whole contents of our Old Testament. Many cultivated men in Athens knew by heart all the Iliad and the Odyssey of Homer. Memory and reverence alike kept the gospel narratives free from the corruption which Renan supposes.

(b) It attributes to Christ and to the apostles an alternate fervor of romantic enthusiasm and a false pretense of miraculous power which are utterly irreconcilable with the manifest sobriety and holiness of their lives and teachings. If Jesus did not work miracles, he was an impostor.

On Ernest Renan, His Life and the Life of Jesus, see A. H. Strong, Christ in Creation, 332-363, especially 356—"Renan attributes the origin of Christianity to the predominance in Palestine of a constitutional susceptibility to mystic excitements. Christ is to him the incarnation of sympathy and tears, a being of tender impulses and passionate ardors, whose native genius it was to play upon the hearts of men. Truth or falsehood made little difference to him; anything that would comfort the poor, or touch the finer feelings of humanity, he availed himself of; ecstasies, visions, melting moods, these were the secrets of his power. Religion was a beneficent superstition, a sweet delusion—excellent as a balm and solace for the ignorant crowd, who never could be philosophers if they tried. And so the gospel river, as one has said, is traced back to a fountain of weeping men and women whose brains had oozed out at their eyes, and the perfection of spirituality is made to be a sort of maudlin monasticism.... How different from the strong and holy love of Christ, which would save men only by bringing them to the truth, and which claims men's imitation only because, without love for God and for the soul, a man is without truth. How inexplicable from this view the fact that a pure Christianity has everywhere quickened the intellect of the nations, and that every revival of it, as at the Reformation, has been followed by mighty forward leaps of civilization. Was Paul a man carried away by mystic dreams and irrational enthusiasms? Let the keen dialectic skill of his epistles and his profound grasp of the great matters of revelation answer. Has the Christian church been a company of puling sentimentalists? Let the heroic deaths for the truth suffered by the martyrs witness. Nay, he must have a low idea of his kind, and a yet lower idea of the God who made them, who can believe that the noblest spirits of the race have risen to greatness by abnegating will and reason, and have gained influence over all ages by resigning themselves to semi-idiocy."

(c) It fails to account for the power and progress of the gospel, as a system directly opposed to men's natural tastes and prepossessions—a system which substitutes truth for romance and law for impulse.

A. H. Strong, Christ in Creation, 358—"And if the later triumphs of Christianity are inexplicable upon the theory of Renan, how can we explain its founding? The sweet swain of Galilee, beloved by women for his beauty, fascinating the unlettered crowd by his gentle speech and his poetic ideals, giving comfort to the sorrowing and hope to the poor, credited with supernatural power which at first he thinks it not worth while to deny and finally gratifies the multitude by pretending to exercise, roused by opposition to polemics and invective until the delightful young rabbi becomes a gloomy giant, an intractable fanatic, a fierce revolutionist, whose denunciation of the powers that be brings him to the Cross,—what is there in him to account for the moral wonder which we call Christianity and the beginnings of its empire in the world? Neither delicious pastorals like those of Jesus' first period, nor apocalyptic fevers like those of his second period, according to Renan's gospel, furnish any rational explanation of that mighty movement which has swept through the earth and has revolutionized the faith of mankind."

Berdoe, Browning, 47—"If Christ were not God, his life at that stage of the world's history could by no possibility have had the vitalizing force and love-compelling power that Renan's pages everywhere disclose. Renan has strengthened faith in Christ's deity while laboring to destroy it."

Renan, in discussing Christ's appearance to Paul on the way to Damascus, explains the inward from the outward, thus precisely reversing the conclusion of Baur. A sudden storm, a flash of lightning, a sudden attack of ophthalmic fever, Paul took as an appearance from heaven. But we reply that so keen an observer and reasoner could not have been thus deceived. Nothing could have made him the apostle to the Gentiles but a sight of the glorified Christ and the accompanying revelation of the holiness of God, his own sin, the sacrifice of the Son of God, its universal efficacy, the obligation laid upon him to proclaim it to the ends of the earth. For reviews of Renan, see Hutton, Essays, 261-281, and Contemp. Thought and Thinkers, 1:227-234; H. B. Smith, Faith and Philosophy, 401-441; Christlieb, Mod. Doubt, 425-447; Pressensé, in Theol. Eclectic, 1:199; Uhlhorn, Mod. Representations of Life of Jesus, 1-33; Bib. Sac, 22:207; 23:353, 529; Present Day Tracts, 3: no. 16, and 4: no. 21; E. G. Robinson, Christian Evidences, 43-48; A. H. Strong, Sermon before Baptist World Congress, 1905.

4th. The Development-theory of Harnack (born 1851).

This holds Christianity to be a historical development from germs which were devoid of both dogma and miracle. Jesus was a teacher of ethics, and the original gospel is most clearly represented by the Sermon on the Mount. Greek influence, and especially that of the Alexandrian philosophy, added to this gospel a theological and supernatural element, and so changed Christianity from a life into a doctrine.

Harnack dates Matthew at 70-75; Mark at 65-70; Luke at 78-93; the fourth gospel at 80-110. He regards both the fourth gospel and the book of Revelation as the works, not of John the Apostle, but of John the Presbyter. He separates the prologue of the fourth gospel from the gospel itself, and considers the prologue as a preface added after its original composition in order to enable the Hellenistic reader to understand it. "The gospel itself," says Harnack, "contains no Logos-idea; it did not develop out of a Logos-idea, such as flourished at Alexandria; it only connects itself with such an idea. The gospel itself is based upon the historic Christ; he is the subject of all its statements. This historical trait can in no way be dissolved by any kind of speculation. The memory of what was actually historical was still too powerful to admit at this point any Gnostic influences. The Logos-idea of the prologue is the Logos of Alexandrine Judaism, the Logos of Philo, and it is derived ultimately from the 'Son of man' in the book of Daniel.... The fourth gospel, which does not proceed from the Apostle John and does not so claim, cannot be used as a historical source in the ordinary sense of that word.... The author has managed with sovereign freedom; has transposed occurrences and has put them in a light that is foreign to them; has of his own accord composed the discourses, and has illustrated lofty thoughts by inventing situations for them. Difficult as it is to recognize, an actual tradition in his work is not wholly lacking. For the history of Jesus, however, it can hardly anywhere be taken into account; only little can be taken from it, and that with caution.... On the other hand it is a source of the first rank for the answer of the question what living views of the person of Jesus, what light and what warmth, the gospel has brought into being." See Harnack's article in Zeitschrift für Theol. u. Kirche, 2:189-231, and his Wesen des Christenthums, 13. Kaftan also, who belongs to the same Ritschlian school with Harnack, tells us in his Truth of the Christian Religion, 1:97, that as the result of the Logos-speculation, "the centre of gravity, instead of being placed in the historical Christ who founded the kingdom of God, is placed in the Christ who as eternal Logos of God was the mediator in the creation of the world." This view is elaborated by Hatch in his Hibbert Lectures for 1888, on the Influence of Greek Ideas and Usages upon the Christian Church.

We object to the Development-theory of Harnack, that

(a) The Sermon on the Mount is not the sum of the gospel, nor its original form. Mark is the most original of the gospels, yet Mark omits the Sermon on the Mount, and Mark is preëminently the gospel of the miracle-worker.

(b) All four gospels lay the emphasis, not on Jesus' life and ethical teaching, but on his death and resurrection. Matthew implies Christ's deity when it asserts his absolute knowledge of the Father (11:27), his universal judgeship (25:32), his supreme authority (28:18), and his omnipresence (28:20), while the phrase "Son of man" implies that he is also "Son of God."

Mat. 11:27—"All things have been delivered unto me of my Father: and no one knoweth the Son, save the Father; neither doth any know the Father, save the Son, and he to whomsoever the Son willeth to reveal him"; 25:32—"and before him shall be gathered all the nations: and he shall separate them one from another, as the shepherd separateth the sheep from the goats"; 28:18—"All authority hath been given unto me in heaven and on earth"; 28:20—"lo, I am with you always, even unto the end of the world." These sayings of Jesus in Matthew's gospel show that the conception of Christ's greatness was not peculiar to John: "I am" transcends time; "with you" transcends space. Jesus speaks "sub specie eternitatis"; his utterance is equivalent to that of John 8:58—"Before Abraham was born, I am," and to that of Hebrews 13:8—"Jesus Christ is the same yesterday and to-day, yea and for ever." He is, as Paul declares in Eph. 1:23, one "that filleth all in all," that is, who is omnipresent.

A. H. Strong, Philos. and Religion, 206—The phrase "Son of man" intimates that Christ was more than man: "Suppose I were to go about proclaiming myself 'Son of man.' Who does not see that it would be mere impertinence, unless I claimed to be something more. 'Son of Man? But what of that? Cannot every human being call himself the same?' When one takes the title 'Son of man' for his characteristic designation, as Jesus did, he implies that there is something strange in his being Son of man; that this is not his original condition and dignity; that it is condescension on his part to be Son of man. In short, when Christ calls himself Son of man, it implies that he has come from a higher level of being to inhabit this low earth of ours. And so, when we are asked 'What think ye of the Christ? whose son is he?' we must answer, not simply, He is Son of man, but also, He is Son of God." On Son of man, see Driver; on Son of God, see Sanday; both in Hastings' Dictionary of the Bible. Sanday: "The Son is so called primarily as incarnate. But that which is the essence of the Incarnation must needs be also larger than the Incarnation. It must needs have its roots in the eternity of Godhead." Gore, Incarnation, 65, 73—"Christ, the final Judge, of the synoptics, is not dissociable from the divine, eternal Being, of the fourth gospel."

(c) The preëxistence and atonement of Christ cannot be regarded as accretions upon the original gospel, since these find expression in Paul who wrote before any of our evangelists, and in his epistles anticipated the Logos-doctrine of John.

(d) We may grant that Greek influence, through the Alexandrian philosophy, helped the New Testament writers to discern what was already present in the life and work and teaching of Jesus; but, like the microscope which discovers but does not create, it added nothing to the substance of the faith.

Gore, Incarnation, 62—"The divinity, incarnation, resurrection of Christ were not an accretion upon the original belief of the apostles and their first disciples, for these are all recognized as uncontroverted matters of faith in the four great epistles of Paul, written at a date when the greater part of those who had seen the risen Christ were still alive. The Alexandrian philosophy was not the source of apostolic doctrine, but only the form in which that doctrine was cast, the light thrown upon it which brought out its meaning. A. H. Strong, Christ in Creation, 146—"When we come to John's gospel, therefore, we find in it the mere unfolding of truth that for substance had been in the world for at least sixty years.... If the Platonizing philosophy of Alexandria assisted in this genuine development of Christian doctrine, then the Alexandrian philosophy was a providential help to inspiration. The microscope does not invent; it only discovers. Paul and John did not add to the truth of Christ; their philosophical equipment was only a microscope which brought into clear view the truth that was there already."

Pfleiderer, Philos. Religion, 1:126—"The metaphysical conception of the Logos, as immanent in the world and ordering it according to law, was filled with religious and moral contents. In Jesus the cosmical principle of nature became a religious principle of salvation." See Kilpatrick's article on Philosophy, in Hastings' Bible Dictionary. Kilpatrick holds that Harnack ignores the self-consciousness of Jesus; does not fairly interpret the Acts in its mention of the early worship of Jesus by the church before Greek philosophy had influenced it; refers to the intellectual peculiarities of the N. T. writers conceptions which Paul insists are simply the faith of all Christian people as such; forgets that the Christian idea of union with God secured through the atoning and reconciling work of a personal Redeemer utterly transcended Greek thought, and furnished the solution of the problem after which Greek philosophy was vainly groping.

(e) Though Mark says nothing of the virgin-birth because his story is limited to what the apostles had witnessed of Jesus' deeds, Matthew apparently gives us Joseph's story and Luke gives Mary's story—both stories naturally published only after Jesus' resurrection.

(f) The larger understanding of doctrine after Jesus' death was itself predicted by our Lord (John 16:12). The Holy Spirit was to bring his teachings to remembrance, and to guide into all the truth (16:13), and the apostles were to continue the work of teaching which he had begun (Acts 1:1).

John 16:12, 13—"I have yet many things to say unto you, but ye cannot bear them now. Howbeit, when he, the Spirit of truth, is come, he shall guide you into all the truth"; Acts 1:1—"The former treatise I made, O Theophilus, concerning all that Jesus began to do and to teach." A. H. Strong, Christ in Creation, 146—"That the beloved disciple, after a half century of meditation upon what he had seen and heard of God manifest in the flesh, should have penetrated more deeply into the meaning of that wonderful revelation is not only not surprising,—it is precisely what Jesus himself foretold. Our Lord had many things to say to his disciples, but then they could not bear them. He promised that the Holy Spirit should bring to their remembrance both himself and his words, and should lead them into all the truth. And this is the whole secret of what are called accretions to original Christianity. So far as they are contained in Scripture, they are inspired discoveries and unfoldings, not mere speculations and inventions. They are not additions, but elucidations, not vain imaginings, but correct interpretations.... When the later theology, then, throws out the supernatural and dogmatic, as coming not from Jesus but from Paul's epistles and from the fourth gospel, our claim is that Paul and John are only inspired and authoritative interpreters of Jesus, seeing themselves and making us see the fulness of the Godhead that dwelt in him."

While Harnack, in our judgment, errs in his view that Paul contributed to the gospel elements which it did not originally possess, he shows us very clearly many of the elements in that gospel which he was the first to recognize. In his Wesen des Christenthums, 111, he tells us that a few years ago a celebrated Protestant theologian declared that Paul, with his Rabbinical theology, was the destroyer of the Christian religion. Others have regarded him as the founder of that religion. But the majority have seen in him the apostle who best understood his Lord and did most to continue his work. Paul, as Harnack maintains, first comprehended the gospel definitely: (1) as an accomplished redemption and a present salvation—the crucified and risen Christ as giving access to God and righteousness and peace therewith; (2) as something new, which does away with the religion of the law; (3) as meant for all, and therefore for Gentiles also, indeed, as superseding Judaism; (4) as expressed in terms which are not simply Greek but also human,—Paul made the gospel comprehensible to the world. Islam, rising in Arabia, is an Arabian religion still. Buddhism remains an Indian religion. Christianity is at home in all lands. Paul put new life into the Roman empire, and inaugurated the Christian culture of the West. He turned a local into a universal religion. His influence however, according to Harnack, tended to the undue exaltation of organization and dogma and O. T. inspiration—points in which, in our judgment, Paul took sober middle ground and saved Christian truth for the world.

2. Genuineness of the Books of the Old Testament

Since nearly one half of the Old Testament is of anonymous authorship and certain of its books may be attributed to definite historic characters only by way of convenient classification or of literary personification, we here mean by genuineness honesty of purpose and freedom from anything counterfeit or intentionally deceptive so far as respects the age or the authorship of the documents.

We show the genuineness of the Old Testament books:

(a) From the witness of the New Testament, in which all but six books of the Old Testament are either quoted or alluded to as genuine.

The N. T. shows coincidences of language with the O. T. Apocryphal books, but it contains only one direct quotation from them; while, with the exception of Judges, Ecclesiastes, Canticles, Esther, Ezra, and Nehemiah, every book in the Hebrew canon is used either for illustration or proof. The single Apocryphal quotation is found in Jude 14 and is in all probability taken from the book of Enoch. Although Volkmar puts the date of this book at 132 A. D., and although some critics hold that Jude quoted only the same primitive tradition of which the author of the book of Enoch afterwards made use, the weight of modern scholarship inclines to the opinion that the book itself was written as early as 170-70 B. C., and that Jude quoted from it; see Hastings' Bible Dictionary: Book of Enoch; Sanday, Bampton Lect. on Inspiration, 95. "If Paul could quote from Gentile poets (Acts 17:28; Titus 1:12), it is hard to understand why Jude could not cite a work which was certainly in high standing among the faithful"; see Schodde, Book of Enoch, 41, with the Introd. by Ezra Abbot. While Jude 14 gives us the only direct and express quotation from an Apocryphal book, Jude 6 and 9 contain allusions to the Book of Enoch and to the Assumption of Moses; see Charles, Assumption of Moses, 62. In Hebrews 1:3, we have words taken from Wisdom 7:26; and Hebrews 11:34-38 is a reminiscence of 1 Maccabees.

(b) From the testimony of Jewish authorities, ancient and modern, who declare the same books to be sacred, and only the same books, that are now comprised in our Old Testament Scriptures.

Josephus enumerates twenty-two of these books "which are justly accredited" (omit θεῖα—Niese, and Hastings' Dict., 3:607). Our present Hebrew Bible makes twenty-four, by separating Ruth from Judges, and Lamentations from Jeremiah. See Josephus, Against Apion, 1:8; Smith's Bible Dictionary, article on the Canon, 1:359, 360. Philo (born 20 B. C.) never quotes an Apocryphal book, although he does quote from nearly all the books of the O. T.; see Ryle, Philo and Holy Scripture. George Adam Smith, Modern Criticism and Preaching, 7—"The theory which ascribed the Canon of the O. T. to a single decision of the Jewish church in the days of its inspiration is not a theory supported by facts. The growth of the O. T. Canon was very gradual. Virtually it began in 621 B. C., with the acceptance by all Judah of Deuteronomy, and the adoption of the whole Law, or first five books of the O. T., under Nehemiah in 445 B. C. Then came the prophets before 200 B. C., and the Hagiographa from a century to two centuries later. The strict definition of the last division was not complete by the time of Christ. Christ seems to testify to the Law, the Prophets, and the Psalms; yet neither Christ nor his apostles make any quotation from Ezra, Nehemiah, Esther, Canticles, or Ecclesiastes, the last of which books were not yet recognized by all the Jewish schools. But while Christ is the chief authority for the O. T., he was also its first critic. He rejected some parts of the Law and was indifferent to many others. He enlarged the sixth and seventh commandments, and reversed the eye for an eye, and the permission of divorce; touched the leper, and reckoned all foods lawful; broke away from literal observance of the Sabbath-day; left no commands about sacrifice, temple-worship, circumcision, but, by institution of the New Covenant, abrogated these sacraments of the Old. The apostles appealed to extra-canonical writings." Gladden, Seven Puzzling Bible Books, 68-96—"Doubts were entertained in our Lord's day as to the canonicity of several parts of the O. T., especially Proverbs, Ecclesiastes, Song of Solomon, Esther."

(c) From the testimony of the Septuagint translation, dating from the first half of the third century, or from 280 to 180 B. C.

MSS. of the Septuagint contain, indeed, the O. T. Apocrypha, but the writers of the latter do not recognize their own work as on a level with the canonical Scriptures, which they regard as distinct from all other books (Ecclesiasticus, prologue, and 48:24; also 24:23-27; 1 Mac. 12:9; 2 Mac. 6:23; 1 Esd. 1:28; 6:1; Baruch 2:21). So both ancient and modern Jews. See Bissell, in Lange's Commentary on the Apocrypha, Introduction, 44. In the prologue to the apocryphal book of Ecclesiasticus, we read of "the Law and the Prophets and the rest of the books," which shows that as early as 130 B. C., the probable date of Ecclesiasticus, a threefold division of the Jewish sacred books was recognized. That the author, however, did not conceive of these books as constituting a completed canon seems evident from his assertion in this connection that his grandfather Jesus also wrote. 1 Mac. 12:9 (80-90 B. C.) speaks of "the sacred books which are now in our hands." Hastings, Bible Dictionary, 3:611—"The O. T. was the result of a gradual process which began with the sanction of the Hexateuch by Ezra and Nehemiah, and practically closed with the decisions of the Council of Jamnia"—Jamnia is the ancient Jabneh, 7 miles south by west of Tiberias, where met a council of rabbins at some time between 90 to 118 A. D. This Council decided in favor of Canticles and Ecclesiastes, and closed the O. T. Canon.

The Greek version of the Pentateuch which forms a part of the Septuagint is said by Josephus to have been made in the reign and by the order of Ptolemy Philadelphus, King of Egypt, about 270 or 280 B. C. "The legend is that it was made by seventy-two persons in seventy-two days. It is supposed, however, by modern critics that this version of the several books is the work not only of different hands but of separate times. It is probable that at first only the Pentateuch was translated, and the remaining books gradually; but the translation is believed to have been completed by the second century B. C." (Century Dictionary, in voce). It therefore furnishes an important witness to the genuineness of our O. T. documents. Driver, Introd. to O. T. Lit., xxxi—"For the opinion, often met with in modern books, that the Canon of the O. T. was closed by Ezra, or in Ezra's time, there is no foundation in antiquity whatever.... All that can reasonably be treated as historical in the accounts of Ezra's literary labors is limited to the Law."

(d) From indications that soon after the exile, and so early as the times of Ezra and Nehemiah (500-450 B. C.), the Pentateuch together with the book of Joshua was not only in existence but was regarded as authoritative.

2 Mac, 2:13-15 intimates that Nehemiah founded a library, and there is a tradition that a "Great Synagogue" was gathered in his time to determine the Canon. But Hastings' Dictionary, 4:644, asserts that "the Great Synagogue was originally a meeting, and not an institution. It met once for all, and all that is told about it, except what we read in Nehemiah, is pure fable of the later Jews." In like manner no dependence is to be placed upon the tradition that Ezra miraculously restored the ancient Scriptures that had been lost during the exile. Clement of Alexandria says: "Since the Scriptures perished in the Captivity of Nebuchadnezzar, Esdras (the Greek form of Ezra) the Levite, the priest, in the time of Artaxerxes, King of the Persians, having become inspired in the exercise of prophecy, restored again the whole of the ancient Scriptures." But the work now divided into 1 and 2 Chronicles, Ezra and Nehemiah, mentions Darius Codomannus (Neh. 12:22), whose date is 336 B. C. The utmost the tradition proves is that about 300 B. C. the Pentateuch was in some sense attributed to Moses; see Bacon, Genesis of Genesis, 35; Bib. Sac., 1863:381, 660, 799; Smith, Bible Dict., art.: Pentateuch; Theological Eclectic, 6:215; Bissell, Hist. Origin of the Bible, 398-403. On the Men of the Great Synagogue, see Wright, Ecclesiastes, 5-12, 475-477.

(e) From the testimony of the Samaritan Pentateuch, dating from the time of Ezra and Nehemiah (500-450 B. C.).

The Samaritans had been brought by the king of Assyria from "Babylon, and from Cuthah and from Avva, and from Hamath and Sepharvaim" (2 K. 17:6, 24, 26), to take the place of the people of Israel whom the king had carried away captive to his own land. The colonists had brought their heathen gods with them, and the incursions of wild beasts which the intermission of tillage occasioned gave rise to the belief that the God of Israel was against them. One of the captive Jewish priests was therefore sent to teach them "the law of the god of the land" and he "taught them how they should fear Jehovah" (2 K. 17:27, 28). The result was that they adopted the Jewish ritual, but combined the worship of Jehovah with that of their graven images (verse 33). When the Jews returned from Babylon and began to rebuild the walls of Jerusalem, the Samaritans offered their aid, but this aid was indignantly refused (Ezra 4 and Nehemiah 4). Hostility arose between Jews and Samaritans—a hostility which continued not only to the time of Christ (John 4:9), but even to the present day. Since the Samaritan Pentateuch substantially coincides with the Hebrew Pentateuch, it furnishes us with a definite past date at which it certainly existed in nearly its present form. It witnesses to the existence of our Pentateuch in essentially its present form as far back as the time of Ezra and Nehemiah.

Green, Higher Criticism of the Pentateuch, 44, 45—"After being repulsed by the Jews, the Samaritans, to substantiate their claim of being sprung from ancient Israel, eagerly accepted the Pentateuch which was brought them by a renegade priest." W. Robertson Smith, in Encyc. Brit., 21:244—"The priestly law, which is throughout based on the practice of the priests of Jerusalem before the captivity, was reduced to form after the exile, and was first published by Ezra as the law of the rebuilt temple of Zion. The Samaritans must therefore have derived their Pentateuch from the Jews after Ezra's reforms, i. e., after 444 B. C. Before that time Samaritanism cannot have existed in a form at all similar to that which we know; but there must have been a community ready to accept the Pentateuch." See Smith's Bible Dictionary, art.: Samaritan Pentateuch; Hastings, Bible Dictionary, art.: Samaria; Stanley Leathes, Structure of the O. T., 1-41.

(f) From the finding of "the book of the law" in the temple, in the eighteenth year of King Josiah, or in 621 B. C.

2 K. 22:8—"And Hilkiah the high priest said unto Shaphan the scribe, I have found the book of the law in the house of Jehovah." 23:2—"The book of the covenant" was read before the people by the king and proclaimed to be the law of the land. Curtis, in Hastings' Bible Dict., 3:596—"The earliest written law or book of divine instruction of whose introduction or enactment an authentic account is given, was Deuteronomy or its main portion, represented as found in the temple in the 18th year of king Josiah (B. C. 621) and proclaimed by the king as the law of the land. From that time forward Israel had a written law which the pious believer was commanded to ponder day and night (Joshua 1:8; Ps. 1:2); and thus the Torah, as sacred literature, formally commenced in Israel. This law aimed at a right application of Mosaic principles." Ryle, in Hastings' Bible Dict., 1:602—"The law of Deuteronomy represents an expansion and development of the ancient code contained in Exodus 20-23, and precedes the final formulation of the priestly ritual, which only received its ultimate form in the last period of revising the structure of the Pentateuch."

Andrew Harper, on Deuteronomy, in Expositor's Bible: "Deuteronomy does not claim to have been written by Moses. He is spoken of in the third person in the introduction and historical framework, while the speeches of Moses are in the first person. In portions where the author speaks for himself, the phrase 'beyond Jordan' means east of Jordan; in the speeches of Moses the phrase 'beyond Jordan' means west of Jordan; and the only exception is Deut. 3:8, which cannot originally have been part of the speech of Moses. But the style of both parts is the same, and if the 3rd person parts are by a later author, the 1st person parts are by a later author also. Both differ from other speeches of Moses in the Pentateuch. Can the author be a contemporary writer who gives Moses' words, as John gave the words of Jesus? No, for Deuteronomy covers only the book of the Covenant, Exodus 20-23. It uses JE but not P, with which JE is interwoven. But JE appears in Joshua and contributes to it an account of Joshua's death. JE speaks of kings in Israel (Gen. 36:31-39). Deuteronomy plainly belongs to the early centuries of the Kingdom, or to the middle of it."

Bacon, Genesis of Genesis, 43-49—"The Deuteronomic law was so short that Shaphan could read it aloud before the king (2 K. 22:10) and the king could read 'the whole of it' before the people (23:2); compare the reading of the Pentateuch for a whole week (Neh. 8:2-18). It was in the form of a covenant; it was distinguished by curses; it was an expansion and modification, fully within the legitimate province of the prophet, of a Torah of Moses codified from the traditional form of at least a century before. Such a Torah existed, was attributed to Moses, and is now incorporated as 'the book of the covenant' in Exodus 20 to 24. The year 620 is therefore the terminus a quo of Deuteronomy. The date of the priestly code is 444 B. C." Sanday, Bampton Lectures for 1893, grants "(1) the presence in the Pentateuch of a considerable element which in its present shape is held by many to be not earlier than the captivity; (2) the composition of the book of Deuteronomy, not long, or at least not very long, before its promulgation by king Josiah in the year 621, which thus becomes a pivot-date in the history of Hebrew literature."

(g) From references in the prophets Hosea (B. C. 743-737) and Amos (759-745) to a course of divine teaching and revelation extending far back of their day.

Hosea 8:12—"I wrote for him the ten thousand things of my law"; here is asserted the existence prior to the time of the prophet, not only of a law, but of a written law. All critics admit the book of Hosea to be a genuine production of the prophet, dating from the eighth century B. C.; see Green, in Presb. Rev., 1886:585-608. Amos 2:4—"they have rejected the law of Jehovah, and have not kept his statutes"; here is proof that, more than a century before the finding of Deuteronomy in the temple, Israel was acquainted with God's law. Fisher, Nature and Method of Revelation, 26, 27—"The lofty plane reached by the prophets was not reached at a single bound.... There must have been a tap-root extending far down into the earth." Kurtz remarks that "the later books of the O. T. would be a tree without roots, if the composition of the Pentateuch were transferred to a later period of Hebrew history." If we substitute for the word "Pentateuch" the words "Book of the covenant," we may assent to this dictum of Kurtz. There is sufficient evidence that, before the times of Hosea and Amos, Israel possessed a written law—the law embraced in Exodus 20-24—but the Pentateuch as we now have it, including Leviticus, seems to date no further back than the time of Jeremiah, 445 B. C. The Levitical law however was only the codification of statutes and customs whose origin lay far back in the past and which were believed to be only the natural expansion of the principles of Mosaic legislation.

Leathes, Structure of O. T., 54—"Zeal for the restoration of the temple after the exile implied that it had long before been the centre of the national polity, that there had been a ritual and a law before the exile." Present Day Tracts, 3:52—Levitical institutions could not have been first established by David. It is inconceivable that he "could have taken a whole tribe, and no trace remain of so revolutionary a measure as the dispossessing them of their property to make them ministers of religion." James Robertson, Early History of Israel: "The varied literature of 850-750 B. C. implies the existence of reading and writing for some time before. Amos and Hosea hold, for the period succeeding Moses, the same scheme of history which modern critics pronounce late and unhistorical. The eighth century B. C. was a time of broad historic day, when Israel had a definite account to give of itself and of its history. The critics appeal to the prophets, but they reject the prophets when these tell us that other teachers taught the same truth before them, and when they declare that their nation had been taught a better religion and had declined from it, in other words, that there had been law long before their day. The kings did not give law. The priests presupposed it. There must have been a formal system of law much earlier than the critics admit, and also an earlier reference in their worship to the great events which made them a separate people." And Dillman goes yet further back and declares that the entire work of Moses presupposes "a preparatory stage of higher religion in Abraham."

(h) From the repeated assertions of Scripture that Moses himself wrote a law for his people, confirmed as these are by evidence of literary and legislative activity in other nations far antedating his time.

Ex. 24:4—"And Moses wrote all the words of Jehovah"; 34:27—"And Jehovah said unto Moses, Write thou these words: for after the tenor of these words I have made a covenant with thee and with Israel"; Num. 33:2—"And Moses wrote their goings out according to their journeys by the commandment of Jehovah"; Deut. 31:9—"And Moses wrote this law, and delivered it unto the priests the sons of Levi, that bare the ark of the covenant of Jehovah, and unto all the elders of Israel"; 22—"So Moses wrote this song the same day, and taught it the children of Israel"; 24-26—"And it came to pass, when Moses had made an end of writing the words of this law in a book, until they were finished, that Moses commanded the Levites, that bare the ark of the covenant of Jehovah, saying, Take this book of the law, and put it by the side of the ark of the covenant of Jehovah your God, that it may be there for a witness against thee." The law here mentioned may possibly be only "the book of the covenant" (Ex.

20-24), and the speeches of Moses in Deuteronomy may have been orally handed down. But the fact that Moses was "instructed in all the wisdom of the Egyptians" (Acts 7:22), together with the fact that the art of writing was known in Egypt for many hundred years before his time, make it more probable that a larger portion of the Pentateuch was of his own composition.

Kenyon, in Hastings' Dict., art.: Writing, dates the Proverbs of Ptah-hotep, the first recorded literary composition in Egypt, at 3580-3536 B. C., and asserts the free use of writing among the Sumerian inhabitants of Babylonia as early as 4000 B. C. The statutes of Hammurabi king of Babylon compare for extent with those of Leviticus, yet they date back to the time of Abraham, 2200 B. C.,— indeed Hammurabi is now regarded by many as the Amraphel of Gen. 14:1. Yet these statutes antedate Moses by 700 years. It is interesting to observe that Hammurabi professes to have received his statutes directly from the Sun-god of Sippar, his capital city. See translation by Winckler, in Der alte Orient, 97; Johns, The Oldest Code of Laws; Kelso, in Princeton Theol. Rev., July, 1905:399-412—Facts "authenticate the traditional date of the Book of the Covenant, overthrow the formula Prophets and Law, restore the old order Law and Prophets, and put into historical perspective the tradition that Moses was the author of the Sinaitic legislation."

As the controversy with regard to the genuineness of the Old Testament books has turned of late upon the claims of the Higher Criticism in general, and upon the claims of the Pentateuch in particular, we subjoin separate notes upon these subjects.

The Higher Criticism in general. Higher Criticism does not mean criticism in any invidious sense, any more than Kant's Critique of Pure Reason was an unfavorable or destructive examination. It is merely a dispassionate investigation of the authorship, date and purpose of Scripture books, in the light of their composition, style and internal characteristics. As the Lower Criticism is a text-critique, the Higher Criticism is a structure-critique. A bright Frenchman described a literary critic as one who rips open the doll to get at the sawdust there is in it. This can be done with a sceptical and hostile spirit, and there can be little doubt that some of the higher critics of the Old Testament have begun their studies with prepossessions against the supernatural, which have vitiated all their conclusions. These presuppositions are often unconscious, but none the less influential. When Bishop Colenso examined the Pentateuch and Joshua, he disclaimed any intention of assailing the miraculous narratives as such; as if he had said: "My dear little fish, you need not fear me; I do not wish to catch you; I only intend to drain the pond in which you live." To many scholars the waters at present seem very low in the Hexateuch and indeed throughout the whole Old Testament.

Shakespeare made over and incorporated many old Chronicles of Plutarch and Holinshed, and many Italian tales and early tragedies of other writers; but Pericles and Titus Andronicus still pass current under the name of Shakespeare. We speak even now of "Gesenius' Hebrew Grammar," although of its twenty-seven editions the last fourteen have been published since his death, and more of it has been written by other editors than Gesenius ever wrote himself. We speak of "Webster's Dictionary," though there are in the "Unabridged" thousands of words and definitions that Webster never saw. Francis Brown: "A modern writer masters older records and writes a wholly new book. Not so with eastern historians. The latest comer, as Renan says, 'absorbs his predecessors without assimilating them, so that the most recent has in its belly the fragments of the previous works in a raw state.' The Diatessaron of Tatian is a parallel to the composite structure of the O. T. books. One passage yields the following: Mat. 21:12a; John 2:14a; Mat. 21:12b; John 2:14b, 15; Mat. 21:12c, 13; John 2:16; Mark 11:16; John 2:17-22; all succeeding each other without a break." Gore, Lux Mundi, 353—"There is nothing materially untruthful, though there is something uncritical, in attributing the whole legislation to Moses acting under the divine command. It would be only of a piece with the attribution of the collection of Psalms to David, and of Proverbs to Solomon."

The opponents of the Higher Criticism have much to say in reply. Sayce, Early History of the Hebrews, holds that the early chapters of Genesis were copied from Babylonian sources, but he insists upon a Mosaic or pre-Mosaic date for the copying. Hilprecht however declares that the monotheistic faith of Israel could never have proceeded "from the Babylonian mountain of gods—that charnel-house full of corruption and dead men's bones." Bissell, Genesis Printed in Colors, Introd., iv—"It is improbable that so many documentary histories existed so early, or if existing that the compiler should have attempted to combine them. Strange that the earlier should be J and should use the word 'Jehovah,' while the later P should use the word 'Elohim,' when 'Jehovah' would have far better suited the Priests' Code.... xiii—The Babylonian tablets contain in a continuous narrative the more prominent facts of both the alleged Elohistic and Jehovistic sections of Genesis, and present them mainly in the Biblical order. Several hundred years before Moses what the critics call two were already one. It is absurd to say that the unity was due to a redactor at the period of the exile, 444 B. C. He who believes that God revealed himself to primitive man as one God, will see in the Akkadian story a polytheistic corruption of the original monotheistic account." We must not estimate the antiquity of a pair of boots by the last patch which the cobbler has added; nor must we estimate the antiquity of a Scripture book by the glosses and explanations added by later editors. As the London Spectator remarks on the Homeric problem: "It is as impossible that a first-rate poem or work of art should be produced without a great master-mind which first conceives the whole, as that a fine living bull should be developed out of beef-sausages." As we shall proceed to show, however, these utterances overestimate the unity of the Pentateuch and ignore some striking evidences of its gradual growth and composite structure.

The Authorship of the Pentateuch in particular. Recent critics, especially Kuenen and Robertson Smith, have maintained that the Pentateuch is Mosaic only in the sense of being a gradually growing body of traditional law, which was codified as late as the time of Ezekiel, and, as the development of the spirit and teachings of the great law-giver, was called by a legal fiction after the name of Moses and was attributed to him. The actual order of composition is therefore: (1) Book of the Covenant (Exodus 20-23); (2) Deuteronomy; (3) Leviticus. Among the reasons assigned for this view are the facts (a) that Deuteronomy ends with an account of Moses' death, and therefore could not have been written by Moses; (b) that in Leviticus Levites are mere servants to the priests, while in Deuteronomy the priests are officiating Levites, or, in other words, all the Levites are priests; (c) that the books of Judges and of 1 Samuel, with their record of sacrifices offered in many places, give no evidence that either Samuel or the nation of Israel had any knowledge of a law confining worship to a local sanctuary. See Kuenen, Prophets and Prophecy in Israel; Wellhausen, Geschichte Israels, Band 1; and art.: Israel, in Encyc. Brit., 13:398, 399, 415; W. Robertson Smith, O. T. in Jewish Church, 306, 386, and Prophets of Israel; Hastings, Bible Dict., arts.: Deuteronomy, Hexateuch, and Canon of the O. T.

It has been urged in reply, (1) that Moses may have written, not autographically, but through a scribe (perhaps Joshua), and that this scribe may have completed the history in Deuteronomy with the account of Moses' death; (2) that Ezra or subsequent prophets may have subjected the whole Pentateuch to recension, and may have added explanatory notes; (3) that documents of previous ages may have been incorporated, in course of its composition by Moses, or subsequently by his successors; (4) that the apparent lack of distinction between the different classes of Levites in Deuteronomy may be explained by the fact that, while Leviticus was written with exact detail for the priests, Deuteronomy is the record of a brief general and oral summary of the law, addressed to the people at large and therefore naturally mentioning the clergy as a whole; (5) that the silence of the book of Judges as to the Mosaic ritual may be explained by the design of the book to describe only general history, and by the probability that at the tabernacle a ritual was observed of which the people in general were ignorant. Sacrifices in other places only accompanied special divine manifestations which made the recipient temporarily a priest. Even if it were proved that the law with regard to a central sanctuary was not observed, it would not show that the law did not exist, any more than violation of the second commandment by Solomon proves his ignorance of the decalogue, or the mediæval neglect of the N. T. by the Roman church proves that the N. T. did not then exist. We cannot argue that "where there was transgression, there was no law" (Watts, New Apologetic, 83, and The Newer Criticism).

In the light of recent research, however, we cannot regard these replies as satisfactory. Woods, in his article on the Hexateuch, Hastings' Dictionary, 2:365, presents a moderate statement of the results of the higher criticism which commends itself to us as more trustworthy. He calls it a theory of stratification, and holds that "certain more or less independent documents, dealing largely with the same series of events, were composed at different periods, or, at any rate, under different auspices, and were afterwards combined, so that our present Hexateuch, which means our Pentateuch with the addition of Joshua, contains these several different literary strata.... The main grounds for accepting this hypothesis of stratification are (1) that the various literary pieces, with very few exceptions, will be found on examination to arrange themselves by common characteristics into comparatively few groups; (2) that an original consecution of narrative may be frequently traced between what in their present form are isolated fragments.

"This will be better understood by the following illustration. Let us suppose a problem of this kind: Given a patchwork quilt, explain the character of the original pieces out of which the bits of stuff composing the quilt were cut. First, we notice that, however well the colors may blend, however nice and complete the whole may look, many of the adjoining pieces do not agree in material, texture, pattern, color, or the like. Ergo, they have been made up out of very different pieces of stuff.... But suppose we further discover that many of the bits, though now separated, are like one another in material, texture, etc., we may conjecture that these have been cut out of one piece. But we shall prove this beyond reasonable doubt if we find that several bits when unpicked fit together, so that the pattern of one is continued in the other; and, moreover, that if all of like character are sorted out, they form, say, four groups, each of which was evidently once a single piece of stuff, though parts of each are found missing, because, no doubt, they have not been required to make the whole. But we make the analogy of the Hexateuch even closer, if we further suppose that in certain parts of the quilt the bits belonging to, say, two of these groups are so combined as to form a subsidiary pattern within the larger pattern of the whole quilt, and had evidently been sewed together before being connected with other parts of the quilt; and we may make it even closer still, if we suppose that, besides the more important bits of stuff, smaller embellishments, borderings, and the like, had been added so as to improve the general effect of the whole."

The author of this article goes on to point out three main portions of the Hexateuch which essentially differ from each other. There are three distinct codes: the Covenant code (C—Ex. 20:22 to 23:33, and 24:3-8), the Deuteronomic code (D), and the Priestly code (P). These codes have peculiar relations to the narrative portions of the Hexateuch. In Genesis, for example, "the greater part of the book is divided into groups of longer or shorter pieces, generally paragraphs or chapters, distinguished respectively by the almost exclusive use of Elohim or Jehovah as the name of God." Let us call these portions J and E. But we find such close affinities between C and JE, that we may regard them as substantially one. "We shall find that the larger part of the narratives, as distinct from the laws, of Exodus and Numbers belong to JE; whereas, with special exceptions, the legal portions belong to P. In the last chapters of Deuteronomy and in the whole of Joshua we find elements of JE. In the latter book we also find elements which connect it with D.

"It should be observed that not only do we find here and there separate pieces in the Hexateuch, shown by their characters to belong to these three sources, JE, D, and P, but the pieces will often be found connected together by an obvious continuity of subject when pieced together, like the bits of patchwork in the illustration with which we started. For example, if we read continuously Gen. 11:27-33; 12:4b, 5; 13:6a, 11b, 12a; 16:1a, 3, 15, 16; 17; 19:29; 21:1a, 2b-5; 23; 25:7-11a—passages mainly, on other grounds, attributed to P, we get an almost continuous and complete, though very concise, account of Abraham's life." We may concede the substantial correctness of the view thus propounded. It simply shows God's actual method in making up the record of his revelation. We may add that any scholar who grants that Moses did not himself write the account of his own death and burial in the last chapter of Deuteronomy, or who recognizes two differing accounts of creation in Genesis 1 and 2, has already begun an analysis of the Pentateuch and has accepted the essential principles of the higher criticism.

In addition to the literature already referred to mention may also be made of Driver's Introd. to O. T., 118-150, and Deuteronomy, Introd.; W. R. Harper, in Hebraica, Oct.-Dec. 1888, and W. H. Green's reply in Hebraica. Jan.-Apr. 1889; also Green, The Unity of the Book of Genesis, Moses and the Prophets, Hebrew Feasts, and Higher Criticism of the Pentateuch; with articles by Green in Presb. Rev., Jan. 1882 and Oct. 1886; Howard Osgood, in Essays on Pentateuchal Criticism, and in Bib. Sac., Oct. 1888, and July, 1893; Watts, The Newer Criticism, and New Apologetic, 83; Presb. Rev., arts. by H. P. Smith, April, 1882, and by F. L. Patton, 1883:341-410; Bib. Sac., April, 1882:291-344, and by G. F. Wright, July, 1898:515-525; Brit. Quar., July, 1881:123; Jan. 1884:138-143; Mead, Supernatural Revelation, 373-385; Stebbins, A Study in the Pentateuch; Bissell, Historic Origin of the Bible, 277-342, and The Pentateuch, its Authorship and Structure; Bartlett, Sources of History in the Pentateuch, 180-216, and The Veracity of the Hexateuch; Murray, Origin and Growth of the Psalms, 58; Payne-Smith, in Present Day Tracts, 3: no. 15; Edersheim, Prophecy and History; Kurtz, Hist. Old Covenant, 1:46; Perowne, in Contemp. Rev., Jan. and Feb. 1888; Chambers, Moses and his Recent Critics; Terry, Moses and the Prophets; Davis, Dictionary of the Bible, art.: Pentateuch; Willis J. Beecher, The Prophets and the Promise; Orr, Problem of the O. T., 326-329.

II. Credibility of the Writers of the Scriptures

We shall attempt to prove this only of the writers of the gospels; for if they are credible witnesses, the credibility of the Old Testament, to which they bore testimony, follows as a matter of course.

1. They are capable or competent witnesses,—that is, they possessed actual knowledge with regard to the facts they professed to relate. (a) They had opportunities of observation and inquiry. (b) They were men of sobriety and discernment, and could not have been themselves deceived. (c) Their circumstances were such as to impress deeply upon their minds the events of which they were witnesses.

2. They are honest witnesses. This is evident when we consider that: (a) Their testimony imperiled all their worldly interests. (b) The moral elevation of their writings, and their manifest reverence for truth and constant inculcation of it, show that they were not wilful deceivers, but good men. (c) There are minor indications of the honesty of these writers in the circumstantiality of their story, in the absence of any expectation that their narratives would be questioned, in their freedom from all disposition to screen themselves or the apostles from censure.

Lessing says that Homer never calls Helen beautiful, but he gives the reader an impression of her surpassing loveliness by portraying the effect produced by her presence. So the evangelists do not describe Jesus' appearance or character, but lead us to conceive the cause that could produce such effects. Gore, Incarnation, 77—"Pilate, Caiaphas, Herod, Judas, are not abused,—they are photographed. The sin of a Judas and a Peter is told with equal simplicity. Such fairness, wherever you find it, belongs to a trustworthy witness."

3. The writings of the evangelists mutually support each other. We argue their credibility upon the ground of their number and of the consistency of their testimony. While there is enough of discrepancy

to show that there has been no collusion between them, there is concurrence enough to make the falsehood of them all infinitely improbable. Four points under this head deserve mention: (a) The evangelists are independent witnesses. This is sufficiently shown by the futility of the attempts to prove that any one of them has abridged or transcribed another. (b) The discrepancies between them are none of them irreconcilable with the truth of the recorded facts, but only present those facts in new lights or with additional detail. (c) That these witnesses were friends of Christ does not lessen the value of their united testimony, since they followed Christ only because they were convinced that these facts were true. (d) While one witness to the facts of Christianity might establish its truth, the combined evidence of four witnesses gives us a warrant for faith in the facts of the gospel such as we possess for no other facts in ancient history whatsoever. The same rule which would refuse belief in the events recorded in the gospels "would throw doubt on any event in history."

No man does or can write his own signature twice precisely alike. When two signatures, therefore, purporting to be written by the same person, are precisely alike, it is safe to conclude that one of them is a forgery. Compare the combined testimony of the evangelists with the combined testimony of our five senses. "Let us assume," says Dr. C. E. Rider, "that the chances of deception are as one to ten when we use our eyes alone, one to twenty when we use our ears alone, and one to forty when we use our sense of touch alone; what are the chances of mistake when we use all these senses simultaneously? The true result is obtained by multiplying these proportions together. This gives one to eight thousand."

4. The conformity of the gospel testimony with experience. We have already shown that, granting the fact of sin and the need of an attested revelation from God, miracles can furnish no presumption against the testimony of those who record such a revelation, but, as essentially belonging to such a revelation, miracles may be proved by the same kind and degree of evidence as is required in proof of any other extraordinary facts. We may assert, then, that in the New Testament histories there is no record of facts contrary to experience, but only a record of facts not witnessed in ordinary experience—of facts, therefore, in which we may believe, if the evidence in other respects is sufficient.

5. Coincidence of this testimony with collateral facts and circumstances. Under this head we may refer to (a) the numberless correspondences between the narratives of the evangelists and contemporary history; (b) the failure of every attempt thus far to show that the sacred history is contradicted by any single fact derived from other trustworthy sources; (c) the infinite improbability that this minute and complete harmony should ever have been secured in fictitious narratives.

6. Conclusion from the argument for the credibility of the writers of the gospels. These writers having been proved to be credible witnesses, their narratives, including the accounts of the miracles and prophecies of Christ and his apostles, must be accepted as true. But God would not work miracles or reveal the future to attest the claims of false teachers. Christ and his apostles must, therefore, have been what they claimed to be, teachers sent from God, and their doctrine must be what they claimed it to be, a revelation from God to men.

On the whole subject, see Ebrard, Wissensch. Kritik der evang. Geschichte; Greenleaf, Testimony of the Evangelists, 30, 31; Starkie on Evidence, 734; Whately, Historic Doubts as to Napoleon Buonaparte; Haley, Examination of Alleged Discrepancies; Smith's Voyage and Shipwreck of St. Paul; Paley, Horse Paulinæ; Birks, in Strivings for the Faith, 37-72—"Discrepancies are like the slight diversities of the different pictures of the stereoscope." Renan calls the land of Palestine a fifth gospel. Weiss contrasts the Apocryphal Gospels, where there is no historical setting and all is in the air, with the evangelists, where time and place are always stated.

No modern apologist has stated the argument for the credibility of the New Testament with greater clearness and force than Paley,—Evidences, chapters 8 and 10—"No historical fact is more certain than that the original propagators of the gospel voluntarily subjected themselves to lives of fatigue, danger, and suffering, in the prosecution of their undertaking. The nature of the undertaking, the character of the persons employed in it, the opposition of their tenets to the fixed expectations of the country in which they at first advanced them, their undissembled condemnation of the religion of all other countries, their total want of power, authority, or force, render it in the highest degree probable that this must have been the case.

"The probability is increased by what we know of the fate of the Founder of the institution, who was put to death for his attempt, and by what we also know of the cruel treatment of the converts to the institution within thirty years after its commencement—both which points are attested by heathen writers, and, being once admitted, leave it very incredible that the primitive emissaries of the religion who exercised their ministry first amongst the people who had destroyed their Master, and afterwards amongst those who persecuted their converts, should themselves escape with impunity or pursue their purpose in ease and safety.

"This probability, thus sustained by foreign testimony, is advanced, I think, to historical certainty by the evidence of our own books, by the accounts of a writer who was the companion of the persons whose sufferings he relates, by the letters of the persons themselves, by predictions of persecutions, ascribed to the Founder of the religion, which predictions would not have been inserted in this history, much less, studiously dwelt upon, if they had not accorded with the event, and which, even if falsely ascribed to him, could only have been so ascribed because the event suggested them; lastly, by incessant exhortations to fortitude and patience, and by an earnestness, repetition and urgency upon the subject which were unlikely to have appeared, if there had not been, at the time, some extraordinary call for the exercise of such virtues. It is also made out, I think, with sufficient evidence, that both the teachers and converts of the religion, in consequence of their new profession, took up a new course of life and conduct.

"The next great question is, what they did this for. It was for a miraculous story of some kind, since for the proof that Jesus of Nazareth ought to be received as the Messiah, or as a messenger for God, they neither had nor could have anything but miracles to stand upon.... If this be so, the religion must be true. These men could not be deceivers. By only not bearing testimony, they might have avoided all these sufferings and lived quietly. Would men in such circumstances pretend to have seen what they never saw, assert facts which they had no knowledge of, go about lying to teach virtue, and though not only convinced of Christ's being an impostor, but having seen the success of his imposture in his crucifixion, yet persist in carrying it on, and so persist as to bring upon themselves, for nothing, and with a full knowledge of the consequences, enmity and hatred, danger and death?"

Those who maintain this, moreover, require us to believe that the Scripture writers were "villains for no end but to teach honesty, and martyrs without the least prospect of honor or advantage." Imposture must have a motive. The self-devotion of the apostles is the strongest evidence of their truth, for even Hume declares that "we cannot make use of a more convincing argument in proof of honesty than to prove that the actions ascribed to any persons are contrary to the course of nature, and that no human motives, in such circumstances, could ever induce them to such conduct."

III. The Supernatural Character of the Scripture Teaching

1. Scripture teaching in general
    A. The Bible is the work of one mind.
    (a) In spite of its variety of authorship and the vast separation of its writers from one another in point of time, there is a unity of subject, spirit, and aim throughout the whole.
    We here begin a new department of Christian evidences. We now turn our attention to internal evidence. The relation of external to internal evidence seems to be suggested in Christ's two questions in Mark 8:27, 29—"Who do men say that I am?... who say ye that I am?" The unity in variety displayed in Scripture is one of the chief internal evidences. This unity is indicated in our word "Bible," in the singular number. Yet the original word was "Biblia," a plural number. The world has come to see a unity in what were once scattered fragments: the many "Biblia" have become one "Bible." In one sense R. W. Emerson's contention is true: "The Bible is not a book,—it is a literature." But we may also say, and with equal truth: "The Bible is not simply a collection of books,—it is a book." The Bible is made up of sixty-six books, by forty writers, of all ranks,—shepherds, fishermen, priests, warriors, statesmen, kings,—composing their works at intervals through a period of seventeen centuries. Evidently no collusion between them is possible. Scepticism tends ever to ascribe to the Scriptures greater variety of authorship and date, but all this only increases the wonder of the Bible's unity. If unity in a half dozen writers is remarkable, in forty it is astounding. "The many diverse instruments of this orchestra play one perfect tune: hence we feel that they are led by one master and composer." Yet it takes the same Spirit who inspired the Bible to teach its unity. The union is not an external or superficial one, but one that is internal and spiritual.
    (b) Not one moral or religious utterance of all these writers has been contradicted or superseded by the utterances of those who have come later, but all together constitute a consistent system.
    Here we must distinguish between the external form and the moral and religious substance. Jesus declares in Mat. 5:21, 22, 27, 28, 33, 34, 38, 39, 43, 44, "Ye have heard that it was said to them of old time ... but I say unto you," and then he seems at first sight to abrogate certain original commands. But he also declares in this connection, Mat. 5:17, 18—"Think not I am come to destroy the law or the prophets: I came not to destroy but to fulfil. For verily I say unto you, Till heaven and earth pass away, one jot or one tittle shall in no wise pass away from the law, till all things be accomplished." Christ's new commandments only bring out the inner meaning of the old. He fulfils them not in their literal form but in their essential spirit. So the New Testament completes the revelation of the Old Testament and makes the Bible a perfect unity. In this unity the Bible stands alone. Hindu, Persian, and Chinese religious books contain no consistent system of faith. There is progress in revelation from the earlier to the later books of the Bible, but this is not progress through successive steps of falsehood; it is rather progress from a less to a more clear and full unfolding of the truth. The whole truth lay germinally in the protevangelium uttered to our first parents (Gen. 3:15—the seed of the woman should bruise the serpent's head).

(c) Each of these writings, whether early or late, has represented moral and religious ideas greatly in advance of the age in which it has appeared, and these ideas still lead the world.

All our ideas of progress, with all the forward-looking spirit of modern Christendom, are due to Scripture. The classic nations had no such ideas and no such spirit, except as they caught them from the Hebrews. Virgil's prophecy, in his fourth Eclogue, of a coming virgin and of the reign of Saturn and of the return of the golden age, was only the echo of the Sibylline books and of the hope of a Redeemer with which the Jews had leavened the whole Roman world; see A. H. Strong, The Great Poets and their Theology, 94-96.

(d) It is impossible to account for this unity without supposing such a supernatural suggestion and control that the Bible, while in its various parts written by human agents, is yet equally the work of a superhuman intelligence.

We may contrast with the harmony between the different Scripture writers the contradictions and refutations which follow merely human philosophies—e. g., the Hegelian idealism and the Spencerian materialism. Hegel is "a name to swear at, as well as to swear by." Dr. Stirling, in his Secret of Hegel, "kept all the secret to himself, if he ever knew it." A certain Frenchman once asked Hegel if he could not gather up and express his philosophy in one sentence for him. "No," Hegel replied, "at least not in French." If Talleyrand's maxim be true that whatever is not intelligible is not French, Hegel's answer was a correct one. Hegel said of his disciples: "There is only one man living who understands me, and he does not."

Goeschel, Gabler, Daub, Marheinecke, Erdmann, are Hegel's right wing, or orthodox representatives and followers in theology; see Sterrett, Hegel's Philosophy of Religion. Hegel is followed by Alexander and Bradley in England, but is opposed by Seth and Schiller. Upton, Hibbert Lectures, 279-300, gives a valuable estimate of his position and influence: Hegel is all thought and no will. Prayer has no effect on God,—it is a purely psychological phenomenon. There is no free-will, and man's sin as much as man's holiness is a manifestation of the Eternal. Evolution is a fact, but it is only fatalistic evolution. Hegel notwithstanding did great service by substituting knowledge of reality for the oppressive Kantian relativity, and by banishing the old notion of matter as a mysterious substance wholly unlike and incompatible with the properties of mind. He did great service also by showing that the interactions of matter and mind are explicable only by the presence of the Absolute Whole in every part, though he erred greatly by carrying that idea of the unity of God and man beyond its proper limits, and by denying that God has given to the will of man any power to put itself into antagonism to His Will. Hegel did great service by showing that we cannot know even the part without knowing the whole, but he erred in teaching, as T. H. Green did, that the relations constitute the reality of the thing. He deprives both physical and psychical existences of that degree of selfhood or independent reality which is essential to both science and religion. We want real force, and not the mere idea of force; real will, and not mere thought.

B. This one mind that made the Bible is the same mind that made the soul, for the Bible is divinely adapted to the soul,

(a) It shows complete acquaintance with the soul.

The Bible addresses all parts of man's nature. There are Law and Epistles for man's reason; Psalms and Gospels for his affections; Prophets and Revelations for his imagination. Hence the popularity of the Scriptures. Their variety holds men. The Bible has become interwoven into modern life. Law, literature, art, all show its moulding influence.

(b) It judges the soul—contradicting its passions, revealing its guilt, and humbling its pride.

No product of mere human nature could thus look down upon human nature and condemn it. The Bible speaks to us from a higher level. The Samaritan woman's words apply to the whole compass of divine revelation; it tells us all things that ever we did (John 4:29). The Brahmin declared that Romans 1, with its description of heathen vices, must have been forged after the missionaries came to India.

(c) It meets the deepest needs of the soul—by solutions of its problems, disclosures of God's character, presentations of the way of pardon, consolations and promises for life and death.

Neither Socrates nor Seneca sets forth the nature, origin and consequences of sin as committed against the holiness of God, nor do they point out the way of pardon and renewal. The Bible teaches us what nature cannot, viz.: God's creatorship, the origin of evil, the method of restoration, the certainty of a future state, and the principle of rewards and punishments there.

(d) Yet it is silent upon many questions for which writings of merely human origin seek first to provide solutions.

Compare the account of Christ's infancy in the gospels with the fables of the Apocryphal New Testament; compare the scant utterances of Scripture with regard to the future state with Mohammed's and Swedenborg's revelations of Paradise. See Alexander McLaren's sermon on The Silence of Scripture, in his book entitled: Christ in the Heart, 131-141.

(e) There are infinite depths and inexhaustible reaches of meaning in Scripture, which difference it from all other books, and which compel us to believe that its author must be divine.

Sir Walter Scott, on his death bed: "Bring me the Book!" "What book?" said Lockhart, his son-in-law. "There is but one book!" said the dying man. Réville concludes an Essay in the Revue des deux Mondes (1864): "One day the question was started, in an assembly, what book a man condemned to lifelong imprisonment, and to whom but one book would be permitted, had better take into his cell with him. The company consisted of Catholics, Protestants, philosophers and even materialists, but all agreed that their choice would fall only on the Bible."

On the whole subject, see Garbett, God's Word Written, 3-56; Luthardt, Saving Truths, 210; Rogers, Superhuman Origin of Bible, 155-181; W. L. Alexander, Connection and Harmony of O. T. and N. T.; Stanley Leathes, Structure of the O. T.; Bernard, Progress of Doctrine in the N. T.; Rainy, Delivery and Development of Doctrine; Titcomb, in Strivings for the Faith; Immer, Hermeneutics, 91; Present Day Tracts, 4: no. 23; 5: no. 28; 6: no. 31; Lee on Inspiration, 26-32.

2. Moral System of the New Testament

The perfection of this system is generally conceded. All will admit that it greatly surpasses any other system known among men. Among its distinguishing characteristics may be mentioned:

(a) Its comprehensiveness,—including all human duties in its code, even the most generally misunderstood and neglected, while it permits no vice whatsoever.

Buddhism regards family life as sinful. Suicide was commended by many ancient philosophers. Among the Spartans to steal was praiseworthy,—only to be caught stealing was criminal. Classic times despised humility. Thomas Paine said that Christianity cultivated "the spirit of a spaniel," and John Stuart Mill asserted that Christ ignored duty to the state. Yet Peter urges Christians to add to their faith manliness, courage, heroism (2 Pet. 1:5—"in your faith supply virtue"), and Paul declares the state to be God's ordinance (Rom. 13:1—"Let every soul be in subjection to the higher powers: for there is no power but of God; and the powers that be are ordained of God"). Patriotic defence of a nation's unity and freedom has always found its chief incitement and ground in these injunctions of Scripture. E. G. Robinson: "Christian ethics do not contain a particle of chaff,—all is pure wheat."

(b) Its spirituality,—accepting no merely external conformity to right precepts, but judging all action by the thoughts and motives from which it springs.

The superficiality of heathen morals is well illustrated by the treatment of the corpse of a priest in Siam: the body is covered with gold leaf, and then is left to rot and shine. Heathenism divorces religion from ethics. External and ceremonial observances take the place of purity of heart. The Sermon on the Mount on the other hand pronounces blessing only upon inward states of the soul. Ps. 51:6—"Behold, thou desirest truth in the inward parts, and in the hidden part thou wilt make me to know wisdom"; Micah 6:8—"what doth Jehovah require of thee, but to do justly, and to love kindness, and to walk humbly with thy God?"

(c) Its simplicity,—inculcating principles rather than imposing rules; reducing these principles to an organic system; and connecting this system with religion by summing up all human duty in the one command of love to God and man.

Christianity presents no extensive code of rules, like that of the Pharisees or of the Jesuits. Such codes break down of their own weight. The laws of the State of New York alone constitute a library of themselves, which only the trained lawyer can master. It is said that Mohammedanism has recorded sixty-five thousand special instances in which the reader is directed to do right. It is the merit of Jesus' system that all its requisitions are reduced to unity. Mark 12:29-31—"Hear, O Israel; The Lord our God, the Lord is one: and thou shalt love the Lord thy God with all thy heart, and with all thy soul, and with all thy mind, and with all thy strength. The second is this: Thou shalt love thy neighbor as thyself. There is none other commandment greater than these." Wendt, Teaching of Jesus, 2:384-814, calls attention to the inner unity of Jesus' teaching. The doctrine that God is a loving Father is applied with unswerving consistency. Jesus confirmed whatever was true in the O. T., and he set aside the unworthy. He taught not so much about God, as about the kingdom of God, and about the ideal fellowship between God and men. Morality was the necessary and natural expression of religion. In Christ teaching and life were perfectly blended. He was the representative of the religion which he taught.

(d) Its practicality,—exemplifying its precepts in the life of Jesus Christ; and, while it declares man's depravity and inability in his own strength to keep the law, furnishing motives to obedience, and the divine aid of the Holy Spirit to make this obedience possible.

Revelation has two sides: Moral law, and provision for fulfilling the moral law that has been broken. Heathen systems can incite to temporary reformations, and they can terrify with fears of retribution. But only God's regenerating grace can make the tree good, in such a way that its fruit will be good also (Mat. 12:33). There is a difference between touching the pendulum of the clock and winding it up,—the former may set it temporarily swinging, but only the latter secures its regular and permanent motion. The moral system of the N. T. is not simply law,—it is also grace: John 1:17—"the law was given through Moses; grace and truth came through Jesus Christ." Dr. William Ashmore's tract represents a Chinaman in a pit. Confucius looks into the pit and says: "If you had done as I told you,

you would never have gotten in." Buddha looks into the pit and says: "If you were up here I would show you what to do." So both Confucius and Buddha pass on. But Jesus leaps down into the pit and helps the poor Chinaman out.

At the Parliament of Religions in Chicago there were many ideals of life propounded, but no religion except Christianity attempted to show that there was any power given to realize these ideals. When Joseph Cook challenged the priests of the ancient religions to answer Lady Macbeth's question: "How cleanse this red right hand?" the priests were dumb. But Christianity declares that "the blood of Jesus his Son cleanseth us from all sin" (1 John 1:7). E. G. Robinson: Christianity differs from all other religions in being (1) a historical religion; (2) in turning abstract law into a person to be loved; (3) in furnishing a demonstration of God's love in Christ; (4) in providing atonement for sin and forgiveness for the sinner; (5) in giving a power to fulfil the law and sanctify the life. Bowne, Philos. of Theism, 249—"Christianity, by making the moral law the expression of a holy Will, brought that law out of its impersonal abstraction, and assured its ultimate triumph. Moral principles may be what they were before, but moral practice is forever different. Even the earth itself has another look, now that it has heaven above it." Frances Power Cobbe, Life, 92—"The achievement of Christianity was not the inculcation of a new, still less of a systematic, morality; but the introduction of a new spirit into morality; as Christ himself said, a leaven into the lump."

We may justly argue that a moral system so pure and perfect, since it surpasses all human powers of invention and runs counter to men's natural tastes and passions, must have had a supernatural, and if a supernatural, then a divine, origin.

Heathen systems of morality are in general defective, in that they furnish for man's moral action no sufficient example, rule, motive, or end. They cannot do this, for the reason that they practically identify God with nature, and know of no clear revelation of his holy will. Man is left to the law of his own being, and since he is not conceived of as wholly responsible and free, the lower impulses are allowed sway as well as the higher, and selfishness is not regarded as sin. As heathendom does not recognize man's depravity, so it does not recognize his dependence upon divine grace, and its virtue is self-righteousness. Heathenism is man's vain effort to lift himself to God; Christianity is God's coming down to man to save him; see Gunsaulus, Transfig. of Christ, 11, 12. Martineau, 1:15, 16, calls attention to the difference between the physiological ethics of heathendom and the psychological ethics of Christianity. Physiological ethics begins with nature; and, finding in nature the uniform rule of necessity and the operation of cause and effect, it comes at last to man and applies the same rule to him, thus extinguishing all faith in personality, freedom, responsibility, sin and guilt. Psychological ethics, on the contrary, wisely begins with what we know best, with man; and finding in him free-will and a moral purpose, it proceeds outward to nature and interprets nature as the manifestation of the mind and will of God.

"Psychological ethics are altogether peculiar to Christendom.... Other systems begin outside and regard the soul as a homogeneous part of the universe, applying to the soul the principle of necessity that prevails outside of it.... In the Christian religion, on the other hand, the interest, the mystery of the world are concentrated in human nature.... The sense of sin—a sentiment that left no trace in Athens— involves a consciousness of personal alienation from the Supreme Goodness; the aspiration after holiness directs itself to a union of affection and will with the source of all Perfection; the agency for transforming men from their old estrangement to new reconciliation is a Person, in whom the divine and human historically blend; and the sanctifying Spirit by which they are sustained at the height of their purer life is a living link of communion between their minds and the Soul of souls.... So Nature, to the Christian consciousness, sank into the accidental and the neutral." Measuring ourselves by human standards, we nourish pride; measuring ourselves by divine standards, we nourish humility. Heathen nations, identifying God with nature or with man, are unprogressive. The flat architecture of the Parthenon, with its lines parallel to the earth, is the type of heathen religion; the aspiring arches of the Gothic cathedral symbolize Christianity.

Sterrett, Studies in Hegel, 33, says that Hegel characterized the Chinese religion as that of Measure, or temperate conduct; Brahmanism as that of Phantasy, or inebriate dream-life; Buddhism as that of Self-involvement; that of Egypt as the imbruted religion of Enigma, symbolized by the Sphinx; that of Greece, as the religion of Beauty; the Jewish as that of Sublimity; and Christianity as the Absolute religion, the fully revealed religion of truth and freedom. In all this Hegel entirely fails to grasp the elements of Will, Holiness, Love, Life, which characterize Judaism and Christianity, and distinguish them from all other religions. R. H. Hutton: "Judaism taught us that Nature must be interpreted by our knowledge of God, not God by our knowledge of Nature." Lyman Abbott: "Christianity is not a new life, but a new power; not a summons to a new life, but an offer of new life; not a reënactment of the old law, but a power of God unto salvation; not love to God and man, but Christ's message that God loves us, and will help us to the life of love."

Beyschlag, N. T. Theology, 5, 6—"Christianity postulates an opening of the heart of the eternal God to the heart of man coming to meet him. Heathendom shows us the heart of man blunderingly grasping the hem of God's garment, and mistaking Nature, his majestic raiment, for himself. Only in the Bible does man press beyond God's external manifestations to God himself." See Wuttke, Christian Ethics, 1:37-173; Porter, in Present Day Tracts, 4: no. 19, pp. 33-64: Blackie, Four Phases of Morals; Faiths of the World (St. Giles Lectures, second series); J. F. Clarke, Ten Great Religions, 2:280-317; Garbett, Dogmatic Faith; Farrar, Witness of History to Christ, 134, and Seekers after God, 181, 182, 320; Curtis on Inspiration, 288. For denial of the all-comprehensive character of Christian Morality, see John Stuart Mill, on Liberty; per contra, see Review of Mill, in Theol. Eclectic, 6:508-512; Row, in Strivings for the Faith, pub. by Christian Evidence Society, 181-220; also, Bampton Lectures, 1877:130-176; Fisher, Beginnings of Christianity, 28-38, 174.

In contrast with the Christian system of morality the defects of heathen systems are so marked and fundamental, that they constitute a strong corroborative evidence of the divine origin of the Scripture revelation. We therefore append certain facts and references with regard to particular heathen systems.

1. Confucianism. Confucius (Kung-fu-tse), B. C. 551-478, contemporary with Pythagoras and Buddha. Socrates was born ten years after Confucius died. Mencius (371-278) was a disciple of Confucius. Matheson, in Faiths of the World (St. Giles Lectures), 73-108, claims that Confucianism was "an attempt to substitute a morality for theology." Legge, however, in Present Day Tracts, 3: no. 18, shows that this is a mistake. Confucius simply left religion where he found it. God, or Heaven, is worshiped in China, but only by the Emperor. Chinese religion is apparently a survival of the worship of the patriarchal family. The father of the family was its only head and priest. In China, though the family widened into the tribe, and the tribe into the nation, the father still retained his sole authority, and, as the father of his people, the Emperor alone officially offered sacrifice to God. Between God and the people the gulf has so widened that the people may be said to have no practical knowledge of God or communication with him. Dr. W. A. P. Martin: "Confucianism has degenerated into a pantheistic medley, and renders worship to an impersonal 'anima mundi,' under the leading forms of visible nature."

Dr. William Ashmore, private letter: "The common people of China have: (1) Ancestor-worship, and the worship of deified heroes: (2) Geomancy, or belief in the controlling power of the elements of nature; but back of these, and antedating them, is (3) the worship of Heaven and Earth, or Father and Mother, a very ancient dualism; this belongs to the common people also, though once a year the Emperor, as a sort of high-priest of his people, offers sacrifice on the altar of Heaven; in this he acts alone. 'Joss' is not a Chinese word at all. It is the corrupted form of the Portuguese word 'Deos.' The word 'pidgin' is similarly an attempt to say 'business' (big-i-ness or bidgin). 'Joss-pidgin' therefore means simply 'divine service,' or service offered to Heaven and Earth, or to spirits of any kind, good or bad. There are many gods, a Queen of Heaven, King of Hades, God of War, god of literature, gods of the hills, valleys, streams, a goddess of small-pox, of child-bearing, and all the various trades have their gods. The most lofty expression the Chinese have is 'Heaven,' or 'Supreme Heaven,' or 'Azure Heaven.' This is the surviving indication that in the most remote times they had knowledge of one supreme, intelligent and personal Power who ruled over all." Mr. Yugoro Chiba has shown that the Chinese classics permit sacrifice by all the people. But it still remains true that sacrifice to "Supreme Heaven" is practically confined to the Emperor, who like the Jewish high-priest offers for his people once a year.

Confucius did nothing to put morality upon a religious basis. In practice, the relations between man and man are the only relations considered. Benevolence, righteousness, propriety, wisdom, sincerity, are enjoined, but not a word is said with regard to man's relations to God. Love to God is not only not commanded—it is not thought of as possible. Though man's being is theoretically an ordinance of God, man is practically a law to himself. The first commandment of Confucius is that of filial piety. But this includes worship of dead ancestors, and is so exaggerated as to bury from sight the related duties of husband to wife and of parent to child. Confucius made it the duty of a son to slay his father's murderer, just as Moses insisted on a strictly retaliatory penalty for bloodshed; see J. A. Farrer, Primitive Manners and Customs, 80. He treated invisible and superior beings with respect, but held them at a distance. He recognized the "Heaven" of tradition; but, instead of adding to our knowledge of it, he stifled inquiry. Dr. Legge: "I have been reading Chinese books for more than forty years, and any general requirement to love God, or the mention of any one as actually loving him, has yet to come for the first time under my eye."

Ezra Abbot asserts that Confucius gave the golden rule in positive as well as negative form; see Harris, Philos. Basis of Theism, 222. This however seems to be denied by Dr. Legge, Religions of China, 1-58. Wu Ting Fang, former Chinese minister to Washington, assents to the statement that Confucius gave the golden rule only in its negative form, and he says this difference is the difference between a passive and an aggressive civilization, which last is therefore dominant. The golden rule, as Confucius gives it, is: "Do not unto others that which you would not they should do unto you." Compare with this, Isocrates: "Be to your parents what you would have your children be to you.... Do not to others the things which make you angry when others do them to you"; Herodotus: "What I punish in another man, I will myself, as far as I can, refrain from"; Aristotle: "We should behave toward our friends as we should wish them to behave toward us"; Tobit, 4:15—"What thou hatest, do to no one"; Philo: "What one hates to endure, let him not do"; Seneca bids us "give as we wish to receive"; Rabbi Hillel: "Whatsoever is hateful to you, do not to another; this is the whole law, and all the rest is explanation."

Broadus, in Am. Com. on Matthew, 161—"The sayings of Confucius, Isocrates, and the three Jewish teachers, are merely negative; that of Seneca is confined to giving, and that of Aristotle to the treatment of friends. Christ lays down a rule for positive action, and that toward all men." He teaches that I am bound to do to others all that they could rightly desire me to do to them. The golden rule therefore requires a supplement, to show what others can rightly desire, namely, God's glory first, and their good as second and incidental thereto. Christianity furnishes this divine and perfect standard; Confucianism is defective in that it has no standard higher than human convention. While Confucianism excludes polytheism, idolatry, and deification of vice, it is a shallow and tantalizing system, because it does not recognize the hereditary corruption of human nature, or furnish any remedy for moral evil except the "doctrines of the sages." "The heart of man," it says, "is naturally perfectly upright and correct." Sin is simply "a disease, to be cured by self-discipline; a debt, to be canceled by meritorious acts; an ignorance, to be removed by study and contemplation." See Bib. Sac., 1883:292, 293; N. Englander, 1883:565; Marcus Dods, in Erasmus and other Essays, 239.

2. THE INDIAN SYSTEMS. Brahmanism, as expressed in the Vedas, dates back to 1000-1500 B. C. As Caird (in Faiths of the World, St. Giles Lectures, lecture 1) has shown, it originated in the contemplation of the power in nature apart from the moral Personality that works in and through nature. Indeed we may say that all heathenism is man's choice of a non-moral in place of a moral God. Brahmanism is a system of pantheism, "a false or illegitimate consecration of the finite." All things are a manifestation of Brahma. Hence evil is deified as well as good. And many thousand gods are worshiped as partial representations of the living principle which moves through all. "How many gods have the Hindus?" asked Dr. Duff of his class. Henry Drummond thought there were about twenty-five. "Twenty-five?" responded the indignant professor; "twenty-five millions of millions!" While the early Vedas present a comparatively pure nature-worship, later Brahmanism becomes a worship of the vicious and the vile, of the unnatural and the cruel. Juggernaut and the suttee did not belong to original Hindu religion.

Bruce, Apologetics, 15—"Pantheism in theory always means polytheism in practice." The early Vedas are hopeful in spirit; later Brahmanism is a religion of disappointment. Caste is fixed and consecrated as a manifestation of God. Originally intended to express, in its four divisions of priest, soldier, agriculturist, slave, the different degrees of unworldliness and divine indwelling, it becomes an iron fetter to prevent all aspiration and progress. Indian religion sought to exalt receptivity, the unity of existence, and rest from self-determination and its struggles. Hence it ascribed to its gods the same character as nature-forces. God was the common source of good and of evil. Its ethics is an ethics of moral indifference. Its charity is a charity for sin, and the temperance it desires is a temperance that will let the intemperate alone. Mozoomdar, for example, is ready to welcome everything in Christianity but its reproof of sin and its demand for righteousness. Brahmanism degrades woman, but it deifies the cow.

Buddhism, beginning with Buddha, 600 B. C., "recalls the mind to its elevation above the finite," from which Brahmanism had fallen away. Buddha was in certain respects a reformer. He protested against caste, and proclaimed that truth and morality are for all. Hence Buddhism, through its possession of this one grain of truth, appealed to the human heart, and became, next to Christianity, the greatest missionary religion. Notice then, first, its universalism. But notice also that this is a false universalism, for it ignores individualism and leads to universal stagnation and slavery. While Christianity is a religion of history, of will, of optimism, Buddhism is a religion of illusion, of quietism, of pessimism; see Nash, Ethics and Revelation, 107-109. In characterizing Buddhism as a missionary religion, we must notice, secondly, its element of altruism. But this altruism is one which destroys the self, instead of preserving it. The future Buddha, out of compassion for a famished tiger, permits the tiger to devour him. "Incarnated as a hare, he jumps into the fire to cook himself for a meal for a beggar,—having previously shaken himself three times, so that none of the insects in his fur should perish with him"; see William James, Varieties of Religious Experience, 283. Buddha would deliver man, not by philosophy, nor by asceticism, but by self-renunciation. All isolation and personality are sin, the guilt of which rests, however, not on man, but on existence in general.

While Brahmanism is pantheistic, Buddhism is atheistic in its spirit. Pfleiderer, Philos. Religion, 1:285—"The Brahmanic Akosmism, that had explained the world as mere seeming, led to the Buddhistic Atheism." Finiteness and separateness are evil, and the only way to purity and rest is by ceasing to exist. This is essential pessimism. The highest morality is to endure that which must be, and to escape from reality and from personal existence as soon as possible. Hence the doctrine of Nirvana. Rhys Davids, in his Hibbert Lectures, claims that early Buddhism meant by Nirvana, not annihilation, but the extinction of the self-life, and that this was attainable during man's present mortal existence. But the term Nirvana now means, to the great mass of those who use it, the loss of all personality and consciousness, and absorption into the general life of the universe. Originally the term denoted only freedom from individual desire, and those who had entered into Nirvana might again come out of it; see Ireland, Blot on the Brain, 238. But even in its original form, Nirvana was sought only from a selfish motive. Self-renunciation and absorption in the whole was not the enthusiasm of benevolence,—it was the refuge of despair. It is a religion without god or sacrifice. Instead of communion with a personal God, Buddhism has in prospect only an extinction of personality, as reward for untold ages of lonely self-conquest, extending through many transmigrations. Of Buddha it has been truly said "That all the all he had for needy man Was nothing, and his best of being was But not to be." Wilkinson, Epic of Paul, 296—"He by his own act dying all the time, In ceaseless effort utterly to cease, Will willing not to will, desire desiring To be desire no more, until at last The fugitive go free, emancipate But by becoming naught." Of Christ Bruce well says: "What a contrast this Healer of disease and Preacher of pardon to the worst, to Buddha, with his religion of despair!"

Buddhism is also fatalistic. It inculcates submission and compassion—merely negative virtues. But it knows nothing of manly freedom, or of active love—the positive virtues of Christianity. It leads men to spare others, but not to help them. Its morality revolves around self, not around God. It has in it no organizing principle, for it recognizes no God, no inspiration, no soul, no salvation, no personal immortality. Buddhism would save men only by inducing them to flee from existence. To the Hindu, family life involves sin. The perfect man must forsake wife and children. All gratification of natural appetites and passions is evil. Salvation is not from sin, but from desire, and from this men can be saved only by escaping from life itself. Christianity buries sin, but saves the man; Buddha would save the man by killing him. Christianity symbolizes the convert's entrance upon a new life by raising him from the baptismal waters; the baptism of Buddhism should be immersion without emersion. The fundamental idea of Brahmanism, extinction of personality, remains the same in Buddhism; the only difference being that the result is secured by active atonement in the former, by passive contemplation in the latter. Virtue, and the knowledge that everything earthly is a vanishing spark of the original light, delivers man from existence and from misery.

Prof. G. H. Palmer, of Harvard, in The Outlook, June 19, 1897—"Buddhism is unlike Christianity in that it abolishes misery by abolishing desire; denies personality instead of asserting it; has many gods, but no one God who is living and conscious; makes a shortening of existence rather than a lengthening of it to be the reward of righteousness. Buddhism makes no provision for family, church, state, science, or art. It gives us a religion that is little, when we want one that is large." Dr. E. Benjamin Andrews: "Schopenhauer and Spencer are merely teachers of Buddhism. They regard the central source of all as unknowable force, instead of regarding it as a Spirit, living and holy. This takes away all impulse to scientific investigation. We need to start from a Person, and not from a thing."

For comparison of the sage of India, Sakya Muni, more commonly called Buddha (properly "the Buddha" = the enlightened; but who, in spite of Edwin Arnold's "Light of Asia," is represented as not pure from carnal pleasures before he began his work), with Jesus Christ, see Bib. Sac., July, 1882:458-498; W. C. Wilkinson, Edwin Arnold, Poetizer and Paganizer; Kellogg, The Light of Asia and the Light of the World. Buddhism and Christianity are compared in Presb. Rev., July, 1883:505-548; Wuttke, Christian Ethics, 1:47-54; Mitchell, in Present Day Tracts, 6: no. 33. See also Oldenberg, Buddha; Lillie, Popular Life of Buddha; Beal, Catena of Buddhist Scriptures, 153—"Buddhism declares itself ignorant of any mode of personal existence compatible with the idea of spiritual perfection, and so far it is ignorant of God"; 157—"The earliest idea of Nirvana seems to have included in it no more than the enjoyment of a state of rest consequent on the extinction of all causes of sorrow." The impossibility of satisfying the human heart with a system of atheism is shown by the fact that the Buddha himself has been apotheosized to furnish an object of worship. Thus Buddhism has reverted to Brahmanism.

Monier Williams: "Mohammed has as much claim to be 'the Light of Asia' as Buddha has. What light from Buddha? Not about the heart's depravity, or the origin of sin, or the goodness, justice, holiness, fatherhood of God, or the remedy for sin, but only the ridding self from suffering by ridding self from life—a doctrine of merit, of self-trust, of pessimism, and annihilation of personality." Christ, himself personal, loving and holy, shows that God is a person of holiness and love. Robert Browning: "He that created love, shall not he love?" Only because Jesus is God, have we a gospel for the world. The claim that Buddha is "the Light of Asia" reminds one of the man who declared the moon to be of greater value than the sun, because it gives light in the darkness when it is needed, while the sun gives light in the daytime when it is not needed.

3. THE GREEK SYSTEMS. Pythagoras (584-504) based morality upon the principle of numbers. "Moral good was identified with unity; evil with multiplicity; virtue was harmony of the soul and its likeness to God. The aim of life was to make it represent the beautiful order of the Universe. The whole practical tendency of Pythagoreanism was ascetic, and included a strict self-control and an earnest culture." Here already we seem to see the defect of Greek morality in confounding the good with the

beautiful, and in making morality a mere self-development. Matheson, Messages of the Old Religions: Greece reveals the intensity of the hour, the value of the present life, the beauty of the world that now is. Its religion is the religion of beautiful humanity. It anticipates the new heaven and the new earth. Rome on the other hand stood for union, incorporation, a universal kingdom. But its religion deified only the Emperor, not all humanity. It was the religion, not of love, but of power, and it identified the church with the state.

Socrates (469-400) made knowledge to be virtue. Morality consisted in subordinating irrational desires to rational knowledge. Although here we rise above a subjectively determined good as the goal of moral effort, we have no proper sense of sin. Knowledge, and not love, is the motive. If men know the right, they will do the right. This is a great overvaluing of knowledge. With Socrates, teaching is a sort of midwifery—not depositing information in the mind, but drawing out the contents of our own inner consciousness. Lewis Morris describes it as the life-work of Socrates to "doubt our doubts away." Socrates holds it right to injure one's enemies. He shows proud self-praise in his dying address. He warns against pederasty, yet compromises with it. He does not insist upon the same purity of family life which Homer describes in Ulysses and Penelope. Charles Kingsley, in Alton Locke, remarks that the spirit of the Greek tragedy was 'man mastered by circumstance'; that of modern tragedy is "man mastering circumstance." But the Greek tragedians, while showing man thus mastered, do still represent him as inwardly free, as in the case of Prometheus, and this sense of human freedom and responsibility appears to some extent in Socrates.

Plato (430-348) held that morality is pleasure in the good, as the truly beautiful, and that knowledge produces virtue. The good is likeness to God,—here we have glimpses of an extra-human goal and model. The body, like all matter, being inherently evil, is a hindrance to the soul,—here we have a glimpse of hereditary depravity. But Plato "reduced moral evil to the category of natural evil." He failed to recognize God as creator and master of matter; failed to recognize man's depravity as due to his own apostasy from God; failed to found morality on the divine will rather than on man's own consciousness. He knew nothing of a common humanity, and regarded virtue as only for the few. As there was no common sin, so there was no common redemption. Plato thought to reach God by intellect alone, when only conscience and heart could lead to him. He believed in a freedom of the soul in a preëxistent state where a choice was made between good and evil, but he believed that, after that antemundane decision had been made, the fates determined men's acts and lives irreversibly. Reason drives two horses, appetite and emotion, but their course has been predetermined.

Man acts as reason prompts. All sin is ignorance. There is nothing in this life but determinism. Martineau, Types, 13, 48, 49, 78, 88—Plato in general has no proper notion of responsibility; he reduces moral evil to the category of natural evil. His Ideas with one exception are not causes. Cause is mind, and mind is the Good. The Good is the apex and crown of Ideas. The Good is the highest Idea, and this highest Idea is a Cause. Plato has a feeble conception of personality, whether in God or in man. Yet God is a person in whatever sense man is a person, and man's personality is reflective self-consciousness. Will in God or man is not so clear. The Right is dissolved into the Good. Plato advocated infanticide and the killing off of the old and the helpless.

Aristotle (384-322) leaves out of view even the element of God-likeness and antemundane evil which Plato so dimly recognized, and makes morality the fruit of mere rational self-consciousness. He grants evil proclivities, but he refuses to call them immoral. He advocates a certain freedom of will, and he recognizes inborn tendencies which war against this freedom, but how these tendencies originated he cannot say, nor how men may be delivered from them. Not all can be moral; the majority must be restrained by fear. He finds in God no motive, and love to God is not so much as mentioned as the source of moral action. A proud, composed, self-centered, and self-contained man is his ideal character. See Nicomachean Ethics, 7:6, and 10:10; Wuttke, Christian Ethics, 1:92-126. Alexander, Theories of Will, 39-54—Aristotle held that desire and reason are the springs of action. Yet he did not hold that knowledge of itself would make men virtuous. He was a determinist. Actions are free only in the sense of being devoid of external compulsion. He viewed slavery as both rational and right. Butcher, Aspects of Greek Genius, 76—"While Aristotle attributed to the State a more complete personality than it really possessed, he did not grasp the depth and meaning of the personality of the individual." A. H. Strong, Christ in Creation, 289—Aristotle had no conception of the unity of humanity. His doctrine of unity did not extend beyond the State. "He said that 'the whole is before the parts,' but he meant by 'the whole' only the pan-Hellenic world, the commonwealth of Greeks; he never thought of humanity, and the word 'mankind' never fell from his lips. He could not understand the unity of humanity, because he knew nothing of Christ, its organizing principle." On Aristotle's conception of God, see James Ten Broeke, in Bap. Quar. Rev., Jan. 1892—God is recognized as personal, yet he is only the Greek Reason, and not the living, loving, providential Father of the Hebrew revelation. Aristotle substitutes the logical for the dynamical in his dealing with the divine causality. God is thought, not power.

Epicurus (342-270) regarded happiness, the subjective feeling of pleasure, as the highest criterion of truth and good. A prudent calculating for prolonged pleasure is the highest wisdom. He regards only this life. Concern for retribution and for a future existence is folly. If there are gods, they have no concern for men. "Epicurus, on pretense of consulting for their ease, complimented the gods, and bowed them out of existence." Death is the falling apart of material atoms and the eternal cessation of consciousness. The miseries of this life are due to imperfection in the fortuitously constructed universe. The more numerous these undeserved miseries, the greater our right to seek pleasure. Alexander, Theories of the Will, 55-75—The Epicureans held that the soul is composed of atoms, yet that the will is free. The atoms of the soul are excepted from the law of cause and effect. An atom may decline or deviate in the universal descent, and this is the Epicurean idea of freedom. This indeterminism was held by all the Greek sceptics, materialists though they were.

Zeno, the founder of the Stoic philosophy (340-264), regarded virtue as the only good. Thought is to subdue nature. The free spirit is self-legislating, self-dependent, self-sufficient. Thinking, not feeling, is the criterion of the true and the good. Pleasure is the consequence, not the end of moral action. There is an irreconcilable antagonism of existence. Man cannot reform the world, but he can make himself perfect. Hence an unbounded pride in virtue. The sage never repents. There is not the least recognition of the moral corruption of mankind. There is no objective divine ideal, or revealed divine will. The Stoic discovers moral law only within, and never suspects his own moral perversion. Hence he shows self-control and justice, but never humility or love. He needs no compassion or forgiveness, and he grants none to others. Virtue is not an actively outworking character, but a passive resistance to irrational reality. Man may retreat into himself. The Stoic is indifferent to pleasure and pain, not because he believes in a divine government, or in a divine love for mankind, but as a proud defiance of the irrational world. He has no need of God or of redemption. As the Epicurean gives himself to enjoyment of the world, the Stoic gives himself to contempt of the world. In all afflictions, each can say, "The door is open." To the Epicurean, the refuge is intoxication; to the Stoic, the refuge is suicide: "If the house smokes, quit it." Wuttke, Christian Ethics, 1:62-161, from whom much of this account of the Greeks systems is condensed, describes Epicureanism and Stoicism as alike making morality subjective, although Epicureanism regarded spirit as determined by nature, while Stoicism regarded nature as determined by spirit.

The Stoics were materialists and pantheists. Though they speak of a personal God, this is a figure of speech. False opinion is at the root of all vice. Chrysippus denied what we now call the liberty of indifference, saying that there could not be an effect without a cause. Man is enslaved to passion. The Stoics could not explain how a vicious man could become virtuous. The result is apathy. Men act only according to character, and this a doctrine of fate. The Stoic indifference or apathy in misfortune is not a bearing of it at all, but rather a cowardly retreat from it. It is in the actual suffering of evil that Christianity finds "the soul of good." The office of misfortune is disciplinary and purifying; see Seth, Ethical Principles, 417. "The shadow of the sage's self, projected on vacancy, was called God, and, as the sage had long since abandoned interest in practical life, he expected his Divinity to do the same."

The Stoic reverenced God just because of his unapproachable majesty. Christianity sees in God a Father, a Redeemer, a carer for our minute wants, a deliverer from our sin. It teaches us to see in Christ the humanity of the divine, affinity with God, God's supreme interest in his handiwork. For the least of his creatures Christ died. Kinship with God gives dignity to man. The individuality that Stoicism lost in the whole, Christianity makes the end of the creation. The State exists to develop and promote it. Paul took up and infused new meaning into certain phrases of the Stoic philosophy about the freedom and royalty of the wise man, just as John adopted and glorified certain phrases of Alexandrian philosophy about the Word. Stoicism was lonely and pessimistic. The Stoics said that the best thing was not to be born; the next best thing was to die. Because Stoicism had no God of helpfulness and sympathy, its virtue was mere conformity to nature, majestic egoism and self-complacency. In the Roman Epictetus (89), Seneca (65), and Marcus Aurelius (121-180), the religious element comes more into the foreground, and virtue appears once more as God-likeness; but it is possible that this later Stoicism was influenced by Christianity. On Marcus Aurelius, see New Englander, July, 1881:415-431; Capes, Stoicism.

4. SYSTEMS OF WESTERN ASIA. Zoroaster (1000 B. C. ?), the founder of the Parsees, was a dualist, at least so far as to explain the existence of evil and of good by the original presence in the author of all things of two opposing principles. Here is evidently a limit put upon the sovereignty and holiness of God. Man is not perfectly dependent upon him, nor is God's will an unconditional law for his creatures. As opposed to the Indian systems, Zoroaster's insistence upon the divine personality furnished a far better basis for a vigorous and manly morality. Virtue was to be won by hard struggle of free beings against evil. But then, on the other hand, this evil was conceived as originally due, not to finite beings themselves, but either to an evil deity who warred against the good, or to an evil principle in the one deity himself. The burden of guilt is therefore shifted from man to his maker. Morality becomes subjective and unsettled. Not love to God or imitation of God, but rather self-love and self-development, furnish the motive and aim of morality. No fatherhood or love is recognized in the deity, and other things besides God (e. g., fire) are worshiped. There can be no depth to the consciousness of

sin, and no hope of divine deliverance.

It is the one merit of Parseeism that it recognizes the moral conflict of the world; its error is that it carries this moral conflict into the very nature of God. We can apply to Parseeism the words of the Conference of Foreign Mission Boards to the Buddhists of Japan: "All religions are expressions of man's sense of dependence, but only one provides fellowship with God. All religions speak of a higher truth, but only one speaks of that truth as found in a loving personal God, our Father. All religions show man's helplessness, but only one tells of a divine Savior, who offers to man forgiveness of sin, and salvation through his death, and who is now a living person, working in and with all who believe in him, to make them holy and righteous and pure." Matheson, Messages of Old Religions, says that Parseeism recognizes an obstructive element in the nature of God himself. Moral evil is reality; but there is no reconciliation, nor is it shown that all things work together for good. See Wuttke, Christian Ethics, 1:47-54; Faiths of the World (St. Giles Lectures), 109-144; Mitchell, in Present Day Tracts, 3: no. 25; Whitney on the Avesta, in Oriental and Linguistic Studies.

Mohammed (570-632 A. D.), the founder of Islam, gives us in the Koran a system containing four dogmas of fundamental immorality, namely, polygamy, slavery, persecution, and suppression of private judgement. Mohammedanism is heathenism in monotheistic form. Its good points are its conscientiousness and its relation to God. It has prospered because it has preached the unity of God, and because it is a book-religion. But both these it got from Judaism and Christianity. It has appropriated the Old Testament saints and even Jesus. But it denies the death of Christ and sees no need of atonement. The power of sin is not recognized. The idea of sin, in Moslems, is emptied of all positive content. Sin is simply a falling short, accounted for by the weakness and shortsightedness of man, inevitable in the fatalistic universe, or not remembered in wrath by the indulgent and merciful Father. Forgiveness is indulgence, and the conception of God is emptied of the quality of justice. Evil belongs only to the individual, not to the race. Man attains the favor of God by good works, based on prophetic teaching. Morality is not a fruit of salvation, but a means. There is no penitence or humility, but only self-righteousness; and this self-righteousness is consistent with great sensuality, unlimited divorce, and with absolute despotism in family, civil and religious affairs. There is no knowledge of the fatherhood of God or of the brotherhood of man. In all the Koran, there is no such declaration as that "God so loved the world" (John 3:16).

The submission of Islam is submission to an arbitrary will, not to a God of love. There is no basing of morality in love. The highest good is the sensuous happiness of the individual. God and man are external to one another. Mohammed is a teacher but not a priest. Mozley, Miracles, 140, 141— "Mohammed had no faith in human nature. There were two things which he thought men could do, and would do, for the glory of God—transact religious forms, and fight, and upon these two points he was severe; but within the sphere of common practical life, where man's great trial lies, his code exhibits the disdainful laxity of a legislator who accomodates his rule to the recipient, and shows his estimate of the recipient by the accommodation which he adopts.... 'Human nature is weak,' said he." Lord Houghton: The Koran is all wisdom, all law, all religion, for all time. Dead men bow before a dead God. "Though the world rolls on from change to change, And realms of thought expand, The letter stands without expanse or range, Stiff as a dead man's hand." Wherever Mohammedanism has gone, it has either found a desert or made one. Fairbairn, in Contemp. Rev., Dec. 1882:866—"The Koran has frozen Mohammedan thought; to obey is to abandon progress." Muir, in Present Day Tracts, 3: no. 14— "Mohammedanism reduces men to a dead level of social depression, despotism, and semi-barbarism. Islam is the work of man; Christianity of God." See also Faiths of the World (St. Giles Lectures, Second Series), 361-396; J. F. Clarke, Ten Great Religions, 1:448-488; 280-317; Great Religions of the World, published by the Harpers; Zwemer, Moslem Doctrine of God.

3. The person and character of Christ

A. The conception of Christ's person as presenting deity and humanity indissolubly united, and the conception of Christ's character, with its faultless and all-comprehending excellence, cannot be accounted for upon any other hypothesis than that they were historical realities.

The stylobate of the Parthenon at Athens rises about three inches in the middle of the 101 feet of the front, and four inches in the middle of the 228 feet of the flanks. A nearly parallel line is found in the entablature. The axes of the columns lean inward nearly three inches in their height of 34 feet, thus giving a sort of pyramidal character to the structure. Thus the architect overcame the apparent sagging of horizontal lines, and at the same time increased the apparent height of the edifice; see Murray, Handbook of Greece, 5th ed., 1884, 1:308, 309; Ferguson, Handbook of Architecture, 268-270. The neglect to counteract this optical illusion has rendered the Madeleine in Paris a stiff and ineffective copy of the Parthenon. The Galilean peasant who should minutely describe these peculiarities of the Parthenon would prove, not only that the edifice was a historical reality, but that he had actually seen it. Bruce, Apologetics, 343—"In reading the memoirs of the evangelists, you feel as one sometimes feels in a picture-gallery. Your eye alights on the portrait of a person whom you do not know. You look at it intently for a few moments and then remark to a companion: 'That must be like the original,—it is so life-like.' " Theodore Parker: "It would take a Jesus to forge a Jesus." See Row, Bampton Lectures, 1877:178-219, and in Present Day Tracts, 4: no. 22; F. W. Farrar, Witness of History to Christ; Barry, Boyle Lecture on Manifold Witness for Christ.

(a) No source can be assigned from which the evangelists could have derived such a conception. The Hindu avatars were only temporary unions of deity with humanity. The Greeks had men half-deified, but no unions of God and man. The monotheism of the Jews found the person of Christ a perpetual stumbling-block. The Essenes were in principle more opposed to Christianity than the Rabbinists.

Herbert Spencer, Data of Ethics, 279—"The coëxistence of a perfect man and an imperfect society is impossible; and could the two coëxist, the resulting conduct would not furnish the ethical standard sought." We must conclude that the perfect manhood of Christ is a miracle, and the greatest of miracles. Bruce, Apologetics, 346, 351—"When Jesus asks: 'Why callest thou me good?' he means: 'Learn first what goodness is, and call no man good till you are sure that he deserves it.' Jesus' goodness was entirely free from religious scrupulosity; it was distinguished by humanity; it was full of modesty and lowliness.... Buddhism has flourished 2000 years, though little is known of its founder. Christianity might have been so perpetuated, but it is not so. I want to be sure that the ideal has been embodied in an actual life. Otherwise it is only poetry, and the obligation to conform to it ceases." For comparison of Christ's incarnation with Hindu, Greek, Jewish, and Essene ideas, see Dorner, Hist. Doct. Person of Christ, Introduction. On the Essenes, see Herzog, Encyclop., art,: Essener; Pressensé, Jesus Christ, Life, Times and Work, 84-87; Lightfoot on Colossians, 349-419; Godet, Lectures in Defence of the Christian Faith.

(b) No mere human genius, and much less the genius of Jewish fishermen, could have originated this conception. Bad men invent only such characters as they sympathize with. But Christ's character condemns badness. Such a portrait could not have been drawn without supernatural aid. But such aid would not have been given to fabrication. The conception can be explained only by granting that Christ's person and character were historical realities.

Between Pilate and Titus 30,000 Jews are said to have been crucified around the walls of Jerusalem. Many of these were young men. What makes one of them stand out on the pages of history? There are two answers: The character of Jesus was a perfect character, and, He was God as well as man. Gore, Incarnation, 63—"The Christ of the gospels, if he be not true to history, represents a combined effort of the creative imagination without parallel in literature. But the literary characteristics of Palestine in the first century make the hypothesis of such an effort morally impossible." The Apocryphal gospels show us what mere imagination was capable of producing. That the portrait of Christ is not puerile, inane, hysterical, selfishly assertive, and self-contradictory, can be due only to the fact that it is the photograph from real life.

For a remarkable exhibition of the argument from the character of Jesus, see Bushnell, Nature and the Supernatural, 276-332. Bushnell mentions the originality and vastness of Christ's plan, yet its simplicity and practical adaptation; his moral traits of independence, compassion, meekness, wisdom, zeal, humility, patience; the combination in him of seemingly opposite qualities. With all his greatness, he was condescending and simple; he was unworldly, yet not austere; he had strong feelings, yet was self-possessed; he had indignation toward sin, yet compassion toward the sinner; he showed devotion to his work, yet calmness under opposition; universal philanthropy, yet susceptibility to private attachments; the authority of a Savior and Judge, yet the gratitude and the tenderness of a son; the most elevated devotion, yet a life of activity and exertion. See chapter on The Moral Miracle, in Bruce, Miraculous Element of the Gospels, 43-78.

B. The acceptance and belief in the New Testament descriptions of Jesus Christ cannot be accounted for except upon the ground that the person and character described had an actual existence.

(a) If these descriptions were false, there were witnesses still living who had known Christ and who would have contradicted them. (b) There was no motive to induce acceptance of such false accounts, but every motive to the contrary. (c) The success of such falsehoods could be explained only by supernatural aid, but God would never have thus aided falsehood. This person and character, therefore, must have been not fictitious but real; and if real, then Christ's words are true, and the system of which his person and character are a part is a revelation from God.

"The counterfeit may for a season Deceive the wide earth; But the lie waxing great comes to labor, And truth has its birth." Matthew Arnold, The Better Part: "Was Christ a man like us? Ah, let us see, If we then too can be Such men as he!" When the blatant sceptic declared: "I do not believe that such a man as Jesus Christ ever lived," George Warren merely replied: "I wish I were like him!" Dwight L. Moody was called a hypocrite, but the stalwart evangelist answered: "Well, suppose I am. How does that make your case any better? I know some pretty mean things about myself; but you cannot say anything against my Master." Goethe: "Let the culture of the spirit advance forever; let the human spirit broaden itself as it will; yet it will never go beyond the height and moral culture of Christianity, as it glitters and shines in the gospels."

Renan, Life of Jesus: "Jesus founded the absolute religion, excluding nothing, determining nothing, save its essence.... The foundation of the true religion is indeed his work. After him, there is nothing left but to develop and fructify." And a Christian scholar has remarked: "It is an astonishing proof of the divine guidance vouchsafed to the evangelists that no man, of their time or since, has been able to touch the picture of Christ without debasing it." We may find an illustration of this in the words of Chadwick, Old and New Unitarianism, 207—"Jesus' doctrine of marriage was ascetic, his doctrine of property was communistic, his doctrine of charity was sentimental, his doctrine of non-resistance was such as commends itself to Tolstoi, but not to many others of our time. With the example of Jesus, it is the same as with his teachings. Followed unreservedly, would it not justify those who say: 'The hope of the race is in its extinction'; and bring all our joys and sorrows to a sudden end?" To this we may answer in the words of Huxley, who declares that Jesus Christ is "the noblest ideal of humanity which mankind has yet worshiped." Gordon, Christ of To-Day, 179—"The question is not whether Christ is good enough to represent the Supreme Being, but whether the Supreme Being is good enough to have Christ for his representative. John Stuart Mill looks upon the Christian religion as the worship of Christ, rather than the worship of God, and in this way he explains the beneficence of its influence."

John Stuart Mill, Essays on Religion, 254—"The most valuable part of the effect on the character which Christianity has produced, by holding up in a divine person a standard of excellence and a model for imitation, is available even to the absolute unbeliever, and can never more be lost to humanity. For it is Christ rather than God whom Christianity has held up to believers as the pattern of perfection for humanity. It is the God incarnate, more than the God of the Jews or of nature, who, being idealized, has taken so great and salutary hold on the modern mind. And whatever else may be taken away from us by rational criticism, Christ is still left: a unique figure, not more unlike all his precursors than all his followers, even those who had the direct benefit of his personal preaching.... Who among his disciples, or among their proselytes, was capable of inventing the sayings ascribed to Jesus, or of imagining the life and character revealed in the Gospels?... About the life and sayings of Jesus there is a stamp of personal originality combined with profundity of insight which, if we abandon the idle expectation of finding scientific precision where something very different was aimed at, must place the Prophet of Nazareth, even in the estimation of those who have no belief in his inspiration, in the very first rank of the men of sublime genius of whom our species can boast. When this preëminent genius is combined with the qualities of probably the greatest moral reformer and martyr to that mission who ever existed upon earth, religion cannot be said to have made a bad choice in pitching on this man as the ideal representative and guide of humanity; nor even now would it be easy, even for an unbeliever, to find a better translation of the rule of virtue from the abstract into the concrete than the endeavor so to live that Christ would approve our life. When to this we add that, to the conception of the rational sceptic, it remains a possibility that Christ actually was ... a man charged with a special, express and unique commission from God to lead mankind to truth and virtue, we may well conclude that the influences of religion on the character, which will remain after rational criticism has done its utmost against the evidences of religion, are well worth preserving, and that what they lack in direct strength as compared with those of a firmer belief is more than compensated by the greater truth and rectitude of the morality they sanction." See also Ullmann, Sinlessness of Jesus; Alexander, Christ and Christianity, 129-157; Schaff, Person of Christ; Young, The Christ in History; George Dana Boardman, The Problem of Jesus.

4. The testimony of Christ to himself—as being a messenger from God and as being one with God

Only one personage in history has claimed to teach absolute truth, to be one with God, and to attest his divine mission by works such as only God could perform.

A. This testimony cannot be accounted for upon the hypothesis that Jesus was an intentional deceiver: for (a) the perfectly consistent holiness of his life; (b) the unwavering confidence with which he challenged investigation of his claims and staked all upon the result; (c) the vast improbability of a lifelong lie in the avowed interests of truth; and (d) the impossibility that deception should have wrought such blessing to the world,—all show that Jesus was no conscious impostor.

Fisher, Essays on the Supernat. Origin of Christianity, 515-538—Christ knew how vast his claims were, yet he staked all upon them. Though others doubted, he never doubted himself. Though persecuted unto death, he never ceased his consistent testimony. Yet he lays claim to humility: Mat. 11:29—"I am meek and lowly in heart." How can we reconcile with humility his constant self-assertion? We answer that Jesus' self-assertion was absolutely essential to his mission, for he and the truth were one: he could not assert the truth without asserting himself, and he could not assert himself without asserting the truth. Since he was the truth, he needed to say so, for men's sake and for the truth's sake, and he could be meek and lowly in heart in saying so. Humility is not self-depreciation, but only the judging of ourselves according to God's perfect standard. "Humility" is derived from "humus". It is the coming down from airy and vain self-exploitation to the solid ground, the hard-pan, of actual fact.

God requires of us only so much humility as is consistent with truth. The self-glorification of the egotist is nauseating, because it indicates gross ignorance or misrepresentation of self. But it is a duty to be self-asserting, just so far as we represent the truth and righteousness of God. There is a noble self-assertion which is perfectly consistent with humility. Job must stand for his integrity. Paul's humility was not of the Uriah Heep variety. When occasion required, he could assert his manhood and his rights, as at Philippi and at the Castle of Antonia. So the Christian should frankly say out the truth that is in him. Each Christian has an experience of his own, and should tell it to others. In testifying to the truth he is only following the example of "Christ Jesus, who before Pontius Pilate witnessed the good confession" (1 Tim. 6:13).

B. Nor can Jesus' testimony to himself be explained upon the hypothesis that he was self-deceived: for this would argue (a) a weakness and folly amounting to positive insanity. But his whole character and life exhibit a calmness, dignity, equipoise, insight, self-mastery, utterly inconsistent with such a theory. Or it would argue (b) a self-ignorance and self-exaggeration which could spring only from the deepest moral perversion. But the absolute purity of his conscience, the humility of his spirit, the self-denying beneficence of his life, show this hypothesis to be incredible.

Rogers, Superhuman Origin of the Bible, 39—If he were man, then to demand that all the world should bow down to him would be worthy of scorn like that which we feel for some straw-crowned monarch of Bedlam. Forrest, The Christ of History and of Experience, 22, 76—Christ never united with his disciples in prayer. He went up into the mountain to pray, but not to pray with them: Luke 9:18—"as he was alone praying, his disciples were with him." The consciousness of preëxistence is the indispensable precondition of the total demand which he makes in the Synoptics. Adamson, The Mind in Christ, 81, 82—We value the testimony of Christians to their communion with God. Much more should we value the testimony of Christ. Only one who, first being divine, also knew that he was divine, could reveal heavenly things with the clearness and certainty that belong to the utterances of Jesus. In him we have something very different from the momentary flashes of insight which leave us in all the greater darkness.

Nash, Ethics and Revelation, 5—"Self-respect is bottomed upon the ability to become what one desires to be; and, if the ability steadily falls short of the task, the springs of self-respect dry up; the motives of happy and heroic action wither. Science, art, generous civic life, and especially religion, come to man's rescue,"—showing him his true greatness and breadth of being in God. The State is the individual's larger self. Humanity, and even the universe, are parts of him. It is the duty of man to enable all men to be men. It is possible for men not only truthfully but also rationally to assert themselves, even in earthly affairs. Chatham to the Duke of Devonshire: "My Lord, I believe I can save this country, and that no one else can." Leonardo da Vinci, in his thirtieth year, to the Duke of Milan: "I can carry through every kind of work in sculpture, in clay, marble, and bronze; also in painting I can execute everything that can be demanded, as well as any one whosoever."

Horace: "Exegi monumentum ære perennius." Savage, Life beyond Death, 209—A famous old minister said once, when a young and zealous enthusiast tried to get him to talk, and failing, burst out with, "Have you no religion at all?" "None to speak of," was the reply. When Jesus perceived a tendency in his disciples to self-glorification, he urged silence; but when he saw the tendency to introspection and inertness, he bade them proclaim what he had done for them (Mat. 8:4; Mark 5:19). It is never right for the Christian to proclaim himself; but, if Christ had not proclaimed himself, the world could never have been saved. Rush Rhees. Life of Jesus of Nazareth, 235-237—"In the teaching of Jesus, two topics have the leading place—the Kingdom of God, and himself. He sought to be Lord, rather than Teacher only. Yet the Kingdom is not one of power, national and external, but one of fatherly love and of mutual brotherhood."

Did Jesus do anything for effect, or as a mere example? Not so. His baptism had meaning for him as a consecration of himself to death for the sins of the world, and his washing of the disciples' feet was the fit beginning of the paschal supper and the symbol of his laying aside his heavenly glory to purify us for the marriage supper of the Lamb. Thomas à Kempis: "Thou art none the holier because thou art praised, and none the worse because thou art censured. What thou art, that thou art, and it avails thee naught to be called any better than thou art in the sight of God." Jesus' consciousness of his absolute sinlessness and of his perfect communion with God is the strongest of testimonies to his divine nature and mission. See Theological Eclectic, 4:137; Liddon, Our Lord's Divinity, 153; J. S. Mill, Essays on Religion, 253; Young, Christ of History; Divinity of Jesus Christ, by Andover Professors, 37-62.

If Jesus, then, cannot be charged with either mental or moral unsoundness, his testimony must be true, and he himself must be one with God and the revealer of God to men.

Neither Confucius nor Buddha claimed to be divine, or the organs of divine revelation, though both were moral teachers and reformers. Zoroaster and Pythagoras apparently believed themselves charged with a divine mission, though their earliest biographers wrote centuries after their death. Socrates claimed nothing for himself which was beyond the power of others. Mohammed believed his extraordinary states of body and soul to be due to the action of celestial beings; he gave forth the Koran as "a warning to all creatures," and sent a summons to the King of Persia and the Emperor of Constantinople, as well as to other potentates, to accept the religion of Islam; yet he mourned when he died that he could not have opportunity to correct the mistakes of the Koran and of his own life. For Confucius or Buddha, Zoroaster or Pythagoras, Socrates or Mohammed to claim all power in heaven and earth, would show insanity or moral perversion. But this is precisely what Jesus claimed. He was either mentally or morally unsound, or his testimony is true. See Baldensperger, Selbstbewusstsein Jesu; E. Ballentine, Christ his own Witness.

IV. The Historical Results of the Propagation of Scripture Doctrine

1. The rapid progress of the gospel in the first centuries of our era shows its divine origin

A. That Paganism should have been in three centuries supplanted by Christianity, is an acknowledged wonder of history.

The conversion of the Roman Empire to Christianity was the most astonishing revolution of faith and worship ever known. Fifty years after the death of Christ, there were churches in all the principal cities of the Roman Empire. Nero (37-68) found (as Tacitus declares) an "ingens multitudo" of Christians to persecute. Pliny writes to Trajan (52-117) that they "pervaded not merely the cities but the villages and country places, so that the temples were nearly deserted." Tertullian (160-230) writes: "We are but of yesterday, and yet we have filled all your places, your cities, your islands, your castles, your towns, your council-houses, even your camps, your tribes, your senate, your forum. We have left you nothing but your temples." In the time of the emperor Valerian (253-268), the Christians constituted half the population of Rome. The conversion of the emperor Constantine (272-337) brought the whole empire, only 300 years after Jesus' death, under the acknowledged sway of the gospel. See McIlvaine and Alexander, Evidences of Christianity.

B. The wonder is the greater when we consider the obstacles to the progress of Christianity:
(a) The scepticism of the cultivated classes; (b) the prejudice and hatred of the common people; and (c) the persecutions set on foot by government.

(a) Missionaries even now find it difficult to get a hearing among the cultivated classes of the heathen. But the gospel appeared in the most enlightened age of antiquity—the Augustan age of literature and historical inquiry. Tacitus called the religion of Christ "exitiabilis superstitio"—"quos per flagitia invisos vulgus Christianos appellabat." Pliny: "Nihil aliud inveni quam superstitionem pravam et immodicam." If the gospel had been false, its preachers would not have ventured into the centres of civilization and refinement; or if they had, they would have been detected. (b) Consider the interweaving of heathen religions with all the relations of life. Christians often had to meet the furious zeal and blind rage of the mob,—as at Lystra and Ephesus. (c) Rawlinson, in his Historical Evidences, claims that the Catacombs of Rome comprised nine hundred miles of streets and seven millions of graves within a period of four hundred years—a far greater number than could have died a natural death—and that vast multitudes of these must have been massacred for their faith. The Encyclopædia Britannica, however, calls the estimate of De Marchi, which Rawlinson appears to have taken as authority, a great exaggeration. Instead of nine hundred miles of streets, Northcote has three hundred fifty. The number of interments to correspond would be less than three millions. The Catacombs began to be deserted by the time of Jerome. The times when they were universally used by Christians could have been hardly more than two hundred years. They did not begin in sand-pits. There were three sorts of tufa: (1) rocky, used for quarrying and too hard for Christian purposes; (2) sandy, used for sand-pits, too soft to permit construction of galleries and tombs; (3) granular, that used by Christians. The existence of the Catacombs must have been well known to the heathen. After Pope Damasus the exaggerated reverence for them began. They were decorated and improved. Hence many paintings are of later date than 400, and testify to papal polity, not to that of early Christianity. The bottles contain, not blood, but wine of the eucharist celebrated at the funeral.

Fisher, Nature and Method of Revelation, 256-258, calls attention to Matthew Arnold's description of the needs of the heathen world, yet his blindness to the true remedy: "On that hard pagan world disgust And secret loathing fell; Deep weariness and sated lust Made human life a hell. In his cool hall, with haggard eyes, The Roman noble lay; He drove abroad, in furious guise, Along the Appian Way; He made a feast, drank fierce and fast, And crowned his hair with flowers,—No easier nor no quicker passed The impracticable hours." Yet with mingled pride and sadness, Mr. Arnold fastidiously rejects more heavenly nutriment. Of Christ he says: "Now he is dead! Far hence he lies, In the lorn Syrian town, And on his grave, with shining eyes, The Syrian stars look down." He sees that the millions "Have such need of joy, And joy whose grounds are true, And joy that should all hearts employ As when the past was new!" The want of the world is: "One mighty wave of thought and joy, Lifting mankind amain." But the poet sees no ground of hope: "Fools! that so often here, Happiness mocked our prayer, I think might make us fear A like event elsewhere,—Make us not fly to dreams, But moderate desire." He sings of the time when Christianity was young: "Oh, had I lived in that great day,

How had its glory new Filled earth and heaven, and caught away My ravished spirit too!" But desolation of spirit does not bring with it any lowering of self-esteem, much less the humility which deplores the presence and power of evil in the soul, and sighs for deliverance. "They that are whole have no need of a physician, but they that are sick" (Mat. 9:12). Rejecting Christ, Matthew Arnold embodies in his verse "the sweetness, the gravity, the strength, the beauty, and the languor of death" (Hutton, Essays, 302).

C. The wonder becomes yet greater when we consider the natural insufficiency of the means used to secure this progress.

(a) The proclaimers of the gospel were in general unlearned men, belonging to a despised nation. (b) The gospel which they proclaimed was a gospel of salvation through faith in a Jew who had been put to an ignominious death. (c) This gospel was one which excited natural repugnance, by humbling men's pride, striking at the root of their sins, and demanding a life of labor and self-sacrifice. (d) The gospel, moreover, was an exclusive one, suffering no rival and declaring itself to be the universal and only religion.

(a) The early Christians were more unlikely to make converts than modern Jews are to make proselytes, in vast numbers, in the principal cities of Europe and America. Celsus called Christianity "a religion of the rabble." (b) The cross was the Roman gallows—the punishment of slaves. Cicero calls it "servitutis extremum summumque supplicium." (c) There were many bad religions: why should the mild Roman Empire have persecuted the only good one? The answer is in part: Persecution did not originate with the official classes; it proceeded really from the people at large. Tacitus called Christians "haters of the human race." Men recognized in Christianity a foe to all their previous motives, ideals, and aims. Altruism would break up the old society, for every effort that centered in self or in the present life was stigmatized by the gospel as unworthy. (d) Heathenism, being without creed or principle, did not care to propagate itself. "A man must be very weak," said Celsus, "to imagine that Greeks and barbarians, in Asia, Europe, and Libya, can ever unite under the same system of religion." So the Roman government would allow no religion which did not participate in the worship of the State. "Keep yourselves from idols," "We worship no other God," was the Christian's answer. Gibbon, Hist. Decline and Fall, 1: chap. 15, mentions as secondary causes: (1) the zeal of the Jews; (2) the doctrine of immortality; (3) miraculous powers; (4) virtues of early Christians; (5) privilege of participation in church government. But these causes were only secondary, and all would have been insufficient without an invincible persuasion of the truth of Christianity. For answer to Gibbon, see Perrone, Prelectiones Theologicæ, 1:133.

Persecution destroys falsehood by leading its advocates to investigate the grounds of their belief; but it strengthens and multiplies truth by leading its advocates to see more clearly the foundations of their faith. There have been many conscientious persecutors: John 16:2—"They shall put you out of the synagogues: yea, the hour cometh, that whosoever killeth you shall think that he offereth service unto God." The Decretal of Pope Urban II reads: "For we do not count them to be homicides, to whom it may have happened, through their burning zeal against the excommunicated, to put any of them to death." St. Louis, King of France, urged his officers "not to argue with the infidel, but to subdue unbelievers by thrusting the sword into them as far as it will go." Of the use of the rack in England on a certain occasion, it was said that it was used with all the tenderness which the nature of the instrument would allow. This reminds us of Isaak Walton's instruction as to the use of the frog: "Put the hook through his mouth and out at his gills; and, in so doing, use him as though you loved him."

Robert Browning, in his Easter Day, 275-288, gives us what purports to be A Martyr's Epitaph, inscribed upon a wall of the Catacombs, which furnishes a valuable contrast to the sceptical and pessimistic strain of Matthew Arnold: "I was born sickly, poor and mean, A slave: no misery could screen The holders of the pearl of price from Cæsar's envy: therefore twice I fought with beasts, and three times saw My children suffer by his law; At length my own release was earned: I was some time in being burned, But at the close a Hand came through The fire above my head, and drew My soul to Christ, whom now I see. Sergius, a brother, writes for me This testimony on the wall—For me, I have forgot it all."

The progress of a religion so unprepossessing and uncompromising to outward acceptance and dominion, within the space of three hundred years, cannot be explained without supposing that divine power attended its promulgation, and therefore that the gospel is a revelation from God.

Stanley, Life and Letters, 1:527—"In the Kremlin Cathedral, whenever the Metropolitan advanced from the altar to give his blessing, there was always thrown under his feet a carpet embroidered with the eagle of old Pagan Rome, to indicate that the Christian Church and Empire of Constantinople had succeeded and triumphed over it." On this whole section, see F. W. Farrar, Witness of History to Christ, 91; McIlvaine, Wisdom of Holy Scripture, 139.

2. The beneficent influence of the Scripture doctrines and precepts, wherever they have had sway, shows their divine origin. Notice:

A. Their influence on civilization in general, securing a recognition of principles which heathenism ignored, such as Garbett mentions: (a) the importance of the individual; (b) the law of mutual love; (c) the sacredness of human life; (d) the doctrine of internal holiness; (e) the sanctity of home; (f) monogamy, and the religious equality of the sexes; (g) identification of belief and practice.

The continued corruption of heathen lands shows that this change is not due to any laws of merely natural progress. The confessions of ancient writers show that it is not due to philosophy. Its only explanation is that the gospel is the power of God.

Garbett, Dogmatic Faith, 177-186; F. W. Farrar, Witness of History to Christ, chap. on Christianity and the Individual; Brace, Gesta Christi, preface, vi—"Practices and principles implanted, stimulated or supported by Christianity, such as regard for the personality of the weakest and poorest; respect for woman; duty of each member of the fortunate classes to raise up the unfortunate; humanity to the child, the prisoner, the stranger, the needy, and even to the brute; unceasing opposition to all forms of cruelty, oppression and slavery; the duty of personal purity, and the sacredness of marriage; the necessity of temperance; obligation of a more equitable division of the profits of labor, and of greater coöperation between employers and employed; the right of every human being to have the utmost opportunity of developing his faculties, and of all persons to enjoy equal political and social privileges; the principle that the injury of one nation is the injury of all, and the expediency and duty of unrestricted trade and intercourse between all countries; and finally, a profound opposition to war, a determination to limit its evils when existing, and to prevent its arising by means of international arbitration."

Max Müller: "The concept of humanity is the gift of Christ." Guizot, History of Civilization, 1: Introd., tells us that in ancient times the individual existed for the sake of the State; in modern times the State exists for the sake of the individual. "The individual is a discovery of Christ." On the relations between Christianity and Political Economy, see A. H. Strong, Philosophy and Religion, pages 443-460; on the cause of the changed view with regard to the relation of the individual to the State, see page 207—"What has wrought the change? Nothing but the death of the Son of God. When it was seen that the smallest child and the lowest slave had a soul of such worth that Christ left his throne and gave up his life to save it, the world's estimate of values changed, and modern history began." Lucian, the Greek satirist and humorist, 160 A. D., said of the Christians: "Their first legislator [Jesus] has put it into their heads that they are all brothers."

It is this spirit of common brotherhood which has led in most countries to the abolition of cannibalism, infanticide, widow-burning, and slavery. Prince Bismarck: "For social well-being I ask nothing more than Christianity without phrases"—which means the religion of the deed rather than of the creed. Yet it is only faith in the historic revelation of God in Christ which has made Christian deeds possible. Shaler, Interpretation of Nature, 232-278—Aristotle, if he could look over society to-day, would think modern man a new species, in his going out in sympathy to distant peoples. This cannot be the result of natural selection, for self-sacrifice is not profitable to the individual. Altruistic emotions owe their existence to God. Worship of God has flowed back upon man's emotions and has made them more sympathetic. Self-consciousness and sympathy, coming into conflict with brute emotions, originate the sense of sin. Then begins the war of the natural and the spiritual. Love of nature and absorption in others is the true Nirvana. Not physical science, but the humanities, are most needed in education.

H. E. Hersey, Introd. to Browning's Christmas Eve, 19— "Sidney Lanier tells us that the last twenty centuries have spent their best power upon the development of personality. Literature, education, government, and religion, have learned to recognize the individual as the unit of force. Browning goes a step further. He declares that so powerful is a complete personality that its very touch gives life and courage and potency. He turns to history for the inspiration of enduring virtue and the stimulus for sustained effort, and he finds both in Jesus Christ." J. P. Cooke, Credentials of Science, 43—The change from the ancient philosopher to the modern investigator is the change from self-assertion to self-devotion, and the great revolution can be traced to the influence of Christianity and to the spirit of humility exhibited and inculcated by Christ. Lewes, Hist. Philos., 1:408—Greek morality never embraced any conception of humanity; no Greek ever attained to the sublimity of such a point of view.

Kidd, Social Evolution, 165, 287—It is not intellect that has pushed forward the world of modern times: it is the altruistic feeling that originated in the cross and sacrifice of Christ. The French Revolution was made possible by the fact that humanitarian ideas had undermined the upper classes themselves, and effective resistance was impossible. Socialism would abolish the struggle for existence on the part of individuals. What security would be left for social progress? Removing all restrictions upon population ensures progressive deterioration. A non-socialist community would outstrip a socialist community where all the main wants of life were secure. The real tendency of society is to bring all the people into rivalry, not only on a footing of political equality, but on conditions of equal social opportunities. The State in future will interfere and control, in order to preserve or secure free competition, rather than to suspend it. The goal is not socialism or State management, but competition in which all shall have equal advantages. The evolution of human society is not primarily intellectual but religious. The winning races are the religious races. The Greeks had more intellect, but we have more civilization and progress. The Athenians were as far above us as we are above the negro race. Gladstone said that we are intellectually weaker than the men of the middle ages. When the intellectual development of any section of the race has for the time being outrun its ethical development, natural selection has apparently weeded it out, like any other unsuitable product. Evolution is developing reverence, with its allied qualities, mental energy, resolution, enterprise, prolonged and concentrated application, simple minded and single minded devotion to duty. Only religion can overpower selfishness and individualism and ensure social progress.

B. Their influence upon individual character and happiness, wherever they have been tested in practice. This influence is seen (a) in the moral transformations they have wrought—as in the case of Paul the apostle, and of persons in every Christian community; (b) in the self-denying labors for human welfare to which they have led—as in the case of Wilberforce and Judson; (c) in the hopes they have inspired in times of sorrow and death.

These beneficent fruits cannot have their source in merely natural causes, apart from the truth and divinity of the Scriptures; for in that case the contrary beliefs would be accompanied by the same blessings. But since we find these blessings only in connection with Christian teaching, we may justly consider this as their cause. This teaching, then, must be true, and the Scriptures must be a divine revelation. Else God has made a lie to be the greatest blessing to the race.

The first Moravian missionaries to the West Indies walked six hundred miles to take ship, worked their passage, and then sold themselves as slaves, in order to get the privilege of preaching to the negroes.... The father of John G. Paton was a stocking-weaver. The whole family, with the exception of the very small children, worked from 6 a. m. to 10 p. m., with one hour for dinner at noon and a half hour each for breakfast and supper. Yet family prayer was regularly held twice a day. In these breathing-spells for daily meals John G. Paton took part of his time to study the Latin Grammar, that he might prepare himself for missionary work. When told by an uncle that, if he went to the New Hebrides, the cannibals would eat him, he replied: "You yourself will soon be dead and buried, and I had as lief be eaten by cannibals as by worms." The Aneityumese raised arrow-root for fifteen years and sold it to pay the £1200 required for printing the Bible in their own language. Universal church-attendance and Bible-study make those South Sea Islands the most heavenly place on earth on the Sabbath-day.

In 1839, twenty thousand negroes in Jamaica gathered to begin a life of freedom. Into a coffin were put the handcuffs and shackles of slavery, relics of the whipping-post and the scourge. As the clock struck twelve at night, a preacher cried with the first stroke: "The monster is dying!" and so with every stroke until the last, when he cried: "The monster is dead!" Then all rose from their knees and sang: "Praise God from whom all blessings flow!"... "What do you do that for?" said the sick Chinaman whom the medical missionary was tucking up in bed with a care which the patient had never received since he was a baby. The missionary took the opportunity to tell him of the love of Christ.... The aged Australian mother, when told that her two daughters, missionaries in China, had both of them been murdered by a heathen mob, only replied: "This decides me; I will go to China now myself, and try to teach those poor creatures what the love of Jesus means."... Dr. William Ashmore: "Let one missionary die, and ten come to his funeral." A shoemaker, teaching neglected boys and girls while he worked at his cobbler's bench, gave the impulse to Thomas Guthrie's life of faith.

We must judge religions not by their ideals, but by their performances. Omar Khayyam and Mozoomdar give us beautiful thoughts, but the former is not Persia, nor is the latter India. "When the microscopic search of scepticism, which has hunted the heavens and sounded the seas to disprove the existence of a Creator, has turned its attention to human society and has found on this planet a place ten miles square where a decent man can live in decency, comfort, and security, supporting and educating his children, unspoiled and unpolluted; a place where age is reverenced, infancy protected, manhood respected, womanhood honored, and human life held in due regard—when sceptics can find such a place ten miles square on this globe, where the gospel of Christ has not gone and cleared the way and laid the foundations and made decency and security possible, it will then be in order for the sceptical literati to move thither and to ventilate their views. But so long as these very men are dependent upon the very religion they discard for every privilege they enjoy, they may well hesitate before they rob the Christian of his hope and humanity of its faith in that Savior who alone has given that hope of eternal life which makes life tolerable and society possible, and robs death of its terrors and the grave of its gloom." On the beneficent influence of the gospel, see Schmidt, Social Results of Early Christianity; D. J. Hill, The Social Influence of Christianity.

Chapter III - Inspiration Of The Scriptures

I. Definition of Inspiration

Inspiration is that influence of the Spirit of God upon the minds of the Scripture writers which made their writings the record of a progressive divine revelation, sufficient, when taken together and interpreted by the same Spirit who inspired them, to lead every honest inquirer to Christ and to salvation.

Notice the significance of each part of this definition: 1. Inspiration is an influence of the Spirit of God. It is not a merely naturalistic phenomenon or psychological vagary, but is rather the effect of the inworking of the personal divine Spirit. 2. Yet inspiration is an influence upon the mind, and not upon the body. God secures his end by awakening man's rational powers, and not by an external or mechanical communication. 3. The writings of inspired men are the record of a revelation. They are not themselves the revelation. 4. The revelation and the record are both progressive. Neither one is complete at the beginning. 5. The Scripture writings must be taken together. Each part must be viewed in connection with what precedes and with what follows. 6. The same Holy Spirit who made the original revelations must interpret to us the record of them, if we are to come to the knowledge of the truth. 7. So used and so interpreted, these writings are sufficient, both in quantity and in quality, for their religious purpose. 8. That purpose is, not to furnish us with a model history or with the facts of science, but to lead us to Christ and to salvation.

(a) Inspiration is therefore to be defined, not by its method, but by its result. It is a general term including all those kinds and degrees of the Holy Spirit's influence which were brought to bear upon the minds of the Scripture writers, in order to secure the putting into permanent and written form of the truth best adapted to man's moral and religious needs.

(b) Inspiration may often include revelation, or the direct communication from God of truth to which man could not attain by his unaided powers. It may include illumination, or the quickening of man's cognitive powers to understand truth already revealed. Inspiration, however, does not necessarily and always include either revelation or illumination. It is simply the divine influence which secures a transmission of needed truth to the future, and, according to the nature of the truth to be transmitted, it may be only an inspiration of superintendence, or it may be also and at the same time an inspiration of illumination or revelation.

(c) It is not denied, but affirmed, that inspiration may qualify for oral utterance of truth, or for wise leadership and daring deeds. Men may be inspired to render external service to God's kingdom, as in the cases of Bezalel and Samson; even though this service is rendered unwillingly or unconsciously, as in the cases of Balaam and Cyrus. All human intelligence, indeed, is due to the inbreathing of that same Spirit who created man at the beginning. We are now concerned with inspiration, however, only as it pertains to the authorship of Scripture.

Gen. 2:7—"And Jehovah God formed man of the dust of the ground, and breathed into his nostrils the breath of life; and man became a living soul"; Ex. 31:2, 3—"I have called by name Bezalel ... and I have filled him with the Spirit of God ... in all manner of workmanship"; Judges 13:24, 25— "called his name Samson: and the child grew, and Jehovah blessed him. And the Spirit of Jehovah began to move him"; Num. 23:5—"And Jehovah put a word in Balaam's mouth, and said, Return unto Balak, and thus shalt thou speak"; 2 Chron. 36:22—"Jehovah stirred up the spirit of Cyrus"; Is. 44:28— "that saith of Cyrus, He is my shepherd"; 45:5—"I will gird thee, though thou hast not known me"; Job 32:8—"there is a spirit in man, and the breath of the Almighty giveth them understanding." These passages show the true meaning of 2 Tim. 3:16—"Every scripture inspired of God." The word θεόπνευστος is to be understood as alluding, not to the flute-player's breathing into his instrument, but to God's original inbreathing of life. The flute is passive, but man's soul is active. The flute gives out only what it receives, but the inspired man under the divine influence is a conscious and free originator of thought and expression. Although the inspiration of which we are to treat is simply the inspiration of the Scripture writings, we can best understand this narrower use of the term by remembering that all real knowledge has in it a divine element, and that we are possessed of complete consciousness only as we live, move, and have our being in God. Since Christ, the divine Logos or Reason, is "the light which lighteth every man" (John 1:9), a special influence of "the spirit of Christ which was in them" (1 Pet. 1:11) rationally accounts for the fact that "men spake from God, being moved by the Holy Spirit" (2 Pet. 1:21).

It may help our understanding of terms above employed if we adduce instances of

(1) Inspiration without revelation, as in Luke or Acts, Luke 1:1-3; (2) Inspiration including revelation, as in the Apocalypse, Rev. 1:1, 11; (3) Inspiration without illumination, as in the prophets, 1 Pet. 1:11; (4) Inspiration including illumination, as in the case of Paul, 1 Cor. 2:12; (5) Revelation without inspiration, as in God's words from Sinai, Ex. 20:1, 22; (6) Illumination without inspiration, as in modern preachers, Eph. 2:20.

Other definitions are those of Park: "Inspiration is such an influence over the writers of the Bible that all their teachings which have a religious character are trustworthy"; of Wilkinson: "Inspiration is help from God to keep the report of divine revelation free from error. Help to whom? No matter to whom, so the result is secured. The final result, viz.: the record or report of revelation, this must be free from error. Inspiration may affect one or all of the agents employed"; of Hovey: "Inspiration was an influence of the Spirit of God on those powers of men which are concerned in the reception, retention and expression of religious truth—an influence so pervading and powerful that the teaching of inspired men was according to the mind of God. Their teaching did not in any instance embrace all truth in respect to God, or man, or the way of life; but it comprised just so much of the truth on any particular subject as could be received in faith by the inspired teacher and made useful to those whom he addressed. In this sense the teaching of the original documents composing our Bible may be pronounced free from error"; of G. B. Foster: "Revelation is the action of God in the soul of his child, resulting in divine self-expression there: Inspiration is the action of God in the soul of his child, resulting in apprehension and appropriation of the divine expression. Revelation has logical but not chronological priority"; of Horton, Inspiration and the Bible, 10-13—"We mean by Inspiration exactly those qualities or characteristics which are the marks or notes of the Bible.... We call our Bible inspired; by which we mean that by reading and studying it we find our way to God, we find his will for us, and we find how we can conform ourselves to his will."

Fairbairn, Christ in Modern Theology, 496, while nobly setting forth the naturalness of revelation, has misconceived the relation of inspiration to revelation by giving priority to the former: "The idea of a written revelation may be said to be logically involved in the notion of a living God. Speech is natural to spirit; and if God is by nature spirit, it will be to him a matter of nature to reveal himself. But if he speaks to man, it will be through men; and those who hear best will be most possessed of God. This possession is termed 'inspiration.' God inspires, man reveals: revelation is the mode or form—word, character, or institution—in which man embodies what he has received. The terms, though not equivalent, are co-extensive, the one denoting the process on its inner side, the other on its outer." This statement, although approved by Sanday, Inspiration, 124, 125, seems to us almost precisely to reverse the right meaning of the words. We prefer the view of Evans, Bib. Scholarship and Inspiration, 54— "God has first revealed himself, and then has inspired men to interpret, record and apply this revelation. In redemption, inspiration is the formal factor, as revelation is the material factor. The men are inspired, as Prof. Stowe said. The thoughts are inspired, as Prof. Briggs said. The words are inspired, as Prof. Hodge said. The warp and woof of the Bible is $\pi\nu\varepsilon\tilde{\upsilon}\mu\alpha$: 'the words that I have spoken unto you are spirit' (John 6:63). Its fringes run off, as was inevitable, into the secular, the material, the psychic." Phillips Brooks, Life, 2:351—"If the true revelation of God is in Christ, the Bible is not properly a revelation, but the history of a revelation. This is not only a fact but a necessity, for a person cannot be revealed in a book, but must find revelation, if at all, in a person. The centre and core of the Bible must therefore be the gospels, as the story of Jesus."

Some, like Priestley, have held that the gospels are authentic but not inspired. We therefore add to the proof of the genuineness and credibility of Scripture, the proof of its inspiration. Chadwick, Old and New Unitarianism, 11—"Priestley's belief in supernatural revelation was intense. He had an absolute distrust of reason as qualified to furnish an adequate knowledge of religious things, and at the same time a perfect confidence in reason as qualified to prove that negative and to determine the contents of the revelation." We might claim the historical truth of the gospels, even if we did not call them inspired. Gore, in Lux Mundi, 341—"Christianity brings with it a doctrine of the inspiration of the Holy Scriptures, but is not based upon it." Warfield and Hodge, Inspiration, 8—"While the inspiration of the Scriptures is true, and being true is fundamental to the adequate interpretation of Scripture, it nevertheless is not, in the first instance, a principle fundamental to the truth of the Christian religion."

On the idea of Revelation, see Ladd, in Journ. Christ. Philos., Jan. 1883:156-178; on Inspiration, ibid., Apr. 1883:225-248. See Henderson on Inspiration (2nd ed.), 58, 205, 249, 303, 310. For other works on the general subject of Inspiration, see Lee, Bannerman, Jamieson, Macnaught; Garbett, God's Word Written; Aids to Faith, essay on Inspiration. Also, Philippi, Glaubenslehre, 1:205; Westcott, Introd. to Study of the Gospels, 27-65; Bib. Sac., 1:97; 4:154; 12:217; 15:29, 314; 25:192-198; Dr. Barrows, in Bib. Sac., 1867:593; 1872:428; Farrar, Science in Theology, 208; Hodge and Warfield, in Presb. Rev., Apr. 1881:225-261; Manly, The Bible Doctrine of Inspiration; Watts, Inspiration; Mead, Supernatural Revelation, 350; Whiton, Gloria Patri, 136; Hastings, Bible Dict., 1:296-299; Sanday, Bampton Lectures on Inspiration.

1. Since we have shown that God has made a revelation of himself to man, we may reasonably presume that he will not trust this revelation wholly to human tradition and misrepresentation, but will also provide a record of it essentially trustworthy and sufficient; in other words, that the same Spirit who originally communicated the truth will preside over its publication, so far as is needed to accomplish its religious purpose.

Since all natural intelligence, as we have seen, presupposes God's indwelling, and since in Scripture the all-prevailing atmosphere, with its constant pressure and effort to enter every cranny and corner of the world, is used as an illustration of the impulse of God's omnipotent Spirit to vivify and energize every human soul (Gen. 2:7; Job 32:8), we may infer that, but for sin, all men would be morally and spiritually inspired (Num. 11:29—"Would that all Jehovah's people were prophets, that Jehovah would put his Spirit upon them!" Is. 59:2—"your iniquities have separated between you and your God"). We have also seen that God's method of communicating his truth in matters of religion is presumably analogous to his method of communicating secular truth, such as that of astronomy or history. There is an original delivery to a single nation, and to single persons in that nation, that it may through them be given to mankind. Sanday, Inspiration, 140—"There is a 'purpose of God according to selection' (Rom. 9:11); there is an 'election' or 'selection of grace'; and the object of that selection was Israel and those who take their name from Israel's Messiah. If a tower is built in ascending tiers, those who stand upon the lower tiers are yet raised above the ground, and some may be raised higher than others, but the full and unimpeded view is reserved for those who mount upward to the top. And that is the place destined for us if we will take it."

If we follow the analogy of God's working in other communications of knowledge, we shall reasonably presume that he will preserve the record of his revelations in written and accessible documents, handed down from those to whom these revelations were first communicated, and we may expect that these documents will be kept sufficiently correct and trustworthy to accomplish their religious purpose, namely, that of furnishing to the honest inquirer a guide to Christ and to salvation. The physician commits his prescriptions to writing; the Clerk of Congress records its proceedings; the State Department of our government instructs our foreign ambassadors, not orally, but by dispatches. There is yet greater need that revelation should be recorded, since it is to be transmitted to distant ages; it contains long discourses; it embraces mysterious doctrines. Jesus did not write himself; for he was the subject, not the mere channel, of revelation. His unconcern about the apostles' immediately committing to writing what they saw and heard is inexplicable, if he did not expect that inspiration would assist them.

We come to the discussion of Inspiration with a presumption quite unlike that of Kuenen and Wellhausen, who write in the interest of almost avowed naturalism. Kuenen, in the opening sentences of his Religion of Israel, does indeed assert the rule of God in the world. But Sanday, Inspiration, 117, says well that "Kuenen keeps this idea very much in the background. He expended a whole volume of 593 large octavo pages (Prophets and Prophecy in Israel, London, 1877) in proving that the prophets were not moved to speak by God, but that their utterances were all their own." The following extract, says Sanday, indicates the position which Dr. Kuenen really held: "We do not allow ourselves to be deprived of God's presence in history. In the fortunes and development of nations, and not least clearly in those of Israel, we see Him, the holy and all-wise Instructor of his human children. But the old contrasts must be altogether set aside. So long as we derive a separate part of Israel's religious life directly from God, and allow the supernatural or immediate revelation to intervene in even one single point, so long also our view of the whole continues to be incorrect, and we see ourselves here and there necessitated to do violence to the well-authenticated contents of the historical documents. It is the supposition of a natural development alone which accounts for all the phenomena" (Kuenen, Prophets and Prophecy in Israel, 585).

2. Jesus, who has been proved to be not only a credible witness, but a messenger from God, vouches for the inspiration of the Old Testament, by quoting it with the formula: "It is written"; by declaring that "one jot or one tittle" of it "shall in no wise pass away," and that "the Scripture cannot be broken."

Jesus quotes from four out of the five books of Moses, and from the Psalms, Isaiah, Malachi, and Zechariah, with the formula, "it is written"; see Mat. 4:4, 6, 7; 11:10; Mark 14:27; Luke 4:4-12. This formula among the Jews indicated that the quotation was from a sacred book and was divinely inspired. Jesus certainly regarded the Old Testament with as much reverence as the Jews of his day. He declared that "one jot or one tittle shall in no wise pass away from the law" (Mat. 5:18). He said that "the scripture cannot be broken" (John 10:35) = "the normative and judicial authority of the Scripture cannot be set aside; notice here [in the singular, ἡ γραφή] the idea of the unity of Scripture" (Meyer). And yet our Lord's use of O. T. Scripture was wholly free from the superstitious literalism which prevailed among the Jews of his day. The phrases "word of God" (John 10:35; Mark 7:13), "wisdom of God" (Luke 11:49) and "oracles of God" (Rom. 3:2) probably designate the original revelations of God and not the record of these in Scripture; cf. 1 Sam. 9:27; 1 Chron. 17:3; Is. 40:8; Mat. 13:19; Luke 3:2; Acts 8:25. Jesus refuses assent to the O. T. law respecting the Sabbath (Mark 2:27 sq.), external defilements (Mark 7:15), divorce (Mark 10:2 sq.). He "came not to destroy but to fulfil" (Mat. 5:17); yet he fulfilled the law by bringing out its inner spirit in his perfect life, rather than by formal and minute obedience to its precepts; see Wendt, Teaching of Jesus, 2:5-35.

The apostles quote the O. T. as the utterance of God (Eph. 4:8—διὸ λέγει, sc. θεός). Paul's insistence upon the form of even a single word, as in Gal. 3:16, and his use of the O. T. for purposes of allegory, as in Gal 4:21-31, show that in his view the O. T. text was sacred. Philo, Josephus and the Talmud, in their interpretations of the O. T., fall continually into a "narrow and unhappy literalism." "The N. T. does not indeed escape Rabbinical methods, but even where these are most prominent they seem to affect the form far more than the substance. And through the temporary and local form the writer constantly penetrates to the very heart of the O. T. teaching;" see Sanday, Bampton Lectures on Inspiration, 87; Henderson, Inspiration, 254.

3. Jesus commissioned his apostles as teachers and gave them promises of a supernatural aid of the Holy Spirit in their teaching, like the promises made to the Old Testament prophets.

Mat. 28:19, 20—"Go ye ... teaching ... and lo, I am with you." Compare promises to Moses (Ex. 3:12), Jeremiah (Jer. 1:5-8), Ezekiel (Ezek. 2 and 3). See also Is. 44:3 and Joel 2:28—"I will pour my Spirit upon thy seed"; Mat. 10:7—"as ye go, preach"; 19—"be not anxious how or what ye shall speak"; John 14:26—"the Holy Spirit ... shall teach you all things"; 15:26, 27—"the Spirit of truth ... shall bear witness of me: and ye also bear witness" = the Spirit shall witness in and through you; 16:13—"he shall guide you into all the truth" = (1) limitation—all the truth of Christ, i. e., not of philosophy or science, but of religion; (2) comprehension—all the truth within this limited range, i. e., sufficiency of Scripture as rule of faith and practice (Hovey); 17:8—"the words which thou gavest me I have given unto them"; Acts 1:4—"he charged them ... to wait for the promise of the Father"; John 20:22—"he breathed on them, and saith unto them, Receive ye the Holy Spirit." Here was both promise and communication of the personal Holy Spirit. Compare Mat. 10:19, 20—"it shall be given you in that hour what ye shall speak. For it is not ye that speak, but the Spirit of your Father that speaketh in you." See Henderson, Inspiration, 247, 248.

Jesus' testimony here is the testimony of God. In Deut. 18:18, it is said that God will put his words into the mouth of the great Prophet. In John 12:49, 50, Jesus says: "I spake not from myself, but the Father that sent me, he hath given me a commandment, what I should say, and what I should speak. And I know that his commandment is life eternal; the things therefore which I speak, even as the Father hath said unto me, so I speak." John 17:7, 8—"all things whatsoever thou hast given me are from thee: for the words which thou gavest me I have given unto them." John 8:40—"a man that hath told you the truth, which I heard from God."

4. The apostles claim to have received this promised Spirit, and under his influence to speak with divine authority, putting their writings upon a level with the Old Testament Scriptures. We have not only direct statements that both the matter and the form of their teaching were supervised by the Holy Spirit, but we have indirect evidence that this was the case in the tone of authority which pervades their addresses and epistles.

Statements:—1 Cor. 2:10, 13—"unto us God revealed them through the Spirit.... Which things also we speak, not in words which man's wisdom teacheth, but which the Spirit teacheth"; 11:23—"I received of the Lord that which also I delivered unto you"; 12:8, 28—the λόγος σοφίας was apparently a gift peculiar to the apostles; 14:37, 38—"the things which I write unto you ... they are the commandment of the Lord"; Gal. 1:12—"neither did I receive it from man, nor was I taught it, but it came to me through revelation of Jesus Christ"; 1 Thess. 4:2, 8—"ye know what charge we gave you through the Lord Jesus.... Therefore he that rejecteth, rejecteth not man, but God, who giveth his Holy Spirit unto you." The following passages put the teaching of the apostles on the same level with O. T. Scripture: 1 Pet. 1:11, 12—"Spirit of Christ which was in them" [O. T. prophets];—[N. T. preachers] "preached the gospel unto you by the Holy Spirit"; 2 Pet. 1:21—O. T. prophets "spake from God, being moved by the Holy Spirit"; 3:2—"remember the words which were spoken before by the holy prophets" [O. T.], "and the commandment of the Lord and Savior through your apostles" [N. T.]; 16—"wrest [Paul's Epistles], as they do also the other scriptures, unto their own destruction." Cf. Ex. 4:14-16; 7:1.

Implications:—2 Tim. 3:16—"Every scripture inspired of God is also profitable"—a clear implication of inspiration, though not a direct statement of it = there is a divinely inspired Scripture. In 1 Cor. 5:3-5, Paul, commanding the Corinthian church with regard to the incestuous person, was arrogant if not inspired. There are more imperatives in the Epistles than in any other writings of the same extent. Notice the continual asseveration of authority, as in Gal. 1:1, 2, and the declaration that disbelief of the record is sin, as in 1 John 5:10, 11. Jude 3—"the faith which was once for all (ἅπαξ) delivered unto the saints." See Kahnis, Dogmatik, 3:122; Henderson, Inspiration (2nd ed.), 34, 234; Conant, Genesis, Introd., xiii, note; Charteris, New Testament Scriptures: They claim truth, unity, authority.

The passages quoted above show that inspired men distinguished inspiration from their own unaided thinking. These inspired men claim that their inspiration is the same with that of the prophets. Rev. 22:6—"the Lord, the God of the spirits of the prophets, sent his angel to show unto his servants the things which must shortly come to pass" = inspiration gave them supernatural knowledge of the future. As inspiration in the O. T. was the work of the pre-incarnate Christ, so inspiration in the N. T. is the work of the ascended and glorified Christ by his Holy Spirit. On the Relative Authority of the Gospels, see Gerhardt, in Am. Journ. Theol., Apl. 1899:275-294, who shows that not the words of Jesus in the gospels are the final revelation, but rather the teaching of the risen and glorified Christ in the Acts and the Epistles. The Epistles are the posthumous works of Christ. Pattison, Making of the Sermon, 23— "The apostles, believing themselves to be inspired teachers, often preached without texts; and the fact that their successors did not follow their example shows that for themselves they made no such claim. Inspiration ceased, and henceforth authority was found in the use of the words of the now complete Scriptures."

5. The apostolic writers of the New Testament, unlike professedly inspired heathen sages and poets, gave attestation by miracles or prophecy that they were inspired by God, and there is reason to believe that the productions of those who were not apostles, such as Mark, Luke, Hebrews, James, and Jude, were recommended to the churches as inspired, by apostolic sanction and authority.

The twelve wrought miracles (Mat. 10:1). Paul's "signs of an apostle" (2 Cor. 13:12) = miracles. Internal evidence confirms the tradition that Mark was the "interpreter of Peter," and that Luke's gospel and the Acts had the sanction of Paul. Since the purpose of the Spirit's bestowment was to qualify those who were to be the teachers and founders of the new religion, it is only fair to assume that Christ's promise of the Spirit was valid not simply to the twelve but to all who stood in their places, and to these not simply as speakers, but, since in this respect they had a still greater need of divine guidance, to them as writers also.

The epistle to the Hebrews, with the letters of James and Jude, appeared in the lifetime of some of the twelve, and passed unchallenged; and the fact that they all, with the possible exception of 2 Peter, were very early accepted by the churches founded and watched over by the apostles, is sufficient evidence that the apostles regarded them as inspired productions. As evidences that the writers regarded their writings as of universal authority, see 1 Cor. 1:2—"unto the church of God which is at Corinth ... with all that call upon the name of our Lord Jesus Christ in every place," etc.; 7:17—"so ordain I in all the churches"; Col. 4:16—"And when this epistle hath been read among you, cause that it be read also in the church of the Laodiceans"; 2 Pet. 3:15, 16—"our beloved brother Paul also, according to the wisdom given to him, wrote unto you." See Bartlett, in Princeton Rev., Jan. 1880:23-57; Bib. Sac., Jan. 1884:204, 205.

Johnson, Systematic Theology, 40—"Miraculous gifts were bestowed at Pentecost on many besides apostles. Prophecy was not an uncommon gift during the apostolic period." There is no antecedent improbability that inspiration should extend to others than to the principal leaders of the church, and since we have express instances of such inspiration in oral utterances (Acts 11:28; 21:9, 10) it seems natural that there should have been instances of inspiration in written utterances also. In some cases this appears to have been only an inspiration of superintendence. Clement of Alexandria says only that Peter neither forbade nor encouraged Mark in his plan of writing the gospel. Irenæus tells us that Mark's gospel was written after the death of Peter. Papias says that Mark wrote down what he remembered to have heard from Peter. Luke does not seem to have been aware of any miraculous aid in his writing, and his methods appear to have been those of the ordinary historian.

6. The chief proof of inspiration, however, must always be found in the internal characteristics of the Scriptures themselves, as these are disclosed to the sincere inquirer by the Holy Spirit. The testimony of the Holy Spirit combines with the teaching of the Bible to convince the earnest reader that this teaching is as a whole and in all essentials beyond the power of man to communicate, and that it must therefore have been put into permanent and written form by special inspiration of God.

Foster, Christian Life and Theology, 105—"The testimony of the Spirit is an argument from identity of effects—the doctrines of experience and the doctrines of the Bible—to identity of cause.... God-wrought experience proves a God-wrought Bible.... This covers the Bible as a whole, if not the whole of the Bible. It is true so far as I can test it. It is to be believed still further if there is no other evidence." Lyman Abbott, in his Theology of an Evolutionist, 105, calls the Bible "a record of man's laboratory work in the spiritual realm, a history of the dawning of the consciousness of God and of the divine life in the soul of man." This seems to us unduly subjective. We prefer to say that the Bible is also God's witness to us of his presence and working in human hearts and in human history—a witness which proves its divine origin by awakening in us experiences similar to those which it describes, and which are beyond the power of man to originate.

G. P. Fisher, in Mag. of Christ. Lit., Dec. 1892:239—"Is the Bible infallible? Not in the sense that all its statements extending even to minutiæ in matters of history and science are strictly accurate. Not in the sense that every doctrinal and ethical statement in all these books is incapable of amendment. The whole must sit in judgment on the parts. Revelation is progressive. There is a human factor as well as a divine. The treasure is in earthen vessels. But the Bible is infallible in the sense that whoever surrenders himself in a docile spirit to its teaching will fall into no hurtful error in matters of faith and charity. Best of all, he will find in it the secret of a new, holy and blessed life, 'hidden with Christ in God' (Col. 3:3). The Scriptures are the witness to Christ.... Through the Scriptures he is truly and adequately made known to us." Denney, Death of Christ, 314—"The unity of the Bible and its inspiration are correlative terms. If we can discern a real unity in it—and I believe we can when we see that it converges upon and culminates in a divine love bearing the sin of the world—then that unity and its inspiration are one and the same thing. And it is not only inspired as a whole, it is the only book that is inspired. It is the only book in the world to which God sets his seal in our hearts when we read in search of an answer to the question, How shall a sinful man be righteous with God?... The conclusion of our study of Inspiration should be the conviction that the Bible gives us a body of doctrine—a 'faith which was once for all delivered unto the saints' (Jude 3)."

III. Theories of Inspiration

1. The Intuition-theory

This holds that inspiration is but a higher development of that natural insight into truth which all men possess to some degree; a mode of intelligence in matters of morals and religion which gives rise to sacred books, as a corresponding mode of intelligence in matters of secular truth gives rise to great works of philosophy or art. This mode of intelligence is regarded as the product of man's own powers, either without special divine influence or with only the inworking of an impersonal God.

This theory naturally connects itself with Pelagian and rationalistic views of man's independence of God, or with pantheistic conceptions of man as being himself the highest manifestation of an all-pervading but unconscious intelligence. Morell and F. W. Newman in England, and Theodore Parker in America, are representatives of this theory. See Morell, Philos. of Religion, 127-179—"Inspiration is only a higher potency of what every man possesses in some degree." See also Francis W. Newman (brother of John Henry Newman), Phases of Faith (= phases of unbelief); Theodore Parker, Discourses of Religion, and Experiences as a Minister: "God is infinite; therefore he is immanent in nature, yet transcending it; immanent in spirit, yet transcending that. He must fill each point of spirit, as of space; matter must unconsciously obey; man, conscious and free, has power to a certain extent to disobey, but obeying, the immanent God acts in man as much as in nature"—quoted in Chadwick, Theodore Parker, 271. Hence Parker's view of Inspiration: If the conditions are fulfilled, inspiration comes in proportion to man's gifts and to his use of those gifts. Chadwick himself, in his Old and New Unitarianism, 68, says that "the Scriptures are inspired just so far as they are inspiring, and no more."

W. C. Gannett, Life of Ezra Stiles Gannett, 196—"Parker's spiritualism affirmed, as the grand truth of religion, the immanence of an infinitely perfect God in matter and mind, and his activity in both spheres." Martineau, Study of Religion, 2:178-180—"Theodore Parker treats the regular results of the human faculties as an immediate working of God, and regards the Principia of Newton as inspired.... What then becomes of the human personality? He calls God not only omnipresent, but omniactive. Is then Shakespeare only by courtesy author of Macbeth?... If this were more than rhetorical, it would be unconditional pantheism." Both nature and man are other names for God. Martineau is willing to grant that our intuitions and ideals are expressions of the Deity in us, but our personal reasoning and striving, he thinks, cannot be attributed to God. The word νοῦς has no plural: intellect, in whatever subject manifested, being all one, just as a truth is one and the same, in however many persons' consciousness it may present itself; see Martineau, Seat of Authority, 403. Palmer, Studies in Theological Definition, 27—"We can draw no sharp distinction between the human mind discovering truth, and the divine mind imparting revelation." Kuenen belongs to this school.

With regard to this theory we remark:

(a) Man has, indeed, a certain natural insight into truth, and we grant that inspiration uses this, so far as it will go, and makes it an instrument in discovering and recording facts of nature or history.

In the investigation, for example, of purely historical matters, such as Luke records, merely natural insight may at times have been sufficient. When this was the case, Luke may have been left to the exercise of his own faculties, inspiration only inciting and supervising the work. George Harris, Moral Evolution, 413—"God could not reveal himself to man, unless he first revealed himself in man. If it should be written in letters on the sky: 'God is good,'—the words would have no meaning, unless goodness had been made known already in human volitions. Revelation is not by an occasional stroke, but by a continuous process. It is not superimposed, but inherent.... Genius is inspired; for the mind which perceives truth must be responsive to the Mind that made things the vehicles of thought." Sanday, Bampton Lectures on Inspiration: "In claiming for the Bible inspiration, we do not exclude the possibility of other lower or more partial degrees of inspiration in other literatures. The Spirit of God has doubtless touched other hearts and other minds ... in such a way as to give insight into truth, besides those which could claim descent from Abraham." Philo thought the LXX translators, the Greek philosophers, and at times even himself, to be inspired. Plato he regards as "most sacred" (ιερωτατος), but all good men are in various degrees inspired. Yet Philo never quotes as authoritative any but the Canonical Books. He attributes to them an authority unique in its kind.

(b) In all matters of morals and religion, however, man's insight into truth is vitiated by wrong affections, and, unless a supernatural wisdom can guide him, he is certain to err himself, and to lead others into error.

1 Cor. 2:14—"Now the natural man receiveth not the things of the Spirit of God: for they are foolishness unto him; and he cannot know them, because they are spiritually judged"; 10—"But unto us God revealed them through the Spirit: for the Spirit searcheth all things, yea, the deep things of God." See quotation from Coleridge, in Shairp, Culture and Religion, 114—"Water cannot rise higher than its source; neither can human reasoning"; Emerson, Prose Works, 1:474; 2:468—"'Tis curious we only believe as deep as we live"; Ullmann, Sinlessness of Jesus, 183, 184. For this reason we hold to a communication of religious truth, at least at times, more direct and objective than is granted by George Adam Smith, Com. on Isaiah, 1:372—"To Isaiah inspiration was nothing more nor less than the possession of certain strong moral and religious convictions, which he felt he owed to the communication of the Spirit of God, and according to which he interpreted, and even dared to foretell, the history of his people and of the world. Our study completely dispels, on the evidence of the Bible itself, that view of inspiration and prediction so long held in the church." If this is meant as a denial of any communication of truth other than the internal and subjective, we set over against it. Num. 12:6-8—"if there be a prophet among you, I the Lord will make myself known unto him in a vision, I will speak with him in a dream. My servant Moses is not so; he is faithful in all my house: with him will I speak mouth to mouth, even manifestly, and not in dark speeches; and the form of Jehovah shall he behold."

(c) The theory in question, holding as it does that natural insight is the only source of religious truth, involves a self-contradiction;—if the theory be true, then one man is inspired to utter what a second is inspired to pronounce false. The Vedas, the Koran and the Bible cannot be inspired to contradict each other.

The Vedas permit thieving, and the Koran teaches salvation by works; these cannot be inspired and the Bible also. Paul cannot be inspired to write his epistles, and Swedenborg also inspired to reject them. The Bible does not admit that pagan teachings have the same divine endorsement with its own. Among the Spartans to steal was praiseworthy; only to be caught stealing was criminal. On the religious consciousness with regard to the personality of God, the divine goodness, the future life, the utility of prayer, in all of which Miss Cobbe, Mr. Greg and Mr. Parker disagree with each other, see Bruce, Apologetics, 143, 144. With Matheson we may grant that the leading idea of inspiration is "the growth of the divine through the capacities of the human," while yet we deny that inspiration confines itself to this subjective enlightenment of the human faculties, and also we exclude from the divine working all those perverse and erroneous utterances which are the results of human sin.

(d) It makes moral and religious truth to be a purely subjective thing—a matter of private opinion—having no objective reality independently of men's opinions regarding it.

On this system truth is what men "trow"; things are what men "think"—words representing only the subjective. "Better the Greek αληθεια = 'the unconcealed' (objective truth)"—Harris, Philos. Basis of Theism, 182. If there be no absolute truth, Lessing's "search for truth" is the only thing left to us. But who will search, if there is no truth to be found? Even a wise cat will not eternally chase its own tail. The exercise within certain limits is doubtless useful, but the cat gives it up so soon as it becomes convinced that the tail cannot be caught. Sir Richard Burton became a Roman Catholic, a Brahmin, and a Mohammedan, successively, apparently holding with Hamlet that "there is nothing either good or bad, but thinking makes it so." This same scepticism as to the existence of objective truth appears in the sayings: "Your religion is good for you, and mine for me"; "One man is born an Augustinian, and another a Pelagian." See Dix, Pantheism, Introd., 12. Richter: "It is not the goal, but the course, that makes us happy."

(e) It logically involves the denial of a personal God who is truth and reveals truth, and so makes man to be the highest intelligence in the universe. This is to explain inspiration by denying its existence; since, if there be no personal God, inspiration is but a figure of speech for a purely natural fact.

The animus of this theory is denial of the supernatural. Like the denial of miracles, it can be maintained only upon grounds of atheism or pantheism. The view in question, as Hutton in his Essays remarks, would permit us to say that the word of the Lord came to Gibbon, amid the ruins of the Coliseum, saying: "Go, write the history of the Decline and Fall!" But, replies Hutton: Such a view is pantheistic. Inspiration is the voice of a living friend, in distinction from the voice of a dead friend, i. e., the influence of his memory. The inward impulse of genius, Shakespeare's for example, is not properly denominated inspiration. See Row, Bampton Lectures for 1877:428-474; Rogers, Eclipse of Faith, 73 sq. and 283 sq.; Henderson, Inspiration (2nd ed.), 443-469, 481-490. The view of Martineau, Seat of Authority, 302, is substantially this. See criticism of Martineau, by Rainy, in Critical Rev., 1:5-20.

2. The Illumination Theory

This regards inspiration as merely an intensifying and elevating of the religious perceptions of the Christian, the same in kind, though greater in degree, with the illumination of every believer by the Holy Spirit. It holds, not that the Bible is, but that it contains, the word of God, and that not the writings, but only the writers, were inspired. The illumination given by the Holy Spirit, however, puts the inspired writer only in full possession of his normal powers, but does not communicate objective truth beyond his ability to discover or understand.

This theory naturally connects itself with Arminian views of mere coöperation with God. It differs from the Intuition-theory by containing several distinctively Christian elements: (1) the influence of a personal God; (2) an extraordinary work of the Holy Spirit; (3) the Christological character of the Scriptures, putting into form a revelation of which Christ is the centre (Rev. 19:10). But while it grants that the Scripture writers were "moved by the Holy Spirit" (φερόμενοι—2 Pet. 1:21), it ignores the complementary fact that the Scripture itself is "inspired of God" (θεόπνευστος—2 Tim. 3:16). Luther's view resembles this; see Dorner, Gesch. prot. Theol., 236, 237. Schleiermacher, with the more orthodox Neander, Tholuck and Cremer, holds it; see Essays by Tholuck, in Herzog, Encyclopädie, and in Noyes, Theological Essays; Cremer, Lexicon N.T., θεόπνευστος, and in Herzog and Hauck, Realencyc., 9:183-203. In France, Sabatier, Philos. Religion, 90, remarks: "Prophetic inspiration is piety raised to the second power"—it differs from the piety of common men only in intensity and energy. See also Godet, in Revue Chrétienne, Jan. 1878.

In England Coleridge propounded this view in his Confessions of an Inquiring Spirit (Works, 5:669)—"Whatever finds me bears witness that it has proceeded from a Holy Spirit; in the Bible there is more that finds me than I have experienced in all other books put together." [Shall we then call Baxter's "Saints' Rest" inspired, while the Books of Chronicles are not?] See also F. W. Robertson, Sermon I; Life and Letters, letter 53, vol. 1:270; 2:143-150—"The other way, some twenty or thirty men in the world's history have had special communication, miraculous and from God; in this way, all may have it, and by devout and earnest cultivation of the mind and heart may have it illimitably increased." Frederick W. H. Myers, Catholic Thoughts on the Bible and Theology, 10-20, emphasizes the idea that the Scriptures are, in their earlier parts, not merely inadequate, but partially untrue, and subsequently superseded by fuller revelations. The leading thought is that of accommodation; the record of revelation is not necessarily infallible. Allen, Religious Progress, 44, quotes Bishop Thirlwall: "If that Spirit by which every man spoke of old is a living and present Spirit, its later lessons may well transcend its earlier";—Pascal's "colossal man" is the race; the first men represented only infancy; we are "the ancients", and we are wiser than our fathers. See also Farrar, Critical History of Free Thought, 473, note 50; Martineau, Studies in Christianity: "One Gospel in Many Dialects."

Of American writers who favor this view, see J. F. Clarke, Orthodoxy, its Truths and Errors, 74; Curtis, Human Element in Inspiration; Whiton, in N. Eng., Jan. 1882:63-72; Ladd, in Andover Review, July, 1885, in What is the Bible? and in Doctrine of Sacred Scripture, 1:759—"a large proportion of its writings inspired"; 2:178, 275, 497—"that fundamental misconception which identifies the Bible and the word of God"; 2:488—"Inspiration, as the subjective condition of Biblical revelation and the predicate of the word of God, is specifically the same illumining, quickening, elevating and purifying work of the Holy Spirit as that which goes on in the persons of the entire believing community." Professor Ladd therefore pares down all predictive prophecy, and regards Isaiah 53, not as directly and solely, but only as typically, Messianic. Clarke, Christian Theology, 35-44—"Inspiration is exaltation, quickening of ability, stimulation of spiritual power; it is uplifting and enlargement of capacity for perception, comprehension and utterance; and all under the influence of a thought, a truth, or an ideal that has taken possession of the soul.... Inspiration to write was not different in kind from the common influence of God upon his people.... Inequality in the Scriptures is plain.... Even if we were convinced that some book would better have been omitted from the Canon, our confidence in the Scriptures would not thereby be shaken. The Canon did not make Scripture, but Scripture made the Canon. The inspiration of the Bible does not prove its excellence, but its excellence proves its inspiration. The Spirit brought the Scriptures to help Christ's work, but not to take his place. Scripture says with Paul: 'Not that we have lordship over your faith, but are helpers of your joy: for in faith ye stand fast' (2 Cor. 1:24)."

E. G. Robinson: "The office of the Spirit in inspiration is not different from that which he performed for Christians at the time the gospels were written.... When the prophets say: 'Thus saith the Lord,' they mean simply that they have divine authority for what they utter." Calvin E. Stowe, History of Books of Bible, 19—"It is not the words of the Bible that were inspired. It is not the thoughts of the Bible that were inspired. It was the men who wrote the Bible who were inspired." Thayer, Changed Attitude toward the Bible, 63—"It was not before the polemic spirit became rife in the controversies which followed the Reformation that the fundamental distinction between the word of God and the record of that word became obliterated, and the pestilent tenet gained currency that the Bible is absolutely free from every error of every sort." Principal Cave, in Homiletical Review, Feb. 1892, admitting errors but none serious in the Bible, proposes a mediating statement for the present controversy, namely, that Revelation implies inerrancy, but that Inspiration does not. Whatever God reveals must be true, but many have become inspired without being rendered infallible. See also Mead, Supernatural Revelation, 291 sq.

With regard to this theory we remark:

(a) There is unquestionably an illumination of the mind of every believer by the Holy Spirit, and we grant that there may have been instances in which the influence of the Spirit, in inspiration, amounted only to illumination.

Certain applications and interpretations of Old Testament Scripture, as for example, John the Baptist's application to Jesus of Isaiah's prophecy (John 1:29—"Behold, the Lamb of God, that taketh away [marg. "beareth"] the sin of the world"), and Peter's interpretation of David's words (Acts 2:27—"thou wilt not leave my soul unto Hades, Neither wilt thou give thy Holy One to see corruption"), may have required only the illuminating influence of the Holy Spirit. There is a sense in which we may say that the Scriptures are inspired only to those who are themselves inspired. The Holy Spirit must show us Christ before we recognize the work of the Spirit in Scripture. The doctrines of atonement and of justification perhaps did not need to be newly revealed to the N. T. writers; illumination as to earlier revelations may have sufficed. But that Christ existed before his incarnation, and that there are personal distinctions in the Godhead, probably required revelation. Edison says that "inspiration is simply perspiration." Genius has been defined as "unlimited power to take pains." But it is more—the power to do spontaneously and without effort what the ordinary man does by the hardest. Every great genius recognizes that this power is due to the inflowing into him of a Spirit greater than his own—the Spirit of divine wisdom and energy. The Scripture writers attribute their understanding of divine things to the Holy Spirit; see next paragraph. On genius, as due to "subliminal uprush," see F. W. H. Myers, Human Personality, 1:70-120.

(b) But we deny that this was the constant method of inspiration, or that such an influence can account for the revelation of new truth to the prophets and apostles. The illumination of the Holy Spirit gives no new truth, but only a vivid apprehension of the truth already revealed. Any original communication of truth must have required a work of the Spirit different, not in degree, but in kind.

The Scriptures clearly distinguish between revelation, or the communication of new truth, and illumination, or the quickening of man's cognitive powers to perceive truth already revealed. No increase in the power of the eye or the telescope will do more than to bring into clear view what is already within its range. Illumination will not lift the veil that hides what is beyond. Revelation, on the other hand, is an "unveiling"—the raising of a curtain, or the bringing within our range of what was hidden before. Such a special operation of God is described in 2 Sam. 23:2, 3—"The Spirit of Jehovah spake by me, And his word was upon my tongue. The God of Israel said, The Rock of Israel spake to me"; Mat. 10:20—"For it is not ye that speak, but the Spirit of your Father that speaketh in you"; 1 Cor. 2:9-13—"Things which eye saw not, and ear heard not, And which entered not into the heart of man, Whatsoever things God prepared for them that love him. But unto us God revealed them through the Spirit: for the Spirit searcheth all things, yea, the deep things of God. For who among men knoweth the things of a man, save the spirit of the man, which is in him? even so the things of God none knoweth, save the Spirit of God. But we received, not the spirit of the world, but the spirit which is from God; that we might know the things that were freely given to us of God."

Clairvoyance and second sight, of which along with many cases of imposition and exaggeration there seems to be a small residuum of proved fact, show that there may be extraordinary operations of our natural powers. But, as in the case of miracle, the inspiration of Scripture necessitated an exaltation of these natural powers such as only the special influence of the Holy Spirit can explain. That the product is inexplicable as due to mere illumination seems plain when we remember that revelation sometimes excluded illumination as to the meaning of that which was communicated, for the prophets are represented in 1 Pet. 1:11 as "searching what time or what manner of time the Spirit of Christ which was in them did point unto, when it testified beforehand the sufferings of Christ, and the glories that should follow them." Since no degree of illumination can account for the prediction of "things that are to come" (John 16:13), this theory tends to the denial of any immediate revelation in prophecy so-called, and the denial easily extends to any immediate revelation of doctrine.

(c) Mere illumination could not secure the Scripture writers from frequent and grievous error. The spiritual perception of the Christian is always rendered to some extent imperfect and deceptive by remaining depravity. The subjective element so predominates in this theory, that no certainty remains even with regard to the trustworthiness of the Scriptures as a whole.

While we admit imperfections of detail in matters not essential to the moral and religious teaching of Scripture, we claim that the Bible furnishes a sufficient guide to Christ and to salvation. The theory we are considering, however, by making the measure of holiness to be the measure of inspiration, renders even the collective testimony of the Scripture writers an uncertain guide to truth. We point out therefore that inspiration is not absolutely limited by the moral condition of those who are inspired.

Knowledge, in the Christian, may go beyond conduct. Balaam and Caiaphas were not holy men, yet they were inspired (Num. 23:5; John 11:49-52). The promise of Christ assured at least the essential trustworthiness of his witnesses (Mat. 10:7, 19, 20; John 14:26; 15:26, 27; 16:13; 17:8). This theory that inspiration is a wholly subjective communication of truth leads to the practical rejection of important parts of Scripture, in fact to the rejection of all Scripture that professes to convey truth beyond the power of man to discover or to understand. Notice the progress from Thomas Arnold (Sermons, 2:185) to Matthew Arnold (Literature and Dogma, 134, 137). Notice also Swedenborg's rejection of nearly one half the Bible (Ruth, Chronicles, Ezra, Nehemiah, Esther, Job, Proverbs, Ecclesiastes, Song of Solomon, and the whole of the N. T. except the Gospels and the Apocalypse), connected with the claim of divine authority for his new revelation. "His interlocutors all Swedenborgize" (R. W. Emerson). On Swedenborg, see Hours with the Mystics, 2:230; Moehler, Symbolism, 436-466; New Englander, Jan. 1874:195; Baptist Review, 1883:143-157; Pond, Swedenborgianism; Ireland, The Blot on the Brain, 1-129.

(d) The theory is logically indefensible, as intimating that illumination with regard to truth can be imparted without imparting truth itself, whereas God must first furnish objective truth to be perceived before he can illuminate the mind to perceive the meaning of that truth.

The theory is analogous to the views that preservation is a continued creation; knowledge is recognition; regeneration is increase of light. In order to preservation, something must first be created which can be preserved; in order to recognition, something must be known which can be recognized or known again; in order to make increase of light of any use, there must first be the power to see. In like manner, inspiration cannot be mere illumination, because the external necessarily precedes the internal, the objective precedes the subjective, the truth revealed precedes the apprehension of that truth. In the case of all truth that surpasses the normal powers of man to perceive or evolve, there must be special communication from God; revelation must go before inspiration; inspiration alone is not revelation. It matters not whether this communication of truth be from without or from within. As in creation, God can work from within, yet the new result is not explicable as mere reproduction of the past. The eye can see only as it receives and uses the external light furnished by the sun, even though it be equally true that without the eye the light of the sun would be nothing worth.

Pfleiderer, Grundriss, 17-19, says that to Schleiermacher revelation is the original appearance of a proper religious life, which life is derived neither from external communication nor from invention and reflection, but from a divine impartation, which impartation can be regarded, not merely as an instructive influence upon man as an intellectual being, but as an endowment determining his whole personal existence—an endowment analogous to the higher conditions of poetic and heroic exaltation. Pfleiderer himself would give the name "revelation" to "every original experience in which man becomes aware of, and is seized by, supersensible truth, truth which does not come from external impartation nor from purposed reflection, but from the unconscious and undivided transcendental ground of the soul, and so is received as an impartation from God through the medium of the soul's human activity." Kaftan, Dogmatik, 51 sq.—"We must put the conception of revelation in place of inspiration. Scripture is the record of divine revelation. We do not propose a new doctrine or inspiration, in place of the old. We need only revelation, and, here and there, providence. The testimony of the Holy Spirit is given, not to inspiration, but to revelation—the truths that touch the human spirit and have been historically revealed."

Allen, Jonathan Edwards, 182—Edwards held that spiritual life in the soul is given by God only to his favorites and dear children, while inspiration may be thrown out, as it were, to dogs and swine—a Balaam, Saul, and Judas. The greatest privilege of apostles and prophets was, not their inspiration, but their holiness. Better to have grace in the heart, than to be the mother of Christ (Luke 11:27, 28). Maltbie D. Babcock, in S. S. Times, 1901:590—"The man who mourns because infallibility cannot be had in a church, or a guide, or a set of standards, does not know when he is well off. How could God develop our minds, our power of moral judgment, if there were no 'spirit to be tried' (1 John 4:1), no necessity for discrimination, no discipline of search and challenge and choice? To give the right answer to a problem is to put him on the side of infallibility so far as that answer is concerned, but it is to do him an ineffable wrong touching his real education. The blessing of life's schooling is not in knowing the right answer in advance, but in developing power through struggle."

Why did John Henry Newman surrender to the Church of Rome? Because he assumed that an external authority is absolutely essential to religion, and, when such an assumption is followed, Rome is the only logical terminus. "Dogma was," he says, "the fundamental principle of my religion." Modern ritualism is a return to this mediæval notion. "Dogmatic Christianity," says Harnack, "is Catholic. It needs an inerrant Bible, and an infallible church to interpret that Bible. The dogmatic Protestant is of the same camp with the sacramental and infallible Catholic." Lyman Abbott: "The new Reformation denies the infallibility of the Bible, as the Protestant Reformation denied the infallibility of the Church. There is no infallible authority. Infallible authority is undesirable.... God has given us something far better,—life.... The Bible is the record of the gradual manifestation of God to man in human experience, in moral laws and their applications, and in the life of Him who was God manifest in the flesh."

Leighton Williams: "There is no inspiration apart from experience. Baptists are not sacramental, nor creedal, but experimental Christians"—not Romanists, nor Protestants, but believers in an inner light. "Life, as it develops, awakens into self-consciousness. That self-consciousness becomes the most reliable witness as to the nature of the life of which it is the development. Within the limits of its own sphere, its authority is supreme. Prophecy is the utterance of the soul in moments of deep religious experience. The inspiration of Scripture writers is not a peculiar thing,—it was given that the same inspiration might be perfected in those who read their writings." Christ is the only ultimate authority, and he reveals himself in three ways, through Scripture, the Reason, and the Church. Only Life saves, and the Way leads through the Truth to the Life. Baptists stand nearer to the Episcopal system of life than to the Presbyterian system of creed. Whiton, Gloria Patri, 136—"The mistake is in looking to the Father above the world, rather than to the Son and the Spirit within the world, as the immediate source of revelation.... Revelation is the unfolding of the life and thought of God within the world. One should not be troubled by finding errors in the Scriptures, any more than by finding imperfections in any physical work of God, as in the human eye."

3. The Dictation-theory

This theory holds that inspiration consisted in such a possession of the minds and bodies of the Scripture writers by the Holy Spirit, that they became passive instruments or amanuenses—pens, not penmen, of God.

This theory naturally connects itself with that view of miracles which regards them as suspensions or violations of natural law. Dorner, Glaubenslehre, 1:624 (transl. 2:186-189), calls it a "docetic view of inspiration. It holds to the abolition of second causes, and to the perfect passivity of the human instrument; denies any inspiration of persons, and maintains inspiration of writings only. This exaggeration of the divine element led to the hypothesis of a multiform divine sense in Scripture, and, in assigning the spiritual meaning, a rationalizing spirit led the way." Representatives of this view are Quenstedt, Theol. Didact., 1:76—"The Holy Ghost inspired his amanuenses with those expressions which they would have employed, had they been left to themselves"; Hooker, Works, 2:383—"They neither spake nor wrote any word of their own, but uttered syllable by syllable as the Spirit put it into their mouths"; Gaussen, Theopneusty, 61—"The Bible is not a book which God charged men already enlightened to make under his protection; it is a book which God dictated to them"; Cunningham, Theol. Lectures, 349—"The verbal inspiration of the Scriptures [which he advocates] implies in general that the words of Scripture were suggested or dictated by the Holy Spirit, as well as the substance of the matter, and this, not only in some portion of the Scriptures, but through the whole." This reminds us of the old theory that God created fossils in the rocks, as they would be had ancient seas existed.

Sanday, Bamp. Lect. on Inspiration, 74, quotes Philo as saying: "A prophet gives forth nothing at all of his own, but acts as interpreter at the prompting of another in all his utterances, and as long as he is under inspiration he is in ignorance, his reason departing from its place and yielding up the citadel of the soul, when the divine Spirit enters into it and dwells in it and strikes at the mechanism of the voice, sounding through it to the clear declaration of that which he prophesieth"; in Gen. 15:12—"About the setting of the sun a trance came upon Abram"—the sun is the light of human reason which sets and gives place to the Spirit of God. Sanday, 78, says also: "Josephus holds that even historical narratives, such as those at the beginning of the Pentateuch which were not written down by contemporary prophets, were obtained by direct inspiration from God. The Jews from their birth regard their Scripture as 'the decrees of God,' which they strictly observe, and for which if need be they are ready to die." The Rabbis said that "Moses did not write one word out of his own knowledge."

The Reformers held to a much freer view than this. Luther said: "What does not carry Christ with it, is not apostolic, even though St. Peter or St. Paul taught it. If our adversaries fall back on the Scripture against Christ, we fall back on Christ against the Scripture." Luther refused canonical authority to books not actually written by apostles or composed, like Mark and Luke, under their direction. So he rejected from the rank of canonical authority Hebrews, James, Jude, 2 Peter and Revelation. Even Calvin doubted the Petrine authorship of 2 Peter, excluded the book of Revelation from the Scripture on which he wrote Commentaries, and also thus ignored the second and third epistles of John; see Prof. R. E. Thompson, in S. S. Times, Dec. 3, 1898:803, 804. The dictation-theory is post-Reformation. H. P. Smith, Bib. Scholarship and Inspiration, 85—"After the Council of Trent, the Roman Catholic polemic became sharper. It became the endeavor of that party to show the necessity of tradition and the untrustworthiness of Scripture alone. This led the Protestants to defend the Bible more tenaciously than before." The Swiss Formula of Consensus in 1675 not only called the Scriptures "the very word of God," but declared the Hebrew vowel-points to be inspired, and some theologians traced them back to Adam. John Owen held to the inspiration of the vowel-points; see Horton, Inspiration and Bible, 8. Of the age which produced the Protestant dogmatic theology, Charles Beard, in the Hibbert Lectures for 1883, says: "I know no epoch of Christianity to which I could more confidently point in illustration of the fact that where there is most theology, there is often least religion."

Of this view we may remark:

(a) We grant that there are instances when God's communications were uttered in an audible voice and took a definite form of words, and that this was sometimes accompanied with the command to commit the words to writing.

For examples, see Ex. 3:4—"God called unto him out of the midst of the bush, and said, Moses, Moses"; 20:22—"Ye yourselves have seen that I have talked with you from heaven"; cf. Heb. 12:19— "the voice of words; which voice they that heard entreated that no word more should be spoken unto them"; Numbers 7:89—"And when Moses went into the tent of meeting to speak with him, then he heard the Voice speaking unto him from above the mercy-seat that was upon the ark of the testimony, from between the two cherubim: and he spake unto him"; 8:1—"And Jehovah spake unto Moses, saying," etc.; Dan. 4:31—"While the word was in the king's mouth, there fell a voice from heaven, saying, O king Nebuchadnezzar, to thee it is spoken: The kingdom is departed from thee"; Acts 9:5— "And he said, Who art thou, Lord? And he said, I am Jesus whom thou persecutest"; Rev. 19:9—"And he saith unto me, Write, Blessed are they that are bidden to the marriage supper of the Lamb"; 21:5— "And he that sitteth on the throne said, Behold, I make all things new"; cf. 1:10, 11—"and I heard behind me a great voice, as of a trumpet saying, What thou seest, write in a book and send it to the seven churches." So the voice from heaven at the baptism, and at the transfiguration, of Jesus (Mat. 3:17, and 17:5; see Broadus, Amer. Com., on these passages).

(b) The theory in question, however, rests upon a partial induction of Scripture facts,— unwarrantably assuming that such occasional instances of direct dictation reveal the invariable method of God's communications of truth to the writers of the Bible.

Scripture nowhere declares that this immediate communication of the words was universal. On 1 Cor. 2:13—οὐκ ἐν διδακτοῖς ἀνθρωπίνης σοφίας, λόγοις, ἀλλ᾽ ἐν διδακτοῖς πνεύματος, the text usually cited as proof of invariable dictation—Meyer says: "There is no dictation here; διδακτοῖς excludes everything mechanical." Henderson, Inspiration (2nd ed.), 333, 349—"As human wisdom did not dictate word for word, so the Spirit did not." Paul claims for Scripture simply a general style of plainness which is due to the influence of the Spirit. Manly: "Dictation to an amanuensis is not teaching." Our Revised Version properly translates the remainder of the verse, 1 Cor. 2:13— "combining spiritual things with spiritual words."

(c) It cannot account for the manifestly human element in the Scriptures. There are peculiarities of style which distinguish the productions of each writer from those of every other, and there are variations in accounts of the same transaction which are inconsistent with the theory of a solely divine authorship.

Notice Paul's anacoloutha and his bursts of grief and indignation (Rom. 5:12 sq., 2 Cor. 11:1 sq.), and his ignorance of the precise number whom he had baptized (1 Cor. 1:16). One beggar or two (Mat. 20:30; cf. Luke 18:35); "about five and twenty or thirty furlongs" (John 6:19); "shed for many" (Mat. 26:28 has περί, Mark 14:24 and Luke 22:20 have ὑπέρ). Dictation of words which were immediately to be lost by imperfect transcription? Clarke, Christian Theology, 33-37—"We are under no obligation to maintain the complete inerrancy of the Scriptures. In them we have the freedom of life, rather than extraordinary precision of statement or accuracy of detail. We have become Christians in spite of differences between the evangelists. The Scriptures are various, progressive, free. There is no authority in Scripture for applying the word 'inspired' to our present Bible as a whole, and theology is not bound to employ this word in defining the Scriptures. Christianity is founded in history, and will stand whether the Scriptures are inspired or not. If special inspiration were wholly disproved, Christ would still be the Savior of the world. But the divine element in the Scriptures will never be disproved."

(d) It is inconsistent with a wise economy of means, to suppose that the Scripture writers should have had dictated to them what they knew already, or what they could inform themselves of by the use of their natural powers.

Why employ eye-witnesses at all? Why not dictate the gospels to Gentiles living a thousand years before? God respects the instruments he has called into being, and he uses them according to their constitutional gifts. George Eliot represents Stradivarius as saying:—"If my hand slacked, I should rob God—since he is fullest good—Leaving a blank instead of violins. God cannot make Antonio Stradivari's violins, Without Antonio." Mark 11:3—"The Lord hath need of him," may apply to man as well as beast.

(e) It contradicts what we know of the law of God's working in the soul. The higher and nobler God's communications, the more fully is man in possession and use of his own faculties. We cannot suppose that this highest work of man under the influence of the Spirit was purely mechanical.

Joseph receives communication by vision (Mat. 1:20); Mary, by words of an angel spoken in her waking moments (Luke 1:28). The more advanced the recipient, the more conscious the communication. These four theories might almost be called the Pelagian, the Arminian, the Docetic, and the Dynamical. Sabatier, Philos. Religion, 41, 42, 87—"In the Gospel of the Hebrews, the Father says at the baptism to Jesus: 'My Son, in all the prophets I was waiting for thee, that thou mightest come, and that I might rest in thee. For thou art my Rest.' Inspiration becomes more and more internal, until in Christ it is continuous and complete. Upon the opposite Docetic view, the most perfect inspiration should have been that of Balaam's ass." Semler represents the Pelagian or Ebionitic view, as Quenstedt represents this Docetic view. Semler localizes and temporalizes the contents of Scripture. Yet, though he carried this to the extreme of excluding any divine authorship, he did good service in leading the way to the historical study of the Bible.

4. The Dynamical Theory

The true view holds, in opposition to the first of these theories, that inspiration is not simply a natural but also a supernatural fact, and that it is the immediate work of a personal God in the soul of man.

It holds, in opposition to the second, that inspiration belongs, not only to the men who wrote the Scriptures, but to the Scriptures which they wrote, so that these Scriptures, when taken together, constitute a trustworthy and sufficient record of divine revelation.

It holds, in opposition to the third theory, that the Scriptures contain a human as well as a divine element, so that while they present a body of divinely revealed truth, this truth is shaped in human moulds and adapted to ordinary human intelligence.

In short, inspiration is characteristically neither natural, partial, nor mechanical, but supernatural, plenary, and dynamical. Further explanations will be grouped under the head of The Union of the Divine and Human Elements in Inspiration, in the section which immediately follows.

If the small circle be taken as symbol of the human element in inspiration, and the large circle as symbol of the divine, then the Intuition-theory would be represented by the small circle alone; the Dictation-theory by the large circle alone; the Illumination-theory by the small circle external to the large, and touching it at only a single point; the Dynamical-theory by two concentric circles, the small included in the large. Even when inspiration is but the exaltation and intensification of man's natural powers, it must be considered the work of God as well as of man. God can work from within as well as from without. As creation and regeneration are works of the immanent rather than of the transcendent God, so inspiration is in general a work within man's soul, rather than a communication to him from without. Prophecy may be natural to perfect humanity. Revelation is an unveiling, and the Röntgen rays enable us to see through a veil. But the insight of the Scripture writers into truth so far beyond their mental and moral powers is inexplicable except by a supernatural influence upon their minds; in other words, except as they were lifted up into the divine Reason and endowed with the wisdom of God.

Although we propose this Dynamical-theory as one which best explains the Scripture facts, we do not regard this or any other theory as of essential importance. No theory of inspiration is necessary to Christian faith. Revelation precedes inspiration. There was religion before the Old Testament, and an oral gospel before the New Testament. God might reveal without recording; might permit record without inspiration; might inspire without vouching for anything more than religious teaching and for the history, only so far as was necessary to that religious teaching. Whatever theory of inspiration we frame, should be the result of a strict induction of the Scripture facts, and not an a priori scheme to which Scripture must be conformed. The fault of many past discussions of the subject is the assumption that God must adopt some particular method of inspiration, or secure an absolute perfection of detail in matters not essential to the religious teaching of Scripture. Perhaps the best theory of inspiration is to have no theory.

Warfield and Hodge, Inspiration, 8—"Very many religious and historical truths must be established before we come to the question of inspiration, as for instance the being and moral government of God, the fallen condition of man, the fact of a redemptive scheme, the general historical truth of the Scriptures, and the validity and authority of the revelation of God's will which they contain, i. e., the general truth of Christianity and of its doctrines. Hence it follows that while the inspiration of the Scriptures is true, and being true is a principle fundamental to the adequate interpretation of Scripture, it nevertheless is not, in the first instance, a principle fundamental to the truth of the Christian religion." Warfield, in Presb. and Ref. Rev., April, 1893:208—"We do not found the whole Christian system on the doctrine of inspiration.... Were there no such thing as inspiration, Christianity would be true, and all its essential doctrines would be credibly witnessed to us"—in the gospels and in the living church. F. L. Patton, Inspiration, 22—"I must take exception to the disposition of some to stake the fortunes of Christianity on the doctrine of inspiration. Not that I yield to any one in profound conviction of the truth and importance of the doctrine. But it is proper for us to bear in mind the immense argumentative advantage which Christianity has, aside altogether from the inspiration of the documents on which it rests." So argue also Sanday, Oracles of God, and Dale, The Living Christ.

IV. The Union of the Divine and Human Elements in Inspiration

1. The Scriptures are the production equally of God and of man, and are therefore never to be regarded as merely human or merely divine.

The mystery of inspiration consists in neither of these terms separately, but in the union of the two. Of this, however, there are analogies in the interpenetration of human powers by the divine efficiency in regeneration and sanctification, and in the union of the divine and human natures in the person of Jesus Christ.

According to "Dalton's law," each gas is as a vacuum to every other: "Gases are mutually passive, and pass into each other as into vacua." Each interpenetrates the other. But this does not furnish a perfect illustration of our subject. The atom of oxygen and the atom of nitrogen, in common air, remain side by side but they do not unite. In inspiration the human and the divine elements do unite. The Lutheran maxim, "Mens humana capax divinæ," is one of the most important principles of a true theology. "The Lutherans think of humanity as a thing made by God for himself and to receive himself. The Reformed think of the Deity as ever preserving himself from any confusion with the creature. They fear pantheism and idolatry" (Bp. of Salisbury, quoted in Swayne, Our Lord's Knowledge, xx).

Sabatier, Philos. Religion, 66—"That initial mystery, the relation in our consciousness between the individual and the universal element, between the finite and the infinite, between God and man,—how can we comprehend their coëxistence and their union, and yet how can we doubt it? Where is the thoughtful man to-day who has not broken the thin crust of his daily life, and caught a glimpse of those profound and obscure waters on which floats our consciousness? Who has not felt within himself a veiled presence, and a force much greater than his own? What worker in a lofty cause has not perceived within his own personal activity, and saluted with a feeling of veneration, the mysterious activity of a universal and eternal Power? 'In Deo vivimus, movemur, et sumus.'... This mystery cannot be dissipated, for without it religion itself would no longer exist." Quackenbos, in Harper's Magazine, July, 1900:264, says that "hypnotic suggestion is but inspiration." The analogy of human influence thus communicated may at least help us to some understanding of the divine.

2. This union of the divine and human agencies in inspiration is not to be conceived of as one of external impartation and reception.

On the other hand, those whom God raised up and providentially qualified to do this work, spoke and wrote the words of God, when inspired, not as from without, but as from within, and that not passively, but in the most conscious possession and the most exalted exercise of their own powers of intellect, emotion, and will.

The Holy Spirit does not dwell in man as water in a vessel. We may rather illustrate the experience of the Scripture writers by the experience of the preacher who under the influence of God's Spirit is carried beyond himself, and is conscious of a clearer apprehension of truth and of a greater ability to utter it than belong to his unaided nature, yet knows himself to be no passive vehicle of a divine communication, but to be as never before in possession and exercise of his own powers. The inspiration of the Scripture writers, however, goes far beyond the illumination granted to the preacher, in that it qualifies them to put the truth, without error, into permanent and written form. This inspiration, moreover, is more than providential preparation. Like miracles, inspiration may use man's natural powers, but man's natural powers do not explain it. Moses, David, Paul, and John were providentially endowed and educated for their work of writing Scripture, but this endowment and education were not inspiration itself, but only the preparation for it.

Beyschlag: "With John, remembrance and exposition had become inseparable." E. G. Robinson; "Novelists do not create characters,—they reproduce with modifications material presented to their memories. So the apostles reproduced their impressions of Christ." Hutton, Essays, 2:231—"The Psalmists vacillate between the first person and the third, when they deliver the purposes of God. As they warm with their spiritual inspiration, they lose themselves in the person of Him who inspires them, and then they are again recalled to themselves." Stanley, Life and Letters, 1:380—"Revelation is not resolved into a mere human process because we are able to distinguish the natural agencies through which it was communicated"; 2:102—"You seem to me to transfer too much to these ancient prophets and writers and chiefs our modern notions of divine origin.... Our notion, or rather, the modern Puritanical notion of divine origin, is of a preternatural force or voice, putting aside secondary agencies, and separated from those agencies by an impassable gulf. The ancient, Oriental, Biblical notion was of a supreme Will acting through those agencies, or rather, being inseparable from them. Our notions of inspiration and divine communications insist on absolute perfection of fact, morals, doctrine. The Biblical notion was that inspiration was compatible with weakness, infirmity, contradiction." Ladd, Philosophy of Mind, 182—"In inspiration the thoughts, feelings, purposes are organized into another One than the self in which they were themselves born. That other One is in themselves. They enter into communication with Him. Yet this may be supernatural, even though natural psychological means are used. Inspiration which is external is not inspiration at all." This last sentence, however, seems to us a needless exaggeration of the true principle. Though God originally inspires from within, he may also communicate truth from without.

3. Inspiration, therefore, did not remove, but rather pressed into its own service, all the personal peculiarities of the writers, together with their defects of culture and literary style.

Every imperfection not inconsistent with truth in a human composition may exist in inspired Scripture. The Bible is God's word, in the sense that it presents to us divine truth in human forms, and is a revelation not for a select class but for the common mind. Rightly understood, this very humanity of the Bible is a proof of its divinity.

Locke: "When God made the prophet, he did not unmake the man." Prof. Day: "The bush in which God appeared to Moses remained a bush, while yet burning with the brightness of God and uttering forth the majesty of the mind of God." The paragraphs of the Koran are called ayat, or "sign," from their supposed supernatural elegance. But elegant literary productions do not touch the heart. The Bible is not merely the word of God; it is also the word made flesh. The Holy Spirit hides himself, that he may show forth Christ (John 3:8); he is known only by his effects—a pattern for preachers, who are ministers of the Spirit (2 Cor. 3:6). See Conant on Genesis, 65.

The Moslem declares that every word of the Koran came by the agency of Gabriel from the seventh heaven, and that its very pronunciation is inspired. Better the doctrine of Martineau, Seat of Authority, 289—"Though the pattern be divine, the web that bears it must still be human." Jackson, James Martineau, 255—"Paul's metaphor of the 'treasure in earthen vessels' (2 Cor. 4:7) you cannot allow to give you guidance; you want, not the treasure only, but the casket too, to come from above, and be of the crystal of the sky. You want the record to be divine, not only in its spirit, but also in its letter." Charles Hodge, Syst. Theol., 1:157—"When God ordains praise out of the mouths of babes, they must speak as babes, or the whole power and beauty of the tribute will be lost."

Evans, Bib. Scholarship and Inspiration, 16, 25—"The πνεῦμα of a dead wind is never changed, as the Rabbis of old thought, into the πνεῦμα of a living spirit. The raven that fed Elijah was nothing more than a bird. Nor does man, when supernaturally influenced, cease to be a man. An inspired man is not God, nor a divinely manipulated automaton"; "In Scripture there may be as much imperfection as, in the parts of any organism, would be consistent with the perfect adaptation of that organism to its destined end. Scripture then, taken together, is a statement of moral and religious truth sufficient for men's salvation, or an infallible and sufficient rule of faith and practice." J. S. Wrightnour: "Inspire means to breathe in, as a flute-player breathes into his instrument. As different flutes may have their own shapes, peculiarities, and what might seem like defects, so here; yet all are breathed into by one Spirit. The same Spirit who inspired them selected those instruments which were best for his purpose, as the Savior selected his apostles. In these writings therefore is given us, in the precise way that is best for us, the spiritual instruction and food that we need. Food for the body is not always given in the most concentrated form, but in the form that is best adapted for digestion. So God gives gold, not in coin ready stamped, but in the quartz of the mine whence it has to be dug and smelted." Remains of Arthur H. Hallam, in John Brown's Rab and his Friends, 274—"I see that the Bible fits in to every fold of the human heart. I am a man, and I believe it is God's book, because it is man's book."

4. In inspiration God may use all right and normal methods of literary composition.

As we recognize in literature the proper function of history, poetry, and fiction; of prophecy, parable, and drama; of personification and proverb; of allegory and dogmatic instruction; and even of myth and legend; we cannot deny the possibility that God may use any one of these methods of communicating truth, leaving it to us to determine in any single case which of these methods he has adopted.

In inspiration, as in regeneration and sanctification, God works "in divers manners" (Heb. 1:1). The Scriptures, like the books of secular literature, must be interpreted in the light of their purpose. Poetry must not be treated as prose, and parable must not be made to "go on all fours," when it was meant to walk erect and to tell one simple story. Drama is not history, nor is personification to be regarded as biography. There is a rhetorical overstatement which is intended only as a vivid emphasizing of important truth. Allegory is a popular mode of illustration. Even myth and legend may convey great lessons not otherwise apprehensible to infantile or untrained minds. A literary sense is needed in our judgments of Scripture, and much hostile criticism is lacking in this literary sense.

Denney, Studies in Theology, 218—"There is a stage in which the whole contents of the mind, as yet incapable of science or history, may be called mythological. And what criticism shows us, in its treatment of the early chapters of Genesis, is that God does not disdain to speak to the mind, nor through it, even when it is at this lowly stage. Even the myth, in which the beginnings of human life, lying beyond human research, are represented to itself by the child-mind of the race, may be made the medium of revelation.... But that does not make the first chapter of Genesis science, nor the third chapter history. And what is of authority in these chapters is not the quasi-scientific or quasi-historical form, but the message, which through them comes to the heart, of God's creative wisdom and power." Gore, in Lux Mundi, 356—"The various sorts of mental or literary activity develop in their different lines out of an earlier condition in which they lie fused and undifferentiated. This we can vaguely call the mythical stage of mental evolution. A myth is not a falsehood; it is a product of mental activity, as instructive and rich as any later product, but its characteristic is that it is not yet distinguished into history and poetry and philosophy." So Grote calls the Greek myths the whole intellectual stock of the age to which they belonged—the common root of all the history, poetry, philosophy, theology, which afterwards diverged and proceeded from it. So the early part of Genesis may be of the nature of myth in which we cannot distinguish the historical germ, though we do not deny that it exists. Robert Browning's Clive and Andrea del Sarto are essentially correct representations of historical characters, though the details in each poem are imaginary.

5. The inspiring Spirit has given the Scriptures to the world by a process of gradual evolution.

As in communicating the truths of natural science, God has communicated the truths of religion by successive steps, germinally at first, more fully as men have been able to comprehend them. The education of the race is analogous to the education of the child. First came pictures, object-lessons, external rites, predictions; then the key to these in Christ, and then didactic exposition in the Epistles.

There have been "divers portions," as well as "divers manners" (Heb. 1:1). The early prophecies like that of Gen. 3:15—the seed of the woman bruising the serpent's head—were but faint glimmerings of the dawn. Men had to be raised up who were capable of receiving and transmitting the divine communications. Moses, David, Isaiah mark successive advances in recipiency and transparency to the heavenly light. Inspiration has employed men of various degrees of ability, culture and religious insight. As all the truths of the calculus lie germinally in the simplest mathematical axiom, so all the truths of salvation may be wrapped up in the statement that God is holiness and love. But not every scholar can evolve the calculus from the axiom. The teacher may dictate propositions which the pupil does not understand: he may demonstrate in such a way that the pupil participates in the process; or, best of all, he may incite the pupil to work out the demonstration for himself. God seems to have used all these methods. But while there are instances of dictation and illumination, and inspiration sometimes includes these, the general method seems to have been such a divine quickening of man's powers that he discovers and expresses the truth for himself.

A. J. Balfour, Foundations of Belief, 339—"Inspiration is that, seen from its divine side, which we call discovery when seen from the human side.... Every addition to knowledge, whether in the individual or the community, whether scientific, ethical or theological, is due to a coöperation between the human soul which assimilates and the divine power which inspires. Neither acts, or could act, in independent isolation. For 'unassisted reason' is a fiction, and pure receptivity it is impossible to conceive. Even the emptiest vessel must limit the quantity and determine the configuration of any liquid with which it may be filled.... Inspiration is limited to no age, to no country, to no people." The early Semites had it, and the great Oriental reformers. There can be no gathering of grapes from thorns, or of figs from thistles. Whatever of true or of good is found in human history has come from God. On the Progressiveness of Revelation, see Orr, Problem of the O. T., 431-478.

6. Inspiration did not guarantee inerrancy in things not essential to the main purpose of Scripture.

Inspiration went no further than to secure a trustworthy transmission by the sacred writers of the truth they were commissioned to deliver. It was not omniscience. It was a bestowal of various kinds and degrees of knowledge and aid, according to need; sometimes suggesting new truth, sometimes presiding over the collection of preëxisting material and guarding from essential error in the final elaboration. As inspiration was not omniscience, so it was not complete sanctification. It involved neither personal infallibility, nor entire freedom from sin.

God can use imperfect means. As the imperfection of the eye does not disprove its divine authorship, and as God reveals himself in nature and history in spite of their shortcomings, so inspiration can accomplish its purpose through both writers and writings in some respects imperfect. God is, in the Bible as he was in Hebrew history, leading his people onward to Christ, but only by a progressive unfolding of the truth. The Scripture writers were not perfect men. Paul at Antioch resisted Peter, "because he stood condemned" (Gal 2:11). But Peter differed from Paul, not in public utterances, nor in written words, but in following his own teachings (cf. Acts 15:6-11); versus Norman Fox, in Bap. Rev., 1885:469-482. Personal defects do not invalidate an ambassador, though they may hinder the reception of his message. So with the apostles' ignorance of the time of Christ's second coming. It was only gradually that they came to understand Christian doctrines; they did not teach the truth all at once; their final utterances supplemented and completed the earlier; and all together furnished only that measure of knowledge which God saw needful for the moral and religious teaching of mankind. Many things are yet unrevealed, and many things which inspired men uttered, they did not, when they uttered them, fully understand.

Pfleiderer, Grundriss, 53, 54—"The word is divine-human in the sense that it has for its contents divine truth in human, historical, and individually conditioned form. The Holy Scripture contains the word of God in a way plain, and entirely sufficient to beget saving faith." Frances Power Cobbe, Life, 87—"Inspiration is not a miraculous and therefore incredible thing, but normal and in accordance with the natural relations of the infinite and finite spirit, a divine inflowing of mental light precisely analogous to that moral influence which divines call grace. As every devout and obedient soul may expect to share in divine grace, so the devout and obedient souls of all the ages have shared, as Parker taught, in divine inspiration. And, as the reception of grace even in large measure does not render us impeccable, so neither does the reception of inspiration render us infallible." We may concede to Miss Cobbe that inspiration consists with imperfection, while yet we grant to the Scripture writers an authority higher than our own.

7. Inspiration did not always, or even generally, involve a direct communication to the Scripture writers of the words they wrote.

Thought is possible without words, and in the order of nature precedes words. The Scripture writers appear to have been so influenced by the Holy Spirit that they perceived and felt even the new truths they were to publish, as discoveries of their own minds, and were left to the action of their own minds in the expression of these truths, with the single exception that they were supernaturally held back from the selection of wrong words, and when needful were provided with right ones. Inspiration is therefore not verbal, while yet we claim that no form of words which taken in its connections would teach essential error has been admitted into Scripture.

Before expression there must be something to be expressed. Thought is possible without language. The concept may exist without words. See experiences of deaf-mutes, in Princeton Rev., Jan. 1881:104-128. The prompter interrupts only when the speaker's memory fails. The writing-master guides the pupil's hand only when it would otherwise go wrong. The father suffers the child to walk alone, except when it is in danger of stumbling. If knowledge be rendered certain, it is as good as direct revelation. But whenever the mere communication of ideas or the direction to proper material would not suffice to secure a correct utterance, the sacred writers were guided in the very selection of their words. Minute criticism proves more and more conclusively the suitableness of the verbal dress to the thoughts expressed; all Biblical exegesis is based, indeed, upon the assumption that divine wisdom has made the outward form a trustworthy vehicle of the inward substance of revelation. See Henderson, Inspiration (2nd ed.), 102, 114; Bib. Sac, 1872:428, 640; William James, Psychology, 1:266 sq.

Watts, New Apologetic, 40, 111, holds to a verbal inspiration: "The bottles are not the wine, but if the bottles perish the wine is sure to be spilled"; the inspiring Spirit certainly gave language to Peter and others at Pentecost, for the apostles spoke with other tongues; holy men of old not only thought, but "spake from God, being moved by the Holy Spirit" (2 Pet. 1:21). So Gordon, Ministry of the Spirit, 171—"Why the minute study of the words of Scripture, carried on by all expositors, their search after the precise shade of verbal significance, their attention to the minutest details of language, and to all the delicate coloring of mood and tense and accent?" Liberal scholars, Dr. Gordon thinks, thus affirm the very doctrine which they deny. Rothe, Dogmatics, 238, speaks of "a language of the Holy Ghost." Oetinger: "It is the style of the heavenly court." But Broadus, an almost equally conservative scholar, in his Com. on Mat. 3:17, says that the difference between "This is my beloved Son," and Luke 3:22— "Thou art my beloved Son," should make us cautious in theorizing about verbal inspiration, and he intimates that in some cases that hypothesis is unwarranted. The theory of verbal inspiration is refuted by the two facts: 1. that the N. T. quotations from the O. T., in 99 cases, differ both from the Hebrew and from the LXX; 2. that Jesus' own words are reported with variations by the different evangelists; see Marcus Dods, The Bible, its Origin and Nature, chapter on Inspiration.

Helen Keller told Phillips Brooks that she had always known that there was a God, but she had not known his name. Dr. Z. F. Westervelt, of the Deaf Mute Institute, had under his charge four children of different mothers. All of these children were dumb, though there was no defect of hearing and the organs of speech were perfect. But their mothers had never loved them and had never talked to them in the loving way that provoked imitation. The children heard scolding and harshness, but this did not attract. So the older members of the church in private and in the meetings for prayer should teach the younger to talk. But harsh and contentious talk will not accomplish the result,—it must be the talk of Christian love. William D. Whitney, in his review of Max Müller's Science of Language, 26-31, combats the view of Müller that thought and language are identical. Major Bliss Taylor's reply to Santa Anna: "General Taylor never surrenders!" was a substantially correct, though a diplomatic and euphemistic, version of the General's actual profane words. Each Scripture writer uttered old truth in the new forms with which his own experience had clothed it. David reached his greatness by leaving off the mere repetition of Moses, and by speaking out of his own heart. Paul reached his greatness by giving up the mere teaching of what he had been taught, and by telling what God's plan of mercy was to all. Augustine: "Scriptura est sensus Scripturæ"—"Scripture is what Scripture means." Among the theological writers who admit the errancy of Scripture writers as to some matters unessential to their moral and spiritual teaching, are Luther, Calvin, Cocceius, Tholuck, Neander, Lange, Stier, Van Oosterzee, John Howe, Richard Baxter, Conybeare, Alford, Mead.

8. Yet, notwithstanding the ever-present human element, the all-pervading inspiration of the Scriptures constitutes these various writings an organic whole.

Since the Bible is in all its parts the work of God, each part is to be judged, not by itself alone, but in its connection with every other part. The Scriptures are not to be interpreted as so many merely human productions by different authors, but as also the work of one divine mind. Seemingly trivial things are to be explained from their connection with the whole. One history is to be built up from the several accounts of the life of Christ. One doctrine must supplement another. The Old Testament is part of a progressive system, whose culmination and key are to be found in the New. The central subject and thought which binds all parts of the Bible together, and in the light of which they are to be interpreted, is the person and work of Jesus Christ.

The Bible says: "There is no God" (Ps. 14:1); but then, this is to be taken with the context: "The fool hath said in his heart." Satan's "it is written," (Mat. 4:6) is supplemented by Christ's "It is written again" (Mat. 4:7). Trivialities are like the hair and nails of the body—they have their place as parts of a complete and organic whole; see Ebrard, Dogmatik, 1:40. The verse which mentions Paul's cloak at Troas (2 Tim. 4:13) is (1) a sign of genuineness—a forger would not invent it; (2) an evidence of temporal need endured for the gospel; (3) an indication of the limits of inspiration,—even Paul must have books and parchments. Col. 2:21—"Handle not, nor taste, nor touch"—is to be interpreted by the context in verse 20—"why ... do ye subject yourselves to ordinances?" and by verse 22—"after the precepts and doctrines of men." Hodge, Syst. Theol., 1:164—"The difference between John's gospel and the book of Chronicles is like that between man's brain and the hair of his head; nevertheless the life of the body is as truly in the hair as in the brain." Like railway coupons, Scripture texts are "Not good if detached."

Crooker, The New Bible and its New Uses, 137-144, utterly denies the unity of the Bible. Prof. A. B. Davidson of Edinburgh says that "A theology of the O. T. is really an impossibility, because the O. T. is not a homogeneous whole." These denials proceed from an insufficient recognition of the principle of evolution in O. T. history and doctrine. Doctrines in early Scripture are like rivers at their source; they are not yet fully expanded; many affluents are yet to come. See Bp. Bull's Sermon, in Works, xv:183; and Bruce, Apologetics, 323—"The literature of the early stages of revelation must share the defects of the revelation which it records and interprets.... The final revelation enables us to see the defects of the earlier.... We should find Christ in the O. T. as we find the butterfly in the caterpillar, and man the crown of the universe in the fiery cloud." Crane, Religion of To-morrow, 224—Every part is to be modified by every other part. No verse is true out of the Book, but the whole Book taken together is true. Gore, in Lux Mundi, 350—"To recognize the inspiration of the Scriptures is to put ourselves to school in every part of them." Robert Browning, Ring and Book, 175 (Pope, 228)—"Truth nowhere lies, yet everywhere, in these; Not absolutely in a portion, yet Evolvable from the whole; evolved at last Painfully, held tenaciously by me." On the Organic Unity of the O. T., see Orr, Problem of the O. T., 27-51.

9. When the unity of the Scripture is fully recognized, the Bible, in spite of imperfections in matters non-essential to its religious purpose, furnishes a safe and sufficient guide to truth and to salvation.

The recognition of the Holy Spirit's agency makes it rational and natural to believe in the organic unity of Scripture. When the earlier parts are taken in connection with the later, and when each part is interpreted by the whole, most of the difficulties connected with inspiration disappear. Taken together, with Christ as its culmination and explanation, the Bible furnishes the Christian rule of faith and practice.

The Bible answers two questions: What has God done to save me? and What must I do to be saved? The propositions of Euclid are not invalidated by the fact that he believed the earth to be flat. The ethics of Plato would not be disproved by his mistakes with regard to the solar system. So religious authority is independent of merely secular knowledge.—Sir Joshua Reynolds was a great painter, and a great teacher of his art. His lectures on painting laid down principles which have been accepted as authority for generations. But Joshua Reynolds illustrates his subject from history and science. It was a day when both history and science were young. In some unimportant matters of this sort, which do not in the least affect his conclusions, Sir Joshua Reynolds makes an occasional slip; his statements are inaccurate. Does he, therefore, cease to be an authority in matters of his art?—The Duke of Wellington said once that no human being knew at what time of day the battle of Waterloo began. One historian gets his story from one combatant, and he puts the hour at eleven in the morning. Another historian gets his information from another combatant, and he puts it at noon. Shall we say that this discrepancy argues error in the whole account, and that we have no longer any certainty that the battle of Waterloo was ever fought at all?

Such slight imperfections are to be freely admitted, while at the same time we insist that the Bible, taken as a whole, is incomparably superior to all other books, and is "able to make thee wise unto salvation" (2 Tim. 3:15). Hooker, Eccl. Polity: "Whatsoever is spoken of God or things pertaining to God otherwise than truth is, though it seem an honor, it is an injury. And as incredible praises given unto men do often abate and impair the credit of their deserved commendation, so we must likewise take great heed lest, in attributing to Scripture more than it can have, the incredibility of that do cause even those things which it hath more abundantly to be less reverently esteemed." Baxter, Works, 21:349—"Those men who think that these human imperfections of the writers do extend further, and may appear in some passages of chronologies or history which are no part of the rule of faith and life, do not hereby destroy the Christian cause. For God might enable his apostles to an infallible recording and preaching of the gospel, even all things necessary to salvation, though he had not made them infallible in every by-passage and circumstance, any more than they were indefectible in life."

The Bible, says Beet, "contains possible errors in small details or allusions, but it gives us with absolute certainty the great facts of Christianity, and upon these great facts, and upon these only, our faith is based." Evans, Bib. Scholarship and Inspiration, 15, 18, 65—"Teach that the shell is part of the kernel and men who find that they cannot keep the shell will throw away shell and kernel together.... This overstatement of inspiration made Renan, Bradlaugh and Ingersoll sceptics.... If in creation God can work out a perfect result through imperfection why cannot he do the like in inspiration? If in Christ God can appear in human weakness and ignorance, why not in the written word?"

We therefore take exception to the view of Watts, New Apologetic, 71—"Let the theory of historical errors and scientific errors be adopted, and Christianity must share the fate of Hinduism. If its inspired writers err when they tell us of earthly things, none will believe when they tell of heavenly things." Watts adduces instances of Spinoza's giving up the form while claiming to hold the substance, and in this way reducing revelation to a phenomenon of naturalistic pantheism. We reply that no a priori theory of perfection in divine inspiration must blind us to the evidence of actual imperfection in Scripture. As in creation and in Christ, so in Scripture, God humbles himself to adopt human and imperfect methods of self-revelation. See Jonathan Edwards, Diary: "I observe that old men seldom have any advantage of new discoveries, because they are beside the way to which they have been so long used. Resolved, if ever I live to years, that I will be impartial to hear the reasons of all pretended discoveries, and receive them if rational, however long soever I have been used to another way of thinking."

Bowne, The Immanence of God, 109, 110—"Those who would find the source of certainty and the seat of authority in the Scriptures alone, or in the church alone, or reason and conscience alone, rather than in the complex and indivisible coworking of all these factors, should be reminded of the history of religious thought. The stiffest doctrine of Scripture inerrancy has not prevented warring interpretations; and those who would place the seat of authority in reason and conscience are forced to admit that outside illumination may do much for both. In some sense the religion of the spirit is a very important fact, but when it sets up in opposition to the religion of a book, the light that is in it is apt to turn to darkness."

10. While inspiration constitutes Scripture an authority more trustworthy than are individual reason or the creeds of the church, the only ultimate authority is Christ himself.

Christ has not so constructed Scripture as to dispense with his personal presence and teaching by his Spirit. The Scripture is the imperfect mirror of Christ. It is defective, yet it reflects him and leads to him. Authority resides not in it, but in him, and his Spirit enables the individual Christian and the collective church progressively to distinguish the essential from the non-essential, and so to perceive the truth as it is in Jesus. In thus judging Scripture and interpreting Scripture, we are not rationalists, but are rather believers in him who promised to be with us alway even unto the end of the world and to lead us by his Spirit into all the truth.

James speaks of the law as a mirror (James 1:23-25—"like unto a man beholding his natural face in a mirror ... looketh into the perfect law"); the law convicts of sin because it reflects Christ. Paul speaks of the gospel as a mirror (2 Cor. 3:18—"we all, beholding as in a mirror the glory of the Lord"); the gospel transforms us because it reflects Christ. Yet both law and gospel are imperfect; they are like mirrors of polished metal, whose surface is often dim, and whose images are obscure; (1 Cor. 13:12—"For now we see in a mirror, darkly; but then face to face"); even inspired men know only in part, and prophesy only in part. Scripture itself is the conception and utterance of a child, to be done away when that which is perfect is come, and we see Christ as he is.

Authority is the right to impose beliefs or to command obedience. The only ultimate authority is God, for he is truth, justice and love. But he can impose beliefs and command obedience only as he is known. Authority belongs therefore only to God revealed, and because Christ is God revealed he can say: "All authority hath been given unto me in heaven and on earth" (Mat. 28:18). The final authority in religion is Jesus Christ. Every one of his revelations of God is authoritative. Both nature and human nature are such revelations. He exercises his authority through delegated and subordinate authorities, such as parents and civil government. These rightfully claim obedience so long as they hold to their own respective spheres and recognize their relation of dependence upon him. "The powers that be are ordained of God" (Rom. 13:1), even though they are imperfect manifestations of his wisdom and righteousness. The decisions of the Supreme Court are authoritative even though the judges are fallible and come short of establishing absolute justice. Authority is not infallibility, in the government either of the family or of the state.

The church of the middle ages was regarded as possessed of absolute authority. But the Protestant Reformation showed how vain were these pretensions. The church is an authority only as it recognizes and expresses the supreme authority of Christ. The Reformers felt the need of some external authority in place of the church. They substituted the Scripture. The phrase "the word of God," which designates the truth orally uttered or affecting the minds of men, came to signify only a book. Supreme authority was ascribed to it. It often usurped the place of Christ. While we vindicate the proper authority of Scripture, we would show that its authority is not immediate and absolute, but mediate and relative, through human and imperfect records, and needing a supplementary and divine teaching to interpret them. The authority of Scripture is not apart from Christ or above Christ, but only in subordination to him and to his Spirit. He who inspired Scripture must enable us to interpret Scripture. This is not a doctrine of rationalism, for it holds to man's absolute dependence upon the enlightening Spirit of Christ. It is not a doctrine of mysticism, for it holds that Christ teaches us only by opening to us the meaning of his past revelations. We do not expect any new worlds in our astronomy, nor do we expect any new Scriptures in our theology. But we do expect that the same Christ who gave the Scriptures will give us new insight into their meaning and will enable us to make new applications of their teachings.

The right and duty of private judgment with regard to Scripture belong to no ecclesiastical caste, but are inalienable liberties of the whole church of Christ and of each individual member of that church. And yet this judgment is, from another point of view, no private judgment. It is not the judgment of arbitrariness or caprice. It does not make the Christian consciousness supreme, if we mean by this term the consciousness of Christians apart from the indwelling Christ. When once we come to Christ, he joins us to himself, he seats us with him upon his throne, he imparts to us his Spirit, he bids us use our reason in his service. In judging Scripture, we make not ourselves but Christ supreme, and recognize him as the only ultimate and infallible authority in matters of religion. We can believe that the total revelation of Christ in Scripture is an authority superior to individual reason or to any single affirmation of the church, while yet we believe that this very authority of Scripture has its limitation, and that Christ himself must teach us what this total revelation is. So the judgment which Scripture encourages us to pass upon its own limitations only induces a final and more implicit reliance upon the living and personal Son of God. He has never intended that Scripture should be a substitute for his own presence, and it is only his Spirit that is promised to lead us into all the truth.

On the authority of Scripture, see A. H. Strong, Christ in Creation, 113-136—"The source of all authority is not Scripture, but Christ.... Nowhere are we told that the Scripture of itself is able to convince the sinner or to bring him to God. It is a glittering sword, but it is 'the sword of the Spirit' (Eph. 6:17); and unless the Spirit use it, it will never pierce the heart. It is a heavy hammer, but only the Spirit can wield it so that it breaks in pieces the flinty rock. It is the type locked in the form, but the paper will never receive an impression until the Spirit shall apply the power. No mere instrument shall have the glory that belongs to God. Every soul shall feel its entire dependence upon him. Only the Holy Spirit can turn the outer word into an inner word. And the Holy Spirit is the Spirit of Christ. Christ comes into direct contact with the soul. He himself gives his witness to the truth. He bears testimony to Scripture, even more than Scripture bears testimony to him."

11. The preceding discussion enables us at least to lay down three cardinal principles and to answer three common questions with regard to inspiration.

Principles: (a) The human mind can be inhabited and energized by God while yet attaining and retaining its own highest intelligence and freedom. (b) The Scriptures being the work of the one God, as well as of the men in whom God moved and dwelt, constitute an articulated and organic unity. (c) The unity and authority of Scripture as a whole are entirely consistent with its gradual evolution and with great imperfection in its non-essential parts.

Questions: (a) Is any part of Scripture uninspired? Answer: Every part of Scripture is inspired in its connection and relation with every other part. (b) Are there degrees of inspiration? Answer: There are degrees of value, but not of inspiration. Each part in its connection with the rest is made completely true, and completeness has no degrees. (c) How may we know what parts are of most value and what is the teaching of the whole? Answer: The same Spirit of Christ who inspired the Bible is promised to take of the things of Christ, and, by showing them to us, to lead us progressively into all the truth.

Notice the value of the Old Testament, revealing as it does the natural attributes of God, as a basis and background for the revelation of mercy in the New Testament. Revelation was in many parts (πολυμερῶς—Heb. 1:1) as well as in many ways. "Each individual oracle, taken by itself, was partial and incomplete" (Robertson Smith, O. T. in Jewish Ch., 21). But the person and the words of Christ sum up and complete the revelation, so that, taken together and in their connection with him, the various parts of Scripture constitute an infallible and sufficient rule of faith and practice. See Browne, Inspiration of the N. T.; Bernard, Progress of Doctrine in the N. T.; Stanley Leathes, Structure of the O. T.; Rainy, Delivery and Development of Doctrine. See A. H. Strong, on Method of Inspiration, in Philosophy and Religion, 148-155.

The divine influence upon the minds of post-biblical writers, leading to the composition of such allegories as Pilgrim's Progress, and such dramas as Macbeth, is to be denominated illumination rather than inspiration, for the reasons that these writings contain error as well as truth in matters of religion and morals; that they add nothing essential to what the Scriptures give us; and that, even in their expression of truth previously made known, they are not worthy of a place in the sacred canon. W. H. P. Faunce: "How far is Bunyan's Pilgrim's Progress true to present Christian experience? It is untrue: 1. In its despair of this world. The Pilgrim has to leave this world in order to be saved. Modern experience longs to do God's will here, and to save others instead of forsaking them. 2. In its agony over sin and frightful conflict. Bunyan illustrates modern experience better by Christiana and her children who go through the Valley and the Shadow of Death in the daytime, and without conflict with Apollyon. 3. In the constant uncertainty of the issue of the Pilgrim's fight. Christian enters Doubting Castle and meets Giant Despair, even after he has won most of his victories. In modern experience, 'at evening time there shall be light'—(Zech. 14:7). 4. In the constant conviction of an absent Christ. Bunyan's Christ is never met this side of the Celestial City. The Cross at which the burden dropped is the symbol of a sacrificial act, but it is not the Savior himself. Modern experience has Christ living in us and with us alway, and not simply a Christ whom we hope to see at the end of the journey."

Beyschlag, N. T. Theol., 2:18—"Paul declares his own prophecy and inspiration to be essentially imperfect (1 Cor. 13:9, 10, 12; cf. 1 Cor. 12:10; 1 Thess. 5:19-21). This admission justifies a Christian criticism even of his views. He can pronounce an anathema on those who preach 'a different gospel' (Gal. 1:8, 9), for what belongs to simple faith, the facts of salvation, are absolutely certain. But where prophetic thought and speech go beyond these facts of salvation, wood and straw may be mingled with the gold, silver and precious stones built upon the one foundation. So he distinguishes his own modest γνώμη from the ἐπιταγὴ κυρίου (1 Cor. 7:25, 40)." Clarke, Christian Theology, 44—"The authority of Scripture is not one that binds, but one that sets free. Paul is writing of Scripture when he says: 'Not that we have lordship over your faith, but are helpers of your joy: for in faith ye stand fast' (2 Cor. 1:24)."

Cremer, in Herzog, Realencyc., 183-203—"The church doctrine is that the Scriptures are inspired, but it has never been determined by the church how they are inspired." Butler, Analogy, part II, chap. III—"The only question concerning the truth of Christianity is, whether it be a real revelation, not whether it be attended with every circumstance which we should have looked for; and concerning the authority of Scripture, whether it be what it claims to be, not whether it be a book of such sort, and so promulgated, as weak men are apt to fancy a book containing a divine revelation should. And therefore, neither obscurity, nor seeming inaccuracy of style, nor various readings, nor early disputes about the authors of particular parts, nor any other things of the like kind, though they had been much more considerable than they are, could overthrow the authority of Scripture; unless the prophets, apostles, or our Lord had promised that the book containing the divine revelation should be secure from these things." W. Robertson Smith: "If am asked why I receive the Scriptures as the word of God and as the only perfect rule of faith and life, I answer with all the Fathers of the Protestant church: 'Because the Bible is the only record of the redeeming love of God; because in the Bible alone I find God drawing nigh to men in Jesus Christ, and declaring his will for our salvation. And the record I know to be true by the witness of his Spirit in my heart, whereby I am assured that none other than God himself is able to speak such words to my soul.' " The gospel of Jesus Christ is the ἅπαξ λεγόμενον of the Almighty. See Marcus Dods, The Bible, its Origin and Nature; Bowne, The Immanence of God, 66-115.

V. Objections to the Doctrine of Inspiration

In connection with a divine-human work like the Bible, insoluble difficulties may be expected to present themselves. So long, however, as its inspiration is sustained by competent and sufficient evidence, these difficulties cannot justly prevent our full acceptance of the doctrine, any more than disorder and mystery in nature warrant us in setting aside the proofs of its divine authorship. These difficulties are lessened with time; some have already disappeared; many may be due to ignorance, and may be removed hereafter; those which are permanent may be intended to stimulate inquiry and to discipline faith.

It is noticeable that the common objections to inspiration are urged, not so much against the religious teaching of the Scriptures, as against certain errors in secular matters which are supposed to be interwoven with it. But if these are proved to be errors indeed, it will not necessarily overthrow the doctrine of inspiration; it will only compel us to give a larger place to the human element in the composition of the Scriptures, and to regard them more exclusively as a text-book of religion. As a rule of religious faith and practice, they will still be the infallible word of God. The Bible is to be judged as a book whose one aim is man's rescue from sin and reconciliation to God, and in these respects it will still be found a record of substantial truth. This will appear more fully as we examine the objections one by one.

"The Scriptures are given to teach us, not how the heavens go, but how to go to heaven." Their aim is certainly not to teach science or history, except so far as science or history is essential to their moral and religious purpose. Certain of their doctrines, like the virgin-birth of Christ and his bodily resurrection, are historical facts, and certain facts, like that of creation, are also doctrines. With regard to these great facts, we claim that inspiration has given us accounts that are essentially trustworthy, whatever may be their imperfections in detail. To undermine the scientific trustworthiness of the Indian Vedas is to undermine the religion which they teach. But this only because their scientific doctrine is an essential part of their religious teaching. In the Bible, religion is not dependent upon physical science. The Scriptures aim only to declare the creatorship and lordship of the personal God. The method of his working may be described pictorially without affecting this substantial truth. The Indian cosmogonies, on the other hand, polytheistic or pantheistic as they are, teach essential untruth, by describing the origin of things as due to a series of senseless transformations without basis of will or wisdom.

So long as the difficulties of Scripture are difficulties of form rather than substance, of its incidental features rather than its main doctrine, we may say of its obscurities as Isocrates said of the work of Heraclitus: "What I understand of it is so excellent that I can draw conclusions from it concerning what I do not understand." "If Bengel finds things in the Bible too hard for his critical faculty, he finds nothing too hard for his believing faculty." With John Smyth, who died at Amsterdam in 1612, we may say: "I profess I have changed, and shall be ready still to change, for the better"; and with John Robinson, in his farewell address to the Pilgrim Fathers: "I am verily persuaded that the Lord hath more truth yet to break forth from his holy word." See Luthardt, Saving Truths, 205; Philippi, Glaubenslehre, 205 sq.; Bap. Rev., April, 1881: art. by O. P. Eaches; Cardinal Newman, in 19th Century, Feb. 1884.

1. Errors in matters of Science

Upon this objection we remark:

(a) We do not admit the existence of scientific error in the Scripture. What is charged as such is simply truth presented in popular and impressive forms.

The common mind receives a more correct idea of unfamiliar facts when these are narrated in phenomenal language and in summary form than when they are described in the abstract terms and in the exact detail of science.

The Scripture writers unconsciously observe Herbert Spencer's principle of style: Economy of the reader's or hearer's attention,—the more energy is expended upon the form the less there remains to grapple with the substance (Essays, 1-47). Wendt, Teaching of Jesus, 1:130, brings out the principle of Jesus' style: "The greatest clearness in the smallest compass." Hence Scripture uses the phrases of common life rather than scientific terminology. Thus the language of appearance is probably used in Gen. 7:19—"all the high mountains that were under the whole heaven were covered"—such would be the appearance, even if the deluge were local instead of universal; in Josh. 10:12, 13—"and the sun stood still"—such would be the appearance, even if the sun's rays were merely refracted so as preternaturally to lengthen the day; in Ps. 93:1—"The world also is established, that it cannot be moved"—such is the appearance, even though the earth turns on its axis and moves round the sun. In narrative, to substitute for "sunset" some scientific description would divert attention from the main subject. Would it be preferable, in the O. T., if we should read: "When the revolution of the earth upon its axis caused the rays of the solar luminary to impinge horizontally upon the retina, Isaac went out to meditate" (Gen. 24:63)? "Le secret d'ennuyer est de tout dire." Charles Dickens, in his American Notes, 72, describes a prairie sunset: "The decline of day here was very gorgeous, tinging the firmament deeply with red and gold, up to the very keystone of the arch above us" (quoted by Hovey, Manual of Christian Theology, 97). Did Dickens therefore believe the firmament to be a piece of solid masonry?

Canon Driver rejects the Bible story of creation because the distinctions made by modern science cannot be found in the primitive Hebrew. He thinks the fluid state of the earth's substance should have been called "surging chaos," instead of "waters" (Gen. 1:2). "An admirable phrase for modern and cultivated minds," replies Mr. Gladstone, "but a phrase that would have left the pupils of the Mosaic writer in exactly the condition out of which it was his purpose to bring them, namely, a state of utter ignorance and darkness, with possibly a little ripple of bewilderment to boot"; see Sunday School Times, April 26, 1890. The fallacy of holding that Scripture gives in detail all the facts connected with a historical narrative has led to many curious arguments. The Gregorian Calendar which makes the year begin in January was opposed by representing that Eve was tempted at the outset by an apple, which was possible only in case the year began in September; see Thayer, Change of Attitude towards the Bible, 46.

(b) It is not necessary to a proper view of inspiration to suppose that the human authors of Scripture had in mind the proper scientific interpretation of the natural events they recorded.

It is enough that this was in the mind of the inspiring Spirit. Through the comparatively narrow conceptions and inadequate language of the Scripture writers, the Spirit of inspiration may have secured the expression of the truth in such germinal form as to be intelligible to the times in which it was first published, and yet capable of indefinite expansion as science should advance. In the miniature picture of creation in the first chapter of Genesis, and in its power of adjusting itself to every advance of scientific investigation, we have a strong proof of inspiration.

The word "day" in Genesis 1 is an instance of this general mode of expression. It would be absurd to teach early races, that deal only in small numbers, about the myriads of years of creation. The child's object-lesson, with its graphic summary, conveys to his mind more of truth than elaborate and exact statement would convey. Conant (Genesis 2:10) says of the description of Eden and its rivers: "Of course the author's object is not a minute topographical description, but a general and impressive conception as a whole." Yet the progress of science only shows that these accounts are not less but more true than was supposed by those who first received them. Neither the Hindu Shasters nor any heathen cosmogony can bear such comparison with the results of science. Why change our interpretations of Scripture so often? Answer: We do not assume to be original teachers of science, but only to interpret Scripture with the new lights we have. See Dana, Manual of Geology, 741-746; Guyot, in Bib. Sac., 1855:324; Dawson, Story of Earth and Man, 32.

This conception of early Scripture teaching as elementary and suited to the childhood of the race would make it possible, if the facts so required, to interpret the early chapters of Genesis as mythical or legendary. God might condescend to "Kindergarten formulas." Goethe said that "We should deal with children as God deals with us: we are happiest under the influence of innocent delusions." Longfellow: "How beautiful is youth! how bright it gleams, With its illusions, aspirations, dreams! Book of beginnings, story without end, Each maid a heroine, and each man a friend!" We might hold with Goethe and with Longfellow, if we only excluded from God's teaching all essential error. The narratives of Scripture might be addressed to the imagination, and so might take mythical or legendary form, while yet they conveyed substantial truth that could in no other way be so well apprehended by early man; see Robert Browning's poem, "Development," in Asolando. The Koran, on the other hand, leaves no room for imagination, but fixes the number of the stars and declares the firmament to be solid. Henry Drummond: "Evolution has given us a new Bible.... The Bible is not a book which has been made,—it has grown."

Bagehot tells us that "One of the most remarkable of Father Newman's Oxford sermons explains how science teaches that the earth goes round the sun, and how Scripture teaches that the sun goes round the earth; and it ends by advising the discreet believer to accept both." This is mental bookkeeping by double entry; see Mackintosh, in Am. Jour. Theology, Jan. 1899:41. Lenormant, in Contemp. Rev., Nov. 1879—"While the tradition of the deluge holds so considerable a place in the legendary memories of all branches of the Aryan race, the monuments and original texts of Egypt, with their many cosmogonic speculations, have not afforded any, even distant, allusion to this cataclysm." Lenormant here wrongly assumed that the language of Scripture is scientific language. If it is the language of appearance, then the deluge may be a local and not a universal catastrophe. G. F. Wright, Ice Age in North America, suggests that the numerous traditions of the deluge may have had their origin in the enormous floods of the receding glacier. In South-western Queensland, the standard gauge at the Meteorological Office registered 10-¾, 20, 35-¾, 10-¾ inches of rainfall, in all 77-¼ inches, in four successive days.

(c) It may be safely said that science has not yet shown any fairly interpreted passage of Scripture to be untrue.

With regard to the antiquity of the race, we may say that owing to the differences of reading between the Septuagint and the Hebrew there is room for doubt whether either of the received chronologies has the sanction of inspiration. Although science has made probable the existence of man upon the earth at a period preceding the dates assigned in these chronologies, no statement of inspired Scripture is thereby proved false.

Usher's scheme of chronology, on the basis of the Hebrew, puts the creation 4004 years before Christ. Hales's, on the basis of the Septuagint, puts it 5411 B. C. The Fathers followed the LXX. But the genealogies before and after the flood may present us only with the names of "leading and representative men." Some of these names seem to stand, not for individuals, but for tribes, e. g.: Gen. 10:16—where Canaan is said to have begotten the Jebusite and the Amorite; 29—Joktan begot Ophir and Havilah. In Gen. 10:6, we read that Mizraim belonged to the sons of Ham. But Mizraim is a dual, coined to designate the two parts, Upper and Lower Egypt. Hence a son of Ham could not bear the name of Mizraim. Gen. 10:13 reads: "And Mizraim begat Ludim." But Ludim is a plural form. The word signifies a whole nation, and "begat" is not employed in a literal sense. So in verses 15, 16: "Canaan begat ... the Jebusite," a tribe; the ancestors of which would have been called Jebus. Abraham, Isaac and Jacob, however, are names, not of tribes or nations, but of individuals; see Prof. Edward König, of Bonn, in S. S. Times, Dec. 14, 1901. E. G. Robinson: "We may pretty safely go back to the time of Abraham, but no further." Bib. Sac., 1899:403—"The lists in Genesis may relate to families and not to individuals."

G. F. Wright, Ant. and Origin of Human Race, lect. II—"When in David's time it is said that 'Shebuel, the son of Gershom, the son of Moses, was ruler over the treasures' (1 Chron. 23:16; 26:24), Gershom was the immediate son of Moses, but Shebuel was separated by many generations from

Gershom. So when Seth is said to have begotten Enosh when he was 105 years old (Gen. 5:6), it is, according to Hebrew usage, capable of meaning that Enosh was descended from the branch of Seth's line which set off at the 105th year, with any number of intermediate links omitted." The appearance of completeness in the text may be due to alteration of the text in the course of centuries; see Bib. Com., 1:30. In the phrase "Jesus Christ, the son of David, the son of Abraham" (Mat. 1:1) thirty-eight to forty generations are omitted. It may be so in some of the Old Testament genealogies. There is room for a hundred thousand years, if necessary (Conant). W. H. Green, in Bib. Sac., April, 1890:303, and in Independent, June 18, 1891—"The Scriptures furnish us with no data for a chronological computation prior to the life of Abraham. The Mosaic records do not fix, and were not intended to fix, the precise date of the Flood or of the Creation.... They give a series of specimen lives, with appropriate numbers attached, to show by selected examples what was the original term of human life. To make them a complete and continuous record, and to deduce from them the antiquity of the race, is to put them to a use they were never intended to serve."

Comparison with secular history also shows that no such length of time as 100,000 years for man's existence upon earth seems necessary. Rawlinson, in Jour. Christ. Philosophy, 1883:339-364, dates the beginning of the Chaldean monarchy at 2400 B. C. Lenormant puts the entrance of the Sanskritic Indians into Hindustan at 2500 B. C. The earliest Vedas are between 1200 and 1000 B. C. (Max Müller). Call of Abraham, probably 1945 B. C. Chinese history possibly began as early as 2356 B. C. (Legge). The old Empire in Egypt possibly began as early as 2650 B. C. Rawlinson puts the flood at 3600 B. C., and adds 2000 years between the deluge and the creation, making the age of the world 1886 + 3600 + 2000 = 7486. S. R. Pattison, in Present Day Tracts, 3: no. 13, concludes that "a term of about 8000 years is warranted by deductions from history, geology, and Scripture." See also Duke of Argyll, Primeval Man, 76-128; Cowles on Genesis, 49-80; Dawson, Fossil Men, 246; Hicks, in Bap. Rev., July, 1884 (15000 years); Zöckler, Urgeschichte der Erde und des Menschen, 137-163. On the critical side, see Crooker, The New Bible and its Uses, 80-102.

Evidence of a geological nature seems to be accumulating, which tends to prove man's advent upon earth at least ten thousand years ago. An arrowhead of tempered copper and a number of human bones were found in the Rocky Point mines, near Gilman, Colorado, 460 feet beneath the surface of the earth, embedded in a vein of silver-bearing ore. More than a hundred dollars worth of ore clung to the bones when they were removed from the mine. On the age of the earth and the antiquity of man, see G. F. Wright, Man and the Glacial Epoch, lectures IV and X, and in McClure's Magazine, June, 1901, and Bib. Sac., 1903:31—"Charles Darwin first talked about 300 million years as a mere trifle of geologic time. His son George limits it to 50 or 100 million; Croll and Young to 60 or 70 million; Wallace to 28 million; Lord Kelvin to 24 million; Thompson and Newcomb to only 10 million." Sir Archibald Geikie, at the British Association at Dover in 1899, said that 100 million years sufficed for that small portion of the earth's history which is registered in the stratified rocks of the crust.

Shaler, Interpretation of Nature, 122, considers vegetable life to have existed on the planet for at least 100 million years. Warren Upham, in Pop. Science Monthly, Dec. 1893:153—"How old is the earth? 100 million years." D. G. Brinton, in Forum, Dec. 1893:454, puts the minimum limit of man's existence on earth at 50,000 years. G. F. Wright does not doubt that man's presence on this continent was preglacial, say eleven or twelve thousand years ago. He asserts that there has been a subsidence of Central Asia and Southern Russia since man's advent, and that Arctic seals are still found in Lake Baikal in Siberia. While he grants that Egyptian civilization may go back to 5000 B. C., he holds that no more than 6000 or 7000 years before this are needed as preparation for history. Le Conte, Elements of Geology, 613—"Men saw the great glaciers of the second glacial epoch, but there is no reliable evidence of their existence before the first glacial epoch. Deltas, implements, lake shores, waterfalls, indicate only 7000 to 10,000 years." Recent calculations of Prof. Prestwich, the most eminent living geologist of Great Britain, tend to bring the close of the glacial epoch down to within 10,000 or 15,000 years.

(d) Even if error in matters of science were found in Scripture, it would not disprove inspiration, since inspiration concerns itself with science only so far as correct scientific views are necessary to morals and religion.

Great harm results from identifying Christian doctrine with specific theories of the universe. The Roman church held that the revolution of the sun around the earth was taught in Scripture, and that Christian faith required the condemnation of Galileo; John Wesley thought Christianity to be inseparable from a belief in witchcraft; opposers of the higher criticism regard the Mosaic authorship of the Pentateuch as "articulus stantis vel cadentis ecclesiæ." We mistake greatly when we link inspiration with scientific doctrine. The purpose of Scripture is not to teach science, but to teach religion, and, with the exception of God's creatorship and preserving agency in the universe, no scientific truth is essential to the system of Christian doctrine. Inspiration might leave the Scripture writers in possession of the scientific ideas of their time, while yet they were empowered correctly to declare both ethical and religious truth. A right spirit indeed gains some insight into the meaning of nature, and so the Scripture writers seem to be preserved from incorporating into their productions much of the scientific error of their day. But entire freedom from such error must not be regarded as a necessary accompaniment of inspiration.

2. Errors in matters of History

To this objection we reply:

(a) What are charged as such are often mere mistakes in transcription, and have no force as arguments against inspiration, unless it can first be shown that inspired documents are by the very fact of their inspiration exempt from the operation of those laws which affect the transmission of other ancient documents.

We have no right to expect that the inspiration of the original writer will be followed by a miracle in the case of every copyist. Why believe in infallible copyists, more than in infallible printers? God educates us to care for his word, and for its correct transmission. Reverence has kept the Scriptures more free from various readings than are other ancient manuscripts. None of the existing variations endanger any important article of faith. Yet some mistakes in transcription there probably are. In 1 Chron. 22:14, instead of 100,000 talents of gold and 1,000,000 talents of silver (= $3,750,000,000), Josephus divides the sum by ten. Dr. Howard Osgood: "A French writer, Revillout, has accounted for the differing numbers in Kings and Chronicles, just as he accounts for the same differences in Egyptian and Assyrian later accounts, by the change in the value of money and debasement of issues. He shows the change all over Western Asia." Per contra, see Bacon, Genesis of Genesis, 45.

In 2 Chron. 13:3, 17, where the numbers of men in the armies of little Palestine are stated as 400,000 and 800,000, and 500,000 are said to have been slain in a single battle, "some ancient copies of the Vulgate and Latin translations of Josephus have 40,000, 80,000, and 50,000"; see Annotated Paragraph Bible, in loco. In 2 Chron. 17:14-19, Jehoshaphat's army aggregates 1,160,000, besides the garrisons of his fortresses. It is possible that by errors in transcription these numbers have been multiplied by ten. Another explanation however, and perhaps a more probable one, is given under (d) below. Similarly, compare 1 Sam. 6:19, where 50,070 are slain, with the 70 of Josephus; 2 Sam. 8:4— "1,700 horsemen," with 1 Chron. 18:4—"7,000 horsemen"; Esther 9:16—75,000 slain by the Jews, with LXX—15,000. In Mat. 27:9, we have "Jeremiah" for "Zechariah"—this Calvin allows to be a mistake; and, if a mistake, then one made by the first copyist, for it appears in all the uncials, all the manuscripts and all the versions except the Syriac Peshito where it is omitted, evidently on the authority of the individual transcriber and translator. In Acts 7:16—"the tomb that Abraham bought"—Hackett regards "Abraham" as a clerical error for "Jacob" (compare Gen. 33:18, 19). See Bible Com., 3:165, 249, 251, 317.

(b) Other so-called errors are to be explained as a permissible use of round numbers, which cannot be denied to the sacred writers except upon the principle that mathematical accuracy was more important than the general impression to be secured by the narrative.

In Numbers 25:9, we read that there fell in the plague 24,000; 1 Cor. 10:8 says 23,000. The actual number was possibly somewhere between the two. Upon a similar principle, we do not scruple to celebrate the Landing of the Pilgrims on December 22nd and the birth of Christ on December 25th. We speak of the battle of Bunker Hill, although at Bunker Hill no battle was really fought. In Ex. 12:40, 41, the sojourn of the Israelites in Egypt is declared to be 430 years. Yet Paul, in Gal. 3:17, says that the giving of the law through Moses was 430 years after the call of Abraham, whereas the call of Abraham took place 215 years before Jacob and his sons went down into Egypt, and Paul should have said 645 years instead of 430. Franz Delitzsch: "The Hebrew Bible counts four centuries of Egyptian sojourn (Gen. 15:13-16), more accurately, 430 years (Ex. 12:40); but according to the LXX (Ex. 12:40) this number comprehends the sojourn in Canaan and Egypt, so that 215 years come to the pilgrimage in Canaan, and 215 to the servitude in Egypt. This kind of calculation is not exclusively Hellenistic; it is also found in the oldest Palestinian Midrash. Paul stands on this side in Gal. 3:17, making, not the immigration into Egypt, but the covenant with Abraham the terminus a quo of the 430 years which end in the Exodus from Egypt and in the legislation"; see also Hovey, Com. on Gal. 3:17. It was not Paul's purpose to write chronology,—so he may follow the LXX, and call the time between the promise to Abraham and the giving of the law to Moses 430 years, rather than the actual 600. If he had given the larger number, it might have led to perplexity and discussion about a matter which had nothing to do with the vital question in hand. Inspiration may have employed current though inaccurate statements as to matters of history, because they were the best available means of impressing upon men's minds truth of a more important sort. In Gen. 15:13 the 430 years is called in round numbers 400 years, and so in Acts 7:6.

(c) Diversities of statement in accounts of the same event, so long as they touch no substantial truth, may be due to the meagreness of the narrative, and might be fully explained if some single fact, now unrecorded, were only known. To explain these apparent discrepancies would not only be beside the purpose of the record, but would destroy one valuable evidence of the independence of the several writers or witnesses.

On the Stokes trial, the judge spoke of two apparently conflicting testimonies as neither of them necessarily false. On the difference between Matthew and Luke as to the scene of the Sermon on the Mount (Mat. 5:1; cf. Luke 6:17) see Stanley, Sinai and Palestine, 360. As to one blind man or two (Mat. 20:30; cf. Luke 18:35) see Bliss, Com. on Luke, 275, and Gardiner, in Bib. Sac., July, 1879:513, 514; Jesus may have healed the blind men during a day's excursion from Jericho, and it might be described as "when they went out," or "as they drew nigh to Jericho." Prof. M. B. Riddle: "Luke 18:35 describes the general movement towards Jerusalem and not the precise detail preceding the miracle; Mat. 20:30 intimates that the miracle occurred during an excursion from the city,—Luke afterwards telling of the final departure"; Calvin holds to two meetings; Godet to two cities; if Jesus healed two blind men, he certainly healed one, and Luke did not need to mention more than one, even if he knew of both; see Broadus on Mat. 20:30. In Mat. 8:28, where Matthew has two demoniacs at Gadara and Luke has only one at Gerasa, Broadus supposes that the village of Gerasa belonged to the territory of the city of Gadara, a few miles to the Southeast of the lake, and he quotes the case of Lafayette: "In the year 1824 Lafayette visited the United States and was welcomed with honors and pageants. Some historians will mention only Lafayette, but others will relate the same visit as made and the same honors as enjoyed by two persons, namely, Lafayette and his son. Will not both be right?" On Christ's last Passover, see Robinson, Harmony, 212; E. H. Sears, Fourth Gospel, Appendix A; Edersheim, Life and Times of the Messiah, 2:507. Augustine: "Locutiones variæ, sed non contrariæ: dlversæ, sed non adversæ."

Bartlett, in Princeton Rev., Jan. 1880:46, 47, gives the following modern illustrations: Winslow's Journal (of Plymouth Plantation) speaks of a ship sent out "by Master Thomas Weston." But Bradford in his far briefer narrative of the matter, mentions it as sent "by Mr. Weston and another." John Adams, in his letters, tells the story of the daughter of Otis about her father's destruction of his own manuscripts. At one time he makes her say: "In one of his unhappy moments he committed them all to the flames"; yet, in the second letter, she is made to say that "he was several days in doing it." One newspaper says: President Hayes attended the Bennington centennial; another newspaper says: the President and Mrs. Hayes; a third: the President and his Cabinet; a fourth: the President, Mrs. Hayes and a majority of his Cabinet. Archibald Forbes, in his account of Napoleon III at Sedan, points out an agreement of narratives as to the salient points, combined with "the hopeless and bewildering discrepancies as to details," even as these are reported by eye-witnesses, including himself, Bismarck, and General Sheridan who was on the ground, as well as others.

Thayer, Change of Attitude, 52, speaks of Luke's "plump anachronism in the matter of Theudas"—Acts 5:36—"For before those days rose up Theudas." Josephus, Antiquities, 20:5:1, mentions an insurrectionary Theudas, but the date and other incidents do not agree with those of Luke. Josephus however may have mistaken the date as easily as Luke, or he may refer to another man of the same name. The inscription on the Cross is given in Mark 15:26, as "The King of the Jews"; in Luke 23:38, as "This is the King of the Jews"; in Mat. 27:37, as "This is Jesus the King of the Jews"; and in John 19:19, as "Jesus of Nazareth the King of the Jews." The entire superscription, in Hebrew, Greek and Latin, may have contained every word given by the several evangelists combined, and may have read "This is Jesus of Nazareth, the King of the Jews," and each separate report may be entirely correct so far as it goes. See, on the general subject, Haley, Alleged Discrepancies; Fisher, Beginnings of Christianity, 406-412.

(d) While historical and archæological discovery in many important particulars goes to sustain the general correctness of the Scripture narratives, and no statement essential to the moral and religious teaching of Scripture has been invalidated, inspiration is still consistent with much imperfection in historical detail and its narratives "do not seem to be exempted from possibilities of error."

The words last quoted are those of Sanday. In his Bampton Lectures on Inspiration, 400, he remarks that "Inspiration belongs to the historical books rather as conveying a religious lesson, than as histories; rather as interpreting, than as narrating plain matter of fact. The crucial issue is that in these last respects they do not seem to be exempted from possibilities of error." R. V. Foster, Systematic Theology, (Cumberland Presbyterian): The Scripture writers "were not inspired to do otherwise than to take these statements as they found them." Inerrancy is not freedom from misstatements, but from error defined as "that which misleads in any serious or important sense." When we compare the accounts of 1 and 2 Chronicles with those of 1 and 2 Kings we find in the former an exaggeration of numbers, a suppression of material unfavorable to the writer's purpose, and an emphasis upon that which is favorable, that contrasts strongly with the method of the latter. These characteristics are so continuous that the theory of mistakes in transcription does not seem sufficient to account for the facts. The author's aim was to draw out the religious lessons of the story, and historical details are to him of comparative unimportance.

H. P. Smith, Bib. Scholarship and Inspiration, 108—"Inspiration did not correct the Chronicler's historical point of view, more than it corrected his scientific point of view, which no doubt made the earth the centre of the solar system. It therefore left him open to receive documents, and to use them, which idealized the history of the past, and described David and Solomon according to the ideas of later times and the priestly class. David's sins are omitted, and numbers are multiplied, to give greater dignity to the earlier kingdom." As Tennyson's Idylls of the King give a nobler picture of King Arthur, and a more definite aspect to his history, than actual records justify, yet the picture teaches great moral and religious lessons, so the Chronicler seems to have manipulated his material in the interest of religion. Matters of arithmetic were minor matters. "Majoribus intentus est."

E. G. Robinson: "The numbers of the Bible are characteristic of a semi-barbarous age. The writers took care to guess enough. The tendency of such an age is always to exaggerate." Two Formosan savages divide five pieces between them by taking two apiece and throwing one away. The lowest tribes can count only with the fingers of their hands; when they use their toes as well, it marks an advance in civilization. To the modern child a hundred is just as great a number as a million. So the early Scriptures seem to use numbers with a childlike ignorance as to their meaning. Hundreds of thousands can be substituted for tens of thousands, and the substitution seems only a proper tribute to the dignity of the subject. Gore, in Lux Mundi, 353—"This was not conscious perversion, but unconscious idealizing of history, the reading back into past records of a ritual development which was really later. Inspiration excludes conscious deception, but it appears to be quite consistent with this sort of idealizing; always supposing that the result read back into the earlier history does represent the real purpose of God and only anticipates the realization."

There are some who contend that these historical imperfections are due to transcription and that they did not belong to the original documents. Watts, New Apologetic, 71, 111, when asked what is gained by contending for infallible original autographs if they have been since corrupted, replies: "Just what we gain by contending for the original perfection of human nature, though man has since corrupted it. We must believe God's own testimony about his own work. God may permit others to do what, as a holy righteous God, he cannot do himself." When the objector declares it a matter of little consequence whether a pair of trousers were or were not originally perfect, so long as they are badly rent just now, Watts replies: "The tailor who made them would probably prefer to have it understood that the trousers did not leave his shop in their present forlorn condition. God drops no stitches and sends out no imperfect work." Watts however seems dominated by an a priori theory of inspiration, which blinds him to the actual facts of the Bible.

Evans, Bib. Scholarship and Inspiration, 40—"Does the present error destroy the inspiration of the Bible as we have it? No. Then why should the original error destroy the inspiration of the Bible, as it was first given? There are spots on yonder sun; do they stop its being the sun? Why, the sun is all the more a sun for the spots. So the Bible." Inspiration seems to have permitted the gathering of such material as was at hand, very much as a modern editor might construct his account of an army movement from the reports of a number of observers; or as a modern historian might combine the records of a past age with all their imperfections of detail. In the case of the Scripture writers, however, we maintain that inspiration has permitted no sacrifice of moral and religious truth in the completed Scripture, but has woven its historical material together into an organic whole which teaches all the facts essential to the knowledge of Christ and of salvation.

When we come to examine in detail what purport to be historical narratives, we must be neither credulous nor sceptical, but simply candid and open-minded. With regard for example to the great age of the Old Testament patriarchs, we are no more warranted in rejecting the Scripture accounts upon the ground that life in later times is so much shorter, than we are to reject the testimony of botanists as to trees of the Sequoia family between four and five hundred feet high, or the testimony of geologists as to Saurians a hundred feet long, upon the ground that the trees and reptiles with which we are acquainted are so much smaller. Every species at its introduction seems to exhibit the maximum of size and vitality. Weismann, Heredity, 6, 30—"Whales live some hundreds of years; elephants two hundred—their gestation taking two years. Giants prove that the plan upon which man is constructed can also be carried out on a scale far larger than the normal one." E. Ray Lankester, Adv. of Science, 205-237, 286—agrees with Weismann in his general theory. Sir George Cornewall Lewis long denied centenarism, but at last had to admit it.

Charles Dudley Warner, in Harper's Magazine, Jan. 1895, gives instances of men 137, 140, and 192 years old. The German Haller asserts that "the ultimate limit of human life does not exceed two centuries: to fix the exact number of years is exceedingly difficult." J. Norman Lockyer, in Nature, regards the years of the patriarchs as lunar years. In Egypt, the sun being used, the unit of time was a year; but in Chaldea, the unit of time was a month, for the reason that the standard of time was the moon. Divide the numbers by twelve, and the lives of the patriarchs come out very much the same length with lives at the present day. We may ask, however, how this theory would work in shortening the lives between Noah and Moses. On the genealogies in Matthew and Luke, see Lord Harvey, Genealogies of our Lord, and his art, in Smith's Bible Dictionary; per contra, see Andrews, Life of Christ, 55 sq. On Quirinius and the enrollment for taxation (Luke 2:2), see Pres. Woolsey, in New Englander, 1869. On the general subject, see Rawlinson, Historical Evidences, and essay in Modern

Scepticism, published by Christian Evidence Society, 1:265; Crooker, New Bible and New Uses, 102-126.

3. Errors in Morality

(a) What are charged as such are sometimes evil acts and words of good men—words and acts not sanctioned by God. These are narrated by the inspired writers as simple matter of history, and subsequent results, or the story itself, is left to point the moral of the tale.

Instances of this sort are Noah's drunkenness (Gen. 9:20-27); Lot's incest (Gen. 19:30-38); Jacob's falsehood (Gen. 27:19-24); David's adultery (2 Sam. 11:1-4); Peter's denial (Mat. 26:69-75). See Lee, Inspiration, 265, note. Esther's vindictiveness is not commended, nor are the characters of the Book of Esther said to have acted in obedience to a divine command. Crane, Religion of To-morrow, 241—"In law and psalm and prophecy we behold the influence of Jehovah working as leaven among a primitive and barbarous people. Contemplating the Old Scriptures in this light, they become luminous with divinity, and we are furnished with the principle by which to discriminate between the divine and the human in the book. Particularly in David do we see a rugged, half-civilized, kingly man, full of gross errors, fleshly and impetuous, yet permeated with a divine Spirit that lifts him, struggling, weeping, and warring, up to some of the loftiest conceptions of Deity which the mind of man has conceived. As an angelic being, David is a caricature; as a man of God, as an example of God moving upon and raising up a most human man, he is a splendid example. The proof that the church is of God, is not its impeccability, but its progress."

(b) Where evil acts appear at first sight to be sanctioned, it is frequently some right intent or accompanying virtue, rather than the act itself, upon which commendation is bestowed.

As Rehab's faith, not her duplicity (Josh. 2:1-24; cf. Heb. 11:31 and James 2:25); Jael's patriotism, not her treachery (Judges 4:17-22; cf. 5:24). Or did they cast in their lot with Israel and use the common stratagems of war (see next paragraph)? Herder: "The limitations of the pupil are also limitations of the teacher." While Dean Stanley praises Solomon for tolerating idolatry, James Martineau, Study, 2:137, remarks: "It would be a ridiculous pedantry to apply the Protestant pleas of private judgment to such communities as ancient Egypt and Assyria.... It is the survival of coercion, after conscience has been born to supersede it, that shocks and revolts us in persecution."

(c) Certain commands and deeds are sanctioned as relatively just—expressions of justice such as the age could comprehend, and are to be judged as parts of a progressively unfolding system of morality whose key and culmination we have in Jesus Christ.

Ex. 20:25—"I gave them statutes that were not good"—as Moses' permission of divorce and retaliation (Deut. 24:1; cf. Mat. 5:31, 32; 19:7-9; Ex. 21:24; cf. Mat. 5:38, 39). Compare Elijah's calling down fire from heaven (2 K. 1:10-12) with Jesus' refusal to do the same, and his intimation that the spirit of Elijah was not the spirit of Christ (Luke 9:52-56); cf. Mattheson, Moments on the Mount, 253-255, on Mat. 17:8—"Jesus only": "The strength of Elias paled before him. To shed the blood of enemies requires less strength than to shed one's own blood, and to conquer by fire is easier than to conquer by love." Hovey: "In divine revelation, it is first starlight, then dawn, finally day." George Washington once gave directions for the transportation to the West Indies and the sale there of a refractory negro who had given him trouble. This was not at variance with the best morality of his time, but it would not suit the improved ethical standards of today. The use of force rather than moral suasion is sometimes needed by children and by barbarians. We may illustrate by the Sunday School scholar's unruliness which was cured by his classmates during the week. "What did you say to him?" asked the teacher. "We didn't say nothing; we just punched his head for him." This was Old Testament righteousness. The appeal in the O. T. to the hope of earthly rewards was suitable to a stage of development not yet instructed as to heaven and hell by the coming and work of Christ; compare Ex. 20:12 with Mat. 5:10; 25:46. The Old Testament aimed to fix in the mind of a selected people the idea of the unity and holiness of God; in order to exterminate idolatry, much other teaching was postponed. See Peabody, Religion of Nature, 45; Mozley, Ruling Ideas of Early Ages; Green, in Presb. Quar., April, 1877:221-252; McIlvaine, Wisdom of Holy Scripture, 328-368; Brit. and For. Evang. Rev., Jan. 1878:1-32; Martineau, Study, 2:137.

When therefore we find in the inspired song of Deborah, the prophetess (Judges 5:30), an allusion to the common spoils of war—"a damsel, two damsels to every man" or in Prov. 31:6, 7—"Give strong drink unto him that is ready to perish, and wine unto the bitter in soul. Let him drink, and forget his poverty, and remember his misery no more"—we do not need to maintain that these passages furnish standards for our modern conduct. Dr. Fisher calls the latter "the worst advice to a person in affliction, or dispirited by the loss of property." They mark past stages in God's providential leading of mankind. A higher stage indeed is already intimated in Prov. 31:4—"it is not for kings to drink wine, Nor for princes to say, Where is strong drink?" We see that God could use very imperfect instruments and could inspire very imperfect men. Many things were permitted for men's "hardness of heart" (Mat. 19:8). The Sermon on the Mount is a great advance on the law of Moses (Mat. 5:21—"Ye have heard that it was said to them of old time"; cf. 22—"But I say unto you").

Robert G. Ingersoll would have lost his stock in trade if Christians had generally recognized that revelation is gradual, and is completed only in Christ. This gradualness of revelation is conceded in the common phrase: "the new dispensation." Abraham Lincoln showed his wisdom by never going far ahead of the common sense of the people. God similarly adapted his legislation to the capacities of each successive age. The command to Abraham to sacrifice his son (Gen. 22:1-19) was a proper test of Abraham's faith in a day when human sacrifice violated no common ethical standard because the Hebrew, like the Roman, "patria potestas" did not regard the child as having a separate individuality, but included the child in the parent and made the child equally responsible for the parent's sin. But that very command was given only as a test of faith, and with the intent to make the intended obedience the occasion of revealing God's provision of a substitute and so of doing away with human sacrifice for all future time. We may well imitate the gradualness of divine revelation in our treatment of dancing and of the liquor traffic.

(d) God's righteous sovereignty affords the key to other events. He has the right to do what he will with his own, and to punish the transgressor when and where he will; and he may justly make men the foretellers or executors of his purposes.

Foretellers, as in the imprecatory Psalms (137:9; cf. Is. 13:16-18 and Jer. 50:16, 29); executors, as in the destruction of the Canaanites (Deut. 7:2, 16). In the former case the Psalm was not the ebullition of personal anger, but the expression of judicial indignation against the enemies of God. We must distinguish the substance from the form. The substance was the denunciation of God's righteous judgments; the form was taken from the ordinary customs of war in the Psalmist's time. See Park, in Bib. Sac., 1862:165; Cowles, Com. on Ps. 137; Perowne on Psalms, Introd., 61; Presb. and Ref. Rev., 1897:490-505; cf. 2 Tim. 4:14—"the Lord will render to him according to his works"—a prophecy, not a curse, ἀποδώσει, not ἀποδώη, as in A. V. In the latter case, an exterminating war was only the benevolent surgery that amputated the putrid limb, and so saved the religious life of the Hebrew nation and of the after-world. See Dr. Thomas Arnold, Essay on the Right Interpretation of Scripture; Fisher, Beginnings of Christianity, 11-24.

Another interpretation of these events has been proposed, which would make them illustrations of the principle indicated in (c) above: E. G. Robinson, Christian Theology, 45—"It was not the imprecations of the Psalm that were inspired of God, but his purposes and ideas of which these were by the times the necessary vehicle; just as the adultery of David was not by divine command, though through it the purpose of God as to Christ's descent was accomplished." John Watson (Ian Maclaren), Cure of Souls, 143—"When the massacre of the Canaanites and certain proceedings of David are flung in the face of Christians, it is no longer necessary to fall back on evasions or special pleading. It can now be frankly admitted that, from our standpoint in this year of grace, such deeds were atrocious, and that they never could have been according to the mind of God, but that they must be judged by their date, and considered the defects of elementary moral processes. The Bible is vindicated, because it is, on the whole, a steady ascent, and because it culminates in Christ."

Lyman Abbott, Theology of an Evolutionist, 56—"Abraham mistook the voice of conscience, calling on him to consecrate his only son to God, and interpreted it as a command to slay his son as a burnt offering. Israel misinterpreted his righteous indignation at the cruel and lustful rites of the Canaanitish religion as a divine summons to destroy the worship by putting the worshipers to death; a people undeveloped in moral judgment could not distinguish between formal regulations respecting camp-life and eternal principles of righteousness, such as, Thou shalt love thy neighbor as thyself, but embodied them in the same code, and seemed to regard them as of equal authority." Wilkinson, Epic of Paul, 281—"If so be such man, so placed ... did in some part That utterance make his own, profaning it, To be his vehicle for sense not meant By the august supreme inspiring Will"—i. e., putting some of his own sinful anger into God's calm predictions of judgment. Compare the stern last words of "Zechariah, the son of Jehoiada, the priest" when stoned to death in the temple court: "Jehovah look upon it and require it" (2 Chron. 24:20-22), with the last words of Jesus: "Father, forgive them, for they know not what they do" (Luke 23:34) and of Stephen: "Lord, lay not this sin to their charge" (Acts 7:60).

(e) Other apparent immoralities are due to unwarranted interpretations. Symbol is sometimes taken for literal fact; the language of irony is understood as sober affirmation; the glow and freedom of Oriental description are judged by the unimpassioned style of Western literature; appeal to lower motives is taken to exclude, instead of preparing for, the higher.

In Hosea 1:2, 3, the command to the prophet to marry a harlot was probably received and executed in vision, and was intended only as symbolic: compare Jer. 25:15-18—"Take this cup ... and cause all the nations ... to drink." Literal obedience would have made the prophet contemptible to those whom he would instruct, and would require so long a time as to weaken, if not destroy, the designed effect; see Ann. Par. Bible, in loco. In 2 K. 6:19, Elisha's deception, so called, was probably only ironical and benevolent; the enemy dared not resist, because they were completely in his power. In the Song of Solomon, we have, as Jewish writers have always held, a highly-wrought dramatic description of the union between Jehovah and his people, which we must judge by Eastern and not by Western literary standards.

Francis W. Newman, in his Phases of Faith, accused even the New Testament of presenting low motives for human obedience. It is true that all right motives are appealed to, and some of these motives are of a higher sort than are others. Hope of heaven and fear of hell are not the highest motives, but they may be employed as preliminary incitements to action, even though only love for God and for holiness will ensure salvation. Such motives are urged both by Christ and by his apostles: Mat. 6:20—"lay up for yourselves treasures in heaven"; 10:28—"fear him who is able to destroy both soul and body in hell"; Jude 23—"some save with fear, snatching them out of the fire." In this respect the N. T. does not differ from the O. T. George Adam Smith has pointed out that the royalists got their texts, "the powers that be" (Rom. 13:1) and "the king as supreme" (1 Pet. 2:13), from the N. T., while the O. T. furnished texts for the defenders of liberty. While the O. T. deals with national life, and the discharge of social and political functions, the N. T. deals in the main with individuals and with their relations to God. On the whole subject, see Hessey, Moral Difficulties of the Bible; Jellett, Moral Difficulties of the O. T.; Faith and Free Thought (Lect. by Christ. Ev. Soc.), 2:173; Rogers, Eclipse of Faith; Butler, Analogy, part ii, chap. iii; Orr, Problem of the O. T., 465-483.

4. Errors of Reasoning

(a) What are charged as such are generally to be explained as valid argument expressed in highly condensed form. The appearance of error may be due to the suppression of one or more links in the reasoning.

In Mat. 22:32, Christ's argument for the resurrection, drawn from the fact that God is the God of Abraham, Isaac, and Jacob, is perfectly and obviously valid, the moment we put in the suppressed premise that the living relation to God which is here implied cannot properly be conceived as something merely spiritual, but necessarily requires a new and restored life of the body. If God is the God of the living, then Abraham, Isaac, and Jacob shall rise from the dead. See more full exposition, under Eschatology. Some of the Scripture arguments are enthymemes, and an enthymeme, according to Arbuthnot and Pope, is "a syllogism in which the major is married to the minnor, and the marriage is kept secret."

(b) Where we cannot see the propriety of the conclusions drawn from given premises, there is greater reason to attribute our failure to ignorance of divine logic on our part, than to accommodation or ad hominem arguments on the part of the Scripture writers.

By divine logic we mean simply a logic whose elements and processes are correct, though not understood by us. In Heb. 7:9, 10 (Levi's paying tithes in Abraham), there is probably a recognition of the organic unity of the family, which in miniature illustrates the organic unity of the race. In Gal. 3:20—"a mediator is not a mediator of one; but God is one"—the law, with its two contracting parties, is contrasted with the promise, which proceeds from the sole fiat of God and is therefore unchangeable. Paul's argument here rests on Christ's divinity as its foundation—otherwise Christ would have been a mediator in the same sense in which Moses was a mediator (see Lightfoot, in loco). In Gal. 4:21-31, Hagar and Ishmael on the one hand, and Sarah and Isaac on the other, illustrate the exclusion of the bondmen of the law from the privileges of the spiritual seed of Abraham. Abraham's two wives, and the two classes of people in the two sons, represent the two covenants (so Calvin). In John 10:34—"I said, Ye are gods," the implication is that Judaism was not a system of mere monotheism, but of theism tending to theanthropism, a real union of God and man (Westcott, Bib. Com., in loco). Godet well remarks that he who doubts Paul's logic will do well first to suspect his own.

(c) The adoption of Jewish methods of reasoning, where it could be proved, would not indicate error on the part of the Scripture writers, but rather an inspired sanction of the method as applied to that particular case.

In Gal. 3:16—"He saith not, And to seeds, as of many; but as of one, And to thy seed, which is Christ." Here it is intimated that the very form of the expression in Gen. 22:18, which denotes unity, was selected by the Holy Spirit as significant of that one person, Christ, who was the true seed of Abraham and in whom all nations were to be blessed. Argument from the form of a single word is in this case correct, although the Rabbins often made more of single words than the Holy Spirit ever intended. Watts, New Apologetic, 69—"F. W. Farrar asserts that the plural of the Hebrew or Greek terms for 'seed' is never used by Hebrew or Greek writers as a designation of human offspring. But see Sophocles, Œdipus at Colonus, 599, 600—γῆς ἐμῆς ἀπηλάθην πρὸς τῶν ἐμαυτοῦ σπερμάτων—'I was driven away from my own country by my own offspring.' " In 1 Cor. 10:1-6—"and the rock was Christ"—the Rabbinic tradition that the smitten rock followed the Israelites in their wanderings is declared to be only the absurd literalizing of a spiritual fact—the continual presence of Christ, as preëxistent Logos, with his ancient people. Per contra, see Row, Rev. and Mod. Theories, 98-128.

(d) If it should appear however upon further investigation that Rabbinical methods have been wrongly employed by the apostles in their argumentation, we might still distinguish between the truth they are seeking to convey and the arguments by which they support it. Inspiration may conceivably make known the truth, yet leave the expression of the truth to human dialectic as well as to human rhetoric.

Johnson, Quotations of the N. T. from the O. T., 137, 138—"In the utter absence of all evidence to the contrary, we ought to suppose that the allegories of the N. T. are like the allegories of literature in general, merely luminous embodiments of the truth.... If these allegories are not presented by their writers as evidences, they are none the less precious, since they illuminate the truth otherwise evinced, and thus render it at once clear to the apprehension and attractive to the taste." If however the purpose of the writers was to use these allegories for proof, we may still see shining through the rifts of their traditional logic the truth which they were striving to set forth. Inspiration may have put them in possession of this truth without altering their ordinary scholastic methods of demonstration and expression. Horton, Inspiration, 108—"Discrepancies and illogical reasonings were but inequalities or cracks in the mirrors, which did not materially distort or hide the Person" whose glory they sought to reflect. Luther went even further than this when he said that a certain argument in the epistle was "good enough for the Galatians."

5. Errors in quoting or interpreting the Old Testament

(a) What are charged as such are commonly interpretations of the meaning of the original Scripture by the same Spirit who first inspired it.

In Eph. 5:14, "arise from the dead, and Christ shall shine upon thee" is an inspired interpretation of Is. 60:1—"Arise, shine; for thy light is come." Ps. 68:18—"Thou hast received gifts among men"—is quoted in Eph. 4:8 as "gave gifts to men." The words in Hebrew are probably a concise expression for "thou hast taken spoil which thou mayest distribute as gifts to men." Eph. 4:8 agrees exactly with the sense, though not with the words, of the Psalm. In Heb. 11:21, "Jacob ... worshiped, leaning upon the top of his staff" (LXX); Gen. 47:31 has "bowed himself upon the bed's head." The meaning is the same, for the staff of the chief and the spear of the warrior were set at the bed's head. Jacob, too feeble to rise, prayed in his bed. Here Calvin says that "the apostle does not hesitate to accommodate to his own purpose what was commonly received,—they were not so scrupulous" as to details. Even Gordon, Ministry of the Spirit, 177, speaks of "a reshaping of his own words by the Author of them." We prefer, with Calvin, to see in these quotations evidence that the sacred writers were insistent upon the substance of the truth rather than upon the form, the spirit rather than the letter.

(b) Where an apparently false translation is quoted from the Septuagint, the sanction of inspiration is given to it, as expressing a part at least of the fulness of meaning contained in the divine original—a fulness of meaning which two varying translations do not in some cases exhaust.

Ps. 4:4—Heb.: "Tremble, and sin not" (= no longer); LXX: "Be ye angry, and sin not." Eph. 4:26 quotes the LXX. The words may originally have been addressed to David's comrades, exhorting them to keep their anger within bounds. Both translations together are needed to bring out the meaning of the original. Ps. 40:6-8—"Mine ears hast thou opened" is translated in Heb. 10:5-7—"a body didst thou prepare for me." Here the Epistle quotes from the LXX. But the Hebrew means literally: "Mine ears hast thou bored"—an allusion to the custom of pinning a slave to the doorpost of his master by an awl driven through his ear, in token of his complete subjection. The sense of the verse is therefore given in the Epistle: "Thou hast made me thine in body and soul—lo, I come to do thy will." A. C. Kendrick: "David, just entering upon his kingdom after persecution, is a type of Christ entering on his earthly mission. Hence David's words are put into the mouth of Christ. For 'ears,' the organs with which we hear and obey and which David conceived to be hollowed out for him by God, the author of the Hebrews substitutes the word 'body,' as the general instrument of doing God's will" (Com. on Heb. 10:5-7).

(c) The freedom of these inspired interpretations, however, does not warrant us in like freedom of interpretation in the case of other passages whose meaning has not been authoritatively made known.

We have no reason to believe that the scarlet thread of Rahab (Josh. 2:18) was a designed prefiguration of the blood of Christ, nor that the three measures of meal in which the woman hid her leaven (Mat. 13:33) symbolized Shem, Ham and Japheth, the three divisions of the human race. C. H. M., in his notes on the tabernacle in Exodus, tells us that "the loops of blue = heavenly grace; the taches of gold = the divine energy of Christ; the rams' skins dyed red = Christ's consecration and devotedness; the badgers' skins = his holy vigilance against temptation"! The tabernacle was indeed a type of Christ (John 1:14—ἐσκήνωσεν. 2:19, 21—"in three days I will raise it up ... but he spake of the temple of his body"); yet it does not follow that every detail of the structure was significant. So each parable teaches some one main lesson,—the particulars may be mere drapery; and while we may use the parables for illustration, we should never ascribe divine authority to our private impressions of their meaning.

Mat. 25:1-13—the parable of the five wise and the five foolish virgins—has been made to teach that the number of the saved precisely equals the number of the lost. Augustine defended persecution from the words in Luke 14:23—"constrain them to come in." The Inquisition was justified by Mat.

13:30—"bind them in bundles to burn them." Innocent III denied the Scriptures to the laity, quoting Heb. 12:20—"If even a beast touch the mountain, it shall be stoned." A Plymouth Brother held that he would be safe on an evangelizing journey because he read in John 19:36—"A bone of him shall not be broken." Mat. 17:8—"they saw no one, save Jesus only"—has been held to mean that we should trust only Jesus. The Epistle of Barnabas discovered in Abraham's 318 servants a prediction of the crucified Jesus, and others have seen in Abraham's three days' journey to Mount Moriah the three stages in the development of the soul. Clement of Alexandria finds the four natural elements in the four colors of the Jewish Tabernacle. All this is to make a parable "run on all fours." While we call a hero a lion, we do not need to find in the man something to correspond to the lion's mane and claws. See Toy, Quotations in the N. T.; Franklin Johnson, Quotations of the N. T. from the O. T.; Crooker, The New Bible and its New Uses, 126-136.

(d) While we do not grant that the New Testament writers in any proper sense misquoted or misinterpreted the Old Testament, we do not regard absolute correctness in these respects as essential to their inspiration. The inspiring Spirit may have communicated truth, and may have secured in the Scriptures as a whole a record of that truth sufficient for men's moral and religious needs, without imparting perfect gifts of scholarship or exegesis.

In answer to Toy, Quotations in the N. T., who takes a generally unfavorable view of the correctness of the N. T. writers, Johnson, Quotations of the N. T. from the O. T., maintains their correctness. On pages x, xi, of his Introduction, Johnson remarks: "I think it just to regard the writers of the Bible as the creators of a great literature, and to judge and interpret them by the laws of literature. They have produced all the chief forms of literature, as history, biography, anecdote, proverb, oratory, allegory, poetry, fiction. They have needed therefore all the resources of human speech, its sobriety and scientific precision on one page, its rainbow hues of fancy and imagination on another, its fires of passion on yet another. They could not have moved and guided men in the best manner had they denied themselves the utmost force and freedom of language; had they refused to employ its wide range of expressions, whether exact or poetic; had they not borrowed without stint its many forms of reason, of terror, of rapture, of hope, of joy, of peace. So also, they have needed the usual freedom of literary allusion and citation, in order to commend the gospel to the judgment, the tastes, and the feelings of their readers."

6. Errors in Prophecy

(a) What are charged as such may frequently be explained by remembering that much of prophecy is yet unfulfilled.

It is sometimes taken for granted that the book of Revelation, for example, refers entirely to events already past. Moses Stuart, in his Commentary, and Warren's Parousia, represent this preterist interpretation. Thus judged, however, many of the predictions of the book might seem to have failed.

(b) The personal surmises of the prophets as to the meaning of the prophecies they recorded may have been incorrect, while yet the prophecies themselves are inspired.

In 1 Pet. 1:10, 11, the apostle declares that the prophets searched "what time or what manner of time the Spirit of Christ which was in them did point unto, when it testified beforehand the sufferings of Christ and the glories that should follow them." So Paul, although he does not announce it as certain, seems to have had some hope that he might live to witness Christ's second coming. See 2 Cor. 5:4—"not for that we would be unclothed, but that we would be clothed upon" (ἐπενδύσασθαι—put on the spiritual body, as over the present one, without the intervention of death); 1 Thess. 4:15, 17—"we that are alive, that are left unto the coming of the Lord." So Mat. 2:15 quotes from Hosea 11:1—"Out of Egypt did I call my son," and applies the prophecy to Christ, although Hosea was doubtless thinking only of the exodus of the people of Israel.

(c) The prophet's earlier utterances are not to be severed from the later utterances which elucidate them, nor from the whole revelation of which they form a part. It is unjust to forbid the prophet to explain his own meaning.

2 Thessalonians was written expressly to correct wrong inferences as to the apostle's teaching drawn from his peculiar mode of speaking in the first epistle. In 2 Thess. 2:2-5 he removes the impression "that the day of the Lord is now present" or "just at hand"; declares that "it will not be, except the falling away come first, and the man of sin be revealed"; reminds the Thessalonians: "when I was yet with you, I told you these things." Yet still, in verse 1, he speaks of "the coming of our Lord Jesus Christ, and our gathering together unto him."

These passages, taken together, show: (1) that the two epistles are one in their teaching; (2) that in neither epistle is there any prediction of the immediate coming of the Lord; (3) that in the second epistle great events are foretold as intervening before that coming; (4) that while Paul never taught that Christ would come during his own lifetime, he hoped at least during the earlier part of his life that it might be so—a hope that seems to have been dissipated in his later years. (See 2 Tim. 4:6—"I am already being offered, and the time of my departure is come.") We must remember, however, that there was a "coming of the Lord" in the destruction of Jerusalem within three or four years of Paul's death. Henry Van Dyke: "The point of Paul's teaching in 1 and 2 Thess. is not that Christ is coming to-morrow, but that he is surely coming." The absence of perspective in prophecy may explain Paul's not at first defining the precise time of the end, and so leaving it to be misunderstood.

The second Epistle to the Thessalonians, therefore, only makes more plain the meaning of the first, and adds new items of prediction. It is important to recognize in Paul's epistles a progress in prophecy, in doctrine, in church polity. The full statement of the truth was gradually drawn out, under the influence of the Spirit, upon occasion of successive outward demands and inward experiences. Much is to be learned by studying the chronological order of Paul's epistles, as well as of the other N. T. books. For evidence of similar progress in the epistles of Peter, compare 1 Pet. 4:7 with 2 Pet. 3:4 sq.

(d) The character of prophecy as a rough general sketch of the future, in highly figurative language, and without historical perspective, renders it peculiarly probable that what at first sight seem to be errors are due to a misinterpretation on our part, which confounds the drapery with the substance, or applies its language to events to which it had no reference.

James 5:9 and Phil. 4:5 are instances of that large prophetic speech which regards the distant future as near at hand, because so certain to the faith and hope of the church. Sanday, Inspiration, 376-378—"No doubt the Christians of the Apostolic age did live in immediate expectation of the Second Coming, and that expectation culminated at the crisis at which the Apocalypse was written. In the Apocalypse, as in every predictive prophecy, there is a double element, one part derived from the circumstances of the present and another pointing forwards to the future.... All these things, in an exact and literal sense have fallen through with the postponement of that great event in which they centre. From the first they were but meant as the imaginative pictorial and symbolical clothing of that event. What measure of real fulfilment the Apocalypse may yet be destined to receive we cannot tell. But in predictive prophecy, even when most closely verified, the essence lies less in the prediction than in the eternal laws of moral and religious truth which the fact predicted reveals or exemplifies." Thus we recognize both the divinity and the freedom of prophecy, and reject the rationalistic theory which would relate the fall of the Beaconsfield government in Matthew's way: "That it might be fulfilled which was spoken by Cromwell, saying: 'Get you gone, and make room for honest men!' " See the more full statement of the nature of prophecy, on pages 132-141. Also Bernard, Progress of Doctrine in the N. T.

7. Certain books unworthy of a place in inspired Scripture

(a) This charge may be shown, in each single case, to rest upon a misapprehension of the aim and method of the book, and its connection with the remainder of the Bible, together with a narrowness of nature or of doctrinal view, which prevents the critic from appreciating the wants of the peculiar class of men to which the book is especially serviceable.

Luther called James "a right strawy epistle." His constant pondering of the doctrine of justification by faith alone made it difficult for him to grasp the complementary truth that we are justified only by such faith as brings forth good works, or to perceive the essential agreement of James and Paul. Prof. R. E. Thompson, in S. S. Times, Dec. 3,1898:803, 804—"Luther refused canonical authority to books not actually written by apostles or composed (as Mark and Luke) under their direction. So he rejected from the rank of canonical authority Hebrews, James, Jude, 2 Peter, Revelation. Even Calvin doubted the Petrine authorship of 2 Peter, excluded the book of Revelation from the Scripture on which he wrote Commentaries, and also thus ignored 2 and 3 John." G. P. Fisher in S. S. Times, Aug. 29, 1891—"Luther, in his preface to the N. T. (Edition of 1522), gives a list of what he considers as the principal books of the N. T. These are John's Gospel and First Epistle, Paul's Epistles, especially Romans and Galatians, and Peter's First Epistle. Then he adds that 'St. James' Epistle is a right strawy Epistle compared with them'—'ein recht strohern Epistel gegen sie,' thus characterizing it not absolutely but only relatively." Zwingle even said of the Apocalypse: "It is not a Biblical book." So Thomas Arnold, with his exaggerated love for historical accuracy and definite outline, found the Oriental imagery and sweeping visions of the book of Revelation so bizarre and distasteful that he doubted their divine authority.

(b) The testimony of church history and general Christian experience to the profitableness and divinity of the disputed books is of greater weight than the personal impressions of the few who criticize them.

Instance the testimonies of the ages of persecution to the worth of the prophecies, which assure God's people that his cause shall surely triumph. Denney, Studies in Theology, 226—"It is at least as likely that the individual should be insensible to the divine message in a book, as that the church should have judged it to contain such a message if it did not do so." Milton, Areopagitica: "The Bible brings in holiest men passionately murmuring against Providence through all the arguments of Epicurus." Bruce, Apologetics, 329—"O. T. religion was querulous, vindictive, philolevitical, hostile toward foreigners, morbidly self-conscious, and tending to self-righteousness. Ecclesiastes shows us how we ought not to feel. To go about crying Vanitas! is to miss the lesson it was meant to teach, namely, that the Old

Covenant was vanity—proved to be vanity by allowing a son of the Covenant to get into so despairing a mood." Chadwick says that Ecclesiastes got into the Canon only after it had received an orthodox postscript.

Pfleiderer, Philos. Religion, 1:193—"Slavish fear and self-righteous reckoning with God are the unlovely features of this Jewish religion of law to which the ethical idealism of the prophets had degenerated, and these traits strike us most visibly in Pharsiaism.... It was this side of the O. T. religion to which Christianity took a critical and destroying attitude, while it revealed a new and higher knowledge of God. For, says Paul, 'ye received not the spirit of bondage again unto fear; but ye received the spirit of adoption' (Rom. 8:15). In unity with God man does not lose his soul but preserves it. God not only commands but gives." Ian Maclaren (John Watson), Cure of Souls, 144—"When the book of Ecclesiastes is referred to the days of the third century B. C., then its note is caught, and any man who has been wronged and embittered by political tyranny and social corruption has his bitter cry included in the book of God."

(c) Such testimony can be adduced in favor of the value of each one of the books to which exception is taken, such as Esther, Job, Song of Solomon, Ecclesiastes, Jonah, James, Revelation.

Esther is the book, next to the Pentateuch, held in highest reverence by the Jews. "Job was the discoverer of infinity, and the first to see the bearing of infinity on righteousness. It was the return of religion to nature. Job heard the voice beyond the Sinai-voice" (Shadow-Cross, 89). Inge, Christian Mysticism, 43—"As to the Song of Solomon, its influence upon Christian Mysticism has been simply deplorable. A graceful romance in honor of true love has been distorted into a precedent and sanction for giving way to hysterical emotions in which sexual imagery has been freely used to symbolize the relation between the soul and its Lord." Chadwick says that the Song of Solomon got into the Canon only after it had received an allegorical interpretation. Gladden, Seven Puzzling Bible Books, 165, thinks it impossible that "the addition of one more inmate to the harem of that royal rake, King Solomon, should have been made the type of the spiritual affection between Christ and his church. Instead of this, the book is a glorification of pure love. The Shulamite, transported to the court of Solomon, remains faithful to her shepherd lover, and is restored to him."

Bruce, Apologetics, 321—"The Song of Solomon, literally interpreted as a story of true love, proof against the blandishments of the royal harem, is rightfully in the Canon as a buttress to the true religion; for whatever made for purity in the relations of the sexes made for the worship of Jehovah—Baal worship and impurity being closely associated." Rutherford, McCheyne, and Spurgeon have taken more texts from the Song of Solomon than from any other portion of Scripture of like extent. Charles G. Finney, Autobiography, 378—"At this time it seemed as if my soul was wedded to Christ in a sense which I never had any thought or conception of before. The language of the Song of Solomon was as natural to me as my breath. I thought I could understand well the state he was in when he wrote that Song, and concluded then, as I have ever thought since, that that Song was written by him after he had been reclaimed from his great backsliding. I not only had all the fulness of my first love, but a vast accession to it. Indeed, the Lord lifted me up so much above anything that I had experienced before, and taught me so much of the meaning of the Bible, of Christ's relations and power and willingness, that I found myself saying to him: I had not known or conceived that any such thing was true." On Jonah, see R. W. Dale, in Expositor, July, 1892, advocating the non-historical and allegorical character of the book. Bib. Sac., 10:737-764—"Jonah represents the nation of Israel as emerging through a miracle from the exile, in order to carry out its mission to the world at large. It teaches that God is the God of the whole earth; that the Ninevites as well as the Israelites are dear to him; that his threatenings of penalty are conditional."

8. Portions of the Scripture books written by others than the persons to whom they are ascribed

The objection rests upon a misunderstanding of the nature and object of inspiration. It may be removed by considering that

(a) In the case of books made up from preëxisting documents, inspiration simply preserved the compilers of them from selecting inadequate or improper material. The fact of such compilation does not impugn their value as records of a divine revelation, since these books supplement each other's deficiencies and together are sufficient for man's religious needs.

Luke distinctly informs us that he secured the materials for his gospel from the reports of others who were eye-witnesses of the events he recorded (Luke 1:1-4). The book of Genesis bears marks of having incorporated documents of earlier times. The account of creation which begins with Gen. 2:4 is evidently written by a different hand from that which penned 1:1-31 and 2:1-3. Instances of the same sort may be found in the books of Chronicles. In like manner, Marshall's Life of Washington incorporates documents by other writers. By thus incorporating them, Marshall vouches for their truth. See Bible Com., 1:2, 22.

Dorner, Hist. Prot. Theology, 1:243—"Luther ascribes to faith critical authority with reference to the Canon. He denies the canonicity of James, without regarding it as spurious. So of Hebrews and

Revelation, though later, in 1545, he passed a more favorable judgment upon the latter. He even says of a proof adduced by Paul in Galatians that it is too weak to hold. He allows that in external matters not only Stephen but even the sacred authors contain inaccuracies. The authority of the O. T. does not seem to him invalidated by the admission that several of its writings have passed through revising hands. What would it matter, he asks, if Moses did not write the Pentateuch? The prophets studied Moses and one another. If they built in much wood, hay and stubble along with the rest, still the foundation abides; the fire of the great day shall consume the former; for in this manner do we treat the writings of Augustine and others. Kings is far more to be believed than Chronicles. Ecclesiastes is forged and cannot come from Solomon. Esther is not canonical. The church may have erred in adopting a book into the Canon. Faith first requires proof. Hence he ejects the Apocryphal books of the O. T. from the Canon. So some parts of the N. T. receive only a secondary, deuterocanonical position. There is a difference between the word of God and the holy Scriptures, not merely in reference to the form, but also in reference to the subject matter."

H. P. Smith, Bib. Scholarship and Inspiration, 94—"The Editor of the Minor Prophets united in one roll the prophetic fragments which were in circulation in his time. Finding a fragment without an author's name he inserted it in the series. It would not have been distinguished from the work of the author immediately preceding. So Zech. 9:1-4 came to go under the name of Zechariah, and Is. 40-66 under the name of Isaiah. Reuss called these 'anatomical studies.' " On the authorship of the book of Daniel, see W. C. Wilkinson, in Homiletical Review, March, 1902:208, and Oct. 1902:305; on Paul, see Hom. Rev., June, 1902:501; on 110th Psalm, Hom. Rev., April, 1902:309.

(b) In the case of additions to Scripture books by later writers, it is reasonable to suppose that the additions, as well as the originals, were made by inspiration, and no essential truth is sacrificed by allowing the whole to go under the name of the chief author.

Mark 16:9-20 appears to have been added by a later hand (see English Revised Version). The Eng. Rev. Vers. also brackets or segregates a part of verse 3 and the whole of verse 4 in John 5 (the moving of the water by the angel), and the whole passage John 7:53-8:11 (the woman taken in adultery). Westcott and Hort regard the latter passage as an interpolation, probably "Western" in its origin (so also Mark 16:9-20). Others regard it as authentic, though not written by John. The closing chapter of Deuteronomy was apparently added after Moses' death—perhaps by Joshua. If criticism should prove other portions of the Pentateuch to have been composed after Moses' time, the inspiration of the Pentateuch would not be invalidated, so long as Moses was its chief author or even the original source and founder of its legislation (John 5:46—"he wrote of me"). Gore, in Lux Mundi, 355—"Deuteronomy may be a republication of the law, in the spirit and power of Moses, and put dramatically into his mouth."

At a spot near the Pool of Siloam, Manasseh is said to have ordered that Isaiah should be sawn asunder with a wooden saw. The prophet is again sawn asunder by the recent criticism. But his prophecy opens (Is. 1:1) with the statement that it was composed during a period which covered the reigns of four kings—Uzziah, Jotham, Ahaz and Hezekiah—nearly forty years. In so long a time the style of a writer greatly changes. Chapters 40-66 may have been written in Isaiah's later age, after he had retired from public life. Compare the change in the style of Zechariah, John and Paul, with that in Thomas Carlyle and George William Curtis. On Isaiah, see Smyth, Prophecy a Preparation for Christ; Bib. Sac., Apr. 1881:230-253; also July, 1881; Stanley, Jewish Ch., 2:646, 647; Nägelsbach, Int. to Lange's Isaiah.

For the view that there were two Isaiahs, see George Adam Smith, Com. on Isaiah, 2:1-25: Isaiah flourished B. C. 740-700. The last 27 chapters deal with the captivity (598-538) and with Cyrus (550), whom they name. The book is not one continuous prophecy, but a number of separate orations. Some of these claim to be Isaiah's own, and have titles, such as "The vision of Isaiah the son of Amos" (1:1); "The word that Isaiah the son of Amos saw" (2:1). But such titles describe only the individual prophecies they head. Other portions of the book, on other subjects and in different styles, have no titles at all. Chapters 40-66 do not claim to be his. There are nine citations in the N. T. from the disputed chapters, but none by our Lord. None of these citations were given in answer to the question: Did Isaiah write chapters 44-66? Isaiah's name is mentioned only for the sake of reference. Chapters 44-66 set forth the exile and captivity as already having taken place. Israel is addressed as ready for deliverance. Cyrus is named as deliverer. There is no grammar of the future like Jeremiah's. Cyrus is pointed out as proof that former prophecies of deliverance are at last coming to pass. He is not presented as a prediction, but as a proof that prediction is being fulfilled. The prophet could not have referred the heathen to Cyrus as proof that prophecy had been fulfilled, had he not been visible to them in all his weight of war. Babylon has still to fall before the exiles can go free. But chapters 40-66 speak of the coming of Cyrus as past, and of the fall of Babylon as yet to come. Why not use the prophetic perfect of both, if both were yet future? Local color, language and thought are all consistent with exilic authorship. All suits the exile, but all is foreign to the subjects and methods of Isaiah, for example, the use of the terms righteous and righteousness. Calvin admits exilic authorship (on Is. 55:3). The passage 56:9-57, however, is an exception and is preëxilic. 40-48 are certainly by one hand, and may be dated 555-538. 2nd Isaiah is not a unity, but consists of a number of pieces written before, during, and after the exile, to comfort the people of God.

(c) It is unjust to deny to inspired Scripture the right exercised by all historians of introducing certain documents and sayings as simply historical, while their complete truthfulness is neither vouched for nor denied.

An instance in point is the letter of Claudius Lysias in Acts 23:26-30—a letter which represents his conduct in a more favorable light than the facts would justify—for he had not learned that Paul was a Roman when he rescued him in the temple (Acts 21:31-33; 22:26-29). An incorrect statement may be correctly reported. A set of pamphlets printed in the time of the French Revolution might be made an appendix to some history of France without implying that the historian vouched for their truth. The sacred historians may similarly have been inspired to use only the material within their reach, leaving their readers by comparison with other Scriptures to judge of its truthfulness and value. This seems to have been the method adopted by the compiler of 1 and 2 Chronicles. The moral and religious lessons of the history are patent, even though there is inaccuracy in reporting some of the facts. So the assertions of the authors of the Psalms cannot be taken for absolute truth. The authors were not sinless models for the Christian,—only Christ is that. But the Psalms present us with a record of the actual experience of believers in the past. It has its human weakness, but we can profit by it, even though it expresses itself at times in imprecations. Jeremiah 20:7—"O lord, thou hast deceived me"—may possibly be thus explained.

9. Sceptical or fictitious Narratives

(a) Descriptions of human experience may be embraced in Scripture, not as models for imitation, but as illustrations of the doubts, struggles, and needs of the soul. In these cases inspiration may vouch, not for the correctness of the views expressed by those who thus describe their mental history, but only for the correspondence of the description with actual fact, and for its usefulness as indirectly teaching important moral lessons.

The book of Ecclesiastes, for example, is the record of the mental struggles of a soul seeking satisfaction without God. If written by Solomon during the time of his religious declension, or near the close of it, it would constitute a most valuable commentary upon the inspired history. Yet it might be equally valuable, though composed by some later writer under divine direction and inspiration. H. P. Smith, Bib. Scholarship and Inspiration, 97—"To suppose Solomon the author of Ecclesiastes is like supposing Spenser to have written In Memoriam." Luther, Keil, Delitzsch, Ginsburg, Hengstenberg all declare it to be a production of later times (330 B. C.). The book shows experience of misgovernment. An earlier writer cannot write in the style of a later one, though the later can imitate the earlier. The early Latin and Greek Fathers quoted the Apocryphal Wisdom of Solomon as by Solomon; see Plumptre, Introd. to Ecclesiastes, in Cambridge Bible. Gore, in Lux Mundi, 355—"Ecclesiastes, though like the book of Wisdom purporting to be by Solomon, may be by another author.... 'A pious fraud' cannot be inspired; an idealizing personification, as a normal type of literature, can be inspired." Yet Bernhard Schäfer, Das Buch Koheleth, ably maintains the Solomonic authorship.

(b) Moral truth may be put by Scripture writers into parabolic or dramatic form, and the sayings of Satan and of perverse men may form parts of such a production. In such cases, inspiration may vouch, not for the historical truth, much less for the moral truth of each separate statement, but only for the correspondence of the whole with ideal fact; in other words, inspiration may guarantee that the story is true to nature, and is valuable as conveying divine instruction.

It is not necessary to suppose that the poetical speeches of Job's friends were actually delivered in the words that have come down to us. Though Job never had had a historical existence, the book would still be of the utmost value, and would convey to us a vast amount of true teaching with regard to the dealings of God and the problem of evil. Fact is local; truth is universal. Some novels contain more truth than can be found in some histories. Other books of Scripture, however, assure us that Job was an actual historical character (Ez. 14:14; James 5:11). Nor is it necessary to suppose that our Lord, in telling the parable of the Prodigal Son (Luke 15:11-32) or that of the Unjust Steward (16:1-8), had in mind actual persons of whom each parable was an exact description.

Fiction is not an unworthy vehicle of spiritual truth. Parable, and even fable, may convey valuable lessons. In Judges 9:14, 15, the trees, the vine, the bramble, all talk. If truth can be transmitted in myth and legend, surely God may make use of these methods of communicating it, and even though Gen. 1-3 were mythical it might still be inspired. Aristotle said that poetry is truer than history. The latter only tells us that certain things happened. Poetry presents to us the permanent passions, aspirations and deeds of men which are behind all history and which make it what it is; see Dewey, Psychology, 197. Though Job were a drama and Jonah an apologue, both might be inspired. David Copperfield, the Apology of Socrates, Fra Lippo Lippi, were not the authors of the productions which bear their names, but Dickens, Plato and Browning, rather. Impersonation is a proper method in literature. The speeches of Herodotus and Thucydides might be analogues to those in Deuteronomy and in the Acts, and yet these last might be inspired.

The book of Job could not have been written in patriarchal times. Walled cities, kings, courts, lawsuits, prisons, stocks, mining enterprises, are found in it. Judges are bribed by the rich to decide against the poor. All this belongs to the latter years of the Jewish Kingdom. Is then the book of Job all a lie? No more than Bunyan's Pilgrim's Progress and the parable of the Good Samaritan are all a lie. The book of Job is a dramatic poem. Like Macbeth or the Ring and the Book, it is founded in fact. H. P. Smith, Biblical Scholarship and Inspiration, 101—"The value of the book of Job lies in the spectacle of a human soul in its direst affliction working through its doubts, and at last humbly confessing its weakness and sinfulness in the presence of its Maker. The inerrancy is not in Job's words or in those of his friends, but in the truth of the picture presented. If Jehovah's words at the end of the book are true, then the first thirty-five chapters are not infallible teaching."

Gore, in Lux Mundi, 355, suggests in a similar manner that the books of Jonah and of Daniel may be dramatic compositions worked up upon a basis of history. George Adam Smith, in the Expositors' Bible, tells us that Jonah flourished 780 B. C., in the reign of Jeroboam II. Nineveh fell in 606. The book implies that it was written after this (3:3—"Nineveh was an exceeding great city"). The book does not claim to be written by Jonah, by an eye-witness, or by a contemporary. The language has Aramaic forms. The date is probably 300 B. C. There is an absence of precise data, such as the sin of Nineveh, the journey of the prophet thither, the place where he was cast out on land, the name of the Assyrian king. The book illustrates God's mission of prophecy to the Gentiles, his care for them, their susceptibility to his word. Israel flies from duty, but is delivered to carry salvation to the heathen. Jeremiah had represented Israel as swallowed up and cast out (Jer. 51:34, 44 sq.—"Nebuchadnezzar the king of Babylon hath devoured me ... he hath, like a monster, swallowed me up, he hath filled his maw with my delicacies; he hath cast me out.... I will bring forth out of his mouth that which he hath swallowed up.") Some tradition of Jonah's proclaiming doom to Nineveh may have furnished the basis of the apologue. Our Lord uses the story as a mere illustration, like the homiletic use of Shakespeare's dramas. "As Macbeth did," "As Hamlet said," do not commit us to the historical reality of Macbeth or of Hamlet. Jesus may say as to questions of criticism: "Man, who made me a judge or a divider over you?" "I came not to judge the world, but to save the world" (Luke 12:14; John 12:47). He had no thought of confirming, or of not confirming, the historic character of the story. It is hard to conceive the compilation of a psalm by a man in Jonah's position. It is not the prayer of one inside the fish, but of one already saved. More than forty years ago President Woolsey of Yale conceded that the book of Jonah was probably an apologue.

(c) In none of these cases ought the difficulty of distinguishing man's words from God's words, or ideal truth from actual truth, to prevent our acceptance of the fact of inspiration; for in this very variety of the Bible, combined with the stimulus it gives to inquiry and the general plainness of its lessons, we have the very characteristics we should expect in a book whose authorship was divine.

The Scripture is a stream in which "the lamb may wade and the elephant may swim." There is need both of literary sense and of spiritual insight to interpret it. This sense and this insight can be given only by the Spirit of Christ, the Holy Spirit, who inspired the various writings to witness of him in various ways, and who is present in the world to take of the things of Christ and show them to us (Mat. 28:20; John 16:13, 14). In a subordinate sense the Holy Spirit inspires us to recognize inspiration in the Bible. In the sense here suggested we may assent to the words of Dr. Charles H. Parkhurst at the inauguration of William Adams Brown as Professor of Systematic Theology in the Union Theological Seminary, November 1, 1898—"Unfortunately we have condemned the word 'inspiration' to a particular and isolated field of divine operation, and it is a trespass upon current usage to employ it in the full urgency of its Scriptural intent in connection with work like your own or mine. But the word voices a reality that lies so close to the heart of the entire Christian matter that we can ill afford to relegate it to any single or technical function. Just as much to-day as back at the first beginnings of Christianity, those who would declare the truths of God must be inspired to behold the truths of God.... The only irresistible persuasiveness is that which is born of vision, and it is not vision to be able merely to describe what some seer has seen, though it were Moses or Paul that was the seer."

10. Acknowledgment of the non-inspiration of Scripture teachers and their writings

This charge rests mainly upon the misinterpretation of two particular passages:

(a) Acts 23:5 ("I wist not, brethren, that he was the high priest") may be explained either as the language of indignant irony: "I would not recognize such a man as high priest"; or, more naturally, an actual confession of personal ignorance and fallibility, which does not affect the inspiration of any of Paul's final teachings or writings.

Of a more reprehensible sort was Peter's dissimulation at Antioch, or practical disavowal of his convictions by separating or withdrawing himself from the Gentile Christians (Gal. 2:11-13). Here was no public teaching, but the influence of private example. But neither in this case, nor in that mentioned above, did God suffer the error to be a final one. Through the agency of Paul, the Holy Spirit set the matter right.

(b) 1 Cor. 7:12, 10 ("I, not the Lord"; "not I, but the Lord"). Here the contrast is not between the apostle inspired and the apostle uninspired, but between the apostle's words and an actual saying of our Lord, as in Mat. 5:32; 19:3-10; Mark 10:11; Luke 16:18 (Stanley on Corinthians). The expressions may be paraphrased:—"With regard to this matter no express command was given by Christ before his ascension. As one inspired by Christ, however, I give you my command."

Meyer on 1 Cor. 7:10—"Paul distinguishes, therefore, here and in verses 12, 25, not between his own and inspired commands, but between those which proceeded from his own (God-inspired) subjectivity and those which Christ himself supplied by his objective word." "Paul knew from the living voice of tradition what commands Christ had given concerning divorce." Or if it should be maintained that Paul here disclaims inspiration,—a supposition contradicted by the following δοκῶ—"I think that I also have the Spirit of God" (verse 40),—it only proves a single exception to his inspiration, and since it is expressly mentioned, and mentioned only once, it implies the inspiration of all the rest of his writings. We might illustrate Paul's method, if this were the case, by the course of the New York Herald when it was first published. Other journals had stood by their own mistakes and had never been willing to acknowledge error. The Herald gained the confidence of the public by correcting every mistake of its reporters. The result was that, when there was no confession of error, the paper was regarded as absolutely trustworthy. So Paul's one acknowledgment of non-inspiration might imply that in all other cases his words had divine authority. On Authority in Religion, see Wilfred Ward, in Hibbert Journal, July, 1903:677-692.

PART IV - THE NATURE, DECREES, AND WORKS OF GOD

Chapter I - The Attributes Of God

In contemplating the words and acts of God, as in contemplating the words and acts of individual men, we are compelled to assign uniform and permanent effects to uniform and permanent causes. Holy acts and words, we argue, must have their source in a principle of holiness; truthful acts and words, in a settled proclivity to truth; benevolent acts and words, in a benevolent disposition.

Moreover, these permanent and uniform sources of expression and action to which we have applied the terms principle, proclivity, disposition, since they exist harmoniously in the same person, must themselves inhere, and find their unity, in an underlying spiritual substance or reality of which they are the inseparable characteristics and partial manifestations.

Thus we are led naturally from the works to the attributes, and from the attributes to the essence, of God.

For all practical purposes we may use the words essence, substance, being, nature, as synonymous with each other. So, too, we may speak of attribute, quality, characteristic, principle, proclivity, disposition, as practically one. As, in cognizing matter, we pass from its effects in sensation to the qualities which produce the sensations, and then to the material substance to which the qualities belong; and as, in cognizing mind, we pass from its phenomena in thought and action to the faculties and dispositions which give rise to these phenomena, and then to the mental substance to which these faculties and dispositions belong; so, in cognizing God, we pass from his words and acts to his qualities or attributes, and then to the substance or essence to which these qualities or attributes belong.

The teacher in a Young Ladies' Seminary described substance as a cushion, into which the attributes as pins are stuck. But pins and cushion alike are substance,—neither one is quality. The opposite error is illustrated from the experience of Abraham Lincoln on the Ohio River. "What is this transcendentalism that we hear so much about?" asked Mr. Lincoln. The answer came: "You see those swallows digging holes in yonder bank? Well, take away the bank from around those holes, and what is left is transcendentalism." Substance is often represented as being thus transcendental. If such representations were correct, metaphysics would indeed be "that, of which those who listen understand nothing, and which he who speaks does not himself understand," and the metaphysician would be the fox who ran into the hole and then pulled in the hole after him. Substance and attributes are correlates,—neither one is possible without the other. There is no quality that does not qualify something; and there is no thing, either material or spiritual, that can be known or can exist without qualities to differentiate it from other things. In applying the categories of substance and attribute to God, we indulge in no merely curious speculation, but rather yield to the necessities of rational thought and show how we must think of God if we think at all. See Shedd, History of Doctrine, 1:240; Kahnis, Dogmatik, 3:172-188.

I. Definition of the term Attributes

The attributes of God are those distinguishing characteristics of the divine nature which are inseparable from the idea of God and which constitute the basis and ground for his various manifestations to his creatures.

We call them attributes, because we are compelled to attribute them to God as fundamental qualities or powers of his being, in order to give rational account of certain constant facts in God's self-revelations.

II. Relation of the divine Attributes to the divine Essence

1. The attributes have an objective existence. They are not mere names for human conceptions of God—conceptions which have their only ground in the imperfection of the finite mind. They are qualities objectively distinguishable from the divine essence and from each other.

The nominalistic notion that God is a being of absolute simplicity, and that in his nature there is no internal distinction of qualities or powers, tends directly to pantheism; denies all reality of the divine perfections; or, if these in any sense still exist, precludes all knowledge of them on the part of finite beings. To say that knowledge and power, eternity and holiness, are identical with the essence of God and with each other, is to deny that we know God at all.

The Scripture declarations of the possibility of knowing God, together with the manifestation of the distinct attributes of his nature, are conclusive against this false notion of the divine simplicity.

Aristotle says well that there is no such thing as a science of the unique, of that which has no analogies or relations. Knowing is distinguishing; what we cannot distinguish from other things we cannot know. Yet a false tendency to regard God as a being of absolute simplicity has come down from mediæval scholasticism, has infected much of the post-reformation theology, and is found even so recently as in Schleiermacher, Rothe, Olshausen, and Ritschl. E. G. Robinson defines the attributes as "our methods of conceiving of God." But this definition is influenced by the Kantian doctrine of relativity and implies that we cannot know God's essence, that is, the thing-in-itself, God's real being. Bowne, Philosophy of Theism, 141—"This notion of the divine simplicity reduces God to a rigid and lifeless stare.... The One is manifold without being many."

The divine simplicity is the starting-point of Philo: God is a being absolutely bare of quality. All quality in finite beings has limitation, and no limitation can be predicated of God who is eternal, unchangeable, simple substance, free, self-sufficient, better than the good and the beautiful. To predicate any quality of God would reduce him to the sphere of finite existence. Of him we can only say that he is, not what he is; see art. by Schürer, in Encyc. Brit., 18:761.

Illustrations of this tendency are found in Scotus Erigena: "Deus nescit se quid est, quia non est quid"; and in Occam: The divine attributes are distinguished neither substantially nor logically from each other or from the divine essence; the only distinction is that of names; so Gerhard and Quenstedt. Charnock, the Puritan writer, identifies both knowledge and will with the simple essence of God. Schleiermacher makes all the attributes to be modifications of power or causality; in his system God and world = the "natura naturans" and "natura naturata" of Spinoza. There is no distinction of attributes and no succession of acts in God, and therefore no real personality or even spiritual being; see Pfleiderer, Prot. Theol. seit Kant, 110. Schleiermacher said: "My God is the Universe." God is causative force. Eternity, omniscience and holiness are simply aspects of causality. Rothe, on the other hand, makes omniscience to be the all-comprehending principle of the divine nature; and Olshausen, on John 1:1, in a similar manner attempts to prove that the Word of God must have objective and substantial being, by assuming that knowing = willing; whence it would seem to follow that, since God wills all that he knows, he must will moral evil. Bushnell and others identify righteousness in God with benevolence, and therefore cannot see that any atonement needs to be made to God. Ritschl also holds that love is the fundamental divine attribute, and that omnipotence and even personality are simply modifications of love; see Mead, Ritschl's Place in the History of Doctrine, 8. Herbert Spencer only carries the principle further when he concludes God to be simple unknowable force.

But to call God everything is the same as to call him nothing. With Dorner, we say that "definition is no limitation." As we rise in the scale of creation from the mere jelly-sac to man, the homogeneous becomes the heterogeneous, there is differentiation of functions, complexity increases. We infer that God, the highest of all, instead of being simple force, is infinitely complex, that he has an infinite variety of attributes and powers. Tennyson, Palace of Art (lines omitted in the later editions): "All nature widens upward: evermore The simpler essence lower lies: More complex is more perfect, owning more Discourse, more widely wise."

Jer. 10:10—God is "the living God"; John 5:26—he "hath life in himself"—unsearchable riches of positive attributes; John 17:23—"thou lovedst me"—manifoldness in unity. This complexity in God is the ground of blessedness for him and of progress for us: 1 Tim. 1:11—"the blessed God"; Jer. 9:23, 24—"let him glory in this, that he knoweth me." The complex nature of God permits anger at the sinner and compassion for him at the same moment: Ps. 7:11—"a God that hath indignation every day"; John 3:16—"God so loved the world"; Ps. 85:10, 11—"mercy and truth are met together." See Julius Müller, Doct. Sin, 2:116 sq.; Schweizer, Glaubenslehre, 1:229-235; Thomasius, Christi Person und Werk, 1:43, 50; Martensen, Dogmatics, 91—"If God were the simple One, τὸ ἀπλῶς ἕν, the mystic abyss in which every form of determination were extinguished, there would be nothing in the Unity to be known." Hence "nominalism is incompatible with the idea of revelation. We teach, with realism, that the attributes of God are objective determinations in his revelation and as such are rooted in his inmost essence."

2. The attributes inhere in the divine essence. They are not separate existences. They are attributes

of God.

While we oppose the nominalistic view which holds them to be mere names with which, by the necessity of our thinking, we clothe the one simple divine essence, we need equally to avoid the opposite realistic extreme of making them separate parts of a composite God.

We cannot conceive of attributes except as belonging to an underlying essence which furnishes their ground of unity. In representing God as a compound of attributes, realism endangers the living unity of the Godhead.

Notice the analogous necessity of attributing the properties of matter to an underlying substance, and the phenomena of thought to an underlying spiritual essence; else matter is reduced to mere force, and mind, to mere sensation,—in short, all things are swallowed up in a vast idealism. The purely realistic explanation of the attributes tends to low and polytheistic conceptions of God. The mythology of Greece was the result of personifying the divine attributes. The nomina were turned into numina, as Max Müller says; see Taylor, Nature on the Basis of Realism, 293. Instance also Christmas Evans's sermon describing a Council in the Godhead, in which the attributes of Justice, Mercy, Wisdom, and Power argue with one another. Robert Hall called Christmas Evans "the one-eyed orator of Anglesey," but added that his one eye could "light an army through a wilderness"; see Joseph Cross, Life and Sermons of Christmas Evans, 112-116; David Rhys Stephen, Memoirs of Christmas Evans, 168-176. We must remember that "Realism may so exalt the attributes that no personal subject is left to constitute the ground of unity. Looking upon Personality as anthropomorphism, it falls into a worse personification, that of omnipotence, holiness, benevolence, which are mere blind thoughts, unless there is one who is the Omnipotent, the Holy, the Good." See Luthardt, Compendium der Dogmatik, 70.

3. The attributes belong to the divine essence as such. They are to be distinguished from those other powers or relations which do not appertain to the divine essence universally.

The personal distinctions (proprietates) in the nature of the one God are not to be denominated attributes; for each of these personal distinctions belongs not to the divine essence as such and universally, but only to the particular person of the Trinity who bears its name, while on the contrary all of the attributes belong to each of the persons.

The relations which God sustains to the world (predicata), moreover, such as creation, preservation, government, are not to be denominated attributes; for these are accidental, not necessary or inseparable from the idea of God. God would be God, if he had never created.

To make creation eternal and necessary is to dethrone God and to enthrone a fatalistic development. It follows that the nature of the attributes is to be illustrated, not alone or chiefly from wisdom and holiness in man, which are not inseparable from man's nature, but rather from intellect and will in man, without which he would cease to be man altogether. Only that is an attribute, of which it can be safely said that he who possesses it would, if deprived of it, cease to be God. Shedd, Dogm. Theol., 1:335—"The attribute is the whole essence acting in a certain way. The centre of unity is not in any one attribute, but in the essence.... The difference between the divine attribute and the divine person is, that the person is a mode of the existence of the essence, while the attribute is a mode either of the relation, or of the operation, of the essence."

4. The attributes manifest the divine essence. The essence is revealed only through the attributes. Apart from its attributes it is unknown and unknowable.

But though we can know God only as he reveals to us his attributes, we do, notwithstanding, in knowing these attributes, know the being to whom these attributes belong. That this knowledge is partial does not prevent its corresponding, so far as it goes, to objective reality in the nature of God.

All God's revelations are, therefore, revelations of himself in and through his attributes. Our aim must be to determine from God's works and words what qualities, dispositions, determinations, powers of his otherwise unseen and unsearchable essence he has actually made known to us; or in other words, what are the revealed attributes of God.

John 1:18—"No man hath seen God at any time; the only begotten Son, who is in the bosom of the Father, he hath declared him"; 1 Tim. 6:16—"whom no man hath seen, nor can see"; Mat. 5:8—"Blessed are the pure in heart: for they shall see God"; 11:27—"neither doth any man know the Father, save the Son, and he to whomsoever the Son willeth to reveal him." C. A. Strong: "Kant, not content with knowing the reality in the phenomena, was trying to know the reality apart from the phenomena; he was seeking to know, without fulfilling the conditions of knowledge; in short, he wished to know without knowing." So Agnosticism perversely regards God as concealed by his own manifestation. On the contrary, in knowing the phenomena we know the object itself. J. C. C. Clarke, Self and the Father, 6—"In language, as in nature, there are no verbs without subjects, but we are always hunting for the noun that has no adjective, and the verb that has no subject, and the subject that has no verb. Consciousness is necessarily a consciousness of self. Idealism and monism would like to see all verbs solid with their subjects, and to write 'I do' or 'I feel' in the mazes of a monogram, but consciousness refuses, and before it says 'Do' or 'Feel' it finishes saying 'I.' " J. G. Holland's Katrina, to her lover: "God is not worshiped in his attributes. I do not love your attributes, but you. Your attributes all meet me otherwhere, Blended in other personalities, Nor do I love nor do I worship them, Nor those who bear them. E'en the spotted pard Will dare a danger which will make you pale; But shall his courage steal my heart from you? You cheat your conscience, for you know That I may like your attributes. Yet love not you."

III. Methods of determining the divine Attributes

We have seen that the existence of God is a first truth. It is presupposed in all human thinking, and is more or less consciously recognized by all men. This intuitive knowledge of God we have seen to be corroborated and explicated by arguments drawn from nature and from mind. Reason leads us to a causative and personal Intelligence upon whom we depend. This Being of indefinite greatness we clothe, by a necessity of our thinking, with all the attributes of perfection. The two great methods of determining what these attributes are, are the Rational and the Biblical.

1. The Rational method. This is threefold:—(a) the via negationis, or the way of negation, which consists in denying to God all imperfections observed in created beings; (b) the via eminentiæ, or the way of climax, which consists in attributing to God in infinite degree all the perfections found in creatures; and (c) the via causalitatis, or the way of causality, which consists in predicating of God those attributes which are required in him to explain the world of nature and of mind.

This rational method explains God's nature from that of his creation, whereas the creation itself can be fully explained only from the nature of God. Though the method is valuable, it has insuperable limitations, and its place is a subordinate one. While we use it continually to confirm and supplement results otherwise obtained, our chief means of determining the divine attributes must be

2. The Biblical method. This is simply the inductive method, applied to the facts with regard to God revealed in the Scriptures. Now that we have proved the Scriptures to be a revelation from God, inspired in every part, we may properly look to them as decisive authority with regard to God's attributes.

The rational method of determining the attributes of God is sometimes said to have been originated by Dionysius the Areopagite, reputed to have been a judge at Athens at the time of Paul and to have died A. D. 95. It is more probably eclectic, combining the results attained by many theologians, and applying the intuitions of perfection and causality which lie at the basis of all religious thinking. It is evident from our previous study of the arguments for God's existence, that from nature we cannot learn either the Trinity or the mercy of God, and that these deficiencies in our rational conclusions with respect to God must be supplied, if at all, by revelation. Spurgeon, Autobiography, 166—"The old saying is 'Go from Nature up to Nature's God.' But it is hard work going up hill. The best thing is to go from Nature's God down to Nature; and, if you once get to Nature's God and believe him and love him, it is surprising how easy it is to hear music in the waves, and songs in the wild whisperings of the winds, and to see God everywhere." See also Kahnis, Dogmatik, 3:181.

IV. Classification of the Attributes

The attributes may be divided into two great classes: Absolute or Immanent, and Relative or Transitive.

By Absolute or Immanent Attributes, we mean attributes which respect the inner being of God, which are involved in God's relations to himself, and which belong to his nature independently of his connection with the universe.

By Relative or Transitive Attributes, we mean attributes which respect the outward revelation of God's being, which are involved in God's relations to the creation, and which are exercised in consequence of the existence of the universe and its dependence upon him.

Under the head of Absolute or Immanent Attributes, we make a three-fold division into Spirituality, with the attributes therein involved, namely, Life and Personality; Infinity, with the attributes therein involved, namely, Self-existence, Immutability, and Unity; and Perfection, with the attributes therein involved, namely, Truth, Love, and Holiness.

Under the head of Relative or Transitive Attributes, we make a three-fold division, according to the order of their revelation, into Attributes having relation to Time and Space, as Eternity and Immensity; Attributes having relation to Creation, as Omnipresence, Omniscience, and Omnipotence; and Attributes having relation to Moral Beings, as Veracity and Faithfulness, or Transitive Truth; Mercy and Goodness, or Transitive Love; and Justice and Righteousness, or Transitive Holiness.

This classification may be better understood from the following schedule:

1. Absolute or Immanent Attributes: A. Spirituality, involving (a) Life, (b) Personality. B. Infinity, involving (a) Self-existence, (b) Immutability, (c) Unity. C. Perfection, involving (a) Truth, (b) Love, (c) Holiness.

2. Relative or Transitive Attributes: A. Related to Time and Space—(a) Eternity, (b) Immensity. B. Related to Creation—(a) Omnipresence, (b) Omniscience, (c) Omnipotence. C. Related to Moral

Beings—(a) Veracity, (b) Mercy, (c) Justice.

It will be observed, upon examination of the preceding schedule, that our classification presents God first as Spirit, then as the infinite Spirit, and finally as the perfect Spirit. This accords with our definition of the term God (see page 52). It also corresponds with the order in which the attributes commonly present themselves to the human mind. Our first thought of God is that of mere Spirit, mysterious and undefined, over against our own spirits. Our next thought is that of God's greatness; the quantitative element suggests itself; his natural attributes rise before us; we recognize him as the infinite One. Finally comes the qualitative element; our moral natures recognize a moral God; over against our error, selfishness and impurity, we perceive his absolute perfection.

It should also be observed that this moral perfection, as it is an immanent attribute, involves relation of God to himself. Truth, love and holiness, as they respectively imply an exercise in God of intellect, affection and will, may be conceived of as God's self-knowing, God's self-loving, and God's self-willing. The significance of this will appear more fully in the discussion of the separate attributes.

Notice the distinction between absolute and relative, between immanent and transitive, attributes. Absolute = existing in no necessary relation to things outside of God. Relative = existing in such relation. Immanent = "remaining within, limited to, God's own nature in their activity and effect, inherent and indwelling, internal and subjective—opposed to emanent or transitive." Transitive = having an object outside of God himself. We speak of transitive verbs, and we mean verbs that are followed by an object. God's transitive attributes are so called, because they respect and affect things and beings outside of God.

The aim of this classification into Absolute and Relative Attributes is to make plain the divine self-sufficiency. Creation is not a necessity, for there is a πλήρωμα in God (Col. 1:19), even before he makes the world or becomes incarnate. And πλήρωμα is not "the filling material," nor "the vessel filled," but "that which is complete in itself," or, in other words, "plenitude," "fulness," "totality," "abundance." The whole universe is but a drop of dew upon the fringe of God's garment, or a breath exhaled from his mouth. He could create a universe a hundred times as great. Nature is but the symbol of God. The tides of life that ebb and flow on the far shores of the universe are only faint expressions of his life. The Immanent Attributes show us how completely matters of grace are Creation and Redemption, and how unspeakable is the condescension of him who took our humanity and humbled himself to the death of the Cross. Ps. 8:3, 4—"When I consider thy heavens ... what is man that thou art mindful of him?" 113:5, 6—"Who is like unto Jehovah our God, that hath his seat on high, that humbleth himself?" Phil. 2:6, 7—"Who, existing in the form of God, ... emptied himself, taking the form of a servant."

Ladd, Theory of Reality, 69—"I know that I am, because, as the basis of all discriminations as to what I am, and as the core of all such self-knowledge, I immediately know myself as will" So as to the non-ego, "that things actually are is a factor in my knowledge of them which springs from the root of an experience with myself as a will, at once active and inhibited, as an agent and yet opposed by another." The ego and the non-ego as well are fundamentally and essentially will. "Matter must be, per se, Force. But this is ... to be a Will" (439). We know nothing of the atom apart from its force (442). Ladd quotes from G. E. Bailey: "The life-principle, varying only in degree, is omnipresent. There is but one indivisible and absolute Omniscience and Intelligence, and this thrills through every atom of the whole Cosmos" (446). "Science has only made the Substrate of material things more and more completely self-like" (449). Spirit is the true and essential Being of what is called Nature (472). "The ultimate Being of the world is a self-conscious Mind and Will, which is the Ground of all objects made known in human experience" (550).

On classification of attributes, see Luthardt, Compendium, 71; Rothe, Dogmatik, 71; Kahnis, Dogmatik, 3:162; Thomasius, Christi Person und Werk, 1:47, 52, 136. On the general subject, see Charnock, Attributes; Bruce, Eigenschaftslehre.

V. Absolute or Immanent Attributes

First division.—Spirituality, and attributes therein involved.

In calling spirituality an attribute of God, we mean, not that we are justified in applying to the divine nature the adjective "spiritual," but that the substantive "Spirit" describes that nature (John 4:24, marg.—"God is spirit"; Rom. 1:20—"the invisible things of him"; 1 Tim. 1:17—"incorruptible, invisible"; Col. 1:15—"the invisible God"). This implies, negatively, that (a) God is not matter. Spirit is not a refined form of matter but an immaterial substance, invisible, uncompounded, indestructible. (b) God is not dependent upon matter. It cannot be shown that the human mind, in any other state than the present, is dependent for consciousness upon its connection with a physical organism. Much less is it true that God is dependent upon the material universe as his sensorium. God is not only spirit, but he is pure spirit. He is not only not matter, but he has no necessary connection with matter (Luke 24:39—"A spirit hath not flesh and bones, as ye behold me having").

John gives us the three characteristic attributes of God when he says that God is "spirit," "light," "love" (John 4:24; 1 John 1:5; 4:8),—not a spirit, a light, a love. Le Conte, in Royce's Conception of God, 45—"God is spirit, for spirit is essential Life and essential Energy, and essential Love, and essential Thought; in a word, essential Person." Biedermann, Dogmatik, 631—"Das Wesen des Geistes als des reinen Gegensatzes zur Materie, ist das reine Sein, das in sich ist, aber nicht da ist." Martineau, Study, 2:366—"The subjective Ego is always here, as opposed to all else, which is variously there.... Without local relations, therefore, the soul is inaccessible." But, Martineau continues, "if matter be but centres of force, all the soul needs may be centres from which to act." Romanes, Mind and Motion, 34—"Because within the limits of human experience mind is only known as associated with brain, it does not follow that mind cannot exist in any other mode." La Place swept the heavens with his telescope, but could not find anywhere a God. "He might just as well," says President Sawyer, "have swept his kitchen with a broom." Since God is not a material being, he cannot be apprehended by any physical means.

Those passages of Scripture which seem to ascribe to God the possession of bodily parts and organs, as eyes and hands, are to be regarded as anthropomorphic and symbolic. "When God is spoken of as appearing to the patriarchs and walking with them, the passages are to be explained as referring to God's temporary manifestations of himself in human form—manifestations which prefigured the final tabernacling of the Son of God in human flesh. Side by side with these anthropomorphic expressions and manifestations, moreover, are specific declarations which repress any materializing conceptions of God; as, for example, that heaven is his throne and the earth his footstool (Is. 66:1), and that the heaven of heavens cannot contain him (1 K. 8:27)."

Ex. 33:18-20 declares that man cannot see God and live; 1 Cor. 2:7-16 intimates that without the teaching of God's Spirit we cannot know God; all this teaches that God is above sensuous perception, in other words, that he is not a material being. The second command of the decalogue does not condemn sculpture and painting, but only the making of images of God. It forbids our conceiving God after the likeness of a thing, but it does not forbid our conceiving God after the likeness of our inward self, i. e., as personal. This again shows that God is a spiritual being. Imagination can be used in religion, and great help can be derived from it. Yet we do not know God by imagination,—imagination only helps us vividly to realize the presence of the God whom we already know. We may almost say that some men have not imagination enough to be religious. But imagination must not lose its wings. In its representations of God, it must not be confined to a picture, or a form, or a place. Humanity tends too much to rest in the material and the sensuous, and we must avoid all representations of God which would identify the Being who is worshiped with the helps used in order to realize his presence; John 4:24—"they that worship him must worship in spirit and truth."

An Egyptian Hymn to the Nile, dating from the 19th dynasty (14th century B. C.), contains these words: "His abode is not known; no shrine is found with painted figures; there is no building that can contain him" (Cheyne, Isaiah, 2:120). The repudiation of images among the ancient Persians (Herod. 1:131), as among the Japanese Shintos, indicates the remains of a primitive spiritual religion. The representation of Jehovah with body or form degrades him to the level of heathen gods. Pictures of the Almighty over the chancels of Romanist cathedrals confine the mind and degrade the conception of the worshiper. We may use imagination in prayer, picturing God as a benignant form holding out arms of mercy, but we should regard such pictures only as scaffolding for the building of our edifice of worship, while we recognize, with the Scripture, that the reality worshiped is immaterial and spiritual. Otherwise our idea of God is brought down to the low level of man's material being. Even man's spiritual nature may be misrepresented by physical images, as when mediæval artists pictured death, by painting a doll-like figure leaving the body at the mouth of the person dying.

The longing for a tangible, incarnate God meets its satisfaction in Jesus Christ. Yet even pictures of Christ soon lose their power. Luther said: "If I have a picture of Christ in my heart, why not one upon canvas?" We answer: Because the picture in the heart is capable of change and improvement, as we ourselves change and improve; the picture upon canvas is fixed, and holds to old conceptions which we should outgrow. Thomas Carlyle: "Men never think of painting the face of Christ, till they lose the impression of him upon their hearts." Swedenborg, in modern times, represents the view that God exists in the shape of a man—an anthropomorphism of which the making of idols is only a grosser and more barbarous form; see H. B. Smith, System of Theology, 9, 10. This is also the doctrine of Mormonism; see Spencer, Catechism of Latter Day Saints. The Mormons teach that God is a man; that he has numerous wives by whom he peoples space with an infinite number of spirits. Christ was a favorite son by a favorite wife, but birth as man was the only way he could come into the enjoyment of real life. These spirits are all the sons of God, but they can realize and enjoy their sonship only through birth. They are about every one of us pleading to be born. Hence, polygamy.

We come now to consider the positive import of the term Spirit. The spirituality of God involves the two attributes of Life and Personality.

1. Life

The Scriptures represent God as the living God.

Jer. 10:10—"He is the living God"; 1 Thess. 1:9—"turned unto God from idols, to serve a living and true God"; John 5:26-"hath life in himself"; cf. 14:6—"I am ... the life," and Heb. 7:16—"the power of an endless life"; Rev. 11:11—"the Spirit of life."

Life is a simple idea, and is incapable of real definition. We know it, however, in ourselves, and we can perceive the insufficiency or inconsistency of certain current definitions of it. We cannot regard life in God as

(a) Mere process, without a subject; for we cannot conceive of a divine life without a God to live it.

Versus Lewes, Problems of Life and Mind, 1:10—"Life and mind are processes; neither is a substance; neither is a force; ... the name given to the whole group of phenomena becomes the personification of the phenomena, and the product is supposed to have been the producer." Here we have a product without any producer—a series of phenomena without any substance of which they are manifestations. In a similar manner we read in Dewey, Psychology, 247—"Self is an activity. It is not something which acts; it is activity.... It is constituted by activities.... Through its activity the soul is." Here it does not appear how there can be activity, without any subject or being that is active. The inconsistency of this view is manifest when Dewey goes on to say: "The activity may further or develop the self," and when he speaks of "the organic activity of the self." So Dr. Burdon Sanderson: "Life is a state of ceaseless change,—a state of change with permanence; living matter ever changes while it is ever the same." "Plus ça change, plus c'est la même chose." But this permanent thing in the midst of change is the subject, the self, the being, that has life.

Nor can we regard life as

(b) Mere correspondence with outward condition and environment; for this would render impossible a life of God before the existence of the universe.

Versus Herbert Spencer, Biology, 1:59-71—"Life is the definite combination of heterogeneous changes, both simultaneous and successive, in correspondence with external coëxistences and sequences." Here we have, at best, a definition of physical and finite life; and even this is insufficient, because the definition recognizes no original source of activity within, but only a power of reaction in response to stimulus from without. We might as well say that the boiling tea-kettle is alive (Mark Hopkins). We find this defect also in Robert Browning's lines in The Ring and the Book (The Pope, 1307): "O Thou—as represented here to me In such conception as my soul allows—Under thy measureless, my atom-width!—Man's mind, what is it but a convex glass Wherein are gathered all the scattered points Picked out of the immensity of sky, To reunite there, be our heaven for earth, Our known Unknown, our God revealed to man?" Life is something more than a passive receptivity.

(c) Life is rather mental energy, or energy of intellect, affection, and will. God is the living God, as having in his own being a source of being and activity, both for himself and others.

Life means energy, activity, movement. Aristotle: "Life is energy of mind." Wordsworth, Excursion, book 5:602—"Life is love and immortality, The Being one, and one the element.... Life, I repeat, is energy of love Divine or human." Prof. C. L. Herrick, on Critics of Ethical Monism, in Denison Quarterly, Dec. 1896:248—"Force is energy under resistance, or self-limited energy, for all parts of the universe are derived from the energy. Energy manifesting itself under self-conditioning or differential forms is force. The change of pure energy into force is creation." Prof. Herrick quotes from S. T. Coleridge, Anima Poetæ: "Space is the name for God; it is the most perfect image of soul—pure soul being to us nothing but unresisted action. Whenever action is resisted, limitation begins—and limitation is the first constituent of body; the more omnipresent it is in a given space, the more that space is body or matter; and thus all body presupposes soul, inasmuch as all resistance presupposes action." Schelling: "Life is the tendency to individualism."

If spirit in man implies life, spirit in God implies endless and inexhaustible life. The total life of the universe is only a faint image of that moving energy which we call the life of God. Dewey, Psychology, 253—"The sense of being alive is much more vivid in childhood than afterwards. Leigh Hunt says that, when he was a child, the sight of certain palings painted red gave him keener pleasure than any experience of manhood." Matthew Arnold: "Bliss was it in that dawn to be alive, But to be young was very heaven." The child's delight in country scenes, and our intensified perceptions in brain fever, show us by contrast how shallow and turbid is the stream of our ordinary life. Tennyson, Two Voices: "'Tis life, whereof our nerves are scant, Oh life, not death, for which we pant; More life, and fuller, that we want." That life the needy human spirit finds only in the infinite God. Instead of Tyndall's: "Matter has in it the promise and potency of every form of life," we accept Sir William Crookes's dictum: "Life has in it the promise and potency of every form of matter." See A. H. Strong, on The Living God, in Philos. and Religion, 180-187.

2. Personality

The Scriptures represent God as a personal being. By personality we mean the power of self-consciousness and of self-determination. By way of further explanation we remark:

(a) Self-consciousness is more than consciousness. This last the brute may be supposed to possess, since the brute is not an automaton. Man is distinguished from the brute by his power to objectify self. Man is not only conscious of his own acts and states, but by abstraction and reflection he recognizes the self which is the subject of these acts and states. (b) Self-determination is more than determination. The brute shows determination, but his determination is the result of influences from without; there is no inner spontaneity. Man, by virtue of his free-will, determines his action from within. He determines self in view of motives, but his determination is not caused by motives; he himself is the cause.

God, as personal, is in the highest degree self-conscious and self-determining. The rise in our own minds of the idea of God, as personal, depends largely upon our recognition of personality in ourselves. Those who deny spirit in man place a bar in the way of the recognition of this attribute of God.

Ex. 3:14—"And God said unto Moses, I AM THAT I AM: and he said, Thus shalt thou say unto the children of Israel, I AM hath sent me unto you." God is not the everlasting "IT IS," or "I WAS," but the everlasting "I AM" (Morris, Philosophy and Christianity, 128); "I AM" implies both personality and presence. 1 Cor. 2:11—"the things of God none knoweth, save the Spirit of God"; Eph. 1:9—"good pleasure which he purposed"; 11—"the counsel of his will." Definitions of personality are the following: Boethius—"Persona est animæ rationalis individua substantia" (quoted in Dorner, Glaubenslehre, 2:415). F. W. Robertson, Genesis 3—"Personality = self-consciousness, will, character." Porter, Human Intellect, 626—"Distinct subsistence, either actually or latently self-conscious and self-determining." Harris, Philos. Basis of Theism: Person = "being, conscious of self, subsisting in individuality and identity, and endowed with intuitive reason, rational sensibility, and free-will." See Harris, 98, 99, quotation from Mansel—"The freedom of the will is so far from being, as it is generally considered, a controvertible question in philosophy, that it is the fundamental postulate without which all action and all speculation, philosophy in all its branches and human consciousness itself, would be impossible."

One of the most astounding announcements in all literature is that of Matthew Arnold, in his "Literature and Dogma," that the Hebrew Scriptures recognize in God only "the power, not ourselves, that makes for righteousness" = the God of pantheism. The "I AM" of Ex. 3:14 could hardly have been so misunderstood, if Matthew Arnold had not lost the sense of his own personality and responsibility. From free-will in man we rise to freedom in God—"That living Will that shall endure, When all that seems shall suffer shock." Observe that personality needs to be accompanied by life—the power of self-consciousness and self-determination needs to be accompanied by activity—in order to make up our total idea of God as Spirit. Only this personality of God gives proper meaning to his punishments or to his forgiveness. See Bib. Sac., April, 1884:217-233; Eichhorn, die Persönlichkeit Gottes.

Illingworth, Divine and Human Personality, 1:25, shows that the sense of personality has had a gradual growth; that its pre-Christian recognition was imperfect; that its final definition has been due to Christianity. In 29-53, he notes the characteristics of personality as reason, love, will. The brute perceives; only the man apperceives, i. e., recognizes his perception as belonging to himself. In the German story, Dreiäuglein, the three-eyed child, had besides her natural pair of eyes one other to see what the pair did, and besides her natural will had an additional will to set the first to going right. On consciousness and self-consciousness, see Shedd, Dogm. Theol., 1:179-189—"In consciousness the object is another substance than the subject; but in self-consciousness the object is the same substance as the subject." Tennyson, in his Palace of Art, speaks of "the abysmal depths of personality." We do not fully know ourselves, nor yet our relation to God. But the divine consciousness embraces the whole divine content of being: "the Spirit searcheth all things, yea, the deep things of God" (1 Cor. 2:10).

We are not fully masters of ourselves. Our self-determination is as limited as is our self-consciousness. But the divine will is absolutely without hindrance; God's activity is constant, intense, infinite; Job 23:13—"What his soul desireth, even that he doeth"; John 5:17—"My Father worketh even until now, and I work." Self-knowledge and self-mastery are the dignity of man; they are also the dignity of God; Tennyson: "Self-reverence, self-knowledge, self-control, These three lead life to sovereign power." Robert Browning, The Last Ride Together: "What act proved all its thought had been? What will but felt the fleshly screen?" Moberly, Atonement and Personality, 6, 161, 216-255— "Perhaps the root of personality is capacity for affection."... Our personality is incomplete; we reason truly only with God helping; our love in higher Love endures; we will rightly, only as God works in us to will and to do; to make us truly ourselves we need an infinite Personality to supplement and energize our own; we are complete only in Christ (Col. 2:9, 10—"In him dwelleth all the fulness of the Godhead bodily, and in him ye are made full.")

Webb, on the Idea of Personality as applied to God, in Jour. Theol. Studies, 2:50—"Self knows itself and what is not itself as two, just because both alike are embraced within the unity of its experience, stand out against this background, the apprehension of which is the very essence of that rationality or personality which distinguishes us from the lower animals. We find that background, God, present in us, or rather, we find ourselves present in it. But if I find myself present in it, then it, as more complete, is simply more personal than I. Our not-self is outside of us, so that we are finite and lonely, but God's not-self is within him, so that there is a mutual inwardness of love and insight of which the most perfect communion among men is only a faint symbol. We are 'hermit-spirits,' as Keble says, and we come to union with others only by realizing our union with God. Personality is not impenetrable in man, for 'in him we live, and move, and have our being' (Acts 17:28), and 'that which hath been made is life in him' (John 1:3, 4).". Palmer, Theologic Definition, 39—"That which has its cause without itself is a thing, while that which has its cause within itself is a person."

Second Division.—Infinity, and attributes therein involved.

By infinity we mean, not that the divine nature has no known limits or bounds, but that it has no limits or bounds. That which has simply no known limits is the indefinite. The infinity of God implies that he is in no way limited by the universe or confined to the universe; he is transcendent as well as immanent. Transcendence, however, must not be conceived as freedom from merely spatial restrictions, but rather as unlimited resource, of which God's glory is the expression.

Ps. 145:3—"his greatness is unsearchable"; Job 11:7-9—"high as heaven ... deeper than Sheol"; Is. 66:1—"Heaven is my throne, and the earth is my footstool"; 1 K. 8:27—"Heaven and the heaven of heavens cannot contain thee"; Rom. 11:33—"how unsearchable are his judgments, and his ways past finding out." There can be no infinite number, since to any assignable number a unit can be added, which shows that this number was not infinite before. There can be no infinite universe, because an infinite universe is conceivable only as an infinite number of worlds or of minds. God himself is the only real Infinite, and the universe is but the finite expression or symbol of his greatness.

We therefore object to the statement of Lotze, Microcosm, 1:446—"The complete system, grasped in its totality, offers an expression of the whole nature of the One.... The Cause makes actual existence its complete manifestation." In a similar way Schurman, Belief in God, 26, 173-178, grants infinity, but denies transcendence: "The infinite Spirit may include the finite, as the idea of a single organism embraces within a single life a plurality of members and functions.... The world is the expression of an ever active and inexhaustible will. That the external manifestation is as boundless as the life it expresses, science makes exceedingly probable. In any event, we have not the slightest reason to contrast the finitude of the world with the infinity of God.... If the natural order is eternal and infinite, as there seems no reason to doubt, it will be difficult to find a meaning for 'beyond' or 'before.' Of this illimitable, ever-existing universe, God is the Inner ground or substance. There is no evidence, neither does any religious need require us to believe, that the divine Being manifest in the universe has any actual or possible existence elsewhere, in some transcendent sphere.... The divine will can express itself only as it does, because no other expression would reveal what it is. Of such a will, the universe is the eternal expression."

In explanation of the term infinity, we may notice:

(a) That infinity can belong to but one Being, and therefore cannot be shared with the universe. Infinity is not a negative but a positive idea. It does not take its rise from an impotence of thought, but is an intuitive conviction which constitutes the basis of all other knowledge.

See Porter, Human Intellect, 651, 652, and this Compendium, pages 59-62. Versus Mansel, Proleg. Logica, chap. 1—"Such negative notions ... imply at once an attempt to think, and a failure in that attempt." On the contrary, the conception of the Infinite is perfectly distinguishable from that of the finite, and is both necessary and logically prior to that of the finite. This is not true of our idea of the universe, of which all we know is finite and dependent. We therefore regard such utterances as those of Lotze and Schurman above, and those of Chamberlin and Caird below, as pantheistic in tendency, although the belief of these writers in divine and human personality saves them from falling into other errors of pantheism.

Prof. T. C. Chamberlin, of the University of Chicago: "It is not sufficient to the modern scientific thought to think of a Ruler outside of the universe, nor of a universe with the Ruler outside. A supreme Being who does not embrace all the activities and possibilities and potencies of the universe seems something less than the supremest Being, and a universe with a Ruler outside seems something less than a universe. And therefore the thought is growing on the minds of scientific thinkers that the supreme Being is the universal Being, embracing and comprehending all things." Caird, Evolution of Religion, 2:62—"Religion, if it would continue to exist, must combine the monotheistic idea with that which it has often regarded as its greatest enemy, the spirit of pantheism." We grant in reply that religion must appropriate the element of truth in pantheism, namely, that God is the only substance, ground and principle of being, but we regard it as fatal to religion to side with pantheism in its denials of God's transcendence and of God's personality.

(b) That the infinity of God does not involve his identity with "the all," or the sum of existence, nor prevent the coëxistence of derived and finite beings to which he bears relation. Infinity implies simply that God exists in no necessary relation to finite things or beings, and that whatever limitation of the divine nature results from their existence is, on the part of God, a self-limitation.

Ps. 113:5, 6—"that humbleth himself to behold the things that are in heaven and in the earth." It is involved in God's infinity that there should be no barriers to his self-limitation in creation and redemption (see page 9, F.). Jacob Boehme said: "God is infinite, for God is all." But this is to make God all imperfection, as well as all perfection. Harris, Philos. Basis Theism: "The relation of the absolute to the finite is not the mathematical relation of a total to its parts, but it is a dynamical and rational relation." Shedd, Dogm. Theol., 1:189-191—"The infinite is not the total; 'the all' is a pseudo-infinite, and to assert that it is greater than the simple infinite is the same error that is committed in mathematics when it is asserted that an infinite number plus a vast finite number is greater than the simple infinite." Fullerton, Conception of the Infinite, 90—"The Infinite, though it involves unlimited possibility of quantity, is not itself a quantitative but rather a qualitative conception." Hovey, Studies of Ethics and Religion, 39-47—"Any number of finite beings, minds, loves, wills, cannot reveal fully an infinite Being, Mind, Love, Will. God must be transcendent as well as immanent in the universe, or he is neither infinite nor an object of supreme worship."

Clarke, Christian Theology, 117—"Great as the universe is, God is not limited to it, wholly absorbed by what he is doing in it, and capable of doing nothing more. God in the universe is not like the life of the tree in the tree, which does all that it is capable of in making the tree what it is. God in the universe is rather like the spirit of a man in his body, which is greater than his body, able to direct his body, and capable of activities in which his body has no share. God is a free spirit, personal, self-directing, unexhausted by his present activities." The Persian poet said truly: "The world is a bud from his bower of beauty; the sun is a spark from the light of his wisdom; the sky is a bubble on the sea of his power." Faber: "For greatness which is infinite makes room For all things in its lap to lie. We should be crushed by a magnificence Short of infinity. We share in what is infinite; 'tis ours, For we and it alike are Thine. What I enjoy, great God, by right of Thee, Is more than doubly mine."

(c) That the infinity of God is to be conceived of as intensive, rather than as extensive. We do not attribute to God infinite extension, but rather infinite energy of spiritual life. That which acts up to the measure of its power is simply natural and physical force. Man rises above nature by virtue of his reserves of power. But in God the reserve is infinite. There is a transcendent element in him, which no self-revelation exhausts, whether creation or redemption, whether law or promise.

Transcendence is not mere outsideness,—it is rather boundless supply within. God is not infinite by virtue of existing "extra flammantia mœnia mundi" (Lucretius) or of filling a space outside of space,—he is rather infinite by being the pure and perfect Mind that passes beyond all phenomena and constitutes the ground of them. The former conception of infinity is simply supra-cosmic, the latter alone is properly transcendent; see Hatch, Hibbert Lectures, 244. "God is the living God, and has not yet spoken his last word on any subject" (G. W. Northrup). God's life "operates unspent." There is "ever more to follow." The legend stamped with the Pillars of Hercules upon the old coins of Spain was Ne plus ultra—"Nothing beyond," but when Columbus discovered America the legend was fitly changed to Plus ultra—"More beyond." So the motto of the University of Rochester is Meliora—"Better things."

Since God's infinite resources are pledged to aid us, we may, as Emerson bids us, "hitch our wagon to a star," and believe in progress. Tennyson, Locksley Hall: "Men, my brothers, men the workers, ever reaping something new. That which they have done but earnest of the things that they shall do." Millet's L'Angelus is a witness to man's need of God's transcendence. Millet's aim was to paint, not air but prayer. We need a God who is not confined to nature. As Moses at the beginning of his ministry cried, "Show me, I pray thee, thy glory" (Ex. 33:18), so we need marked experiences at the beginning of the Christian life, in order that we may be living witnesses to the supernatural. And our Lord promises such manifestations of himself: John 14:21—"I will love him, and will manifest myself unto him."

Ps. 71:15—"My mouth shall tell of thy righteousness, And of thy salvation all the day; For I know not the numbers thereof" = it is infinite. Ps. 89:2—"Mercy shall be built up forever" = ever growing manifestations and cycles of fulfilment—first literal, then spiritual. Ps. 113:4-6—"Jehovah is high above all nations, And his glory above the heavens. Who is like unto Jehovah our God, That hath his seat on high, That humbleth himself [stoopeth down] to behold The things that are in heaven and in the earth?" Mal. 2:15—"did he not make one, although he had the residue of the Spirit?" = he might have created many wives for Adam, though he did actually create but one. In this "residue of the Spirit," says Caldwell, Cities of our Faith, 370, "there yet lies latent—as winds lie calm in the air of a summer noon, as heat immense lies cold and hidden in the mountains of coal—the blessing and the life of nations, the infinite enlargement of Zion."

Is. 52:10—"Jehovah hath made bare his holy arm" = nature does not exhaust or entomb God; nature is the mantle in which he commonly reveals himself; but he is not fettered by the robe he wears—he can thrust it aside, and make bare his arm in providential interpositions for earthly deliverance, and in mighty movements of history for the salvation of the sinner and for the setting up of his own kingdom. See also John 1:16—"of his fulness we all received, and grace for grace" = "Each blessing appropriated became the foundation of a greater blessing. To have realized and used one measure of grace was to have gained a larger measure in exchange for it χάριν ἀντὶ χάριτος"; so Westcott, in Bib. Com., in loco. Christ can ever say to the believer, as he said to Nathanael (John 1:50): "thou shalt see greater things than these."

Because God is infinite, he can love each believer as much as if that single soul were the only one for whom he had to care. Both in providence and in redemption the whole heart of God is busy with plans for the interest and happiness of the single Christian. Threatenings do not half reveal God, nor his promises half express the "eternal weight of glory" (2 Cor. 4:17). Dante, Paradiso, 19:40-63—God "Could not upon the universe so write The impress of his power, but that his word Must still be left in distance infinite." To "limit the Holy One of Israel" (Ps. 78:41—marg.) is falsehood as well as sin.

This attribute of infinity, or of transcendence, qualifies all the other attributes, and so is the foundation for the representations of majesty and glory as belonging to God (see Ex. 33:18; Ps. 19:1; Is. 6:3; Mat. 6:13; Acts 7:2; Rom. 1:23; 9:23; Heb. 1:3; 1 Pet. 4:14; Rev. 21:23). Glory is not itself a divine attribute; it is rather a result—an objective result—of the exercise of the divine attributes. This glory exists irrespective of the revelation and recognition of it in the creation (John 17:5). Only God can worthily perceive and reverence his own glory. He does all for his own glory. All religion is founded on the glory of God. All worship is the result of this immanent quality of the divine nature. Kedney, Christian Doctrine, 1:360-373, 2:354, apparently conceives of the divine glory as an eternal material environment of God, from which the universe is fashioned. This seems to contradict both the spirituality and the infinity of God. God's infinity implies absolute completeness apart from anything external to himself. We proceed therefore to consider the attributes involved in infinity.

Of the attributes involved in Infinity, we mention:

1. Self-existence
   By self-existence we mean
   (a) That God is "causa sui," having the ground of his existence in himself. Every being must have the ground of its existence either in or out of itself. We have the ground of our existence outside of us. God is not thus dependent. He is a se; hence we speak of the aseity of God.

   God's self-existence is implied in the name "Jehovah" (Ex. 6:3) and in the declaration "I AM THAT I AM" (Ex. 3:14), both of which signify that it is God's nature to be. Self-existence is certainly incomprehensible to us, yet a self-existent person is no greater mystery than a self-existent thing, such as Herbert Spencer supposes the universe to be; indeed it is not so great a mystery, for it is easier to derive matter from mind than to derive mind from matter. See Porter, Human Intellect, 661. Joh. Angelus Silesius: "Gott ist das was Er ist; Ich was Ich durch Ihn bin; Doch kennst du Einen wohl, So kennst du mich und Ihn." Martineau, Types, 1:302—"A cause may be eternal, but nothing that is caused can be so." He protests against the phrase "causa sui." So Shedd, Dogm. Theol., 1:338, objects to the phrase "God is his own cause," because God is the uncaused Being. But when we speak of God as "causa sui," we do not attribute to him beginning of existence. The phrase means rather that the ground of his existence is not outside of himself, but that he himself is the living spring of all energy and of all being.

   But lest this should be misconstrued, we add
   (b) That God exists by the necessity of his own being. It is his nature to be. Hence the existence of God is not a contingent but a necessary existence. It is grounded, not in his volitions, but in his nature.

   Julius Müller, Doctrine of Sin, 2:126, 130, 170, seems to hold that God is primarily will, so that the essence of God is his act: "God's essence does not precede his freedom"; "if the essence of God were for him something given, something already present, the question 'from whence it was given?' could not be evaded; God's essence must in this case have its origin in something apart from him, and thus the true conception of God would be entirely swept away." But this implies that truth, reason, love, holiness, equally with God's essence, are all products of will. If God's essence, moreover, were his act, it would be in the power of God to annihilate himself. Act presupposes essence; else there is no God to act. The will by which God exists, and in virtue of which he is causa sui, is therefore not will in the sense of volition, but will in the sense of the whole movement of his active being. With Müller's view Thomasius and Delitzsch are agreed. For refutation of it, see Philippi, Glaubenslehre, 2:63.

   God's essence is not his act, not only because this would imply that he could destroy himself, but also because before willing there must be being. Those who hold God's essence to be simple activity are impelled to this view by the fear of postulating some dead thing in God which precedes all exercise of faculty. So Miller, Evolution of Love, 43—"Perfect action, conscious and volitional, is the highest generalization, the ultimate unit, the unconditioned nature, of infinite Being"; i. e., God's nature is subjective action, while external nature is his objective action. A better statement, however, is that of Bowne, Philos. of Theism, 170—"While there is a necessity in the soul, it becomes controlling only through freedom; and we may say that everyone must constitute himself a rational soul.... This is absolutely true of God."

2. Immutability

By this we mean that the nature, attributes, and will of God are exempt from all change. Reason teaches us that no change is possible in God, whether of increase or decrease, progress or deterioration, contraction or development. All change must be to better or to worse. But God is absolute perfection, and no change to better is possible. Change to worse would be equally inconsistent with perfection. No cause for such change exists, either outside of God or in God himself.

Psalm 102:27—"thou art the same"; Mal. 3:6—"I, Jehovah, change not"; James 1:17—"with whom can be no variation, neither shadow that is cast by turning." Spenser, Faerie Queen, Cantos of Mutability, 8:2—"Then 'gin I think on that which nature sayde, Of that same time when no more change shall be, But steadfast rest of all things, firmly stayed Upon the pillours of eternity; For all that moveth doth in change delight, But henceforth all shall rest eternally With him that is the God of Sabaoth hight; Oh thou great Sabaoth God, grant me that Sabbath's sight!" Bowne, Philos. of Theism, 146, defines immutability as "the constancy and continuity of the divine nature which exists through all the divine acts as their law and source."

The passages of Scripture which seem at first sight to ascribe change to God are to be explained in one of three ways:

(a) As illustrations of the varied methods in which God manifests his immutable truth and wisdom in creation.

Mathematical principles receive new application with each successive stage of creation. The law of cohesion gives place to chemical law, and chemistry yields to vital forces, but through all these changes there is a divine truth and wisdom which is unchanging, and which reduces all to rational order. John Caird, Fund. Ideas of Christianity, 2:140—"Immutability is not stereotyped sameness, but impossibility of deviation by one hair's breadth from the course which is best. A man of great force of character is continually finding new occasions for the manifestation and application of moral principle. In God infinite consistency is united with infinite flexibility. There is no iron-bound impassibility, but rather an infinite originality in him."

(b) As anthropomorphic representations of the revelation of God's unchanging attributes in the changing circumstances and varying moral conditions of creatures.

Gen. 6:6—"it repented Jehovah that he had made man"—is to be interpreted in the light of Num. 23:19—"God is not a man, that he should lie: neither the son of man, that he should repent." So cf. 1 Sam. 15:11 with 15:29. God's unchanging holiness requires him to treat the wicked differently from the righteous. When the righteous become wicked, his treatment of them must change. The sun is not fickle or partial because it melts the wax but hardens the clay,—the change is not in the sun but in the objects it shines upon. The change in God's treatment of men is described anthropomorphically, as if it were a change in God himself,—other passages in close conjunction with the first being given to correct any possible misapprehension. Threats not fulfilled, as in Jonah 3:4, 10, are to be explained by their conditional nature. Hence God's immutability itself renders it certain that his love will adapt itself to every varying mood and condition of his children, so as to guide their steps, sympathize with their sorrows, answer their prayers. God responds to us more quickly than the mother's face to the changing moods of her babe. Godet, in The Atonement, 338—"God is of all beings the most delicately and infinitely sensitive."

God's immutability is not that of the stone, that has no internal experience, but rather that of the column of mercury, that rises and falls with every change in the temperature of the surrounding atmosphere. When a man bicycling against the wind turns about and goes with the wind instead of going against it, the wind seems to change, though it is blowing just as it was before. The sinner struggles against the wind of prevenient grace until he seems to strike against a stone wall. Regeneration is God's conquest of our wills by his power, and conversion is our beginning to turn round and to work with God rather than against God. Now we move without effort, because we have God at our back; Phil. 2:12, 13—"work out your own salvation ... for it is God who worketh in you." God has not changed, but we have changed; John 3:8—"The wind bloweth where it will ... so is every one that is born of the Spirit." Jacob's first wrestling with the Angel was the picture of his lifelong self-will, opposing God; his subsequent wrestling in prayer was the picture of a consecrated will, working with God (Gen. 32:24-28). We seem to conquer God, but he really conquers us. He seems to change, but it is we who change after all.

(c) As describing executions, in time, of purposes eternally existing in the mind of God. Immutability must not be confounded with immobility. This would deny all those imperative volitions of God by which he enters into history. The Scriptures assure us that creation, miracles, incarnation, regeneration, are immediate acts of God. Immutability is consistent with constant activity and perfect freedom.

The abolition of the Mosaic dispensation indicates no change in God's plan; it is rather the execution of his plan. Christ's coming and work were no sudden makeshift, to remedy unforeseen defects in the Old Testament scheme: Christ came rather in "the fulness of the time" (Gal. 4:4), to fulfill the "counsel" of God (Acts 2:23). Gen. 8:1—"God remembered Noah" = interposed by special act for Noah's deliverance, showed that he remembered Noah. While we change, God does not. There is no fickleness or inconstancy in him. Where we once found him, there we may find him still, as Jacob did at Bethel (Gen. 35:1, 6, 9). Immutability is a consolation to the faithful, but a terror to God's enemies (Mal. 3:6—"I, Jehovah, change not; therefore ye, O sons of Jacob, are not consumed"; Ps. 7:11—"a God that hath indignation every day"). It is consistent with constant activity in nature and in grace (John 5:17—"My Father worketh even until now, and I work"; Job 23:13, 14—"he is in one mind, and who can turn him?... For he performeth that which is appointed for me: and many such things are with him"). If God's immutability were immobility, we could not worship him, any more than the ancient Greeks were able to worship Fate. Arthur Hugh Clough: "It fortifies my soul to know, That, though I perish, Truth is so: That, howsoe'er I stray and range, Whate'er I do, Thou dost not change. I steadier step when I recall That, if I slip, Thou dost not fall." On this attribute see Charnock, Attributes, 1:310-362; Dorner, Gesammelte Schriften, 188-377; translated in Bib. Sac., 1879:28-59, 209-223.

3. Unity

By this we mean (a) that the divine nature is undivided and indivisible (unus); and (b) that there is but one infinite and perfect Spirit (unicus).

Deut. 6:4—"Hear, O Israel: Jehovah our God is one Jehovah"; Is. 44:6—"besides me there is no God"; John 5:44—"the only God"; 17:3—"the only true God"; 1 Cor. 8:4—"no God but one"; 1 Tim. 1:17—"the only God"; 6:15—"the blessed and only Potentate"; Eph. 4:5, 6—"one Lord, one faith, one baptism, one God and Father of all, who is over all, and through all, and in all." When we read in Mason, Faith of the Gospel, 25—"The unity of God is not numerical, denying the existence of a second; it is integral, denying the possibility of division," we reply that the unity of God is both,—it includes both the numerical and the integral elements.

Humboldt, in his Cosmos, has pointed out that the unity and creative agency of the heavenly Father have given unity to the order of nature, and so have furnished the impulse to modern physical science. Our faith in a "universe" rests historically upon the demonstration of God's unity which has been given by the incarnation and death of Christ. Tennyson, In Memoriam: "That God who ever lives and loves, One God, one law, one element, And one far off divine event To which the whole creation moves." See A. H. Strong, Christ in Creation, 184-187. Alexander McLaren: "The heathen have many gods because they have no one that satisfies hungry hearts or corresponds to their unconscious ideals. Completeness is not reached by piecing together many fragments. The wise merchantman will gladly barter a sack full of 'goodly pearls' for the one of great price. Happy they who turn away from the many to embrace the One!"

Against polytheism, tritheism, or dualism, we may urge that the notion of two or more Gods is self-contradictory; since each limits the other and destroys his godhood. In the nature of things, infinity and absolute perfection are possible only to one. It is unphilosophical, moreover, to assume the existence of two or more Gods, when one will explain all the facts. The unity of God is, however, in no way inconsistent with the doctrine of the Trinity; for, while this doctrine holds to the existence of hypostatical, or personal, distinctions in the divine nature, it also holds that this divine nature is numerically and eternally one.

Polytheism is man's attempt to rid himself of the notion of responsibility to one moral Lawgiver and Judge by dividing up his manifestations, and attributing them to separate wills. So Force, in the terminology of some modern theorizers, is only God with his moral attributes left out. "Henotheism" (says Max Müller, Origin and Growth of Religion, 285) "conceives of each individual god as unlimited by the power of other gods. Each is felt, at the time, as supreme and absolute, notwithstanding the limitations which to our minds must arise from his power being conditioned by the power of all the gods."

Even polytheism cannot rest in the doctrine of many gods, as an exclusive and all-comprehending explanation of the universe. The Greeks believed in one supreme Fate that ruled both gods and men. Aristotle: "God, though he is one, has many names, because he is called according to states into which he is ever entering anew." The doctrine of God's unity should teach men to give up hope of any other God, to reveal himself to them or to save them. They are in the hands of the one and only God, and therefore there is but one law, one gospel, one salvation; one doctrine, one duty, one destiny. We cannot rid ourselves of responsibility by calling ourselves mere congeries of impressions or mere victims of circumstance. As God is one, so the soul made in God's image is one also. On the origin of polytheism, see articles by Tholuck, in Bib. Repos., 2:84, 246, 441, and Max Müller, Science of Religion, 124.

Moberly, Atonement and Personality, 83—"The Alpha and Omega, the beginning and end and sum and meaning of Being, is but One. We who believe in a personal God do not believe in a limited God. We do not mean one more, a bigger specimen of existences, amongst existences. Rather, we mean that the reality of existence itself is personal: that Power, that Law, that Life, that Thought, that Love, are ultimately, in their very reality, identified in one supreme, and that necessarily a personal Existence.

Now such supreme Being cannot be multiplied: it is incapable of a plural: it cannot be a generic term. There cannot be more than one all-inclusive, more than one ultimate, more than one God. Nor has Christian thought, at any point, for any moment, dared or endured the least approach to such a thought or phrase as 'two Gods.' If the Father is God, and the Son God, they are both the same God wholly, unreservedly. God is a particular, an unique, not a general, term. Each is not only God, but is the very same 'singularis unicus et totus Deus.' They are not both generically God, as though 'God' could be an attribute or predicate; but both identically God, the God, the one all-inclusive, indivisible, God.... If the thought that wishes to be orthodox had less tendency to become tritheistic, the thought that claims to be free would be less Unitarian."

Third Division.—Perfection, and attributes therein involved.

By perfection we mean, not mere quantitative completeness, but qualitative excellence. The attributes involved in perfection are moral attributes. Right action among men presupposes a perfect moral organization, a normal state of intellect, affection and will. So God's activity presupposes a principle of intelligence, of affection, of volition, in his inmost being, and the existence of a worthy object for each of these powers of his nature. But in eternity past there is nothing existing outside or apart from God. He must find, and he does find, the sufficient object of intellect, affection, and will, in himself. There is a self-knowing, a self-loving, a self-willing, which constitute his absolute perfection. The consideration of the immanent attributes is, therefore, properly concluded with an account of that truth, love, and holiness, which render God entirely sufficient to himself.

Mat. 5:48—"Ye therefore shall be perfect, as your heavenly Father is perfect"; Rom. 12:2— "perfect will of God"; Col. 1:28—"perfect in Christ"; cf. Deut. 32:4—"The Rock, his work is perfect"; Ps. 18:30—"As for God, his way is perfect."

1. Truth

By truth we mean that attribute of the divine nature in virtue of which God's being and God's knowledge eternally conform to each other.

In further explanation we remark:

A. Negatively:

(a) The immanent truth of God is not to be confounded with that veracity and faithfulness which partially manifest it to creatures. These are transitive truth, and they presuppose the absolute and immanent attribute.

Deut 32:4—"A God of faithfulness and without iniquity, Just and right is he"; John 17:3—"the only true God" (ἀληθινόν); 1 John 5:20—"we know him that is true" (τὸν ἀληθινόν). In both these passages ἀληθινός describes God as the genuine, the real, as distinguished from ἀληθής, the veracious (compare John 6:32—"the true bread"; Heb. 8:2—"the true tabernacle"). John 14:6—"I am ... the truth." As "I am ... the life" signifies, not "I am the living one," but rather "I am he who is life and the source of life," so "I am ... the truth" signifies, not "I am the truthful one," but "I am he who is truth and the source of truth"—in other words, truth of being, not merely truth of expression. So 1 John 5:7—"the Spirit is the truth." Cf. 1 Esdras 1:38—"The truth abideth and is forever strong, and it liveth and ruleth forever" = personal truth? See Godet on John 1:18; Shedd, Dogm. Theol., 1:181.

Truth is God perfectly revealed and known. It may be likened to the electric current which manifests and measures the power of the dynamo. There is no realm of truth apart from the world-ground, just as there is no law of nature that is independent of the Author of nature. While we know ourselves only partially, God knows himself fully. John Caird, Fund. Ideas of Christianity, 1:192—"In the life of God there are no unrealized possibilities. The presupposition of all our knowledge and activity is that absolute and eternal unity of knowing and being which is only another expression for the nature of God. In one sense, he is all reality, and the only reality, whilst all finite existence is but a becoming, which never is." Lowrie, Doctrine of St. John, 57-63—"Truth is reality revealed. Jesus is the Truth, because in him the sum of the qualities hidden in God is presented and revealed to the world, God's nature in terms of an active force and in relation to his rational creation." This definition however ignores the fact that God is truth, apart from and before all creation. As an immanent attribute, truth implies a conformity of God's knowledge to God's being, which antedates the universe; see B. (b) below.

(b) Truth in God is not a merely active attribute of the divine nature. God is truth, not only in the sense that he is the being who truly knows, but also in the sense that he is the truth that is known. The passive precedes the active; truth of being precedes truth of knowing.

Plato: "Truth is his (God's) body, and light his shadow." Hollaz (quoted in Thomasius, Christi Person und Werk, 1:137) says that "truth is the conformity of the divine essence with the divine intellect." See Gerhard, loc. ii:152; Kahnis, Dogmatik, 2:272, 279; 3:193—"Distinguish in God the personal self-consciousness [spirituality, personality—see pages 252, 253] from the unfolding of this in the divine knowledge, which can have no other object but God himself. So far, now, as self-knowing in God is absolutely identical with his being is he the absolutely true. For truth is the knowledge which answers to the being, and the being which answers to the knowledge."

Royce, World and Individual, 1:270—"Truth either may mean that about which we judge, or it may mean the correspondence between our ideas and their objects." God's truth is both object of his knowledge and knowledge of his object. Miss Clara French, The Dramatic Action and Motive of King John: "You spell Truth with a capital, and make it an independent existence to be sought for and absorbed; but, unless truth is God, what can it do for man? It is only a personality that can touch a personality." So we assent to the poet's declaration that "Truth, crushed to earth, shall rise again," only because Truth is personal. Christ, the Revealer of God, is the Truth. He is not simply the medium but also the object of all knowledge; Eph. 4:20—"ye did not so learn Christ" = ye knew more than the doctrine about Christ,—ye knew Christ himself; John 17:3—"this is life eternal that they should know thee the only true God, and him whom thou didst send, even Jesus Christ."

B. Positively:

(a) All truth among men, whether mathematical, logical, moral, or religious, is to be regarded as having its foundation in this immanent truth of the divine nature and as disclosing facts in the being of God.

There is a higher Mind than our mind. No apostle can say "I am the truth," though each of them can say "I speak the truth." Truth is not a scientific or moral, but a substantial, thing—"nicht Schulsache, sondern Lebenssache." Here is the dignity of education, that knowledge of truth is knowledge of God. The laws of mathematics are disclosures to us, not of the divine reason merely, for this would imply truth outside of and before God, but of the divine nature. J. W. A. Stewart: "Science is possible because God is scientific." Plato: "God geometrizes." Bowne: "The heavens are crystalized mathematics." The statement that two and two make four, or that virtue is commendable and vice condemnable, expresses an everlasting principle in the being of God. Separate statements of truth are inexplicable apart from the total revelation of truth, and this total revelation is inexplicable apart from One who is truth and who is thus revealed. The separate electric lights in our streets are inexplicable apart from the electric current which throbs through the wires, and this electric current is itself inexplicable apart from the hidden dynamo whose power it exactly expresses and measures. The separate lights of truth are due to the realizing agency of the Holy Spirit; the one unifying current which they partially reveal is the outgoing work of Christ, the divine Logos; Christ is the one and only Revealer of him who dwells "in light unapproachable; whom no man hath seen, nor can see" (1 Tim. 6:16).

Prof. H. E. Webster began his lectures "by assuming the Lord Jesus Christ and the multiplication-table." But this was tautology, because the Lord Jesus Christ, the Truth, the only revealer of God, includes the multiplication-table. So Wendt, Teaching of Jesus, 1:257; 2:202, unduly narrows the scope of Christ's revelation when he maintains that with Jesus truth is not the truth which corresponds to reality but rather the right conduct which corresponds to the duty prescribed by God. "Grace and truth" (John 1:17) then means the favor of God and the righteousness which God approves. To understand Jesus is impossible without being ethically like him. He is king of truth, in that he reveals this righteousness, and finds obedience for it among men. This ethical aspect of the truth, we would reply, important as it is, does not exclude but rather requires for its complement and presupposition that other aspect of the truth as the reality to which all being must conform and the conformity of all being to that reality. Since Christ is the truth of God, we are successful in our search for truth only as we recognize him. Whether all roads lead to Rome depends upon which way your face is turned. Follow a point of land out into the sea, and you find only ocean. With the back turned upon Jesus Christ all following after truth leads only into mist and darkness. Aristotle's ideal man was "a hunter after truth." But truth can never be found disjoined from love, nor can the loveless seeker discern it. "For the loving worm within its clod Were diviner than a loveless God" (Robert Browning). Hence Christ can say: John 18:37—"Every one that is of the truth heareth my voice."

(b) This attribute therefore constitutes the principle and guarantee of all revelation, while it shows the possibility of an eternal divine self-contemplation apart from and before all creation. It is to be understood only in the light of the doctrine of the Trinity.

To all this doctrine, however, a great school of philosophers have opposed themselves. Duns Scotus held that God's will made truth as well as right. Descartes said that God could have made it untrue that the radii of a circle are all equal. Lord Bacon said that Adam's sin consisted in seeking a good in itself, instead of being content with the merely empirical good. Whedon, On the Will, 316—"Infinite wisdom and infinite holiness consist in, and result from, God's volitions eternally." We reply that, to make truth and good matters of mere will, instead of regarding them as characteristics of God's being, is to deny that anything is true or good in itself. If God can make truth to be falsehood, and injustice to be justice, then God is indifferent to truth or falsehood, to good or evil, and he ceases thereby to be God. Truth is not arbitrary,—it is matter of being—the being of God. There are no regulative principles of knowledge which are not transcendental also. God knows and wills truth, because he is truth. Robert Browning, A Soul's Tragedy, 214—"Were't not for God, I mean, what hope of truth—Speaking truth, hearing truth—would stay with Man?" God's will does not make truth, but truth rather makes God's will. God's perfect knowledge in eternity past has an object. That object must be himself. He is the truth Known, as well as the truthful Knower. But a perfect objective must be personal. The doctrine of the Trinity is the necessary complement to the doctrine of the Attributes. Shedd, Dogm. Theol., 1:183—"The pillar of cloud becomes a pillar of fire." See A. H. Strong, Christ in Creation, 102-112.

On the question whether it is ever right to deceive, see Paine, Ethnic Trinities, 300-339. Plato said that the use of such medicines should be restricted to physicians. The rulers of the state may lie for the public good, but private people not: "officiosum mendacium." It is better to say that deception is justifiable only where the person deceived has, like a wild beast or a criminal or an enemy in war, put himself out of human society and deprived himself of the right to truth. Even then deception is a sad necessity which witnesses to an abnormal condition of human affairs. With James Martineau, when asked what answer he would give to an intending murderer when truth would mean death, we may say: "I suppose I should tell an untruth, and then should be sorry for it forever after." On truth as an attribute of God, see Bib. Sac., Oct. 1877:735; Finney, Syst. Theol., 661; Janet, Final Causes, 416.

2. Love

By love we mean that attribute of the divine nature in virtue of which God is eternally moved to self-communication.

1 John 4:8—"God is love"; 3:16—"hereby know we love, because he laid down his life for us"; John 17:24—"thou lovedst me before the foundation of the world"; Rom. 15:30—"the love of the Spirit."

In further explanation we remark:

A. Negatively:

(a) The immanent love of God is not to be confounded with mercy and goodness toward creatures. These are its manifestations, and are to be denominated transitive love.

Thomasius, Christi Person und Werk, 1:138, 139—"God's regard for the happiness of his creatures flows from this self-communicating attribute of his nature. Love, in the true sense of the word, is living good-will, with impulses to impartation and union; self-communication (bonum communicativum sui); devotion, merging of the ego in another, in order to penetrate, fill, bless this other with itself, and in this other, as in another self, to possess itself, without giving up itself or losing itself. Love is therefore possible only between persons, and always presupposes personality. Only as Trinity has God love, absolute love; because as Father, Son, and Holy Ghost he stands in perfect self-impartation, self-devotion, and communion with himself." Julius Müller, Doct. Sin, 2:136—"God has in himself the eternal and wholly adequate object of his love, independently of his relation to the world."

In the Greek mythology, Eros was one of the oldest and yet one of the youngest of the gods. So Dante makes the oldest angel to be the youngest, because nearest to God the fountain of life. In 1 John 2:7, 8, "the old commandment" of love is evermore "a new commandment," because it reflects this eternal attribute of God. "There is a love unstained by selfishness, Th' outpouring tide of self-abandonment, That loves to love, and deems its preciousness Repaid in loving, though no sentiment Of love returned reward its sacrament; Nor stays to question what the loved one will, But hymns its overture with blessings immanent; Rapt and sublimed by love's exalting thrill, Loves on, through frown or smile, divine, immortal still." Clara Elizabeth Ward: "If I could gather every look of love, That ever any human creature wore, And all the looks that joy is mother of, All looks of grief that mortals ever bore, And mingle all with God-begotten grace, Methinks that I should see the Savior's face."

(b) Love is not the all-inclusive ethical attribute of God. It does not include truth, nor does it include holiness.

Ladd, Philosophy of Conduct, 352, very properly denies that benevolence is the all-inclusive virtue. Justness and Truth, he remarks, are not reducible to benevolence. In a review of Ladd's work in Bib. Sac., Jan. 1903:185, C. M. Mead adds: "He comes to the conclusion that it is impossible to resolve all the virtues into the generic one of love or benevolence without either giving a definition of benevolence which is unwarranted and virtually nullifies the end aimed at, or failing to recognize certain virtues which are as genuinely virtues as benevolence itself. Particularly is it argued that the virtues of the will (courage, constancy, temperance), and the virtues of judgment (wisdom, justness, trueness), get no recognition in this attempt to subsume all virtues under the one virtue of love. 'The unity of the virtues is due to the unity of a personality, in active and varied relations with other persons' (361). If benevolence means wishing happiness to all men, then happiness is made the ultimate good, and eudæmonism is accepted as the true ethical philosophy. But if, on the other hand, in order to avoid this conclusion, benevolence is made to mean wishing the highest welfare to all men, and the highest welfare is conceived as a life of virtue, then we come to the rather inane conclusion that the essence of virtue is to wish that men may be virtuous." See also art. by Vos, in Presb. and Ref. Rev., Jan. 1892:1-37.

(c) Nor is God's love a mere regard for being in general, irrespective of its moral quality.

Jonathan Edwards, in his treatise On the Nature of Virtue, defines virtue as regard for being in general. He considers that God's love is first of all directed toward himself as having the greatest quantity of being, and only secondarily directed toward his creatures whose quantity of being is infinitesimal as compared with his. But we reply that being in general is far too abstract a thing to elicit or justify love. Charles Hodge said truly that, if obligation is primarily due to being in general, then there is no more virtue in loving God than there is in loving Satan. Virtue, we hold, must consist, not in love for being in general, but in love for good being, that is, in love for God as holy. Love has no moral value except as it is placed upon a right object and is proportioned to the worth of that object. "Love of being in general" makes virtue an irrational thing, because it has no standard of conduct. Virtue is rather the love of God as right and as the source of right.

G. S. Lee, The Shadow-cross, 38—"God is love, and law is the way he loves us. But it is also true that God is law, and love is the way he rules us." Clarke, Christian Theology, 88—"Love is God's desire to impart himself, and so all good, to other persons, and to possess them for his own spiritual fellowship." The intent to communicate himself is the intent to communicate holiness, and this is the "terminus ad quem" of God's administration. Drummond, in his Ascent of Man, shows that Love began with the first cell of life. Evolution is not a tale of battle, but a love-story. We gradually pass from selfism to otherism. Evolution is the object of nature, and altruism is the object of evolution. Man = nutrition, looking to his own things; Woman = reproduction, looking to the things of others. But the greatest of these is love. The mammalia = the mothers, last and highest, care for others. As the mother gives love, so the father gives righteousness. Law, once a latent thing, now becomes active. The father makes a sort of conscience for those beneath him. Nature, like Raphael, is producing a Holy Family.

Jacob Boehme: "Throw open and throw out thy heart. For unless thou dost exercise thy heart, and the love of thy heart, upon every man in the world, thy self-love, thy pride, thy envy, thy distaste, thy dislike, will still have dominion over thee.... In the name and in the strength of God, love all men. Love thy neighbor as thyself, and do to thy neighbor as thou doest to thyself. And do it now. For now is the accepted time, and now is the day of salvation." These expressions are scriptural and valuable, if they are interpreted ethically, and are understood to inculcate the supreme duty of loving the Holy One, of being holy as he is holy, and of seeking to bring all intelligent beings into conformity with his holiness.

(d) God's love is not a merely emotional affection, proceeding from sense or impulse, nor is it prompted by utilitarian considerations.

Of the two words for love in the N. T., φιλέω designates an emotional affection, which is not and cannot be commanded (John 11:36—"Behold how he loved him!"), while ἀγαπάω expresses a rational and benevolent affection which springs from deliberate choice (John 3:16—"God so loved the world"; Mat. 19:19—"Thou shall love thy neighbor as thyself"; 5:44—"Love your enemies"). Thayer, N. T. Lex., 653—Ἀγαπᾶν "properly denotes a love founded in admiration, veneration, esteem, like the Lat. diligere, to be kindly disposed to one, to wish one well; but φιλεῖν denotes an inclination prompted by sense and emotion, Lat. amare.... Hence men are said ἀγαπᾶν God, not φιλεῖν." In this word ἀγάπη, when used of God, it is already implied that God loves, not for what he can get, but for what he can give. The rationality of his love involves moreover a subordination of the emotional element to a higher law than itself, namely, that of holiness. Even God's self-love must have a reason and norm in the perfections of his own being.

B. Positively:

(a) The immanent love of God is a rational and voluntary affection, grounded in perfect reason and deliberate choice.

Ritschl, Justification and Reconciliation, 3:277—"Love is will, aiming either at the appropriation of an object, or at the enrichment of its existence, because moved by a feeling of its worth.... Love is to persons; it is a constant will; it aims at the promotion of the other's personal end, whether known or conjectured; it takes up the other's personal end and makes it part of his own. Will, as love, does not give itself up for the other's sake; it aims at closest fellowship with the other for a common end." A. H. Strong, Christ in Creation, 388-405—"Love is not rightfully independent of the other faculties, but is subject to regulation and control.... We sometimes say that religion consists in love.... It would be more strictly true to say that religion consists in a new direction of our love, a turning of the current toward God which once flowed toward self.... Christianity rectifies the affections, before excessive, impulsive, lawless,—gives them worthy and immortal objects, regulates their intensity in some due proportion to the value of the things they rest upon, and teaches the true methods of their manifestation. In true religion love forms a copartnership with reason.... God's love is no arbitrary, wild, passionate torrent of emotion ... and we become like God by bringing our emotions, sympathies, affections, under the dominion of reason and conscience."

(b) Since God's love is rational, it involves a subordination of the emotional element to a higher law than itself, namely, that of truth and holiness.

Phil. 1:9—"And this I pray, that your love may abound yet more and more in knowledge and all discernment." True love among men illustrates God's love. It merges self in another instead of making that other an appendage to self. It seeks the other's true good, not merely his present enjoyment or advantage. Its aim is to realize the divine idea in that other, and therefore it is exercised for God's sake and in the strength which God supplies. Hence it is a love for holiness, and is under law to holiness. So God's love takes into account the highest interests, and makes infinite sacrifice to secure them. For the sake of saving a world of sinners, God "spared not his own Son, but delivered him up for us all" (Rom. 8:32), and "Jehovah hath laid on him the iniquity of us all" (Is. 53:6). Love requires a rule or standard for its regulation. This rule or standard is the holiness of God. So once more we see that love cannot include holiness, because it is subject to the law of holiness. Love desires only the best for its object, and the best is God. The golden rule does not bid us give what others desire, but what they need: Rom. 15:2—"Let each one of us please his neighbor for that which is good, unto edifying."

(c) The immanent love of God therefore requires and finds a perfect standard in his own holiness, and a personal object in the image of his own infinite perfections. It is to be understood only in the light of the doctrine of the Trinity.

As there is a higher Mind than our mind, so there is a greater Heart than our heart. God is not simply the loving One—he is also the Love that is loved. There is an infinite life of sensibility and affection in God. God has feeling, and in an infinite degree. But feeling alone is not love. Love implies not merely receiving but giving, not merely emotion but impartation. So the love of God is shown in his eternal giving. James 1:5—"God, who giveth," or "the giving God" (τοῦ διδόντος Θεοῦ) = giving is not an episode in his being—it is his nature to give. And not only to give, but to give himself. This he does eternally in the self-communications of the Trinity; this he does transitively and temporally in his giving of himself for us in Christ, and to us in the Holy Spirit.

Jonathan Edwards, Essay on Trinity (ed. G. P. Fisher), 79—"That in John God is love shows that there are more persons than one in the Deity, for it shows love to be essential and necessary to the Deity, so that his nature consists in it, and this supposes that there is an eternal and necessary object, because all love respects another that is the beloved. By love here the apostle certainly means something beside that which is commonly called self-love: that is very improperly called love, and is a thing of an exceeding diverse nature from the affection or virtue of love the apostle is speaking of." When Newman Smyth, Christian Ethics, 226-239, makes the first characteristic of love to be self-affirmation, and when Dorner, Christian Ethics, 73, makes self-assertion an essential part of love, they violate linguistic usage by including under love what properly belongs to holiness.

(d) The immanent love of God constitutes a ground of the divine blessedness. Since there is an infinite and perfect object of love, as well as of knowledge and will, in God's own nature, the existence of the universe is not necessary to his serenity and joy.

Blessedness is not itself a divine attribute; it is rather a result of the exercise of the divine attributes. It is a subjective result of this exercise, as glory is an objective result. Perfect faculties, with perfect objects for their exercise, ensure God's blessedness. But love is especially its source. Acts 20:35—"It is more blessed to give than to receive." Happiness (hap, happen) is grounded in circumstances; blessedness, in character. Love precedes creation and is the ground of creation. Its object therefore cannot be the universe, for that does not exist, and, if it did exist, could not be a proper object of love for the infinite God. The only sufficient object of his love is the image of his own perfections, for that alone is equal to himself. Upton, Hibbert Lectures, 264—"Man most truly realizes his own nature, when he is ruled by rational, self-forgetful love. He cannot help inferring that the highest thing in the individual consciousness is the dominant thing in the universe at large." Here we may assent, if we remember that not the love itself but that which is loved must be the dominant thing, and we shall see that to be not love but holiness.

Jones, Robert Browning, 219—"Love is for Browning the highest, richest conception man can form. It is our idea of that which is perfect; we cannot even imagine anything better. And the idea of evolution necessarily explains the world as the return of the highest to itself. The universe is homeward bound.... All things are potentially spirit, and all the phenomena of the world are manifestations of love.... Man's reason is not, but man's love is, a direct emanation from the inmost being of God" (345). Browning should have applied to truth and holiness the same principle which he recognized with regard to love. But we gratefully accept his dicta: "He that created love, shall not he love?... God! thou art Love! I build my faith on that."

(e) The love of God involves also the possibility of divine suffering, and the suffering on account of sin which holiness necessitates on the part of God is itself the atonement.

Christ is "the Lamb that hath been slain from the foundation of the world" (Rev. 13:8); 1 Pet. 1:19, 20—"precious blood, as of a lamb without blemish and without spot, even the blood of Christ: who was foreknown indeed before the foundation of the world." While holiness requires atonement, love provides it. The blessedness of God is consistent with sorrow for human misery and sin. God is passible, or capable of suffering. The permission of moral evil in the decree of creation was at cost to God. Scripture attributes to him emotions of grief and anger at human sin (Gen. 6:6—"it grieved him at his heart"; Rom. 1:18—"wrath of God"; Eph. 4:30—"grieve not the Holy Spirit of God"); painful sacrifice in the gift of Christ (Rom. 8:32—"spared not his own son"; cf. Gen. 22:16—"hast not withheld thy son") and participation in the suffering of his people (Is. 63:9—"in all their affliction he was afflicted"); Jesus Christ in his sorrow and sympathy, his tears and agony, is the revealer of God's feelings toward the race, and we are urged to follow in his steps, that we may be perfect, as our Father in heaven is perfect. We cannot, indeed, conceive of love without self-sacrifice, nor of self-sacrifice without suffering. It would seem, then, that as immutability is consistent with imperative volitions in human history, so the blessedness of God may be consistent with emotions of sorrow.

But does God feel in proportion to his greatness, as the mother suffers more than the sick child whom she tends? Does God suffer infinitely in every suffering of his creatures? We must remember that God is infinitely greater than his creation, and that he sees all human sin and woe as part of his great plan. We are entitled to attribute to him only such passibleness as is consistent with infinite perfection. In combining passibleness with blessedness, then, we must allow blessedness to be the controlling element, for our fundamental idea of God is that of absolute perfection. Martensen, Dogmatics, 101— "This limitation is swallowed up in the inner life of perfection which God lives, in total independence of his creation, and in triumphant prospect of the fulfilment of his great designs. We may therefore say with the old theosophic writers: 'In the outer chambers is sadness, but in the inner ones is unmixed joy.' " Christ was "anointed ... with the oil of gladness above his fellows," and "for the joy that was set before him endured the cross" (Heb. 1:9; 12:2). Love rejoices even in pain, when this brings good to those beloved. "Though round its base the rolling clouds are spread, Eternal sunshine settles on its head."

In George Adam Smith's Life of Henry Drummond, 11, Drummond cries out after hearing the confessions of men who came to him: "I am sick of the sins of these men! How can God bear it?" Simon, Reconciliation, 338-343, shows that before the incarnation, the Logos was a sufferer from the sins of men. This suffering however was kept in check and counterbalanced by his consciousness as a factor in the Godhead, and by the clear knowledge that men were themselves the causes of this suffering. After he became incarnate he suffered without knowing whence all the suffering came. He had a subconscious life into which were interwoven elements due to the sinful conduct of the race whose energy was drawn from himself and with which in addition he had organically united himself. If this is limitation, it is also self-limitation which Christ could have avoided by not creating, preserving, and redeeming mankind. We rejoice in giving away a daughter in marriage, even though it costs pain. The highest blessedness in the Christian is coincident with agony for the souls of others. We partake of Christ's joy only when we know the fellowship of his sufferings. Joy and sorrow can coëxist, like Greek fire, that burns under water.

Abbé Gratry, La Morale et la Loi de l'Histoire, 165, 166—"What! Do you really suppose that the personal God, free and intelligent, loving and good, who knows every detail of human torture, and hears every sigh—this God who sees, who loves as we do, and more than we do—do you believe that he is present and looks pitilessly on what breaks your heart, and what to him must be the spectacle of Satan reveling in the blood of humanity? History teaches us that men so feel for sufferers that they have been drawn to die with them, so that their own executioners have become the next martyrs. And yet you represent God, the absolute goodness, as alone impassible? It is here that our evangelical faith comes in. Our God was made man to suffer and to die! Yes, here is the true God. He has suffered from the beginning in all who have suffered. He has been hungry in all who have hungered. He has been immolated in all and with all who have offered up their lives. He is the Lamb slain from the foundation of the world." Similarly Alexander Vinet, Vital Christianity, 240, remarks that "The suffering God is not simply the teaching of modern divines. It is a New Testament thought, and it is one that answers all the doubts that arise at the sight of human suffering. To know that God is suffering with it makes that suffering more awful, but it gives strength and life and hope, for we know that, if God is in it, suffering is the road to victory. If he shares our suffering we shall share his crown," and we can say with the Psalmist, 68:19—"Blessed be God, who daily beareth our burden, even the God who is our salvation," and with Isaiah 63:9—"In all their affliction he was afflicted, and the angel of his presence saved them."

Borden P. Bowne, Atonement: "Something like this work of grace was a moral necessity with God. It was an awful responsibility that was taken when our human race was launched with its fearful possibilities of good and evil. God thereby put himself under infinite obligation to care for his human family; and reflections on his position as Creator and Ruler, instead of removing, only make more manifest this obligation. So long as we conceive God as sitting apart in supreme ease and self-satisfaction, he is not love at all, but only a reflection of our selfishness and vulgarity. So long as we conceive him as bestowing blessing upon us out of his infinite fulness, but at no real cost to himself, he sinks below the moral heroes of our race. There is ever a higher thought possible, until we see God taking the world upon his heart, entering into the fellowship of our sorrow, and becoming the supreme burden bearer and leader in self-sacrifice. Then only are the possibilities of grace and condescension and love and moral heroism filled up, so that nothing higher remains. And the work of Christ, so far as it was a historical event, must be viewed not merely as a piece of history, but also as a manifestation of that cross which was hidden in the divine love from the foundation of the world, and which is involved in the existence of the human world at all."

Royce, Spirit of Modern Philosophy, 264—"The eternal resolution that, if the world will be tragic, it shall still, in Satan's despite, be spiritual, is the very essence of the eternal joy of that World-Spirit of whose wisdom ours is but a fragmentary reflection.... When you suffer, your sufferings are God's sufferings,—not his external work nor his external penalty, nor the fruit of his neglect, but identically his own personal woe. In you God himself suffers, precisely as you do, and has all your reason for overcoming this grief." Henry N. Dodge, Christus Victor: "O Thou, that from eternity Upon thy wounded heart hast borne Each pang and cry of misery Wherewith our human hearts are torn, Thy love upon the grievous cross Doth glow, the beacon-light of time, Forever sharing pain and loss With every man in every clime. How vast, how vast Thy sacrifice, As ages come and ages go, Still waiting till it shall suffice To draw the last cold heart and slow!"

On the question, Is God passible? see Bennett Tyler, Sufferings of Christ; A Layman, Sufferings of Christ; Woods, Works, 1:299-317; Bib. Sac., 11:744; 17:422-424; Emmons, Works, 4:201-208; Fairbairn, Place of Christ, 483-487; Bushnell, Vic. Sacrifice, 59-93; Kedney, Christ. Doctrine Harmonized, 1:185-245; Edward Beecher, Concord of Ages, 81-204; Young, Life and Light of Men, 20-43, 147-150; Schaff, Hist. Christ. Church, 2:191; Crawford, Fatherhood of God, 43, 44; Anselm, Proslogion, cap. 8; Upton, Hibbert Lectures, 268; John Caird, Fund. Ideas of Christianity, 2:117, 118, 137-142. Per

contra, see Shedd, Essays and Addresses, 277, 279 note; Woods, in Lit. and Theol. Rev., 1834:43-61; Harris, God the Creator and Lord of All, 1:201. On the Biblical conception of Love in general, see article by James Orr, in Hastings' Bible Dictionary.

3. Holiness

Holiness is self-affirming purity. In virtue of this attribute of his nature, God eternally wills and maintains his own moral excellence. In this definition are contained three elements: first, purity; secondly, purity willing; thirdly, purity willing itself.

Ex. 15:11—"glorious in holiness"; 19:10-16—the people of Israel must purify themselves before they come into the presence of God; Is. 6:3—"Holy, holy, holy, is Jehovah of hosts"—notice the contrast with the unclean lips, that must be purged with a coal from the altar (verses 5-7); 2 Cor, 7:1—"cleanse ourselves from all defilement of flesh and spirit, perfecting holiness in the fear of God"; 1 Thess. 3:13—"unblamable in holiness"; 4:7—"God called us not for uncleanness, but in sanctification"; Heb. 12:29—"our God is a consuming fire"—to all iniquity. These passages show that holiness is the opposite to impurity, that it is itself purity. The development of the conception of holiness in Hebrew history was doubtless a gradual one. At first it may have included little more than the idea of separation from all that is common, small and mean. Physical cleanliness and hatred of moral evil were additional elements which in time became dominant. We must remember however that the proper meaning of a term is to be determined not by the earliest but by the latest usage. Human nature is ethical from the start, and seeks to express the thought of a rule or standard of obligation, and of a righteous Being who imposes that rule or standard. With the very first conceptions of majesty and separation which attach to the apprehension of divinity in the childhood of the race there mingles at least some sense of the contrast between God's purity and human sin. The least developed man has a conscience which condemns some forms of wrong doing, and causes a feeling of separation from the power or powers above. Physical defilement becomes the natural symbol of moral evil. Places and vessels and rites are invested with dignity as associated with or consecrated to the Deity.

That the conception of holiness clears itself of extraneous and unessential elements only gradually, and receives its full expression only in the New Testament revelation and especially in the life and work of Christ, should not blind us to the fact that the germs of the idea lie far back in the very beginnings of man's existence upon earth. Even then the sense of wrong within had for its correlate a dimly recognized righteousness without. So soon as man knows himself as a sinner he knows something of the holiness of that God whom he has offended. We must take exception therefore to the remark of Schurman, Belief in God, 231—"The first gods were probably non-moral beings," for Schurman himself had just said: "A God without moral character is no God at all." Dillmann, in his O. T. Theology, very properly makes the fundamental thought of O. T. religion, not the unity or the majesty of God, but his holiness. This alone forms the ethical basis for freedom and law. E. G. Robinson, Christian Theology—"The one aim of Christianity is personal holiness. But personal holiness will be the one absorbing and attainable aim of man, only as he recognizes it to be the one preëminent attribute of God. Hence everything divine is holy—the temple, the Scriptures, the Spirit." See articles on Holiness in O. T., by J. Skinner, and on Holiness in N. T., by G. B. Stevens, in Hastings' Bible Dictionary.

The development of the idea of holiness as well as the idea of love was prepared for before the advent of man. A. H. Strong, Education and Optimism: "There was a time when the past history of life upon the planet seemed one of heartless and cruel slaughter. The survival of the fittest had for its obverse side the destruction of myriads. Nature was 'red in tooth and claw with ravine.' But further thought has shown that this gloomy view results from a partial induction of facts. Paleontological life was marked not only by a struggle for life, but by a struggle for the life of others. The beginnings of altruism are to be seen in the instinct of reproduction, and in the care of offspring. In every lion's den and tiger's lair, in every mother eagle's feeding of her young, there is a self-sacrifice which faintly shadows forth man's subordination of personal interests to the interests of others. But in the ages before man can be found incipient justice as well as incipient love. The struggle for one's own life has its moral side as well as the struggle for the life of others. The instinct of self-preservation is the beginning of right, righteousness, justice, and law, on earth. Every creature owes it to God to preserve its own being. So we can find an adumbration of morality even in the predatory and internecine warfare of the geologic ages. The immanent God was even then preparing the way for the rights, the dignity, the freedom of humanity." And, we may add, was preparing the way for the understanding by men of his own fundamental attribute of holiness. See Henry Drummond, Ascent of Man; Griffith-Jones, Ascent through Christ.

In further explanation we remark:

A. Negatively, that holiness is not

(a) Justice, or purity demanding purity from creatures. Justice, the relative or transitive attribute, is indeed the manifestation and expression of the immanent attribute of holiness, but it is not to be confounded with it.

Quenstedt, Theol., 8:1:34, defines holiness as "summa omnisque labis expers to Deo puritas, puritatem debitam exigens a creaturis"—a definition of transitive holiness, or justice, rather than of the immanent attribute. Is. 5:16—"Jehovah of hosts is exalted in justice, and God the Holy One is sanctified in righteousness"—Justice is simply God's holiness in its judicial activity. Though holiness is commonly a term of separation and expresses the inherent opposition of God to all that is sinful, it is also used as a term of union, as in Lev. 11:44—"be ye holy; for I am holy." When Jesus turned from the young ruler (Mark 10:23) he illustrated the first; John 8:29 illustrates the second: "he that sent me is with me." Lowrie, Doctrine of St. John, 51-57—"'God is light' (1 John 1:5) indicates the character of God, moral purity as revealed, as producing joy and life, as contrasted with doing ill, walking in darkness, being in a state of perdition."

Universal human conscience is itself a revelation of the holiness of God, and the joining everywhere of suffering with sin is the revelation of God's justice. The wrath, anger, jealousy of God show that this reaction of God's nature is necessary. God's nature is itself holy, just, and good. Holiness is not replaced by love, as Ritschl holds, since there is no self-impartation without self-affirmation. Holiness not simply demands in law, but imparts in the Holy Spirit; see Pfleiderer, Grundriss, 79—versus Ritschl's doctrine that holiness is God's exaltation, and that it includes love; see also Pfleiderer, Die Ritschlische Theologie, 53-63. Santayana, Sense of Beauty, 69—"If perfection is the ultimate justification of being, we may understand the ground of the moral dignity of beauty. Beauty is a pledge of the possible conformity between the soul and nature, and consequently a ground of faith in the supremacy of the good." We would regard nature however as merely the symbol and expression of God, and so would regard beauty as a ground of faith in his supremacy. What Santayana says of beauty is even more true of holiness. Wherever we see it, we recognize in it a pledge of the possible conformity between the soul and God, and consequently a ground of faith in the supremacy of God.

(b) Holiness is not a complex term designating the aggregate of the divine perfections. On the other hand, the notion of holiness is, both in Scripture and in Christian experience, perfectly simple, and perfectly distinct from that of other attributes.

Dick, Theol., 1:275—Holiness = venerableness, i. e., "no particular attribute, but the general character of God as resulting from his moral attributes." Wardlaw calls holiness the union of all the attributes, as pure white light is the union of all the colored rays of the spectrum (Theology, 1:618-634). So Nitzsch, System of Christ. Doct., 166; H. W. Beecher: "Holiness = wholeness." Approaching this conception is the definition of W. N. Clarke, Christian Theology, 83—"Holiness is the glorious fulness of the goodness of God, consistently held as the principle of his own action, and the standard for his creatures." This implies, according to Dr. Clarke, 1. An inward character of perfect goodness; 2. That character as the consistent principle of his own action; 3. The goodness which is the principle of his own action is also the standard for theirs. In other words, holiness is 1. character; 2. self-consistency; 3. requirement. We object to this definition that it fails to define. We are not told what is essential to this character; the definition includes in holiness that which properly belongs to love; it omits all mention of the most important elements in holiness, namely purity and right.

A similar lack of clear definition appears in the statement of Mark Hopkins, Law of Love, 105—"It is this double aspect of love, revealing the whole moral nature, and turning every way like the flaming sword that kept the way of the tree of life, that is termed holiness." As has been shown above, holiness is contrasted in Scripture, not with mere finiteness or littleness or misfortune or poverty or even unreality, but only with uncleanness and sinfulness. E. G. Robinson, Christ. Theology, 80—"Holiness in man is the image of God's. But it is clear that holiness in man is not in proportion to the other perfections of his being—to his power, his knowledge, his wisdom, though it is in proportion to his rectitude of will—and therefore cannot be the sum of all perfections.... To identify holiness with the sum of all perfections is to make it mean mere completeness of character."

(c) Holiness is not God's self-love, in the sense of supreme regard for his own interest and happiness. There is no utilitarian element in holiness.

Buddeus, Theol. Dogmat., 2:1:36, defines holiness as God's self-love. But God loves and affirms self, not as self, but as the holiest. There is no self-seeking in God. Not the seeking of God's interests, but love for God as holy, is the principle and source of holiness in man. To call holiness God's self-love is to say that God is holy because of what he can make by it, i. e., to deny that holiness has any independent existence. See Thomasius, Christi Person und Werk, 1:155.

We would not deny, but would rather maintain, that there is a proper self-love which is not selfishness. This proper self-love, however, is not love at all. It is rather self-respect, self-preservation, self-vindication, and it constitutes an important characteristic of holiness. But to define holiness as merely God's love for himself, is to leave out of the definition the reason for this love in the purity and righteousness of the divine nature. God's self-respect implies that God respects himself for something in his own being. What is that something? Is holiness God's "moral excellence" (Hopkins), or God's "perfect goodness" (Clarke)? But what is this moral excellence or perfect goodness? We have here the method and the end described, but not the motive and ground. God does not love himself for his love, but he loves himself for his holiness. Those who maintain that love is self-affirming as well as self-communicating, and therefore that holiness is God's love for himself, must still admit that this self-affirming love which is holiness conditions and furnishes the standard for the self-communicating love which is benevolence.

G. B. Stevens, Johannine Theology, 364, tells us that "God's righteousness is the self-respect of perfect love." Miller, Evolution of Love, 53—"Self-love is that kind of action which in a perfect being actualizes, in a finite being seeks to actualize, a perfect or ideal self." In other words, love is self-affirmation. But we object that self-love is not love at all, because there is in it no self-communicating. If holiness is in any sense a form or manifestation of love—a question which we have yet to consider—it is certainly not a unitarian and utilitarian self-love, which would be identical with selfishness, but rather an affection which implies trinitarian otherness and the maintenance of self as an ideal object. This appears to be the meaning of Jonathan Edwards, in his Essay on the Trinity (ed. Fisher), 79—"All love respects another that is the beloved. By love the apostle certainly means something beside that which is commonly called self-love: that is very improperly called love, and is a thing of an exceeding diverse nature from the affection or virtue of love the apostle is speaking of." Yet we shall see that while Jonathan Edwards denies holiness to be a unitarian and utilitarian self-love, he regards its very essence to be God's trinitarian love for himself as a being of perfect moral excellence.

Ritschl's lack of trinitarian conviction makes it impossible for him to furnish any proper ground for either love or holiness in the nature of God. Ritschl holds that Christ as a person is an end in himself; he realized his own ideal; he developed his own personality; he reached his own perfection in his work for man; he is not merely a means toward the end of man's salvation. But when Ritschl comes to his doctrine of God, he is strangely inconsistent with all this, for he fails to represent God as having any end in himself, and deals with him simply as a means toward the kingdom of God as an end. Garvie, Ritschlian Theology, 256, 278, 279, well points out that personality means self-possession as well as self-communication, distinction from others as well as union with others. Ritschl does not see that God's love is primarily directed towards his Son, and only secondarily directed toward the Christian community. So he ignores the immanent Trinity. Before self-communication there must be self-maintenance. Otherwise God gives up his independence and makes created existence necessary.

(d) Holiness is not identical with, or a manifestation of, love. Since self-maintenance must precede self-impartation, and since benevolence has its object, motive, standard and limit in righteousness, holiness the self-affirming attribute can in no way be resolved into love the self-communicating.

That holiness is a form of love is the doctrine of Jonathan Edwards, Essay on the Trinity (ed. Fisher), 97—"'Tis in God's infinite love to himself that his holiness consists. As all creature holiness is to be resolved into love, as the Scripture teaches us, so doth the holiness of God himself consist in infinite love to himself. God's holiness is the infinite beauty and excellence of his nature, and God's excellency consists in his love to himself." In his treatise on The Nature of Virtue, Jonathan Edwards defines virtue as regard for being in general. He considers that God's love is first of all directed toward himself as having the greatest quantity of being, and only secondarily directed towards his creatures whose quantity of being is infinitesimal as compared with his. God therefore finds his chief end in himself, and God's self-love is his holiness. This principle has permeated and dominated subsequent

New England theology, from Samuel Hopkins, Works, 2:9-66, who maintains that holiness = love of being in general, to Horace Bushnell, Vicarious Sacrifice, who declares: "Righteousness, transferred into a word of the affections, is love; and love, translated back into a word of the conscience, is righteousness; the eternal law of right is only another conception of the law of love; the two principles, right and love, appear exactly to measure each other." So Park, Discourses, 155-180.

Similar doctrine is taught by Dorner, Christian Ethics, 73, 93, 184—"Love unites existence for self with existence for others, self-assertion and self-impartation.... Self-love in God is not selfishness, because he is the original and necessary seat of good in general, universal good. God guards his honor even in giving himself to others.... Love is the power and desire to be one's self while in another, and while one's self to be in another who is taken into the heart as an end.... I am to love my neighbor only as myself.... Virtue however requires not only good will, but the willing of the right thing." So Newman Smyth, Christian Ethics, 226-239, holds that 1. Love is self-affirmation. Hence he maintains that holiness or self-respect is involved in love. Righteousness is not an independent excellence to be contrasted with or put in opposition to benevolence; it is an essential part of love. 2. Love is self-impartation. The only limit is ethical. Here is an ever deepening immanence, yet always some transcendence of God, for God cannot deny himself. 3. Love is self-finding in another. Vicariousness belongs to love. We reply to both Dorner and Smyth that their acknowledgment that love has its condition, limit, motive, object and standard, shows that there is a principle higher than love, and which regulates love. This principle is recognized as ethical. It is identical with the right. God cannot deny himself because he is fundamentally the right. This self-affirmation is holiness, and holiness cannot be a part of love, or a form of love, because it conditions and dominates love. To call it benevolence is to ignore its majestic distinctness and to imperil its legitimate supremacy.

God must first maintain his own being before he can give to another, and this self-maintenance must have its reason and motive in the worth of that which is maintained. Holiness cannot be love, because love is irrational and capricious except as it has a standard by which it is regulated, and this standard cannot be itself love, but must be holiness. We agree with Clarke, Christian Theology, 92, that "love is the desire to impart holiness." Love is a means to holiness, and holiness is therefore the supreme good and something higher than mere love. It is not true, vice versa, that holiness is the desire to impart love, or that holiness is a means to love. Instead then of saying, with Clarke, that "holiness is central in God, but love is central in holiness," we should prefer to say: "Love is central in God, but holiness is central in love," though in this case we should use the term love as including self-love. It is still better not to use the word love at all as referring to God's regard for himself. In ordinary usage, love means only regard for another and self-communication to that other. To embrace in it God's self-affirmation is to misinterpret holiness and to regard it as a means to an end, instead of making it what it really is, the superior object, and the regulative principle, of love.

That which lays down the norm or standard for love must be the superior of love. When we forget that "Righteousness and justice are the foundation of his throne" (Ps. 97:2), we lose one of the chief landmarks of Christian doctrine and involve ourselves in a mist of error. Rev. 4:3—"there was a rainbow round about the throne" = in the midst of the rainbow of pardon and peace there is a throne of holiness and judgment. In Mat. 6:9, 10, "Thy kingdom come" is not the first petition, but rather, "Hallowed be thy name." It is a false idea of the divine simplicity which would reduce the attributes to one. Self-assertion is not a form of self-impartation. Not sentiency, a state of the sensibility, even though it be the purest benevolence, is the fundamental thing, but rather activity of will and a right direction of that will. Hodge, Essays, 133-136, 262-273, shows well that holy love is a love controlled by holiness. Holiness is not a mere means to happiness. To be happy is not the ultimate reason for being holy. Right and wrong are not matters of profit and loss. To be told that God is only benevolence, and that he punishes only when the happiness of the universe requires it, destroys our whole allegiance to God and does violence to the constitution of our nature.

That God is only love has been called "the doctrine of the papahood of God." God is "a summer ocean of kindliness, never agitated by storms" (Dale, Ephesians, 59). But Jesus gives us the best idea of God, and in him we find, not only pity, but at times moral indignation. John 17:11—"Holy Father" = more than love. Love can be exercised by God only when it is right love. Holiness is the track on which the engine of love must run. The track cannot be the engine. If either includes the other, then it is holiness that includes love, since holiness is the maintenance of God's perfection, and perfection involves love. He that is holy affirms himself also as the perfect love. If love were fundamental, there would be nothing to give, and so love would be vain and worthless. There can be no giving of self, without a previous self-affirming. God is not holy because he loves, but he loves because he is holy. Love cannot direct itself; it is under bonds to holiness. Justice is not dependent on love for its right to be. Stephen G. Barnes: "Mere good will is not the sole content of the law; it is insufficient in times of fiery trial; it is inadequate as a basis for retribution. Love needs justice, and justice needs love; both are commanded in God's law and are perfectly revealed in God's character."

There may be a friction between a man's two hands, and there may be a conflict between a man's conscience and his will, between his intellect and his affection. Force is God's energy under resistance, the resistance as well as the energy being his. So, upon occasion of man's sin, holiness and love in God become opposite poles or forces. The first and most serious effect of sin is not its effect upon man, but its effect upon God. Holiness necessarily requires suffering, and love endures it. This eternal suffering of God on account of sin is the atonement, and the incarnate Christ only shows what has been in the heart of God from the beginning. To make holiness a form of love is really to deny its existence, and with this to deny that any atonement is necessary for man's salvation. If holiness is the same as love, how is it that the classic world, that knew of God's holiness, did not also know of his love? The ethics here reminds one of Abraham Lincoln's meat broth that was made of the shadow of a pigeon that died of starvation. Holiness that is only good will is not holiness at all, for it lacks the essential elements of purity and righteousness.

At the railway switching grounds east of Rochester, there is a man whose duty it is to move a bar of iron two or three inches to the left or to the right. So he determines whether a train shall go toward New York or toward Washington, toward New Orleans or San Francisco. Our conclusion at this point in our theology will similarly determine what our future system will be. The principle that holiness is a manifestation of love, or a form of benevolence, leads to the conclusions that happiness is the only good, and the only end; that law is a mere expedient for the securing of happiness; that penalty is simply deterrent or reformatory in its aim; that no atonement needs to be offered to God for human sin; that eternal retribution cannot be vindicated, since there is no hope of reform. This view ignores the testimony of conscience and of Scripture that sin is intrinsically ill-deserving, and must be punished on that account, not because punishment will work good to the universe,—indeed, it could not work good to the universe, unless it were just and right in itself. It ignores the fact that mercy is optional with God, while holiness is invariable; that punishment is many times traced to God's holiness, but never to God's love; that God is not simply love but light—moral light—and therefore is "a consuming fire" (Heb. 12:29) to all iniquity. Love chastens (Heb. 12:6), but only holiness punishes (Jer. 10:24—"correct me, but in measure; not in thine anger"; Ez. 28:22—"I shall have executed judgments in her, and shall be sanctified in her"; 36:21, 22—in judgment "I do not this for your sake, but for my holy name"; 1 John 1:5—"God is light, and in him is no darkness"—moral darkness; Rev. 15:1, 4—"the wrath of God ... thou only art holy ... thy righteous acts have been made manifest"; 16:5—"righteous art thou ... because thou didst thus judge"; 19:2—"true and righteous are his judgments; for he hath judged the great harlot"). See Hovey, God with Us, 187-221; Philippi, Glaubenslehre, 2:80-82; Thomasius, Christi Person und Werk, 154, 155, 346-353; Lange, Pos. Dogmatik, 203.

B. Positively, that holiness is

(a) Purity of substance.—In God's moral nature, as necessarily acting, there are indeed the two elements of willing and being. But the passive logically precedes the active; being comes before willing; God is pure before he wills purity. Since purity, however, in ordinary usage is a negative term and means only freedom from stain or wrong, we must include in it also the positive idea of moral rightness. God is holy in that he is the source and standard of the right.

E. G. Robinson, Christian Theology, 80—"Holiness is moral purity, not only in the sense of absence of all moral stain, but of complacency in all moral good." Shedd, Dogm. Theology, 1:362— "Holiness in God is conformity to his own perfect nature. The only rule for the divine will is the divine reason; and the divine reason prescribes everything that is befitting an infinite Being to do. God is not under law, nor above law. He is law. He is righteous by nature and necessity.... God is the source and author of law for all moral beings." We may better Shedd's definition by saying that holiness is that attribute in virtue of which God's being and God's will eternally conform to each other. In thus maintaining that holy being logically precedes holy willing, we differ from the view of Lotze, Philos. of Religion, 139—"Such will of God no more follows from his nature as secondary to it, or precedes it as primary to it than, in motion, direction can be antecedent or subsequent to velocity." Bowne, Philos. of Theism, 16—"God's nature = a fixed law of activity or mode of manifestation.... But laws of thought are no limitation, because they are simply modes of thought-activity. They do not rule intellect, but only express what intellect is."

In spite of these utterances of Lotze and of Bowne, we must maintain that, as truth of being logically precedes truth of knowing, and as a loving nature precedes loving emotions, so purity of substance precedes purity of will. The opposite doctrine leads to such utterances as that of Whedon (On the Will, 316): "God is holy, in that he freely chooses to make his own happiness in eternal right. Whether he could not make himself equally happy in wrong is more than we can say.... Infinite wisdom and infinite holiness consist in, and result from, God's volitions eternally." Whedon therefore believes, not in God's unchangeableness, but in God's unchangingness. He cannot say whether motives may not at some time prove strongest for divine apostasy to evil. The essential holiness of God affords no basis for certainty. Here we have to rely on our faith, more than on the object of faith; see H. B. Smith, Review of Whedon, in Faith and Philosophy, 355-399. As we said with regard to truth, so here we say with regard to holiness, that to make holiness a matter of mere will, instead of regarding it as a characteristic of God's being, is to deny that anything is holy in itself. If God can make impurity to be purity, then God in himself is indifferent to purity or impurity, and he ceases therefore to be God. Robert Browning, A Soul's Tragedy, 223—"I trust in God—the Right shall be the Right And other than the Wrong, while He endures." P. S. Moxom: "Revelation is a disclosure of the divine righteousness. We do not add to the thought when we say that it is also a disclosure of the divine love, for love is a manifestation or realization of that rightness of relations which righteousness is." H. B. Smith, System, 223-231—"Virtue = love for both happiness and holiness, yet holiness as ultimate,—love to the highest Person and to his ends and objects."

(b) Energy of will.—This purity is not simply a passive and dead quality; it is the attribute of a personal being; it is penetrated and pervaded by will. Holiness is the free moral movement of the Godhead.

As there is a higher Mind than our mind, and a greater Heart than our heart, so there is a grander Will than our will. Holiness contains this element of will, although it is a will which expresses nature, instead of causing nature. It is not a still and moveless purity, like the whiteness of the new-fallen snow, or the stainless blue of the summer sky. It is the most tremendous of energies, in unsleeping movement. It is "a glassy sea" (Rev. 15:2), but "a glassy sea mingled with fire." A. J. Gordon: "Holiness is not a dead-white purity, the perfection of the faultless marble statue. Life, as well as purity, enters into the idea of holiness. They who are 'without fault before the throne' are they who 'follow the Lamb whithersoever he goeth'—holy activity attending and expressing their holy state." Martensen, Christian Ethics, 62, 63—"God is the perfect unity of the ethically necessary and the ethically free"; "God cannot do otherwise than will his own essential nature." See Thomasius, Christi Person und Werk, 141; and on the Holiness of Christ, see Godet, Defence of the Christian Faith, 203-241.

The centre of personality is will. Knowing has its end in feeling, and feeling has its end in willing. Hence I must make feeling subordinate to willing, and happiness to righteousness. I must will with God and for God, and must use all my influence over others to make them like God in holiness. William James, Will to Believe, 123—"Mind must first get its impression from the object; then define what that object is and what active measures its presence demands; and finally react.... All faiths and philosophies, moods and systems, subserve and pass into a third stage, the stage of action." What is true of man is even more true of God. All the wills of men combined, aye, even the whole moving energy of humanity in all climes and ages, is as nothing compared with the extent and intensity of God's willing. The whole momentum of God's being is behind moral law. That law is his self-expression. His beneficent yet also his terrible arm is ever defending and enforcing it. God must maintain his holiness, for this is his very Godhead. If he did not maintain it, love would have nothing to give away, or to make others partakers of.

Does God will the good because it is the good, or is the good good because God wills it? In the former case, there would seem to be a good above God; in the latter case, good is something arbitrary and changeable. Kaftan, Dogmatik, 186, 187, says that neither of these is true; he holds that there is no a priori good before the willing of it, and he also holds that will without direction is not will; the good is good for God, not before, but in, his self-determination. Dorner, System Doctrine, 1:432, holds on the contrary that both these are true, because God has no mere simple form of being, whether necessary or free, but rather a manifoldly diverse being, absolutely correlated however, and reciprocally conditioning itself,—that is, a trinitarian being, both necessary and free. We side with Dorner here, and claim that the belief that God's will is the executive of God's being is necessary to a correct ethics and to a correct theology. Celsus justified polytheism by holding that whatever is a part of God reveals God, serves God, and therefore may rationally be worshiped. Christianity he excepted from this wide toleration, because it worshiped a jealous God who was not content to be one of many. But this jealousy really signifies that God is a Being to whom moral distinctions are real. The God of Celsus, the God of pantheism, is not jealous, because he is not the Holy One, but simply the Absolute. The category of the ethical is merged in the category of being; see Bruce, Apologetics, 16. The great lack of modern theology is precisely this ethical lack; holiness is merged in benevolence; there is no proper recognition of God's righteousness. John 17:25—"O righteous Father, the world knew thee not"—is a text as true to-day as in Jesus' time. See Issel, Begriff der Heiligkeit in N. T., 41, 84, who defines holiness in God as "the ethical perfection of God in its exaltation above all that is sinful," and holiness in men as "the condition corresponding to that of God, in which man keeps himself pure from sin."

(c) Self-affirmation.—Holiness is God's self-willing. His own purity is the supreme object of his regard and maintenance. God is holy, in that his infinite moral excellence affirms and asserts itself as the highest possible motive and end. Like truth and love, this attribute can be understood only in the light of the doctrine of the Trinity.

Holiness is purity willing itself. We have an analogy in man's duty of self-preservation, self-respect, self-assertion. Virtue is bound to maintain and defend itself, as in the case of Job. In his best moments, the Christian feels that purity is not simply the negation of sin, but the affirmation of an inward and divine principle of righteousness. Thomasius, Christi Person und Werk, 1:137—"Holiness is the perfect agreement of the divine willing with the divine being; for as the personal creature is holy when it wills and determines itself as God wills, so is God the holy one because he wills himself as what he is (or, to be what he is). In virtue of this attribute, God excludes from himself everything that contradicts his nature, and affirms himself in his absolutely good being—his being like himself." Tholuck on Romans, 5th ed., 151—"The term holiness should be used to indicate a relation of God to himself. That is holy which, undisturbed from without, is wholly like itself." Dorner, System of Doctrine, 1:456—"It is the part of goodness to protect goodness." We shall see, when we consider the doctrine of the Trinity, that that doctrine has close relations to the doctrine of the immanent attributes. It is in the Son that God has a perfect object of will, as well as of knowledge and love.

The object of God's willing in eternity past can be nothing outside of himself. It must be the highest of all things. We see what it must be, only when we remember that the right is the unconditional imperative of our moral nature. Since we are made in his image we must conclude that God eternally wills righteousness. Not all God's acts are acts of love, but all are acts of holiness. The self-respect, self-preservation, self-affirmation, self-assertion, self-vindication, which we call God's holiness, is only faintly reflected in such utterances as Job 27:5, 6—"Till I die I will not put away mine integrity from me. My righteousness I hold fast, and will not let it go"; 31:37—"I would declare unto him the number of my steps; as a prince would I go near unto him." The fact that the Spirit of God is denominated the Holy Spirit should teach us what is God's essential nature, and the requisition that we should be holy as he is holy should teach us what is the true standard of human duty and object of human ambition. God's holiness moreover, since it is self-affirmation, furnishes the guarantee that God's love will not fail to secure its end, and that all things will serve his purpose. Rom. 11:36—"For of him, and through him, and unto him, are all things. To him be the glory for ever. Amen." On the whole subject of Holiness, as an attribute of God, see A. H. Strong, Philosophy and Religion, 188-200, and Christ in Creation, 388-405; Delitzsch, art. Heiligkeit, in Herzog, Realencyclop.; Baudissin, Begriff der Heiligkeit im A. T.,—synopsis in Studien und Kritiken, 1880:169; Robertson Smith, Prophets of Israel, 224-234; E. B. Coe, in Presb. and Ref. Rev., Jan. 1890:42-47; and articles on Holiness in O. T., and Holiness in N. T., in Hastings' Bible Dictionary.

VI. Relative or Transitive Attributes
First Division.—Attributes having relation to Time and Space.

1. Eternity
By this we mean that God's nature (a) is without beginning or end; (b) is free from all succession of time; and (c) contains in itself the cause of time.

Deut. 32:40—"For I lift up my hand to heaven, And say, As I live forever...."; Ps. 90:2—"Before the mountains ... from everlasting ... thou art God"; 102:27—"thy years shall have no end"; Is. 41:4—"I Jehovah, the first, and with the last"; 1 Cor. 2:7—πρὸ τῶν αἰώνων—"before the worlds" or "ages" = πρὸ καταβολῆς κόσμου—"before the foundation of the world" (Eph. 1:4). 1 Tim. 1:17—Βασιλεῖ τῶν αἰώνων—"King of the ages" (so also Rev. 15:8). 1 Tim. 6:16—"who only hath immortality." Rev. 1:8—"the Alpha and the Omega." Dorner: "We must not make Kronos (time) and Uranos (space) earlier divinities before God." They are among the "all things" that were "made by him " (John 1:3). Yet time and space are not substances; neither are they attributes (qualities of substance); they are rather relations of finite existence. (Porter, Human Intellect, 568, prefers to call time and space "correlates to beings and events.") With finite existence they come into being; they are not mere regulative conceptions of our minds; they exist objectively, whether we perceive them or not. Ladd: "Time is the mental presupposition of the duration of events and of objects. Time is not an entity, or it would be necessary to suppose some other time in which it endures. We think of space and time as unconditional, because they furnish the conditions of our knowledge. The age of a son is conditioned on the age of his father. The conditions themselves cannot be conditioned. Space and time are mental forms, but not only that. There is an extra-mental something in the case of space and time, as in the case of sound."

Ex. 3:14—"I am"—involves eternity. Ps. 102:12-14—"But thou, O Jehovah, wilt abide forever.... Thou wilt arise, and have mercy upon Zion; for it is time to have pity upon her.... For thy servants ... have pity upon her dust" = because God is eternal, he will have compassion upon Zion: he will do this, for even we, her children, love her very dust. Jude 25—"glory, majesty, dominion and power, before all time, and now, and for evermore." Pfleiderer, Philos. Religion, 1:165—"God is 'King of the æons' (1 Tim. 1:17), because he distinguishes, in his thinking, his eternal inner essence from his changeable working in the world. He is not merged in the process." Edwards the younger describes timelessness as "the immediate and invariable possession of the whole unlimited life together and at once." Tyler, Greek Poets, 148—"The heathen gods had only existence without end. The Greeks seem never to have conceived of existence without beginning." On precognition as connected with the so-called future already existing, and on apparent time progression as a subjective human sensation and not inherent in the universe as it exists in an infinite Mind, see Myers, Human Personality, 2:262 sq. Tennyson, Life,

1:322—"For was and is and will be are but is: And all creation is one act at once, The birth of light; but we that are not all, As parts, can see but parts, now this, now that, And live perforce from thought to thought, and make The act a phantom of succession: there Our weakness somehow shapes the shadow, Time."

Augustine: "Mundus non in tempore, sed cum tempore, factus est." There is no meaning to the question: Why did creation take place when it did rather than earlier? or the question: What was God doing before creation? These questions presuppose an independent time in which God created—a time before time. On the other hand, creation did not take place at any time, but God gave both the world and time their existence. Royce, World and Individual, 2:111-115—"Time is the form of the will, as space is the form of the intellect (cf. 124, 133). Time runs only in one direction (unlike space), toward fulfilment of striving or expectation. In pursuing its goals, the self lives in time. Every now is also a succession, as is illustrated in any melody. To God the universe is 'totum simul', as to us any succession is one whole. 233—Death is a change in the time-span—the minimum of time in which a succession can appear as a completed whole. To God 'a thousand years' are 'as one day' (2 Pet. 3:8). 419—God, In his totality as the Absolute Being, is conscious not, in time, but of time, and of all that infinite time contains. In time there follow, in their sequence, the chords of his endless symphony. For him is this whole symphony of life at once.... You unite present, past and future in a single consciousness whenever you hear any three successive words, for one is past, another is present, at the same time that a third is future. So God unites in timeless perception the whole succession of finite events.... The single notes are not lost in the melody. You are in God, but you are not lost in God." Mozart, quoted in Wm. James, Principles of Psychology, 1:255—"All the inventing and making goes on in me as in a beautiful strong dream. But the best of all is the hearing of it all at once."

Eternity is infinity in its relation to time. It implies that God's nature is not subject to the law of time. God is not in time. It is more correct to say that time is in God. Although there is logical succession in God's thoughts, there is no chronological succession.

Time is duration measured by successions. Duration without succession would still be duration, though it would be immeasurable. Reid, Intellectual Powers, essay 3, chap. 5—"We may measure duration by the succession of thoughts in the mind, as we measure length by inches or feet, but the notion or idea of duration must be antecedent to the mensuration of it, as the notion of length is antecedent to its being measured." God is not under the law of time. Solly, The Will, 254—"God looks through time as we look through space." Murphy, Scientific Bases, 90—"Eternity is not, as men believe, Before and after us, an endless line. No, 'tis a circle. Infinitely great—All the circumference with creations thronged: God at the centre dwells, beholding all. And as we move in this eternal round, The finite portion which alone we see Behind us, is the past; what lies before We call the future. But to him who dwells Far at the centre, equally remote From every point of the circumference, Both are alike, the future and the past." Vaughan (1655): "I saw Eternity the other night. Like a great ring of pure and endless light. And calm as it was bright; and round beneath it Time in hours, days, years, Driven by the spheres, Like a vast shadow moved, in which the world And all her train were hurled."

We cannot have derived from experience our idea of eternal duration in the past, for experience gives us only duration that has had beginning. The idea of duration as without beginning must therefore be given us by intuition. Case, Physical Realism, 379, 380—"Time is the continuance, or continual duration, of the universe." Bradley, Appearance and Reality, 39—Consider time as a stream—under a spatial form: "If you take time as a relation between units without duration, then the whole time has no duration, and is not time at all. But if you give duration to the whole time, then at once the units themselves are found to possess it, and they cease to be units." The now is not time, unless it turns past into future, and this is a process. The now then consists of nows, and these nows are undiscoverable. The unit is nothing but its own relation to something beyond, something not discoverable. Time therefore is not real, but is appearance.

John Caird, Fund. Ideas, 1:185—"That which grasps and correlates objects in space cannot itself be one of the things of space; that which apprehends and connects events as succeeding each other in time must itself stand above the succession or stream of events. In being able to measure them, it cannot be flowing with them. There could not be for self-consciousness any such thing as time, if it were not, in one aspect of it, above time, if it did not belong to an order which is or has in it an element which is eternal.... As taken up into thought, succession is not successive." A. H. Strong, Historical Discourse, May 9, 1900—"God is above space and time, and we are in God. We mark the passage of time, and we write our histories. But we can do this, only because in our highest being we do not belong to space and time, but have in us a bit of eternity. John Caird tells us that we could not perceive the flowing of the stream if we were ourselves a part of the current; only as we have our feet planted on solid rock, can we observe that the water rushes by. We belong to God; we are akin to God; and while the world passes away and the lust thereof, he that doeth the will of God abideth forever." J. Estlin Carpenter and P. H. Wicksteed, Studies in Theology, 10—"Dante speaks of God as him in whom 'every where and every when are focused in a point', that is, to whom every season is now and every place is here."

Amiel's Journal: "Time is the supreme illusion. It is the inner prism by which we decompose being and life, the mode by which we perceive successively what is simultaneous in idea.... Time is the successive dispersion of being, just as speech is the successive analysis of an intuition, or of an act of the will. In itself it is relative and negative, and it disappears within the absolute Being.... Time and space are fragments of the Infinite for the use of finite creatures. God permits them that he may not be alone. They are the mode under which creatures are possible and conceivable.... If the universe subsists, it is because the eternal Mind loves to perceive its own content, in all its wealth and expression, especially in its stages of preparation.... The radiations of our mind are imperfect reflections from the great show of fireworks set in motion by Brahma, and great art is great only because of its conformities with the divine order—with that which is."

Yet we are far from saying that time, now that it exists, has no objective reality to God. To him, past, present, and future are "one eternal now," not in the sense that there is no distinction between them, but only in the sense that he sees past and future as vividly as he sees the present. With creation time began, and since the successions of history are veritable successions, he who sees according to truth must recognize them.

Thomas Carlyle calls God "the Eternal Now." Mason, Faith of the Gospel, 30—"God is not contemptuous of time.... One day is with the Lord as a thousand years. He values the infinitesimal in time, even as he does in space. Hence the patience, the long-suffering, the expectation, of God." We are reminded of the inscription on the sun-dial, in which it is said of the hours: "Pereunt et imputantur"— "They pass by, and they are charged to our account." A certain preacher remarked on the wisdom of God which has so arranged that the moments of time come successively and not simultaneously, and thus prevent infinite confusion! Shedd, Dogm. Theol., 1:344, illustrates God's eternity by the two ways in which a person may see a procession: first from a doorway in the street through which the procession is passing; and secondly, from the top of a steeple which commands a view of the whole procession at the same instant.

S. E. Meze, quoted in Royce, Conception of God, 40—"As if all of us were cylinders, with their ends removed, moving through the waters of some placid lake. To the cylinders the waters seem to move. What has passed is a memory, what is to come is doubtful. But the lake knows that all the water is equally real, and that it is quiet, immovable, unruffled. Speaking technically, time is no reality. Things seem past and future, and, in a sense, non-existent to us, but, in fact, they are just as genuinely real as the present is." Yet even here there is an order. You cannot play a symphony backward and have music. This qualification at least must be put upon the words of Berkeley; "A succession of ideas I take to constitute time, and not to be only the sensible measure thereof, as Mr. Locke and others think."

Finney, quoted in Bib. Sac., Oct. 1877:722—"Eternity to us means all past, present and future duration. But to God it means only now. Duration and space, as they respect his existence, mean infinitely different things from what they do when they respect our existence. God's existence and his acts, as they respect finite existence, have relation to time and space. But as they respect his own existence, everything is here and now. With respect to all finite existences, God can say: I was, I am, I shall be, I will do; but with respect to his own existence, all that he can say is: I am, I do."

Edwards the younger, Works, 1:386, 387—"There is no succession in the divine mind; therefore no new operations take place. All the divine acts are from eternity, nor is there any time with God. The effects of these divine acts do indeed all take place in time and in a succession. If it should be said that on this supposition the effects take place not till long after the acts by which they are produced, I answer that they do so in our view, but not in the view of God. With him there is no time; no before or after with respect to time: nor has time any existence in the divine mind, or in the nature of things independently of the minds and perceptions of creatures; but it depends on the succession of those perceptions." We must qualify this statement of the younger Edwards by the following from Julius Müller: "If God's working can have no relation to time, then all bonds of union between God and the world are snapped asunder."

It is an interesting question whether the human spirit is capable of timeless existence, and whether the conception of time is purely physical. In dreams we seem to lose sight of succession; in extreme pain an age is compressed into a minute. Does this throw light upon the nature of prophecy? Is the soul of the prophet rapt into God's timeless existence and vision? It is doubtful whether Rev. 10:6—"there shall be time no longer" can be relied upon to prove the affirmative; for the Rev. Vers. marg. and the American Revisers translate "there shall be delay no longer." Julius Müller, Doct. Sin, 2:147—"All self-consciousness is a victory over time." So with memory; see Dorner, Glaubenslehre, 1:471. On "the death-vision of one's whole existence," see Frances Kemble Butler's experience in Shedd, Dogm. Theol., 1:351—"Here there is succession and series, only so exceedingly rapid as to seem simultaneous." This rapidity however is so great as to show that each man can at the last be judged in an instant. On space and time as unlimited, see Porter, Hum. Intellect, 564-566. On the conception of eternity, see Mansel, Lectures, Essays and Reviews, 111-126, and Modern Spiritualism, 255-292; New Englander, April, 1875: art. on the Metaphysical Idea of Eternity. For practical lessons from the Eternity of God, see Park, Discourses, 137-154; Westcott, Some Lessons of the Rev. Vers., (Pott, N. Y., 1897), 187—with comments on αἰῶνες in Eph. 3:21, Heb. 11:3, Rev. 4; 10, 11—"the universe under the aspect of time."

2. Immensity

By this we mean that God's nature (a) is without extension; (b) is subject to no limitations of space; and (c) contains in itself the cause of space.

1 Kings 8:27—"behold, heaven and the heaven of heavens cannot contain thee." Space is a creation of God; Rom. 8:39—"nor height nor depth, nor any other creature." Zahn, Bib. Dogmatik, 149—"Scripture does not teach the immanence of God in the world, but the immanence of the world in God." Dante does not put God, but Satan at the centre; and Satan, being at the centre, is crushed with the whole weight of the universe. God is the Being who encompasses all. All things exist in him. E. G. Robinson: "Space is a relation; God is the author of relations and of our modes of thought; therefore God is the author of space. Space conditions our thought, but it does not condition God's thought."

Jonathan Edwards: "Place itself is mental, and within and without are mental conceptions.... When I say the material universe exists only in the mind, I mean that it is absolutely dependent on the conception of the mind for its existence, and does not exist as spirits do, whose existence does not consist in, nor in dependence on, the conception of other minds." H. M. Stanley, on Space and Science, in Philosophical Rev., Nov. 1898:615—"Space is not full of things, but things are spaceful.... Space is a form of dynamic appearance." Bradley carries the ideality of space to an extreme, when, in his Appearance and Reality, 35-38, he tells us: Space is not a mere relation, for it has parts, and what can be the parts of a relation? But space is nothing but a relation, for it is lengths of lengths of—nothing that we can find. We can find no terms either inside or outside. Space, to be space, must have space outside itself. Bradley therefore concludes that space is not reality but only appearance.

Immensity is infinity in its relation to space. God's nature is not subject to the law of space. God is not in space. It is more correct to say that space is in God. Yet space has an objective reality to God. With creation space began to be, and since God sees according to truth, he recognizes relations of space in his creation.

Many of the remarks made in explanation of time apply equally to space. Space is not a substance nor an attribute, but a relation. It exists so soon as extended matter exists, and exists as its necessary condition, whether our minds perceive it or not. Reid, Intellectual Powers, essay 2, chap. 9—"Space is not so properly an object of sense, as a necessary concomitant of the objects of sight and touch." When we see or touch body, we get the idea of space in which the body exists, but the idea of space is not furnished by the sense; it is an a priori cognition of the reason. Experience furnishes the occasion of its evolution, but the mind evolves the conception by its own native energy.

Anselm, Proslogion, 19—"Nothing contains thee, but thou containest all things." Yet it is not precisely accurate to say that space is in God, for this expression seems to intimate that God is a greater space which somehow includes the less. God is rather unspatial and is the Lord of space. The notion that space and the divine immensity are identical leads to a materialistic conception of God. Space is not an attribute of God, as Clarke maintained, and no argument for the divine existence can be constructed from this premise (see pages 85, 86). Martineau, Types, 1:138, 139, 170—"Malebranche said that God is the place of all spirits, as space is the place of all bodies.... Descartes held that there is no such thing as empty space. Nothing cannot possibly have extension. Wherever extension is, there must be something extended. Hence the doctrine of a plenum, A vacuum is inconceivable." Lotze, Outlines of Metaphysics, 87—"According to the ordinary view ... space exists, and things exist in it; according to our view, only things exist, and between them nothing exists, but space exists in them."

Case, Physical Realism, 379, 380—"Space is the continuity, or continuous extension, of the universe as one substance." Ladd: "Is space extended? Then it must be extended in some other space. That other space is the space we are talking about. Space then is not an entity, but a mental presupposition of the existence of extended substance. Space and time are neither finite nor infinite. Space has neither circumference nor centre,—its centre would be everywhere. We cannot imagine space at all. It is simply a precondition of mind enabling us to perceive things." In Bib. Sac., 1890:415-444, art.: Is Space a Reality? Prof. Mead opposes the doctrine that space is purely subjective, as taught by Bowne; also the doctrine that space is a certain order of relations among realities; that space is nothing apart from things; but that things, when they exist, exist in certain relations, and that the sum, or system, of these relations constitutes space.

We prefer the view of Bowne, Metaphysics, 127, 137, 143, that "Space is the form of objective experience, and is nothing in abstraction from that experience.... It is a form of intuition, and not a mode of existence. According to this view, things are not in space and space-relations, but appear to be. In themselves they are essentially non-spatial; but by their interactions with one another, and with the mind, they give rise to the appearance of a world of extended things in a common space. Space-predicates, then, belong to phenomena only, and not to things-in-themselves.... Apparent reality exists spatially; but proper ontological reality exists spacelessly and without spatial predicates." For the view that space is relative, see also Cocker, Theistic Conception of the World, 66-96; Calderwood, Philos. of the Infinite, 331-335. Per contra, see Porter, Human Intellect, 662; Hazard, Letters on Causation in Willing, appendix; Bib. Sac., Oct. 1877:723; Gear, in Bap. Rev., July, 1880:434; Lowndes, Philos. of Primary Beliefs, 144-161.

Second Division.—Attributes having relation to Creation.

1. Omnipresence

By this we mean that God, in the totality of his essence, without diffusion or expansion, multiplication or division, penetrates and fills the universe in all its parts.

Ps. 139:7 sq.—"Whither shall I go from thy Spirit? Or whither shall I flee from thy presence?" Jer. 23:23, 24—"Am I a God at hand, saith Jehovah, and not a God afar off?... Do not I fill heaven and earth?" Acts 17:27, 28—"he is not far from each one of us: for in him we live, and move, and have our being." Faber: "For God is never so far off As even to be near. He is within. Our spirit is The home he holds most dear. To think of him as by our side Is almost as untrue As to remove his shrine beyond Those skies of starry blue. So all the while I thought myself Homeless, forlorn and weary, Missing my joy, I walked the earth Myself God's sanctuary." Henri Amiel: "From every point on earth we are equally near to heaven and the infinite." Tennyson, The Higher Pantheism: "Speak to him then, for he hears, and spirit with spirit can meet; Closer is he than breathing, and nearer than hands and feet." "As full, as perfect, in a hair as heart."

The atheist wrote: "God is nowhere," but his little daughter read it: "God is now here," and it converted him. The child however sometimes asks: "If God is everywhere, how is there any room for us?" and the only answer is that God is not a material but a spiritual being, whose presence does not exclude finite existence but rather makes such existence possible. This universal presence of God had to be learned gradually. It required great faith in Abraham to go out from Ur of the Chaldees, and yet to hold that God would be with him in a distant land (Heb. 11:8). Jacob learned that the heavenly ladder followed him wherever he went (Gen. 28:15). Jesus taught that "neither in this mountain, nor in Jerusalem, shall ye worship the Father" (John 4:21). Our Lord's mysterious comings and goings after his resurrection were intended to teach his disciples that he was with them "always, even unto the end of the world" (Mat. 28:20). The omnipresence of Jesus demonstrates, a fortiori, the omnipresence of God.

In explanation of this attribute we may say:

(a) God's omnipresence is not potential but essential.—We reject the Socinian representation that God's essence is in heaven, only his power on earth. When God is said to "dwell in the heavens," we are to understand the language either as a symbolic expression of exaltation above earthly things, or as a declaration that his most special and glorious self-manifestations are to the spirits of heaven.

Ps. 123:1—"O thou that sittest in the heavens"; 113:5—"That hath his seat on high"; Is. 57:15—"the high and lofty One that inhabiteth eternity." Mere potential omnipresence is Deistic as well as Socinian. Like birds in the air or fish in the sea, "at home, abroad, We are surrounded still with God." We do not need to go up to heaven to call him down, or into the abyss to call him up (Rom. 10:6, 7). The best illustration is found in the presence of the soul in every part of the body. Mind seems not confined to the brain. Natural realism in philosophy, as distinguished from idealism, requires that the mind should be at the point of contact with the outer world, instead of having reports and ideas brought to it in the brain; see Porter, Human Intellect, 149. All believers in a soul regard the soul as at least present in all parts of the brain, and this is a relative omnipresence no less difficult in principle than its presence in all parts of the body. An animal's brain may be frozen into a piece solid as ice, yet, after thawing, it will act as before: although freezing of the whole body will cause death. If the immaterial principle were confined to the brain we should expect freezing of the brain to cause death. But if the soul may be omnipresent in the body or even in the brain, the divine Spirit may be omnipresent in the universe. Bowne, Metaphysics, 136—"If finite things are modes of the infinite, each thing must be a mode of the entire infinite; and the infinite must be present in its unity and completeness in every finite thing, just as the entire soul is present in all its acts." This idealistic conception of the entire mind as present in all its thoughts must be regarded as the best analogue to God's omnipresence in the universe. We object to the view that this omnipresence is merely potential, as we find it in Clarke, Christian Theology, 74—"We know, and only know, that God is able to put forth all his power of action, without regard to place.... Omnipresence is an element in the immanence of God.... A local God would be no real God. If he is not everywhere, he is not true God anywhere. Omnipresence is implied in all providence, in all prayer, in all communion with God and reliance on God."

So long as it is conceded that consciousness is not confined to a single point in the brain, the question whether other portions of the brain or of the body are also the seat of consciousness may be regarded as a purely academic one, and the answer need not affect our present argument. The principle of omnipresence is granted when once we hold that the soul is conscious at more than one point of the physical organism. Yet the question suggested above is an interesting one and with regard to it psychologists are divided. Paulsen, Einleitung in die Philosophie (1892), 138-159, holds that consciousness is correlated with the sum-total of bodily processes, and with him agree Fechner and Wundt. "Pflüger and Lewes say that as the hemispheres of the brain owe their intelligence to the consciousness which we know to be there, so the intelligence of the spinal cord's acts must really be due to the invisible presence of a consciousness lower in degree." Professor Brewer's rattlesnake, after several hours of decapitation, still struck at him with its bloody neck, when he attempted to seize it by the tail. From the reaction of the frog's leg after decapitation may we not infer a certain consciousness? "Robin, on tickling the breast of a criminal an hour after decapitation, saw the arm and hand move toward the spot." Hudson, Demonstration of a Future Life, 239-249, quotes from Hammond, Treatise on Insanity, chapter 2, to prove that the brain is not the sole organ of the mind. Instinct does not reside exclusively in the brain; it is seated in the medulla oblongata, or in the spinal cord, or in both these organs. Objective mind, as Hudson thinks, is the function of the physical brain, and it ceases when the brain loses its vitality. Instinctive acts are performed by animals after excision of the brain, and by human beings born without brain. Johnson, in Andover Rev., April, 1890:421—"The brain is not the only seat of consciousness. The same evidence that points to the brain as the principal seat of consciousness points to the nerve-centres situated in the spinal cord or elsewhere as the seat of a more or less subordinate consciousness or intelligence." Ireland, Blot on the Brain, 26—"I do not take it for proved that consciousness is entirely confined to the brain."

In spite of these opinions, however, we must grant that the general consensus among psychologists is upon the other side. Dewey, Psychology, 349—"The sensory and motor nerves have points of meeting in the spinal cord. When a stimulus is transferred from a sensory nerve to a motor without the conscious intervention of the mind, we have reflex action.... If something approaches the eye, the stimulus is transferred to the spinal cord, and instead of being continued to the brain and giving rise to a sensation, it is discharged into a motor nerve and the eye is immediately closed.... The reflex action in itself involves no consciousness." William James, Psychology, 1:16, 66, 134, 214—"The cortex of the brain is the sole organ of consciousness in man.... If there be any consciousness pertaining to the lower centres, it is a consciousness of which the self knows nothing.... In lower animals this may not be so much the case.... The seat of the mind, so far as its dynamical relations are concerned, is somewhere in the cortex of the brain." See also C. A. Strong, Why the Mind has a Body, 40-50.

(b) God's omnipresence is not the presence of a part but of the whole of God in every place.— This follows from the conception of God as incorporeal We reject the materialistic representation that God is composed of material elements which can be divided or sundered. There is no multiplication or diffusion of his substance to correspond with the parts of his dominions. The one essence of God is present at the same moment in all.

1 Kings 8:27—"the heaven and the heaven of heavens cannot contain (circumscribe) thee." God must be present in all his essence and all his attributes in every place. He is "totus in omni parte." Alger, Poetry of the Orient: "Though God extends beyond Creation's rim, Each smallest atom holds the whole of him." From this it follows that the whole Logos can be united to and be present in the man Christ Jesus, while at the same time he fills and governs the whole universe; and so the whole Christ can be united to, and can be present in, the single believer, as fully as if that believer were the only one to receive of his fulness.

A. J. Gordon: "In mathematics the whole is equal to the sum of its parts. But we know of the Spirit that every part is equal to the whole. Every church, every true body of Jesus Christ, has just as much of Christ as every other, and each has the whole Christ." Mat. 13:20—"where two or three are gathered together in my name, there am I in the midst of them." "The parish priest of austerity Climbed up in a high church steeple, To be nearer God so that he might Hand his word down to the people. And in sermon script he daily wrote What he thought was sent from heaven, And he dropt it down on the people's heads Two times one day in seven. In his age God said, 'Come down and die,' And he cried out from the steeple, 'Where art thou, Lord?' And the Lord replied, 'Down here among my people.' "

(c) God's omnipresence is not necessary but free.—We reject the pantheistic notion that God is bound to the universe as the universe is bound to God. God is immanent in the universe, not by compulsion, but by the free act of his own will, and this immanence is qualified by his transcendence.

God might at will cease to be omnipresent, for he could destroy the universe; but while the universe exists, he is and must be in all its parts. God is the life and law of the universe,—this is the truth in pantheism. But he is also personal and free,—this pantheism denies. Christianity holds to a free, as well as to an essential, omnipresence—qualified and supplemented, however, by God's transcendence. The boasted truth in pantheism is an elementary principle of Christianity, and is only the stepping-stone to a nobler truth—God's personal presence with his church. The Talmud contrasts the worship of an idol and the worship of Jehovah: "The idol seems so near, but is so far, Jehovah seems so far, but is so near!" God's omnipresence assures us that he is present with us to hear, and present in every heart and in the ends of the earth to answer, prayer. See Rogers, Superhuman Origin of the Bible, 10; Bowne, Metaphysics, 136; Charnock, Attributes, 1:363-405.

The Puritan turned from the moss-rose bud, saying: "I have learned to call nothing on earth lovely." But this is to despise not only the workmanship but the presence of the Almighty. The least thing in nature is worthy of study because it is the revelation of a present God. The uniformity of nature and the reign of law are nothing but the steady will of the omnipresent God. Gravitation is God's omnipresence in space, as evolution is God's omnipresence in time. Dorner, System of Doctrine, 1:73- "God being omnipresent, contact with him may be sought at any moment in prayer and contemplation; indeed, it will always be true that we live and move and have our being in him, as the perennial and omnipresent source of our existence." Rom. 10:6-8—"Say not in thy heart, Who shall ascend into heaven? (that is, to bring Christ down:) or, Who shall descend into the abyss? (that is, to bring Christ up from the dead.) But what saith it? The word is nigh thee, in thy mouth, and in thy heart." Lotze, Metaphysics, § 256, quoted in Illingworth, Divine Immanence, 135, 136. Sunday-school scholar: "Is God in my pocket?" "Certainly." "No, he isn't, for I haven't any pocket." God is omnipresent so long as there is a universe, but he ceases to be omnipresent when the universe ceases to be.

2. Omniscience

By this we mean God's perfect and eternal knowledge of all things which are objects of knowledge, whether they be actual or possible, past, present, or future.

God knows his inanimate creation: Ps. 147:4—"counteth the number of the stars; He calleth them all by their names." He has knowledge of brute creatures: Mat. 10:29—sparrows—"not one of them shall fall on the ground without your Father." Of men and their works: Ps. 33:13-15—"beholdeth all the sons of men ... considereth all their works." Of hearts of men and their thoughts: Acts 15:8—"God, who knoweth the heart"; Ps. 139:2—"understandest my thought afar off." Of our wants: Mat. 6:8—"knoweth what things ye have need of." Of the least things: Mat. 10:30—"the very hairs of your head are all numbered." Of the past: Mal. 3:16—"book of remembrance." Of the future: Is. 46:9, 10—"declaring the end from the beginning." Of men's future free acts: Is. 44:28—"that saith of Cyrus, He is my shepherd and shall perform all my pleasure." Of men's future evil acts: Acts 2:23—"him, being delivered up by the determinate counsel and foreknowledge of God." Of the ideally possible: 1 Sam. 23:12—"Will the men of Keilah deliver up me and my men into the hands of Saul? And Jehovah said, They will deliver thee up" (sc. if thou remainest); Mat. 11:23—"if the mighty works had been done in Sodom which were done in thee, it would have remained." From eternity: Acts 15:18—"the Lord, who maketh these things known from of old." Incomprehensible: Ps. 139:6—"Such knowledge is too wonderful for me"; Rom. 11:33—"O the depth of the riches both of the wisdom and the knowledge of God." Related to wisdom: Ps. 104:24—"In wisdom hast thou made them all"; Eph. 3:10—"manifold wisdom of God."

Job 7:20—"O thou watcher of men"; Ps. 56:8—"Thou numberest my wanderings" = my whole life has been one continuous exile; "Put thou my tears into thy bottle" = the skin bottle of the east,— there are tears enough to fill one; "Are they not in thy book?" = no tear has fallen to the ground unnoted,—God has gathered them all. Paul Gerhardt: "Du zählst wie oft ein Christe wein', Und was sein Kummer sei; Kein stilles Thränlein ist so klein, Du hebst und legst es bei." Heb. 4:13—"there is no creature that is not manifest in his sight: but all things are naked and laid open before the eyes of him with whom we have to do"—τετραχηλισμένα—with head bent back and neck laid bare, as animals slaughtered in sacrifice, or seized by the throat and thrown on the back, so that the priest might discover whether there was any blemish. Japanese proverb: "God has forgotten to forget."

(a) The omniscience of God may be argued from his omnipresence, as well as from his truth or self-knowledge, in which the plan of creation has its eternal ground, and from prophecy, which expresses God's omniscience.

It is to be remembered that omniscience, as the designation of a relative and transitive attribute, does not include God's self-knowledge. The term is used in the technical sense of God's knowledge of all things that pertain to the universe of his creation. H. A. Gordon: "Light travels faster than sound. You can see the flash of fire from the cannon's mouth, a mile away, considerably before the noise of the discharge reaches the ear. God flashed the light of prediction upon the pages of his word, and we see it. Wait a little and we see the event itself."

Royce, The Conception of God, 9—"An omniscient being would be one who simply found presented to him, not by virtue of fragmentary and gradually completed processes of inquiry, but by virtue of an all-embracing, direct and transparent insight into his own truth—who found thus presented to him, I say, the complete, the fulfilled answer to every genuinely rational question."

Browning, Ferishtah's Fancies, Plot-culture: "How will it fare shouldst thou impress on me That certainly an Eye is over all And each, to make the minute's deed, word, thought As worthy of reward and punishment? Shall I permit my sense an Eye-viewed shame, Broad daylight perpetration,—so to speak,—I had not dared to breathe within the Ear, With black night's help around me?"

(b) Since it is free from all imperfection, God's knowledge is immediate, as distinguished from the knowledge that comes through sense or imagination; simultaneous, as not acquired by successive observations, or built up by processes of reasoning; distinct, as free from all vagueness or confusion;

true, as perfectly corresponding to the reality of things; eternal, as comprehended in one timeless act of the divine mind.

An infinite mind must always act, and must always act in an absolutely perfect manner. There is in God no sense, symbol, memory, abstraction, growth, reflection, reasoning,—his knowledge is all direct and without intermediaries. God was properly represented by the ancient Egyptians, not as having eye, but as being eye. His thoughts toward us are "more than can be numbered" (Ps. 40:5), not because there is succession in them, now a remembering and now a forgetting, but because there is never a moment of our existence in which we are out of his mind; he is always thinking of us. See Charnock, Attributes, 1:406-497. Gen. 16:13—"Thou art a God that seeth." Mivart, Lessons from Nature, 374—"Every creature of every order of existence, while its existence is sustained, is so complacently contemplated by God, that the intense and concentrated attention of all men of science together upon it could but form an utterly inadequate symbol of such divine contemplation." So God's scrutiny of every deed of darkness is more searching than the gaze of a whole Coliseum of spectators, and his eye is more watchful over the good than would be the united care of all his hosts in heaven and earth.

Armstrong, God and the Soul: "God's energy is concentrated attention, attention concentrated everywhere. We can attend to two or three things at once; the pianist plays and talks at the same time; the magician does one thing while he seems to do another. God attends to all things, does all things, at once." Marie Corelli, Master Christian, 104—"The biograph is a hint that every scene of human life is reflected in a ceaseless moving panorama some where, for the beholding of some one." Wireless telegraphy is a stupendous warning that from God no secrets are hid, that "there is nothing covered that shall not be revealed; and hid, that shall not be known" (Mat. 10:26). The Röntgen rays, which take photographs of our insides, right through our clothes, and even in the darkness of midnight, show that to God "the night shineth as the day" (Ps. 139:12).

Professor Mitchel's equatorial telescope, slowly moving by clockwork, toward sunset, suddenly touched the horizon and disclosed a boy in a tree stealing apples, but the boy was all unconscious that he was under the gaze of the astronomer. Nothing was so fearful to the prisoner in the French cachot as the eye of the guard that never ceased to watch him in perfect silence through the loophole in the door. As in the Roman empire the whole world was to a malefactor one great prison, and in his flight to the most distant lands the emperor could track him, so under the government of God no sinner can escape the eye of his Judge. But omnipresence is protective as well as detective. The text Gen. 16:13—"Thou, God, seest me"—has been used as a restraint from evil more than as a stimulus to good. To the child of the devil it should certainly be the former. But to the child of God it should as certainly be the latter. God should not be regarded as an exacting overseer or a standing threat, but rather as one who understands us, loves us, and helps us. Ps. 139:17, 18—"How precious also are thy thoughts unto me, O God! How great is the sum of them! If I should count them, they are more in number than the sand: When I awake, I am still with thee."

(c) Since God knows things as they are, he knows the necessary sequences of his creation as necessary, the free acts of his creatures as free, the ideally possible as ideally possible.

God knows what would have taken place under circumstances not now present; knows what the universe would have been, had he chosen a different plan of creation; knows what our lives would have been, had we made different decisions in the past (Is. 48:18—"Oh that thou hadst hearkened ... then had thy peace been as a river"). Clarke, Christian Theology, 77—"God has a double knowledge of his universe. He knows it as it exists eternally in his mind, as his own idea; and he knows it as actually existing in time and space, a moving, changing, growing universe, with perpetual process of succession. In his own idea, he knows it all at once; but he is also aware of its perpetual becoming, and with reference to events as they occur he has foreknowledge, present knowledge, and knowledge afterwards.... He conceives of all things simultaneously, but observes all things in their succession."

Royce, World and Individual, 2:374—holds that God does not temporally foreknow anything except as he is expressed in finite beings, but yet that the Absolute possesses a perfect knowledge at one glance of the whole of the temporal order, present, past and future. This, he says, is not foreknowledge, but eternal knowledge. Priestley denied that any contingent event could be an object of knowledge. But Reid says the denial that any free action can be foreseen involves the denial of God's own free agency, since God's future actions can be foreseen by men; also that while God foresees his own free actions, this does not determine those actions necessarily. Tennyson, In Memoriam, 26—"And if that eye which watches guilt And goodness, and hath power to see Within the green the mouldered tree, And towers fallen as soon as built—Oh, if indeed that eye foresee Or see (in Him is no before) In more of life true life no more And Love the indifference to be, Then might I find, ere yet the morn Breaks hither over Indian seas, That Shadow waiting with the keys, To shroud me from my proper scorn."

(d) The fact that there is nothing in the present condition of things from which the future actions of free creatures necessarily follow by natural law does not prevent God from foreseeing such actions, since his knowledge is not mediate, but immediate. He not only foreknows the motives which will occasion men's acts, but he directly foreknows the acts themselves. The possibility of such direct knowledge without assignable grounds of knowledge is apparent if we admit that time is a form of finite thought to which the divine mind is not subject.

Aristotle maintained that there is no certain knowledge of contingent future events. Socinus, in like manner, while he admitted that God knows all things that are knowable, abridged the objects of the divine knowledge by withdrawing from the number those objects whose future existence he considered as uncertain, such as the determinations of free agents. These, he held, cannot be certainly foreknown, because there is nothing in the present condition of things from which they will necessarily follow by natural law. The man who makes a clock can tell when it will strike. But free-will, not being subject to mechanical laws, cannot have its acts predicted or foreknown. God knows things only in their causes—future events only in their antecedents. John Milton seems also to deny God's foreknowledge of free acts: "So, without least impulse or shadow of fate, Or aught by me immutably foreseen, They trespass."

With this Socinian doctrine some Arminians agree, as McCabe, in his Foreknowledge of God, and in his Divine Nescience of Future Contingencies a Necessity. McCabe, however, sacrifices the principle of free will, in defence of which he makes this surrender of God's foreknowledge, by saying that in cases of fulfilled prophecy, like Peter's denial and Judas's betrayal, God brought special influences to bear to secure the result,—so that Peter's and Judas's wills acted irresponsibly under the law of cause and effect. He quotes Dr. Daniel Curry as declaring that "the denial of absolute divine foreknowledge is the essential complement of the Methodist theology, without which its philosophical incompleteness is defenceless against the logical consistency of Calvinism." See also article by McCabe in Methodist Review, Sept. 1892:760-773. Also Simon, Reconciliation, 287—"God has constituted a creature, the actions of which he can only know as such when they are performed. In presence of man, to a certain extent, even the great God condescends to wait; nay more, has himself so ordained things that he must wait, inquiring, 'What will he do?' "

So Dugald Stewart: "Shall we venture to affirm that it exceeds the power of God to permit such a train of contingent events to take place as his own foreknowledge shall not extend to?" Martensen holds this view, and Rothe, Theologische Ethik, 1:212-234, who declares that the free choices of men are continually increasing the knowledge of God. So also Martineau, Study of Religion, 2:279—"The belief in the divine foreknowledge of our future has no basis in philosophy. We no longer deem it true that even God knows the moment of my moral life that is coming next. Even he does not know whether I shall yield to the secret temptation at midday. To him life is a drama of which he knows not the conclusion." Then, says Dr. A. J. Gordon, there is nothing so dreary and dreadful as to be living under the direction of such a God. The universe is rushing on like an express-train in the darkness without headlight or engineer; at any moment we may be plunged into the abyss. Lotze does not deny God's foreknowledge of free human actions, but he regards as insoluble by the intellect the problem of the relation of time to God, and such foreknowledge as "one of those postulates as to which we know not how they can be fulfilled." Bowne, Philosophy of Theism, 159—"Foreknowledge of a free act is a knowledge without assignable grounds of knowing. On the assumption of a real time, it is hard to find a way out of this difficulty.... The doctrine of the ideality of time helps us by suggesting the possibility of an all-embracing present, or an eternal now, for God. In that case the problem vanishes with time, its condition."

Against the doctrine of the divine nescience we urge not only our fundamental conviction of God's perfection, but the constant testimony of Scripture. In Is. 41:21, 22, God makes his foreknowledge the test of his Godhead in the controversy with idols. If God cannot foreknow free human acts, then "the Lamb that hath been slain from the foundation of the world" (Rev. 13:8) was only a sacrifice to be offered in case Adam should fall, God not knowing whether he would or not, and in case Judas should betray Christ, God not knowing whether he would or not. Indeed, since the course of nature is changed by man's will when he burns towns and fells forests, God cannot on this theory predict even the course of nature. All prophecy is therefore a protest against this view.

How God foreknows free human decisions we may not be able to say, but then the method of God's knowledge in many other respects is unknown to us. The following explanations have been proposed. God may foreknow free acts:—

1. Mediately, by foreknowing the motives of these acts, and this either because these motives induce the acts, (1) necessarily, or (2) certainly. This last "certainly" is to be accepted, if either; since motives are never causes, but are only occasions, of action. The cause is the will, or the man himself. But it may be said that foreknowing acts through their motives is not foreknowing at all, but is reasoning or inference rather. Moreover, although intelligent beings commonly act according to motives previously dominant, they also at critical epochs, as at the fall of Satan and of Adam, choose between motives, and in such cases knowledge of the motives which have hitherto actuated them gives no clue to their next decisions. Another statement is therefore proposed to meet these difficulties, namely, that God may foreknow free acts:—

2. Immediately, by pure intuition, inexplicable to us. Julius Müller, Doctrine of Sin, 2:203, 225—"If God can know a future event as certain only by a calculation of causes, it must be allowed that he

cannot with certainty foreknow any free act of man; for his foreknowledge would then be proof that the act in question was the necessary consequence of certain causes, and was not in itself free. If, on the contrary, the divine knowledge be regarded as intuitive, we see that it stands in the same immediate relation to the act itself as to its antecedents, and thus the difficulty is removed." Even upon this view there still remains the difficulty of perceiving how there can be in God's mind a subjective certitude with regard to acts in respect to which there is no assignable objective ground of certainty. Yet, in spite of this difficulty, we feel bound both by Scripture and by our fundamental idea of God's perfection to maintain God's perfect knowledge of the future free acts of his creatures. With President Pepper we say: "Knowledge of contingency is not necessarily contingent knowledge." With Whedon: "It is not calculation, but pure knowledge." See Dorner, System of Doct., 1:332-337; 2:58-62; Jahrbuch für deutsche Theologie, 1858:601-605; Charnock, Attributes, 1:429-446; Solly, The Will, 240-254. For a valuable article on the whole subject, though advocating the view that God foreknows acts by foreknowing motives, see Bib. Sac., Oct. 1883:655-694. See also Hill, Divinity, 517.

(e) Prescience is not itself causative. It is not to be confounded with the predetermining will of God. Free actions do not take place because they are foreseen, but they are foreseen because they are to take place.

Seeing a thing in the future does not cause it to be, more than seeing a thing in the past causes it to be. As to future events, we may say with Whedon: "Knowledge takes them, not makes them." Foreknowledge may, and does, presuppose predetermination, but it is not itself predetermination. Thomas Aquinas, in his Summa, 1:38:1:1, says that "the knowledge of God is the cause of things"; but he is obliged to add: "God is not the cause of all things that are known by God, since evil things that are known by God are not from him." John Milton, Paradise Lost, book 3—"Foreknowledge had no influence on their fault, Which had no less proved certain unforeknown."

(f) Omniscience embraces the actual and the possible, but it does not embrace the self-contradictory and the impossible, because these are not objects of knowledge.

God does not know what the result would be if two and two made five, nor does he know "whether a chimæra ruminating in a vacuum devoureth second intentions"; and that, simply for the reason that he cannot know self-contradiction and nonsense. These things are not objects of knowledge. Clarke, Christian Theology, 80—"Can God make an old man in a minute? Could he make it well with the wicked while they remained wicked? Could he create a world in which $2 + 2 = 5$?" Royce, Spirit of Modern Philosophy, 366—"Does God know the whole number that is the square root of 65? or what adjacent hills there are that have no valleys between them? Does God know round squares, and sugar salt-lumps, and Snarks and Boojums and Abracadabras?"

(g) Omniscience, as qualified by holy will, is in Scripture denominated "wisdom." In virtue of his wisdom God chooses the highest ends and uses the fittest means to accomplish them.

Wisdom is not simply "estimating all things at their proper value" (Olmstead); it has in it also the element of counsel and purpose. It has been defined as "the talent of using one's talents." It implies two things: first, choice of the highest end; secondly, choice of the best means to secure this end. J. C. C. Clarke, Self and the Father, 39—"Wisdom is not invented conceptions, or harmony of theories with theories; but is humble obedience of mind to the reception of facts that are found in things." Thus man's wisdom, obedience, faith, are all names for different aspects of the same thing. And wisdom in God is the moral choice which makes truth and holiness supreme. Bowne, Principles of Ethics, 261—"Socialism pursues a laudable end by unwise or destructive means. It is not enough to mean well. Our methods must take some account of the nature of things, if they are to succeed. We cannot produce well-being by law. No legislation can remove inequalities of nature and constitution. Society cannot produce equality, any more than it can enable a rhinoceros to sing, or legislate a cat into a lion."

3. Omnipotence

By this we mean the power of God to do all things which are objects of power, whether with or without the use of means.

Gen. 17:1—"I am God Almighty." He performs natural wonders: Gen. 1:1-3—"Let there be Light"; Is. 44:24—"stretcheth forth the heavens alone"; Heb. 1:3—"upholding all things by the word of his power." Spiritual wonders: 2 Cor. 4:6—"God, that said, Light shall shine out of darkness, who shined in our hearts"; Eph. 1:19—"exceeding greatness of his power to us-ward who believe"; Eph. 3:20—"able to do exceeding abundantly." Power to create new things: Mat. 3:9—"able of these stones to raise up children unto Abraham". Rom. 4:17—"giveth life to the dead, and calleth the things that are not, as though they were." After his own pleasure: Ps. 115:3—"He hath done whatsoever he hath pleased"; Eph. 1:11—"worketh all things after the counsel of his will." Nothing impossible: Gen 18:14—"Is anything too hard for Jehovah?" Mat. 19:26—"with God all things are possible." E. G. Robinson, Christian Theology, 73—"If all power in the universe is dependent on his creative will for its existence, it is impossible to conceive any limit to his power except that laid on it by his own will. But this is only negative proof; absolute omnipotence is not logically demonstrable, though readily enough recognized as a just conception of the infinite God, when propounded on the authority of a positive revelation."

The omnipotence of God is illustrated by the work of the Holy Spirit, which in Scripture is compared to wind, water and fire. The ordinary manifestations of these elements afford no criterion of the effects they are able to produce. The rushing mighty wind at Pentecost was the analogue of the wind-Spirit who bore everything before him on the first day of creation (Gen. 1:2; John 3:8; Acts 2:2). The pouring out of the Spirit is likened to the flood of Noah when the windows of heaven were opened and there was not room enough to receive that which fell (Mal. 3:10). And the baptism of the Holy Spirit is like the fire that shall destroy all impurity at the end of the world (Mat. 3:11; 2 Pet. 3:7-13). See A. H. Strong, Christ in Creation, 307-310.

(a) Omnipotence does not imply power to do that which is not an object of power; as, for example, that which is self-contradictory or contradictory to the nature of God.

Self-contradictory things: "facere factum infectum"—the making of a past event to have not occurred (hence the uselessness of praying: "May it be that much good was done"); drawing a shorter than a straight line between two given points; putting two separate mountains together without a valley between them. Things contradictory to the nature of God: for God to lie, to sin, to die. To do such things would not imply power, but impotence. God has all the power that is consistent with infinite perfection—all power to do what is worthy of himself. So no greater thing can be said by man than this: "I dare do all that may become a man; Who dares do more is none." Even God cannot make wrong to be right, nor hatred of himself to be blessed. Some have held that the prevention of sin in a moral system is not an object of power, and therefore that God cannot prevent sin in a moral system. We hold the contrary; see this Compendium: Objections to the Doctrine of Decrees.

Dryden, Imitation of Horace, 3:29:71—"Over the past not heaven itself has power; What has been has, and I have had my hour"—words applied by Lord John Russell to his own career. Emerson, The Past: "All is now secure and fast, Not the gods can shake the Past." Sunday-school scholar: "Say, teacher, can God make a rock so big that he can't lift it?" Seminary Professor: "Can God tell a lie?" Seminary student: "With God all things are possible."

(b) Omnipotence does not imply the exercise of all his power on the part of God. He has power over his power; in other words, his power is under the control of wise and holy will. God can do all he will, but he will not do all he can. Else his power is mere force acting necessarily, and God is the slave of his own omnipotence.

Schleiermacher held that nature not only is grounded in the divine causality, but fully expresses that causality; there is no causative power in God for anything that is not real and actual. This doctrine does not essentially differ from Spinoza's natura naturans and natura naturata. See Philippi, Glaubenslehre, 2:62-66. But omnipotence is not instinctive; it is a power used according to God's pleasure. God is by no means encompassed by the laws of nature, or shut up to a necessary evolution of his own being, as pantheism supposes. As Rothe has shown, God has a will-power over his nature-power, and is not compelled to do all that he can do. He is able from the stones of the street to "raise up children unto Abraham," but he has not done it. In God are unopened treasures, an inexhaustible fountain of new beginnings, new creations, new revelations. To suppose that in creation he has expended all the inner possibilities of his being is to deny his omnipotence. So Job 26:14—"Lo, these are but the outskirts of his ways: And how small a whisper do we hear of him! But the thunder of his power who can understand?" See Rogers, Superhuman Origin of the Bible, 10; Hodgson, Time and Space, 579, 580.

1 Pet. 5:6—"Humble yourselves therefore under the mighty hand of God"—his mighty hand of providence, salvation, blessing—"that he may exalt you in due time; casting all your anxiety upon him, because he careth for you." "The mighty powers held under mighty control"—this is the greatest exhibition of power. Unrestraint is not the highest freedom. Young men must learn that self-restraint is the true power. Prov. 16:32—"He that is slow to anger is better than the mighty; And he that ruleth his spirit, than he that taketh a city." Shakespeare, Coriolanus, 2:3—"We have power in ourselves to do it, but it is a power that we have no power to do." When dynamite goes off, it all goes off: there is no reserve. God uses as much of his power as he pleases: the remainder of wrath in himself, as well as in others, he restrains.

(c) Omnipotence in God does not exclude, but implies, the power of self-limitation. Since all such self-limitation is free, proceeding from neither external nor internal compulsion, it is the act and manifestation of God's power. Human freedom is not rendered impossible by the divine omnipotence, but exists by virtue of it. It is an act of omnipotence when God humbles himself to the taking of human flesh in the person of Jesus Christ.

Thomasius: "If God is to be over all and in all, he cannot himself be all." Ps. 113: 5, 6—"Who is like unto Jehovah our God.... That humbleth himself to behold the things that are in heaven and in the earth?" Phil. 2:7, 8—"emptied himself ... humbled himself." See Charnock, Attributes, 2:5-107. President Woolsey showed true power when he controlled his indignation and let an offending student go free. Of Christ on the cross, says Moberly, Atonement and Personality, 116—"It was the power [to retain his life, to escape suffering], with the will to hold it unused, which proved him to be what he was, the obedient and perfect man." We are likest the omnipotent One when we limit ourselves for love's sake. The attribute of omnipotence is the ground of trust, as well as of fear, on the part of God's creatures. Isaac Watts: "His every word of grace is strong As that which built the skies; The voice that rolls the stars along Speaks all the promises."

Third Division.—Attributes having relation to Moral Beings.

1. Veracity and Faithfulness, or Transitive Truth

By veracity and faithfulness we mean the transitive truth of God, in its twofold relation to his creatures in general and to his redeemed people in particular.

Ps. 138:2—"I will ... give thanks unto thy name for thy lovingkindness and for thy truth: For thou hast magnified thy word above all thy name"; John 3:33—"hath set his seal to this, that God is true"; Rom. 3:4—"let God be found true, but every man a liar"; Rom. 1:25—"the truth of God"; John 14:17—"the Spirit of truth"; 1 John 5:7—"the Spirit is the truth"; 1 Cor. 1:9—"God is faithful"; 1 Thess. 5:24—"faithful is he that calleth you"; 1 Pet. 4:19—"a faithful Creator"; 2 Cor. 1:20—"how many soever be the promises of God, in him is the yea"; Num. 23:19—"God is not a man that he should lie"; Tit. 1:2—"God, who cannot lie, promised"; Heb. 6:18—"in which it is impossible for God to lie."

(a) In virtue of his veracity, all his revelations to creatures consist with his essential being and with each other.

In God's veracity we have the guarantee that our faculties in their normal exercise do not deceive us; that the laws of thought are also laws of things; that the external world, and second causes in it, have objective existence; that the same causes will always produce the same effects; that the threats of the moral nature will be executed upon the unrepentant transgressor; that man's moral nature is made in the image of God's; and that we may draw just conclusions from what conscience is in us to what holiness is in him. We may therefore expect that all past revelations, whether in nature or in his word, will not only not be contradicted by our future knowledge, but will rather prove to have in them more of truth than we ever dreamed. Man's word may pass away, but God's word abides forever (Mat. 5:18—"one jot or one tittle shall in no wise pass away from the law"; Is. 40:8—"the word of God shall stand forever").

Mat. 6:16—"be not as the hypocrites." In God the outer expression and the inward reality always correspond. Assyrian wills were written on a small tablet encased in another upon which the same thing was written over again. Breakage, or falsification, of the outer envelope could be corrected by reference to the inner. So our outer life should conform to the heart within, and the heart within to the outer life. On the duty of speaking the truth, and the limitations of the duty, see Newman Smyth, Christian Ethics, 386-403—"Give the truth always to those who in the bonds of humanity have a right to the truth; conceal it, or falsify it, only when the human right to the truth has been forfeited, or is held in abeyance, by sickness, weakness, or some criminal intent."

(b) In virtue of his faithfulness, he fulfills all his promises to his people, whether expressed in words or implied in the constitution he has given them.

In God's faithfulness we have the sure ground of confidence that he will perform what his love has led him to promise to those who obey the gospel. Since his promises are based, not upon what we are or have done, but upon what Christ is and has done, our defects and errors do not invalidate them, so long as we are truly penitent and believing: 1 John 1:9—"faithful and righteous to forgive us our sins" = faithful to his promise, and righteous to Christ. God's faithfulness also ensures a supply for all the real wants of our being, both here and hereafter, since these wants are implicit promises of him who made us: Ps. 84:11—"No good thing will he withhold from them that walk uprightly"; 91:4—"His truth is a shield and a buckler"; Mat. 6:33—"all these things shall be added unto you"; 1 Cor. 2:9—"Things which eye saw not, and ear heard not, And which entered not into the heart of man, Whatsoever things God prepared for them that love him."

Regulus goes back to Carthage to die rather than break his promise to his enemies. George William Curtis economizes for years, and gives up all hope of being himself a rich man, in order that he may pay the debts of his deceased father. When General Grant sold all the presents made to him by the crowned heads of Europe, and paid the obligations in which his insolvent son had involved him, he said: "Better poverty and honor, than wealth and disgrace." Many a business man would rather die than fail to fulfil his promise and let his note go to protest. "Maxwelton braes are bonnie, Where early falls the dew, And 'twas there that Annie Laurie Gave me her promise true; Which ne'er forget will I; And for bonnie Annie Laurie I'd lay me down and dee." Betray the man she loves? Not "Till a' the seas gang dry, my dear, And the rocks melt wi'the sun." God's truth will not be less than that of mortal man. God's veracity is the natural correlate to our faith.

2. Mercy and Goodness, or Transitive Love

By mercy and goodness we mean the transitive love of God in its two-fold relation to the disobedient and to the obedient portions of his creatures.

Titus 3:4—"his love toward man"; Rom. 2:4—"goodness of God"; Mat. 5:44, 45—"love your enemies ... that ye may be sons of your Father"; John 3:16—"God so loved the world"; 2 Pet. 1:3—"granted unto us all things that pertain unto life and godliness"; Rom. 8:32—"freely give us all things"; John 4:10—"Herein is love, not that we loved God, but that he loved us, and sent his Son to be the propitiation for our sins."

(a) Mercy is that eternal principle of God's nature which leads him to seek the temporal good and eternal salvation of those who have opposed themselves to his will, even at the cost of infinite self-sacrifice.

Martensen: "Viewed in relation to sin, eternal love is compassionate grace." God's continued importation of natural life is a foreshadowing, in a lower sphere, of what he desires to do for his creatures in the higher sphere—the communication of spiritual and eternal life through Jesus Christ. When he bids us love our enemies, he only bids us follow his own example. Shakespeare, Titus Andronicus, 2:2—"Wilt thou draw near the nature of the gods? Draw near them, then, in being merciful." Twelfth Night, 3:4—"In nature there's no blemish but the mind; None can be called deformed but the unkind. Virtue is beauty."

(b) Goodness is the eternal principle of God's nature which leads him to communicate of his own life and blessedness to those who are like him in moral character. Goodness, therefore, is nearly identical with the love of complacency; mercy, with the love of benevolence.

Notice, however, that transitive love is but an outward manifestation of immanent love. The eternal and perfect object of God's love is in his own nature. Men become subordinate objects of that love only as they become connected and identified with its principal object, the image of God's perfections in Christ. Only in the Son do men become sons of God. To this is requisite an acceptance of Christ on the part of man. Thus it can be said that God imparts himself to men just so far as men are willing to receive him. And as God gives himself to men, in all his moral attributes, to answer for them and to renew them in character, there is truth in the statement of Nordell (Examiner, Jan. 17, 1884) that "the maintenance of holiness is the function of divine justice; the diffusion of holiness is the function of divine love." We may grant this as substantially true, while yet we deny that love is a mere form or manifestation of holiness. Self-impartation is different from self-affirmation. The attribute which moves God to pour out is not identical with the attribute which moves him to maintain. The two ideas of holiness and of love are as distinct as the idea of integrity on the one hand and of generosity on the other. Park: "God loves Satan, in a certain sense, and we ought to." Shedd: "This same love of compassion God feels toward the non-elect; but the expression of that compassion is forbidden for reasons which are sufficient for God, but are entirely unknown to the creature." The goodness of God is the basis of reward, under God's government. Faithfulness leads God to keep his promises; goodness leads him to make them.

Edwards, Nature of Virtue, in Works, 2:263—Love of benevolence does not presuppose beauty in its object. Love of complacence does presuppose beauty. Virtue is not love to an object for its beauty. The beauty of intelligent beings does not consist in love for beauty, or virtue in love for virtue. Virtue is love for being in general, exercised in a general good will. This is the doctrine of Edwards. We prefer to say that virtue is love, not for being in general, but for good being, and so for God, the holy One. The love of compassion is perfectly compatible with hatred of evil and with indignation against one who commits it. Love does not necessarily imply approval, but it does imply desire that all creatures should fulfil the purpose of their existence by being morally conformed to the holy One; see Godet, in The Atonement, 339.

Rom. 5:8—"God commendeth his own love toward us, in that, while we were yet sinners, Christ died for us." We ought to love our enemies, and Satan is our worst enemy. We ought to will the good of Satan, or cherish toward him the love of benevolence, though not the love of complacence. This does not involve a condoning of his sin, or an ignoring of his moral depravity, as seems implied in the verses of Wm. C. Gannett: "The poem hangs on the berry-bush When comes the poet's eye; The street begins to masquerade When Shakespeare passes by. The Christ sees white in Judas' heart And loves his traitor well; The God, to angel his new heaven, Explores his deepest hell."

3. Justice and Righteousness, or Transitive Holiness

By justice and righteousness we mean the transitive holiness of God, in virtue of which his treatment of his creatures conforms to the purity of his nature,—righteousness demanding from all moral beings conformity to the moral perfection of God, and justice visiting non-conformity to that perfection with penal loss or suffering.

Gen. 18:25—"shall not the Judge of all the earth do right?" Deut. 32:4—"All his ways are justice; A God of faithfulness and without iniquity, Just and right is he"; Ps. 5:5—"Thou hatest all workers of iniquity"; 7:9-12—"the righteous God trieth the hearts ... saveth the upright ... is a righteous judge, Yea, a God that hath indignation every day"; 18:24-26—"Jehovah recompensed me according to my righteousness.... With the merciful, thou wilt show thyself merciful ... with the perverse thou wilt show thyself froward"; Mat. 5:48—"Ye therefore shall be perfect, as your heavenly Father is perfect"; Rom. 2:6—"will render to every man according to his works"; 1 Pet. 1:16—"Ye shall be holy; for I am holy." These passages show that God loves the same persons whom he hates. It is not true that he hates the sin, but loves the sinner; he both hates and loves the sinner himself, hates him as he is a living and wilful antagonist of truth and holiness, loves him as he is a creature capable of good and ruined by his transgression.

There is no abstract sin that can be hated apart from the persons in whom that sin is represented and embodied. Thomas Fuller found it difficult to starve the profaneness but to feed the person of the impudent beggar who applied to him for food. Mr. Finney declared that he would kill the slave-catcher, but would love him with all his heart. In our civil war Dr. Kirk said: "God knows that we love the rebels, but God also knows that we will kill them if they do not lay down their arms." The complex nature of God not only permits but necessitates this same double treatment of the sinner, and the earthly father experiences the same conflict of emotions when his heart yearns over the corrupt son whom he is compelled to banish from the household. Moberly, Atonement and Personality, 7—"It is the sinner who is punished, not the sin."

(a) Since justice and righteousness are simply transitive holiness—righteousness designating this holiness chiefly in its mandatory, justice chiefly in its punitive, aspect,—they are not mere manifestations of benevolence, or of God's disposition to secure the highest happiness of his creatures, nor are they grounded in the nature of things as something apart from or above God.

Cremer, N. T. Lexicon: δίκαιος = "the perfect coincidence existing between God's nature, which is the standard for all, and his acts." Justice and righteousness are simply holiness exercised toward creatures. The same holiness which exists in God in eternity past manifests itself as justice and righteousness, so soon as intelligent creatures come into being. Much that was said under Holiness as an immanent attribute of God is equally applicable here. The modern tendency to confound holiness with love shows itself in the merging of justice and righteousness in mere benevolence. Instances of this tendency are the following: Ritschl, Unterricht, § 16—"The righteousness of God denotes the manner in which God carries out his loving will in the redemption of humanity as a whole and of individual men; hence his righteousness is indistinguishable from his grace"; see also Ritschl, Rechtf. und Versöhnung, 2:113; 3:296. Prof. George M. Forbes: "Only right makes love moral; only love makes right moral." Jones, Robert Browning, 70—"Is it not beneficence that places death at the heart of sin? Carlyle forgot this. God is not simply a great taskmaster. The power that imposes law is not an alien power." D'Arcy, Idealism and Theology, 237-240—"How can self-realization be the realization of others? Why must the true good be always the common good? Why is the end of each the end of all?... We need a concrete universal which will unify all persons."

So also, Harris, Kingdom of Christ on Earth, 39-42; God the Creator, 287, 290, 302—"Love, as required and regulated by reason, may be called righteousness. Love is universal good will or benevolence, regulated in its exercise by righteousness. Love is the choice of God and man as the objects of trust and service. This choice involves the determination of the will to seek universal well-being, and in this aspect it is benevolence. It also involves the consent of the will to the reason, and the determination to regulate all action in seeking well-being by its truths, laws, and ideals; and in this aspect it is righteousness.... Justice is the consent of the will to the law of love, in its authority, its requirements, and its sanctions. God's wrath is the necessary reaction of this law of love in the constitution and order of the universe against the wilful violator of it, and Christ's sufferings atone for sin by asserting and maintaining the authority, universality, and inviolability of God's law of love in his redemption of men and his forgiveness of their sins.... Righteousness cannot be the whole of love, for this would shut us up to the merely formal principle of the law without telling us what the law requires. Benevolence cannot be the whole of love, for this would shut us up to hedonism, in the form of utilitarianism, excluding righteousness from the character of God and man."

Newman Smyth also, in his Christian Ethics, 227-231, tells us that "love, as self-affirming, is righteousness; as self-imparting, is benevolence; as self-finding in others, is sympathy. Righteousness, as subjective regard for our own moral being, is holiness; as objective regard for the persons of others, is justice. Holiness is involved in love as its essential respect to itself; the heavenly Father is the holy Father (John 17:11). Love contains in its unity a trinity of virtue. Love affirms its own worthiness, imparts to others its good, and finds its life again in the well-being of others. The ethical limit of self-impartation is found in self-affirmation. Love in self-bestowal cannot become suicidal. The benevolence of love has its moral bounds in the holiness of love. True love in God maintains its transcendence, and excludes pantheism."

The above doctrine, quoted for substance from Newman Smyth, seems to us unwarrantably to include in love what properly belongs to holiness. It virtually denies that holiness has any independent existence as an attribute of God. To make holiness a manifestation of love seems to us as irrational as to say that self-affirmation is a form of self-impartation. The concession that holiness regulates and limits love shows that holiness cannot itself be love, but must be an independent and superior attribute. Right furnishes the rule and law for love, but it is not true that love furnishes the rule and law for right. There is no such double sovereignty as this theory would imply. The one attribute that is independent and supreme is holiness, and love is simply the impulse to communicate this holiness.

William Ashmore: "Dr. Clarke lays great emphasis on the character of 'a good God.'... But he is more than a merely good God; he is a just God, and a righteous God, and a holy God—a God who is 'angry with the wicked,' even while ready to forgive them, if they are willing to repent in his way, and not in their own. He is the God who brought in a flood upon the world of the ungodly; who rained down fire and brimstone from heaven; and who is to come in 'flaming fire, taking vengeance on them that know not God' and obey not the gospel of his son.... Paul reasoned about both the 'goodness' and the 'severity' of God."

(b) Transitive holiness, as righteousness, imposes law in conscience and Scripture, and may be called legislative holiness. As justice, it executes the penalties of law, and may be called distributive or judicial holiness. In righteousness God reveals chiefly his love of holiness; in justice, chiefly his hatred of sin.

The self-affirming purity of God demands a like purity in those who have been made in his image. As God wills and maintains his own moral excellence, so all creatures must will and maintain the moral excellence of God. There can be only one centre in the solar system,—the sun is its own centre and the centre for all the planets also. So God's purity is the object of his own will,—it must be the object of all the wills of all his creatures also. Bixby, Crisis in Morals, 282—"It is not rational or safe for the hand to separate itself from the heart. This is a universe, and God is the heart of the great system. Altruism is not the result of society, but society is the result of altruism. It begins in creatures far below man. The animals which know how to combine have the greatest chance of survival. The unsociable animal dies out. The most perfect organism is the most sociable. Right is the debt which the part owes to the whole." This seems to us but a partial expression of the truth. Right is more than a debt to others,—it is a debt to one's self, and the self-affirming, self-preserving, self-respecting element constitutes the limit and standard of all outgoing activity. The sentiment of loyalty is largely a reverence for this principle of order and stability in government. Ps. 145:5—"Of the glorious majesty of thine honor, And of thy wondrous works, will I meditate"; 97:2—"Clouds and darkness are round about him: Righteousness and justice are the foundation of his throne."

John Milton, Eikonoklastes: "Truth and justice are all one; for truth is but justice in our knowledge, and justice is but truth in our practice.... For truth is properly no more than contemplation, and her utmost efficiency is but teaching; but justice in her very essence is all strength and activity, and hath a sword put into her hand to use against all violence and oppression on the earth. She it is who accepts no person, and exempts none from the severity of her stroke." A. J. Balfour, Foundations of Belief, 326—"Even the poet has not dared to represent Jupiter torturing Prometheus without the dim figure of Avenging Fate waiting silently in the background.... Evolution working out a nobler and nobler justice is proof that God is just. Here is 'preferential action'." S. S. Times, June 9, 1900—"The natural man is born with a wrong personal astronomy. Man should give up the conceit of being the centre of all things. He should accept the Copernican theory, and content himself with a place on the edge of things—the place he has always really had. We all laugh at John Jasper and his thesis that 'the sun do move.' The Copernican theory is leaking down into human relations, as appears from the current phrase: 'There are others'."

(c) Neither justice nor righteousness, therefore, is a matter of arbitrary will. They are revelations of the inmost nature of God, the one in the form of moral requirement, the other in the form of judicial sanction. As God cannot but demand of his creatures that they be like him in moral character, so he cannot but enforce the law which he imposes upon them. Justice just as much binds God to punish as it binds the sinner to be punished.

All arbitrariness is excluded here. God is what he is—infinite purity. He cannot change. If creatures are to attain the end of their being, they must be like God in moral purity. Justice is nothing but the recognition and enforcement of this natural necessity. Law is only the transcript of God's nature. Justice does not make law,—it only reveals law. Penalty is only the reaction of God's holiness against that which is its opposite. Since righteousness and justice are only legislative and retributive holiness, God can cease to demand purity and to punish sin only when he ceases to be holy, that is, only when he ceases to be God. "Judex damnatur cum nocens absolvitur."

Simon, Reconciliation, 141—"To claim the performance of duty is as truly obligatory as it is obligatory to perform the duty which is prescribed." E. H. Johnson, Systematic Theology, 84— "Benevolence intends what is well for the creature; justice insists on what is fit. But the well-for-us and the fit-for-us precisely coincide. The only thing that is well for us is our normal employment and development; but to provide for this is precisely what is fitting and therefore due to us. In the divine nature the distinction between justice and benevolence is one of form." We criticize this utterance as not sufficiently taking into account the nature of the right. The right is not merely the fit. Fitness is only general adaptation which may have in it no ethical element, whereas right is solely and exclusively ethical. The right therefore regulates the fit and constitutes its standard. The well-for-us is to be determined by the right-for-us, but not vice versa. George W. Northrup: "God is not bound to bestow the same endowments upon creatures, nor to keep all in a state of holiness forever, nor to redeem the fallen, nor to secure the greatest happiness of the universe. But he is bound to purpose and to do what his absolute holiness requires. He has no attribute, no will, no sovereignty, above this law of his being. He cannot lie, he cannot deny himself, he cannot look upon sin with complacency, he cannot acquit the guilty without an atonement."

(d) Neither justice nor righteousness bestows rewards. This follows from the fact that obedience is due to God, instead of being optional or a gratuity. No creature can claim anything for his obedience. If God rewards, he rewards in virtue of his goodness and faithfulness, not in virtue of his justice or his righteousness. What the creature cannot claim, however, Christ can claim, and the rewards which are goodness to the creature are righteousness to Christ. God rewards Christ's work for us and in us.

Bruch, Eigenschaftslehre, 280-282, and John Austin, Province of Jurisprudence, 1:88-93, 220-223, both deny, and rightly deny, that justice bestows rewards. Justice simply punishes infractions of law. In Mat. 25:34—"inherit the kingdom"—inheritance implies no merit; 46—the wicked are adjudged to eternal punishment; the righteous, not to eternal reward, but to eternal life. Luke 17:7-10—"when ye shall have done all the things that are commanded you, say, We are unprofitable servants; we have done that which it was our duty to do." Rom. 6:23—punishment is the "wages of sin": but salvation is "the gift of God"; 2:6—God rewards, not on account of man's work but "according to his works." Reward is thus seen to be in Scripture a matter of grace to the creature; only to the Christ who works for us in atonement, and in us in regeneration and sanctification, is reward a matter of debt (see also John 6:27 and 2 John 8). Martineau, Types, 2:86, 244, 249—"Merit is toward man; virtue toward God."

All mere service is unprofitable, because it furnishes only an equivalent to duty, and there is no margin. Works of supererogation are impossible, because our all is due to God. He would have us rise into the region of friendship, realize that he has been treating us not as Master but as Father, enter into a relation of uncalculating love. With this proviso that rewards are matters of grace, not of debt, we may assent to the maxim of Solon: "A republic walks upon two feet—just punishment for the unworthy and due reward for the worthy." George Harris, Moral Evolution, 139—"Love seeks righteousness, and is satisfied with nothing other than that." But when Harris adopts the words of the poet: "The very wrath from pity grew, From love of men the hate of wrong," he seems to us virtually to deny that God hates evil for any other reason than because of its utilitarian disadvantages, and to imply that good has no independent existence in his nature. Bowne, Ethics, 171—"Merit is desert of reward, or better, desert of moral approval." Tennyson: "For merit lives from man to man, And not from man, O Lord, to thee." Baxter: "Desert is written over the gate of hell; but over the gate of heaven only, The Gift of God."

(e) Justice in God, as the revelation of his holiness, is devoid of all passion or caprice. There is in God no selfish anger. The penalties he inflicts upon transgression are not vindictive but vindicative. They express the revulsion of God's nature from moral evil, the judicial indignation of purity against impurity, the self-assertion of infinite holiness against its antagonist and would-be destroyer. But because its decisions are calm, they are irreversible.

Anger, within certain limits, is a duty of man. Ps. 97:10—"ye that love Jehovah, hate evil"; Eph. 4:28—"Be ye angry, and sin not." The calm indignation of the judge, who pronounces sentence with tears, is the true image of the holy anger of God against sin. Weber, Zorn Gottes, 28, makes wrath only the jealousy of love. It is more truly the jealousy of holiness. Prof. W. A. Stevens, Com. on 1 Thess. 2:10—"Holily and righteously are terms that describe the same conduct in two aspects; the former, as conformed to God's character in itself; the latter, as conformed to his law; both are positive." Lillie, on 2 Thess. 1:6—"Judgment is 'a righteous thing with God.' Divine justice requires it for its own satisfaction." See Shedd, Dogm. Theol., 1:175-178, 365-385; Trench, Syn. N. T., 1:180, 181.

Of Gaston de Foix, the old chronicler admirably wrote: "He loved what ought to be loved, and hated what ought to be hated, and never had miscreant with him." Compare Ps. 101:5, 6—"Him that hath a high look and a proud heart will I not suffer. Mine eyes shall be upon the faithful of the land, that they may dwell with me." Even Horace Bushnell spoke of the "wrath-principle" in God. 1 K. 11:9—"And Jehovah was angry with Solomon" because of his polygamy. Jesus' anger was no less noble than his love. The love of the right involved hatred of the wrong. Those may hate who hate evil for its hatefulness and for the sake of God. Hate sin in yourself first, and then you may hate it in itself and in the world. Be angry only in Christ and with the wrath of God. W. C. Wilkinson, Epic of Paul, 264—"But we must purge ourselves of self-regard, Or we are sinful in abhorring sin." Instance Judge Harris's pity, as he sentenced the murderer; see A. H. Strong, Philosophy and Religion, 192, 193.

Horace's "Ira furor brevis est"—"Anger is a temporary madness"—is true only of selfish and sinful anger. Hence the man who is angry is popularly called "mad." But anger, though apt to become sinful, is not necessarily so. Just anger is neither madness, nor is it brief. Instance the judicial anger of the church of Corinth in inflicting excommunication: 2 Cor. 7:11—"what indignation, yea what fear, yea what longing, yea what zeal, yea what avenging!" The only revenge permissible to the Christian church is that in which it pursues and exterminates sin. To be incapable of moral indignation against wrong is to lack real love for the right. Dr. Arnold of Rugby was never sure of a boy who only loved good; till the boy also began to hate evil, Dr. Arnold did not feel that he was safe. Herbert Spencer said that good nature with Americans became a crime. Lecky, Democracy and Liberty: "There is one thing worse than corruption, and that is acquiescence in corruption."

Colestock, Changing Viewpoint, 139—"Xenophon intends to say a very commendable thing of Cyrus the Younger, when he writes of him that no one had done more good to his friends or more harm to his enemies." Luther said to a monkish antagonist: "I will break in pieces your heart of brass and pulverize your iron brains." Shedd, Dogmatic Theology, 1:175-178—"Human character is worthless in proportion as abhorrence of sin is lacking in it. It is related of Charles II that 'he felt no gratitude for benefits, and no resentment for wrongs; he did not love anyone, and he did not hate anyone.' He was indifferent toward right and wrong, and the only feeling he had was contempt." But see the death-bed scene of the "merry monarch," as portrayed in Bp. Burnet, Evelyn's Memoirs, or the Life of Bp. Ken. Truly "The end of mirth is heaviness" (Prov. 14:13).

Stout, Manual of Psychology, 22—"Charles Lamb tells us that his friend George Dyer could never be brought to say anything in condemnation of the most atrocious crimes, except that the criminal must have been very eccentric." Professor Seeley: "No heart is pure that is not passionate." D. W. Simon, Redemption of Man, 249, 250, says that God's resentment "is a resentment of an essentially altruistic character." If this means that it is perfectly consistent with love for the sinner, we can accept the statement; if it means that love is the only source of the resentment, we regard the statement as a misinterpretation of God's justice, which is but the manifestation of his holiness and is not a mere expression of his love. See a similar statement of Lidgett, Spiritual Principle of the Atonement, 251—"Because God is love, his love coëxists with his wrath against sinners, is the very life of that wrath, and is so persistent that it uses wrath as its instrument, while at the same time it seeks and supplies a propitiation." This statement ignores the fact that punishment is never in Scripture regarded as an expression of God's love, but always of God's holiness. When we say that we love God, let us make sure that it is the true God, the God of holiness, that we love, for only this love will make us like him.

The moral indignation of a whole universe of holy beings against moral evil, added to the agonizing self-condemnations of awakened conscience in all the unholy, is only a faint and small reflection of the awful revulsion of God's infinite justice from the impurity and selfishness of his creatures, and of the intense, organic, necessary, and eternal reaction of his moral being in self-vindication and the punishment of sin; see Jer. 44:4—"Oh, do not this abominable thing that I hate!" Num. 32:23—"be sure your sin will find you out"; Heb. 10:30, 31—"For we know him that said, Vengeance belongeth unto me, I will recompense. And again, The Lord shall judge his people. It is a fearful thing to fall into the hands of the living God." On justice as an attribute of a moral governor, see N. W. Taylor, Moral Government, 2:253-293; Owen, Dissertation on Divine Justice, in Works, 10:483-624.

VII. Rank and Relations of the several Attributes

The attributes have relations to each other. Like intellect, affection and will in man, no one of them is to be conceived of as exercised separately from the rest. Each of the attributes is qualified by all the others. God's love is immutable, wise, holy. Infinity belongs to God's knowledge, power, justice. Yet this is not to say that one attribute is of as high rank as another. The moral attributes of truth, love, holiness, are worthy of higher reverence from men, and they are more jealously guarded by God, than the natural attributes of omnipresence, omniscience, and omnipotence. And yet even among the moral attributes one stands as supreme. Of this and of its supremacy we now proceed to speak.

Water is not water unless composed of oxygen and hydrogen. Oxygen cannot be resolved into hydrogen, nor hydrogen into oxygen. Oxygen has its own character, though only in combination with hydrogen does it appear in water. Will in man never acts without intellect and sensibility, yet will, more than intellect or sensibility, is the manifestation of the man. So when God acts, he manifests not one attribute alone, but his total moral excellence. Yet holiness, as an attribute of God, has rights peculiar to itself; it determines the attitude of the affections; it more than any other faculty constitutes God's moral being.

Clarke, Christian Theology, 83,92—"God would not be holy if he were not love, and could not be love if he were not holy. Love is an element in holiness. If this were lacking, there would be no perfect character as principle of his own action or as standard for us. On the other hand only the perfect being can be love. God must be free from all taint of selfishness in order to be love. Holiness requires God to act as love, for holiness is God's self-consistency. Love is the desire to impart holiness. Holiness makes God's character the standard for his creatures; but love, desiring to impart the best good, does the same.

All work of love is work of holiness, and all work of holiness is work of love. Conflict of attributes is impossible, because holiness always includes love, and love always expresses holiness. They never need reconciliation with each other."

The general correctness of the foregoing statement is impaired by the vagueness of its conception of holiness. The Scriptures do not regard holiness as including love, or make all the acts of holiness to be acts of love. Self-affirmation does not include self-impartation, and sin necessitates an exercise of holiness which is not also an exercise of love. But for the Cross, and God's suffering for sin of which the Cross is the expression, there would be conflict between holiness and love. The wisdom of God is most shown, not in reconciling man and God, but in reconciling the holy God with the loving God.

1. Holiness the fundamental attribute in God

That holiness is the fundamental attribute in God, is evident:

(a) From Scripture,—in which God's holiness is not only most constantly and powerfully impressed upon the attention of man, but is declared to be the chief subject of rejoicing and adoration in heaven.

It is God's attribute of holiness that first and most prominently presents itself to the mind of the sinner, and conscience only follows the method of Scripture: 1 Pet. 1:16—"Ye shall be holy; for I am holy"; Heb. 12:14—"the sanctification without which no man shall see the lord"; cf. Luke 5:8—"Depart from me; for I am a sinful man, O Lord." Yet this constant insistence upon holiness cannot be due simply to man's present state of sin, for in heaven, where there is no sin, there is the same reiteration: Is. 6:3—"Holy, holy, holy, is Jehovah of hosts"; Rev. 4:8—"Holy, holy, holy is the Lord God, the Almighty." Of no other attribute is it said that God's throne rests upon it: Ps. 97:2—"Righteousness and justice are the foundation of his throne"; 99:4, 5, 9—"The king's strength also loveth justice.... Exalt ye Jehovah our God.... holy is he." We would substitute the word holiness for the word love in the statement of Newman Smyth, Christian Ethics, 45—"We assume that love is lord in the divine will, not that the will of God is sovereign over his love. God's omnipotence, as Dorner would say, exists for his love."

(b) From our own moral constitution,—in which conscience asserts its supremacy over every other impulse and affection of our nature. As we may be kind, but must be righteous, so God, in whose image we are made, may be merciful, but must be holy.

See Bishop Butler's Sermons upon Human Nature, Bohn's ed., 385-414, showing "the supremacy of conscience in the moral constitution of man." We must be just, before we are generous. So with God, justice must be done always; mercy is optional with him. He was not under obligation to provide a redemption for sinners: 2 Pet. 2:4—"God spared not angels when they sinned, but cast them down to hell." Salvation is a matter of grace, not of debt. Shedd, Discourses and Essays, 277-298—"The quality of justice is necessary exaction; but 'the quality of mercy is not (con)strained' " [cf. Denham: "His mirth is forced and strained"]. God can apply the salvation, after he has wrought it out, to whomsoever he will: Rom. 9:18—"he hath mercy on whom he will." Young, Night-Thoughts, 4:233—"A God all mercy is a God unjust." Emerson: "Your goodness must have some edge to it; else it is none." Martineau, Study, 2:100—"No one can be just without subordinating Pity to the sense of Right."

We may learn of God's holiness a priori. Even the heathen could say "Fiat justitia, ruat cœlum," or "pereat mundus." But, for our knowledge of God's mercy, we are dependent upon special revelation. Mercy, like omnipotence, may exist in God without being exercised. Mercy is not grace but debt, if God owes the exercise of it either to the sinner or to himself; versus G. B. Stevens, in New Eng., 1888:421-443. "But justice is an attribute which not only exists of necessity, but must be exercised of necessity; because not to exercise it would be injustice"; see Shedd, Dogm. Theol., 1:218, 219, 389, 390; 2:402, and Sermons to Nat. Man, 366. If it be said that, by parity of reasoning, for God not to exercise mercy is to show himself unmerciful,—we reply that this is not true so long as higher interests require that exercise to be withheld. I am not unmerciful when I refuse to give the poor the money needed to pay an honest debt; nor is the Governor unmerciful when he refuses to pardon the condemned and unrepentant criminal. Mercy has its conditions, as we proceed to show, and it does not cease to be when these conditions do not permit it to be exercised. Not so with justice: justice must always be exercised; when it ceases to be exercised, it also ceases to be.

The story of the prodigal shows a love that ever reaches out after the son in the far country, but which is ever conditioned by the father's holiness and restrained from acting until the son has voluntarily forsaken his riotous living. A just father may banish a corrupt son from the household, yet may love him so tenderly that his banishment causes exquisite pain. E. G. Robinson: "God, Christ and the Holy Spirit have a conscience, that is, they distinguish between right and wrong." E. H. Johnson, Syst. Theology, 85, 86—"Holiness is primary as respects benevolence; for (a) Holiness is itself moral excellence, while the moral excellence of benevolence can be explained. (b) Holiness is an attribute of being, while benevolence is an attribute of action; but action presupposes and is controlled by being. (c) Benevolence must take counsel of holiness, since for a being to desire aught contrary to holiness would be to wish him harm, while that which holiness leads God to seek, benevolence finds best for the creature. (d) The Mosaic dispensation elaborately symbolized, and the Christian dispensation makes provision to meet, the requirements of holiness as supreme; James 3:17—'First pure, then [by consequence] peaceable.' "

We are "to do justly," as well as "to love kindness, and to walk humbly with" our God (Micah 6:8). Dr. Samuel Johnson: "It is surprising to find how much more kindness than justice society contains." There is a sinful mercy. A School Commissioner finds it terrible work to listen to the pleas of incompetent teachers begging that they may not be dismissed, and he can nerve himself for it only by remembering the children whose education may be affected by his refusal to do justice. Love and pity are not the whole of Christian duty, nor are they the ruling attributes of God.

(c) From the actual dealings of God,—in which holiness conditions and limits the exercise of other attributes. Thus, for example, in Christ's redeeming work, though love makes the atonement, it is violated holiness that requires it; and in the eternal punishment of the wicked, the demand of holiness for self-vindication overbears the pleading of love for the sufferers.

Love cannot be the fundamental attribute of God, because love always requires a norm or standard, and this norm or standard is found only in holiness; Phil. 1:9—"And this I pray, that your love may abound yet more in knowledge and all discernment"; see A. H. Strong, Christ in Creation, 388-405. That which conditions all is highest of all. Holiness shows itself higher than love, in that it conditions love. Hence God's mercy does not consist in outraging his own law of holiness, but in enduring the penal affliction by which that law of holiness is satisfied. Conscience in man is but the reflex of holiness in God. Conscience demands either retribution or atonement. This demand Christ meets by his substituted suffering. His sacrifice assuages the thirst of conscience in man, as well as the demand of holiness in God: John 6:55—"For my flesh is meat indeed, and my blood is drink indeed." See Shedd, Discourses and Essays, 280, 291, 292; Dogmatic Theology, 1:377, 378—"The sovereignty and freedom of God in respect to justice relates not to the abolition, nor to the relaxation, but to the substitution, of punishment. It does not consist in any power to violate or waive legal claims. The exercise of the other attributes of God is regulated and conditioned by that of justice.... Where then is the mercy of God, in case justice is strictly satisfied by a vicarious person? There is mercy in permitting another person to do for the sinner what the sinner is bound to do for himself; and greater mercy in providing that person; and still greater mercy in becoming that person."

Enthusiasm, like fire, must not only burn, but must be controlled. Man invented chimneys to keep in the heat but to let out the smoke. We need the walls of discretion and self-control to guide the flaming of our love. The holiness of God is the regulating principle of his nature. The ocean of his mercy is bounded by the shores of his justice. Even if holiness be God's self-love, in the sense of God's self-respect or self-preservation, still this self-love must condition love to creatures. Only as God maintains himself in his holiness, can he have anything of worth to give; love indeed is nothing but the self-communication of holiness. And if we say, with J. M. Whiton, that self-affirmation in a universe in which God is immanent is itself a form of self-impartation, still this form of self-impartation must condition and limit that other form of self-impartation which we call love to creatures. See Thomasius, Christi Person und Werk, 1:137-155, 346-353; Patton, art. on Retribution and the Divine Goodness, in Princeton Rev., Jan. 1878:8-16; Owen, Dissertation on the Divine Justice, in Works, 10: 483-624.

(d) From God's eternal purpose of salvation,—in which justice and mercy are reconciled only through the foreseen and predetermined sacrifice of Christ. The declaration that Christ is "the Lamb ... slain from the foundation of the world" implies the existence of a principle in the divine nature which requires satisfaction, before God can enter upon the work of redemption. That principle can be none other than holiness.

Since both mercy and justice are exercised toward sinners of the human race, the otherwise inevitable antagonism between them is removed only by the atoning death of the God-man. Their opposing claims do not impair the divine blessedness, because the reconciliation exists in the eternal counsels of God. This is intimated in Rev. 13:8—"the Lamb that hath been slain from the foundation of the world." This same reconciliation is alluded to in Ps. 85:10—"Mercy and truth are met together; Righteousness and peace have kissed each other"; and in Rom. 3:26—"that he might himself be just, and the justifier of him that hath faith in Jesus." The atonement, then, if man was to be saved, was necessary, not primarily on man's account, but on God's account. Shedd, Discourses and Essays, 279—The sacrifice of Christ was an "atonement ab intra, a self-oblation on the part of Deity himself, by which to satisfy those immanent and eternal imperatives of the divine nature which without it must find their satisfaction in the punishment of the transgressor, or else be outraged." Thus God's word of redemption, as well as his word of creation, is forever "settled in heaven" (Ps. 119:89). Its execution on the cross was "according to the pattern" on high. The Mosaic sacrifice prefigured the sacrifice of Christ; but the sacrifice of Christ was but the temporal disclosure of an eternal fact in the nature of God. See Kreibig, Versöhnung, 155, 156.

God requires satisfaction because he is holiness, but he makes satisfaction because he is love. The

Judge himself, with all his hatred of transgression, still loves the transgressor, and comes down from the bench to take the criminal's place and bear his penalty. But this is an eternal provision and an eternal sacrifice. Heb. 9:14—"the blood of Christ, who through the eternal Spirit offered himself without blemish unto God." Matheson, Voices of the Spirit, 215, 216—"Christ's sacrifice was offered through the Spirit. It was not wrung from a reluctant soul through obedience to outward law; it came from the inner heart, from the impulse of undying love. It was a completed offering before Calvary began; it was seen by the Father before it was seen by the world. It was finished in the Spirit, ere it began in the flesh, finished in the hour when Christ exclaimed: 'not as I will, but as thou wilt' (Mat. 26:39)."

Lang, Homer, 506—"Apollo is the bringer of pestilence and the averter of pestilence, in accordance with the well-known rule that the two opposite attributes should be combined in the same deity." Lord Bacon, Confession of Faith: "Neither angel, man nor world, could stand or can stand one moment in God's sight without beholding the same in the face of a Mediator; and therefore before him, with whom all things are present, the Lamb of God was slain before all worlds; without which eternal counsel of his, it was impossible for him to have descended to any work of creation." Orr, Christian View of God and the World, 819—"Creation is built on redemption lines"—which is to say that incarnation and atonement were included in God's original design of the world.

2. The holiness of God the ground of moral obligation

A. Erroneous Views. The ground of moral obligation is not

(a) In power,—whether of civil law (Hobbes, Gassendi), or of divine will (Occam, Descartes). We are not bound to obey either of these, except upon the ground that they are right. This theory assumes that nothing is good or right in itself, and that morality is mere prudence.

Civil law: See Hobbes, Leviathan, part i, chap. 6 and 13; part ii, chap. 30; Gassendi, Opera, 6:120. Upon this view, might makes right; the laws of Nero are always binding; a man may break his promise when civil law permits; there is no obligation to obey a father, a civil governor, or God himself, when once it is certain that the disobedience will be hidden, or when the offender is willing to incur the punishment. Martineau, Seat of Authority, 67—"Mere magnitude of scale carries no moral quality; nor could a whole population of devils by unanimous ballot confer righteousness upon their will, or make it binding upon a single Abdiel." Robert Browning, Christmas Eve, xvii—"Justice, good, and truth were still Divine if, by some demon's will, Hatred and wrong had been proclaimed Law through the world, and right misnamed."

Divine will: See Occam, lib. 2, quæs. 19 (quoted in Porter, Moral Science, 125); Descartes (referred to in Hickok, Moral Science, 27, 28); Martineau, Types, 148—"Descartes held that the will of God is not the revealer but the inventor of moral distinctions. God could have made Euclid a farrago of lies, and Satan a model of moral perfection." Upon this view, right and wrong are variable quantities. Duns Scotus held that God's will makes not only truth but right. God can make lying to be virtuous and purity to be wrong. If Satan were God, we should be bound to obey him. God is essentially indifferent to right and wrong, good and evil. We reply that behind the divine will is the divine nature, and that in the moral perfection of that nature lies the only ground of moral obligation. God pours forth his love and exerts his power in accordance with some determining principle in his own nature. That principle is not happiness. Finney, Syst. Theology, 936, 937—"Could God's command make it obligatory upon us to will evil to him? If not, then his will is not the ground of moral obligation. The thing that is most valuable, namely, the highest good of God and of the universe must be both the end and the ground. It is the divine reason and not the divine will that perceives and affirms the law of conduct. The divine will publishes, but does not originate, the rule. God's will could not make vice to be virtuous."

As between power or utility on the one hand, and right on the other hand, we must regard right as the more fundamental. We do not, however, as will be seen further on, place the ground of moral obligation even in right, considered as an abstract principle; but place it rather in the moral excellence of him who is the personal Right and therefore the source of right. Character obliges, and the master often bows in his heart to the servant, when this latter is the nobler man.

(b) Nor in utility,—whether our own happiness or advantage present or eternal (Paley), for supreme regard for our own interest is not virtuous; or the greatest happiness or advantage to being in general (Edwards), for we judge conduct to be useful because it is right, not right because it is useful. This theory would compel us to believe that in eternity past God was holy only because of the good he got from it,—that is, there was no such thing as holiness in itself, and no such thing as moral character in God.

Our own happiness: Paley, Mor. and Pol. Philos., book i, chap. vii—"Virtue is the doing good to mankind, in obedience to the will of God, and for the sake of everlasting happiness." This unites (a) and (b). John Stuart Mill and Dr. N. W. Taylor held that our own happiness is the supreme end. These writers indeed regard the highest happiness as attained only by living for others (Mill's altruism), but they can assign no reason why one who knows no other happiness than the pleasures of sense should not adopt the maxim of Epicurus, who, according to Lucretius, taught that "ducit quemque voluptas." This theory renders virtue impossible; for a virtue which is mere regard to our own interest is not virtue but prudence. "We have a sense of right and wrong independently of all considerations of happiness or its loss." James Mill held that the utility is not the criterion of the morality but itself constitutes the morality. G. B. Foster well replies that virtue is not mere egoistic sagacity, and the moral act is not simply a clever business enterprise. All languages distinguish between virtue and prudence. To say that the virtues are great utilities is to confound the effect with the cause. Carlyle says that a man can do without happiness. Browning, Red Cotton Nightcap Country: "Thick heads ought to recognize The devil, that old stager, at his trick Of general utility, who leads Downward perhaps, but fiddles all the way." This is the morality of Mother Goose: "He put in his thumb, And pulled out a plum, And said, 'What a good boy am I!' "

E. G. Robinson, Principles and Practice of Morality, 160—"Utility has nothing ultimate in itself, and therefore can furnish no ground of obligation. Utility is mere fitness of one thing to minister to something else." To say that things are right because they are useful, is like saying that things are beautiful because they are pleasing. Martineau, Types of Ethical Theory, 2:170, 511, 556—"The moment the appetites pass into the self-conscious state, and become ends instead of impulses, they draw to themselves terms of censure.... So intellectual conscientiousness, or strict submission of the mind to evidence, has its inspiration in pure love of truth, and would not survive an hour if entrusted to the keeping either of providence or of social affection.... Instincts, which provide for they know not what, are proof that want is the original impulse to action, instead of pleasure being the end." On the happiness theory, appeals to self-interest on behalf of religion ought to be effective,—as a matter of fact few are moved by them.

Dewey, Psychology, 300, 362—"Emotion turned inward eats up itself. Live on feelings rather than on the things to which feelings belong, and you defeat your own end, exhaust your power of feeling, commit emotional suicide. Hence arise cynicism, the nil admirari spirit, restless searching for the latest sensation. The only remedy is to get outside of self, to devote self to some worthy object, not for feeling's sake but for the sake of the object.... We do not desire an object because it gives us pleasure, but it gives us pleasure because it satisfies the impulse which, in connection with the idea of the object, constitutes the desire.... Pleasure is the accompaniment of the activity or development of the self."

Salter, First Steps in Philosophy, 150—"It is right to aim at happiness. Happiness is an end. Utilitarianism errs in making happiness the only and the highest end. It exalts a state of feeling into the supremely desirable thing. Intuitionalism gives the same place to a state of will. The truth includes both. The true end is the highest development of being, self and others, the realization of the divine idea, God in man." Bowne, Principles of Ethics, 96—"The standard of appeal is not the actual happiness of the actual man but the normal happiness of the normal man.... Happiness must have a law. But then also the law must lead to happiness.... The true ethical aim is to realize the good. But then the contents of this good have to be determined in accordance with an inborn ideal of human worth and dignity.... Not all good, but the true good, not the things which please, but the things which should please, are to be the aim of action."

Bixby, Crisis of Morals, 223—"The Utilitarian is really asking about the wisest method of embodying the ideal. He belongs to that second stage in which the moral artist considers through what material and in what form and color he may best realize his thought. What the ideal is, and why it is the highest, he does not tell us. Morality begins, not in feeling, but in reason. And reason is impersonal. It discerns the moral equality of personalities." Genung, Epic of the Inner Life, 20—Job speaks out his character like one of Robert Browning's heroes. He teaches that "there is a service of God which is not work for reward: it is a heart-loyalty, a hunger after God's presence, which survives loss and chastisement; which in spite of contradictory seeming cleaves to what is godlike as the needle seeks the pole; and which reaches up out of the darkness and hardness of this life into the light and love beyond."

Greatest good of being: Not only Edwards, but Priestley, Bentham, Dwight, Finney, Hopkins, Fairchild, hold this view. See Edwards, Works, 2:261-304—"Virtue is benevolence toward being in general"; Dwight, Theology, 3:150-162—"Utility the foundation of Virtue"; Hopkins, Law of Love, 7-28; Fairchild, Moral Philosophy; Finney, Syst. Theol., 42-135. This theory regards good as a mere state of the sensibility, instead of consisting in purity of being. It forgets that in eternity past "love for being in general" = simply God's self-love, or God's regard for his own happiness. This implies that God is holy only for a purpose; he is bound to be unholy, if greater good would result; that is, holiness has no independent existence in his nature. We grant that a thing is often known to be right by the fact that it is useful; but this is very different from saying that its usefulness makes it right. "Utility is only the setting of the diamond, which marks, but does not make, its value." "If utility be a criterion of rectitude, it is only because it is a revelation of the divine nature." See British Quarterly, July, 1877, on Matthew Arnold and Bishop Butler. Bp. Butler, Nature of Virtue, in Works, Bohn's ed., 334—"Benevolence is the true self-love." Love and holiness are obligatory in themselves, and not because they promote the general good. Cicero well said that they who confounded the honestum with the utile deserved to be banished from society. See criticism on Porter's Moral Science, in Lutheran Quarterly, Apr. 1885:325-

331; also F. L. Patton, on Metaphysics of Oughtness, in Presb. Rev., 1886:127-150.

Encyc. Britannica, 7:690, on Jonathan Edwards—"Being in general, being without any qualities, is too abstract a thing to be the primary cause of love. The feeling which Edwards refers to is not love, but awe or reverence, and moreover necessarily a blind awe. Properly stated therefore, true virtue, according to Edwards, would consist in a blind awe of being in general,—only this would be inconsistent with his definition of virtue as existing in God. In reality, as he makes virtue merely the second object of love, his theory becomes identical with that utilitarian theory with which the names of Hume, Bentham and Mill are associated." Hodge, Essays, 275—"If obligation is due primarily to being in general, then there is no more virtue in loving God—willing his good—than there is in loving Satan. But love to Christ differs in its nature from benevolence toward the devil." Plainly virtue consists, not in love for mere being, but in love for good being, or in other words, in love for the holy God. Not the greatest good of being, but the holiness of God, is the ground of moral obligation.

Dr. E. A. Park interprets the Edwardian theory as holding that virtue is love to all beings according to their value, love of the greater therefore more than the less, "love to particular beings in a proportion compounded of the degree of being and the degree of virtue or benevolence to being which they have." Love is choice. Happiness, says Park, is not the sole good, much less the happiness of creatures. The greatest good is holiness, though the last good aimed at is happiness. Holiness is disinterested love—free choice of the general above the private good. But we reply that this gives us no reason or standard for virtue. It does not tell us what is good nor why we should choose it. Martineau, Types, 2:70, 77, 471, 484—"Why should I promote the general well-being? Why should I sacrifice myself for others? Only because this is godlike. It Would never have been prudent to do right, had it not been something infinitely more.... It is not fitness that makes an act moral, but it is its morality that makes it fit."

Herbert Spencer must be classed as a utilitarian. He says that justice requires that "every man be free to do as he wills provided he infringes not the equal freedom of every other man." But, since this would permit injury to another by one willing to submit to injury in return, Mr. Spencer limits the freedom to "such actions as subserve life." This is practically equivalent to saying that the greatest sum of happiness is the ultimate end. On Jonathan Edwards, see Robert Hall, Works, 1:43 sq.; Alexander, Moral Science, 194-198; Bib. Repertory (Princeton Review), 25:22; Bib. Sacra, 9:176, 197; 10:403, 705.

(c) Nor in the nature of things (Price),—whether by this we mean their fitness (Clarke), truth (Wollaston), order (Jouffroy), relations (Wayland), worthiness (Hickok), sympathy (Adam Smith), or abstract right (Haven and Alexander); for this nature of things is not ultimate, but has its ground in the nature of God. We are bound to worship the highest; if anything exists beyond and above God, we are bound to worship that,—that indeed is God.

See Wayland, Moral Science, 33-48; Hickok, Moral Science, 27-34; Haven, Moral Philosophy, 27-50; Alexander, Moral Science, 159-198. In opposition to all the forms of this theory, we urge that nothing exists independently of or above God. "If the ground of morals exist independently of God, either it has ultimately no authority, or it usurps the throne of the Almighty. Any rational being who kept the law would be perfect without God, and the moral centre of all intelligences would be outside of God" (Talbot). God is not a Jupiter controlled by Fate. He is subject to no law but the law of his own nature. Noblesse oblige,—character rules,—purity is the highest. And therefore to holiness all creatures, voluntarily or involuntarily, are constrained to bow. Hopkins, Law of Love, 77—"Right and wrong have nothing to do with things, but only with actions; nothing to do with any nature of things existing necessarily, but only with the nature of persons." Another has said: "The idea of right cannot be original, since right means conformity to some standard or rule." This standard or rule is not an abstraction, but an existing being—the infinitely perfect God.

Faber: "For right is right, since God is God; And right the day must win; To doubt would be disloyalty, To falter would be sin." Tennyson: "And because right is right, to follow right Were wisdom in the scorn of consequence." Right is right, and I should will the right, not because God wills it, but because God is it. E. G. Robinson, Principles and Practice of Morality, 178-180—"Utility and relations simply reveal the constitution of things and so represent God. Moral law was not made for purposes of utility, nor do relations constitute the reason for obligation. They only show what the nature of God is who made the universe and revealed himself in it. In his nature is found the reason for morality." S. S. Times, Oct. 17, 1891—"Only that is level which conforms to the curvature of the earth's surface. A straight line tangent to the earth's curve would at its ends be much further from the earth's centre than at its middle. Now equity means levelness. The standard of equity is not an impersonal thing, a 'nature of things' outside of God. Equity or righteousness is no more to be conceived independently of the divine centre of the moral world than is levelness comprehensible apart from the earth's centre."

Since God finds the rule and limitation of his action solely in his own being, and his love is conditioned by his holiness, we must differ from such views as that of Moxom: "Whether we define God's nature as perfect holiness or perfect love is immaterial, since his nature is manifested only through his action, that is, through his relation to other beings. Most of our reasoning on the divine standard of righteousness, or the ultimate ground of moral obligation, is reasoning in a circle, since we must always go back to God for the principle of his action; which principle we can know only by means of his action. God, the perfectly righteous Being, is the ideal standard of human righteousness. Righteousness in man therefore is conformity to the nature of God. God, in agreement with his perfect nature, always wills the perfectly good toward man. His righteousness is an expression of his love; his love is a manifestation of his righteousness."

So Newman Smyth: "Righteousness is the eternal genuineness of the divine love. It is not therefore an independent excellence, to be contrasted with, or even put in opposition to, benevolence; it is an essential part of love." In reply to which we urge as before that that which is the object of love, that which limits and conditions love, that which furnishes the norm and reason for love, cannot itself be love, nor hold merely equal rank with love. A double standard is as irrational in ethics as in commerce, and it leads in ethics to the same debasement of the higher values, and the same unsettling of relations, as has resulted in our currency from the attempt to make silver regulate gold at the same time that gold regulates silver.

B. The Scriptural View.—According to the Scriptures, the ground of moral obligation is the holiness of God, or the moral perfection of the divine nature, conformity to which is the law of our moral being (Robinson, Chalmers, Calderwood, Gregory, Wuttke). We show this:

(a) From the commands: "Ye shall be holy," where the ground of obligation assigned is simply and only: "for I am holy" (1 Pet. 1:16); and "Ye therefore shall be perfect," where the standard laid down is: "as your heavenly Father is perfect" (Mat. 5:48). Here we have an ultimate reason and ground for being and doing right, namely, that God is right, or, in other words, that holiness is his nature.

(b) From the nature of the love in which the whole law is summed up (Mat. 22:37—"Thou shalt love the Lord thy God"; Rom. 13:10—"love therefore is the fulfilment of the law"). This love is not regard for abstract right or for the happiness of being, much less for one's own interest, but it is regard for God as the fountain and standard of moral excellence, or in other words, love for God as holy. Hence this love is the principle and source of holiness in man.

(c) From the example of Christ, whose life was essentially an exhibition of supreme regard for God, and of supreme devotion to his holy will. As Christ saw nothing good but what was in God (Mark 10:18—"none is good save one, even God"), and did only what he saw the Father do (John 5:19; see also 30—"I seek not mine own will, but the will of him that sent me"), so for us, to be like God is the sum of all duty, and God's infinite moral excellence is the supreme reason why we should be like him.

For statements of the correct view of the ground of moral obligation, see E. G. Robinson, Principles and Practice of Morality, 138-180; Chalmers, Moral Philosophy, 412-420; Calderwood, Moral Philosophy; Gregory, Christian Ethics, 112-122; Wuttke, Christian Ethics, 2:80-107; Talbot, Ethical Prolegomena, in Bap. Quar., July, 1877:257-274—"The ground of all moral law is the nature of God, or the ethical nature of God in relation to the like nature in man, or the imperativeness of the divine nature." Plato: "The divine will is the fountain of all efficiency; the divine reason is the fountain, of all law; the divine nature is the fountain of all virtue." If it be said that God is love as well as holiness, we ask: Love to what? And the only answer is: Love to the right, or to holiness. To ask why right is a good, is no more sensible than to ask why happiness is a good. There must be something ultimate. Schiller said there are people who want to know why ten is not twelve. We cannot study character apart from conduct, nor conduct apart from character. But this does not prevent us from recognizing that character is the fundamental thing and that conduct is only the expression of it.

The moral perfection of the divine nature includes truth and love, but since it is holiness that conditions the exercise of every other attribute, we must conclude that holiness is the ground of moral obligation. Infinity also unites with holiness to make it the perfect ground, but since the determining element is holiness, we call this, and not infinity, the ground of obligation. J. H. Harris, Baccalaureate Sermon, Bucknell University, 1890—"As holiness is the fundamental attribute of God, so holiness is the supreme good of man. Aristotle perceived this when he declared the chief good of man to be energizing according to virtue. Christianity supplies the Holy Spirit and makes this energizing possible." Holiness is the goal of man's spiritual career; see 1 Thess. 3:13—"to the end he may establish your hearts unblamable in holiness before our God and Father."

Arthur H. Hallam, in John Brown's Rab and his Friends, 272—"Holiness and happiness are two notions of one thing.... Unless therefore the heart of a created being is at one with the heart of God, it cannot but be miserable." It is more true to say that holiness and happiness are, as cause and effect, inseparably bound together. Martineau, Types, 1:xvi; 2:70-77—"Two classes of facts it is indispensable for us to know: what are the springs of voluntary conduct, and what are its effects"; Study, 1:26—"Ethics must either perfect themselves in Religion, or disintegrate themselves into Hedonism." William Law remarks: "Ethics are not external but internal. The essence of a moral act does not lie in its result, but in the motive from which it springs. And that again is good or bad, according as it conforms to the character of God." For further discussion of the subject see our chapter on The Law of God. See also Thornwell, Theology, 1:363-373; Hinton, Art of Thinking, 47-62; Goldwin Smith, in Contemporary Review, March, 1882, and Jan. 1884; H. B. Smith, System of Theology, 195-231, esp. 223.

Chapter II - Doctrine Of The Trinity

In the nature of the one God there are three eternal distinctions which are represented to us under the figure of persons, and these three are equal. This tripersonality of the Godhead is exclusively a truth of revelation. It is clearly, though not formally, made known in the New Testament, and intimations of it may be found in the Old.

The doctrine of the Trinity may be expressed in the six following statements: 1. In Scripture there are three who are recognized as God. 2. These three are so described in Scripture that we are compelled to conceive of them as distinct persons. 3. This tripersonality of the divine nature is not merely economic and temporal, but is immanent and eternal. 4. This tripersonality is not tritheism; for while there are three persons, there is but one essence. 5. The three persons, Father, Son and Holy Spirit, are equal. 6. Inscrutable yet not self-contradictory, this doctrine furnishes the key to all other doctrines.—These statements we proceed now to prove and to elucidate.

Reason shows us the Unity of God; only revelation shows us the Trinity of God, thus filling out the indefinite outlines of this Unity and vivifying it. The term "Trinity" is not found in Scripture, although the conception it expresses is Scriptural. The invention of the term is ascribed to Tertullian. The Montanists first defined the personality of the Spirit, and first formulated the doctrine of the Trinity. The term "Trinity" is not a metaphysical one. It is only a designation of four facts: (1) the Father is God; (2) the Son is God; (3) the Spirit is God; (4) there is but one God.

Park: "The doctrine of the Trinity does not on the one hand assert that three persons are united in one person, or three beings in one being, or three Gods in one God (tritheism); nor on the other hand that God merely manifests himself in three different ways (modal trinity, or trinity of manifestations); but rather that there are three eternal distinctions in the substance of God." Smyth, preface to Edwards, Observations on the Trinity: "The church doctrine of the Trinity affirms that there are in the Godhead three distinct hypostases or subsistences—the Father, the Son and the Holy Spirit—each possessing one and the same divine nature, though in a different manner. The essential points are (1) the unity of essence; (2) the reality of immanent or ontological distinctions." See Park on Edwards's View of the Trinity, in Bib. Sac., April, 1881:333. Princeton Essays, 1:28—"There is one God; Father, Son, and Holy Spirit are this one God; there is such a distinction between Father, Son and Holy Spirit as to lay a sufficient ground for the reciprocal use of the personal pronouns." Joseph Cook: "(1) The Father, the Son, and the Holy Ghost are one God; (2) each has a peculiarity incommunicable to the others; (3) neither is God without the others; (4) each, with the others, is God."

We regard the doctrine of the Trinity as implicitly held by the apostles and as involved in the New Testament declarations with regard to Father, Son and Holy Spirit, while we concede that the doctrine had not by the New Testament writers been formulated. They held it, as it were in solution; only time, reflection, and the shock of controversy and opposition, caused it to crystalize into definite and dogmatic form. Chadwick, Old and New Unitarianism, 59, 60, claims that the Jewish origin of Christianity shows that the Jewish Messiah could not originally have been conceived of as divine. If Jesus had claimed this, he would not have been taken before Pilate,—the Jews would have dispatched him. The doctrine of the Trinity, says Chadwick, was not developed until the Council of Nice, 325. E. G. Robinson: "There was no doctrine of the Trinity in the Patristic period, as there was no doctrine of the Atonement before Anselm." The Outlook, Notes and Queries, March 30, 1901—"The doctrine of the Trinity cannot be said to have taken final shape before the appearance of the so-called Athanasian Creed in the 8th or 9th century. The Nicene Creed, formulated in the 4th century, is termed by Dr. Schaff, from the orthodox point of view, 'semi-trinitarian.' The earliest time known at which Jesus was deified was, after the New Testament writers, in the letters of Ignatius, at the beginning of the second century."

Gore, Incarnation, 179—"The doctrine of the Trinity is not so much heard, as overheard, in the statements of Scripture." George P. Fisher quotes some able and pious friend of his as saying: "What meets us in the New Testament is the disjecta membra of the Trinity." G. B. Foster: "The doctrine of the Trinity is the Christian attempt to make intelligible the personality of God without dependence upon the world." Charles Kingsley said that, whether the doctrine of the Trinity is in the Bible or no, it ought to be there, because our spiritual nature cries out for it. Shedd, Dogmatic Theology, 1:250—"Though the doctrine of the Trinity is not discoverable by human reason, it is susceptible of a rational defense, when revealed." On New England Trinitarianism, see New World, June, 1896:272-295—art. by Levi L.

Paine. He says that the last phase of it is represented by Phillips Brooks, James M. Whiton and George A. Gordon. These hold to the essential divineness of humanity and preëminently of Christ, the unique representative of mankind, who was, in this sense, a true incarnation of Deity. See also, L. L. Paine, Evolution of Trinitarianism, 141, 287.

Neander declared that the Trinity is not a fundamental doctrine of Christianity. He was speaking however of the speculative, metaphysical form which the doctrine has assumed in theology. But he speaks very differently of the devotional and practical form in which the Scriptures present it, as in the baptismal formula and in the apostolic benediction. In regard to this he says: "We recognize therein the essential contents of Christianity summed up in brief." Whiton, Gloria Patri, 10, 11, 55, 91, 92—"God transcendent, the Father, is revealed by God immanent, the Son. This one nature belongs equally to God, to Christ, and to mankind, and in this fact is grounded the immutableness of moral distinctions and the possibility of moral progress.... The immanent life of the universe is one with the transcendent Power; the filial stream is one with its paternal Fount. To Christ supremely belongs the name of Son, which includes all that life that is begotten of God. In Christ the before unconscious Sonship of the world awakes to consciousness of the Father. The Father is the Life transcendent, above all; the Son is Life immanent, through all; the Holy Spirit is the Life individualized, in all. In Christ we have collectivism; in the Holy Spirit we have individualism; as Bunsen says: 'The chief power in the world is personality.' "

For treatment of the whole doctrine, see Dorner, System of Doctrine, 1:344-465; Twesten, Dogmatik, and translation in Bib. Sac., 3:502; Ebrard, Dogmatik, 1:145-199; Thomasius, Christi Person und Werk, 1:57-135; Kahnis, Dogmatik, 3:203-229; Shedd, Dogm. Theol., 1:248-333, and History of Doctrine, 1:246-385; Farrar, Science and Theology, 138; Schaff, Nicene Doctrine of the Holy Trinity, in Theol. Eclectic, 4:209. For the Unitarian view, see Norton, Statement of Reasons, and J. F. Clarke, Truths and Errors of Orthodoxy.

I. In Scriptures there are Three who are recognized as God

1. Proofs from the New Testament
    A. The Father is recognized as God.
    The Father is recognized as God,—and that in so great a number of passages (such as John 6:27—"him the Father, even God, hath sealed," and 1 Pet. 1:2—"foreknowledge of God the Father") that we need not delay to adduce extended proof.
    B. Jesus Christ is recognized as God.
    (a) He is expressly called God.
    In John 1:1—Θεός ἦν ὁ λόγος—the absence of the article shows Θεός to be the predicate (cf. 4:24—πνεῦμα ὁ Θεός). This predicate precedes the verb by way of emphasis, to indicate progress in the thought = "the Logos was not only with God, but was God" (see Meyer and Luthardt, Comm. in loco). "Only ὁ λόγος can be the subject, for in the whole Introduction the question is, not who God is, but who the Logos is" (Godet).
    Westcott in Bible Commentary, in loco—"The predicate stands emphatically first. It is necessarily without the article, inasmuch as it describes the nature of the Word and does not identify his person. It would be pure Sabellianism to say: 'The Word was ὁ Θεός.' Thus in verse 1 we have set forth the Word in his absolute eternal being, (a) his existence: beyond time; (b) his personal existence: in active communion with God; (c) his nature: God in essence." Marcus Dods, in Expositor's Greek Testament, in loco: "The Word is distinguishable from God, yet Θεὸς ἦν ὁ λόγος—the word was God, of divine nature; not 'a God,' which to a Jewish ear would have been abominable, nor yet identical with all that can be called God, for then the article would have been inserted (cf. 1 John 3:4)."
    In John 1:18, μονογενὴς θεός—"the only begotten God"—must be regarded as the correct reading, and as a plain ascription of absolute Deity to Christ. He is not simply the only revealer of God, but he is himself God revealed.
    John 1:18—"No man hath seen God at any time; the only begotten God, who is in the bosom of the Father, he hath declared him." In this passage, although Tischendorf (8th ed.) has μονογενὴς υἱός, Westcott and Hort (with ℵ*BC*L Pesh. Syr.) read μονογενὴς Θεός and the Rev. Vers. puts "the only begotten God" in the margin, though it retains "the only begotten Son" in the text. Harnack says the reading μονογενὴς θεός is "established beyond contradiction"; see Westcott, Bib. Com. on John, pages 32, 33. Here then we have a new and unmistakable assertion of the deity of Christ. Meyer says that the apostles actually call Christ God only in John 1:1 and 20:28, and that Paul never so recognizes him. But Meyer is able to maintain his position only by calling the doxologies to Christ, in 2 Tim. 4:18, Heb. 13:21 and 2 Pet. 3:18, post-apostolic. See Thayer, N. T. Lexicon, on Θεός, and on μονογενής.
    In John 20:28, the address of Thomas Ὁ κύριός μου καὶ ὁ θεός μου—"My Lord and my God"—since it was unrebuked by Christ, is equivalent to an assertion on his own part of his claim to Deity.
    John 20:28—"Thomas answered and said unto him, My Lord and my God." This address cannot

be interpreted as a sudden appeal to God in surprise and admiration, without charging the apostle with profanity. Nor can it be considered a mere exhibition of overwrought enthusiasm, since it was accepted by Christ. Contrast the conduct of Paul and Barnabas when the heathen at Lystra were bringing sacrifice to them as Jupiter and Mercury (Acts 14:11-18). The words of Thomas, as addressed directly to Christ and as accepted by Christ, can be regarded only as a just acknowledgment on the part of Thomas that Christ was his Lord and his God. Alford, Commentary, in loco: "The Socinian view that these words are merely an exclamation is refuted (1) by the fact that no such exclamations were in use among the Jews; (2) by the εἶπεν αὐτῷ; (3) by the impossibility of referring the ὁ κύριός μου to another than Jesus: see verse 13; (4) by the N. T. usage of expressing the vocative by the nominative with an article; (5) by the psychological absurdity of such a supposition: that one just convinced of the presence of him whom he dearly loved should, instead of addressing him, break out into an irrelevant cry; (6) by the further absurdity of supposing that, if such were the case, the Apostle John, who of all the sacred writers most constantly keeps in mind the object for which he is writing, should have recorded anything so beside that object; (7) by the intimate conjunction of πεπίστευκας." Cf. Mat. 5:34—"Swear not ... by the heaven"—swearing by Jehovah is not mentioned, because no Jew did so swear. This exclamation of Thomas, the greatest doubter among the twelve, is the natural conclusion of John's gospel. The thesis "the Word was God" (John 1:1) has now become part of the life and consciousness of the apostles. Chapter 21 is only an Epilogue, or Appendix, written later by John, to correct the error that he was not to die; see Westcott, Bible Com., in loco. The Deity of Christ is the subject of the apostle who best understood his Master. Lyman Beecher: "Jesus Christ is the acting Deity of the universe."

In Rom. 9:5, the clause ὁ ὢν ἐπὶ πάντων Θεὸς εὐλογητός cannot be translated "blessed be the God over all," for ὢν is superfluous if the clause is a doxology; "εὐλογητός precedes the name of God in a doxology, but follows it, as here, in a description" (Hovey). The clause can therefore be justly interpreted only as a description of the higher nature of the Christ who had just been said, τὸ κατὰ σάρκα, or according to his lower nature, to have had his origin from Israel (see Tholuck, Com. in loco).

Sanday, Com. on Rom. 9:5—"The words would naturally refer to Christ, unless 'God' is so definitely a proper name that it would imply a contrast in itself. We have seen that this is not so." Hence Sanday translates: "of whom is the Christ as concerning the flesh, who is over all, God blessed forever". See President T. Dwight, in Jour. Soc. Bib. Exegesis, 1881:22-55; per contra, Ezra Abbot, in the same journal, 1881:1-19, and Denney, in Expositor's Gk. Test., in loco.

In Titus 2:13, ἐπιφάνειαν τῆς δόξης τοῦ μεγάλου Θεοῦ καὶ σωτῆρος ἡμῶν Ἰησοῦ Χριστοῦ we regard (with Ellicott) as "a direct, definite, and even studied declaration of Christ's divinity" = "the ... appearing of the glory of our great God and Savior Jesus Christ" (so English Revised Version). Ἐπιφάνεια is a term applied specially to the Son and never to the Father, and μεγάλου is uncalled for if used of the Father, but peculiarly appropriate if used of Christ. Upon the same principles we must interpret the similar text 2 Pet. 1:1 (see Huther, in Meyer's Com.: "The close juxtaposition indicates the author's certainty of the oneness of God and Jesus Christ").

Titus 2:13—"looking for the blessed hope and appearing of the glory of our great God and Savior, Jesus Christ"—so the English Revised Version. The American Revisers however translate: "the glory of the great God and Savior"; and Westcott and Hort bracket the word ἡμῶν. These considerations somewhat lessen the cogency of this passage as a proof-text, yet upon the whole the balance of argument seems to us still to incline in favor of Ellicott's interpretation as given above.

In Heb. 1:8, πρὸς δὲ τὸν υἱόν; ὁ θρόνος σου, ὁ Θεὸς, εἰς τὸν αἰῶνα is quoted as an address to Christ, and verse 10 which follows—"Thou, Lord, in the beginning hast laid the foundation of the earth"—by applying to Christ an Old Testament ascription to Jehovah, shows that ὁ Θεός, in verse 8, is used in the sense of absolute Godhead.

It is sometimes objected that the ascription of the name God to Christ proves nothing as to his absolute deity, since angels and even human judges are called gods, as representing God's authority and executing his will. But we reply that, while it is true that the name is sometimes so applied, it is always with adjuncts and in connections which leave no doubt of its figurative and secondary meaning. When, however, the name is applied to Christ, it is, on the contrary, with adjuncts and in connections which leave no doubt that it signifies absolute Godhead. See Ex. 4:16—"thou shalt be to him as God"; 7:1— "See, I have made thee as God to Pharaoh"; 22:28—"Thou shalt not revile God, [marg., the judges], nor curse a ruler of thy people"; Ps. 82:1—"God standeth in the congregation of God; he judgeth among the gods" [among the mighty]; 6—"I said, Ye are gods, And all of you sons of the Most High"; 7— "Nevertheless ye shall die like men, And fall like one of the princes." Cf. John 10:34-36—"If he called them gods, unto whom the word of God came" (who were God's commissioned and appointed representatives), how much more proper for him who is one with the Father to call himself God.

As in Ps. 82:7 those who had been called gods are represented as dying, so in Ps. 97:7—"Worship him, all ye gods"—they are bidden to fall down before Jehovah. Ann. Par. Bible: "Although the deities of the heathen have no positive existence, they are often described in Scripture as if they had, and are represented as bowing down before the majesty of Jehovah." This verse is quoted in Heb. 1:6—"let all the angels of God worship him"—i. e., Christ. Here Christ is identified with Jehovah. The quotation is made from the Septuagint, which has "angels" for "gods." "Its use here is in accordance with the spirit of the Hebrew word, which includes all that human error might regard as objects of worship." Those who are figuratively and rhetorically called "gods" are bidden to fall down in worship before him who is the true God, Jesus Christ. See Dick, Lectures on Theology, 1:314; Liddon, Our Lord's Divinity, 10.

In 1 John 5:20—ἐσμεν ἐν τῷ ἀληθινῷ, ἐν τῷ υἱῷ αὐτοῦ Ἰησοῦ Χριστῷ. οὗτος ἐστιν ὁ ἀληθινὸς Θεός—"it would be a flat repetition, after the Father had been twice called ὁ ἀληθινός, to say now again: 'this is ὁ ἀληθινὸς Θεός.' Our being in God has its basis in Christ his Son, and this also makes it more natural that οὗτος should be referred to υἱῷ. But ought not ὁ ἀληθενός then to be without the article (as in John 1:1—Θεός ἦν ὁ λόγος)? No, for it is John's purpose in 1 John 5:20 to say, not what Christ is, but who he is. In declaring what one is, the predicate must have no article; in declaring who one is, the predicate must have the article. St. John here says that this Son, on whom our being in the true God rests, is this true God himself" (see Ebrard, Com. in loco).

Other passages might be here adduced, as Col. 2:9—"in him dwelleth all the fulness of the Godhead bodily"; Phil 2:6—"existing in the form of God"; but we prefer to consider these under other heads as indirectly proving Christ's divinity. Still other passages once relied upon as direct statements of the doctrine must be given up for textual reasons. Such are Acts 20:28, where the correct reading is in all probability not ἐκκλησίαν τοῦ Θεοῦ, but ἐκκλησίαν τοῦ Κυρίου (so ACDE Tregelles and Tischendorf; B and א, however, have τοῦ Θεοῦ. The Rev. Vers. continues to read "church of God"; Amer. Revisers, however, read "church of the Lord"—see Ezra Abbot's investigation in Bib. Sac., 1876: 313-352); and 1 Tim. 3:16, where ὅς is unquestionably to be substituted for Θεός, though even here ἐφανερώθη intimates preëxistence.

Rev. George E. Ellis, D. D., before the Unitarian Club, Boston, November, 1882—"Fifty years of study, thought and reading given largely to the Bible and to the literature which peculiarly relates to it, have brought me to this conclusion, that the book—taken with the especial divine quality and character claimed for it, and so extensively assigned to it, as inspired and infallible as a whole, and in all its contents—is an Orthodox book. It yields what is called the Orthodox creed. The vast majority of its readers, following its letter, its obvious sense, its natural meaning, and yielding to the impression which some of its emphatic texts make upon them, find in it Orthodoxy. Only that kind of ingenious, special, discriminative, and in candor I must add, forced treatment, which it receives from us liberals can make the book teach anything but Orthodoxy. The evangelical sects, so called, are clearly right in maintaining that their view of Scripture and of its doctrines draws a deep and wide division of creed between them and ourselves. In that earnest controversy by pamphlet warfare between Drs. Channing and Ware on the one side, and Drs. Worcester and Woods and Professor Stuart on the other—a controversy which wrought up the people of our community sixty years ago more than did our recent political campaign—I am fully convinced that the liberal contestants were worsted. Scripture exegesis, logic and argument were clearly on the side of the Orthodox contestants. And this was so, mainly because the liberal party put themselves on the same plane with the Orthodox in their way of regarding and dealing with Scripture texts in their bearing upon the controversy. Liberalism cannot vanquish Orthodoxy, if it yields to the latter in its own way of regarding and treating the whole Bible. Martin Luther said that the Papists burned the Bible because it was not on their side. Now I am not about to attack the Bible because it is not on my side; but I am about to object as emphatically as I can against a character and quality assigned to the Bible, which it does not claim for itself, which cannot be certified for it: and the origin and growth and intensity of the fond and superstitious influences resulting in that view we can trace distinctly to agencies accounting for, but not warranting, the current belief. Orthodoxy cannot readjust its creeds till it readjusts its estimate of the Scriptures. The only relief which one who professes the Orthodox creed can find is either by forcing his ingenuity into the proof-texts or indulging his liberty outside of them."

With this confession of a noted Unitarian it is interesting to compare the opinion of the so-called Trinitarian, Dr. Lyman Abbott, who says that the New Testament nowhere calls Christ God, but everywhere calls him man, as in 1 Tim. 2:5—"for there is one God, one mediator also between God and men, himself man, Christ Jesus." On this passage Prof. L. L. Paine remarks in the New World, Dec. 1894—"That Paul ever confounded Christ with God himself, or regarded him as in any way the Supreme Divinity, is a position invalidated not only by direct statements, but also by the whole drift of his epistles."

(b) Old Testament descriptions of God are applied to him.

This application to Christ of titles and names exclusively appropriated to God is inexplicable, if Christ was not regarded as being himself God. The peculiar awe with which the term "Jehovah" was set apart by a nation of strenuous monotheists as the sacred and incommunicable name of the one self-existent and covenant-keeping God forbids the belief that the Scripture writers could have used it as the designation of a subordinate and created being.

Mat. 3:3—"Make ye ready the way of the Lord"—is a quotation from Is. 40:3—"Prepare ye ... the way of Jehovah." John 12:41—"These things said Isaiah, because he saw his glory; and he spake of him" [i. e., Christ]—refers to Is. 6:1—"In the year that King Uzziah died I saw the Lord sitting upon a throne." So in Eph. 4:7, 8—"measure of the gift of Christ ... led captivity captive"—is an application to Christ of what is said of Jehovah in Ps. 68:18. In 1 Pet. 3:15, moreover, we read, with all the great uncials, several of the Fathers, and all the best versions: "sanctify in your hearts Christ as Lord"; here the apostle borrows his language from Is. 8:13, where we read: "Jehovah of hosts, him shall ye sanctify." When we remember that, with the Jews, God's covenant-title was so sacred that for the Kethib (= "written") Jehovah there was always substituted the Keri (= "read"—imperative) Adonai, in order to avoid pronunciation of the great Name, it seems the more remarkable that the Greek equivalent of "Jehovah" should have been so constantly used of Christ. Cf. Rom. 10:9—"confess ... Jesus as Lord"; 1 Cor. 12:3—"no man can say, Jesus is Lord, but in the Holy Spirit." We must remember also the indignation of the Jews at Christ's assertion of his equality and oneness with the Father. Compare Goethe's, "Wer darf ihn nennen?" with Carlyle's, "the awful Unnameable of this Universe." The Jews, it has been said, have always vibrated between monotheism and moneytheism. Yet James, the strongest of Hebrews, in his Epistle uses the word 'Lord' freely and alternately of God the Father and of Christ the Son. This would have been impossible if James had not believed in the community of essence between the Son and the Father.

It is interesting to note that 1 Maccabees does not once use the word Θεός or κύριος, or any other direct designation of God unless it be οὐρανός (cf. "swear ... by the heaven"—Mat. 5:34). So the book of Esther contains no mention of the name of God, though the apocryphal additions to Esther, which are found only in Greek, contain the name of God in the first verse, and mention it in all eight times. See Bissell, Apocrypha, in Lange's Commentary; Liddon, Our Lord's Divinity, 93; Max Müller on Semitic Monotheism, in Chips from a German Workshop, 1:337.

(c) He possesses the attributes of God.

Among these are life, self-existence, immutability, truth, love, holiness, eternity, omnipresence, omniscience, omnipotence. All these attributes are ascribed to Christ in connections which show that the terms are used in no secondary sense, nor in any sense predicable of a creature.

Life: John 1:4—"In him was life"; 14:6—"I am ... the life." Self-existence: John 5:26—"have life in himself"; Heb. 7:16—"power of an endless life." Immutability: Heb. 13:8—"Jesus Christ is the same yesterday and to-day, yea and forever." Truth: John 14:6—"I am ... the truth"; Rev. 3:7—"he that is true." Love: 1 John 3:16—"Hereby know we love" (τὴν ἀγάπην = the personal Love, as the personal Truth) "because he laid down his life for us." Holiness: Luke 1:35—"that which is to be born shall be called holy, the Son of God"; John 6:69—"thou art the Holy One of God"; Heb. 7:26—"holy, guileless, undefiled, separated from sinners."

Eternity: John 1:1—"In the beginning was the Word." Godet says ἐν ἀρχῇ = not "in eternity," but "in the beginning of the creation"; the eternity of the Word being an inference from the ἦν—the Word was, when the world was created: cf. Gen. 1:1—"In the beginning God created." But Meyer says, ἐν ἀρχῇ here rises above the historical conception of "in the beginning" in Genesis (which includes the beginning of time itself) to the absolute conception of anteriority to time; the creation is something subsequent. He finds a parallel in Prov. 8:23—ἐν ἀρχῇ πρὸ τοῦ τὴν γῆν ποιῆσαι. The interpretation "in the beginning of the gospel" is entirely unexegetical; so Meyer. So John 17:5—"glory which I had with thee before the world was"; Eph. 1:4—"chose us in him before the foundation of the world." Dorner also says that ἐν ἀρχῇ in John 1:1 is not "the beginning of the world," but designates the point back of which it is impossible to go, i. e., eternity; the world is first spoken of in verse 3. John 8:58—"Before Abraham was born, I am"; cf. 1:15; Col. 1:17—"he is before all things"; Heb. 1:11—the heavens "shall perish; but thou continuest"; Rev. 21:6—"I am the Alpha and the Omega, the beginning and the end."

Omnipresence: Mat. 28:20—"I am with you always"; Eph. 1:23—"the fulness of him that filleth all in all." Omniscience: Mat. 9:4—"Jesus knowing their thoughts"; John 2:24, 25—"knew all men ... knew what was in man"; 16:30—"knowest all things"; Acts 1:24—"Thou, Lord, who knowest the hearts of all men"—a prayer offered before the day of Pentecost and showing the attitude of the disciples toward their Master; 1 Cor. 4:5—"until the Lord come, who will both bring to light the hidden things of darkness, and make manifest the counsels of the hearts"; Col. 2:3—"in whom are all the treasures of wisdom and knowledge hidden." Omnipotence: Mat. 27:18—"All authority hath been given unto me in heaven and on earth"; Rev. 1:8—"the Lord God, which is and which was and which is to come, the Almighty."

Beyschlag, N. T. Theology, 1:249-260, holds that Jesus' preëxistence is simply the concrete form given to an ideal conception. Jesus traces himself back, as everything else holy and divine was traced back in the conceptions of his time, to a heavenly original in which it preëxisted before its earthly appearance; e. g.: the tabernacle, in Heb. 8:5; Jerusalem, in Gal. 4:25 and Rev. 21:10; the kingdom of God in Mat. 13:24; much more the Messiah, in John 6:62—"ascending where he was before"; 8:58—"Before Abraham was born, I am"; 17:4, 5—"glory which I had with thee before the world was" 17:24—"thou lovedst me before the foundation of the world." This view that Jesus existed before creation only ideally in the divine mind, means simply that God foreknew him and his coming. The view is refuted by the multiplied intimations of a personal, in distinction from an ideal, preëxistence.

Lowrie, Doctrine of St. John, 115—"The words 'In the beginning' (John 1:1) suggest that the author is about to write a second book of Genesis, an account of a new creation." As creation presupposes a Creator, the preëxistence of the personal Word is assigned as the explanation of the being of the universe. The ἦν indicates absolute existence, which is a loftier idea than that of mere preëxistence, although it includes this. While John the Baptist and Abraham are said to have arisen, appeared, come into being, it is said that the Logos was, and that the Logos was God. This implies coëternity with the Father. But, if the view we are combating were correct, John the Baptist and Abraham preëxisted, equally with Christ. This is certainly not the meaning of Jesus in John 8:58— "Before Abraham was born, I am"; cf. Col. 1:17—"he is before all things"—"αὐτός emphasizes the personality, while ἔστιν declares that the preëxistence is absolute existence" (Lightfoot); John 1:15— "He that cometh after me is become before me: for he was before me" = not that Jesus was born earlier than John the Baptist, for he was born six months later, but that he existed earlier. He stands before John in rank, because he existed long before John in time; 6:62—"the Son of man ascending where he was before"; 16:28—"I came out from the Father, and am come into the world." So Is. 9:6, 7, calls Christ "Everlasting Father" = eternity is an attribute of the Messiah. T. W. Chambers, in Jour. Soc. Bib. Exegesis, 1881:169-171—"Christ is the Everlasting One, 'whose goings forth have been from of old, even from the days of eternity' (Micah 5:2). 'Of the increase of his government ... there shall be no end,' just because of his existence there has been no beginning."

(d) The works of God are ascribed to him.

We do not here speak of miracles, which may be wrought by communicated power, but of such works as the creation of the world, the upholding of all things, the final raising of the dead, and the judging of all men. Power to perform these works cannot be delegated, for they are characteristic of omnipotence.

Creation: John 1:3—"All things were made through him"; 1 Cor. 8:6—"one lord, Jesus Christ, through whom are all things"; Col. 1:16—"all things have been created through him, and unto him"; Heb, 1:10—"Thou, Lord, in the beginning didst lay the foundation of the earth, And the heavens are the works of thy hands"; 3:3, 4—"he that built all things is God" = Christ, the builder of the house of Israel, is the God who made all things; Rev. 3:14—"the beginning of the creation of God" (cf. Plato: "Mind is the ἀρχή of motion"). Upholding: Col. 1:17—"in him all things consist" (marg. "hold together"); Heb. 1:3—"upholding all things by the word of his power." Raising the dead and judging the world: John 5:27-29—"authority to execute judgment ... all that are in the tombs shall hear his voice, and shall come forth"; Mat. 25:31, 32—"sit on the throne of his glory; and before him shall be gathered all the nations." If our argument were addressed wholly to believers, we might also urge Christ's work in the world as Revealer of God and Redeemer from sin, as a proof of his deity. [On the works of Christ, see Liddon, Our Lord's Divinity, 153; per contra, see Examination of Liddon's Bampton Lectures, 72.]

Statements of Christ's creative and of his upholding activity are combined in John 1:3, 4—Πάντα δι' αὐτοῦ ἐγένετο, καὶ χωρὶς αὐτοῦ ἐγένετο οὐδὲ ἕν. ὃ γέγονεν ἐν αὐτῷ ζωὴ ἦν—"All things were made through him; and without him was not anything made. That which hath been made was life in him" (marg.). Westcott: "It would be difficult to find a more complete consent of ancient authorities in favor of any reading than that which supports this punctuation." Westcott therefore adopts it. The passage shows that the universe 1. exists within the bounds of Christ's being; 2. is not dead, but living; 3. derives its life from him; see Inge, Christian Mysticism, 46. Creation requires the divine presence, as well as the divine agency. God creates through Christ. All things were made, not ὑπὸ αὐτοῦ—"by him," but δι' αὐτοῦ—"through him." Christian believers "Behind creation's throbbing screen Catch movements of the great Unseen."

Van Oosterzee, Christian Dogmatics, iv, lvi—"That which many a philosopher dimly conjectured, namely, that God did not produce the world in an absolute, immediate manner, but in some way or other, mediately, here presents itself to us with the lustre of revelation, and exalts so much the more the claim of the Son of God to our deep and reverential homage." Would that such scientific men as Tyndall and Huxley might see Christ in nature, and, doing his will, might learn of the doctrine and be led to the Father! The humblest Christian who sees Christ's hand in the physical universe and in human history knows more of the secret of the universe than all the mere scientists put together.

Col 1:17—"In him all things consist," or "hold together," means nothing less than that Christ is the principle of cohesion in the universe, making it a cosmos instead of a chaos. Tyndall said that the attraction of the sun upon the earth was as inconceivable as if a horse should draw a cart without traces. Sir Isaac Newton: "Gravitation must be caused by an agent acting constantly according to certain laws." Lightfoot: "Gravitation is an expression of the mind of Christ." Evolution also is a method of his operation. The laws of nature are the habits of Christ, and nature itself is but his steady and constant will. He binds together man and nature in one organic whole, so that we can speak of a "universe." Without him there would be no intellectual bond, no uniformity of law, no unity of truth. He is the principle of induction, that enables us to argue from one thing to another. The medium of interaction between things is also the medium of intercommunication between minds. It is fitting that he who draws and holds together the physical and intellectual, should also draw and hold together the moral universe, drawing all men to himself (John 12:32) and so to God, and reconciling all things in heaven and earth (Col. 1:20). In Christ "the law appears, Drawn out in living characters," because he is the ground and source of all law, both in nature and in humanity. See A. H. Strong, Christ in Creation, 6-12.

(e) He receives honor and worship due only to God.

In addition to the address of Thomas, in John 20:28, which we have already cited among the proofs that Jesus is expressly called God, and in which divine honor is paid to him, we may refer to the prayer and worship offered by the apostolic and post-apostolic church.

John 5:23—"that all may honor the Son, even as they honor the Father"; 14:14—"If ye shall ask me [so אB and Tisch. 8th ed.] anything in my name, that will I do"; Acts 7:59—"Stephen, calling upon the Lord, and saying, Lord Jesus, receive my spirit" (cf. Luke 23:46—Jesus' words: "Father, into thy hands I commend my spirit"); Rom. 10:9—"confess with thy mouth Jesus as Lord"; 13—"whosoever shall call upon the name of the Lord shall be saved" (cf. Gen. 4:26—"Then began men to call upon the name of Jehovah"); 1 Cor. 11:24, 25—"this do in remembrance of me" = worship of Christ; Heb. 1:6—"let all the angels of God worship him"; Phil. 2:10, 11—"in the name of Jesus every knee should bow ... every tongue should confess that Jesus Christ is Lord"; Rev. 5:12-14—"Worthy is the Lamb that hath been slain to receive the power...."; 2 Pet. 3:18—"Lord and Savior Jesus Christ. To him be the glory"; 2 Tim. 4:18 and Heb. 13:21—"to whom be the glory for ever and ever"—these ascriptions of eternal glory to Christ imply his deity. See also 1 Pet. 3:15—"Sanctify in your hearts Christ as Lord," and Eph. 5:21—"subjecting yourselves one to another in the fear of Christ." Here is enjoined an attitude of mind towards Christ which would be idolatrous if Christ were not God. See Liddon, Our Lord's Divinity, 266, 366.

Foster, Christian Life and Theology, 154—"In the eucharistic liturgy of the 'Teaching' we read: 'Hosanna to the God of David'; Ignatius styles him repeatedly God 'begotten and unbegotten, come in the flesh'; speaking once of 'the blood of God', in evident allusion to Acts 20:28; the epistle to Diognetus takes up the Pauline words and calls him the 'architect and world-builder by whom [God] created the heavens', and names him God (chap. vii); Hermas speaks of him as 'the holy preëxistent Spirit, that created every creature', which style of expression is followed by Justin, who calls him God, as also all the later great writers. In the second epistle of Clement (130-160, Harnack), we read: 'Brethren, it is fitting that you should think of Jesus Christ as of God—as the Judge of the living and the dead.' And Ignatius describes him as 'begotten and unbegotten, passible and impassible, ... who was before the eternities with the Father.' "

These testimonies only give evidence that the Church Fathers saw in Scripture divine honor ascribed to Christ. They were but the precursors of a host of later interpreters. In a lull of the awful massacre of Armenian Christians at Sassouan, one of the Kurdish savages was heard to ask: "Who was that 'Lord Jesus' that they were calling to?" In their death agonies, the Christians, like Stephen of old, called upon the name of the Lord. Robert Browning quoted, in a letter to a lady in her last illness, the words of Charles Lamb, when "in a gay fancy with some friends as to how he and they would feel if the greatest of the dead were to appear suddenly in flesh and blood once more—on the first suggestion, 'And if Christ entered this room?' changed his tone at once and stuttered out as his manner was when moved: 'You see—if Shakspere entered, we should all rise; if He appeared, we must kneel.' " On prayer to Jesus, see Liddon, Bampton Lectures, note F; Bernard, in Hastings' Bib. Dict., 4:44; Zahn, Skizzen aus dem Leben der alten Kirche, 9, 288.

(f) His name is associated with that of God upon a footing of equality.

We do not here allude to 1 John 5:7 (the three heavenly witnesses), for the latter part of this verse is unquestionably spurious; but to the formula of baptism, to the apostolic benedictions, and to those passages in which eternal life is said to be dependent equally upon Christ and upon God, or in which spiritual gifts are attributed to Christ equally with the Father.

The formula of baptism: Mat. 28:19—"baptising them into the name of the father and of the Son and of the Holy Spirit"; cf. Acts 2:38—"be baptised every one of you in the name of Jesus Christ"; Rom. 6:3—"baptized into Christ Jesus." "In the common baptismal formula the Son and the Spirit are coördinated with the Father, and εἰς ὄνομα has religious significance." It would be both absurd and profane to speak of baptizing into the name of the Father and of Moses.

The apostolic benedictions: 1 Cor. 1:3—"Grace to you and peace from God our Father and the Lord Jesus Christ"; 2 Cor. 13:14—"The grace of the Lord Jesus Christ, and the love of God, and the communion of the Holy Spirit, be with you all." "In the benedictions grace is something divine, and Christ has power to impart it. But why do we find 'God,' instead of simply 'the Father,' as in the baptismal formula? Because it is only the Father who does not become man or have a historical existence. Elsewhere he is specially called 'God the Father,' to distinguish him from God the Son and God the Holy Spirit (Gal. 1:3; Eph. 3:14; 6:23)."

Other passages: John 5:23—"that all may honor the Son, even as they honor the Father"; John 14:1—"believe in God, believe also in me"—double imperative (so Westcott, Bible Com., in loco); 17:3—"this is life eternal, that they should know thee the only true God, and him whom thou didst send, even Jesus Christ"; Mat. 11:27—"no one knoweth the Son, save the Father; neither doth any know the Father, save the Son, and he to whomsoever the Son willeth to reveal him"; 1 Cor. 12:4-6—"the same Spirit ... the same Lord [Christ] ... the same God" [the Father] bestow spiritual gifts, e. g., faith: Rom. 10:17—"belief cometh of hearing, and hearing by the word of Christ"; peace: Col. 3:15—"let the peace of Christ rule in your hearts." 2 Thess. 2:16, 17—"now our lord Jesus Christ himself, and God our Father ... comfort your hearts"—two names with a verb in the singular intimate the oneness of the Father and the Son (Lillie). Eph. 5:5—"kingdom of Christ and God"; Col. 3:1—"Christ ... seated on the right hand of God" = participation in the sovereignty of the universe,—the Eastern divan held not only the monarch but his son; Rev. 20:6—"priests of God and of Christ"; 22:3—"the throne of God and of the Lamb"; 16—"the root and the offspring of David" = both the Lord of David and his son. Hackett: "As the dying Savior said to the Father, 'Into thy hands I commend my spirit' (Luke 23:46), so the dying Stephen said to the Savior, 'receive my spirit' (Acts 7:59)."

(g) Equality with God is expressly claimed.

Here we may refer to Jesus' testimony to himself, already treated of among the proofs of the supernatural character of the Scripture teaching (see pages 189, 190). Equality with God is not only claimed for himself by Jesus, but it is claimed for him by his apostles.

John 5:18—"called God his own Father, making himself equal with God"; Phil. 2:6—"who, existing in the form of God, counted not the being on an equality with God a thing to be grasped"—counted not his equality with God a thing to be forcibly retained. Christ made and left upon his contemporaries the impression that he claimed to be God. The New Testament has left, upon the great mass of those who have read it, the impression that Jesus Christ claims to be God. If he is not God, he is a deceiver or is self-deceived, and, in either case, *Christus, si non Deus, non bonus.* See Nicoll, Life of Jesus Christ, 187.

(h) Further proof of Christ's deity may be found in the application to him of the phrases: "Son of God," "Image of God"; in the declarations of his oneness with God; in the attribution to him of the fulness of the Godhead.

Mat. 26:63, 64—"I adjure thee by the living God, that thou tell us whether thou art the Christ, the Son of God. Jesus saith unto him, Thou hast said"—it is for this testimony that Christ dies. Col. 1:15—"the image of the invisible God"; Heb. 1:3—"the effulgence of his [the Father's] glory, and the very image of his substance"; John 10:30—"I and the Father are one"; 14:9—"he that hath seen me hath seen the Father"; 17:11, 22—"that they may be one, even as we are"—ἕ, not εἱς; unum, not unus; one substance, not one person. "Unum is antidote to the Arian, sumus to the Sabellian heresy." Col. 2:9—"in him dwelleth all the fulness of the Godhead bodily"; cf. 1:19—"for it was the pleasure of the Father that in him should all the fulness dwell;" or (marg.) "for the whole fulness of God was pleased to dwell in him." John 16:15—"all things whatsoever the Father hath are mine"; 17:10—"all things that are mine are thine, and thine are mine."

Meyer on John 10:30—"I and the Father are one"—"Here the Arian understanding of a mere ethical harmony as taught in the words 'are one' is unsatisfactory, because irrelevant to the exercise of power. Oneness of essence, though not contained in the words themselves, is, by the necessities of the argument, presupposed in them." Dalman, The Words of Jesus: "Nowhere do we find that Jesus called himself the Son of God in such a sense as to suggest a merely religious and ethical relation to God—a relation which others also possessed and which they were capable of attaining or were destined to acquire." We may add that while in the lower sense there are many "sons of God," there is but one "only begotten Son."

(i) These proofs of Christ's deity from the New Testament are corroborated by Christian experience.

Christian experience recognizes Christ as an absolutely perfect Savior, perfectly revealing the Godhead and worthy of unlimited worship and adoration; that is, it practically recognizes him as Deity. But Christian experience also recognizes that through Christ it has introduction and reconciliation to God as one distinct from Jesus Christ, as one who was alienated from the soul by its sin, but who is now reconciled through Jesus's death. In other words, while recognizing Jesus as God, we are also compelled to recognize a distinction between the Father and the Son through whom we come to the Father.

Although this experience cannot be regarded as an independent witness to Jesus' claims, since it only tests the truth already made known in the Bible, still the irresistible impulse of every person whom Christ has saved to lift his Redeemer to the highest place, and bow before him in the lowliest worship, is strong evidence that only that interpretation of Scripture can be true which recognizes Christ's absolute Godhead. It is the church's consciousness of her Lord's divinity, indeed, and not mere speculation upon the relations of Father, Son, and Holy Ghost, that has compelled the formulation of the Scripture doctrine of the Trinity.

In the letter of Pliny to Trajan, it is said of the early Christians "quod essent soliti carmen Christo quasi Deo dicere invicem." The prayers and hymns of the church show what the church has believed Scripture to teach. Dwight Moody is said to have received his first conviction of the truth of the gospel from hearing the concluding words of a prayer, "For Christ's sake, Amen," when awakened from physical slumber in Dr. Kirk's church, Boston. These words, wherever uttered, imply man's dependence and Christ's deity. See New Englander, 1878:432. In Eph. 4:32, the Revised Version substitutes "in Christ" for "for Christ's sake." The exact phrase "for Christ's sake" is not found in the N. T. in connection with prayer, although the O. T. phrase "for my name's sake" (Ps. 25:11) passes into the N. T. phrase "in the name of Jesus" (Phil. 2:10); cf. Ps. 72:15—"men shall pray for him continually" = the words of the hymn: "For him shall endless prayer be made, And endless blessings crown his head." All this is proof that the idea of prayer for Christ's sake is in Scripture, though the phrase is absent.

A caricature scratched on the wall of the Palatine palace in Rome, and dating back to the third century, represents a human figure with an ass's head, hanging upon a cross, while a man stands before it in the attitude of worship. Under the effigy is this ill-spelled inscription: "Alexamenos adores his God."

This appeal to the testimony of Christian consciousness was first made by Schleiermacher. William E. Gladstone: "All I write, and all I think, and all I hope, is based upon the divinity of our Lord, the one central hope of our poor, wayward race." E. G. Robinson: "When you preach salvation by faith in Christ, you preach the Trinity." W. G. T. Shedd: "The construction of the doctrine of the Trinity started, not from the consideration of the three persons, but from belief in the deity of one of them." On the worship of Christ in the authorized services of the Anglican church, see Stanley, Church and State, 333-335; Liddon, Divinity of our Lord, 514.

In contemplating passages apparently inconsistent with those now cited, in that they impute to Christ weakness and ignorance, limitation and subjection, we are to remember, first, that our Lord was truly man, as well as truly God, and that this ignorance and weakness may be predicated of him as the God-man in whom deity and humanity are united; secondly, that the divine nature itself was in some way limited and humbled during our Savior's earthly life, and that these passages may describe him as he was in his estate of humiliation, rather than in his original and present glory; and, thirdly, that there is an order of office and operation which is consistent with essential oneness and equality, but which permits the Father to be spoken of as first and the Son as second. These statements will be further elucidated in the treatment of the present doctrine and in subsequent examination of the doctrine of the Person of Christ.

There are certain things of which Christ was ignorant: Mark 13:32—"of that day or that hour knoweth no one, not even the angels in heaven, neither the Son, but the Father." He was subject to physical fatigue: John 4:6—"Jesus therefore, being wearied with his journey, sat thus by the well." There was a limitation connected with Christ's taking of human flesh: Phil. 2:7—"emptied himself, taking the form of a servant, being made in the likeness of men"; John 14:28—"the Father is greater than I." There is a subjection, as respects order of office and operation, which is yet consistent with equality of essence and oneness with God; 1 Cor. 15:28—"then shall the Son also himself be subjected to him that did subject all things unto him, that God may be all in all." This must be interpreted consistently with John 17:5—"glorify thou me with thine own self with the glory which I had with thee before the world was," and with Phil. 2:6, where this glory is described as being "the form of God" and "equality with God."

Even in his humiliation, Christ was the Essential Truth, and ignorance in him never involved error or false teaching. Ignorance on his part might make his teaching at times incomplete,—it never in the smallest particular made his teaching false. Yet here we must distinguish between what he intended to teach and what was merely incidental to his teaching. When he said: Moses "wrote of me" (John 5:46) and "David in the Spirit called him Lord" (Mat. 22:43), if his purpose was to teach the authorship of the Pentateuch and of the 110th Psalm, we should regard his words as absolutely authoritative. But it is possible that he intended only to locate the passages referred to, and if so, his words cannot be used to exclude critical conclusions as to their authorship. Adamson, The Mind in Christ, 136—"If he spoke of Moses or David, it was only to identify the passage. The authority of the earlier dispensation did not rest upon its record being due to Moses, nor did the appropriateness of the Psalm lie in its being uttered by David. There is no evidence that the question of authorship ever came before him." Adamson rather more precariously suggests that "there may have been a lapse of memory in Jesus' mention of 'Zachariah, son of Barachiah' (Mat. 23:35), since this was a matter of no spiritual import."

For assertions of Jesus' knowledge, see John 2:24, 25—"he knew all men ... he needed not that any one should bear witness concerning man; for he himself knew what was in man"; 6:64—"Jesus knew from the beginning who they were that believed not, and who it was that should betray him"; 12:33—"this he said, signifying by what manner of death he should die"; 21:19—"Now this he spake, signifying by what manner of death he [Peter] should glorify God"; 13:1—"knowing that his hour was come that he should depart"; Mat. 25:31—"when the Son of man shall come in his glory, and all the angels with him, then shall he sit on the throne of his glory" = he knew that he was to act as final judge of the human race. Other instances are mentioned by Adamson, The Mind in Christ, 24-49: 1. Jesus' knowledge of Peter (John 1:42); 2. his finding Philip (1:43); 3. his recognition of Nathanael (1:47-50); 4. of the woman of Samaria (4:17-19, 39); 5. miraculous draughts of fishes (Luke 5:6-9; John 21:6); 6. death of Lazarus (John 11:14); 7. the ass's colt (Mat. 21:2); 8. of the upper room (Mark 14:15); 9. of Peter's denial (Mat. 26:34); 10. of the manner of his own death (John 12:33; 18:32); 11. of the manner of Peter's death (John 21:19); 12. of the fall of Jerusalem (Mat. 24:2).

On the other hand there are assertions and implications of Jesus' ignorance: he did not know the day of the end (Mark 13:32), though even here he intimates his superiority to angels; 5:30-34—"Who touched my garments?" though even here power had gone forth from him to heal; John 11:34—"Where have ye laid him?" though here he is about to raise Lazarus from the dead; Mark 11:13—"seeing a fig tree afar off having leaves, he came, if haply he might find anything thereon" = he did not know that it had no fruit, yet he had power to curse it. With these evidences of the limitations of Jesus' knowledge, we must assent to the judgment of Bacon, Genesis of Genesis, 33—"We must decline to stake the authority of Jesus on a question of literary criticism"; and of Gore, Incarnation, 195—"That the use by our Lord of such a phrase as 'Moses wrote of me' binds us to the Mosaic authorship of the Pentateuch as a whole, I do not think we need to yield." See our section on The Person of Christ; also Rush Rhees, Life of Jesus, 243, 244. Per contra, see Swayne, Our Lord's Knowledge as Man; and Crooker, The New Bible, who very unwisely claims that belief in a Kenosis involves the surrender of Christ's authority and atonement.

It is inconceivable that any mere creature should say, "God is greater than I am," or should be spoken of as ultimately and in a mysterious way becoming "subject to God." In his state of humiliation Christ was subject to the Spirit (Acts 1:2—"after that he had given commandment through the Holy Spirit"; 10:38—"God anointed him with the Holy Spirit ... for God was with him"; Heb.9:14—"through the eternal Spirit offered himself without blemish unto God"), but in his state of exaltation Christ is Lord of the Spirit (κυρίου πνεύματος—2 Cor. 3:18—Meyer), giving the Spirit and working through the Spirit. Heb. 2:7, marg.—"Thou madest him for a little while lower than the angels." On the whole subject, see Shedd, Hist. Doctrine, 262, 351; Thomasius, Christi Person und Werk, 1:61-64; Liddon, Our Lord's Divinity, 127, 207, 458; per contra, see Examination of Liddon, 252, 294; Professors of Andover Seminary, Divinity of Christ.

C. The Holy Spirit is recognized as God.

(a) He is spoken of as God; (b) the attributes of God are ascribed to him, such as life, truth, love, holiness, eternity, omnipresence, omniscience, omnipotence; (c) he does the works of God, such as creation, regeneration, resurrection; (d) he receives honor due only to God; (e) he is associated with God on a footing of equality, both in the formula of baptism and in the apostolic benedictions.

(a) Spoken of as God. Acts 5:3, 4—"lie to the Holy Spirit ... not lied unto men, but unto God"; 1 Cor. 3:16—"ye are a temple of God ... the Spirit of God dwelleth in you"; 6:19—"your body is a temple of the Holy Spirit"; 12:4-6 "same Spirit ... same Lord ... same God, who worketh all things in all"—"The divine Trinity is here indicated in an ascending climax, in such a way that we pass from the Spirit who bestows the gifts to the Lord [Christ] who is served by means of them, and finally to God, who as the absolute first cause and possessor of all Christian powers works the entire sum of all charismatic gifts in all who are gifted" (Meyer in loco).

(b) Attributes of God. Life: Rom. 8:2—"Spirit of life." Truth: John 16:13 "Spirit of truth." Love: Rom. 15:30—"love of the Spirit." Holiness: Eph. 4:30—"the Holy Spirit of God." Eternity: Heb. 9:14—"the eternal Spirit." Omnipresence: Ps. 139:7—"Whither shall I go from thy Spirit?" Omniscience: 1 Cor. 12:11—"all these [including gifts of healings and miracles] worketh the one and the same Spirit, dividing to each one severally even as he will."

(c) Works of God. Creation: Gen. 1:2, marg.—"Spirit of God was brooding upon the face of the waters." Casting out of demons: Mat. 12:28—"But if I by the Spirit of God cast out demons." Conviction of sin: John 16:8—"convict the world in respect of sin." Regeneration: John 3:8—"born of the Spirit"; Tit. 3:5—"renewing of the Holy Spirit." Resurrection: Rom. 8:11—"give life also to your mortal bodies through his Spirit"; 1 Cor. 15:45—"The last Adam became a life-giving spirit."

(d) Honor due to God. 1 Cor. 3:16—"ye are a temple of God ... the Spirit of God dwelleth in you"—he who inhabits the temple is the object of worship there. See also the next item.

(e) Associated with God. Formula of baptism: Mat. 28:19—"baptizing them into the name of the Father and of the Son and of the Holy Spirit." If the baptismal formula is worship, then we have here worship paid to the Spirit. Apostolic benedictions: 2 Cor. 13:14—"The grace of the Lord Jesus Christ and the love of God, and the communion of the Holy Spirit be with you all." If the apostolic benedictions are prayers, then we have here a prayer to the Spirit. 1 Pet. 1:2—"foreknowledge of God the Father ... sanctification of the Spirit ... sprinkling of the blood of Jesus Christ."

On Heb. 9:14, Kendrick, Com. in loco, interprets: "Offers himself by virtue of an eternal spirit which dwells within him and imparts to his sacrifice a spiritual and an eternal efficacy. The 'spirit' here spoken of was not, then, the 'Holy Spirit'; it was not his purely divine nature; it was that blending of his divine nature with his human personality which forms the mystery of his being, that 'spirit of holiness' by virtue of which he was declared 'the Son of God with power,' on account of his resurrection from the dead." Hovey adds a note to Kendrick's Commentary, *in loco*, as follows: "This adjective 'eternal' naturally suggests that the word 'Spirit' refers to the higher and divine nature of Christ. His truly human nature, on its spiritual side, was indeed eternal as to the future, but so also is the spirit of every man. The unique and superlative value of Christ's self-sacrifice seems to have been due to the impulse of the divine side of his nature." The phrase "eternal spirit" would then mean his divinity. To both these interpretations we prefer that which makes the passage refer to the Holy Spirit, and we cite in support of this view Acts 1:2—"he had given commandment through the Holy Spirit unto the apostles"; 10:38—"God anointed him with the Holy Spirit." On 1 Cor. 2:10, Mason, Faith of the Gospel, 63, remarks: "The Spirit of God finds nothing even in God which baffles his scrutiny. His 'search' is not a seeking for knowledge yet beyond him.... Nothing but God could search the depths of God."

As spirit is nothing less than the inmost principle of life, and the spirit of man is man himself, so the spirit of God must be God (see 1 Cor. 2:11—Meyer). Christian experience, moreover, expressed as it is in the prayers and hymns of the church, furnishes an argument for the deity of the Holy Spirit similar to that for the deity of Jesus Christ. When our eyes are opened to see Christ as a Savior, we are compelled to recognize the work in us of a divine Spirit who has taken of the things of Christ and has shown them to us; and this divine Spirit we necessarily distinguish both from the Father and from the Son. Christian experience, however, is not an original and independent witness to the deity of the Holy Spirit: it simply shows what the church has held to be the natural and unforced interpretation of the Scriptures, and so confirms the Scripture argument already adduced.

The Holy Spirit is God himself personally present in the believer. E. G. Robinson: "If 'Spirit of God' no more implies deity than does 'angel of God,' why is not the Holy Spirit called simply the angel or messenger, of God?" Walker, The Spirit and the Incarnation, 337—"The Holy Spirit is God in his innermost being or essence, the principle of life of both the Father and the Son; that in which God, both as Father and Son, does everything, and in which he comes to us and is in us increasingly through his manifestations. Through the working and indwelling of this Holy Spirit, God in his person of Son was fully incarnate in Christ." Gould, Am. Com. on 1 Cor. 2:11—"For who among men knoweth the things of a man, save the spirit of the man, which is in him? even so the things of God none knoweth, save the Spirit of God"—"The analogy must not be pushed too far, as if the Spirit of God and God were coëxtensive terms, as the corresponding terms are, substantially, in man. The point of the analogy is evidently self-knowledge, and in both cases the contrast is between the spirit within and anything outside." Andrew Murray, Spirit of Christ, 140—"We must not expect always to feel the power of the Spirit when it works. Scripture links power and weakness in a wonderful way, not as succeeding each other but as existing together. 'I was with you in weakness ... my preaching was in power' (1 Cor. 2:3); 'when I am weak then am I strong' (2 Cor. 12:10). The power is the power of God given to faith, and faith grows strong in the dark.... He who would command nature must first and most absolutely obey her.... We want to get possession of the Power, and use it. God wants the Power to get possession of us, and use us."

This proof of the deity of the Holy Spirit is not invalidated by the limitations of his work under the Old Testament dispensation. John 7:39—"for the Holy Spirit was not yet"—means simply that the Holy Spirit could not fulfill his peculiar office as Revealer of Christ until the atoning work of Christ should be accomplished.

John 7:39 is to be interpreted in the light of other Scriptures which assert the agency of the Holy Spirit under the old dispensation (Ps. 51:11—"take not thy holy Spirit from me") and which describe his peculiar office under the new dispensation (John 16:14, 15—"he shall take of mine, and shall declare it unto you"). Limitation in the manner of the Spirit's work in the O. T. involved a limitation in the extent and power of it also. Pentecost was the flowing forth of a tide of spiritual influence which had hitherto been dammed up. Henceforth the Holy Spirit was the Spirit of Jesus Christ, taking of the things of Christ and showing them, applying his finished work to human hearts, and rendering the hitherto localized Savior omnipresent with his scattered followers to the end of time.

Under the conditions of his humiliation, Christ was a servant. All authority in heaven and earth was given him only after his resurrection. Hence he could not send the Holy Spirit until he ascended. The mother can show off her son only when he is fully grown. The Holy Spirit could reveal Christ only when there was a complete Christ to reveal. The Holy Spirit could fully sanctify, only after the example and motive of holiness were furnished in Christ's life and death. Archer Butler: "The divine Artist could not fitly descend to make the copy, before the original had been provided."

And yet the Holy Spirit is "the eternal Spirit" (Heb. 9:14), and he not only existed, but also wrought, in Old Testament times. 2 Pet. 1:21—"men spake from God, being moved by the Holy Spirit"—seems to fix the meaning of the phrase "the Holy Spirit," where it appears in the O. T. Before

Christ "the Holy Spirit was not yet" (John 7:39), just as before Edison electricity was not yet. There was just as much electricity in the world before Edison as there is now. Edison has only taught us its existence and how to use it. Still we can say that, before Edison, electricity, as a means of lighting, warming and transporting people, had no existence. So until Pentecost, the Holy Spirit, as the revealer of Christ, "was not yet." Augustine calls Pentecost the dies natalis, or birthday, of the Holy Spirit; and for the same reason that we call the day when Mary brought forth her firstborn son the birthday of Jesus Christ, though before Abraham was born, Christ was. The Holy Spirit had been engaged in the creation, and had inspired the prophets, but officially, as Mediator between men and Christ, "the Holy Spirit was not yet." He could not show the things of Christ until the things of Christ were ready to be shown. See Gordon, Ministry of the Spirit, 19-25; Prof. J. S. Gubelmann, Person and Work of the Holy Spirit in O. T. Times. For proofs of the deity of the Holy Spirit, see Walker, Doctrine of the Holy Spirit; Hare, Mission of the Comforter; Parker, The Paraclete; Cardinal Manning, Temporal Mission of the Holy Ghost; Dick, Lectures on Theology, 1:341-350. Further references will be given in connection with the proof of the Holy Spirit's personality.

2. Intimations of the Old Testament

The passages which seem to show that even in the Old Testament there are three who are implicitly recognized as God may be classed under four heads:

A. Passages which seem to teach plurality of some sort in the Godhead.

(a) The plural noun סיהלא is employed, and that with a plural verb—a use remarkable, when we consider that the singular לא was also in existence; (b) God uses plural pronouns in speaking of himself; (c) Jehovah distinguishes himself from Jehovah; (d) a Son is ascribed to Jehovah; (e) the Spirit of God is distinguished from God; (f) there are a threefold ascription and a threefold benediction.

(a) Gen. 20:13—"God caused [plural] me to wander from my father's house"; 35:7—"built there an altar, and called the place El-Beth-el; because there God was revealed [plural] unto him." (b) Gen. 1:26—"Let us make man in our image, after our likeness"; 3:22—"Behold, the man is become as one of us"; 11:7—"Come, let us go down, and there confound their language"; Is. 6:8—"Whom shall I send, and who will go for us?" (c) Gen. 19:24—"Then Jehovah rained upon Sodom and upon Gomorrah brimstone and fire from Jehovah out of heaven"; Hos. 1:7—"I will have mercy upon the house of Judah, and will save them by Jehovah, their God"; cf. 2 Tim. 1:18—"The Lord grant unto him to find mercy of the Lord in that day"—though Ellicott here decides adversely to the Trinitarian reference. (d) Ps. 2:7—"Thou art my son; this day have I begotten thee"; Prov. 30:4—"Who hath established all the ends of the earth? What is his name, and what is his son's name, if thou knowest?" (e) Gen. 1:1 and 2, marg.—"God created ... the Spirit of God was brooding"; Ps. 33:6—"By the word of Jehovah were the heavens made, And all the host of them by the breath [spirit] of his mouth"; Is. 48:16—"the Lord Jehovah hath sent me, and his Spirit"; 63:7, 10—"loving kindnesses of Jehovah ... grieved his holy Spirit." (f) Is. 6:3—the trisagion: "Holy, holy, holy"; Num. 6:24-26—"Jehovah bless thee, and keep thee: Jehovah make his face to shine upon thee, and be gracious unto thee: Jehovah lift up his countenance upon thee, and give thee peace."

It has been suggested that as Baal was worshiped in different places and under different names, as Baal-Berith, Baal-hanan, Baal-peor, Baal-zeebub, and his priests could call upon any one of these as possessing certain personified attributes of Baal, while yet the whole was called by the plural term "Baalim," and Elijah could say: "Call ye upon your Gods," so "Elohim" may be the collective designation of the God who was worshiped in different localities; see Robertson Smith, Old Testament in the Jewish Church, 229. But this ignores the fact that Baal is always addressed in the singular, never in the plural, while the plural "Elohim" is the term commonly used in addresses to God. This seems to show that "Baalim" is a collective term, while "Elohim" is not. So when Ewald, Lehre von Gott, 2:333, distinguishes five names of God, corresponding to five great periods of the history of Israel, viz., the "Almighty" of the Patriarchs, the "Jehovah" of the Covenant, the "God of Hosts" of the Monarchy, the "Holy One" of the Deuteronomist and the later prophetic age, and the "Our Lord" of Judaism, he ignores the fact that these designations are none of them confined to the times to which they are attributed, though they may have been predominantly used in those times.

The fact that סיהלא is sometimes used in a narrower sense, as applicable to the Son (Ps. 45:6; cf. Heb. 1:8), need not prevent us from believing that the term was originally chosen as containing an allusion to a certain plurality in the divine nature. Nor is it sufficient to call this plural a simple pluralis majestaticus; since it is easier to derive this common figure from divine usage than to derive the divine usage from this common figure—especially when we consider the constant tendency of Israel to polytheism.

Ps. 45:6; cf. Heb. 1:8—"of the Son he saith, Thy throne, O God, is for ever and ever." Here it is God who calls Christ "God" or "Elohim." The term Elohim has here acquired the significance of a singular. It was once thought that the royal style of speech was a custom of a later date than the time of Moses. Pharaoh does not use it. In Gen. 41:41-44, he says: "I have set thee over all the land of Egypt ...

I am Pharaoh." But later investigations seem to prove that the plural for God was used by the Canaanites before the Hebrew occupation. The one Pharaoh is called "my gods" or "my god," indifferently. The word "master" is usually found in the plural in the O. T. (cf. Gen. 24:9, 51; 39:19; 40:1). The plural gives utterance to the sense of awe. It signifies magnitude or completeness. (See The Bible Student, Aug. 1900:67.)

This ancient Hebrew application of the plural to God is often explained as a mere plural of dignity, = one who combines in himself many reasons for adoration (מיהלא from הלא to fear, to adore). Oehler, O. T. Theology, 1:128-130, calls it a "quantitative plural," signifying unlimited greatness. The Hebrews had many plural forms, where we should use the singular, as "heavens" instead of "heaven," "waters" instead of "water." We too speak of "news," "wages," and say "you" instead of "thou"; see F. W. Robertson, on Genesis, 12. But the Church Fathers, such as Barnabas, Justin Martyr, Irenæus, Theophilus, Epiphanius, and Theodoret, saw in this plural an allusion to the Trinity, and we are inclined to follow them. When finite things were pluralized to express man's reverence, it would be far more natural to pluralize the name of God. And God's purpose in securing this pluralization may have been more far-reaching and intelligent than man's. The Holy Spirit who presided over the development of revelation may well have directed the use of the plural in general, and even the adoption of the plural name Elohim in particular, with a view to the future unfolding of truth with regard to the Trinity.

We therefore dissent from the view of Hill, Genetic Philosophy, 323, 330—"The Hebrew religion, even much later than the time of Moses, as it existed in the popular mind, was, according to the prophetic writings, far removed from a real monotheism, and consisted in the wavering acceptance of the preëminence of a tribal God, with a strong inclination towards a general polytheism. It is impossible therefore to suppose that anything approaching the philosophical monotheism of modern theology could have been elaborated or even entertained by primitive man.... 'Thou shalt have no other gods before me' (Ex. 20:3), the first precept of Hebrew monotheism, was not understood at first as a denial of the hereditary polytheistic faith, but merely as an exclusive claim to worship and obedience." E. G. Robinson says, in a similar strain, that "we can explain the idolatrous tendencies of the Jews only on the supposition that they had lurking notions that their God was a merely national god. Moses seems to have understood the doctrine of the divine unity, but the Jews did not."

To the views of both Hill and Robinson we reply that the primitive intuition of God is not that of many, but that of One. Paul tells us that polytheism is a later and retrogressive stage of development, due to man's sin (Rom. 1:19-25). We prefer the statement of McLaren: "The plural Elohim is not a survival from a polytheistic stage, but expresses the divine nature in the manifoldness of its fulnesses and perfections, rather than in the abstract unity of its being"—and, we may add, expresses the divine nature in its essential fulness, as a complex of personalities. See Conant, Gesenius' Hebrew Grammar, 108; Green, Hebrew Grammar, 306; Girdlestone, O. T. Synonyms, 38, 53; Alexander on Psalm 11:7; 29:1; 58:11.

B. Passages relating to the Angel of Jehovah.

(a) The angel of Jehovah identifies himself with Jehovah; (b) he is identified with Jehovah by others; (c) he accepts worship due only to God. Though the phrase "angel of Jehovah" is sometimes used in the later Scriptures to denote a merely human messenger or created angel, it seems in the Old Testament, with hardly more than a single exception, to designate the pre-incarnate Logos, whose manifestations in angelic or human form foreshadowed his final coming in the flesh.

(a) Gen. 22:11, 16—"the angel of Jehovah called unto him [Abraham, when about to sacrifice Isaac] ... By myself have I sworn, saith Jehovah"; 31:11, 13—"the angel of God said unto me [Jacob] ... I am the God of Beth-el." (b) Gen. 16:9, 13—"angel of Jehovah said unto her ... and she called the name of Jehovah that spake unto her, Thou art a God that seeth"; 48:15, 16—"the God who hath fed me ... the angel who hath redeemed me." (c) Ex. 3:2, 4, 5—"the angel of Jehovah appeared unto him ... God called unto him out of the midst of the bush ... put off thy shoes from off thy feet"; Judges 13:20-22— "angel of Jehovah ascended.... Manoah and his wife ... fell on their faces ... Manoah said ... We shall surely die, because we have seen God."

The "angel of the Lord" appears to be a human messenger in Haggai 1:13—"Haggai, Jehovah's messenger"; a created angel in Mat. 1:20—"an angel of the Lord [called Gabriel] appeared unto" Joseph; in Acts 3:26—"an angel of the Lord spake unto Philip"; and in 12:7—"an angel of the Lord stood by him" (Peter). But commonly, in the O.T., the "angel of Jehovah" is a theophany, a self-manifestation of God. The only distinction is that between Jehovah in himself and Jehovah in manifestation. The appearances of "the angel of Jehovah" seem to be preliminary manifestations of the divine Logos, as in Gen. 18:2, 13—"three men stood over against him [Abraham] ... And Jehovah said unto Abraham"; Dan. 3:25, 28—"the aspect of the fourth is like a son of the gods.... Blessed be the God ... who hath sent his angel." The N.T. "angel of the Lord" does not permit, the O.T. "angel of the Lord" requires, worship (Rev. 22:8, 9—"See thou do it not"; cf. Ex. 3:5—"put off thy shoes"). As supporting this interpretation, see Hengstenberg, Christology, 1:107-123; J. Pye Smith, Scripture Testimony to the Messiah. As opposing it, see Hofmann, Schriftbeweis, 1:329, 378; Kurtz, History of Old Covenant,

1:181. On the whole subject, see Bib. Sac., 1879:593-615.

C. Descriptions of the divine Wisdom and Word.

(a) Wisdom is represented as distinct from God, and as eternally existing with God; (b) the Word of God is distinguished from God, as executor of his will from everlasting.

(a) Prov. 8:1—"Doth not wisdom cry?" Cf. Mat. 11:19—"wisdom is justified by her works"; Luke 7:35—"wisdom is justified of all her children"; 11:49—"Therefore also said the wisdom of God, I will send unto them prophets and apostles"; Prov. 8:22, 30, 31—"Jehovah possessed me in the beginning of his way, Before his works of old.... I was by him, as a master workman: And I was daily his delight.... And my delight was with the sons of men"; cf. 3:19—"Jehovah by wisdom founded the earth," and Heb. 1:2—"his Son ... through whom ... he made the worlds." (b) Ps. 107:20—"He sendeth his word, and healeth them"; 119:89—"For ever, O Jehovah, Thy word is settled in heaven"; 147:15-18—"He sendeth out his commandment.... He sendeth out his word."

In the Apocryphal book entitled Wisdom, 7:26, 28, wisdom is described as "the brightness of the eternal light," "the unspotted mirror of God's majesty," and "the image of his goodness"—reminding us of Heb. 1:3—"the effulgence of his glory, and the very image of his substance." In Wisdom, 9:9, 10, wisdom is represented as being present with God when he made the world, and the author of the book prays that wisdom may be sent to him out of God's holy heavens and from the throne of his glory. In 1 Esdras 4:35-38, Truth in a similar way is spoken of as personal: "Great is the Truth and stronger than all things. All the earth calleth upon the Truth, and the heaven blesseth it; all works shake and tremble at it, and with it is no unrighteous thing. As for the Truth, it endureth and is always strong; it liveth and conquereth forevermore."

It must be acknowledged that in none of these descriptions is the idea of personality clearly developed. Still less is it true that John the apostle derived his doctrine of the Logos from the interpretations of these descriptions in Philo Judæus. John's doctrine (John 1:1-18) is radically different from the Alexandrian Logos-idea of Philo. This last is a Platonizing speculation upon the mediating principle between God and the world. Philo seems at times to verge towards a recognition of personality in the Logos, though his monotheistic scruples lead him at other times to take back what he has given, and to describe the Logos either as the thought of God or as its expression in the world. But John is the first to present to us a consistent view of this personality, to identify the Logos with the Messiah, and to distinguish the Word from the Spirit of God.

Dorner, in his History of the Doctrine of the Person of Christ, 1:13-45, and in his System of Doctrine, 1:348, 349, gives the best account of Philo's doctrine of the Logos. He says that Philo calls the Logos ἀρχάγγελος, ἀρχιερεύς, δεύτερος θεός. Whether this is anything more than personification is doubtful, for Philo also calls the Logos the κόσμος νοητός. Certainly, so far as he makes the Logos a distinct personality, he makes him also a subordinate being. It is charged that the doctrine of the Trinity owes its origin to the Platonic philosophy in its Alexandrian union with Jewish theology. But Platonism had no Trinity. The truth is that by the doctrine of the Trinity Christianity secured itself against false heathen ideas of God's multiplicity and immanence, as well as against false Jewish ideas of God's unity and transcendence. It owes nothing to foreign sources.

We need not assign to John's gospel a later origin, in order to account for its doctrine of the Logos, any more than we need to assign a later origin to the Synoptics in order to account for their doctrine of a suffering Messiah. Both doctrines were equally unknown to Philo. Philo's Logos does not and cannot become man. So says Dorner. Westcott, in Bible Commentary on John, Introd., xv-xviii, and on John 1:1—"The theological use of the term [in John's gospel] appears to be derived directly from the Palestinian Memra, and not from the Alexandrian Logos." Instead of Philo's doctrine being a stepping-stone from Judaism to Christianity, it was a stumbling-stone. It had no doctrine of the Messiah or of the atonement. Bennett and Adeny, Bib. Introd., 340—"The difference between Philo and John may be stated thus: Philo's Logos is Reason, while John's is Word; Philo's is impersonal, while John's is personal; Philo's is not incarnate, while John's is incarnate; Philo's is not the Messiah, while John's is the Messiah."

Philo lived from B. C. 10 or 20 to certainly A. D. 40, when he went at the head of a Jewish embassy to Rome, to persuade the Emperor to abstain from claiming divine honor from the Jews. In his De Opifice Mundi he says: "The Word is nothing else but the intelligible world." He calls the Word the "chainband," "pilot," "steersman," of all things. Gore, Incarnation, 69—"Logos in Philo must be translated 'Reason.' But in the Targums, or early Jewish paraphrases of the O. T., the 'Word' of Jehovah (Memra, Devra) is constantly spoken of as the efficient instrument of the divine action, in cases where the O. T. speaks of Jehovah himself, 'The Word of God' had come to be used personally, as almost equivalent to God manifesting himself, or God in action." George H. Gilbert, in Biblical World, Jan. 1899:44—"John's use of the term Logos was suggested by Greek philosophy, while at the same time the content of the word is Jewish."

Hatch, Hibbert Lectures, 174-208—"The Stoics invested the Logos with personality. They were Monists and they made λόγος and ὕλη the active and the passive forms of the one principle. Some made

God a mode of matter—natura naturata; others made matter a mode of God—natura naturans = the world a self-evolution of God. The Platonic forms, as manifold expressions of a single λόγος, were expressed by a singular term, Logos, rather than the Logoi, of God. From this Logos proceed all forms of mind or reason. So held Philo: 'The mind is an offshoot from the divine and happy soul (of God), an offshoot not separated from him, for nothing divine is cut off and disjoined, but only extended.' Philo's Logos is not only form but force—God's creative energy—the eldest-born of the 'I am,' which robes itself with the world as with a vesture, the high priest's robe, embroidered with all the forces of the seen and unseen worlds."

Wendt, Teaching of Jesus, 1:53—"Philo carries the transcendence of God to its logical conclusions. The Jewish doctrine of angels is expanded in his doctrine of the Logos. The Alexandrian philosophers afterwards represented Christianity as a spiritualized Judaism. But a philosophical system dominated by the idea of the divine transcendence never could have furnished a motive for missionary labors like those of Paul. Philo's belief in transcendence abated his redemptive hopes. But, conversely, the redemptive hopes of orthodox Judaism saved it from some of the errors of exclusive transcendence." See a quotation from Siegfried, in Schürer's History of the Jewish People, article on Philo: "Philo's doctrine grew out of God's distinction and distance from the world. It was dualistic. Hence the need of mediating principles, some being less than God and more than creature. The cosmical significance of Christ bridged the gulf between Christianity and contemporary Greek thought. Christianity stands for a God who is revealed. But a Logos-doctrine like that of Philo may reveal less than it conceals. Instead of God incarnate for our salvation, we may have merely a mediating principle between God and the world, as in Arianism."

The preceding statement is furnished in substance by Prof. William Adams Brown. With it we agree, adding only the remark that the Alexandrian philosophy gave to Christianity, not the substance of its doctrine, but only the terminology for its expression. The truth which Philo groped after, the Apostle John seized and published, as only he could, who had heard, seen, and handled "the Word of life" (1 John 1:1). "The Christian doctrine of the Logos was perhaps before anything else an effort to express how Jesus Christ was God (Θεός), and yet in another sense was not God (ὁ θεός); that is to say, was not the whole Godhead" (quoted in Marcus Dods, Expositors' Bible, on John 1:1). See also Kendrick, in Christian Review, 26:369-399; Gloag, in Presb. and Ref. Rev., 1891:45-57; Réville, Doctrine of the Logos in John and Philo; Godet on John, Germ. transl., 13, 135; Cudworth, Intellectual System, 2:320-333; Pressensé, Life of Jesus Christ, 83; Hagenbach, Hist. Doct., 1:114-117; Liddon, Our Lord's Divinity, 59-71; Conant on Proverbs, 53.

D. Descriptions of the Messiah.

(a) He is one with Jehovah; (b) yet he is in some sense distinct from Jehovah.

(a) Is. 9:6—"unto us a child is born, unto us a son is given ... and his name shall be called Wonderful Counselor, Mighty God, Everlasting Father, Prince of Peace"; Micah 5:2—"thou Bethlehem ... which art little ... out of thee shall one come forth unto me that is to be ruler in Israel; whose goings forth are from of old, from everlasting." (b) Ps. 45:6, 7—"Thy throne, O God, is for ever and ever.... Therefore God, thy God, hath anointed thee"; Mal 3:1—"I send my messenger, and he shall prepare the way before me: and the Lord, whom ye seek, will suddenly come to his temple; and the messenger of the covenant, whom ye desire." Henderson, in his Commentary on this passage, points out that the Messiah is here called "the Lord" or "the Sovereign"—a title nowhere given in this form (with the article) to any but Jehovah; that he is predicted as coming to the temple as its proprietor; and that he is identified with the angel of the covenant, elsewhere shown to be one with Jehovah himself.

It is to be remembered, in considering this, as well as other classes of passages previously cited, that no Jewish writer before Christ's coming had succeeded in constructing from them a doctrine of the Trinity. Only to those who bring to them the light of New Testament revelation do they show their real meaning.

Our general conclusion with regard to the Old Testament intimations must therefore be that, while they do not by themselves furnish a sufficient basis for the doctrine of the Trinity, they contain the germ of it, and may be used in confirmation of it when its truth is substantially proved from the New Testament.

That the doctrine of the Trinity is not plainly taught in the Hebrew Scriptures is evident from the fact that Jews unite with Mohammedans in accusing trinitarians of polytheism. It should not surprise us that the Old Testament teaching on this subject is undeveloped and obscure. The first necessity was that the Unity of God should be insisted on. Until the danger of idolatry was past, a clear revelation of the Trinity might have been a hindrance to religious progress. The child now, like the race then, must learn the unity of God before it can profitably be taught the Trinity,—else it will fall into tritheism; see Gardiner, O. T. and N. T., 49. We should not therefore begin our proof of the Trinity with a reference to passages in the Old Testament. We should speak of these passages, indeed, as furnishing intimations of the doctrine rather than proof of it. Yet, after having found proof of the doctrine in the New Testament, we may expect to find traces of it in the Old which will corroborate our conclusions. As a matter of fact, we shall see that traces of the idea of a Trinity are found not only in the Hebrew Scriptures but in some of the heathen religions as well. E. G. Robinson: "The doctrine of the Trinity underlay the O. T., unperceived by its writers, was first recognized in the economic revelation of Christianity, and was first clearly enunciated in the necessary evolution of Christian doctrine."

II. These Three are so described in Scripture that we are compelled to conceive of them as distinct Persons

1. The Father and the Son are persons distinct from each other
    (a) Christ distinguishes the Father from himself as "another"; (b) the Father and the Son are distinguished as the begetter and the begotten; (c) the Father and the Son are distinguished as the sender and the sent.
    (a) John 5:32, 37—"It is another that beareth witness of me ... the Father that sent me, he hath borne witness of me." (b) Ps. 2:7—"Thou art my Son; this day have I begotten thee"; John 1:14—"the only begotten from the Father"; 18—"the only begotten Son"; 3:16—"gave his only begotten Son." (c) John 10:36—"say ye of him, whom the Father sanctified and sent into the world, Thou blasphemest; because I said, I am the Son of God?"; Gal 4:4—"when the fulness of the time came, God sent forth his Son." In these passages the Father is represented as objective to the Son, the Son to the Father, and both the Father and Son to the Spirit.

2. The Father and the Son are persons distinct from the Spirit
    (a) Jesus distinguishes the Spirit from himself and from the Father; (b) the Spirit proceeds from the Father; (c) the Spirit is sent by the Father and by the Son.
    (a) John 14:16, 17—"I will pray the Father, and he shall give you another Comforter, that he may be with you for ever, even the Spirit of truth"—or "Spirit of the truth," = he whose work it is to reveal and apply the truth, and especially to make manifest him who is the truth. Jesus had been their Comforter: he now promises them another Comforter. If he himself was a person, then the Spirit is a person. (b) John 15:26—"the Spirit of truth which proceedeth from the Father." (c) John 14:26—"the Comforter, even the Holy Spirit, whom the Father will send in my name"; 15:26—"when the Comforter is come, whom I will send unto you from the Father"; Gal. 4:6—"God sent forth the Spirit of his Son into our hearts." The Greek church holds that the Spirit proceeds from the Father only; the Latin church, that the Spirit proceeds both from the Father and from the Son. The true formula is: The Spirit proceeds from the Father through or by (not "and") the Son. See Hagenbach, History of Doctrine, 1:262, 263. Moberly, Atonement and Personality, 195—"The Filioque is a valuable defence of the truth that the Holy Spirit is not simply the abstract second Person of the Trinity, but rather the Spirit of the incarnate Christ, reproducing Christ in human hearts, and revealing in them the meaning of true manhood."

3. The Holy Spirit is a person
    A. Designations proper to personality are given him.
    (a) The masculine pronoun ἐκεῖνος, though πνεῦμα is neuter; (b) the name παράκλητος, which cannot be translated by "comfort", or be taken as the name of any abstract influence. The Comforter, Instructor, Patron, Guide, Advocate, whom this term brings before us, must be a person. This is evident from its application to Christ in 1 John 2:1—"we have an Advocate—παράκλητον—with the Father, Jesus Christ the righteous."
    (a) John 16:14—"He (ἐκεῖνος) shall glorify me"; in Eph. 1:14 also, some of the best authorities, including Tischendorf (8th ed.), read ὅς, the masculine pronoun: "who is an earnest of our inheritance." But in John 14:16-18, παράκλητος is followed by the neuters ὁ and αὐτό, because πνεῦμα had intervened. Grammatical and not theological considerations controlled the writer. See G. B. Stevens, Johannine Theology, 189-217, especially on the distinction between Christ and the Holy Spirit. The Holy Spirit is another person than Christ, in spite of Christ's saying of the coming of the Holy Spirit: "I come unto you." (b) John 16:7—"if I go not away, the Comforter will not come unto you." The word παράκλητος, as appears from 1 John 2:1, quoted above, is a term of broader meaning than merely "Comforter." The Holy Spirit is, indeed, as has been said, "the mother-principle in the Godhead," and "as one whom his mother comforteth" so God by his Spirit comforts his children (Is. 66:13). But the Holy Spirit is also an Advocate of God's claims in the soul, and of the soul's interests in prayer (Rom. 8:26—"maketh intercession for us"). He comforts not only by being our advocate, but by being our instructor, patron, and guide; and all these ideas are found attaching to the word παράκλητος in good Greek usage. The word indeed is a verbal adjective, signifying "called to one's aid," hence a "helper"; the idea of encouragement is included in it, as well as those of comfort and of advocacy. See Westcott, Bible Com., on John 14:16; Cremer, Lexicon of N. T. Greek, in voce.
    T. Dwight, in S. S. Times, on John 14:16—"The fundamental meaning of the word παράκλητος, which is a verbal adjective, is 'called to one's aid,' and thus, when used as a noun, it conveys the idea of

'helper.' This more general sense probably attaches to its use in John's Gospel, while in the Epistle (1 John 2:1, 2) it conveys the idea of Jesus acting as advocate on our behalf before God as a Judge." So the Latin advocatus signifies one "called to"—i. e., called in to aid, counsel, plead. In this connection Jesus says: "I will not leave you orphans" (John 14:18). Cumming, Through the Eternal Spirit, 228—"As the orphaned family, in the day of the parent's death, need some friend who shall lighten their sense of loss by his own presence with them, so the Holy Spirit is 'called in' to supply the present love and help which the Twelve are losing in the death of Jesus." A. A. Hodge, Pop. Lectures, 237—"The Roman 'client,' the poor and dependent man, called in his 'patron' to help him in all his needs. The patron thought for, advised, directed, supported, defended, supplied, restored, comforted his client in all his complications. The client, though weak, with a powerful patron, was socially and politically secure forever."

B. His name is mentioned in immediate connection with other persons, and in such a way as to imply his own personality.

(a) In connection with Christians; (b) in connection with Christ; (c) in connection with the Father and the Son. If the Father and the Son are persons, the Spirit must be a person also.

(a) Acts 15:28—"it seemed good to the Holy Spirit, and to us." (b) John 16:14—"He shall glorify me: for he shall take of mine, and shall declare it unto you"; cf. 17:4—"I glorified thee on the earth." (c) Mat. 28:29—"baptizing them into the name of the Father and of the Son and of the Holy Spirit"; 2 Cor. 13:14—"the grace of the Lord Jesus Christ, and the love of God, and the communion of the Holy Spirit, be with you all"; Jude 21—"praying in the Holy Spirit, keep yourselves in the love of God, looking for the mercy of our Lord Jesus Christ." 1 Pet. 1:1, 2—"elect ... according to the foreknowledge of God the Father, in sanctification of the Spirit, unto obedience and sprinkling of the blood of Jesus Christ." Yet it is noticeable in all these passages that there is no obtrusion of the Holy Spirit's personality, as if he desired to draw attention to himself. The Holy Spirit shows, not himself, but Christ. Like John the Baptist, he is a mere voice, and so is an example to Christian preachers, who are themselves "made ... sufficient as ministers ... of the Spirit" (2 Cor. 3:6). His leading is therefore often unperceived; he so joins himself to us that we infer his presence only from the new and holy exercises of our own minds; he continues to work in us even when his presence is ignored and his purity is outraged by our sins.

C. He performs acts proper to personality.

That which searches, knows, speaks, testifies, reveals, convinces, commands, strives, moves, helps, guides, creates, recreates, sanctifies, inspires, makes intercession, orders the affairs of the church, performs miracles, raises the dead—cannot be a mere power, influence, efflux, or attribute of God, but must be a person.

Gen. 1:2, marg.—"the Spirit of God was brooding upon the face of the waters"; 6:3—"My Spirit shalt not strive with man for ever"; Luke 12:12—"the Holy Spirit shall teach you in that very hour what ye ought to say"; John 3:8—"born of the Spirit"—here Bengel translates: "the Spirit breathes where he wills, and thou hearest his voice"—see also Gordon, Ministry of the Spirit, 166; 16:8—"convict the world in respect of sin, and of righteousness, and of judgment"; Acts 2:4—"the Spirit gave them utterance"; 8:29—"the Spirit said unto Philip, Go near"; 10:19, 20—"the Spirit said unto him [Peter], Behold, three men seek thee.... go with them ... for I have sent them"; 13:2—"the Holy Spirit said, Separate me Barnabas and Saul"; 16:6, 7—"forbidden of the Holy Spirit ... Spirit of Jesus suffered them not"; Rom. 8:11—"give life also to your mortal bodies through his Spirit"; 26—"the Spirit also helpeth our infirmity ... maketh intercession for us"; 15:19—"in the power of signs and wonders, in the power of the Holy Spirit"; 1 Cor. 2:10, 11—"the Spirit searcheth all things.... things of God none knoweth, save the Spirit of God"; 12:8-11—distributes spiritual gifts "to each one severally even as he will"— here Meyer calls attention to the words "as he will," as proving the personality of the Spirit; 2 Pet. 1:21—"men spake from God, being moved by the Holy Spirit"; 1 Pet. 1:2—"sanctification of the Spirit." How can a person be given in various measures? We answer, by being permitted to work in our behalf with various degrees of power. Dorner: "To be power does not belong to the impersonal."

D. He is affected as a person by the acts of others.

That which can be resisted, grieved, vexed, blasphemed, must be a person; for only a person can perceive insult and be offended. The blasphemy against the Holy Ghost cannot be merely blasphemy against a power or attribute of God, since in that case blasphemy against God would be a less crime than blasphemy against his power. That against which the unpardonable sin can be committed must be a person.

Is. 63:10—"they rebelled and grieved his holy Spirit"; Mat. 12:31—"Every sin and blasphemy shall be forgiven unto men; but the blasphemy against the Spirit shall not be forgiven"; Acts 5:3, 4, 9— "lie to the Holy Ghost ... thou hast not lied unto men but unto God.... agreed together to try the Spirit of the Lord"; 7:51—"ye do always resist the Holy Spirit"; Eph. 4:30—"grieve not the Holy Spirit of God." Satan cannot be "grieved." Selfishness can be angered, but only love can be grieved. Blaspheming the Holy Spirit is like blaspheming one's own mother. The passages just quoted show the Spirit's possession of an emotional nature. Hence we read of "the love of the Spirit" (Rom. 15:30). The unutterable sighings of the Christian in intercessory prayer (Rom. 8:26, 27) reveal the mind of the Spirit, and show the infinite depths of feeling which are awakened in God's heart by the sins and needs of men. These deep desires and emotions which are only partially communicated to us, and which only God can understand, are conclusive proof that the Holy Spirit is a person. They are only the overflow into us of the infinite fountain of divine love to which the Holy Spirit unites us.

As Christ in the garden "began to be sorrowful and sore troubled" (Mat. 26:37), so the Holy Spirit is sorrowful and sore troubled at the ignoring, despising, resisting of his work, on the part of those whom he is trying to rescue from sin and to lead out into the freedom and joy of the Christian life. Luthardt, in S. S. Times, May 26, 1888—"Every sin can be forgiven—even the sin against the Son of man—except the sin against the Holy Spirit. The sin against the Son of man can be forgiven because he can be misconceived. For he did not appear as that which he really was. Essence and appearance, truth and reality, contradicted each other." Hence Jesus could pray: "Father, forgive them, for they know not what they do" (Luke 23:34). The office of the Holy Spirit, however, is to show to men the nature of their conduct, and to sin against him is to sin against light and without excuse. See A. H. Strong, Christ in Creation, 297-313. Salmond, in Expositor's Greek Testament, on Eph. 4:30—"What love is in us points truly, though tremulously, to what love is in God. But in us love, in proportion as it is true and sovereign, has both its wrath-side and its grief-side; and so must it be with God, however difficult for us to think it out."

E. He manifests himself in visible form as distinct from the Father and the Son, yet in direct connection with personal acts performed by them.

Mat. 3:16, 17—"Jesus, when he was baptized, went up straightway from the water: and lo, the heavens were opened unto him, and he saw the Spirit of God descending as a dove, and coming upon him; and lo, a voice out of the heavens, saying, This is my beloved Son, in whom I am well pleased"; Luke 3:21, 22—"Jesus also having been baptized, and praying, the heaven was opened, and the Holy Spirit descended in a bodily form, as a dove, upon him, and a voice came out of heaven, Thou art my beloved Son; in thee I am well pleased." Here are the prayer of Jesus, the approving voice of the Father, and the Holy Spirit descending in visible form to anoint the Son of God for his work. "I ad Jordanem, et videbis Trinitatem."

F. This ascription to the Spirit of a personal subsistence distinct from that of the Father and of the Son cannot be explained as personification; for:

(a) This would be to interpret sober prose by the canons of poetry. Such sustained personification is contrary to the genius of even Hebrew poetry, in which Wisdom itself is most naturally interpreted as designating a personal existence. (b) Such an interpretation would render a multitude of passages either tautological, meaningless, or absurd,—as can be easily seen by substituting for the name Holy Spirit the terms which are wrongly held to be its equivalents; such as the power, or influence, or efflux, or attribute of God. (c) It is contradicted, moreover, by all those passages in which the Holy Spirit is distinguished from his own gifts.

(a) The Bible is not primarily a book of poetry, although there is poetry in it. It is more properly a book of history and law. Even if the methods of allegory were used by the Psalmists and the Prophets, we should not expect them largely to characterize the Gospels and Epistles; 1 Cor. 13:4—"Love suffereth long, and is kind"—is a rare instance in which Paul's style takes on the form of poetry. Yet it is the Gospels and Epistles which most constantly represent the Holy Spirit as a person. (b) Acts 10:38—"God anointed him [Jesus] with the Holy Spirit and with power" = anointed him with power and with power? Rom. 15:13—"abound in hope, in the power of the Holy Spirit" = in the power of the power of God? 19—"in the power of signs and wonders, in the power of the Holy Spirit" = in the power of the power of God? 1 Cor. 2:4—"demonstration of the Spirit and of power" = demonstration of power and of power? (c) Luke 1:35—"the Holy Spirit shall come upon thee, and the power of the Most High shall overshadow thee"; 4:14—"Jesus returned in the power of the Spirit into Galilee"; 1 Cor. 12:4, 8, 11—after mention of the gifts of the Spirit, such as wisdom, knowledge, faith, healings, miracles, prophecy, discerning of spirits, tongues, interpretation of tongues, all these are traced to the Spirit who bestows them: "all these worketh the one and the same Spirit, dividing to each one severally even as he will." Here is not only giving, but giving discreetly, in the exercise of an independent will such as belongs only to a person. Rom. 8:26—"the Spirit himself maketh intercession for us"—must be interpreted, if the Holy Spirit is not a person distinct from the Father, as meaning that the Holy Spirit intercedes with himself.

"The personality of the Holy Spirit was virtually rejected by the Arians, as it has since been by Schleiermacher, and it has been positively denied by the Socinians" (E. G. Robinson). Gould, Bib. Theol. N. T., 83, 96—"The Twelve represent the Spirit as sent by the Son, who has been exalted that he may send this new power out of the heavens. Paul represents the Spirit as bringing to us the Christ. In the Spirit Christ dwells in us. The Spirit is the historic Jesus translated into terms of universal Spirit. Through the Spirit we are in Christ and Christ in us. The divine Indweller is to Paul alternately Christ and the Spirit. The Spirit is the divine principle incarnate in Jesus and explaining his preëxistence (2

Cor. 3:17, 18). Jesus was an incarnation of the Spirit of God."

This seeming identification of the Spirit with Christ is to be explained upon the ground that the divine essence is common to both and permits the Father to dwell in and to work through the Son, and the Son to dwell in and to work through the Spirit. It should not blind us to the equally patent Scriptural fact that there are personal relations between Christ and the Holy Spirit, and work done by the latter in which Christ is the object and not the subject; John 16:14—"He shall glorify me: for he shall take of mine, and shall declare it unto you." The Holy Spirit is not some thing, but some one; not αὐτό, but Αὐτός; Christ's alter ego, or other self. We should therefore make vivid our belief in the personality of Christ and of the Holy Spirit by addressing each of them frequently in the prayers we offer and in such hymns as "Jesus, lover of my soul," and "Come, Holy Spirit, heavenly Dove!" On the personality of the Holy Spirit, see John Owen, in Works, 3:64-92; Dick, Lectures on Theology, 1:341-350.

III. This Tripersonality of the Divine Nature is not merely economic and temporal, but is immanent and eternal

1. Scripture proof that these distinctions of personality are eternal

We prove this (a) from those passages which speak of the existence of the Word from eternity with the Father; (b) from passages asserting or implying Christ's preëxistence; (c) from passages implying intercourse between the Father and the Son before the foundation of the world; (d) from passages asserting the creation of the world by Christ; (e) from passages asserting or implying the eternity of the Holy Spirit.

(a) John 1:1, 2—"In the beginning was the Word, and the Word was with God, and the Word was God"; cf. Gen. 1:1—"In the beginning God created the heavens and the earth"; Phil. 2:6—"existing in the form of God ... on an equality with God." (b) John 8:58—"before Abraham was born, I am"; 1:18—"the only begotten Son, who is in the bosom of the Father" (R. V.); Col. 1:15-17—"firstborn of all creation" or "before every creature ... he is before all things." In these passages "am" and "is" indicate an eternal fact; the present tense expresses permanent being. Rev. 22:13, 14—"I am the Alpha and the Omega, the first and the last, the beginning and the end." (c) John 17:5—"Father, glorify thou me with thine own self with the glory which I had with thee before the world was"; 24—"Thou lovedst me before the foundation of the world." (d) John 1:3—"All things were made through him"; 1 Cor. 8:6—"one Lord, Jesus Christ, through whom are all things"; Col. 1:16—"all things have been created through him and unto him"; Heb. 1:2—"through whom also he made the worlds"; 10—"Thou, Lord, in the beginning didst lay the foundation of the earth, and the heavens are the works of thy hands." (e) Gen. 1:2—"the Spirit of God was brooding"—existed therefore before creation; Ps. 33:6—"by the word of Jehovah were the heavens made; and all the host of them by the breath [Spirit] of his mouth"; Heb. 9:14—"through the eternal Spirit."

With these passages before us, we must dissent from the statement of Dr. E. G. Robinson: "About the ontologic Trinity we know absolutely nothing. The Trinity we can contemplate is simply a revealed one, one of economic manifestations. We may suppose that the ontologic underlies the economic." Scripture compels us, in our judgment, to go further than this, and to maintain that there are personal relations between the Father, the Son, and the Holy Spirit independently of creation and of time; in other words we maintain that Scripture reveals to us a social Trinity and an intercourse of love apart from and before the existence of the universe. Love before time implies distinctions of personality before time. There are three eternal consciousnesses and three eternal wills in the divine nature. We here state only the fact,—the explanation of it, and its reconciliation with the fundamental unity of God is treated in our next section. We now proceed to show that the two varying systems which ignore this tripersonality are unscriptural and at the same time exposed to philosophical objection.

2. Errors refuted by the foregoing passages

A. The Sabellian.

Sabellius (of Ptolemais in Pentapolis, 250) held that Father, Son, and Holy Spirit are mere developments or revelations to creatures, in time, of the otherwise concealed Godhead—developments which, since creatures will always exist, are not transitory, but which at the same time are not eternal a parte ante. God as united to the creation is Father; God as united to Jesus Christ is Son; God as united to the church is Holy Spirit. The Trinity of Sabellius is therefore an economic and not an immanent Trinity—a Trinity of forms or manifestations, but not a necessary and eternal Trinity in the divine nature.

Some have interpreted Sabellius as denying that the Trinity is eternal a parte post, as well as a parte ante, and as holding that, when the purpose of these temporary manifestations is accomplished, the Triad is resolved into the Monad. This view easily merges in another, which makes the persons of the Trinity mere names for the ever shifting phases of the divine activity.

The best statement of the Sabellian doctrine, according to the interpretation first mentioned, is that of Schleiermacher, translated with comments by Moses Stuart, in Biblical Repository, 6:1-16. The one unchanging God is differently reflected from the world on account of the world's different receptivities. Praxeas of Rome (200) Noetus of Smyrna (230), and Beryl of Arabia (250) advocated substantially the same views. They were called Monarchians (μόνη ἀρχή), because they believed not in the Triad, but only in the Monad. They were called Patripassians, because they held that, as Christ is only God in human form, and this God suffers, therefore the Father suffers. Knight, Colloquia Peripatetica, xlii, suggests a connection between Sabellianism and Emanationism. See this Compendium, on Theories which oppose Creation.

A view similar to that of Sabellius was held by Horace Bushnell, in his God in Christ, 113-115, 130 sq., 172-175, and Christ in Theology, 119, 120—"Father, Son and Holy Spirit, being incidental to the revelation of God, may be and probably are from eternity to eternity, inasmuch as God may have revealed himself from eternity, and certainly will reveal himself so long as there are minds to know him. It may be, in fact, the nature of God to reveal himself, as truly as it is of the sun to shine or of living mind to think." He does not deny the immanent Trinity, but simply says we know nothing about it. Yet a Trinity of Persons in the divine essence itself he called plain tritheism. He prefers "instrumental Trinity" to "modal Trinity" as a designation of his doctrine. The difference between Bushnell on the one hand, and Sabellius and Schleiermacher on the other, seems then to be the following: Sabellius and Schleiermacher hold that the One becomes three in the process of revelation, and the three are only media or modes of revelation. Father, Son, and Spirit are mere names applied to these modes of the divine action, there being no internal distinctions in the divine nature. This is modalism, or a modal Trinity. Bushnell stands by the Trinity of revelation alone, and protests against any constructive reasonings with regard to the immanent Trinity. Yet in his later writings he reverts to Athanasius and speaks of God as eternally "threeing himself"; see Fisher, Edwards on the Trinity, 73.

Lyman Abbott, in The Outlook, proposes as illustration of the Trinity, 1. the artist working on his pictures; 2. the same man teaching pupils how to paint; 3. the same man entertaining his friends at home. He has not taken on these types of conduct. They are not masks (personæ), nor offices, which he takes up and lays down. There is a threefold nature in him: he is artist, teacher, friend. God is complex, and not simple. I do not know him, till I know him in all these relations. Yet it is evident that Dr. Abbott's view provides no basis for love or for society within the divine nature. The three persons are but three successive aspects or activities of the one God. General Grant, when in office, was but one person, even though he was a father, a President, and a commander in chief of the army and navy of the United States.

It is evident that this theory, in whatever form it may be held, is far from satisfying the demands of Scripture. Scripture speaks of the second person of the Trinity as existing and acting before the birth of Jesus Christ, and of the Holy Spirit as existing and acting before the formation of the church. Both have a personal existence, eternal in the past as well as in the future—which this theory expressly denies.

A revelation that is not a self-revelation of God is not honest. Stuart: Since God is revealed as three, he must be essentially or immanently three, back of revelation; else the revelation would not be true. Dorner: A Trinity of revelation is a misrepresentation, if there is not behind it a Trinity of nature. Twesten properly arrives at the threeness by considering, not so much what is involved in the revelation of God to us, as what is involved in the revelation of God to himself. The unscripturalness of the Sabellian doctrine is plain, if we remember that upon this view the Three cannot exist at once: when the Father says "Thou art my beloved Son" (Luke 3:22), he is simply speaking to himself; when Christ sends the Holy Spirit, he only sends himself. John 1:1—"In the beginning was the Word, and the Word was with God, and the Word was God"—"sets aside the false notion that the Word become personal first at the time of creation, or at the incarnation" (Westcott, Bib. Com. in loco).

Mason, Faith of the Gospel, 50, 51—"Sabellius claimed that the Unity became a Trinity by expansion. Fatherhood began with the world. God is not eternally Father, nor does he love eternally. We have only an impersonal, unintelligible God, who has played upon us and confused our understanding by showing himself to us under three disguises. Before creation there is no Fatherhood, even in germ."

According to Pfleiderer, Philos. Religion, 2:269, Origen held that the Godhead might be represented by three concentric circles; the widest, embracing the whole being, is that of the Father; the next, that of the Son, which extends to the rational creation; and the narrowest is that of the Spirit, who rules in the holy men of the church. King, Reconstruction of Theology, 192, 194—"To affirm social relations in the Godhead is to assert absolute Tritheism.... Unitarianism emphasizes the humanity of Christ, to preserve the unity of God; the true view emphasizes the divinity of Christ, to preserve the unity."

L. L. Paine, Evolution of Trinitarianism, 141, 287, says that New England Trinitarianism is characterized by three things: 1. Sabellian Patripassianism; Christ is all the Father there is, and the Holy Spirit is Christ's continued life; 2. Consubstantiality, or community of essence, of God and man; unlike the essential difference between the created and the uncreated which Platonic dualism maintained, this theory turns moral likeness into essential likeness; 3. Philosophical monism, matter itself being but an evolution of Spirit.... In the next form of the scientific doctrine of evolution, the divineness of man becomes a vital truth, and out of it arises a Christology that removes Jesus of Nazareth indeed out of the order of absolute Deity, but at the same time exalts him to a place of moral eminence that is secure and supreme.

Against this danger of regarding Christ as a merely economic and temporary manifestation of God we can guard only by maintaining the Scriptural doctrine of an immanent Trinity. Moberly, Atonement and Personality, 86, 165—"We cannot incur any Sabellian peril while we maintain—what is fatal to Sabellianism—that that which is revealed within the divine Unity is not only a distinction of aspects or of names, but a real reciprocity of mutual relation. One 'aspect' cannot contemplate, or be loved by, another.... Sabellianism degrades the persons of Deity into aspects. But there can be no mutual relation between aspects. The heat and the light of flame cannot severally contemplate and be in love with one another." See Bushnell's doctrine reviewed by Hodge, Essays and Reviews, 433-473. On the whole subject, see Dorner, Hist. Doct. Person of Christ, 2:152-169; Shedd, Hist. Doctrine, 1:259; Baur, Lehre von der Dreieinigkeit, 1:256-305; Thomasius, Christi Person und Werk 1:83.

B. The Arian.

Arius (of Alexandria; condemned by Council of Nice, 325) held that the Father is the only divine being absolutely without beginning; the Son and the Holy Spirit, through whom God creates and recreates, having been themselves created out of nothing before the world was; and Christ being called God, because he is next in rank to God, and is endowed by God with divine power to create.

The followers of Arius have differed as to the precise rank and claims of Christ. While Socinus held with Arius that worship of Christ was obligatory, the later Unitarians have perceived the impropriety of worshiping even the highest of created beings, and have constantly tended to a view of the Redeemer which regards him as a mere man, standing in a peculiarly intimate relation to God.

For statement of the Arian doctrine, see J. Freeman Clarke, Orthodoxy, Its Truths and Errors. Per contra, see Schäffer, in Bib. Sac., 21:1, article on Athanasius and the Arian controversy. The so-called Athanasian Creed, which Athanasius never wrote, is more properly designated as the Symbolum Quicumque. It has also been called, though facetiously, "the Anathemasian Creed." Yet no error in doctrine can be more perilous or worthy of condemnation than the error of Arius (1 Cor. 16:22—"If any man loveth not the Lord, let him be anathema"; 1 John 2:23—"Whosoever denieth the Son, the same hath not the Father"; 4:3—"every spirit that confesseth not Jesus is not of God: and this is the spirit of the antichrist"). It regards Christ as called God only by courtesy, much as we give to a Lieutenant Governor the title of Governor. Before the creation of the Son, the love of God, if there could be love, was expended on himself. Gwatkin, Studies of Arianism: "The Arian Christ is nothing but a heathen idol, invented to maintain a heathenish Supreme in heathen isolation from the world. The nearer the Son is pulled down towards man by the attenuation of his Godhead, the more remote from man becomes the unshared Godhead of the Father. You have an Être Suprême who is practically unapproachable, a mere One-and-all, destitute of personality."

Gore, Incarnation, 90, 91, 110, shows the immense importance of the controversy with regard to ὁμοούσιον and ὁμοιούσιον. Carlyle once sneered that "the Christian world was torn in pieces over a diphthong." But Carlyle afterwards came to see that Christianity itself was at stake, and that it would have dwindled away to a legend, if the Arians had won. Arius appealed chiefly to logic, not to Scripture. He claimed that a Son must be younger than his Father. But he was asserting the principle of heathenism and idolatry, in demanding worship for a creature. The Goths were easily converted to Arianism. Christ was to them a hero-god, a demigod, and the later Goths could worship Christ and heathen idols impartially.

It is evident that the theory of Arius does not satisfy the demands of Scripture. A created God, a God whose existence had a beginning and therefore may come to an end, a God made of a substance which once was not, and therefore a substance different from that of the Father, is not God, but a finite creature. But the Scripture speaks of Christ as being in the beginning God, with God, and equal with God.

Luther, alluding to John 1:1, says: "'The Word was God' is against Arius; 'the Word was with God' is against Sabellius." The Racovian Catechism, Quaes. 183, 184, 211, 236, 237, 245, 246, teaches that Christ is to be truly worshiped, and they are denied to be Christians who refuse to adore him. Davidis was persecuted and died in prison for refusing to worship Christ; and Socinus was charged, though probably unjustly, with having caused his imprisonment. Bartholomew Legate, an Essexman and an Arian, was burned to death at Smithfield, March 13, 1613. King James I asked him whether he did not pray to Christ. Legate's answer was that "indeed he had prayed to Christ in the days of his ignorance, but not for these last seven years"; which so shocked James that "he spurned at him with his foot." At the stake Legate still refused to recant, and so was burned to ashes amid a vast conflux of people. The very next month another Arian named Whiteman was burned at Burton-on-Trent.

It required courage, even a generation later, for John Milton, in his Christian Doctrine, to declare himself a high Arian. In that treatise he teaches that "the Son of God did not exist from all eternity, is not coëval or coëssential or coëqual with the Father, but came into existence by the will of God to be the next being to himself, the first-born and best beloved, the Logos or Word through whom all creation should take its beginnings." So Milton regards the Holy Spirit as a created being, inferior to the Son and possibly confined to our heavens and earth. Milton's Arianism, however, is characteristic of his later, rather than his earlier, writings; compare the Ode on Christ's Nativity with Paradise Lost, 3:383-391; and see Masson's Life of Milton, 1:39; 6:823, 824; A. H. Strong, Great Poets and their Theology, 260-262.

Dr. Samuel Clarke, when asked whether the Father who had created could not also destroy the Son, said that he had not considered the question. Ralph Waldo Emerson broke with his church and left the ministry because he could not celebrate the Lord's Supper,—it implied a profounder reverence for Jesus than he could give him. He wrote: "It seemed to me at church to-day, that the Communion Service, as it is now and here celebrated, is a document of the dullness of the race. How these, my good neighbors, the bending deacons, with their cups and plates, would have straightened themselves to sturdiness, if the proposition came before them to honor thus a fellow-man"; see Cabot's Memoir, 314. Yet Dr. Leonard Bacon said of the Unitarians that "it seemed as if their exclusive contemplation of Jesus Christ in his human character as the example for our imitation had wrought in them an exceptional beauty and Christlikeness of living."

Chadwick, Old and New Unitarian Belief, 20, speaks of Arianism as exalting Christ to a degree of inappreciable difference from God, while Socinus looked upon him only as a miraculously endowed man, and believed in an infallible book. The term "Unitarians," he claims, is derived from the "Uniti," a society in Transylvania, in support of mutual toleration between Calvinists, Romanists, and Socinians. The name stuck to the advocates of the divine Unity, because they were its most active members. B. W. Lockhart: "Trinity guarantees God's knowableness. Arius taught that Jesus was neither human nor divine, but created in some grade of being between the two, essentially unknown to man. An absentee God made Jesus his messenger, God himself not touching the world directly at any point, and unknown and unknowable to it. Athanasius on the contrary asserted that God did not send a messenger in Christ, but came himself, so that to know Christ is really to know God who is essentially revealed in him. This gave the Church the doctrine of God immanent, or Immanuel, God knowable and actually known by men, because actually present." Chapman, Jesus Christ and the Present Age, 14—"The world was never further from Unitarianism than it is to-day; we may add that Unitarianism was never further from itself." On the doctrines of the early Socinians, see Princeton Essays, 1:195. On the whole subject, see Blunt, Dict. of Heretical Sects, art.: Arius; Guericke, Hist. Doctrine, 1:313, 319. See also a further account of Arianism in the chapter of this Compendium on the Person of Christ.

IV. This Tripersonality is not Tritheism; for, while there are three Persons, there is but one Essence

(a) The term "person" only approximately represents the truth. Although this word, more nearly than any other single word, expresses the conception which the Scriptures give us of the relation between the Father, the Son, and the Holy Spirit, it is not itself used in this connection in Scripture, and we employ it in a qualified sense, not in the ordinary sense in which we apply the word "person" to Peter, Paul, and John.

The word "person" is only the imperfect and inadequate expression of a fact that transcends our experience and comprehension. Bunyan: "My dark and cloudy words, they do but hold The truth, as cabinets encase the gold." Three Gods, limiting each other, would deprive each other of Deity. While we show that the unity is articulated by the persons, it is equally important to remember that the persons are limited by the unity. With us personality implies entire separation from all others—distinct individuality. But in the one God there can be no such separation. The personal distinctions in him must be such as are consistent with essential unity. This is the merit of the statement in the Symbolum Quicumque (or Athanasian Creed, wrongly so called): "The Father is God, the Son is God, the Holy Ghost is God; and yet there are not three Gods but one God. So likewise the Father is Lord, the Son is Lord, the Holy Ghost is Lord; yet there are not three Lords but one Lord. For as we are compelled by Christian truth to acknowledge each person by himself to be God and Lord, so we are forbidden by the same truth to say that there are three Gods or three Lords." See Hagenbach, History of Doctrine, 1:270. We add that the personality of the Godhead as a whole is separate and distinct from all others, and in this respect is more fully analogous to man's personality than is the personality of the Father or of the Son.

The church of Alexandria in the second century chanted together: "One only is holy, the Father; One only is holy, the Son; One only is holy, the Spirit." Moberly, Atonement and Personality, 154, 167, 168—"The three persons are neither three Gods, nor three parts of God. Rather are they God threefoldly, tri-personally.... The personal distinction in Godhead is a distinction within, and of, Unity: not a distinction which qualifies Unity, or usurps the place of it, or destroys it. It is not a relation of mutual exclusiveness, but of mutual inclusiveness. No one person is or can be without the others.... The personality of the supreme or absolute Being cannot be without self-contained mutuality of relations such as Will and Love. But the mutuality would not be real, unless the subject which becomes object, and the object which becomes subject, were on each side alike and equally Personal.... The Unity of all-comprehending inclusiveness is a higher mode of unity than the unity of singular distinctiveness.... The disciples are not to have the presence of the Spirit instead of the Son, but to have the Spirit is to have the Son. We mean by the Personal God not a limited alternative to unlimited abstracts, such as Law, Holiness, Love, but the transcendent and inclusive completeness of them all. The terms Father and Son are certainly terms which rise more immediately out of the temporal facts of the incarnation than out of the eternal relations of the divine Being. They are metaphors, however, which mean far more in the spiritual than they do in the material sphere. Spiritual hunger is more intense than physical hunger. So sin, judgment, grace, are metaphors. But in John 1:1-18 'Son' is not used, but 'Word.' "

(b) The necessary qualification is that, while three persons among men have only a specific unity of nature or essence—that is, have the same species of nature or essence,—the persons of the Godhead have a numerical unity of nature or essence—that is, have the same nature or essence. The undivided essence of the Godhead belongs equally to each of the persons; Father, Son, and Holy Spirit, each possesses all the substance and all the attributes of Deity. The plurality of the Godhead is therefore not a plurality of essence, but a plurality of hypostatical, or personal, distinctions. God is not three and one, but three in one. The one indivisible essence has three modes of subsistence.

The Trinity is not simply a partnership, in which each member can sign the name of the firm; for this is unity of council and operation only, not of essence. God's nature is not an abstract but an organic unity. God, as living, cannot be a mere Monad. Trinity is the organism of the Deity. The one divine Being exists in three modes. The life of the vine makes itself known in the life of the branches, and this union between vine and branches Christ uses to illustrate the union between the Father and himself. (See John 15:10—"If ye keep my commandments, ye shall abide in my love; even as I have kept my Father's commandments, and abide in his love"; cf. verse 5—"I am the vine, ye are the branches; he that abideth in me, and I in him, the same beareth much fruit"; 17:22, 23—"That they may be one, even as we are one; I in them, and thou in me.") So, in the organism of the body, the arm has its own life, a different life from that of the head or the foot, yet has this only by partaking of the life of the whole. See Dorner, System of Doctrine, 1:450-453—"The one divine personality is so present in each of the distinctions, that these, which singly and by themselves would not be personal, yet do participate in the one divine personality, each in its own manner. This one divine personality is the unity of the three modes of subsistence which participate in itself. Neither is personal without the others. In each, in its manner, is the whole Godhead."

The human body is a complex rather than a simple organism, a unity which embraces an indefinite number of subsidiary and dependent organisms. The one life of the body manifests itself in the life of the nervous system, the life of the circulatory system, and the life of the digestive system. The complete destruction of either one of these systems destroys the other two. Psychology as well as physiology reveals to us the possibility of a three-fold life within the bounds of a single being. In the individual man there is sometimes a double and even a triple consciousness. Herbert Spencer, Autobiography, 1:459; 2:204—"Most active minds have, I presume, more or less frequent experiences of double consciousness—one consciousness seeming to take note of what the other is about, and to applaud or blame." He mentions an instance in his own experience. "May there not be possible a bi-cerebral thinking, as there is a binocular vision?... In these cases it seems as though there were going on, quite apart from the consciousness which seemed to constitute myself, some process of elaborating coherent thoughts—as though one part of myself was an independent originator over whose sayings and doings I had no control, and which were nevertheless in great measure consistent; while the other part of myself was a passive spectator or listener, quite unprepared for many of the things that the first part said, and which were nevertheless, though unexpected, not illogical." This fact that there can be more than one consciousness in the same personality among men should make us slow to deny that there can be three consciousnesses in the one God.

Humanity at large is also an organism, and this fact lends new confirmation to the Pauline statement of organic interdependence. Modern sociology is the doctrine of one life constituted by the union of many. "Unus homo, nullus homo" is a principle of ethics as well as of sociology. No man can have a conscience to himself. The moral life of one results from and is interpenetrated by the moral life of all. All men moreover live, move and have their being in God. Within the bounds of the one universal and divine consciousness there are multitudinous finite consciousnesses. Why then should it be thought incredible that in the nature of this one God there should be three infinite consciousnesses? Baldwin, Psychology, 53, 54—"The integration of finite consciousnesses in an all-embracing divine consciousness may find a valid analogy in the integration of subordinate consciousnesses in the unit-personality of man. In the hypnotic state, multiple consciousnesses may be induced in the same nervous organism. In insanity there is a secondary consciousness at war with that which normally dominates." Schurman, Belief in God, 26, 161—"The infinite Spirit may include the finite, as the idea of a single organism embraces within a single life a plurality of members and functions.... All souls are parts or functions of the eternal life of God, who is above all, and through all, and in all, and in whom we live, and move, and have our being." We would draw the conclusion that, as in the body and soul of man, both as an individual and as a race, there is diversity in unity, so in the God in whose image man is made, there is diversity in unity, and a triple consciousness and will are consistent with, and even find their perfection in, a single essence.

By the personality of God we mean more than we mean when we speak of the personality of the Son and the personality of the Spirit. The personality of the Godhead is distinct and separate from all others, and is, in this respect, like that of man. Hence Shedd, Dogm. Theol., 1:194, says "it is preferable to speak of the personality of the essence rather than of the person of the essence; because the essence is not one person, but three persons.... The divine essence cannot be at once three persons and one person, if 'person' is employed in one signification; but it can be at once three persons and one personal Being." While we speak of the one God as having a personality in which there are three persons, we would not call this personality a superpersonality, if this latter term is intended to intimate that God's personality is less than the personality of man. The personality of the Godhead is inclusive rather than exclusive.

With this qualification we may assent to the words of D'Arcy, Idealism and Theology, 93, 94, 218, 230, 236, 254—"The innermost truth of things, God, must be conceived as personal; but the ultimate Unity, which is his, must be believed to be superpersonal. It is a unity of persons, not a personal unity. For us personality is the ultimate form of unity. It is not so in him. For in him all persons live and move and have their being.... God is personal and also superpersonal. In him there is a transcendent unity that can embrace a personal multiplicity.... There is in God an ultimate superpersonal unity in which all persons are one—[all human persons and the three divine persons].... Substance is more real than quality, and subject is more real than substance. The most real of all is the concrete totality, the all-inclusive Universal.... What human love strives to accomplish—the overcoming of the opposition of person to person—is perfectly attained in the divine Unity.... The presupposition on which philosophy is driven back—[that persons have an underlying ground of unity] is identical with that which underlies Christian theology." See Pfleiderer and Lotze on personality, in this Compendium, p. 104.

(c) This oneness of essence explains the fact that, while Father, Son, and Holy Spirit, as respects their personality, are distinct subsistences, there is an intercommunion of persons and an immanence of one divine person in another which permits the peculiar work of one to be ascribed, with a single limitation, to either of the others, and the manifestation of one to be recognized in the manifestation of another. The limitation is simply this, that although the Son was sent by the Father, and the Spirit by the Father and the Son, it cannot be said vice versa that the Father is sent either by the Son, or by the Spirit. The Scripture representations of this intercommunion prevent us from conceiving of the distinctions called Father, Son, and Holy Spirit as involving separation between them.

Dorner adds that "in one is each of the others." This is true with the limitation mentioned in the text above. Whatever Christ does, God the Father can be said to do; for God acts only in and through Christ the Revealer. Whatever the Holy Spirit does, Christ can be said to do; for the Holy Spirit is the Spirit of Christ. The Spirit is the omnipresent Jesus, and Bengel's dictum is true: "Ubi Spiritus, ibi Christus." Passages illustrating this intercommunion are the following: Gen. 1:1—"God created"; cf. Heb. 1:2—"through whom [the Son] also he made the worlds"; John 5:17, 19—"My Father worketh even until now, and I work.... The Son can do nothing of himself, but what he seeth the Father doing; for what things soever he doeth, these the Son also doeth in like manner"; 14:9—"he that hath seen me hath seen the Father"; 11—"I am in the Father and the Father in me"; 18—"I will not leave you desolate: I come unto you" (by the Holy Spirit); 15:26—"when the Comforter is come, whom I will send unto you from the Father, even the Spirit of truth"; 17:21—"that they may all be one; even as thou, Father, art in me, and I in thee"; 2 Cor. 5:19—"God was in Christ reconciling"; Titus 2:10—"God our Savior"; Heb. 12:23—"God the Judge of all"; cf. John 5:22—"neither doth the father judge any man, but he hath given all judgment unto the Son"; Acts 17:31—"judge the world in righteousness by the man whom he hath ordained."

It is this intercommunion, together with the order of personality and operation to be mentioned hereafter, which explains the occasional use of the term "Father" for the whole Godhead; as in Eph. 4:6—"one God and Father of all, who is over all through all [in Christ], and in you all" [by the Spirit]. This intercommunion also explains the designation of Christ as "the Spirit," and of the Spirit as "the Spirit of Christ," as in 1 Cor. 15:45—"the last Adam became a life-giving Spirit"; 2 Cor. 3:17—"Now the Lord is the Spirit"; Gal. 4:6—"sent forth the Spirit of his Son"; Phil. 1:19—"supply of the Spirit of Jesus Christ" (see Alford and Lange on 2 Cor. 3:17, 18). So the Lamb, in Rev. 5:6, has "seven horns and seven eyes, which are the seven Spirits of God, sent forth into all the earth" = the Holy Spirit, with his manifold powers, is the Spirit of the omnipotent, omniscient, and omnipresent Christ. Theologians have designated this intercommunion by the terms περιχώρησις, circumincessio, intercommunicatio, circulatio, inexistentia. The word οὐσία was used to denote essence, substance, nature, being; and the words πρόσωπον and ὑπόστασις for person, distinction, mode of subsistence. On the changing uses of the words πρόσωπον and ὑπόστασις see Dorner, Glaubenslehre, 2:321, note 2. On the meaning of the word 'person' in connection with the Trinity, see John Howe, Calm Discourse of the Trinity; Jonathan Edwards, Observations on the Trinity; Shedd, Dogm. Theol., 1:194, 267-275, 299, 300.

The Holy Spirit is Christ's alter ego, or other self. When Jesus went away, it was an exchange of his presence for his omnipresence; an exchange of limited for unlimited power; an exchange of companionship for indwelling. Since Christ comes to men in the Holy Spirit, he speaks through the apostles as authoritatively as if his own lips uttered the words. Each believer, in having the Holy Spirit, has the whole Christ for his own; see A. J. Gordon, Ministry of the Spirit. Gore, Incarnation, 218—"The persons of the Holy Trinity are not separable individuals. Each involves the others; the coming of each is the coming of the others. Thus the coming of the Spirit must have involved the coming of the Son. But the specialty of the Pentecostal gift appears to be the coming of the Holy Spirit out of the uplifted and glorified manhood of the incarnate Son. The Spirit is the life-giver, but the life with which he works in the church is the life of the Incarnate, the life of Jesus."

Moberly, Atonement and Personality, 85—"For centuries upon centuries, the essential unity of God had been burnt and branded in upon the consciousness of Israel. It had to be completely established first, as a basal element of thought, indispensable, unalterable, before there could begin the disclosure to man of the reality of the eternal relations within the one indivisible being of God. And when the disclosure came, it came not as modifying, but as further interpreting and illumining, that unity which it absolutely presupposed." E. G. Robinson, Christian Theology, 238—"There is extreme difficulty in giving any statement of a triunity that shall not verge upon tritheism on the one hand, or upon mere modalism on the other. It was very natural that Calvin should be charged with Sabellianism, and John Howe with tritheism."

V. The Three Persons, Father, Son, and Holy Spirit, are equal
In explanation, notice that:

1. These titles belong to the Persons
(a) The Father is not God as such; for God is not only Father, but also Son and Holy Spirit. The term "Father" designates that hypostatical distinction in the divine nature in virtue of which God is related to the Son, and through the Son and the Spirit to the church and the world. As author of the believer's spiritual as well as natural life, God is doubly his Father; but this relation which God sustains to creatures is not the ground of the title. God is Father primarily in virtue of the relation which he sustains to the eternal Son; only as we are spiritually united to Jesus Christ do we become children of God.

(b) The Son is not God as such; for God is not only Son, but also Father and Holy Spirit. "The Son" designates that distinction in virtue of which God is related to the Father, is sent by the Father to redeem the world, and with the Father sends the Holy Spirit.

(c) The Holy Spirit is not God as such; for God is not only Holy Spirit, but also Father and Son. "The Holy Spirit" designates that distinction in virtue of which God is related to the Father and the Son, and is sent by them to accomplish the work of renewing the ungodly and of sanctifying the church.

Neither of these names designates the Monad as such. Each designates rather that personal distinction which forms the eternal basis and ground for a particular self-revelation. In the sense of being the Author and Provider of men's natural life, God is the Father of all. But even this natural sonship is mediated by Jesus Christ; see 1 Cor. 8:6—"one Lord, Jesus Christ through whom are all things, and we through him." The phrase "Our Father," however, can be used with the highest truth only by the regenerate, who have been newly born of God by being united to Christ through the power of the Holy Spirit. See Gal. 3:26—"For ye are all sons of God, through faith, in Jesus Christ"; 4:4-6—"God sent forth his Son ... that we might receive the adoption of sons ... sent forth the Spirit of his Son into our hearts, crying, Abba, Father"; Eph. 1:5—"foreordained as unto adoption as sons through Jesus Christ." God's love for Christ is the measure of his love for those who are one with Christ. Human nature in Christ is lifted up into the life and communion of the eternal Trinity. Shedd, Dogm. Theol., 1:306-310.

Human fatherhood is a reflection of the divine, not, vice versa, the divine a reflection of the human; cf. Eph. 3:14, 15—"the Father, from whom every fatherhood πατριά in heaven and on earth is named." Chadwick, Unitarianism, 77-83, makes the name "Father" only a symbol for the great Cause of organic evolution, the Author of all being. But we may reply with Stearns, Evidence of Christian Experience, 177—"to know God outside of the sphere of redemption is not to know him in the deeper meaning of the term 'Father'. It is only through the Son that we know the Father: Mat. 11:27—'Neither doth any know the Father, save the Son, and he to whomsoever the Son willeth to reveal him.'"

Whiton, Gloria Patri, 38—"The Unseen can be known only by the seen which comes forth from it. The all-generating or Paternal Life which is hidden from us can be known only by the generated or

Filial Life in which it reveals itself. The goodness and righteousness which inhabits eternity can be known only by the goodness and righteousness which issues from it in the successive births of time. God above the world is made known only by God in the world. God transcendent, the Father, is revealed by God immanent, the Son." Faber: "O marvellous, O worshipful! No song or sound is heard, But everywhere and every hour, In love, in wisdom and in power, the Father speaks his dear eternal Word." We may interpret this as meaning that self-expression is a necessity of nature to an infinite Mind. The Word is therefore eternal. Christ is the mirror from which are flashed upon us the rays of the hidden Luminary. So Principal Fairbairn says: "Theology must be on its historical side Christocentric, but on its doctrinal side Theocentric."

Salmond, Expositor's Greek Testament, on Eph. 1:5—"By 'adoption' Paul does not mean the bestowal of the full privileges of the family on those who are sons by nature, but the acceptance into the family of those who are not sons originally and by right in the relation proper of those who are sons by birth. Hence υἱοθεσία is never affirmed of Christ, for he alone is Son of God by nature. So Paul regards our sonship, not as lying in the natural relation in which men stand to God as his children, but as implying a new relation of grace, founded on a covenant relation of God and on the work of Christ (Gal. 4:5 sq.)."

2. Qualified sense of these titles

Like the word "person", the names Father, Son, and Holy Spirit are not to be confined within the precise limitations of meaning which would be required if they were applied to men.

(a) The Scriptures enlarge our conceptions of Christ's Sonship by giving to him in his preëxistent state the names of the Logos, the Image, and the Effulgence of God.—The term "Logos" combines in itself the two ideas of thought and word, of reason and expression. While the Logos as divine thought or reason is one with God, the Logos as divine word or expression is distinguishable from God. Words are the means by which personal beings express or reveal themselves. Since Jesus Christ was "the Word" before there were any creatures to whom revelations could be made, it would seem to be only a necessary inference from this title that in Christ God must be from eternity expressed or revealed to himself; in other words, that the Logos is the principle of truth, or self-consciousness, in God.—The term "Image" suggests the ideas of copy or counterpart. Man is the image of God only relatively and derivatively. Christ is the Image of God absolutely and archetypally. As the perfect representation of the Father's perfections, the Son would seem to be the object and principle of love in the Godhead.—The term "Effulgence," finally, is an allusion to the sun and its radiance. As the effulgence of the sun manifests the sun's nature, which otherwise would be unrevealed, yet is inseparable from the sun and ever one with it, so Christ reveals God, but is eternally one with God. Here is a principle of movement, of will, which seems to connect itself with the holiness, or self-asserting purity, of the divine nature.

Smyth, Introd. to Edwards' Observations on the Trinity: "The ontological relations of the persons of the Trinity are not a mere blank to human thought." John 1:1—"In the beginning was the Word"—means more than "in the beginning was the x, or the zero." Godet indeed says that Logos = "reason" only in philosophical writings, but never in the Scriptures. He calls this a Hegelian notion. But both Plato and Philo had made this signification a common one. On λόγος as = reason + speech, see Lightfoot on Colossians, 143, 144. Meyer interprets it as "personal subsistence, the self-revelation of the divine essence, before all time immanent in God." Neander, Planting and Training, 369—Logos = "the eternal Revealer of the divine essence." Bushnell: "Mirror of creative imagination"; "form of God."

Word = 1. Expression; 2. Definite expression; 3. Ordered expression; 4. Complete expression. We make thought definite by putting it into language. So God's wealth of ideas is in the Word formed into an ordered Kingdom, a true Cosmos; see Mason, Faith of the Gospel, 76. Max Müller: "A word is simply a spoken thought made audible as sound. Take away from a word the sound, and what is left is simply the thought of it." Whiton, Gloria Patri, 72, 73—"The Greek saw in the word the abiding thought behind the passing form. The Word was God and yet finite—finite only as to form, infinite as to what the form suggests or expresses. By Word some form must be meant, and any form is finite. The Word is the form taken by the infinite Intelligence which transcends all forms." We regard this identification of the Word with the finite manifestation of the Word as contradicted by John 1:1, where the Word is represented as being with God before creation, and by Phil. 2:6, where the Word is represented as existing in the form of God before his self-limitation in human nature. Scripture requires us to believe in an objectification of God to himself in the person of the Word prior to any finite manifestation of God to men. Christ existed as the Word, and the Word was with God, before the Word was made flesh and before the world came into being; in other words, the Logos was the eternal principle of truth or self-consciousness in the nature of God.

Passages representing Christ as the Image of God are Col. 1:15—"who is the image of the invisible God"; 2 Cor. 4:4—"Christ, who is the image of God" (εἰκών); Heb. 1:3—"the very image of his substance" (χαρακτὴρ τῆς ὑποστάσεως αὐτοῦ); here χαρακτήρ means "impress," "counterpart." Christ is the perfect image of God, as men are not. He therefore has consciousness and will. He possesses all the attributes and powers of God. The word "Image" suggests the perfect equality with God which the title "Son" might at first seem to deny. The living Image of God which is equal to himself and is the object of his infinite love can be nothing less than personal. As the bachelor can never satisfy his longing for companionship by lining his room with mirrors which furnish only a lifeless reflection of himself, so God requires for his love a personal as well as an infinite object. The Image is not precisely the repetition of the original. The stamp from the seal is not precisely the reproduction of the seal. The letters on the seal run backwards and can be easily read only when the impression is before us. So Christ is the only interpretation and revelation of the hidden Godhead. As only in love do we come to know the depths of our own being, so it is only in the Son that "God is love" (1 John 4:8).

Christ is spoken of as the Effulgence of God in Heb. 1:3—"who being the effulgence of his glory" (ἀπαύγασμα τῆς δόξης); cf. 2 Cor. 4:6—"shined in our hearts, to give the light of the knowledge of the glory of God in the face of Jesus Christ." Notice that the radiance of the sun is as old as the sun itself, and without it the sun would not be sun. So Christ is coëqual and coëternal with the Father. Ps. 84:11—"Jehovah God is a sun." But we cannot see the sun except by the sunlight. Christ is the sunlight which streams forth from the Sun and which makes the Sun visible. If there be an eternal Sun, there must be also an eternal Sunlight, and Christ must be eternal. Westcott on Hebrews 1:3—"The use of the absolute timeless term ὤν, 'being', guards against the thought that the Lord's sonship was by adoption, and not by nature. ἀπαύγασμα does not express personality, and χαρακτήρ does not express coëssentiality. The two words are related exactly as ὁμοούσιος and μονογενής, and like those must be combined to give the fulness of the truth. The truth expressed thus antithetically holds good absolutely.... In Christ the essence of God is made distinct; in Christ the revelation of God's character is seen." On Edwards's view of the Trinity, together with his quotations from Ramsey's Philosophical Principles, from which he seems to have derived important suggestions, see Allen, Jonathan Edwards, 338-376; G. P. Fisher, Edwards's Essay on the Trinity, 110-116.

(b) The names thus given to the second person of the Trinity, if they have any significance, bring him before our minds in the general aspect of Revealer, and suggest a relation of the doctrine of the Trinity to God's immanent attributes of truth, love, and holiness. The prepositions used to describe the internal relations of the second person to the first are not prepositions of rest, but prepositions of direction and movement. The Trinity, as the organism of Deity, secures a life-movement of the Godhead, a process in which God evermore objectifies himself and in the Son gives forth of his fulness. Christ represents the centrifugal action of the deity. But there must be centripetal action also. In the Holy Spirit the movement is completed, and the divine activity and thought returns into itself. True religion, in reuniting us to God, reproduces in us, in our limited measure, this eternal process of the divine mind. Christian experience witnesses that God in himself is unknown; Christ is the organ of external revelation; the Holy Spirit is the organ of internal revelation—only he can give us an inward apprehension or realization of the truth. It is "through the eternal Spirit" that Christ "offered himself without blemish unto God," and it is only through the Holy Spirit that the church has access to the Father, or fallen creatures can return to God.

Here we see that God is Life, self-sufficient Life, Infinite Life, of which the life of the universe is but a faint reflection, a rill from the fountain, a drop from the ocean. Since Christ is the only Revealer, the only outgoing principle in the Godhead, it is he in whom the whole creation comes to be and holds together. He is the Life of nature: all natural beauty and grandeur, all forces molecular and molar, all laws of gravitation and evolution, are the work and manifestation of the omnipresent Christ. He is the Life of humanity: the intellectual and moral impulses of man, so far as they are normal and uplifting, are due to Christ; he is the principle of progress and improvement in history. He is the Life of the church: the one and only Redeemer and spiritual Head of the race is also its Teacher and Lord.

All objective revelation of God is the work of Christ. But all subjective manifestation of God is the work of the Holy Spirit. As Christ is the principle of outgoing, so the Holy Spirit is the principle of return to God. God would take up finite creatures into himself, would breath into them his breath, would teach them to launch their little boats upon the infinite current of his life. Our electric cars can go up hill at great speed so long as they grip the cable. Faith is the grip which connects us with the moving energy of God. "The universe is homeward bound," because the Holy Spirit is ever turning objective revelation into subjective revelation, and is leading men consciously or unconsciously to appropriate the thought and love and purpose of Him in whom all things find their object and end; "for of him and through him, and unto him, are all things" (Rom. 11:36),—here there is allusion to the Father as the source, the Son as the medium, and the Spirit as the perfecting and completing agent, in God's operations. But all these external processes are only signs and finite reflections of a life-process internal to the nature of God.

Meyer on John 1:1—"the Word was with God": "πρὸς τὸν θεόν does not = παρὰ τῷ θεῷ, but expresses the existence of the Logos in God in respect of intercourse. The moral essence of this essential fellowship is love, which excludes any merely modalistic conception." Marcus Dods, Expositor's Greek Testament, in loco: "This preposition implies intercourse and therefore separate personality."

Mason, Faith of the Gospel, 62—"And the Word was toward God" = his face is not outwards, as if he were merely revealing, or waiting to reveal, God to the creation. His face is turned inwards. His whole Person is directed toward God, motion corresponding to motion, thought to thought.... In him God stands revealed to himself. Contrast the attitude of fallen Adam, with his face averted from God. Godet, on John 1:1—"Πρὸς τὸν θεόν intimates not only personality but movement.... The tendency of the Logos ad extra rests upon an anterior and essential relation ad intra. To reveal God, one must know him; to project him outwardly, one must have plunged into his bosom." Compare John 1:18—"the only begotten Son, who is in the bosom of the Father" (R. V.) where we find, not ἐν τῷ κόλπῳ, but εἰς τὸν κόλπον. As ἦν εἰς τὴν πόλιν means "went into the city and was there," so the use of these prepositions indicates in the Godhead movement as well as rest. Dorner, System of Doctrine, 3:193, translates πρός by "hingewandt zu," or "turned toward." The preposition would then imply that the Revealer, who existed in the beginning, was ever over against God, in the life-process of the Trinity, as the perfect objectification of himself. "Das Aussichselbstsein kraft des Durchsichselbstsein mit dem Fürsichselbstsein zusammenschliesst." Dorner speaks of "das Aussensichoderineinemandernsein; Sichgeltendmachen des Ausgeschlossenen; Sichnichtsogesetzthaben; Stehenbleibenwollen."

There is in all human intelligence a threefoldness which points toward a trinitarian life in God. We can distinguish a Wissen, a Bewusstsein, a Selbstbewusstein. In complete self-consciousness there are the three elements: 1. We are ourselves; 2. We form a picture of ourselves; 3. We recognize this picture as the picture of ourselves. The little child speaks of himself in the third person: "Baby did it." The objective comes before the subject; "me" comes first, and "I" is a later development; "himself" still holds its place, rather than "heself." But this duality belongs only to undeveloped intelligence; it is characteristic of the animal creation; we revert to it in our dreams; the insane are permanent victims of it; and since sin is moral insanity, the sinner has no hope until, like the prodigal, he "comes to himself" (Luke 15:17). The insane person is mente alienatus, and we call physicians for the insane by the name of alienists. Mere duality gives us only the notion of separation. Perfect self-consciousness whether in man or in God requires a third unifying element. And in God mediation between the "I" and the "Thou" must be the work of a Person also, and the Person who mediates between the two must be in all respects the equal of either, or he could not adequately interpret the one to the other; see Mason, Faith of the Gospel, 57-59.

Shedd, Dogm. Theol., 1:179-189, 276-283—"It is one of the effects of conviction by the Holy Spirit to convert consciousness into self-consciousness.... Conviction of sin is the consciousness of self as the guilty author of sin. Self-consciousness is trinal, while mere consciousness is dual.... One and the same human spirit subsists in two modes or distinctions—subject and object ... The three hypostatical consciousnesses in their combination and unity constitute the one consciousness of God ... as the three persons make one essence."

Dorner considers the internal relations of the Trinity (System, 1:412 sq.) in three aspects: 1. Physical. God is causa sui. But effect that equals cause must itself be causative. Here would be duality, were it not for a third principle of unity. Trinitas dualitatem ad unitatem reducit. 2. Logical. Self-consciousness sets self over against self. Yet the thinker must not regard self as one of many, and call himself "he," as children do; for the thinker would then be, not self-conscious, but mente alienatus, "beside himself." He therefore "comes to himself" in a third, as the brute cannot. 3. Ethical. God—self-willing right. But right based on arbitrary will is not right. Right based on passive nature is not right either. Right as being—Father. Right as willing—Son. Without the latter principle of freedom, we have a dead ethic, a dead God, an enthroned necessity. The unity of necessity and freedom is found by God, as by the Christian, in the Holy Spirit. The Father—I; the Son—Me; the Spirit the unity of the two; see C. C. Everett, Essays, Theological and Literary, 32. There must be not only Sun and Sunlight, but an Eye to behold the Light. William James, in his Psychology, distinguishes the Me, the self as known, from the I, the self as knower.

But we need still further to distinguish a third principle, a subject-object, from both subject and object. The subject cannot recognize the object as one with itself except through a unifying principle which can be distinguished from both. We may therefore regard the Holy Spirit as the principle of self-consciousness in man as well as in God. As there was a natural union of Christ with humanity prior to his redeeming work, so there is a natural union of the Holy Spirit with all men prior to his regenerating work: Job 32:18—"there is a spirit in man, And the breath of the Almighty giveth them understanding." Kuyper, Work of the Holy Spirit, teaches that the Holy Spirit constitutes the principle of life in all living things, and animates all rational beings, as well as regenerates and sanctifies the elect of God. Matheson, Voices of the Spirit, 75, remarks on Job 34:14, 15—"If he gather unto himself his Spirit and his breath; all flesh shall perish together"—that the Spirit is not only necessary to man's salvation, but also to keep up even man's natural life.

Ebrard, Dogmatik, 1:172, speaks of the Son as the centrifugal, while the Holy Spirit is the centripetal movement of the Godhead. God apart from Christ is unrevealed (John 1:18—"No man hath seen God at any time"); Christ is the organ of external revelation (18—"the only begotten Son, who is in the bosom of the Father, he hath declared him"); the Holy Spirit is the organ of internal revelation (1 Cor. 2:10—"unto us Christ revealed them through the Spirit"). That the Holy Spirit is the principle of all movement towards God appears from Heb. 9:14—Christ "through the eternal Spirit offered himself without blemish unto God"; Eph. 2:28—"access in one Spirit unto the Father"; Rom. 8:26—"the Spirit also helpeth our infirmity ... the Spirit himself maketh intercession for us"; John 4:24—"God is a Spirit: and they that worship him must worship in spirit"; 16:8-11—"convict the world in respect of sin, and of righteousness, and of judgment." See Twesten, Dogmatik, on the Trinity; also Thomasius, Christi Person und Werk, 1:111. Mason, Faith of the Gospel, 68—"It is the joy of the Son to receive, his gladness to welcome most those wishes of the Father which will cost most to himself. The Spirit also has his joy in making known,—in perfecting fellowship and keeping the eternal love alive by that incessant sounding of the deeps which makes the heart of the Father known to the Son, and the heart of the Son known to the Father." We may add that the Holy Spirit is the organ of internal revelation even to the Father and to the Son.

(c) In the light of what has been said, we may understand somewhat more fully the characteristic differences between the work of Christ and that of the Holy Spirit. We may sum them up in the four statements that, first, all outgoing seems to be the work of Christ, all return to God the work of the Spirit; secondly, Christ is the organ of external revelation, the Holy Spirit the organ of internal revelation; thirdly, Christ is our advocate in heaven, the Holy Spirit is our advocate in the soul; fourthly, in the work of Christ we are passive, in the work of the Spirit we are active. Of the work of Christ we shall treat more fully hereafter, in speaking of his Offices as Prophet, Priest, and King. The work of the Holy Spirit will be treated when we come to speak of the Application of Redemption in Regeneration and Sanctification. Here it is sufficient to say that the Holy Spirit is represented in the Scriptures as the author of life—in creation, in the conception of Christ, in regeneration, in resurrection; and as the giver of light—in the inspiration of Scripture writers, in the conviction of sinners, in the illumination and sanctification of Christians.

Gen. 1:2—"The Spirit of God was brooding"; Luke 1:35—to Mary: "The Holy Spirit shall come upon thee", John 3:8—"born of the Spirit"; Ps. 37:9, 14—"Come from the four winds, O breath.... I will put my Spirit in you, and ye shall live"; Rom. 8:11—"give life also to your mortal bodies through his Spirit." 1 John 2:1—"an advocate (παράκλητον) with the Father, Jesus Christ the righteous"; John 14:16, 17—"another Comforter (παράκλητον), that he may be with you for ever, even the Spirit of truth"; Rom. 8:26—"the Spirit himself maketh intercession for us." 2 Pet. 1:21—"men spake from God, being moved by the Holy Spirit"; John 16:8—"convict the world in respect of sin"; 13—"when he, the Spirit of truth, is come, he shall guide you into all the truth"; Rom. 8:14—"as many as are led by the Spirit of God, these are sons of God."

McCosh: The works of the Spirit are Conviction, Conversion, Sanctification, Comfort. Donovan: The Spirit is the Spirit of conviction, enlightenment, quickening, in the sinner; and of revelation, remembrance, witness, sanctification, consolation, to the saint. The Spirit enlightens the sinner, as the flash of lightning lights the traveler stumbling on the edge of a precipice at night; enlightens the Christian, as the rising sun reveals a landscape which was all there before, but which was hidden from sight until the great luminary made it visible. "The morning light did not create The lovely prospect it revealed; It only showed the real state Of what the darkness had concealed." Christ's advocacy before the throne is like that of legal counsel pleading in our stead; the Holy Spirit's advocacy in the heart is like the mother's teaching her child to pray for himself.

J. W. A. Stewart: "Without the work of the Holy Spirit redemption would have been impossible, as impossible as that fuel should warm without being lighted, or that bread should nourish without being eaten. Christ is God entering into human history, but without the Spirit Christianity would be only history. The Holy Spirit is God entering into human hearts. The Holy Spirit turns creed into life. Christ is the physician who leaves the remedy and then departs. The Holy Spirit is the nurse who applies and administers the remedy, and who remains with the patient until the cure is completed." Matheson, Voices of the Spirit, 78—"It is in vain that the mirror exists in the room, if it is lying on its face; the sunbeams cannot reach it till its face is upturned to them. Heaven lies about thee not only in thine infancy but at all times. But it is not enough that a place is prepared for thee; thou must be prepared for the place. It is not enough that thy light has come; thou thyself must arise and shine. No outward shining can reveal, unless thou art thyself a reflector of its glory. The Spirit must set thee on thy feet, that thou mayest hear him that speaks to thee (Ez. 2:2)."

The Holy Spirit reveals not himself but Christ. John 16:14—"He shall glorify me: for he shall take of mine, and shall declare it unto you." So should the servants of the Spirit hide themselves while they make known Christ. E. H. Johnson, The Holy Spirit, 40—"Some years ago a large steam engine all of glass was exhibited about the country. When it was at work one would see the piston and the valves go; but no one could see what made them go. When steam is hot enough to be a continuous elastic vapor, it is invisible." So we perceive the presence of the Holy Spirit, not by visions or voices, but by the effect he produces within us in the shape of new knowledge, new love, and new energy of our own powers.

Denney, Studies in Theology, 161—"No man can bear witness to Christ and to himself at the same time. Esprit is fatal to unction; no man can give the impression that he himself is clever and also that Christ is mighty to save. The power of the Holy Spirit is felt only when the witness is unconscious of self, and when others remain unconscious of him." Moule, Veni Creator, 8—"The Holy Spirit, as Tertullian says, is the vicar of Christ. The night before the Cross, the Holy Spirit was present to the mind of Christ as a person."

Gore, in Lux Mundi, 318—"It was a point in the charge against Origen that his language seemed to involve an exclusion of the Holy Spirit from nature, and a limitation of his activity to the church. The whole of life is certainly his. And yet, because his special attribute is holiness, it is in rational natures, which alone are capable of holiness, that he exerts his special influence. A special inbreathing of the divine Spirit gave to man his proper being." See Gen. 2:7—"Jehovah God ... breathed into his nostrils the breath of life; and man became a living soul"; John 3:8—"The Spirit breatheth where it will ... so is every one that is born of the Spirit." E. H. Johnson, on The Offices of the Holy Spirit, in Bib. Sac., July, 1892:381-382—"Why is he specially called the Holy, when Father and Son are also holy, unless because he produces holiness, i. e., makes the holiness of God to be ours individually? Christ is the principle of collectivism, the Holy Spirit the principle of individualism. The Holy Spirit shows man the Christ in him. God above all = Father; God through all = Son; God in all = Holy Spirit (Eph. 4:6)."

The doctrine of the Holy Spirit has never yet been scientifically unfolded. No treatise on it has appeared comparable to Julius Müller's Doctrine of Sin, or to I. A. Dorner's History of the Doctrine of the Person of Christ. The progress of doctrine in the past has been marked by successive stages. Athanasius treated of the Trinity; Augustine of sin; Anselm of the atonement; Luther of justification; Wesley of regeneration; and each of these unfoldings of doctrine has been accompanied by religious awakening. We still wait for a complete discussion of the doctrine of the Holy Spirit, and believe that widespread revivals will follow the recognition of the omnipotent Agent in revivals. On the relations of the Holy Spirit to Christ, see Owen, in Works, 3:152-159; on the Holy Spirit's nature and work, see works by Faber, Smeaton, Tophel, G. Campbell Morgan, J. D. Robertson, Biederwolf; also C. E. Smith, The Baptism of Fire; J. D. Thompson, The Holy Comforter; Bushnell, Forgiveness and Law, last chapter; Bp. Andrews, Works, 3:107-400; James S. Candlish, Work of the Holy Spirit; Redford, Vox Dei; Andrew Murray, The Spirit of Christ; A. J. Gordon, Ministry of the Spirit; Kuyper, Work of the Holy Spirit; J. E. Cumming, Through the Eternal Spirit; Lechler, Lehre vom Heiligen Geiste; Arthur, Tongue of Fire; A. H. Strong, Philosophy and Religion, 250-258, and Christ in Creation, 297-313.

3. Generation and procession consistent with equality

That the Sonship of Christ is eternal, is intimated in Psalm 2:7. "This day have I begotten thee" is most naturally interpreted as the declaration of an eternal fact in the divine nature. Neither the incarnation, the baptism, the transfiguration, nor the resurrection marks the beginning of Christ's Sonship, or constitutes him Son of God. These are but recognitions or manifestations of a preëxisting Sonship, inseparable from his Godhood. He is "born before every creature" (while yet no created thing existed—see Meyer on Col. 1:15) and "by the resurrection of the dead" is not made to be, but only "declared to be," "according to the Spirit of holiness" (= according to his divine nature) "the Son of God with power" (see Philippi and Alford on Rom. 1:3, 4). This Sonship is unique—not predicable of, or shared with, any creature. The Scriptures intimate, not only an eternal generation of the Son, but an eternal procession of the Spirit.

Psalm 2:7—"I will tell of the decree: Jehovah said unto me, Thou art my Son; This day I have begotten thee" see Alexander, Com. in loco; also Com. on Acts 13:33—"'To-day' refers to the date of the decree itself; but this, as a divine act, was eternal,—and so must be the Sonship which it affirms." Philo says that "to-day" with God means "forever." This begetting of which the Psalm speaks is not the resurrection, for while Paul in Acts 13:33 refers to this Psalm to establish the fact of Jesus' Sonship, he refers in Acts 13:34, 35 to another Psalm, the sixteenth, to establish the fact that this Son of God was to rise from the dead. Christ is shown to be Son of God by his incarnation (Heb. 1:5, 6—"when he again bringeth in the firstborn into the world he saith, And let all the angels of God worship him"), his baptism (Mat. 3:17—"This is my beloved Son"), his transfiguration (Mat. 17:5—"This is my beloved Son"), his resurrection (Acts 13:34, 35—"as concerning that he raised him up from the dead ... he saith also in another psalm, Thou wilt not give thy Holy One to see corruption"). Col. 1:15—"the firstborn of all creation"—πρωτότοκος πάσης κτίσεως = "begotten first before all creation" (Julius Müller, Proof-texts, 14); or "first-born before every creature, i. e., begotten, and that antecedently to everything that was created" (Ellicott, Com. in loco). "Herein" (says Luthardt, Compend. Dogmatik, 81, on Col. 1:15) "is indicated an antemundane origin from God—a relation internal to the divine nature." Lightfoot, on Col. 1:15, says that in Rabbi Bechai God is called the "primogenitus mundi."

On Rom. 1:4 (ὁρισθέντος = "manifested to be the mighty Son of God") see Lange's Com., notes by Schaff on pages 56 and 61. Bruce, Apologetics, 404—"The resurrection was the actual introduction of Christ into the full possession of divine Sonship so far as thereto belonged, not only the inner of a holy spiritual essence, but also the outer of an existence in power and heavenly glory." Allen, Jonathan Edwards, 353, 354—"Calvin waves aside eternal generation as an 'absurd fiction.' But to maintain the deity of Christ merely on the ground that it is essential to his making an adequate atonement for sin, is to involve the rejection of his deity if ever the doctrine of atonement becomes obnoxious.... Such was the process by which, in the mind of the last century, the doctrine of the Trinity was undermined. Not to ground the distinctions of the divine essence by some immanent eternal necessity was to make easy the denial of what has been called the ontological Trinity, and then the rejection of the economical Trinity was not difficult or far away."

If Westcott and Hort's reading ὁ μονογενὴς Θεός, "the only begotten God," in John 1:18, is correct, we have a new proof of Christ's eternal Sonship. Meyer explains ἑαυτοῦ in Rom. 8:3—"God, sending his own Son," as an allusion to the metaphysical Sonship. That this Sonship is unique, is plain from John 1:14, 18—"the only begotten from the Father ... the only begotten Son who is in the bosom of the father"; Rom. 8:32—"his own Son"; Gal. 4:4—"sent forth his Son"; cf. Prov. 8:22-31—"When he marked out the foundations of the earth; Then I was by him as a master workman"; 30:4—"Who hath established all the ends of the earth? What is his name, and what is his son's name, if thou knowest?" The eternal procession of the Spirit seems to be implied in John 15:26—"the Spirit of truth which proceedeth from the Father"—see Westcott, Bib. Com., in loco; Heb. 9:14—"the eternal Spirit." Westcott here says that παρά (not ἐξ) shows that the reference is to the temporal mission of the Holy Spirit, not to the eternal procession. At the same time he maintains that the temporal corresponds to the eternal.

The Scripture terms "generation" and "procession," as applied to the Son and to the Holy Spirit, are but approximate expressions of the truth, and we are to correct by other declarations of Scripture any imperfect impressions which we might derive solely from them. We use these terms in a special sense, which we explicitly state and define as excluding all notion of inequality between the persons of the Trinity. The eternal generation of the Son to which we hold is

(a) Not creation, but the Father's communication of himself to the Son. Since the names, Father, Son, and Holy Spirit are not applicable to the divine essence, but are only applicable to its hypostatical distinctions, they imply no derivation of the essence of the Son from the essence of the Father.

The error of the Nicene Fathers was that of explaining Sonship as derivation of essence. The Father cannot impart his essence to the Son and yet retain it. The Father is fons trinitatis, not fons deitatis. See Shedd, Hist. Doct., 1:308-311, and Dogm. Theol., 1:287-299; per contra, see Bib. Sac., 41:698-760.

(b) Not a commencement of existence, but an eternal relation to the Father,—there never having been a time when the Son began to be, or when the Son did not exist as God with the Father.

If there had been an eternal sun, it is evident that there must have been an eternal sunlight also. Yet an eternal sunlight must have evermore proceeded from the sun. When Cyril was asked whether the Son existed before generation, he answered: "The generation of the Son did not precede his existence, but he always existed, and that by generation."

(c) Not an act of the Father's will, but an internal necessity of the divine nature,—so that the Son is no more dependent upon the Father than the Father is dependent upon the Son, and so that, if it be consistent with deity to be Father, it is equally consistent with deity to be Son.

The sun is as dependent upon the sunlight as the sunlight is upon the sun; for without sunlight the sun is no true sun. So God the Father is as dependent upon God the Son, as God the Son is dependent upon God the Father; for without Son the Father would be no true Father. To say that aseity belongs only to the Father is logically Arianism and Subordinationism proper, for it implies a subordination of the essence of the Son to the Father. Essential subordination would be inconsistent with equality. See Thomasius, Christi Person und Werk, 1:115. Palmer, Theol. Definitions, 66, 67, says that Father = independent life; Son begotten = independent life voluntarily brought under limitations; Spirit = necessary consequence of existence of the other two.... The words and actions whereby we design to affect others are "begotten." The atmosphere of unconscious influence is not "begotten," but "proceeding."

(d) Not a relation in any way analogous to physical derivation, but a life-movement of the divine nature, in virtue of which Father, Son, and Holy Spirit, while equal in essence and dignity, stand to each other in an order of personality, office, and operation, and in virtue of which the Father works through the Son, and the Father and the Son through the Spirit.

The subordination of the person of the Son to the person of the Father, or in other words an order of personality, office, and operation which permits the Father to be officially first, the Son second, and the Spirit third, is perfectly consistent with equality. Priority is not necessarily superiority. The possibility of an order, which yet involves no inequality, may be illustrated by the relation between man and woman. In office man is first and woman second, but woman's soul is worth as much as man's; see 1 Cor. 11:3—"the head of every man is Christ; and the head of the woman is the man: and the head of Christ is God." On John 14:28—"the Father is greater than I"—see Westcott, Bib. Com., in loco.

Edwards, Observations on the Trinity (edited by Smyth), 22—"In the Son the whole deity and glory of the Father is as it were repeated or duplicated. Everything in the Father is repeated or expressed again, and that fully, so that there is properly no inferiority." Edwards, Essay on the Trinity (edited by Fisher), 110-116—"The Father is the Deity subsisting in the prime, unoriginated, and most absolute manner, or the Deity in its direct existence. The Son is the Deity generated by God's understanding, or having an Idea of himself and subsisting in that Idea. The Holy Ghost is the Deity subsisting in act, or the divine essence flowing out and breathed forth in God's infinite love to and delight in himself. And I believe the whole divine essence does truly and distinctly subsist both in the divine Idea and in the divine Love, and each of them are properly distinct persons.... We find no other attributes of which it is said in Scripture that they are God, or that God is they, but λόγος and ἀγάπη, the Reason and the Love of God, Light not being different from Reason.... Understanding may be predicated of this Love.... It is not a blind Love.... The Father has Wisdom or Reason by the Son's being in him.... Understanding is in the Holy Spirit, because the Son is in him." Yet Dr. Edwards A. Park declared eternal generation to be "eternal nonsense," and is thought to have hid Edwards's unpublished Essay on the Trinity for many years because it taught this doctrine.

The New Testament calls Christ θεός, but not ὁ θεός. We frankly recognize an eternal subordination of Christ to the Father, but we maintain at the same time that this subordination is a subordination of order, office, and operation, not a subordination of essence. "Non de essentia dicitur, sed de ministeriis." E. G. Robinson: "An eternal generation is necessarily an eternal subordination and dependence. This seems to be fully admitted even by the most orthodox of the Anglican writers, such as Pearson and Hooker. Christ's subordination to the Father is merely official, not essential." Whiton, Gloria Patri, 42, 96—"The early Trinitarians by eternal Sonship meant, first, that it is of the very nature of Deity to issue forth into visible expression. Thus next, that this outward expression of God is not something other than God, but God himself, in a self-expression as divine as the hidden Deity. Thus they answered Philip's cry, 'show us the Father, and it sufficeth us' (John 14:8), and thus they affirmed Jesus' declaration, they secured Paul's faith that God has never left himself without witness. They meant, 'he that hath seen me hath seen the Father' (John 14:9).... The Father is the Life transcendent, the divine Source, 'above all'; the Son is the Life immanent, the divine Stream, 'through all'; the Holy Spirit is the Life individualized, 'in all' (Eph. 4:6). The Holy Spirit has been called 'the executive of the Godhead.' " Whiton is here speaking of the economic Trinity; but all this is even more true of the immanent Trinity. On the Eternal Sonship, see Weiss, Bib. Theol. N. T., 424, note; Treffrey, Eternal Sonship of our Lord; Princeton Essays, 1:30-56; Watson, Institutes, 1:530-577; Bib. Sac., 27:268. On the procession of the Spirit, see Shedd, Dogm. Theol., 1:300-304, and History of Doctrine, 1:387; Dick, Lectures on Theology, 1:347-350.

The same principles upon which we interpret the declaration of Christ's eternal Sonship apply to the procession of the Holy Spirit from the Father through the Son, and show this to be not inconsistent with the Spirit's equal dignity and glory.

We therefore only formulate truth which is concretely expressed in Scripture, and which is recognized by all ages of the church in hymns and prayers addressed to Father, Son, and Holy Spirit, when we assert that in the nature of the one God there are three eternal distinctions, which are best described as persons, and each of which is the proper and equal object of Christian worship.

We are also warranted in declaring that, in virtue of these personal distinctions or modes of subsistence, God exists in the relations, respectively, first, of Source, Origin, Authority, and in this relation is the Father; secondly, of Expression, Medium, Revelation, and in this relation is the Son; thirdly, of Apprehension, Accomplishment, Realization, and in this relation is the Holy Spirit.

John Owen, Works, 3:64-92—"The office of the Holy Spirit is that of concluding, completing, perfecting. To the Father we assign opera naturæ; to the Son, opera gratiæ procuratæ; to the Spirit, opera gratiæ applicatæ." All God's revelations are through the Son or the Spirit, and the latter includes the former. Kuyper, Work of the Holy Spirit, designates the three offices respectively as those of Causation, Construction, Consummation; the Father brings forth, the Son arranges, the Spirit perfects. Allen, Jonathan Edwards, 365-373—"God is Life, Light, Love. As the Fathers regarded Reason both in God and man as the personal, omnipresent second Person of the Trinity, so Jonathan Edwards regarded Love both in God and in man as the personal, omnipresent third Person of the Trinity. Hence the Father is never said to love the Spirit as he is said to love the Son—for this love is the Spirit. The Father and the Son are said to love men, but the Holy Spirit is never said to love them, for love is the Holy Spirit. But why could not Edwards also hold that the Logos or divine Reason also dwelt in humanity, so that manhood was constituted in Christ and shared with him in the consubstantial image of the Father? Outward nature reflects God's light and has Christ in it,—why not universal humanity?"

Moberly, Atonement and Personality, 136, 202, speaks of "1. God, the Eternal, the Infinite, in his infinity, as himself; 2. God, as self-expressed within the nature and faculties of man—body, soul, and spirit—the consummation and interpretation and revelation of what true manhood means and is, in its very truth, in its relation to God; 3. God, as Spirit of Beauty and Holiness, which are himself present in things created, animate and inanimate, and constituting in them their divine response to God; constituting above all in created personalities the full reality of their personal response. Or again: 1. What a man is invisibly in himself; 2. his outward material projection or expression as body; and 3. the response which that which he is through his bodily utterance or operation makes to him, as the true echo or expression of himself." Moberly seeks thus to find in man's nature an analogy to the inner processes of the divine.

VI. Inscrutable, yet not self-contradictory, this Doctrine furnishes the Key to all other Doctrines

1. The mode of this triune existence is inscrutable

It is inscrutable because there are no analogies to it in our finite experience. For this reason all attempts are vain adequately to represent it;

(a) From inanimate things—as the fountain, the stream, and the rivulet trickling from it (Athanasius); the cloud, the rain, and the rising mist (Boardman); color, shape, and size (F. W. Robertson); the actinic, luminiferous, and calorific principles in the ray of light (Solar Hieroglyphics, 34).

Luther: "When logic objects to this doctrine that it does not square with her rules, we must say; 'Mulier taceat in ecclesia.' " Luther called the Trinity a flower, in which might be distinguished its form, its fragrance, and its medicinal efficacy; see Dorner, Gesch. prot. Theol., 189. In Bap. Rev., July, 1880:434, Geer finds an illustration of the Trinity in infinite space with its three dimensions. For analogy of the cloud, rain, mist, see W. E. Boardman, Higher Christian Life. Solar Hieroglyphics, 34 (reviewed in New Englander, Oct. 1874:789)—"The Godhead is a tripersonal unity, and the light is a trinity. Being immaterial and homogeneous, and thus essentially one in its nature, the light includes a plurality of constituents, or in other words is essentially three in its constitution, its constituent principles being the actinic, the luminiferous, and the calorific; and in glorious manifestation the light is one, and is the created, constituted, and ordained emblem of the tripersonal God"—of whom it is said that "God is light, and in him is no darkness at all" (1 John 1:5). The actinic rays are in themselves invisible; only as the luminiferous manifest them, are they seen; only as the calorific accompany them, are they felt.

Joseph Cook: "Sunlight, rainbow, heat—one solar radiance; Father, Son, Holy Spirit, one God. As the rainbow shows what light is when unfolded, so Christ reveals the nature of God. As the rainbow is unraveled light, so Christ is unraveled God, and the Holy Spirit, figured by heat, is Christ's continued life." Ruder illustrations are those of Oom Paul Krüger: the fat, the wick, the flame, in the candle; and of Augustine: the root, trunk, branches, all of one wood, in the tree. In Geer's illustration, mentioned above, from the three dimensions of space, we cannot demonstrate that there is not a fourth, but besides length, breadth, and thickness, we cannot conceive of its existence. As these three exhaust, so far as we know, all possible modes of material being, so we cannot conceive of any fourth person in the Godhead.

(b) From the constitution or processes of our own minds—as the psychological unity of intellect, affection, and will (substantially held by Augustine); the logical unity of thesis, antithesis, and synthesis (Hegel); the metaphysical unity of subject, object, and subject-object (Melanchthon, Olshausen, Shedd).

Augustine: "Mens meminit sui, intelligit se, diligit se; si hoc cernimus, Trinitatem cernimus."... I exist, I am conscious, I will; I exist as conscious and willing, I am conscious of existing and willing, I will to exist and be conscious; and these three functions, though distinct, are inseparable and form one life, one mind, one essence.... "Amor autem alicujus amantis est, et amore aliquid amatur. Ecce tria sunt, amans, et quod amatur, et amor. Quid est ergo amor, nisi quædam vita duo aliqua copulans, vel copulare appetens, amantem scilicet et quod amatur." Calvin speaks of Augustine's view as "a speculation far from solid." But Augustine himself had said: "If asked to define the Trinity, we can only say that it is not this or that." John of Damascus: "All we know of the divine nature is that it is not to be known." By this, however, both Augustine and John of Damascus meant only that the precise mode of God's triune existence is unrevealed and inscrutable.

Hegel, Philos. Relig., transl., 3:99, 100—"God is, but is at the same time the Other, the self-differentiating, the Other in the sense that this Other is God himself and has potentially the Divine nature in it, and that the abolishing of this difference, of this otherness, this return, this love, is Spirit." Hegel calls God "the absolute Idea, the unity of Life and Cognition, the Universal that thinks itself and thinkingly recognizes itself in an infinite Actuality, from which, as its Immediacy, it no less distinguishes itself again"; see Schwegler, History of Philosophy, 321, 331. Hegel's general doctrine is that the highest unity is to be reached only through the fullest development and reconciliation of the deepest and widest antagonism. Pure being is pure nothing; we must die to live. Light is thesis, Darkness is antithesis, Shadow is synthesis, or union of both. Faith is thesis, Unbelief is antithesis, Doubt is synthesis, or union of both. Zweifel comes from Zwei, as doubt from δύο. Hegel called Napoleon "ein Weltgeist zu Pferde"—"a world-spirit on horseback." Ladd, Introd. to Philosophy, 202, speaks of "the monotonous tit-tat-too of the Hegelian logic." Ruskin speaks of it as "pure, definite, and highly finished nonsense." On the Hegelian principle good and evil cannot be contradictory to each other; without evil there could be no good. Stirling well entitled his exposition of the Hegelian Philosophy "The Secret of Hegel," and his readers have often remarked that, if Stirling discovered the secret, he never made it known.

Lord Coleridge told Robert Browning that he could not understand all his poetry. "Ah, well," replied the poet, "if a reader of your calibre understands ten per cent. of what I write, he ought to be content." When Wordsworth was told that Mr. Browning had married Miss Barrett, he said: "It is a good thing that these two understand each other, for no one else understands them." A pupil once brought to Hegel a passage in the latter's writings and asked for an interpretation. The philosopher examined it and replied: "When that passage was written, there were two who knew its meaning—God and myself. Now, alas! there is but one, and that is God." Heinrich Heine, speaking of the effect of Hegelianism upon the religious life of Berlin, says: "I could accommodate myself to the very enlightened Christianity, filtrated from all superstition, which could then be had in the churches, and which was free from the divinity of Christ, like turtle soup without turtle." When German systems of philosophy die, their ghosts take up their abode in Oxford. But if I see a ghost sitting in a chair and then sit down boldly in the chair, the ghost will take offence and go away. Hegel's doctrine of God as the only begotten Son is translated in the Journ. Spec. Philos., 15:395-404.

The most satisfactory exposition of the analogy of subject, object, and subject-object is to be found in Shedd, History of Doctrine, 1:365, note 2. See also Olshausen on John 1:1; H. N. Day, Doctrine of Trinity in Light of Recent Psychology, in Princeton Rev., Sept. 1882:156-179; Morris, Philosophy and Christianity, 122-163. Moberly, Atonement and Personality, 174, has a similar analogy: 1. A man's invisible self; 2. the visible expression of himself in a picture or poem; 3. the response of this picture or poem to himself. The analogy of the family is held to be even better, because no man's personality is complete in itself; husband, wife, and child are all needed to make perfect unity. Allen, Jonathan Edwards, 372, says that in the early church the Trinity was a doctrine of reason; in the Middle Ages it was a mystery; in the 18th century it was a meaningless or irrational dogma; again in the 19th century it becomes a doctrine of the reason, a truth essential to the nature of God. To Allen's characterization of the stages in the history of the doctrine we would add that even in our day we cannot say that a complete exposition of the Trinity is possible. Trinity is a unique fact, different aspects of which may be illustrated, while, as a whole, it has no analogies. The most we can say is that human nature, in its processes and powers, points towards something higher than itself, and that Trinity in God is needed in order to constitute that perfection of being which man seeks as an object of love, worship and service.

No one of these furnishes any proper analogue of the Trinity, since in no one of them is there found the essential element of tripersonality. Such illustrations may sometimes be used to disarm objection, but they furnish no positive explanation of the mystery of the Trinity, and, unless carefully guarded, may lead to grievous error.

2. The Doctrine of the Trinity is not self-contradictory

This it would be, only if it declared God to be three in the same numerical sense in which he is said to be one. This we do not assert. We assert simply that the same God who is one with respect to his essence is three with respect to the internal distinctions of that essence, or with respect to the modes of his being. The possibility of this cannot be denied, except by assuming that the human mind is in all respects the measure of the divine.

The fact that the ascending scale of life is marked by increasing differentiation of faculty and function should rather lead us to expect in the highest of all beings a nature more complex than our own. In man many faculties are united in one intelligent being, and the more intelligent man is, the more distinct from each other these faculties become; until intellect and affection, conscience and will assume a relative independence, and there arises even the possibility of conflict between them. There is nothing irrational or self-contradictory in the doctrine that in God the leading functions are yet more markedly differentiated, so that they become personal, while at the same time these personalities are united by the fact that they each and equally manifest the one indivisible essence.

Unity is as essential to the Godhead as threeness. The same God who in one respect is three, in another respect is one. We do not say that one God is three Gods, nor that one person is three persons, nor that three Gods are one God, but only that there is one God with three distinctions in his being. We do not refer to the faculties of man as furnishing any proper analogy to the persons of the Godhead; we rather deny that man's nature furnishes any such analogy. Intellect, affection, and will in man are not distinct personalities. If they were personalized, they might furnish such an analogy. F. W. Robertson, Sermons, 3:58, speaks of the Father, Son, and Holy Spirit as best conceived under the figure of personalized intellect, affection and will. With this agrees the saying of Socrates, who called thought the soul's conversation with itself. See D. W. Simon, in Bib. Sac., Jan. 1887.

Ps. 86:11—"Unite my heart to fear thy name"—intimates a complexity of powers in man, and a possible disorganization due to sin. Only the fear and love of God can reduce our faculties to order and give us peace, purity, and power. When William after a long courtship at length proposed marriage, Mary said that she "unanimously consented." "Thou shalt love the Lord thy God with all thy heart, and with all thy soul, and with all thy strength, and with all thy mind" (Luke 10:27). Man must not lead a dual life, a double life, like that of Dr. Jekyll and Mr. Hyde. The good life is the unified life. H. H. Bawden: "Theoretically, symmetrical development is the complete criterion. This is the old Greek conception of the perfect life. The term which we translate 'temperance' or 'self-control' is better expressed by 'whole-mindedness.' "

Illingworth, Personality Divine and Human, 54-80—"Our sense of divine personality culminates in the doctrine of the Trinity. Man's personality is essentially triune, because it consists of a subject, an object, and their relation. What is potential and unrealized triunity in man is complete in God.... Our own personality is triune, but it is a potential unrealized triunity, which is incomplete in itself and must go beyond itself for completion, as for example in the family.... But God's personality has nothing potential or unrealized about it.... Trinity is the most intelligible mode of conceiving of God as personal."

John Caird, Fundamental Ideas of Christianity, 1:59, 80—"The parts of a stone are all precisely alike; the parts of a skilful mechanism are all different from one another. In which of the two cases is the unity more real—in that in which there is an absence of distinction, or in that in which there is essential difference of form and function, each separate part having an individuality and activity of its own? The highest unities are not simple but complex." Gordon, Christ of To-day, 106—"All things and persons are modes of one infinite consciousness. Then it is not incredible that there should be three consciousnesses in God. Over against the multitudinous finite personalities are three infinite personalities. This socialism in Deity may be the ground of human society."

The phenomena of double and even of triple consciousness in one and the same individual confirm this view. This fact of more than one consciousness in a finite creature points towards the possibility of a threefold consciousness in the nature of God. Romanes, Mind and Motion, 102, intimates that the social organism, if it attained the highest level of psychical perfection, might be endowed with personality, and that it now has something resembling it—phenomena of thought and conduct which compel us to conceive of families and communities and nations as having a sort of moral personality which implies responsibility and accountability. "The Zeitgeist," he says, "is the product of a kind of collective psychology, which is something other than the sum of all the individual minds of a generation." We do not maintain that any one of these fragmentary or collective consciousnesses attains personality in man, at least in the present life. We only maintain that they indicate that a larger and more complex life is possible than that of which we have common experience, and that there is no necessary contradiction in the doctrine that in the nature of the one and perfect God there are three personal distinctions. R. H. Hutton: "A voluntary self-revelation of the divine mind may be expected to reveal even deeper complexities of spiritual relations in his eternal nature and essence than are found to exist in our humanity—the simplicity of a harmonized complexity, not the simplicity of absolute unity."

3. The doctrine of the Trinity has important relations to other doctrines
    A. It is essential to any proper theism.

Neither God's independence nor God's blessedness can be maintained upon grounds of absolute unity. Anti-trinitarianism almost necessarily makes creation indispensable to God's perfection, tends to a belief in the eternity of matter, and ultimately leads, as in Mohammedanism, and in modern Judaism and Unitarianism, to Pantheism. "Love is an impossible exercise to a solitary being." Without Trinity we cannot hold to a living Unity in the Godhead.

Brit. and For. Evang. Rev., Jan. 1882:35-63—"The problem is to find a perfect objective, congruous and fitting, for a perfect intelligence, and the answer is: 'a perfect intelligence.' " The author of this article quotes James Martineau, the Unitarian philosopher, as follows: "There is only one resource left for completing the needful Objectivity for God, viz., to admit in some form the coëval existence of matter, as the condition or medium of the divine agency or manifestation. Failing the proof [of the absolute origination of matter] we are left with the divine cause, and the material condition of all nature, in eternal co-presence and relation, as supreme object and rudimentary object." See also Martineau, Study, 1:405—"In denying that a plurality of self-existences is possible, I mean to speak only of self-existent causes. A self-existence which is not a cause is by no means excluded, so far as I can see, by a self-existence which is a cause; nay, is even required for the exercise of its causality." Here we see that Martineau's Unitarianism logically drove him into Dualism. But God's blessedness, upon this principle, requires not merely an eternal universe but an infinite universe, for nothing less will afford fit object for an infinite mind. Yet a God who is necessarily bound to the universe, or by whose side a universe, which is not himself, eternally exists, is not infinite, independent, or free. The only exit from this difficulty is in denying God's self-consciousness and self-determination, or in other words, exchanging our theism for dualism, and our dualism for pantheism.

E. H. Johnson, in Bib. Sac., July, 1892:379, quotes from Oxenham's Catholic Doctrine of the Atonement, 108, 109—"Forty years ago James Martineau wrote to George Macdonald: 'Neither my intellectual preference nor my moral admiration goes heartily with the Unitarian heroes, sects or productions, of any age. Ebionites, Arians, Socinians, all seem to me to contrast unfavorably with their opponents, and to exhibit a type of thought far less worthy, on the whole, of the true genius of Christianity.' In his paper entitled A Way out of the Unitarian Controversy, Martineau says that the Unitarian worships the Father; the Trinitarian worships the Son: 'But he who is the Son in one creed is the Father in the other.... The two creeds are agreed in that which constitutes the pith and kernel of both. The Father is God in his primeval essence. But God, as manifested, is the Son.' " Dr. Johnson adds: "So Martineau, after a lifelong service in a Unitarian pulpit and professorship, at length publicly accepts for truth the substance of that doctrine which, in common with the church, he has found so profitable, and tells Unitarians that they and we alike worship the Son, because all that we know of God was revealed by act of the Son." After he had reached his eightieth year, Martineau withdrew from the Unitarian body, though he never formally united with any Trinitarian church.

H. C. Minton, in Princeton Rev., 1903:655-659, has quoted some of Martineau's most significant utterances, such as the following: "The great strength of the orthodox doctrine lies, no doubt, in the appeal it makes to the inward 'sense of sin,'—that sad weight whose burden oppresses every serious soul. And the great weakness of Unitarianism has been its insensibility to this abiding sorrow of the human consciousness. But the orthodox remedy is surely the most terrible of all mistakes, viz., to get rid of the burden, by throwing it on Christ or permitting him to take it.... For myself I own that the literature to which I turn for the nurture and inspiration of Faith, Hope and Love is almost exclusively the product of orthodox versions of the Christian religion. The Hymns of the Wesleys, the Prayers of the Friends, the Meditations of Law and Tauler, have a quickening and elevating power which I rarely feel in the books on our Unitarian shelves.... Yet I can less than ever appropriate, or even intellectually excuse, any distinctive article of the Trinitarian scheme of salvation."

Whiton, Gloria Patri, 23-26, seeks to reconcile the two forms of belief by asserting that "both Trinitarians and Unitarians are coming to regard human nature as essentially one with the divine. The Nicene Fathers builded better than they knew, when they declared Christ homoousios with the Father. We assert the same of mankind." But here Whiton goes beyond the warrant of Scripture. Of none but the only begotten Son can it be said that before Abraham was born he was, and that in him dwelleth all the fulness of the Godhead bodily (John 8:57; Col. 2:9).

Unitarianism has repeatedly demonstrated its logical insufficiency by this "facilis descensus Averno," this lapse from theism into pantheism. In New England the high Arianism of Channing degenerated into the half-fledged pantheism of Theodore Parker, and the full-fledged pantheism of Ralph Waldo Emerson. Modern Judaism is pantheistic in its philosophy, and such also was the later Arabic philosophy of Mohammedanism. Single personality is felt to be insufficient to the mind's conception of Absolute Perfection. We shrink from the thought of an eternally lonely God. "We take refuge in the term 'Godhead.' The literati find relief in speaking of 'the gods.' " Twesten (translated in Bib. Sac., 3:502)—"There may be in polytheism an element of truth, though disfigured and misunderstood. John of Damascus boasted that the Christian Trinity stood midway between the abstract monotheism of the Jews and the idolatrous polytheism of the Greeks." Twesten, quoted in Shedd, Dogm. Theology, 1:255—"There is a πλήρωμα in God. Trinity does not contradict Unity, but only that solitariness which is inconsistent with the living plenitude and blessedness ascribed to God in Scripture, and which God possesses in himself and independently of the finite." Shedd himself remarks: "The attempt of the Deist and the Socinian to construct the doctrine of divine Unity is a failure, because it fails to construct the doctrine of the divine Personality. It contends by implication that God can be self-knowing as a single subject merely, without an object; without the distinctions involved in the subject contemplating, the object contemplated, and the perception of the identity of both."

Mason, Faith of the Gospel, 75—"God is no sterile and motionless unit." Bp. Phillips Brooks: "Unitarianism has got the notion of God as tight and individual as it is possible to make it, and is dying of its meagre Deity." Unitarianism is not the doctrine of one God—for the Trinitarian holds to this; it is rather the unipersonality of this one God. The divine nature demands either an eternal Christ or an eternal creation. Dr. Calthorp, the Unitarian, of Syracuse, therefore consistently declares that "Nature and God are the same." It is the old worship of Baal and Ashtaroth—the deification of power and pleasure. For "Nature" includes everything—all bad impulses as well as good. When a man discovers gravity, he has not discovered God, but only one of the manifestations of God.

Gordon, Christ of To-day, 112—"The supreme divinity of Jesus Christ is but the sovereign expression in human history of the great law of difference in identity that runs through the entire universe and that has its home in the heart of the Godhead." Even James Freeman Clarke, in his Orthodoxy, its Truths and Errors, 436, admits that "there is an essential truth hidden in the idea of the Trinity. While the church doctrine, in every form which it has taken, has failed to satisfy the human intellect, the human heart has clung to the substance contained in them all." William Adams Brown: "If

God is by nature love, he must be by nature social. Fatherhood and Sonship must be immanent in him. In him the limitations of finite personality are removed." But Dr. Brown wrongly adds: "Not the mysteries of God's being, as he is in himself, but as he is revealed, are opened to us in this doctrine." Similarly P. S. Moxom: "I do not know how it is possible to predicate any moral quality of a person who is absolutely out of relation to other persons. If God were conceived of as solitary in the universe, he could not be characterized as righteous." But Dr. Moxom erroneously thinks that these other moral personalities must be outside of God. We maintain that righteousness, like love, requires only plurality of persons within the God-head. See Thomasius, Christi Person und Werk, 1:105, 156. For the pantheistic view, see Strauss, Glaubenslehre, 1:462-524.

W. L. Walker, Christian Theism, 317, quotes Dr. Paul Carus, Primer of Philosophy, 101—"We cannot even conceive of God without attributing trinity to him. An absolute unity would be non-existence. God, if thought of as real and active, involves an antithesis, which may be formulated as God and World, or natura naturans and natura naturata, or in some other way. This antithesis implies already the trinity-conception. When we think of God, not only as that which is eternal and immutable in existence, but also as that which changes, grows, and evolves, we cannot escape the result and we must progress to a triune God-idea. The conception of a God-man, of a Savior, of God revealed in evolution, brings out the antithesis of God Father and God Son, and the very conception of this relation implies God the Spirit that proceeds from both." This confession of an economic Trinity is a rational one only as it implies a Trinity immanent and eternal.

B. It is essential to any proper revelation.

If there be no Trinity, Christ is not God, and cannot perfectly know or reveal God. Christianity is no longer the one, all-inclusive, and final revelation, but only one of many conflicting and competing systems, each of which has its portion of truth, but also its portion of error. So too with the Holy Spirit. "As God can be revealed only through God, so also can he be appropriated only through God. If the Holy Spirit be not God, then the love and self-communication of God to the human soul are not a reality." In other words, without the doctrine of the Trinity we go back to mere natural religion and the far-off God of deism,—and this is ultimately exchanged for pantheism in the way already mentioned.

Martensen, Dogmatics, 104; Thomasius, Christi Person und Werk, 156. If Christ be not God, he cannot perfectly know himself, and his testimony to himself has no independent authority. In prayer the Christian has practical evidence of the Trinity, and can see the value of the doctrine; for he comes to God the Father, pleading the name of Christ, and taught how to pray aright by the Holy Spirit. It is impossible to identify the Father with either the Son or the Spirit. See Rom. 8:27—"he that searcheth the hearts [i. e., God] knoweth what is the mind of the Spirit, because he maketh intercession for the saints according to the will of God." See also Godet on John 1:18—"No man hath seen God at any time; the only begotten Son, who is in the bosom of the Father, he hath declared him"; notice here the relation between ὁ ὤν and ἐξηγήσατο. Napoleon I: "Christianity says with simplicity, 'No man hath seen God, except God.' " John 16:15—"All things whatsoever the Father hath are mine: therefore said I, that he taketh of mine, and shall declare it unto you"; here Christ claims for himself all that belongs to God, and then declares that the Holy Spirit shall reveal him. Only a divine Spirit can do this, even as only a divine Christ can put out an unpresumptuous hand to take all that belongs to the Father. See also Westcott, on John 14:9—"he that hath seen me hath seen the Father; how sayest thou, Show us the Father?"

The agnostic is perfectly correct in his conclusions, if there be no Christ, no medium of communication, no principle of revelation in the Godhead. Only the Son has revealed the Father. Even Royce, in his Spirit of Modern Philosophy, speaks of the existence of an infinite Self, or Logos, or World-mind, of which all individual minds are parts or bits, and of whose timeless choice we partake. Some such principle in the divine nature must be assumed, if Christianity is the complete and sufficient revelation of God's will to men. The Unitarian view regards the religion of Christ as only "one of the day's works of humanity"—an evanescent moment in the ceaseless advance of the race. The Christian on the other hand regards Christ as the only Revealer of God, the only God with whom we have to do, the final authority in religion, the source of all truth and the judge of all mankind. "Heaven and earth shall pass away, but my words shall not pass away" (Mat. 24:35). The resurrection of just and unjust shall be his work (John 5:28), and future retribution shall be "the wrath of the Lamb" (Rev. 6:16). Since God never thinks, says, or does any thing, except through Christ, and since Christ does his work in human hearts only through the Holy Spirit, we may conclude that the doctrine of the Trinity is essential to any proper revelation.

C. It is essential to any proper redemption.

If God be absolutely and simply one, there can be no mediation or atonement, since between God and the most exalted creature the gulf is infinite. Christ cannot bring us nearer to God than he is himself. Only one who is God can reconcile us to God. So, too, only one who is God can purify our souls. A God who is only unity, but in whom is no plurality, may be our Judge, but, so far as we can see, cannot be our Savior or our Sanctifier.

"God is the way to himself." "Nothing human holds good before God, and nothing but God himself can satisfy God." The best method of arguing with Unitarians, therefore, is to rouse the sense of sin; for the soul that has any proper conviction of its sins feels that only an infinite Redeemer can ever save it. On the other hand, a slight estimate of sin is logically connected with a low view of the dignity of Christ. Twesten, translated in Bib. Sac., 3:510—"It would seem to be not a mere accident that Pelagianism, when logically carried out, as for example among the Socinians, has also always led to Unitarianism." In the reverse order, too, it is manifest that rejection of the deity of Christ must tend to render more superficial men's views of the sin and guilt and punishment from which Christ came to save them, and with this to deaden religious feeling and to cut the sinews of all evangelistic and missionary effort (John 12:44; Heb. 10:26). See Arthur, on the Divinity of our Lord in relation to his work of Atonement, in Present Day Tracts, 6: no. 35; Ellis, quoted by Watson, Theol. Inst., 23; Gunsaulus, Transfig. of Christ, 13—"We have tried to see God in the light of nature, while he said: 'In thy light shall we see light' (Ps. 36:9)." We should see nature in the light of Christ. Eternal life is attained only through the knowledge of God in Christ (John 16:9). Hence to accept Christ is to accept God; to reject Christ is to turn one's back on God: John 12:44—"He that believeth on me, believeth not on me, but on him that sent me"; Heb. 10:26, 29—"there remaineth no more a sacrifice for sin ... [for him] who hath trodden under foot the Son of God."

In The Heart of Midlothian, Jeanie Deans goes to London to secure pardon for her sister. She cannot in her peasant attire go direct to the King, for he will not receive her. She goes to a Scotch housekeeper in London; through him to the Duke of Argyle; through him to the Queen; through the Queen she gets pardon from the King, whom she never sees. This was mediæval mediatorship. But now we come directly to Christ, and this suffices us, because he is himself God (The Outlook). A man once went into the cell of a convicted murderer, at the request of the murderer's wife and pleaded with him to confess his crime and accept Christ, but the murderer refused. The seeming clergyman was the Governor, with a pardon which he had designed to bestow in case he found the murderer penitent. A. H. Strong, Christ in Creation, 86—"I have heard that, during our Civil War, a swaggering, drunken, blaspheming officer insulted and almost drove from the dock at Alexandria, a plain unoffending man in citizen's dress; but I have also heard that that same officer turned pale, fell on his knees, and begged for mercy, when the plain man demanded his sword, put him under arrest and made himself known as General Grant. So we may abuse and reject the Lord Jesus Christ, and fancy that we can ignore his claims and disobey his commands with impunity; but it will seem a more serious thing when we find at the last that he whom we have abused and rejected is none other than the living God before whose judgment bar we are to stand."

Henry B. Smith began life under Unitarian influences, and had strong prejudices against evangelical doctrine, especially the doctrines of human depravity and of the divinity of Christ. In his Senior year in College he was converted. Cyrus Hamlin says: "I regard Smith's conversion as the most remarkable event in College in my day." Doubts of depravity vanished with one glimpse into his own heart; and doubts about Christ's divinity could not hold their own against the confession: "Of one thing I feel assured: I need an infinite Savior." Here is the ultimate strength of Trinitarian doctrine. When the Holy Spirit convinces a man of his sin, and brings him face to face with the outraged holiness and love of God, he is moved to cry from the depths of his soul: "None but an infinite Savior can ever save me!" Only in a divine Christ—Christ for us upon the Cross, and Christ in us by his Spirit—can the convicted soul find peace and rest. And so every revival of true religion gives a new impulse to the Trinitarian doctrine. Henry B. Smith wrote in his later life: "When the doctrine of the Trinity was abandoned, other articles of the faith, such as the atonement and regeneration, have almost always followed, by logical necessity, as, when one draws the wire from a necklace of gems, the gems all fall asunder."

D. It is essential to any proper model for human life.

If there be no Trinity immanent in the divine nature, then Fatherhood in God has had a beginning and it may have an end; Sonship, moreover, is no longer a perfection, but an imperfection, ordained for a temporary purpose. But if fatherly giving and filial receiving are eternal in God, then the law of love requires of us conformity to God in both these respects as the highest dignity of our being.

See Hutton, Essays, 1:232—"The Trinity tells us something of God's absolute and essential nature; not simply what he is to us, but what he is in himself. If Christ is the eternal Son of the Father, God is indeed and in essence a Father; the social nature, the spring of love is of the very essence of the eternal Being; the communication of life, the reciprocation of affection dates from beyond time, belongs to the very being of God. The Unitarian idea of a solitary God profoundly affects our conception of God, reduces it to mere power, identifies God with abstract cause and thought. Love is grounded in power, not power in love. The Father is merged in the omniscient and omnipotent genius of the universe." Hence 1 John 2:23—"Whosoever denieth the Son, the same hath not the Father." D'Arcy, Idealism and Theology, 204—"If God be simply one great person, then we have to think of him as waiting until the whole process of creation has been accomplished before his love can find an object upon which to bestow itself. His love belongs, in that case, not to his inmost essence, but to his relation to some of his creatures. The words 'God is love' (1 John 4:8) become a rhetorical exaggeration, rather than the expression of a truth about the divine nature."

Hutton, Essays, 1:239—"We need also the inspiration and help of a perfect filial will. We cannot conceive of the Father as sharing in that dependent attitude of spirit which is our chief spiritual want. It is a Father's perfection to originate—a Son's to receive. We need sympathy and aid in this receptive life; hence, the help of the true Son. Humility, self-sacrifice, submission, are heavenly, eternal, divine. Christ's filial life to the root of all filial life in us. See Gal. 2:19, 20—'it is no longer I that live, but Christ liveth in me: and that life which I now live in the flesh I live in faith, the faith which is in the Son of God, who loved me, and gave himself up for me.'" Thomas Erskine of Linlathen, The Spiritual Order, 233—"There is nothing degrading in this dependence, for we share it with the eternal Son." Gore, Incarnation, 162—"God can limit himself by the conditions of manhood, because the Godhead contains in itself eternally the prototype of human self-sacrifice and self-limitation, for God is love." On the practical lessons and uses of the doctrine of the Trinity, see Presb. and Ref. Rev., Oct 1902:524-550—art. by R. M. Edgar; also sermon by Ganse, in South Church Lectures, 300-310. On the doctrine in general, see Robie, in Bib. Sac., 27:262-289; Pease, Philosophy of Trinitarian Doctrine; N. W. Taylor, Revealed Theology, 1:133; Schultz, Lehre von der Gottheit Christi.

On heathen trinities, see Bib. Repos., 6:116; Christlieb, Mod. Doubt and Christian Belief, 266, 267—"Lao-tse says, 600 B. C., 'Tao, the intelligent principle of all being, is by nature one; the first begat the second; both together begat the third; these three made all things.' " The Egyptian triad of Abydos was Osiris, Isis his wife, and Horus their Son. But these were no true persons; for not only did the Son proceed from the Father, but the Father proceeded from the Son; the Egyptian trinity was pantheistic in its meaning. See Renouf, Hibbert Lectures, 29; Rawlinson, Religions of the Ancient World, 46, 47. The Trinity of the Vedas was Dyaus, Indra, Agni. Derived from the three dimensions of space? Or from the family—father, mother, son? Man creates God in his own image, and sees family life in the Godhead?

The Brahman Trimurti or Trinity, to the members of which are given the names Brahma, Vishnu, Siva—source, supporter, end—is a personification of the pantheistic All, which dwells equally in good and evil, in god and man. The three are represented in the three mystic letters of the syllable Om, or Aum, and by the image at Elephanta of three heads and one body; see Hardwick, Christ and Other Masters, 1:276. The places of the three are interchangeable. Williams: "In the three persons the one God is shown; Each first in place, each last, not one alone; Of Siva, Vishnu, Brahma, each may be, First, second, third, among the blessed three." There are ten incarnations of Vishnu for men's salvation in various times of need; and the one Spirit which temporarily invests itself with the qualities of matter is reduced to its original essence at the end of the æon (Kalpa). This is only a grosser form of Sabellianism, or of a modal Trinity. According to Renouf it is not older than A. D. 1400. Buddhism in later times had its triad. Buddha, or Intelligence, the first principle, associated with Dharma, or Law, the principle of matter, through the combining influence of Sangha, or Order, the mediating principle. See Kellogg, The Light of Asia and the Light of the World, 184, 355. It is probably from a Christian source.

The Greek trinity was composed of Zeus, Athena, and Apollo. Apollo or Loxias (λόγος) utters the decisions of Zeus. "These three surpass all the other gods in moral character and in providential care over the universe. They sustain such intimate and endearing relations to each other, that they may be said to 'agree in one' "; see Tyler, Theol. of Greek Poets, 170, 171; Gladstone, Studies of Homer, vol. 2, sec. 2. Yet the Greek trinity, while it gives us three persons, does not give us oneness of essence. It is a system of tritheism. Plotinus, 300 A. D., gives us a philosophical Trinity in his τὸ ἕν, ὁ νοῦς, ἡ ψυχή.

Watts, New Apologetic, 195—The heathen trinities are "residuary fragments of the lost knowledge of God, not different stages in a process of theological evolution, but evidence of a moral and spiritual degradation." John Caird, Fund. Ideas of Christianity, 92—"In the Vedas the various individual divinities are separated by no hard and fast distinction from each other. They are only names for one indivisible whole, of which the particular divinity invoked at any one time is the type or representative. There is a latent recognition of a unity beneath all the multiplicity of the objects of adoration. The personal or anthropomorphic element is never employed as it is in the Greek and Roman mythology. The personality ascribed to Mitra or Varuna or Indra or Agni is scarcely more real than our modern smiling heaven or whispering breeze or sullen moaning restless sea. 'There is but one,' they say, 'though the poets call him by different names.' The all-embracing heaven, mighty nature, is the reality behind each of these partial manifestations. The pantheistic element which was implicit in the Vedic phase of Indian religion becomes explicit in Brahmanism, and in particular in the so-called Indian systems of philosophy and in the great Indian epic poems. They seek to find in the flux and variety of things the permanent underlying essence. That is Brahma. So Spinoza sought rest in the one eternal substance, and he wished to look at all things 'under the form of eternity.' All things and beings are forms of one whole, of the infinite substance which we call God." See also L. L. Paine, Ethnic Trinities.

The gropings of the heathen religions after a trinity in God, together with their inability to construct a consistent scheme of it, are evidence of a rational want in human nature which only the Christian doctrine is able to supply. This power to satisfy the inmost needs of the believer is proof of its truth. We close our treatment with the words of Jeremy Taylor: "He who goes about to speak of the mystery of the Trinity, and does it by words and names of man's invention, talking of essence and existences, hypostases and personalities, priority in coëquality, and unity in pluralities, may amuse himself and build a tabernacle in his head, and talk something—he knows not what; but the renewed man, that feels the power of the Father, to whom the Son is become wisdom, sanctification, and redemption, in whose heart the love of the Spirit of God is shed abroad—this man, though he understand nothing of what is unintelligible, yet he alone truly understands the Christian doctrine of the Trinity."

Chapter III - The Decrees Of God

I. Definition of Decrees

By the decrees of God we mean that eternal plan by which God has rendered certain all the events of the universe, past, present, and future. Notice in explanation that:

(a) The decrees are many only to our finite comprehension; in their own nature they are but one plan, which embraces not only effects but also causes, not only the ends to be secured but also the means needful to secure them.

In Rom. 8:28—"called according to his purpose"—the many decrees for the salvation of many individuals are represented as forming but one purpose of God. Eph. 1:11—"foreordained according to the purpose of him who worketh all things after the counsel of his will"—notice again the word "purpose," in the singular. Eph. 3:11—"according to the eternal purpose which he purposed in Christ Jesus our Lord." This one purpose or plan of God includes both means and ends, prayer and its answer, labor and its fruit. Tyrolese proverb: "God has his plan for every man." Every man, as well as Jean Paul, is "der Einzige"—the unique. There is a single plan which embraces all things; "we use the word 'decree' when we think of it partitively" (Pepper). See Hodge, Outlines of Theology, 1st ed., 165; 2d ed., 200—"In fact, no event is isolated—to determine one involves determination of the whole concatenation of causes and effects which constitutes the universe." The word "plan" is preferable to the word "decrees," because "plan" excludes the ideas of (1) plurality, (2) short-sightedness, (3) arbitrariness, (4) compulsion.

(b) The decrees, as the eternal act of an infinitely perfect will, though they have logical relations to each other, have no chronological relation. They are not therefore the result of deliberation, in any sense that implies short-sightedness or hesitancy.

Logically, in God's decree the sun precedes the sunlight, and the decree to bring into being a father precedes the decree that there shall be a son. God decrees man before he decrees man's act; he decrees the creation of man before he decrees man's existence. But there is no chronological succession. "Counsel" in Eph. 1:11—"the counsel of his will"—means, not deliberation, but wisdom.

(c) Since the will in which the decrees have their origin is a free will, the decrees are not a merely instinctive or necessary exercise of the divine intelligence or volition, such as pantheism supposes.

It belongs to the perfection of God that he have a plan, and the best possible plan. Here is no necessity, but only the certainty that infinite wisdom will act wisely. God's decrees are not God; they are not identical with his essence; they do not flow from his being in the same necessary way in which the eternal Son proceeds from the eternal Father. There is free will in God, which acts with infinite certainty, yet without necessity. To call even the decree of salvation necessary is to deny grace, and to make an unfree God. See Dick, Lectures on Theology, 1:355; lect. 34.

(d) The decrees have reference to things outside of God. God does not decree to be holy, nor to exist as three persons in one essence.

Decrees are the preparation for external events—the embracing of certain things and acts in a plan. They do not include those processes and operations within the Godhead which have no reference to the universe.

(e) The decrees primarily respect the acts of God himself, in Creation, Providence, and Grace; secondarily, the acts of free creatures, which he foresees will result therefrom.

While we deny the assertion of Whedon, that "the divine plan embraces only divine actions," we grant that God's plan has reference primarily to his own actions, and that the sinful acts of men, in particular, are the objects, not of a decree that God will efficiently produce them, but of a decree that God will permit men, in the exercise of their own free will, to produce them.

(f) The decree to act is not the act. The decrees are an internal exercise and manifestation of the divine attributes, and are not to be confounded with Creation, Providence, and Redemption, which are the execution of the decrees.

The decrees are the first operation of the attributes, and the first manifestation of personality of which we have any knowledge within the Godhead. They presuppose those essential acts or movements within the divine nature which we call generation and procession. They involve by way of consequence that execution of the decrees which we call Creation, Providence, and Redemption, but they are not to be confounded with either of these.

(g) The decrees are therefore not addressed to creatures; are not of the nature of statute law; and lay neither compulsion nor obligation upon the wills of men.

So ordering the universe that men will pursue a given course of action is a very different thing from declaring, ordering, or commanding that they shall. "Our acts are in accordance with the decrees, but not necessarily so—we can do otherwise and often should" (Park). The Frenchman who fell into the water and cried: "I will, drown,—no one shall help me!" was very naturally permitted to drown; if he had said: "I shall drown,—no one will help me!" he might perchance have called some friendly person to his aid.

(h) All human acts, whether evil or good, enter into the divine plan and so are objects of God's decrees, although God's actual agency with regard to the evil is only a permissive agency.

No decree of God reads: "You shall sin." For (1) no decree is addressed to you; (2) no decree with respect to you says shall; (3) God cannot cause sin, or decree to cause it. He simply decrees to create, and himself to act, in such a way that you will, of your own free choice, commit sin. God determines upon his own acts, foreseeing what the results will be in the free acts of his creatures, and so he determines those results. This permissive decree is the only decree of God with respect to sin. Man of himself is capable of producing sin. Of himself he is not capable of producing holiness. In the production of holiness two powers must concur, God's will and man's will, and God's will must act first. The decree of good, therefore, is not simply a permissive decree, as in the case of evil. God's decree, in the former case, is a decree to bring to bear positive agencies for its production, such as circumstances, motives, influences of his Spirit. But, in the case of evil, God's decrees are simply his arrangement that man may do as he pleases, God all the while foreseeing the result.

Permissive agency should not be confounded with conditional agency, nor permissive decree with conditional decree. God foreordained sin only indirectly. The machine is constructed not for the sake of the friction, but in spite of it. In the parable Mat. 13:24-30, the question "Whence then hath it tares?" is answered, not by saying, "I decreed the tares." but by saying: "An enemy hath done this." Yet we must take exception to Principal Fairbairn, Place of Christ in Theology, 456, when he says: "God did not permit sin to be; it is, in its essence, the transgression of his law, and so his only attitude toward it is one of opposition. It is, because man has contradicted and resisted his will." Here the truth of God's opposition to sin is stated so sharply as almost to deny the decree of sin in any sense. We maintain that God does decree sin in the sense of embracing in his plan the foreseen transgressions of men, while at the same time we maintain that these foreseen transgressions are chargeable wholly to men and not at all to God.

(i) While God's total plan with regard to creatures is called predestination, or foreordination, his purpose so to act that certain will believe and be saved is called election, and his purpose so to act that certain will refuse to believe and be lost is called reprobation. We discuss election and reprobation, in a later chapter, as a part of the Application of Redemption.

God's decrees may be divided into decrees with respect to nature, and decrees with respect to moral beings. These last we call foreordination, or predestination; and of these decrees with respect to moral beings there are two kinds, the decree of election, and the decree of reprobation; see our treatment of the doctrine of Election. George Herbert: "We all acknowledge both thy power and love To be exact, transcendent, and divine; Who dost so strongly and so sweetly move. While all things have their will— yet none but thine. For either thy command or thy permission Lays hands on all; they are thy right and left. The first puts on with speed and expedition; The other curbs sin's stealing pace and theft. Nothing escapes them both; all must appear And be disposed and dressed and tuned by thee Who sweetly temperest all. If we could hear Thy skill and art, what music it would be!" On the whole doctrine, see Shedd, Presb. and Ref. Rev., Jan. 1890:1-25.

II. Proof of the Doctrine of Decrees

1. From Scripture

A. The Scriptures declare that all things are included in the divine decrees. B. They declare that special things and events are decreed; as, for example, (a) the stability of the physical universe; (b) the outward circumstances of nations; (c) the length of human life; (d) the mode of our death; (e) the free acts of men, both good acts and evil acts. C. They declare that God has decreed (a) the salvation of believers; (b) the establishment of Christ's kingdom; (c) the work of Christ and of his people in establishing it.

A. Is. 14:26, 27—"This is the purpose that is purposed upon the whole earth; and this is the hand that is stretched out upon all the nations; for Jehovah of hosts hath purposed ... and his hand is stretched out, and who shall turn it back?" 46:10, 11—"declaring the end from the beginning, and from ancient times the things that are not yet done, saying, My counsel shall stand, and I will do all my pleasure ... yea, I have spoken, I will also bring it to pass; I have purposed, I will also do it." Dan. 4:35—"doeth according to his will in the army of heaven, and among the inhabitants of the earth; and none can stay his hand, or say unto him, What doest thou?" Eph. 1:11—"the purpose of him who worketh all things after the counsel of his will."

B. (a) Ps. 119:89-91—"For ever, O Jehovah, thy word is settled in heaven. Thy faithfulness is unto all generations: Thou hast established the earth and it abideth. They abide this day according to thine ordinances; For all things are thy servants." (b) Acts 17:26—"he made of one every nation of men to dwell on all the face of the earth, having determined their appointed seasons, and the bounds of their habitation"; cf. Zach. 5:1—"came four chariots out from between two mountains; and the mountains were mountains of brass"—the fixed decrees from which proceed God's providential dealings? (c) Job 14:5—"Seeing his days are determined, The number of his months is with thee, And thou hast determined his bounds that he cannot pass." (d) John 21:19—"this he spake, signifying by what manner of death he should glorify God." (e) Good acts: Is. 44:28—"that saith of Cyrus, He is my shepherd and shall perform all my pleasure, even saying of Jerusalem, She shall be built; and of the temple, Thy foundation shall be laid"; Eph. 2:10—"For we are his workmanship, created in Christ Jesus for good works, which God afore prepared that we should walk in them." Evil acts: Gen. 50:20—"as for you, ye meant evil against me; but God meant it for good, to bring to pass, as it is this day, to save much people alive"; 1 K. 12:15—"So the king hearkened not unto the people, for it was a thing brought about of Jehovah"; 24—"for this thing is of me"; Luke 22:23—"For the Son of man indeed goeth, as it hath been determined: but woe unto that man through whom he is betrayed"; Acts 2:23—"him, being delivered up by the determinate counsel and foreknowledge of God, ye by the hand of lawless men did crucify and slay"; 4:27, 28—"of a truth in this city against thy holy Servant Jesus, who thou didst anoint, both Herod and Pontius Pilate, with the Gentiles and the people of Israel, were gathered together, to do whatsoever thy hand and thy counsel foreordained to come to pass"; Rom. 9:17—"For the scripture saith unto Pharaoh, For this very purpose did I raise thee up, that I might show in thee my power"; 1 Pet 2:3—"They stumble at the word, being disobedient: whereunto also they were appointed"; Rev. 17:17—"For God did put in their hearts to do his mind, and to come to one mind, and to give their kingdom unto the beast, until the words of God should be accomplished."

C. (a) 1 Cor. 2:7—"the wisdom which hath been hidden, which God foreordained before the worlds unto our glory"; Eph 3:10, 11—"manifold wisdom of God, according to the eternal purpose which he purposed in Christ Jesus our lord." Ephesians 1 is a pæan in praise of God's decrees. (b) The greatest decree of all is the decree to give the world to Christ. Ps. 2:7, 8—"I will tell of the decree:... I will give thee the nations for thine inheritance"; cf. verse 6—"I have set my king Upon my holy hill of Zion"; 1 Cor. 15:25—"he must reign, till he hath put all his enemies under his feet." (c) This decree we are to convert into our decree; God's will is to be executed through our wills. Phil. 2:12, 13—"work out your own salvation with fear and trembling; for it is God who worketh in you both to will and to work, for his good pleasure." Rev. 5:1, 7—"I saw in the right hand of him that sat on the throne a book written within and on the back, close sealed with seven seals.... And he [the Lamb] came, and he taketh it out of the right hand of him that sat on the throne"; verse 9—"Worthy art thou to take the book, and to open the seals thereof"—Christ alone has the omniscience to know, and the omnipotence to execute, the divine decrees. When John weeps because there is none in heaven or earth to loose the seals and to read the book of God's decrees, the Lion of the tribe of Judah prevails to open it. Only Christ conducts the course of history to its appointed end. See A. H. Strong, Christ in Creation, 268-283, on The Decree of God as the Great Encouragement to Missions.

2. From Reason

A. From the Divine Foreknowledge.

Foreknowledge implies fixity, and fixity implies decree.—From eternity God foresaw all the events of the universe as fixed and certain. This fixity and certainty could not have had its ground either in blind fate or in the variable wills of men, since neither of these had an existence. It could have had its ground in nothing outside the divine mind, for in eternity nothing existed besides the divine mind. But for this fixity there must have been a cause; if anything in the future was fixed, something must have fixed it. This fixity could have had its ground only in the plan and purpose of God. In fine, if God foresaw the future as certain, it must have been because there was something in himself which made it certain; or, in other words, because he had decreed it.

We object therefore to the statement of E. G. Robinson, Christian Theology, 74—"God's knowledge and God's purposes both being eternal, one cannot be conceived as the ground of the other, nor can either be predicated to the exclusion of the other as the cause of things, but, correlative and eternal, they must be coequal quantities in thought." We reply that while decree does not chronologically precede, it does logically precede, foreknowledge. Foreknowledge is not of possible events, but of what is certain to be. The certainty of future events which God foreknew could have had its ground only in his decree, since he alone existed to be the ground and explanation of this certainty. Events were fixed only because God had fixed them. Shedd, Dogm. Theol., 1:397—"An event must be made certain, before it can be known as a certain event." Turretin, Inst. Theol., loc. 3, quaes. 12, 18— "Præcipuum fundamentum scientiæ divinæ circa futura contingentia est decretum solum."

Decreeing creation implies decreeing the foreseen results of creation.—To meet the objection that God might have foreseen the events of the universe, not because he had decreed each one, but only because he had decreed to create the universe and institute its laws, we may put the argument in another form. In eternity there could have been no cause of the future existence of the universe, outside of God himself, since no being existed but God himself. In eternity God foresaw that the creation of the world and the institution of its laws would make certain its actual history even to the most insignificant details. But God decreed to create and to institute these laws. In so decreeing he necessarily decreed all that was to come. In fine, God foresaw the future events of the universe as certain, because he had decreed to create; but this determination to create involved also a determination of all the actual results of that creation; or, in other words, God decreed those results.

E. G. Robinson, Christian Theology, 84—"The existence of divine decrees may be inferred from the existence of natural law." Law = certainty = God's will. Positivists express great contempt for the doctrine of the eternal purpose of God, yet they consign us to the iron necessity of physical forces and natural laws. Dr. Robinson also points out that decrees are "implied in the prophecies. We cannot conceive that all events should have converged toward the one great event—the death of Christ—without the intervention of an eternal purpose." E. H. Johnson, Outline Syst. Theol., 2d ed., 251, note—"Reason is confronted by the paradox that the divine decrees are at once absolute and conditional; the resolution of the paradox is that God absolutely decreed a conditional system—a system, however, the workings of which he thoroughly foreknows." The rough unhewn stone and the statue into which it will be transformed are both and equally included in the plan of the sculptor.

No undecreed event can be foreseen.—We grant that God decrees primarily and directly his own acts of creation, providence, and grace; but we claim that this involves also a secondary and indirect decreeing of the acts of free creatures which he foresees will result therefrom. There is therefore no such thing in God as scientia media, or knowledge of an event that is to be, though it does not enter into the divine plan; for to say that God foresees an undecreed event, is to say that he views as future an event that is merely possible; or, in other words, that he views an event not as it is.

We recognize only two kinds of knowledge: (1) Knowledge of undecreed possibles, and (2) foreknowledge of decreed actuals. Scientia media is a supposed intermediate knowledge between these two, namely (3) foreknowledge of undecreed actuals. See further explanations below. We deny the existence of this third sort of knowledge. We hold that sin is decreed in the sense of being rendered certain by God's determining upon a system in which it was foreseen that sin would exist. The sin of man can be foreknown, while yet God is not the immediate cause of it. God knows possibilities, without having decreed them at all. But God cannot foreknow actualities unless he has by his decree made them to be certainties of the future. He cannot foreknow that which is not there to be foreknown. Royce, World and Individual, 2:374, maintains that God has, not foreknowledge, but only eternal knowledge, of temporal things. But we reply that to foreknow how a moral being will act is no more impossible than to know how a moral being in given circumstances would act.

Only knowledge of that which is decreed is foreknowledge.—Knowledge of a plan as ideal or possible may precede decree; but knowledge of a plan as actual or fixed must follow decree. Only the latter knowledge is properly foreknowledge. God therefore foresees creation, causes, laws, events, consequences, because he has decreed creation, causes, laws, events, consequences; that is, because he has embraced all these in his plan. The denial of decrees logically involves the denial of God's foreknowledge of free human actions; and to this Socinians, and some Arminians, are actually led.

An Arminian example of this denial is found in McCabe, Foreknowledge of God, and Divine Nescience of Future Contingencies a Necessity. Per contra, see notes on God's foreknowledge, in this Compendium, pages 283-286. Pepper: "Divine volition stands logically between two divisions and kinds of divine knowledge." God knew free human actions as possible, before he decreed them; he knew them as future, because he decreed them. Logically, though not chronologically, decree comes before foreknowledge. When I say, "I know what I will do," it is evident that I have determined already, and that my knowledge does not precede determination, but follows it and is based upon it. It is therefore not correct to say that God foreknows his decrees. It is more true to say that he decrees his foreknowledge. He foreknows the future which he has decreed, and he foreknows it because he has decreed it. His decrees are eternal, and nothing that is eternal can be the object of foreknowledge. G. F. Wright, in Bib. Sac., 1877:723—"The knowledge of God comprehended the details and incidents of every possible plan. The choice of a plan made his knowledge determinate as foreknowledge."

There are therefore two kinds of divine knowledge: (1) knowledge of what may be—of the possible (scientia simplicis intelligentiæ); and (2) knowledge of what is, and is to be, because God has decreed it (scientia visionis). Between these two Molina, the Spanish Jesuit, wrongly conceived that there was (3) a middle knowledge of things which were to be, although God had not decreed them (scientia media). This would of course be a knowledge which God derived, not from himself, but from his creatures! See Dick, Theology, 1:351. A. S. Carman: "It is difficult to see how God's knowledge can be caused from eternity by something that has no existence until a definite point of time." If it be said that what is to be will be "in the nature of things," we reply that there is no "nature of things" apart from God, and that the ground of the objective certainty, as well as of the subjective certitude corresponding to it, is to be found only in God himself.

But God's decreeing to create, when he foresees that certain free acts of men will follow, is a decreeing of those free acts, in the only sense in which we use the word decreeing, viz., a rendering certain, or embracing in his plan. No Arminian who believes in God's foreknowledge of free human acts has good reason for denying God's decrees as thus explained. Surely God did not foreknow that Adam would exist and sin, whether God determined to create him or not. Omniscience, then, becomes foreknowledge only on condition of God's decree. That God's foreknowledge of free acts is intuitive does not affect this conclusion. We grant that, while man can predict free action only so far as it is rational (i. e., in the line of previously dominant motive), God can predict free action whether it is rational or not. But even God cannot predict what is not certain to be. God can have intuitive foreknowledge of free human acts only upon condition of his own decree to create; and this decree to create, in foresight of all that will follow, is a decree of what follows. For the Arminian view, see Watson, Institutes, 2:375-398, 422-448. Per contra, see Hill, Divinity, 512-582; Fiske, in Bib. Sac., April, 1862; Bennett Tyler, Memoir and Lectures, 214-254; Edwards the younger, 1:398-420; A. H. Strong, Philosophy and Religion, 98-101.

B. From the Divine Wisdom.

It is the part of wisdom to proceed in every undertaking according to a plan. The greater the undertaking, the more needful a plan. Wisdom, moreover, shows itself in a careful provision for all possible circumstances and emergencies that can arise in the execution of its plan. That many such circumstances and emergencies are uncontemplated and unprovided for in the plans of men, is due only to the limitations of human wisdom. It belongs to infinite wisdom, therefore, not only to have a plan, but to embrace all, even the minutest details, in the plan of the universe.

No architect would attempt to build a Cologne cathedral without a plan; he would rather, if possible, have a design for every stone. The great painter does not study out his picture as he goes along; the plan is in his mind from the start; preparations for the last effects have to be made from the beginning. So in God's work every detail is foreseen and provided for; sin and Christ entered into the original plan of the universe. Raymond, Syst. Theol., 2:156, says this implies that God cannot govern the world unless all things be reduced to the condition of machinery; and that it cannot be true, for the reason that God's government is a government of persons and not of things. But we reply that the wise statesman governs persons and not things, yet just in proportion to his wisdom he conducts his administration according to a preconceived plan. God's power might, but God's wisdom would not, govern the universe without embracing all things, even the least human action, in his plan.

C. From the Divine Immutability.

What God does, he always purposed to do. Since with him there is no increase of knowledge or power, such as characterizes finite beings, it follows that what under any given circumstances he permits or does, he must have eternally decreed to permit or do. To suppose that God has a multitude of plans, and that he changes his plan with the exigencies of the situation, is to make him infinitely dependent upon the varying wills of his creatures, and to deny to him one necessary element of perfection, namely, immutability.

God has been very unworthily compared to a chess-player, who will checkmate his opponent whatever moves he may make (George Harris). So Napoleon is said to have had a number of plans before each battle, and to have betaken himself from one to another as fortune demanded. Not so with God. Job 23:13—"he is in one mind, and who can turn him?" James 1:17-"the Father of lights, with whom can be no variation, neither shadow that is cast by turning." Contrast with this Scripture McCabe's statement in his Foreknowledge of God, 62—"This new factor, the godlike liberty of the human will, is capable of thwarting, and in uncounted instances does thwart, the divine will, and compel the great I AM to modify his actions, his purposes, and his plans, in the treatment of individuals and of communities."

D. From the Divine Benevolence.

The events of the universe, if not determined by the divine decrees, must be determined either by chance or by the wills of creatures. It is contrary to any proper conception of the divine benevolence to suppose that God permits the course of nature and of history, and the ends to which both these are moving, to be determined for myriads of sentient beings by any other force or will than his own. Both reason and revelation, therefore, compel us to accept the doctrine of the Westminster Confession, that "God did from all eternity, by the most just and holy counsel of his own will, freely and unchangeably ordain whatsoever comes to pass."

It would not be benevolent for God to put out of his own power that which was so essential to the happiness of the universe. Tyler, Memoir and Lectures, 231-243—"The denial of decrees involves denial of the essential attributes of God, such as omnipotence, omniscience, benevolence; exhibits him as a disappointed and unhappy being; implies denial of his universal providence; leads to a denial of the greater part of our own duty of submission; weakens the obligations of gratitude." We give thanks to God for blessings which come to us through the free acts of others; but unless God has purposed these blessings, we owe our thanks to these others and not to God. Dr. A. J. Gordon said well that a universe without decrees would be as irrational and appalling as would be an express-train driving on in the darkness without headlight or engineer, and with no certainty that the next moment it might not plunge into the abyss. And even Martineau, Study, 2:108, in spite of his denial of God's foreknowledge of man's free acts, is compelled to say: "It cannot be left to mere created natures to play unconditionally with the helm of even a single world and steer it uncontrolled into the haven or on to the reefs; and some security must be taken for keeping the deflections within tolerable bounds." See also Emmons, Works, 4:273-401: and Princeton Essays, 1:57-73.

III. Objections to the Doctrine of Decrees

1. That they are inconsistent with the free agency of man
    To this we reply that:
    A. The objection confounds the decrees with the execution of the decrees. The decrees are, like foreknowledge, an act eternal to the divine nature, and are no more inconsistent with free agency than foreknowledge is. Even foreknowledge of events implies that those events are fixed. If this absolute fixity and foreknowledge is not inconsistent with free agency, much less can that which is more remote from man's action, namely, the hidden cause of this fixity and foreknowledge—God's decrees—be inconsistent with free agency. If anything be inconsistent with man's free agency, it must be, not the decrees themselves, but the execution of the decrees in creation and providence.

    On this objection, see Tyler, Memoir and Lectures, 244-249; Forbes, Predestination and Free Will, 3—"All things are predestinated by God, both good and evil, but not prenecessitated, that is, causally preördained by him—unless we would make God the author of sin. Predestination is thus an indifferent word, in so far as the originating author of anything is concerned; God being the originator of good, but the creature, of evil. Predestination therefore means that God included in his plan of the world every act of every creature, good or bad. Some acts he predestined causally, others permissively. The certainty of the fulfilment of all God's purposes ought to be distinguished from their necessity." This means simply that God's decree is not the cause of any act or event. God's decrees may be executed by the causal efficiency of his creatures, or they may be executed by his own efficiency. In either case it is, if anything, the execution, and not the decree, that is inconsistent with human freedom.

    B. The objection rests upon a false theory of free agency—namely, that free agency implies indeterminateness or uncertainty; in other words, that free agency cannot coëxist with certainty as to the results of its exercise. But it is necessity, not certainty, with which free agency is inconsistent. Free agency is the power of self-determination in view of motives, or man's power (a) to chose between motives, and (b) to direct his subsequent activity according to the motive thus chosen. Motives are never a cause, but only an occasion; they influence, but never compel; the man is the cause, and herein is his freedom. But it is also true that man is never in a state of indeterminateness; never acts without motive, or contrary to all motives; there is always a reason why he acts, and herein is his rationality. Now, so far as man acts according to previously dominant motive—see (b) above—we may by knowing his motive predict his action, and our certainty what that action will be in no way affects his freedom. We may even bring motives to bear upon others, the influence of which we foresee, yet those who act upon them may act in perfect freedom. But if man, influenced by man, may still be free, then man, influenced by divinely foreseen motives, may still be free, and the divine decrees, which simply render certain man's actions, may also be perfectly consistent with man's freedom.

    We must not assume that decreed ends can be secured only by compulsion. Eternal purposes do not necessitate efficient causation on the part of the purposer. Freedom may be the very means of fulfilling the purpose. E. G. Robinson, Christian Theology, 74—"Absolute certainty of events, which is all that omniscience determines respecting them, is not identical with their necessitation." John Milton, Christian Doctrine: "Future events which God has foreseen will happen certainly, but not of necessity. They will happen certainly, because the divine prescience will not be deceived; but they will not happen necessarily, because prescience can have no influence on the object foreknown, inasmuch as it is only an intransitive action."

    There is, however, a smaller class of human actions by which character is changed, rather than expressed, and in which the man acts according to a motive different from that which has previously been dominant—see (a) above. These actions are also are foreknown by God, although they cannot be predicted by man. Man's freedom in them would be inconsistent with God's decrees, if the previous certainty of their occurrence were, not certainty, but necessity; or, in other words, if God's decrees were in all cases decrees efficiently to produce the acts of his creatures. But this is not the case. God's decrees may be executed by man's free causation, as easily as by God's; and God's decreeing this free causation, in decreeing to create a universe of which he foresees that this causation will be a part, in no way interferes with the freedom of such causation, but rather secures and establishes it. Both consciousness and conscience witness that God's decrees are not executed by laying compulsion upon the free wills of men.

The farmer who, after hearing a sermon on God's decrees, took the break-neck road instead of the safe one to his home and broke his wagon in consequence, concluded before the end of his journey that he at any rate had been predestinated to be a fool, and that he had made his calling and election sure. Ladd, Philosophy of Conduct, 146, 187, shows that the will is free, first, by man's consciousness of ability, and, secondly, by man's consciousness of imputability. By nature, he is potentially self-determining; as matter of fact, he often becomes self-determining.

Allen, Religious Progress, 110—"The coming church must embrace the sovereignty of God and the freedom of the will; total depravity and the divinity of human nature; the unity of God and the triune distinctions in the Godhead; gnosticism and agnosticism; the humanity of Christ and his incarnate deity; the freedom of the Christian man and the authority of the church; individualism and solidarity; reason and faith; science and theology; miracle and uniformity of law; culture and piety; the authority of the Bible as the word of God with absolute freedom of Biblical criticism; the gift of administration as in the historic episcopate and the gift of prophecy as the highest sanction of the ministerial commission; the apostolic succession but also the direct and immediate call which knows only the succession of the Holy Ghost." Without assenting to these latter clauses we may commend the comprehensive spirit of this utterance, especially with reference to the vexed question of the relation of divine sovereignty to human freedom.

It may aid us, in estimating the force of this objection, to note the four senses in which the term "freedom" may be used. It may be used as equivalent to (1) physical freedom, or absence of outward constraint; (2) formal freedom, or a state of moral indeterminateness; (3) moral freedom, or self-determinateness in view of motives; (4) real freedom, or ability to conform to the divine standard. With the first of these we are not now concerned, since all agree that the decrees lay no outward constraint upon men. Freedom in the second sense has no existence, since all men have character. Free agency, or freedom in the third sense, has just been shown to be consistent with the decrees. Freedom in the fourth sense, or real freedom, is the special gift of God, and is not to be confounded with free agency. The objection mentioned above rests wholly upon the second of these definitions of free agency. This we have shown to be false, and with this the objection itself falls to the ground.

Ritschl, Justification and Reconciliation, 133-188, gives a good definition of this fourth kind of freedom: "Freedom is self-determination by universal ideals. Limiting our ends to those of family or country is a refined or idealized selfishness. Freedom is self-determination by universal love for man or by the kingdom of God. But the free man must then be dependent on God in everything, because the kingdom of God is a revelation of God." John Caird, Fundamental Ideas of Christianity, 1:133—"In being determined by God we are self-determined; i. e., determined by nothing alien to us, but by our noblest, truest self. The universal life lives in us. The eternal consciousness becomes our own; for 'he that abideth in love abideth in God and God abideth in him' (1 John 4:16)."

Moberly, Atonement and Personality, 226—"Free will is not the independence of the creature, but is rather his self-realization in perfect dependence. Freedom is self-identity with goodness. Both goodness and freedom are, in their perfectness, in God. Goodness in a creature is not distinction from, but correspondence with, the goodness of God. Freedom in a creature is correspondence with God's own self-identity with goodness. It is to realize and to find himself, his true self, in Christ, so that God's love in us has become a divine response, adequate to, because truly mirroring, God." G. S. Lee, The Shadow Christ, 32—."The ten commandments could not be chanted. The Israelites sang about Jehovah and what he had done, but they did not sing about what he told them to do, and that is why they never did it. The conception of duty that cannot sing must weep until it learns to sing. This is Hebrew history."

"There is a liberty, unsung By poets and by senators unpraised, Which monarchs cannot grant nor all the powers Of earth and hell confederate take away; A liberty which persecution, fraud, Oppressions, prisons, have no power to bind; Which whoso tastes can be enslaved no more. 'T is liberty of heart, derived from heaven, Bought with his blood who gave it to mankind, And sealed with the same token." Robert Herrick: "Stone walls do not a prison make, Nor iron bars a cage; Minds innocent and quiet take That for a hermitage. If I have freedom in my love, And in my soul am free, Angels alone that soar above Enjoy such liberty."

A more full discussion of the doctrine of the Will is given under Anthropology, Vol. II. It is sufficient here to say that the Arminian objections to the decrees arise almost wholly from erroneously conceiving of freedom as the will's power to decide, in any given case, against its own character and all the motives brought to bear upon it. As we shall hereafter see, this is practically to deny that man has character, or that the will by its right or wrong moral action gives to itself, as well as to the intellect and affections, a permanent bent or predisposition to good or evil. It is to extend the power of contrary choice, a power which belongs to the sphere of transient volition, over all those permanent states of intellect, affection, and will which we call the moral character, and to say that we can change directly by a single volition that which, as a matter of fact, we can change only indirectly through process and means. Yet even this exaggerated view of freedom would seem not to exclude God's decrees, or prevent a practical reconciliation of the Arminian and Calvinistic views, so long as the Arminian grants God's foreknowledge of free human acts, and the Calvinist grants that God's decree of these acts is not necessarily a decree that God will efficiently produce them. For a close approximation of the two views, see articles by Raymond and by A. A. Hodge, respectively, on the Arminian and the Calvinistic Doctrines of the Will, in McClintock and Strong's Cyclopædia, 10:989, 992.

We therefore hold to the certainty of human action, and so part company with the Arminian. We cannot with Whedon (On the Will), and Hazard (Man a Creative First Cause), attribute to the will the freedom of indifference, or the power to act without motive. We hold with Calderwood, Moral Philosophy, 188, that action without motive, or an act of pure will, is unknown in consciousness (see, however, an inconsistent statement of Calderwood on page 188 of the same work). Every future human act will not only be performed with a motive, but will certainly be one thing rather than another; and God knows what it will be. Whatever may be the method of God's foreknowledge, and whether it be derived from motives or be intuitive, that foreknowledge presupposes God's decree to create, and so presupposes the making certain of the free acts that follow creation.

But this certainty is not necessity. In reconciling God's decrees with human freedom, we must not go to the other extreme, and reduce human freedom to mere determinism, or the power of the agent to act out his character in the circumstances which environ him. Human action is not simply the expression of previously dominant affections; else Neither Satan nor Adam could have fallen, nor could the Christian ever sin. We therefore part company with Jonathan Edwards and his Treatise on the Freedom of the Will, as well as with the younger Edwards (Works, 1:420), Alexander (Moral Science, 107), and Charles Hodge (Syst. Theology, 2:278), all of whom follow Jonathan Edwards in identifying sensibility with the will, in regarding affections as the causes of volitions, and in speaking of the connection between motive and action as a necessary one. We hold, on the contrary, that sensibility and will are two distinct powers, that affections are occasions but never causes of volitions, and that, while motives may infallibly persuade, they never compel the will. The power to make the decision other than it is resides in the will, though it may never be exercised. With Charnock, the Puritan (Attributes, 1:448-450), we say that "man hath a power to do otherwise than that which God foreknows he will do." Since, then, God's decrees are not executed by laying compulsion upon human wills, they are not inconsistent with man's freedom. See Martineau, Study, 2:237, 249, 258, 261; also article by A. H. Strong, on Modified Calvinism, or Remainders of Freedom in Man, in Baptist Review, 1883:219-243; reprinted in the author's Philosophy and Religion, 114-128.

2. That they take away all motive for human exertion

To this we reply that:

(a) They cannot thus influence men, since they are not addressed to men, are not the rule of human action, and become known only after the event. This objection is therefore the mere excuse of indolence and disobedience.

Men rarely make this excuse in any enterprise in which their hopes and their interests are enlisted. It is mainly in matters of religion that men use the divine decrees as an apology for their sloth and inaction. The passengers on an ocean steamer do not deny their ability to walk to starboard or to larboard, upon the plea that they are being carried to their destination by forces beyond their control. Such a plea would be still more irrational in a case where the passengers' inaction, as in case of fire, might result in destruction to the ship.

(b) The objection confounds the decrees of God with fate. But it is to be observed that fate is unintelligent, while the decrees are framed by a personal God in infinite wisdom; fate is indistinguishable from material causation and leaves no room for human freedom, while the decrees exclude all notion of physical necessity; fate embraces no moral ideas or ends, while the decrees make these controlling in the universe.

North British Rev., April, 1870—"Determinism and predestination spring from premises which lie in quite separate regions of thought. The predestinarian is obliged by his theology to admit the existence of a free will in God, and, as a matter of fact, he does admit it in the devil. But the final consideration which puts a great gulf between the determinist and the predestinarian is this, that the latter asserts the reality of the vulgar notion of moral desert. Even if he were not obliged by his interpretation of Scripture to assert this, he would be obliged to assert it in order to help out his doctrine of eternal reprobation."

Hawthorne expressed his belief in human freedom when he said that destiny itself had often been worsted in the attempt to get him out to dinner. Benjamin Franklin, in his Autobiography, quotes the Indian's excuse for getting drunk: "The Great Spirit made all things for some use, and whatsoever use they were made for, to that use they must be put. The Great Spirit made rum for Indians to get drunk with, and so it must be." Martha, in Isabel Carnaby, excuses her breaking of dishes by saying: "It seems as if it was to be. It is the thin edge of the wedge that in time will turn again and rend you." Seminary professor: "Did a man ever die before his time?" Seminary student: "I never knew of such a case." The decrees of God, considered as God's all-embracing plan, leave room for human freedom.

(c) The objection ignores the logical relation between the decree of the end and the decree of the means to secure it. The decrees of God not only ensure the end to be obtained, but they ensure free human action as logically prior thereto. All conflict between the decrees and human exertion must therefore be apparent and not real. Since consciousness and Scripture assure us that free agency exists, it must exist by divine decree; and though we may be ignorant of the method in which the decrees are executed, we have no right to doubt either the decrees or the freedom. They must be held to be consistent, until one of them is proved to be a delusion.

The man who carries a vase of gold-fish does not prevent the fish from moving unrestrainedly within the vase. The double track of a railway enables a formidable approaching train to slip by without colliding with our own. Our globe takes us with it, as it rushes around the sun, yet we do our ordinary work without interruption. The two movements which at first sight seem inconsistent with each other are really parts of one whole. God's plan and man's effort are equally in harmony. Myers, Human Personality, 2:272, speaks of "molecular motion amid molar calm."

Dr. Duryea: "The way of life has two fences. There is an Arminian fence to keep us out of Fatalism; and there is a Calvinistic fence to keep us out of Pelagianism. Some good brethren like to walk on the fences. But it is hard in that way to keep one's balance. And it is needless, for there is plenty of room between the fences. For my part I prefer to walk in the road." Archibald Alexander's statement is yet better: "Calvinism is the broadest of systems. It regards the divine sovereignty and the freedom of the human will as the two sides of a roof which come together at a ridgepole above the clouds. Calvinism accepts both truths. A system which denies either one of the two has only half a roof over its head."

Spurgeon, Autobiography, 1:176, and The Best Bread, 109—"The system of truth revealed in the Scriptures is not simply one straight line but two, and no man will ever get a right view of the gospel until he knows how to look at the two lines at once.... These two facts [of divine sovereignty and of human freedom] are parallel lines; I cannot make them unite, but you cannot make them cross each other." John A. Broadus: "You can see only two sides of a building at once; if you go around it, you see two different sides, but the first two are hidden. This is true if you are on the ground. But if you get up upon the roof or in a balloon, you can see that there are four sides, and you can see them all together. So our finite minds can take in sovereignty and freedom alternately, but not simultaneously. God from above can see them both, and from heaven we too may be able to look down and see."

(d) Since the decrees connect means and ends together, and ends are decreed only as the result of means, they encourage effort instead of discouraging it. Belief in God's plan that success shall reward toil, incites to courageous and persevering effort. Upon the very ground of God's decree, the Scripture urges us to the diligent use of means.

God has decreed the harvest only as the result of man's labor in sowing and reaping; God decrees wealth to the man who works and saves; so answers are decreed to prayer, and salvation to faith. Compare Paul's declaration of God's purpose (Acts 27:22, 24—"there shall be no loss of life among you.... God hath granted thee all them that sail with thee") with his warning to the centurion and sailors to use the means of safety (verse 31—"Except these abide in the ship, ye cannot be saved"). See also Phil. 2:12, 13—"work out your own salvation with fear and trembling, for it is God who worketh in you both to will and to work, for his good pleasure"; Eph. 2:10—"we are his workmanship, created in Christ Jesus for good works, which God afore prepared that we should walk in them"; Deut. 29:29—"the secret things belong unto Jehovah our God: but the things that are revealed belong unto us and to our children for ever, that we may do all the words of this law." See Bennet Tyler, Memoir and Lectures, 252-354.

Ps. 59:10 (A. V.)—"The God of my mercy shall prevent me"—shall anticipate, or go before, me; Is. 65:24—"before they call, I will answer; and while they are yet speaking, I will hear"; Ps. 23:2—"He leadeth me"; John 10:3—"calleth his own sheep by name, and leadeth them out." These texts describe prevenient grace in prayer, in conversion, and in Christian work. Plato called reason and sensibility a mismatched pair, one of which was always getting ahead of the other. Decrees and freedom seem to be mismatched, but they are not so. Even Jonathan Edwards, with his deterministic theory of the will, could, in his sermon on Pressing into the Kingdom, insist on the use of means, and could appeal to men as if they had the power to choose between the motives of self and of God. God's sovereignty and human freedom are like the positive and the negative poles of the magnet,—they are inseparable from one another, and are both indispensable elements in the attraction of the gospel.

Peter Damiani, the great monk-cardinal, said that the sin he found it hardest to uproot was his disposition to laughter. The homage paid to asceticism is the homage paid to the conqueror. But not all conquests are worthy of homage. Better the words of Luther: "If our God may make excellent large pike and good Rhenish wine, I may very well venture to eat and drink. Thou mayest enjoy every pleasure in the world that is not sinful; thy God forbids thee not, but rather wills it. And it is pleasing to the dear God whenever thou rejoicest or laughest from the bottom of thy heart." But our freedom has its limits. Martha Baker Dunn: "A man fishing for pickerel baits his hook with a live minnow and throws him into the water. The little minnow seems to be swimming gaily at his own free will, but just the moment he attempts to move out of his appointed course he begins to realize that there is a hook in his back. That is what we find out when we try to swim against the stream of God's decrees."

3. That they make God the author of sin

To this we reply:

(a) They make God, not the author of sin, but the author of free beings who are themselves the authors of sin. God does not decree efficiently to work evil desires or choices in men. He decrees sin only in the sense of decreeing to create and preserve those who will sin; in other words, he decrees to create and preserve human wills which, in their own self-chosen courses, will be and do evil. In all this, man attributes sin to himself and not to God, and God hates, denounces, and punishes sin.

Joseph's brethren were none the less wicked for the fact that God meant their conduct to result in good (Gen. 50:20). Pope Leo X and his indulgences brought on the Reformation, but he was none the less guilty. Slaveholders would have been no more excusable, even if they had been able to prove that the negro race was cursed in the curse of Canaan (Gen. 9:25—"Cursed be Canaan; a servant of servants shall he be unto his brethren"). Fitch, in Christian Spectator, 3:601—"There can be and is a purpose of God which is not an efficient purpose. It embraces the voluntary acts of moral beings, without creating those acts by divine efficiency." See Martineau, Study, 2:107, 136.

Mat. 26:24—"The Son of man goeth even as it is written of him: but woe unto that man through whom the Son of man is betrayed! good were it for that man if he had not been born." It was appointed that Christ should suffer, but that did not make men less free agents, nor diminish the guilt of their treachery and injustice. Robert G. Ingersoll asked: "Why did God create the devil?" We reply that God did not create the devil,—it was the devil who made the devil. God made a holy and free spirit who abused his liberty, himself created sin, and so made himself a devil.

Pfleiderer, Philos. Religion, 1:299—"Evil has been referred to 1. an extra-divine principle—to one or many evil spirits, or to fate, or to matter—at all events to a principle limiting the divine power; 2. a want or defect in the Deity himself, either his imperfect wisdom or his imperfect goodness; 3. human culpability, either a universal imperfection of human nature, or particular transgressions of the first men." The third of these explanations is the true one: the first is irrational; the second is blasphemous. Yet this second is the explanation of Omar Khayyám, Rubáiyat, stanzas 80, 81—"Oh Thou, who didst with pitfall and with gin Beset the road I was to wander in, Thou wilt not with predestined evil round Enmesh, and then impute my fall to sin. Oh Thou, who man of baser earth didst make, And ev'n with Paradise devise the snake: For all the sin wherewith the face of man Is blackened—man's forgiveness give—and take!" And David Harum similarly says: "If I've done anything to be sorry for, I'm willing to be forgiven."

(b) The decree to permit sin is therefore not an efficient but a permissive decree, or a decree to permit, in distinction from a decree to produce by his own efficiency. No difficulty attaches to such a decree to permit sin, which does not attach to the actual permission of it. But God does actually permit sin, and it must be right for him to permit it. It must therefore be right for him to decree to permit it. If God's holiness and wisdom and power are not impugned by the actual existence of moral evil, they are not impugned by the original decree that it should exist.

Jonathan Edwards, Works, 2:100—"The sun is not the cause of the darkness that follows its setting, but only the occasion"; 254—"If by the author of sin be meant the sinner, the agent, or the actor of sin, or the doer of a wicked thing—so it would be a reproach and blasphemy to suppose God to be the author of sin.... But if by author of sin is meant the permitter or non-hinderer of sin, and at the same time a disposer of the state of events in such a manner, for wise, holy, and most excellent ends and purposes, that sin, if it be permitted and not hindered, will most certainly follow, I do not deny that God is the author of sin: it is no reproach to the Most High to be thus the author of sin." On the objection that the doctrine of decrees imputes to God two wills, and that he has foreordained what he has forbidden, see Bennet Tyler, Memoir and Lectures, 250-252—"A ruler may forbid treason; but his command does not oblige him to do all in his power to prevent disobedience to it. It may promote the good of his kingdom to suffer the treason to be committed, and the traitor to be punished according to law. That in view of this resulting good he chooses not to prevent the treason, does not imply any contradiction or opposition of will in the monarch."

An ungodly editor excused his vicious journalism by saying that he was not ashamed to describe anything which Providence had permitted to happen. But "permitted" here had an implication of causation. He laid the blame of the evil upon Providence. He was ashamed to describe many things that were good and which God actually caused, while he was not ashamed to describe the immoral things which God did not cause, but only permitted men to cause. In this sense we may assent to Jonathan

Edwards's words: "The divine Being is not the author of sin, but only disposes things in such a manner that sin will certainly ensue." These words are found in his treatise on Original Sin. In his Essay on Freedom of the Will, he adds a doctrine of causation which we must repudiate: "The essence of virtue and vice, as they exist in the disposition of the heart, and are manifested in the acts of the will, lies not in their Cause but in their Nature." We reply that sin could not be condemnable in its nature, if God and not man were its cause.

Robert Browning, Mihrab Shah: "Wherefore should any evil hap to man—From ache of flesh to agony of soul—Since God's All-mercy mates All-potency? Nay, why permits he evil to himself—man's sin, accounted such? Suppose a world purged of all pain, with fit inhabitant—Man pure of evil in thought, word and deed—were it not well? Then, wherefore otherwise?" Fairbairn answers the question, as follows, in his Christ in Modern Theology, 456—"Evil once intended may be vanquished by being allowed; but were it hindered by an act of annihilation, then the victory would rest with the evil which had compelled the Creator to retrace his steps. And, to carry the prevention backward another stage, if the possibility of evil had hindered the creative action of God, then he would have been, as it were, overcome by its very shadow. But why did he create a being capable of sinning? Only so could he create a being capable of obeying. The ability to do good implies the capability of doing evil. The engine can neither obey nor disobey, and the creature who was without this double ability might be a machine, but could be no child. Moral perfection can be attained, but cannot be created; God can make a being capable of moral action, but not a being with all the fruits of moral action garnered within him."

(c) The difficulty is therefore one which in substance clings to all theistic systems alike—the question why moral evil is permitted under the government of a God infinitely holy, wise, powerful, and good. This problem is, to our finite powers, incapable of full solution, and must remain to a great degree shrouded in mystery. With regard to it we can only say:

Negatively,—that God does not permit moral evil because he is not unalterably opposed to sin; nor because moral evil was unforeseen and independent of his will; nor because he could not have prevented it in a moral system. Both observation and experience, which testify to multiplied instances of deliverance from sin without violation of the laws of man's being, forbid as to limit the power of God.

Positively,—we seem constrained to say that God permits moral evil because moral evil, though in itself abhorrent to his nature, is yet the incident of a system adapted to his purpose of self-revelation; and further, because it is his wise and sovereign will to institute and maintain this system of which moral evil is an incident, rather than to withhold his self-revelation or to reveal himself through another system in which moral evil should be continually prevented by the exercise of divine power.

There are four questions which neither Scripture nor reason enables us completely to solve and to which we may safely say that only the higher knowledge of the future state will furnish the answers. These questions are, first, how can a holy God permit moral evil? secondly, how could a being created pure ever fall? thirdly, how can we be responsible for inborn depravity? fourthly, how could Christ justly suffer? The first of these questions now confronts us. A complete theodicy (Θεός, God, and δική, justice) would be a vindication of the justice of God in permitting the natural and moral evil that exists under his government. While a complete theodicy is beyond our powers, we throw some light upon God's permission of moral evil by considering (1) that freedom of will is necessary to virtue; (2) that God suffers from sin more than does the sinner; (3) that, with the permission of sin, God provided a redemption; and, (4) that God will eventually overrule all evil for good.

It is possible that the elect angels belong to a moral system in which sin is prevented by constraining motives. We cannot deny that God could prevent sin in a moral system. But it is very doubtful whether God could prevent sin in the best moral system. The most perfect freedom is indispensable to the attainment of the highest virtue. Spurgeon: "There could have been no moral government without permission to sin. God could have created blameless puppets, but they could have had no virtue." Behrends: "If moral beings were incapable of perversion, man would have had all the virtue of a planet,—that is, no virtue at all." Sin was permitted, then, only because it could be overruled for the greatest good. This greatest good, we may add, is not simply the highest nobility and virtue of the creature, but also the revelation of the Creator. But for sin, God's justice and God's mercy alike would have been unintelligible to the universe. E. G. Robinson: "God could not have revealed his character so well without moral evil as with moral evil."

Robert Browning, Christmas Eve, tells us that it was God's plan to make man in his own image: "To create man, and then leave him Able, his own word saith, to grieve him; But able to glorify him too, As a mere machine could never do, That prayed or praised, all unaware Of its fitness for aught but praise or prayer, Made perfect as a thing of course." Upton, Hibbert Lectures, 268-270, 324, holds that sin and wickedness is an absolute evil, but an evil permitted to exist because the effacement of it would mean the effacement at the same time both for God and man, of the possibility of reaching the highest spiritual good. See also Martineau, Study of Religion, 2:108; Momerie, Origin of Evil; St. Clair, Evil Physical and Moral; Voysey, Mystery of Pain, Death and Sin.

C. G. Finney, Skeletons of a Course of Theological Studies, 26, 27—"Infinite goodness, knowledge and power imply only that, if a universe were made, it would be the best that was naturally possible." To say that God could not be the author of a universe in which there is so much of evil, he says, "assumes that a better universe, upon the whole, was a natural possibility. It assumes that a universe of moral beings could, under a moral government administered in the wisest and best manner, be wholly restrained from sin; but this needs proof, and never can be proved.... The best possible universe may not be the best conceivable universe. Apply the legal maxim, 'The defendant is to have the benefit of the doubt, and that in proportion to the established character of his reputation.' There is so much clearly indicating the benevolence of God, that we may believe in his benevolence, where we cannot see it."

For advocacy of the view that God cannot prevent evil in a moral system, see Birks, Difficulties of Belief, 17; Young, The Mystery, or Evil not from God; Bledsoe, Theodicy; N. W. Taylor, Moral Government, 1:288-349; 2:327-356. According to Dr. Taylor's view, God has not a complete control over the moral universe; moral agents can do wrong under every possible influence to prevent it; God prefers, all things considered, that all his creatures should be holy and happy, and does all in his power to make them so; the existence of sin is not on the whole for the best; sin exists because God cannot prevent it in a moral system; the blessedness of God is actually impaired by the disobedience of his creatures. For criticism of these views, see Tyler, Letters on the New Haven Theology, 129, 219. Tyler argues that election and non-election imply power in God to prevent sin; that permitting is not mere submitting to something which he could not possibly prevent. We would add that as a matter of fact God has preserved holy angels, and that there are "just men" who have been "made perfect" (Heb. 12:23) without violating the laws of moral agency. We infer that God could have so preserved Adam. The history of the church leads us to believe that there is no sinner so stubborn that God cannot renew his heart,—even a Saul can be turned into a Paul. We hesitate therefore to ascribe limits to God's power. While Dr. Taylor held that God could not prevent sin in a moral system, that is, in any moral system, Dr. Park is understood to hold the greatly preferable view that God cannot prevent sin in the best moral system. Flint, Christ's Kingdom upon Earth, 59—"The alternative is, not evil or no evil, but evil or the miraculous prevention of evil." See Shedd, Dogm. Theol., 1:406-422.

But even granting that the present is the best moral system, and that in such a system evil cannot be prevented consistently with God's wisdom and goodness, the question still remains how the decree to initiate such a system can consist with God's fundamental attribute of holiness. Of this insoluble mystery we must say as Dr. John Brown, in Spare Hours, 273, says of Arthur H. Hallam's Theodicæa Novissima: "As was to be expected, the tremendous subject remains where he found it. His glowing love and genius cast a gleam here and there across its gloom, but it is as brief as the lightning in the collied night—the jaws of darkness do devour it up—this secret belongs to God. Across its deep and dazzling darkness, and from out its abyss of thick cloud, 'all dark, dark, irrecoverably dark,' no steady ray has ever or will ever come; over its face its own darkness must brood, till he to whom alone the darkness and the light are both alike, to whom the night shineth as the day, says 'Let there be light!' "

We must remember, however, that the decree of redemption is as old as the decree of the apostasy. The provision of salvation in Christ shows at how great a cost to God was permitted the fall of the race in Adam. He who ordained sin ordained also an atonement for sin and a way of escape from it. Shedd, Dogm. Theol., 1:388—"The permission of sin has cost God more than it has man. No sacrifice and suffering on account of sin has been undergone by any man, equal to that which has been endured by an incarnate God. This shows that God is not acting selfishly in permitting it." On the permission of moral evil, see Butler, Analogy, Bohn's ed., 177, 232—"The Government of God, and Christianity, as Schemes imperfectly Comprehended"; Hill, System of Divinity, 528-559; Ulrici, art.: Theodicée, in Herzog's Encyclopädie; Cunningham, Historical Theology, 2:416-489; Patton, on Retribution and the Divine Purpose, in Princeton Rev., 1878:16-23; Bib. Sac, 20:471-488; Wood, The Witness of Sin.

IV. Concluding Remarks

1. Practical uses of the doctrine of decrees

(a) It inspires humility by its representation of God's unsearchable counsels and absolute sovereignty. (b) It teaches confidence in him who has wisely ordered our birth, our death, and our surroundings, even to the minutest particulars, and has made all things work together for the triumph of his kingdom and the good of those who love him; (c) It shows the enemies of God that, as their sins have been foreseen and provided for in God's plan, so they can never, while remaining in their sins, hope to escape their decreed and threatened penalty. (d) It urges the sinner to avail himself of the appointed means of grace, if he would be counted among the number of those for whom God has decreed salvation.

This doctrine is one of those advanced teachings of Scripture which requires for its understanding a matured mind and a deep experience. The beginner in the Christian life may not see its value or even its truth, but with increasing years it will become a staff to lean upon. In times of affliction, obloquy, and persecution, the church has found in the decrees of God, and in the prophecies in which these decrees are published, her strong consolation. It is only upon the basis of the decrees that we can believe that "all things work together for good" (Rom. 8:28) or pray "Thy will be done" (Mat. 6:10).

It is a striking evidence of the truth of the doctrine that even Arminians pray and sing like Calvinists. Charles Wesley, the Arminian, can write: "He wills that I should holy be—What can withstand his will? The counsel of his grace in me He surely will fulfill." On the Arminian theory, prayer that God will soften hard hearts is out of place,—the prayer should be offered to the sinner; for it is his will, not God's, that is in the way of his salvation. And yet this doctrine of Decrees, which at first sight might seem to discourage effort, is the greatest, in fact is the only effectual, incentive to effort. For this reason Calvinists have been the most strenuous advocates of civil liberty. Those who submit themselves most unreservedly to the sovereignty of God are most delivered from the fear of man. Whitefield the Calvinist, and not Wesley the Arminian, originated the great religious movement in which the Methodist church was born (see McFetridge, Calvinism in History, 153), and Spurgeon's ministry has been as fruitful in conversions as Finney's. See Froude, Essay on Calvinism; Andrew Fuller, Calvinism and Socinianism compared in their Practical Effects; Atwater, Calvinism in Doctrine and Life, in Princeton Review, 1876:73; J. A. Smith, Historical Lectures.

Calvinism logically requires the separation of Church and State: though Calvin did not see this, the Calvinist Roger Williams did. Calvinism logically requires a republican form of government: Calvin introduced laymen into the government of the church, and the same principle requires civil liberty as its correlate. Calvinism holds to individualism and the direct responsibility of the individual to God. In the Netherlands, in Scotland, in England, in America, Calvinism has powerfully influenced the development of civil liberty. Ranke: "John Calvin was virtually the founder of America." Motley: "To the Calvinists more than to any other class of men, the political liberties of Holland, England and America are due." John Fiske, The Beginnings of New England: "Perhaps not one of the mediæval popes was more despotic than Calvin; but it is not the less true that the promulgation of his theology was one of the longest steps that mankind have taken towards personal freedom.... It was a religion fit to inspire men who were to be called to fight for freedom, whether in the marshes of the Netherlands or on the moors of Scotland."

Æsop, when asked what was the occupation of Zeus, replied: "To humble the exalted and to exalt the humble." "I accept the universe," said Margaret Fuller. Some one reported this remark to Thomas Carlyle. "Gad! she'd better!" he replied. Dr. John Watson (Ian McLaren): "The greatest reinforcement religion could have in our time would be a return to the ancient belief in the sovereignty of God." Whittier: "All is of God that is and is to be, And God is good. Let this suffice us still Resting in childlike trust upon his will Who moves to his great ends unthwarted by the ill." Every true minister preaches Arminianism and prays Calvinism. This means simply that there is more, in God's love and in God's purposes, than man can state or comprehend. Beecher called Spurgeon a camel with one hump— Calvinism. Spurgeon called Beecher a camel without any hump: "He does not know what he believes, and you never know where to find him."

Arminians sing: "Other refuge have I none; Hangs my helpless soul on thee"; yet John Wesley wrote to the Calvinist Toplady, the author of the hymn: "Your God is my devil." Calvinists replied that it was better to have the throne of the universe vacant than to have it filled by such a pitiful nonentity as the Arminians worshiped. It was said of Lord Byron that all his life he believed in Calvinism, and hated it. Oliver Wendell Holmes similarly, in all his novels except Elsie Venner, makes the orthodox thinblooded and weakkneed, while his heretics are all strong in body. Dale, Ephesians, 52—"Of the two extremes, the suppression of man which was the offense of Calvinism, and the suppression of God which was the offense against which Calvinism so fiercely protested, the fault and error of Calvinism was the nobler and grander.... The most heroic forms of human courage, strength and righteousness have been found in men who in their theology seemed to deny the possibility of human virtue and made the will of God the only real force in the universe."

2. True method of preaching the doctrine

(a) We should most carefully avoid exaggeration or unnecessarily obnoxious statement. (b) We should emphasize the fact that the decrees are not grounded in arbitrary will, but in infinite wisdom. (c) We should make it plain that whatever God does or will do, he must from eternity have purposed to do. (d) We should illustrate the doctrine so far as possible by instances of completeness and far-sightedness in human plans of great enterprises. (e) We may then make extended application of the truth to the encouragement of the Christian and the admonition of the unbeliever.

For illustrations of foresight, instance Louis Napoleon's planning the Suez Canal, and declaring his policy as Emperor, long before he ascended the throne of France. For instances of practical treatment of the theme in preaching, see Bushnell, Sermon on Every Man's Life a Plan of God, in Sermons for the New Life; Nehemiah Adams, Evenings with the Doctrines, 243; Spurgeon's Sermon on Ps. 44:3—"Because thou hadst a favor unto them." Robert Browning, Rabbi Ben Ezra: "Grow old along with me! The best is yet to be, The last of life, for which the first was made: Our times are in his hand Who saith 'A whole I planned, Youth shows but half; trust God: See all nor be afraid!' "

Shakespeare, King Lear, 1:2—"This is the excellent foppery of the world that when we are sick in fortune (often the surfeit of our own behavior) we make guilty of our disasters the sun, the moon and the stars, as if we were villains by necessity, fools by heavenly compulsion, and all that we are evil in by a divine thrusting on; an admirable evasion of man to lay his disposition to the charge of a star!" All's Well: "Our remedies oft in ourselves do lie Which we ascribe to heaven: the fated sky Gives us free scope; only doth backward pull Our slow designs, when we ourselves are dull." Julius Cæsar, 1:2—"Men at some time are masters of their fates: The fault, dear Brutus, is not in our stars, But in ourselves, that we are underlings."

www.ingramcontent.com/pod-product-compliance
Lightning Source LLC
Chambersburg PA
CBHW060328100426
42812CB00003B/920